A DEEPER VISION

ROBERT ROYAL

A Deeper Vision

The Catholic Intellectual Tradition in the Twentieth Century

IGNATIUS PRESS SAN FRANCISCO

Cover photograph by Eva Muntean

Cover design by John Herreid

ISBN 978-1-58617-990-8
Library of Congress Control Number 2014949946
Printed in the United States of America ∞

And for all this, nature is never spent;
there lives the dearest freshness deep down things.

—Gerard Manley Hopkins

Faith does not merely gaze at Jesus, but sees things as Jesus himself sees them, with his own eyes: it is a participation in his way of seeing. In many areas in our lives we trust others who know more than we do. We trust the architect who builds our home, the pharmacist who gives us medicine for healing, the lawyer who defends us in court. We also need someone trustworthy and knowledgeable where God is concerned. Jesus, the Son of God, is the one who makes God known to us (cf. Jn 1:18). Christ's life, his way of knowing the Father and living in complete and constant relationship with him, opens up new and inviting vistas for human experience.

—*Lumen Fidei*

CONTENTS

INTRODUCTION

Jesus Christ, my child, did not come to tell us tales.
During the little time that he had.
What is three years in the life of a world.
In the eternity of this world.
He didn't have any time to waste, he didn't waste his time telling us tales and playing charades for us to figure out.
Very witty charades.
Very clever.
A wizard's riddles.
Full of double-entendres and tricks and stupid subtleties and complexities.
No, he didn't waste his time and he didn't take pains,
He didn't have the time,
His pains, his great, his very great pain.
He didn't waste, he didn't expend all of that, all of his being, everything.
He didn't spend himself, spend everything, he didn't make this enormous, this terrible expense
Of self, of his being, (of) everything.
To come afterwards, with this, by means of this, at this price,
To come at this price with some code to decipher
To decode.
Tricks, silly nonsense, quid pro quos, clever little antics like a fortuneteller from the town.
Like a village clown.
Like a traveling acrobat, a charlatan in his cart.
Like the town prankster, like the funniest guy in the tavern.[1]

[1] Charles Péguy, *The Portal of the Mystery of Hope*, trans. David Louis Schindler, Jr. (Grand Rapids, Mich.: Eerdmans, 1996), 67–68.

These lines by Charles Péguy, a great genius amid many others in twentieth-century Catholicism, express one of the deepest truths about Christianity. In myriad ways, it is a faith that is quite straightforward, almost deceptively simple. A God who came into the world and proclaimed a universal mission of salvation has to be someone who can be broadly understood by everyone. He cannot be a God solely for philosophers, theologians, biblical scholars, psychologists, political theorists, poets, or intellectuals. Neither is his saving action a theory:

> He had an errand to run for us on behalf of his father.
> He did for us what he was sent to do and he went back.
> He came, he paid (what a price!), and he left.
> He didn't come recount for us extraordinary stories.
> Nothing is simpler than the word of God.
> He told us things that were quite ordinary.
> Very ordinary.
> The incarnation, salvation, redemption, the word of God.
> Three or four mysteries.
> Prayer, the seven sacraments.
> Nothing is as simple as God's glory.[2]

But Péguy obviously knows—and is consciously playing on—the vast intellectual tradition that has grown up within Catholicism because of "The incarnation, salvation, redemption, the word of God. / Three or four mysteries." In his efforts to make people realize in very concrete terms what a direct act the Incarnation was—it is like a son being sent to the bakery for a loaf of bread, as he says elsewhere—he himself wrote thousands of pages of prose and poetry. In his poem *Eve* (almost twenty thousand lines long), the last eighty pages describe all the things we will *not* need on our deathbeds, among which:

> It will not be an Aristotelian who slips
> Under those thick laurel trees,
> And it will not be his thin lips
> That will give us the kiss of peace.

[2] Ibid., 69.

Quite other lips, a bit more Catholic
Will plant the kiss on our cheeks.
A hand less blind, more apostolic,
Will find us beneath the broad beech.[3]

Péguy disliked the dominant Catholic Scholastic philosophy (based in Aristotle and Aquinas) that existed in his day. But, as subsequent events in both the Church and the world have shown, although we may not need Aristotle or Aquinas on our deathbeds, we seem not to do well without them—or something very like them that gives us rational moorings—in our everyday lives. The great Irish novelist James Joyce, a lapsed Catholic, claimed to read a page of Aquinas every day, in Latin, to keep his mind sharp because Thomas' reasoning was "like a sharp sword".[4] (Joyce's later descent into impenetrable wordplay may make one question whether the tonic always works.) Even Péguy recognized as well as anyone the value of a clear mind like Aristotle's. And he had a clear enough mind himself to know that philosophy and theology and other intellectual disciplines are natural human acts that will perennially spring into full bloom, particularly when questions of God and eternity present themselves. His own meditations resulted in a quite vivid and sophisticated version of the French philosopher Henri Bergson's thought, for example, which seemed to him to solve various modern problems through its unique combination of closeness to life as it is actually lived and careful analysis that avoids mere intellectualism.

Such paradoxes are quite common to the Catholic intellectual tradition. And in the twentieth century, as in other centuries, they often enough gave rise to leaden treatises, empty sermonizing, and conventional piety—but also to philosophy, art, theology, poetry, fiction, drama, history, and spiritual writing equal to anything produced in any other tradition, religious or secular. Hardly anyone knows about this today, even among Catholics. This strange state of affairs owes something to the fact that in the last third of the twentieth century—that is, in the years following the Second Vatican Council

[3] Charles Péguy, *Oeuvres poétiques complètes* (Paris: Bibliothèque de la Pléiade, 1957), 1154. Author's translation.

[4] Richard Ellmann, *James Joyce* (New York: Oxford University Press, 1965), 353.

(1962–1965)—notions of what was Catholic became confused and contested as they had not been earlier. Before that earthshaking event, which had consequences far beyond Catholicism, even secular observers often said: "At least Catholics know what they believe." And talented Catholics who made creative use of that rich tradition were often recognized in secular institutions. To take just one example, the French Catholic philosopher Jacques Maritain (a protégé of Péguy's as a young man and a prolific and original thinker) was invited to lecture on aesthetics at the National Gallery of Art in Washington in 1950 and, around the very same time, on political philosophy by the University of Chicago as well.[5] Within twenty-five years, however, the kind of Aristotelian-Thomistic philosophy Maritain practiced so brilliantly in essence disappeared, even from Catholic universities, and the secular world turned back to an old view that Catholicism was some kind of anti-rational fundamentalism. No Catholic would likely be honored, as Maritain once was, by prestigious secular institutions today.

The Great Disruption

It is always difficult to ascribe causes to large-scale social changes, but the story of the modern Catholic intellectual tradition is also inextricably woven together with the seismic shift in global culture often associated with the year 1968, which Francis Fukuyama—a non-Catholic—has seen as the beginning of "the great disruption".[6] That year was a kind of watershed that featured not only the youth rebellion (and sexual revolution) in America and Europe, but the strong emergence of liberation theology in Latin America, *tercermundismo* and anti-colonialism in other parts of the developing world, and a general decline in respect for authority and institutions virtually everywhere. (It was also the year in which, in the encyclical *Humanae Vitae*—a radically countercultural and unpopular move—Paul VI repeated the constant Christian teaching since ancient times that

[5] These lectures resulted in two quite lively books that are still of considerable significance: *Creative Intuition in Art and Poetry* (New York: Pantheon Books, 1953); and *Man and the State* (Chicago: University of Chicago Press, 1951).

[6] Francis Fukuyama, *The Great Disruption: Human Nature and the Reconstitution of Social Order* (New York: Free Press, 1999).

artificial contraception is morally impermissible—but that is a story for later.) Radical doubt that philosophy and theology and related disciplines could give some sort of secure knowledge—a doubt that had existed earlier but had been confined to small and specialized groups—also seemed to emerge as almost a default cultural position. Even where "spirituality" continued to exist or people said in large percentages that they still believed in God, that belief tended more and more to be untethered to any institution and to morph into a kind of do-it-yourself perspective on faith and morals. Needless to say, none of this much helped Catholicism, which has always rested on tradition, authority (pope and bishops), an institution (the Church), and a developed body of thought.

Perhaps even more significant than the external changes, however, there were factors internal to Catholicism itself that led to a loss of familiarity with the Catholic intellectual tradition. Catholicism is by its nature and long practice a kind of community of memory, a Church that holds onto what she believes was revealed by God. And the pope and the bishops—since ancient times represented as shepherds protecting their flocks—are authoritative figures, a magisterium, who set boundaries on what they judge to be compatible or incompatible with the tradition. The "opening to the world" at Vatican II led to a much-needed decentralization: bishops were affirmed as successors to the apostles in their own dioceses and authoritative in their "collegiality" with the pope. And the Church rightly moved from an overly institutional and legalistic to a more communitarian and pastoral model that also affirmed the active role of laypeople in the Church and the world.

In the uncertainty of the postconciliar years, cultural currents that were quite distant from Catholicism also entered the Church. Bishops who maintained the ancient positions on faith and morals came to be seen as merely resisting liberal trends. Innovation became for some more important than fidelity—or (creating even greater confusion for ordinary people) it was argued that innovation was a kind of deeper fidelity. And contrary to the intentions of the Council, pope and bishops often found themselves with diminished authority, like their secular counterparts in government, medicine, law, and culture. In these circumstances, it became more difficult to identify what was distinctly Catholic even in the Church herself.

The highly influential Jesuit theologian Karl Rahner once described the Second Vatican Council as a "decisive break" with what went before and even went so far as to say it was one of three such major disjunctions in the history of the Church.[7] The first came with the Council of Jerusalem (Acts 15), the first-century meeting of the apostles and other disciples that many regard as the point of emergence of the new religion, Christianity, from Judaism. The second began with the Roman Emperor Constantine's official acceptance of Christianity, which began a long period in which Church and secular powers were intermingled. And the third, in the twentieth century, brought a new, indeed radical, reorientation—though toward what was not entirely clear, even to Rahner.

While Vatican II was certainly a massive and fresh impulse in the life of the Church, almost everyone today recognizes how much continuity there was and is between the pre- and postconciliar Church. To begin with, the same Creed that was recited at Masses prior to the Council is still being recited today. The manifold changes in liturgy, theology, biblical criticism, and everyday Catholic life that have roots in the Council are still all in the service of the basic affirmations of the faith. Rahner was right in that the Council was a major turning point, but wrong in suggesting—as he did to some people—that the Church had undergone a transformation that simply broke with virtually the entirety of her previous existence. That many quite well educated Catholics somehow came to believe in a disjunction like this—and that the new situation is somehow superior to what was experienced by the generations of Catholics who lived prior to it—is a sign that something went strangely awry among the faithful and even among quite brilliant Catholic minds.

The debate over continuity versus discontinuity persists into the new millennium. One recent scholar has described the choices facing the Council Fathers:

> At stake were almost two different visions of Catholicism: from commands to invitations, from laws to ideals, from definition to mystery, from threats to persuasion, from coercion to conscience, from

[7] Karl Rahner, S.J., "Towards a Fundamental Theological Interpretation of Vatican II", *Theological Studies* 40, no. 4 (1979): 716–27.

> monologue to dialogue, from ruling to serving, from withdrawn to integrated, from vertical to horizontal, from exclusion to inclusion, from hostility to friendship, from rivalry to partnership, from suspicion to trust, from static to ongoing, from passive acceptance to active engagement, from fault-finding to appreciation, from prescriptive to principled, from behavior modification to inner appropriation.[8]

Of course, both elements on either side of these alleged pairs of opposites belong in a fully Catholic vision—"both-and", as has often been said, is one of the marks of Catholicity, not "either-or". (Yet as the postconciliar period showed, there are limits to "both-and". The harder task for the third Christian millennium may lie in discerning when fidelity to the full truth may require saying "no" in order to realize a larger "yes".) Christ commands and threatens as much as he invites and persuades in the New Testament—the words of the founder of Christianity himself are both demanding and consoling, not merely one or the other, as has long been recognized. And they set up the standard. The impulse to raise one side of each pair over the other has led, in a very tangible sense, not only to a lack of fidelity to the Scriptures but to a narrowing and dispersal of the accumulated wisdom of Catholicity into all-too-familiar modern culture clashes between "liberals" and "conservatives". The Catholic Church did well to open herself up at Vatican II to new social and intellectual currents, but just as not everything that went before was wrong, not everything that came after was right.

In the twentieth century, the Catholic Church still faced the age-old questions: eternal truths and contemporary applications, Christian unity and inescapable diversity, God's word and man's response. As in the past, such topics had to be handled with a combination of continuity and innovation: continuity, because Truth, though never finally possessed in this life, is always the same and is with us from age to age; innovation, because—perhaps especially in the twentieth century—a new set of temporal realities emerged that no one, Catholic or not, had ever faced before in quite the same terms. The digital revolution alone has altered global culture in ways we are still struggling to understand.

[8]John W. O'Malley, *What Happened at Vatican II* (Cambridge, Mass.: Belknap Press of Harvard University Press, 2008), 307.

Further Paradoxes

Among the strange paradoxes of the century, the Church was more cohesive and better defined when she faced massive threats, particularly ideologies like Communism, Nazism, and Fascism. When those opponents disappeared, Catholicism often seemed to lose identity and become indistinguishable from other modern philanthropic activities. It is a symptom of this phenomenon that Catholicism succeeded against the Soviet Union, for example, but had a harder time gaining purchase on the open societies of the West. As the British philosopher Elizabeth Anscombe, the distinguished translator and interpreter of the great modern thinker Ludwig Wittgenstein, remarked at the conclusion of a powerful defense of papal teaching on sexuality: "The teaching which I have rehearsed is indeed against the grain of the world, against the current of our time. But that, after all, is what the Church as teacher is for. The truths that are acceptable to a time—as, that we owe it as a debt of justice to provide out of our superfluity for the destitute and the starving—these will be proclaimed not only by the Church: the Church teaches *also* those truths that are hateful to the spirit of an age."[9] But such voices, especially among world-class Catholic thinkers, became increasingly rare as the twentieth century wore on.

Instead, after Vatican II, a dense jungle of diverse currents of thought came within Catholic academic circles, which more and more seemed to operate like their secular counterparts at non-Catholic institutions of higher learning. This clearly raised the intellectual bar at many such colleges and universities. But it also made it more difficult to see what was distinctively Catholic thinking in various fields, even though the metaphysical and ethical foundations in Augustine, Aquinas, and other great figures remained somewhere in the background. The specialists in various disciplines now only rarely had time to look deeply into the work of colleagues pursuing other modes of thought, and their labors therefore looked like isolated

[9] This lecture has been often reprinted and may be found, with related materials, in G. E. M. Anscombe, *Faith in a Hard Ground: Essays on Religion, Philosophy and Ethics*, ed. Luke Gormally and Mary Geach, St. Andrews Studies in Philosophy and Public Affairs (Exeter, U.K., and Charlottesville, Va.: Imprint Academic, 2008), 191.

"intellectual" specialties—in the bad sense that Péguy had identified. It is not at all uncommon in the twenty-first century to find that a Catholic theologian formed in one school of thought knows little even of other Catholic theological currents, let alone of artistic or literary achievements by contemporary Catholics. And vice versa.

A Justification of the Present Book

If there is any justification for a single person trying to cover the various areas dealt with in the present volume—and in a way addressed to non-specialists—it lies in the simple fact that no one has tried to bring together the main strands that make up the modern Catholic intellectual tradition. Perhaps the principal reason that the Catholic intellectual tradition goes largely unacknowledged today is that it has just become too big to be easily grasped. But it is not an impossible task, I believe, to take a synoptic view of the main disciplines informed by Catholic thought, within some sharp limits.

I am quite aware of the dangers involved in this effort. Several years ago, I asked a colleague, a non-Catholic with a doctorate in philosophy from one of the most prestigious state universities, what he thought of Father Frederick Copleston's *A History of Philosophy*, a massive eleven-volume, over five-thousand-page achievement and a landmark of twentieth-century Catholic intellectual life. To my surprise, he had nothing but praise: "Look, it is the best thing out there by miles. And everybody knows it. The only problem is that everybody also thinks it is great—except in the area where he is a specialist. But philosophers differ so much even within single philosophical currents that you can't always even get them to agree on the general outlines of a philosopher's thought. Who else covers so much territory so well?"

I am not so foolish as to invite comparisons of the present volume with the towering achievement by Father Copleston. Several friends who heard about the project, including some bishops, assumed I would put together a multi-author encyclopedia of some kind, since it was obvious that no one person could reasonably claim expertise even in a single one of the subjects to which the following chapters are devoted. Even a whole lifetime would not be enough to understand a figure such as Hans Urs von Balthasar or Karl Rahner, a complex movement like phenomenology or modern Thomism, or the intricacies of literature written in several languages by Catholics in the century just past. I am quite aware of these challenges, to say nothing of the limits of my own abilities, perhaps even more than my readers will be. But there are several reasons, if not full justifications, for an ambitious work like the present one.

To begin with, as my colleague noted, there is real value in a survey of a large intellectual field by a single person. Sections written by various authors would have inevitably clashed with one another—Thomists with phenomenologists, Balthasarians with Rahnerians—and might leave readers not only with conflicting interpretations but with real doubts about how the various pieces fit together under the Catholic rubric, if at all. I have my opinions and sometimes sharp judgments about the material offered here, but since I do not have a professional stake in many of these conflicts, I hope I have tried to present differing positions in as accurate and as sympathetic a light as possible. I have tried to do so using as little technical language as possible (although there are a few places where that is unavoidable) and in the hope of explaining at least why the great minds presented here did what they did. To the experts in each of these areas, let me say in advance that I realize there is a great deal more to be said than what I have sifted out. Without sharp limitations, a book of this kind would quickly have become unwieldy and unreadable—indeed, impossible.

But while I hope to have given as fair an account as I can of the various elements included here, I believe I have also presented them from a certain standpoint: that of a Catholicism opened up to the modern world by the Second Vatican Council—and the steps that led up to it—but one that consciously seeks to affirm what is perennially and robustly Catholic. There is a large difference between a confident Catholicism—with its rich theological, moral, and cultural tradition going back into the Ancient Middle East, Egypt, and beyond by way of its Jewish roots, and with its dynamic appropriation of cultural power from Greece, Rome, northern Europe, the Americas, the Far East, and various modern currents of thought—and one in which that richness is bracketed in favor of privileging, instead, the moment in which one happens to find oneself because of its seeming power or inevitability.

Further, even though at the end of the day it is important to thrash out what is true and what is not, there is an earlier, necessary phase of understanding of what has gone before that helps bring the deeper questions before us in their fullness. As Aristotle once wisely remarked:

> For those who wish to get clear of difficulties it is advantageous to discuss the difficulties well; for the subsequent free play of thought implies the solution of the previous difficulties, and it is not possible to untie a knot of which one does not know.... One should have surveyed all the difficulties beforehand, both for the purposes we have stated and because people who inquire without first stating the difficulties are like those who do not know where they have to go; besides, a man does not otherwise know even whether he has at any given time found what he is looking for or not; for the end is not clear to such a man, while to him who has first discussed the difficulties it is clear. Further, he who has heard all the contending arguments, as if they were the parties to a case, must be in a better position for judging.[10]

One of the reasons Aristotle was absorbed into Catholic thought is that he is so Catholic *avant la lettre*, precisely in this recognition of the importance of examining how others have approached various questions prior to our own efforts to engage them.

Despite appearances, Catholicism has repeatedly returned to this procedure and is likely to be doing so again even now. As the great Catholic historian Christopher Dawson remarked before the crisis of the 1960s, but with a historian's prescience about the precariousness of modern culture: "The Church as a divine society possesses an internal principle of life which is capable of assimilating the most diverse materials and imprinting her own image upon them. Inevitably in the course of history there are times when this spiritual energy is temporarily weakened or obscured, and then the Church tends to be judged as a human organization and identified with the faults and limitations of its members. But always the time comes when she renews her strength and once more puts forth her inherent divine

[10] Aristotle, *The Metaphysics*, trans. W.D. Ross in *The Basic Works of Aristotle*, ed. Richard McKeon (New York: Modern Library, 2001), 716.

energy in the conversion of new peoples and the transformation of old cultures."[11]

If I had to state in a single phrase the perspective from which the following pages proceed, it is this: a *theological anthropology* on the model broadly outlined by John Paul II, which is to say, a view of man and the world as only fully explicable by the data of revelation, but one that also affirms the modern emphasis on human freedom, the rights of conscience, and the value of reason. That perspective should be a common point of departure for Catholics today, even for those who may disagree with John Paul II about specific questions. In short, I hope to have written from a vision of faith and reason—*Fides et Ratio*, to borrow the title of one of his most fertile encyclicals—that is both Catholic and intellectually defensible. This approach both preserves the concreteness of God's work, as Péguy understood it, and is properly modern in the way it seeks understanding of that work.

Intimately connected to this larger vision is a crucial question that still has not received an adequate answer and that runs through all of the following chapters: How does the Catholic Church in the twenty-first century integrate her renewed emphasis on community and pastoral awareness with the equally important and urgent renewal of firm defense of dogmas in faith and morals. Catholicism is not and has never been mere philanthropy, and it is not true to itself, as Anscombe noted, unless it both defines and promulgates its own truths, which shape what it means fully to love God and neighbor. Without those truths, the Church becomes something like a doctor who has a good bedside manner but knows little medicine. She can be comforting and pastoral but cannot really cure and save.

The Modern Context

This book does not move very far outside the *Catholic intellectual* (emphasis on both qualifiers) tradition in the twentieth century. And by design, it does not deal much with American Catholic thought, which I hope to treat in another volume. Still, before entering that

[11] Christopher Dawson, *The Historic Reality of Christian Culture* (New York: Harper, 1960), 103.

arena, a brief survey of the world in which that tradition functioned may be useful for the understanding of why some ideas emerged, since thought never arises in a pure intellectual void. The general lines are fairly well known. In the developed world, we tend to focus on the progress that has been made in respect for human rights, raising the material level of existence for the people, and widespread literacy that—for the first time in human history—allows almost everyone to be an active protagonist in his own life. Despite the problems that come with all human endeavors, these are real achievements for Catholics and for anyone who believes in the dignity of all human persons, made "in the image and likeness of God", and in the need to promote authentic human flourishing.

But there is another side to the story of which Catholics, perhaps more than most, are aware in very concrete terms. After the French Revolution, which as it transformed itself into the Terror notably persecuted and martyred many who had had no part in sustaining the old monarchical order, the Church faced a wholly new social situation. The former system of state churches slowly gave way to secular democracies that were at best indifferent and at worst hostile to religion. France was only the beginning. Germany passed quickly from a collection of jurisdictions to the unity of the Second Reich (1871–1918), which under Bismarck conducted a *Kulturkampf* ("Culture War", 1871–1878) against the Church. In Italy, the unification of the nation in 1870 and the disappearance of the Papal States caused several popes to regard themselves as "prisoners of the Vatican", in self-imposed isolation in the Leonine City, which the new Italian government allowed the papacy to retain. The situation was not regularized until the papacy of Pius XI and the Lateran Accords of 1929.

And there is much more. The Lateran Accords were negotiated with Mussolini's Fascist government, which in some respects made more trouble for the Church after the agreements than before, though the Church operated with relative freedom in Italy compared to in the rest of Europe. The anti-clerical laws in France passed at the beginning of the 1900s by the socialist government of Émile Combes closed at least ten thousand Catholic schools and outlawed religious congregations. Germany's crisis between the two world wars led to the rise of Adolf Hitler, who sought to wipe out

Europe's Jews. But it is often forgotten that even though he was raised a Catholic, Hitler also intended to "crush the Church like a toad". The Third Reich was quite happy to intimidate, imprison, and murder Catholic priests in the meantime, over two thousand of whom wound up in German work camps. Elsewhere, notably in the Spanish Civil War, almost all the bishops were slaughtered along with whole convents, monasteries, and seminaries. When Communism came to the nations of Central and Eastern Europe after World War II, the Church in largely Catholic areas such as Slovakia, Poland, and Hungary, among others, endured yet another round of serious persecution and deaths, until the peaceful demise of the Soviet system in 1989. Communist persecution of Catholics in China, Vietnam, and Cuba persisted into the new millennium. On many public fronts, Catholicism faced immediate and armed attacks in the twentieth century, to say nothing of intellectual and social opposition. It, therefore, needed to discern quite carefully what was and was not good in modern culture.

Culture itself, as John Paul II emphasized, became a central influence in the latter part of the twentieth century as perhaps never before, partly owing to the decline of "high" culture and what must frankly be described as the debasement of popular culture, which had earlier been a vehicle for a reasonably sound world view for the masses. The novelist Mario Vargas Llosa, winner of the 2010 Nobel Prize in Literature, has argued that we have come to the point where culture is now an anti-culture or is so attenuated as to be virtually nonexistent.[12] It is worth adding that a certain scientism—a belief that empirical experiments are the only source of true knowledge—has also demolished even some of the humane secular elements in culture. It is as if all the world has become disillusioned, like Charles Ryder in Evelyn Waugh's *Brideshead Revisited* who flees the Catholic Marchmain family in the middle of that novel, saying, "Henceforth I live in a world of three dimensions—with the aid of my five senses." Ryder hastens to add, "I have since learned that there is no such world."[13] But many people in late modernity are not so sure, including no small number of Catholics.

[12] Mario Vargas Llosa, *La civilización del espectáculo* (Alfaguara: Mexico City, 2012).
[13] Evelyn Waugh, *Brideshead Revisited* (Boston: Little, Brown, 1976), 195.

The Shape of This Book

The plan of this book is simple. It begins with an account of some of the main currents in twentieth-century Catholic philosophy. This represents not a personal choice but the fact that without philosophy there is no theology. And without theology there is no such thing as a Catholic *intellectual* tradition. When John Paul II published his encyclical *Fides et Ratio*, less than two years before the start of the new millennium, he was affirming something that had roots in the Catholic tradition going back to the Gospels themselves: both faith *and* reason are necessary to a Catholic understanding of God and his world. Since Catholics believe God is the Creator of everything, the truths of faith and those of reason cannot contradict one another, for they refer ultimately to the one who is Truth. And truth allows for different avenues of approach. John Paul II gave a nod to Aquinas as a model for how to be a Catholic thinker, but he also made clear that Catholicism has no official philosophy. In the shift from Thomism, dominant in Catholic philosophy prior to Vatican II, to the other philosophies that later became more prominent, the pope himself—a practitioner of personalism and phenomenology—and Joseph Ratzinger—his successor (as Benedict XVI) and an Augustinian—were living examples of the philosophical pluralism that arose within the Church. The gains and losses of that shift are part of the main storyline in twentieth-century Catholic philosophy. In the end, however, Catholicism is by nature a faith that needs what John Paul II called "a philosophy of *genuinely metaphysical* range" (*Fides et Ratio*, 83). Rediscovering that dimension among the pluralism inside and the skepticism and relativism outside of Catholicism remains an urgent task for any Catholicism worthy of the name.

Theology, of course, also has relations with several of the other cultural dimensions examined here. Catholic theology is dependent on a prior revelation. As Aquinas would say, in technical terms it is a "subalternate science". Its data are the data of revelation just as the data of physics are the facts we observe in the empirical world. The "three or four mysteries" of which Péguy spoke can never be fully explained by theology because by definition a mystery is not a problem that can be "solved". It is something that is presented to us and lies beyond our ability to grasp fully. A person may deny that the

Christian revelation is true or even that communication from God as such is possible—or possible to understand—the standard atheist or agnostic premises. But the proper distinctions having been made, that is not the Catholic position, and careful attention both to revealed truths and to truths accessible to reason essentially defines Catholic theology. As John Paul II mentions in *Fides et Ratio*, the dialogue between faith and reason is never finally concluded. How that dialogue transpired over several tumultuous decades after Vatican II is a fascinating and little-known story.

Furthermore, the development of Catholic theology is not shaped solely by the efforts of individual theologians working on various problems. It is also significantly, and sometimes sharply, directed by authoritative statements from the Church's magisterium, or teaching office. To outsiders, this may seem as though mere arbitrary exercises of power are used to prevent thought, roughly parallel to what would be the case if a secular government tried to interfere with the work of a research professor. There have been cases in Church history—most notably Galileo's—when the Church has let herself be twisted sideways and gone beyond her proper competence in such matters, as a fuller Catholicism understands. And that has unfortunately cast habitual suspicion on her other authoritative statements for some people. But the parallels with the secular case are not quite appropriate because *Catholic* theology takes as its proper material of study the revelation found in the Bible and the tradition of understanding that revelation (even as it adds, with Aquinas, that the "argument from authority based on human reason"[14] is the weakest of all arguments).

After Vatican II, the Church went through a period of catching up with modern Scripture studies. She also had useful criticisms and contributions to make to a method developed outside of her purview. Revelation is something larger than Scripture for Catholics: the reality of the history of Israel and the life of Christ and the witness of tradition, in addition to the actual biblical texts themselves, all have to be factored into any Catholic understanding of what God

[14] Thomas Aquinas, *Summa Theologiae*, trans. Fathers of the English Dominican Province (New York et al.: Benziger Bros., 1947, hereafter abbreviated *ST*), I, q. 1, a. 8 ad 2; p. 5.

has done. But since scriptural studies underwent several revolutionary phases in Catholic circles during the twentieth century, those too need to be addressed here because of their significant impact on how scholars in various fields understood revelation to have occurred and also how they debated the place of newly won perspectives on the theological and philosophical enterprise. This process is, even in the second decade of the twenty-first century, still only in its early stages. History, archaeology, textual criticism, and other disciplines await full integration into other fields of thought.

For a Catholic account of the Catholic intellectual tradition in the twentieth century, something also has to be said about liturgy. Since it is a firm Catholic principle that *lex orandi, lex credendi*, changes in various practices clearly reflect some prior changes in thought; however, it is often forgotten that they produce such changes as well. For example, it has often been said that the shift from Latin to the vernacular in the Mass, which was not mandated by the Second Vatican Council incidentally, gave lay people the notion that if something as basic as the Mass could change so drastically, then pretty much anything else could as well. Any real Catholic, traditionalist or progressive, would have to say there is something wrong with that attitude. But perhaps even worse than this attitude was the loss of mystery and elevation, also universally admitted, owing to the kinds of vernacular translations we have had. Some languages—Italian, for example—seem to retain some of the dignity of the old liturgy. But English has fared quite poorly. Whatever the intentions of the translators—and ideological suspicions are not entirely unfounded—ours is not a great era for exalted language. Much of the English Mass oscillates between the banal and the maudlin, even after the "reform of the reform" by Benedict XVI.

A similar problem has crept into contemporary translations of Scripture. It was inevitable and even necessary that the real achievements of modern scriptural scholars be reflected in newer translations. But it was doubtless also inevitable that those translations, at their best, though better from the standpoint of technical accuracy (happily the Good News Bibles and other gimmicky versions died a mercifully quick natural death), would not exactly rise to the level of the old King James or Lutheran Bibles or even the serviceable Douay-Rheims English version. The great Anglo-Catholic poet

T.S. Eliot said of the Protestant New English Bible, which used "dynamic equivalence" rather than strict construal, that it "astonishes in its combination of the vulgar, the trivial and the pedantic".[15] Catholics fared little better. At the very moment when the Catholic Church was for the first time really encouraging laymen to read the Bible themselves and be inspired by direct contact with the living Word of God, the Church was slow to provide the kinds of translations that might lift the hearts and minds of literate laypeople. The beautiful opening of Psalm 23 came out clunkily in the widely used *Jerusalem Bible*: "Yahweh is my shepherd, I lack nothing." The highly gifted British convert Ronald Knox also flubbed: "The Lord is my shepherd. How can I lack anything?" The New American Bible, which appeared first in 1970 and then, revised, in 1986, did all right, "The Lord is my shepherd, I shall not want." But when even one of the best-known and loved lines gets such uneven treatment, it is a clear indication of a much wider problem of contemporary culture and its effects on the basics of belief.

Some of the main divisions of the subject in these pages may evoke skepticism. Do things like literature, culture, and historical studies really play a central role in an intellectual tradition? I thought so before I began writing, and my look into the kind of work produced in these three fields in the twentieth century convinced me still further. One of the main themes that will emerge later in the text is the cultural situation of an intellectual tradition in an age when the intellect itself has come to be distrusted, partly because of the use that has been made of it. I am not the first or the only person to have noticed that the kind of culture we now inhabit, which seems to limit reason to scientific and technical fields and to put all other manifestations of human thought into the category of fantasy, may need to undergo a very public, broad-based shift before it will even be possible to consider faith as something more than mere emotion or wish fulfillment. Literature and other cultural creations, with their ability to bring before us things that the dominant cultural forces may have marginalized or brought to premature closure, are particularly helpful under such conditions.

[15] T.S. Eliot, "Letter: Review of the New English Bible", *Sunday Telegraph*, December 16, 1962, p. 7.

Some readers may remain doubtful that history, literature, and cultural studies can do the work that hard-nosed philosophy or theology can do. The past, we often hear, is just too complex, too susceptible to ideological distortions and anachronisms, and too *past* to be of much use in trying to sort out our problems today. If we take this view to its logical conclusions, however, faith rooted in sacred history, the stories of the Bible, and the traditions of the Jewish people and of the Church—which is one of the distinguishing features of Judaism and Christianity—simply becomes impossible. Whatever uncertainties, gaps, and conflicts of interpretation may exist with respect to biblical history and significant events in Catholic history, without some effort to hold on to the golden thread of the tradition and the action of Divine Providence in history amid the various twists and turns of the labyrinth, there simply is no maintaining the Catholic faith. Some of the literary figures examined here help to recover a living sense of Catholicity precisely within modern contexts. A need to do that even more effectively may in fact be one of the most difficult problems—and significant opportunities—for the Catholic intellectual tradition, as I hope I have shown in the concluding chapters.

So this is no exercise in what centuries ago Malebranche had already dismissed as mere "polymathy". A central question that faces anyone who wants to present Catholicism in the modern world is whether any discursive account has much value beyond that of mere curiosity. Much of what the Catholic intellectual tradition faces today is the sheer stubborn assumption, fueled directly and indirectly by figures like Nietzsche, that Catholicism and all comprehensive explanations of human life are "idols"—partial, credulous, overconfident, power-seeking, compensatory, and discredited at the outset beyond all recall because nothing can be credited that is the result of any fallible human agent. Despite the depressing aspect this cultural attitude sometimes presents, it has an oddly salutary effect as well for those of us not inclined to place our trust in professors.

Jesus Christ did not argue much for himself or his Father or the whole sacred history that Catholicism presupposes. Rather, he did something that still has reverberations all over the world and will have into the future. After all the rational efforts, in the end, as Péguy and other great modern figures have noted, the Catholic intellectual tradition is held to a high—the highest—standard:

He spoke to us without digressions or complications.
He didn't put on airs, embellish things.
He spoke uniformly, like a simple man, crudely, like a man from town.
A man from the village.
Like a man in the street who doesn't search for his words and doesn't make a fuss.
When he chats.
Also, given that he spoke to us and that he spoke to us directly,
Given that he spoke to us in parables,
Which we call similitudes in Latin,
Since he didn't come to tell us tales,
Since he always spoke to us directly and plainly
To the letter,
On the level,
Always in response, we must always hear him and listen to him literally.
Directly and fully on the level.
Our brother, our big Brother did not trick us for the pleasure of being clever.
We ought not to trick him for the pleasure of playing the fool.
And it would be tricking him to look for mischief where he didn't put it.
To hear, to search, to want to hear; to imagine;
To warp;
To hear his word other than how he said it.
Even to listen other than how he spoke.[16]

[16] Péguy, *Portal*, 69–70.

Part One

FAITH AND REASON

Chapter 1

The Thomist Revival and Preconciliar Catholic Thought

In the summer of 1901, on the very threshold of the twentieth century, Jacques Maritain and Raïssa Oumansov, his future wife, were strolling through the Jardin des Plantes in Paris. It was not the usual lovers' scene. They were both studying sciences at the Sorbonne and were in deep despair over the bleak picture of life entailed by scientific materialism. They swore a mutual suicide pact: if they could not find something more worthy to live for, they preferred to die, together. But things moved on swiftly from there. Charles Péguy took them to the lectures of Henri Bergson at the Collège de France, where they and many others heard that there might be other dimensions, more human and philosophically defensible dimensions, to reality. They read in Maurice Maeterlinck, a popular Belgian novelist, about a holy man—also a kind of novelist—named Léon Bloy, who lived in Paris near Sacre Coeur. They visited this poor and highly eccentric figure. In June 1906, Bloy was their godfather as they were received into the Catholic Church, not knowing what would follow, but prepared even to give up the life of the mind, if necessary, for an authentic and fuller existence.

This strange story, involving the most influential Catholic philosopher in the twentieth century, reflects what might be called the characteristic struggle to maintain both a life of faith and a life of reason in the century just past. The last sentence in Bloy's novel *La femme pauvre* would be quoted by many Catholics—sometimes the most intellectually adventurous—during the following decades: "The only sadness is not to be saints" ("Il n'y a qu'une tristesse, c'est de n'être pas des saints"). Some would take this to mean that holiness has nothing to do with the head, that it is all a matter of Pascal's famous contention that the heart has its own reasons and it is the heart that responds to God. In the face of rational objections to the mere idea of the divine, it is an understandable reaction. But it is not a wholly Catholic reaction, in that Catholicism, more than any of the other forms of Christianity, has always insisted on a connection of the head with the heart in response to God.

At the other end of the twentieth century, in September 1998, just two years before the beginning of the third Christian millennium, Pope John Paul II issued *Fides et Ratio*, one of the most far-seeing encyclicals of his globally influential papacy. As the name ("On Faith and Reason") implies, the text—the fruit of his lifelong efforts as an academically trained philosopher and concerned pastor—aimed to bolster belief, of course. But it also asserted strong claims, in a skeptical postmodern age, for the powers of reason. (His successor, Benedict XVI, was to make a similar argument—pointing out the importance of believing in a God who is rational in order to avoid religious extremism and violence—in a controversial 2006 speech[1] at the University of Regensburg, where he had taught as a young professor.) Catholicism, unlike several other religious traditions, has long recognized the importance of philosophy for theology. But it would no doubt have surprised Voltaire or other intellectuals since the Enlightenment that the Catholic Church and the popes of Rome would, at the end of two thousand years of Christianity, be championing reason in a strong sense at the very moment when most secular thinkers believed it to have quite limited scope.

Fides et Ratio was also, however, the product of a complex development within the Catholic Church over the whole course of the twentieth century, in which Catholic philosophy shifted from a heavy emphasis on the thought of Thomas Aquinas—the place where Maritain made his greatest contributions, for which he is cited by the pope (*FR* 74)—to an eclectic mix of various ancient and modern philosophical currents. Some of those currents, instead of encouraging the pursuit of perennial philosophic questions—*Who am I? Where have I come from and where am I going? Why is there evil? What is there after this life?*, as John Paul summed them up—limit themselves to technical issues of ordinary language or logical consistency

[1] James V. Schall, *The Regensburg Lecture* (South Bend, Ind.: St. Augustine's Press, 2007), contains text and commentary.

and declare more ambitious uses of reason illegitimate. John Paul II called upon philosophy—and philosophers, inside and outside the Church—to become more adventurous and ambitious and to regain confidence in the powers of reason to lay hold of all things, human and divine. For him, this was not only an abstract intellectual issue. He had suffered under both Nazism and Communism in his native Poland and was instrumental in bringing down the Soviet bloc in 1989. Wrong notions of truth or weak rational responses to dangerous ideologies had led to something like one hundred million deaths in the twentieth century.

Just prior to the twentieth century, another papal encyclical, Leo XIII's *Aeterni Patris* (1879), had addressed a similar crisis by encouraging the study of the great medieval thinker Saint Thomas Aquinas. Contrary to widespread impressions, Thomism had not been particularly prominent in Catholic philosophical training prior to Leo's efforts. In the nineteenth century, Catholic philosophers often drew on Descartes, Christian Wolff, Immanuel Kant, or other modern figures in somewhat disjointed and unsystematic efforts to explain Catholic beliefs. Leo's encyclical engendered a "Thomist revival" that provided Catholic philosophers with powerful intellectual tools well beyond the mid-point of the twentieth century. The kinds of Thomism that emerged ranged from the supple and creative to the rigid and plodding, from varieties of "the strict observance" to exotic and innovative hybrids involving modern thought.[2] But Leo, too, believed that philosophical renewal was needed to meet modern public questions and anticipated—in *Rerum Novarum*, the 1891 encyclical that started the tradition of modern Catholic social thought—the bloody results that would follow if such renewal were not swiftly put in place.

The studies of Karol Wojtyła (later John Paul II) in philosophy at the seminary and, years after, as he prepared for academic teaching reflected the main arc in twentieth-century Catholic philosophy as a whole. In 1949, he wrote his doctoral dissertation in Rome under Réginald Garrigou-Lagrange, a notoriously strict Thomist and

[2] Cf. Russell Hittinger, "Two Modernisms, Two Thomisms: Reflections on the Centenary of Pius X's Letter against the Modernists", *Nova et Vetera*, Eng. ed., vol. 5, no. 4 (2007): 843–80.

earlier a mentor to Maritain as well.[3] In the dissertation, which later commentators have rightly seen as an expression of the future pope's constant pastoral and contemplative side, Wojtyła chose to use Aquinas to explicate the Spanish mystic Saint John of the Cross.[4] But Garrigou-Lagrange himself was a gifted commentator on the spiritual life,[5] which suggests that strict Thomism did not always lead to mere formulaic aridity or rationalism. Wojtyła's second doctorate (*Habilitationsschrift*), however, the one most European countries require for appointment as a full professor, engaged the prominent modern philosophy known as phenomenology: *An Evaluation of the Possibility of Constructing a Christian Ethics Based on the System of Max Scheler.*[6]

Wojtyła studied Scheler's system quite carefully and came to the conclusion that it was inadequate. The emotional dimension that Scheler emphasized—something that needed to be taken into account in any comprehensive view of human life—was not fully up to the modern task, at least not without some of the sturdier Thomist truths as a supplement, a position sometimes referred to as phenomenological or Lublin Thomism because the University of Lublin in Poland, where Wojtyła taught, was a center for approaches of this sort.[7] Quite apart from the merits of the future pope's analysis, it is telling that one of the greatest Catholic leaders in recent history chose to explore these sorts of modern philosophical challenges in a flexible yet firm way. It also says much about the larger Catholic dialogue between faith and reason that Leo XIII set in motion.

In keeping with the broad spirit of both Aquinas and the phenomenological method, John Paul's *Fides et Ratio* offers a frank opening to other kinds of philosophy:

[3] For one view of this figure, see Richard Peddicord, *The Sacred Monster of Thomism: An Introduction to the Life and Legacy of Reginald Garrigou-Lagrange, O.P.* (South Bend, Ind.: St. Augustine's Press, 2005).

[4] Karol Wojtyła, *Faith according to St. John of the Cross*, trans. Jordan Aumann, O.P. (San Francisco: Ignatius Press, 1981).

[5] See, for instance, his massive three-volume work, *The Three Ages of the Interior Life: Prelude of Eternal Life*, trans. M. Timothea Doyle (St. Louis, Mo., and London: Herder, 1947–1948); and his *Christian Perfection and Contemplation according to St. Thomas Aquinas and St. John of the Cross*, trans. M. Timothea Doyle (St. Louis, Mo.: Herder, 1937).

[6] Published in Polish as *Zagadnienie podmiotu moralności* (Lublin: Catholic University of Lublin Press, 1991). Several translations into other European languages exist, but not English.

[7] Cf. Rocco Buttiglione, *Karol Wojtyła: The Thought of the Man Who Became Pope John Paul II*, trans. Paolo Guietti and Francesca Murphy (Grand Rapids, Mich.: Eerdmans, 1997).

> The Church has no philosophy of her own nor does she canonize any one particular philosophy in preference to others. The underlying reason for this reluctance is that, even when it engages theology, philosophy must remain faithful to its own principles and methods. Otherwise there would be no guarantee that it would remain oriented to truth and that it was moving towards truth by way of a process governed by reason. A philosophy which did not proceed in the light of reason according to its own principles and methods would serve little purpose. At the deepest level, the autonomy which philosophy enjoys is rooted in the fact that reason is by its nature oriented to truth and is equipped moreover with the means necessary to arrive at truth. A philosophy conscious of this as its "constitutive status" cannot but respect the demands and the data of revealed truth. (*FR* 49)

The final claim is, to say the least, not at all obvious to many modern philosophers. John Paul II was aware that several currents in contemporary philosophy, even contemporary Catholic philosophy, regard reason as weak, uncertain, self-contradictory, even self-undermining. But his whole aim in writing appears in his opening sentence: "Faith and reason are like two wings on which the human spirit rises to the contemplation of truth; and God has placed in the human heart a desire to know the truth—in a word, to know himself—so that, by knowing and loving God, men and women may also come to the fullness of truth about themselves."

In passing, he mentions the importance of Aquinas,

> Although he made much of the supernatural character of faith, the Angelic Doctor did not overlook the importance of its reasonableness; indeed he was able to plumb the depths and explain the meaning of this reasonableness. Faith is in a sense an "exercise of thought"; and human reason is neither annulled nor debased in assenting to the contents of faith, which are in any case attained by way of free and informed choice. This is why the Church has been justified in consistently proposing Saint Thomas as a master of thought and a model of the right way to do theology. (*FR* 43)

As is evident in their writings, Aquinas and his great contemporaries welcomed and tried to integrate truths from every source available to them in the High Middle Ages: Greek and Latin, Jewish and Muslim. That is, in part, what it means to be Catholic, which is to say, "universal". Leo XIII and John Paul II, each in his own way, encouraged precisely this kind of openness—an openness precisely to *truth*, as opposed to a characteristically modern open-ended, inconclusive "search for truth"—which led to remarkable developments in Catholic thought in the twentieth century.

A Century of Thought

Viewed from our perspective in the early twenty-first century, the whole phenomenon sometimes looks like a failed project that has degenerated into incoherence. Unleashing thought as Leo XIII did led to a process beyond the capacity of anyone to predict—or control. If Thomism dominated Catholic philosophy for roughly the first two-thirds of the twentieth century, it split quite early into competing schools and factions that were not even always on speaking terms (there were major figures who never read each other). The strict Thomism of some official Catholic institutions tried to remain rigidly close to the master himself but found itself with proliferating and differing interpretations of what that original philosophy in fact had been. Many who resisted strict Thomism (mostly in European seminaries) saw it as aiming to reply to problems about our knowledge of the world and the existence of God raised by figures like Descartes and Kant—the central modern philosophical problems, in other words, questions that Aquinas had never addressed in the modern terms of debate. The critics thought this approach mistaken because it replied to modern rationalism with another rationalism that drew on, but was foreign to, the richness of Thomas. Others took a different tack and sought to integrate certain modern thinkers into Thomism, giving rise to hybrids such as transcendental Thomism (basically Thomas + Kant) and existential Thomism (Thomas + contemporary awareness of the mystery of being). In a 1974 speech at the University of Chicago, Dom Hélder Câmara, Archbishop of Olinda and Recife in Brazil, went so far as to invoke Thomas in the context of liberation theology: "We must take the categories of our age and do with Marx what Aquinas did with Aristotle."[8]

[8] Cf. Arthur McGovern, *Marxism: An American Christian Perspective* (Maryknoll: Orbis, 1980), 2.

Marxism and liberation theology receded with the collapse of the Soviet Union, but Thomist-inspired experiments continue—and continue to be contested.

In the second half of the twentieth century, Catholic philosophy also moved beyond these variations on Thomism into other forms of philosophy. It is quite common now for philosophy departments at Catholic universities to be populated with analytic philosophers, existentialists, poststructuralists and postmodernists, Heideggerians, Whiteheadeans, Teilhardians, Wittgensteinians, Derrideans, Foucauldians, Rawlsians, and others—lying at various angles to Catholicity. In one way, this phenomenon attests to a certain cultural vitality: Catholic thinkers in the twentieth century were not at all reluctant to use the various tools of the non-Catholic culture in interpreting the ancient tenets of the faith. In another way, however, this seeming richness might be looked upon as a dispersion. The tools borrowed from the secular culture seem to have created a discord of voices that make any straightforward philosophical understanding of revelation—always a difficult task anyway—all but impossible. In addition, all this borrowing seemed to blur the distinction between the sacred and the secular, giving rise to further confusions.

It is worth taking a closer look at these developments as a way of understanding both the intellectual gains and losses within one of the great religions and their sometimes considerable, if little known, effects on the contemporary world. The phenomenon is too varied and large for exhaustive treatment, but the main lines of development are relatively clear, as are the questions that the Catholic dialogue between faith and reason sought to answer.

The Thomist Revival

Since the Second Vatican Council (1962–1965), which rightly or wrongly has come to be thought of as a liberalizing movement in the Catholic Church, the revival of Thomism, on the rare occasions when it is even noticed, has frequently been viewed as a narrow and restrictive movement identified with the most reactionary and rigid elements in the Church. This myth contains a kernel of truth, particularly in terms of the ways that the teaching of Thomism took place in European seminaries during the first half of the twentieth century, to judge by some who lived through the experience. A frequent complaint is that simplistic and uninspiring Latin "manuals" of Thomist philosophy were drilled into young seminarians, who had little idea what such dry and abstruse material had to do with Catholicism or their future pastoral duties. There was almost no contact with the brilliant texts of Thomas himself. But the belief that this was all there was to modern Thomism cannot survive the slightest acquaintance with what was actually achieved by the many and diverse thinkers who belonged to a vigorous and creative current in Catholic thought that has continued well into the twenty-first century.[9]

The best-known figures, such as Jacques Maritain and Étienne Gilson, were in their day influential and highly respected even in prestigious non-Catholic intellectual circles. Both lectured extensively at institutions such as Harvard, Princeton, the University of Chicago, the University of Virginia, and other centers of secular learning in addition to Catholic universities. And with good reason: their work—often moving, deep, and eloquent—ranges boldly over subjects as diverse as metaphysics, history, political philosophy, social questions, spirituality, education, and aesthetics. It was only natural, for example, that Jacques Maritain would try to address the crisis in political philosophy posed by the two world wars and the intellectual fault lines—primarily mistaken notions of the human person and society—that enabled the rise of totalitarian movements such as Fascism, Nazism, and Communism. In the process, he virtually invented the mature form of the social philosophy that lies behind all the modern Christian democrat parties, the very parties that reconstructed Europe after the world wars. Maritain was also the principal drafter of the U.N. Universal Declaration of Human Rights. He and the philosophy he developed have, in this and many other ways, had immense influence on the whole modern world order.[10]

And there were other large currents within Thomism that sought to grapple with problems that arose in modern conditions. Naturally,

[9] The discussion of the Thomist revival in this chapter draws on the excellent survey by Gerald A. McCool, *The Neo-Thomists*, Marquette Studies in Philosophy 3 (Milwaukee: Marquette University Press, Association of Jesuit University Presses, 1994).

[10] See Roberto Papini, *The Christian Democrat International*, trans. Robert Royal (Lanham, Md.: Rowman & Littlefield, 1997).

not all of these proved to be equally fruitful, but it is perhaps a testimony to the perceived richness of Thomist thought that creative figures like Maurice Blondel, Henri Bergson, Pierre Rousselot, Joseph Maréchal, Karl Rahner, Bernard Lonergan, and many others drew on Thomas. Adapting Thomism to contemporary uses clearly meant going beyond and outside the questions that Thomas himself addressed, and this led to no little infighting among various schools. In some ways, this should not come as a surprise. Leo XIII did not seek a mere return to the past when he recommended the study of Aquinas in *Aeterni Patris*. He had long been engaged in modern public questions going back to his days as bishop of Perugia, and he recommended Thomas because he thought the Angelic Doctor was a rich source of precisely the kind of insight and careful thought the Church and the world needed as they approached the twentieth century. *Aeterni Patris* is sometimes read in retrospect as primarily an attempt to restore Aristotelian-Thomist theories of knowledge and metaphysics, as opposed to the more skeptical paths of post-Kantian thought. But Leo seems to have considered such studies as preliminaries to a much larger social renewal. As one scholar has noted: "In Leo's own work—some 110 encyclicals and other teaching letters—Thomas is rarely discussed or referenced apart from the social-political problems."[11]

In *Aeterni Patris*, Leo quotes Cardinal Cajetan (1469–1534), a formidable thinker in his own right, in saying that Thomas had received, ordered, and integrated previous Christian wisdom in such a way that he "seems to have inherited the intellect of all" (*AP* 17). In the spirit of Thomas, Leo concluded that "we hold that every word of wisdom, every useful thing by whomsoever discovered or planned, ought to be received with a willing and grateful mind." And the pope recommended that a full and balanced Thomism should be developed "for the defense and beauty of the Catholic faith, for the good of society, and for the advantage of all the sciences"(*AP* 31). Leo's language can be a little florid, in the manner of his day, but clearly he hoped that, just as Thomas had harmonized the newly rediscovered Greek and other forms of learning with Christian thought in his time, his modern students might do something similar for their own.

[11] Hittinger, "Two Modernisms, Two Thomisms", 859.

Leo's encyclical had institutional aims as well. A year after it was published, he appointed three cardinals to a special commission headquartered in Grottaferrata outside of Rome with simple orders to produce new scholarly editions of Aquinas. At the time, it was probably thought that this work would be completed in just a few years. In 2003, the Leonine Commission, as it came to be called because of Leo's role in its creation, was still going strong and moved to Paris, where it is producing careful editions and commentaries and benefiting from a library that includes over a half million digitized pages of manuscripts. The commission's leadership has evolved over the years to represent various regions of the world. The mere fact of its existence gives scholars a place to send newly discovered manuscripts and provides various other researchers with a chance to apply the new discoveries to old questions about dating, purposes of composition, and intended audiences for Thomas' vast output.[12]

Another important institutional development to come out of *Aeterni Patris* was the Higher Institute of Philosophy in Louvain, Belgium. Gioacchino Pecci, the future Leo XIII, had once been the papal nuncio in Belgium. When *Aeterni Patris* appeared, Désiré Mercier, a seminary professor, proposed that the Catholic University of Louvain set up a chair in Thomistic philosophy. In 1882, just three years later, the Belgian bishops named Mercier to that chair. Mercier created the Higher Institute of Philosophy in 1889. He was serious about a dynamic engagement with the world and the vigorous pursuit of truth under the aegis of Saint Thomas, and his faculty were no mere followers of a party line. As hard as it is to believe, now that we have such a wealth of learning on the subject, little was known then about the Middle Ages, let alone the various currents of medieval philosophy. Mercier hired first-rate historians like Maurice De Wulf and other able professors who had studied and taught at major European universities. He also encouraged engagement with modern philosophy and science. In addition, courses were taught in the vernacular, not Latin—which Rome permitted reluctantly—

[12] Many of the results of these collective scholarly labors are reflected in Jean-Pierre Torrell, *Thomas Aquinas*, vol. 1: *The Person and His Work*, trans. Robert Royal, 2nd ed., rev. and expanded (Washington, D.C.: Catholic University of America Press, 2005).

and the Institute published *La Revue néo-scolastique* in French. Whatever might be said about other Catholic centers of study, the Institute did highly creative work.

The Roman Scene

It is sometimes the case that policies established in the capital are more vigorously pursued in the provinces. Rome's academies reacted in a more mixed fashion to Leo's initiative, perhaps because there were already strong and conflicting interests in its Catholic educational institutions. As early as the 1820s, the dynamic Neapolitan Jesuit Luigi Taparelli d'Azeglio, then rector of the Gregorian University, met with strong resistance when he tried to make Thomas' work the organizing philosophy for the seminary program. The Society of Jesus had had an uneven history of using Saint Thomas and happened at that time to be divided between enthusiasts and significant figures such as Salvatore Tongiorgi and Domenico Palmieri, who thought fundamental notions that Thomas had borrowed from Aristotle such as matter and substantial form had been exploded by modern science, though other elements in Thomas were still useful.

Taparelli became Jesuit provincial in Naples a few years later and was actually removed from office because of resistance to his efforts to promote Aquinas. Some of the resistance stemmed from partisans of different currents in an amorphous body of ancient and modern philosophies that had taken up residence in Catholic institutions. In France, Lamennais, de Maistre, and de Bonald, reacting against the radicalism of the French Revolution, pursued a kind of traditionalism that emphasized faith over reason. Germany, with its vigorous modern forms of idealism, looked more to the great figures in that tradition than to Thomism for philosophical illumination. An adventurous global movement called ontologism—a philosophy of a kind of direct intuition of the divine that drew on Plato and Saint Augustine—was promoted by thinkers such as Casimir Ubaghs (Belgium), Louis Branchereau and Flavien Hugonin (France), Carlo Vercellone and Vincenzo Gioberti (Italy), and partly in the work of the great Antonio Rosmini (who had some of his work placed on the Index of Forbidden Books in 1849 but was beatified by Benedict XVI in 2007). Ontologism came into conflict with the Neoscholastics, and then-Bishop Pecci worked to have it condemned at Vatican I. In faraway America, the prominent Catholic convert and intellectual leader Orestes Brownson stood accused of having absorbed the poison. And then there were other, quite eminent figures, such as Cardinal Newman in England, who valued Saint Thomas but were wary of what seemed an over-reliance on only one strand in Christian philosophy, namely, medieval Scholasticism.

Yet Leo had supporters in Rome. As bishop of Perugia, he had ordained a young Corsican, Tommaso Zigliara, and appointed him as a professor at the diocesan seminary, a center of Thomistic studies. Zigliara was a Dominican and a strong expositor of the Aristotelian side of Thomas. In 1870, he became a professor, then regent at the Dominican College in Rome, in good time for the publication of *Aeterni Patris*. Leo also had on hand in Rome another vigorous Dominican, Alberto Lepidi, who combined a solid Thomistic outlook with an appreciation of the Augustinian-Platonic side of Thomas, a dimension less recognized then than it is today after the labors of the Leonine Commission. And Leo had some help from the Jesuits as well. In the aftermath of his ignominious escape from Rome in 1848 during one of the recurrent revolutionary periods in nineteenth-century Europe, Pius IX asked the Jesuits to create and staff a new publication, *La Civiltà Cattolica*, which has remained to this day a kind of unofficial mouthpiece of the Holy See, especially on public matters. Taparelli returned as one of the founders (his brother, Massimo d'Azeglio, was a prominent Italian politician and novelist). He was joined by Joseph Kleutgen, an expert on Germany, Carlo Maria Curci, and Matteo Liberatore, a brilliant Italian writer. All of these figures were solid Thomists—though Liberatore and Kleutgen were Suárezians, subscribing to an interpretation of Thomas that stemmed from Francisco Suárez, S.J. (1548–1617). This perspective was common among the Jesuits but did not recognize some of Thomas' differences with Aristotle, particularly his introduction of "existence" rather than "form" as the primordial act and several other crucial elements that helped make Aristotle's philosophy more compatible with various Christian teachings.

Scholarly journals such as the *Archiv für Literatur- und Kirchengeschichte* were founded in Rome and the prestigious *Beiträge zur*

Geschichte der Philosophie des Mittelalters in Germany. In 1893, the French Dominicans inaugurated the *Revue thomiste* in Toulouse. Developments in English were slower: *Blackfriars* started to appear in England in 1920, and *The Thomist* in America in 1939. The Leonine Commission was working near Rome. But for various reasons the Gregorian University did not participate as much in this new flowering. Its newer professors tended to be strict Thomists, but much less imaginative and original than others at the time. They wrote manuals of Scholastic philosophy widely used in Catholic institutions around the world, but these were in Latin and rarely read by Catholics, let alone scholars more generally, outside of seminaries. Further, these Neoscholastics were divided among strict Thomists, Suárezians, and Scotists. These divisions were not clearly understood at the time, but they would grow as time passed and as historical study also revealed the deep differences that had already existed among philosophers in the Middles Ages. The Roman professors were good and careful thinkers, but they did not engage the modern world in the ways that Leo had hoped would be the case. They were not, therefore, a significant force in advancing Leo's overarching vision.

Leo's ambitiousness can best be appreciated in light of his immediate predecessor and successor. On the social front, he seemed to confirm Lord Acton's observation that Thomas Aquinas was the "first Whig". Pius IX, who ruled as pope before him, is now remembered as an archconservative and is sometimes referred to, in a pun on the Italian for "ninth" as "Pio No-No". Actually, he began as a kind of political liberalizer. But when his minister of the interior in the Papal States, a Protestant named Pellegrino Rossi, was assassinated, Caesar-like, by a Roman mob, he turned in a more reactionary direction. His famous Syllabus of Errors, issued on the Feast of the Immaculate Conception in 1864, proclaimed among other things that it was madness (*deliramenta*) to think that "the Roman Pontiff can, and ought to, reconcile himself and come to terms with progress, liberalism and modern civilization." He also decried the separation of church and state. By contrast, Leo, though he became pope after the Papal States were lost to Italian Unification in 1870, supported a *Ralliement* for Catholics to the French Republic and in his great 1891 encyclical *Rerum Novarum* laid out a social program rooted in Thomist social principles with a certain progressive and modern cast that has shaped Catholic social teaching ever since. On the more strictly doctrinal front, too, Leo occupies a forward-looking place. His successor, Pius X, in 1907 issued the encyclical *Pascendi Domenici Gregis*, which imposed loyalty oaths and sought to eliminate "modernism" from the Church in ways that produced resistance even from faithful and well-intentioned Catholics.

In any event, at the opening of the twentieth century, Leo's initiatives had led to a network of institutions well organized to teach and propagate Thomism: the Institut Catholique in Paris; the Jesuit house of studies at Maria Laach in Germany; the Catholic University of Austria; the University of Fribourg in Switzerland, which benefited from the presence of one of the greatest historians of medieval philosophy, Pierre Mandonnet; Alberto Lepidi, prior to his move to Rome, was Regent of Studies at the Dominican House in Flavigny, which became famous as Le Saulchoir in Belgium, where it moved owing to persecution by the socialist administration in France. Ambroise Gardeil, who helped found Le Saulchoir, had studied with a student of Albert Lepidi and continued the emphasis on the Platonic side of Thomas. Mandonnet, A. G. Sertillanges, and M.-D. Roland-Gosselin taught there, and two of the greatest later luminaries, Marie-Dominique Chenu and Yves Congar—of whom more shortly—studied with them. Gardeil himself taught Réginald Garrigou-Lagrange, later the teacher of Jacques Maritain.[13]

Gardeil and Le Saulchoir felt the need to respond to certain currents in the religious life of France. Kantianism, which from one angle is a sort of culmination of the Cartesian project, with its strict limits on what is knowable by human reason, became a major challenge at the beginning of the twentieth century in France. In keeping with the eclectic nature of Catholic philosophy prior to the Neoscholastic revival, there were even figures such as Maurice Blondel, a sincere Catholic layman, who believed that the turn to the contents of the mind, in the classic Kantian manner, could be quite helpful in bolstering Catholic belief. For many Thomists, beginning philosophical reflection on the basis of the contents of the mind made it impossible to reach what Kant called *noumena*, "the things in themselves". That was certainly Kant's own view. But Blondel made an

[13] Cf. Marie-Dominique Chenu, *Une école de théologie: Le Saulchoir* (Paris: Cerf, 1985).

interesting move—one that would find echoes in later existential and phenomenological currents in Catholic philosophy and in transcendental Thomism. A recognition of the limits of our rational knowledge pointed to the need for other avenues of truth, which opened the door not only to revelation but even to the specific historical revelation of the Bible. In two works, *L'Action* and especially his *Lettre sur les exigences de la pensée contemporaine en matière d'apologétique,*[14] Blondel made the case that what he called the "intrinsic apologetic" of examining our inner drives shows that human beings cannot be content with anything less than God himself. The very dynamics of the mind point beyond themselves toward something that can then be seen, justifiably, as an exact answer to human need, thus making it possible, even in modern conditions, for the traditional "extrinsic apologetics" to get a fair hearing.

Another major problem, clearly in Leo's mind in *Aeterni Patris,* was the way that modern scientific thought had given the impression that everything could be broken down into analyzable parts. Leo and his advisers did not deny that the scientific method had its uses. Indeed, as has already been mentioned above, they wanted to embrace those legitimate advances toward undeniable human goods, as had the best Catholic thinkers for centuries. But, to put it bluntly, the new science, at least as a growing number of scientists and others came to think of it, left no room for life as traditionally understood, to say nothing of the characteristic human things that had occupied philosophers since philosophy first began. Plants and animals were regarded as elaborate machines; in the eighteenth century, Julien Offray de La Mettrie published a book entitled *L'Homme machine* (The machine man) in which he defined man as a machine "perpendicularly walking." A few years later when Pierre Laplace was asked by Napoleon where God came into his system, he famously replied, "Sire, I have no need of that hypothesis." That way of looking at the world obviously left no room for mind, freedom, will, spirit, sin, virtue, heaven, hell, and many other things characteristic not only of Christian thought but of the best secular thinking as well. In France,

[14] English translations worth consulting: *The Letter on Apologetics, and History and Dogma,* trans. Alexander Dru and Illtyd Trethowan (Grand Rapids, Mich.: Eerdmans, 1994); *Action,* trans. Oliva Blanchette (South Bend, Ind.: University of Notre Dame Press, 2003).

Auguste Comte had raised a kind of science-inspired positivism to the level of a new religion.

One of the great and influential figures who replied to this whole climate of philosophical thought in the first half of the twentieth century was Henri Bergson, a friend and teacher of both Charles Péguy and Jacques Maritain. Though Bergson's notions of the *élan vital* and "creative intuition" have not worn well, his thought at least had the virtue of pointing out a glaring problem in the way that abstraction, as then practiced, divorced modern thought from reality—and life. Bergson proposed instead an eloquent, humane engagement with reality in its concreteness and fullness, not merely with ideas. His philosophy seemed to open windows in a philosophical room that had grown musty from being closed in on itself and to allow in fresh air. Many people—from society women to undergraduates, in Paris and elsewhere in Europe and America—who felt choked by dominant philosophical and scientific assumptions responded with great enthusiasm to this attractive argument for human things. Though Jacques Maritain's first book,[15] which appeared later, would be an attack on Bergsonism as a philosophy, his subsequent work still acknowledged Bergson by name as one of the figures who had sought to preserve a whole set of realities that had to be defended if human life itself was not to be reduced to a mere play of atoms and forces. For Bergson, it was not possible to get a hold on the concrete, living, and dynamic realities of human life by way of abstract concepts, which by their very nature were both removed from those realities and fixed. For at least a first understanding of the kinds of realities that cannot be left out of any true account of what it means to be a human being, said Bergson, we need something like an organic intellectual *intuition* rather than a rational analysis.

[15] Maritain wrote two books critical of Bergsonism, the more important being *La philosophie bergsonienne*, which went through several editions in which Maritain softened his criticisms somewhat. Interestingly, one of the leaders of the neo-Thomist revival, A.-G. Sertillanges, produced a critical treatment, *Henri Bergson et le catholicisme* (Paris: Flammarion, 1941), but left open the possibility that some of Bergson's positions could be reconciled with Catholic thought. Bergson actually would have become a Catholic at the end of his life had he not wished to abandon French Jews, of which he was one, during the Nazi occupation in World War II. He died as a result of standing in line in the cold to register with the occupiers. A good short appraisal of Bergson is Leszek Kołakowski's *Bergson* (New York: Oxford University Press, 1985).

The two main modern philosophical positions—the turn inward and scientific reductionism—are common modern philosophical problems that faced all the neo-Thomists (as well as the Catholic philosophers who turned to other traditions of thought in the twentieth century). It is not surprising, then, that, quite different from Thomas' own approach to philosophical matters, epistemology and the conditions of our knowledge about characteristically human things, on the one hand, and a move to reconceptualize being, on the other, bulked large in their writings and teaching. Indeed, it would not be an exaggeration to say that already by the 1920s Neoscholasticism was set on two specifically modern paths: a transcendental Thomism that partly accepted the need for the inward turn and an existential Thomism that rejected that turn while emphasizing a different notion of being. Joseph Maréchal in Belgium and Karl Rahner in Germany (with Bernard Lonergan in Canada, to some extent) were eminent members of the first group; Jacques Maritain and Étienne Gilson in France were among the leading lights in the second group.

Existential Thomism: Maritain, Simon, Gilson

Jacques Maritain (1882–1973) was certainly the most influential, and perhaps the greatest, of the Neoscholastic philosophers. A genial personality and an eloquent writer, he formed friendships with many French artists, poets, musicians, and secular intellectuals. That breadth of human scope is reflected in the ways he combined a rigorous Thomism with more than the usual range of intellectual, social, and aesthetic concerns. He came to Thomism by an unusual path. His family background was secular and Republican, which in France is often associated with militant anti-Catholicism. Indeed, his maternal grandfather was the prominent Republican statesman Jules Favre. Though he had tensions with his family, this heritage meant that, when Maritain converted to Catholicism, he brought a living link with France's secular and non-Catholic achievements to his work that enriched its connections to the modern world in multiple ways. At the university, he met Raïssa Oumansov, a young Jewish woman who had come with her family from Russia to Paris. As noted earlier, they both felt that the world presented by modern scientific materialism was possibly true but unbearable, and they therefore made a pact that if they could not find something worth living for, they would commit suicide together. Maritain studied biology, but he then came under the influence of Charles Péguy, himself a remarkable Catholic figure who, among many other things, was a student and brilliant expositor of Bergson.[16] All of them were also affected by an eccentric, prophet-like figure, Léon Bloy, who would later become their godfather when the Maritains entered the Church.[17]

For the Maritains, as for many others at the beginning of the twentieth century, Bergson represented a way of philosophizing that made room for life, intuition, and meaning. But Maritain began to study Aquinas at the behest of Raïssa's spiritual director, Humbert Clérissac, O.P., which moved him away from his enthusiasm for Bergsonism in strictly philosophical terms. Maritain would always maintain respect, gratitude, and affection toward the man who had led him out of despair—and who would approach the Catholic Church himself later in life. But Maritain thought that in moving away from an overemphasis on abstraction in philosophy, Bergson had lost a grip on crucial distinctions. In Bergson, Maritain argued, there were no essences, just intuition of the concrete and individual. Concepts for Bergson were merely empty forms useful for practical goals. Therefore, the study of being and metaphysics became impossible. Change was the only reality, and God and the world were collapsed into each other. Needless to say, under this dispensation, Christian dogmas could not refer to anything real. As Maritain put it with a young man's bravado: "A poor peasant who believes that God created heaven and earth and who believes in the Holy Sacrament of the Altar knows more about truth, being, and substance than Plotinus, Spinoza, and the whole of Bergsonism."[18]

[16] Bergson was to say of Péguy: "He had a marvelous gift for stepping beyond the materiality of beings, going beyond it and penetrating to the soul. Thus it is that he knew my most secret thought, such as I have never expressed it, such as I would have wished to express it": Charles Péguy, *Basic Verities*, trans. Anne and Julian Green (New York: Pantheon, 1943), 9.

[17] For the Maritains' early life, see Jean-Luc Barré, *Jacques and Raïssa Maritain: Beggars for Heaven*, trans. Bernard E. Doering (Notre Dame, Ind.: University of Notre Dame Press, 2005). For a brief overview of the life and the works, the best introduction is Ralph McInerny, *The Very Rich Hours of Jacques Maritain: A Spiritual Life* (Notre Dame, Ind.: University of Notre Dame Press, 2003). Jude P. Dougherty, *Jacques Maritain: An Intellectual Profile* (Washington, D.C.: Catholic University of America Press, 2003), is insightful.

[18] *La philosophie bergsonienne* (Paris: Rivière, 1914), 306.

Partly because of his early experiences outside the Church, Maritain, more than any other single figure among the Neoscholastics, addressed the full range of modern problems envisioned by Leo XIII's call for renewal. Maritain himself noted that the obligations of the true modern Thomist were twofold:

> We must defend the traditional wisdom and the continuity of the *Philosophia Perennis* against the prejudices of modern individualism, in so far as it values, seeks and delights in novelty for its own sake, and is interested in a system of thought only in so far as it is a creation, the creation of a novel conception of the world. But equally we must show that this wisdom is eternally young and always inventive, and involves a fundamental need, inherent in its very being, to grow and renew itself. And so doing we must combat the prejudices of those who would fix it at a particular stage of its development and fail to understand its essentially progressive nature.[19]

Maritain could not only write brilliantly and movingly, as in the passage just cited, but he followed his own advice and addressed himself to a truly staggering number of topics: epistemology, metaphysics, existentialism, ethics, political philosophy, education, history, art and poetry, science, Judaism, Protestantism, and practical politics. He was also prodigiously productive. The French edition of the complete works[20] of Jacques and Raïssa Maritain (he always gave her credit for much of what he achieved) runs to sixteen volumes of about 1200 pages each.

Two of his major titles, *The Degrees of Knowledge* and *The Range of Reason*, in themselves indicate the amplitude of his purely philosophical scope. In *The Degrees of Knowledge*,[21] probably his masterwork and arguably the greatest work of the Thomist revival, he coined the term "eidetic intuition". As the very words indicate, he was hoping to suggest the way the mind executes a conceptual grasp of the *eidos*, or "form", of things—and therefore has a grip on large categories—and at the same time has an intuition more concrete than is allowed

[19] Jacques Maritain, *A Preface to Metaphysics* (New York: Omega Mentor, 1962), 10.

[20] Jacques et Raïssa Maritain, *Oeuvres complètes* (Fribourg, Switz.: Éditions Universitaires; Paris: Éditions Saint-Paul, 1982–1999).

[21] First published in French, as *Distinguer pour unir, ou, Les degrés du savoir* (Paris: Desclée de Brouwer, 1932), and trans. Bernard Wall and Margot R. Adamson as *The Degrees of Knowledge* (London: G. Bles, Centenary Press, 1937).

by most theories of abstraction. The mere fact that he introduced the term "intuition" here indicates a debt to Bergson. But, unlike Bergson, Maritain began with the intuition of being, not motion, as the source of intelligibility.[22] He would refine these notions in *Existence and the Existent*[23] as further study of Saint Thomas, by Maritain and others, made it clear in the first half of the twentieth century that the historical Thomas had placed an emphasis on the intelligibility of existence before that of essence. Contact with the real had to precede concepts. Working at the very edge of our understanding of how it is we come to know that things exist and what those things are, Maritain made room both for a kind of intuition, but an intuition that also led to conceptual knowledge and, with it, to stable ideas of form, clear distinctions among kinds of things, and the proper place of scientific, moral, aesthetic, and religious knowledge—and for the real possibility of metaphysics. By these distinctions (the French title of *The Degrees of Knowledge* started out as *Distinguish to Unite: The Degrees of Knowledge*), Maritain was even able to conclude with pages explaining how mystical experience was related to, but not of the same as, conceptual knowledge of God.

Perhaps the most important result of all these distinctions was Maritain's identification of the three degrees of abstraction as they existed in Aristotle and the application of those distinctions to the modern

[22] In *A Preface to Metaphysics*, Maritain takes pains to explain what this intuition is and is not: "It is a very simple sight, superior to any discursive reasoning or demonstration, because it is the source of demonstration. It is a sight whose content and implication no words of human speech can exhaust or adequately express and in which in a moment of decisive emotion, as it were, of spiritual conflagration, the soul is in contact, a living, penetrating, and illuminating contact, with a reality which it touches and which takes hold of it.... The characteristics of intuition as I have just described them may seem at first sight those of M. Bergson's intuition. They seem so, in truth, but with the important difference that he denies that his intuition is intellectual. I, on the other hand, have just maintained that the object par excellence of intuition is being, but that that intuition is intellectual. This is remote indeed from the Bergsonian philosophy" (50–51). At the same time, this intellectual intuition has to be distinguished from conceptual knowledge. Kant, says Maritain, never had it: "What is the explanation of this? That it is difficult. It is not indeed difficult like an operation which it is hard to perform, whose successful performance demands expert skill. For there is nothing simpler. It was precisely because he sought it by a technique, an intellectual technique of extreme subtlety, that Kant failed to attain it" (52). Maritain compares this intuition to *hearing* and *listening* to being, rather than "composing answers" (53).

[23] *Existence and the Existent*, trans. Lewis Galantière and Gerald B. Phelan (New York: Pantheon, 1948).

context. For many modern thinkers, there is merely a physical world that we mysteriously come to know and may describe by means of mathematics and science. Because of the more precise distinctions that Thomistic-Aristotelian thought brings to such questions, we can see that there is indeed a first degree of abstraction in the physical sciences—the sciences of the mobile, *perinoetical* knowledge, in Maritain's terminology, when we are looking at empirical facts themselves; *dianoetical* when we raise that knowledge to a true philosophy of nature, a second degree of abstraction from these sciences in physico-mathematical categories such as number, quantity, and extension; and beyond both, as its name attests, a meta-physics that deals with fundamental matters, *ananoetical* in the sense that it relies, not on direct observation, but on indirect knowledge of creatures and analogical reasoning. Furthermore, metaphysics does not, as in some of its mistaken uses in the past, replace the necessary empirical study of nature and the development of physico-mathematical studies; rather, it contextualizes the findings in science and directs them according to what was classically know as wisdom, a kind of science in itself with its own rules. These distinctions do not rely on any Catholic or even "religious" position, since they were already present in the pre-Christian pagan, Aristotle, in Maritain's view, and go a long way toward restoring many characteristically human realities. Nonetheless, they also open up a path for the specific revelation on which theology reflects, since, in distinguishing a proper understanding of each science, they also show certain questions that cannot be answered by any merely rational investigation and therefore invite solutions that are supra-rational without contradicting the properly rational.

In a historical perspective, Maritain was immensely influential, probably the most prominent Catholic philosopher of the twentieth century prior to the Second Vatican Council. Two of his greatest and most enduring books were given as lecture series. *Man and the State* originated from the 1949 Walgreen Lectures at the University of Chicago, and *Creative Intuition in Art and Poetry* from the 1952 A. W. Mellon Lectures at the National Gallery of Art in Washington, D.C. In addition, Charles de Gaulle persuaded Maritain to serve as French ambassador to the Holy See after World War II, a post from which he was able to influence the early steps toward the creation of the European Union. He also was one of the principal authors of the

U.N. Universal Declaration of Human Rights. Few philosophers in history have had as direct an influence on the public affairs of their time as Maritain.

In this and many other respects, he was fulfilling Leo XIII's central goal in calling for a revival of Thomism in *Aeterni Patris*: a renewal of the modern social order on sound philosophical and theological lines. Beginning right after World War I, Maritain was not only publishing foundational philosophical work, but was concerned with artistic questions (*Art et scolastique*, 1920; *Georges Rouault*, 1926; *Réponse à Cocteau*, 1926) as well as with prayer (*De la vie d'oraison*, 1922) and the Catholic-Protestant dispute. Maritain consciously pursued studies of poetry and art because he believed someone needed to counteract pernicious *cultural* influences, such as André Gide's, in France. He even founded a book series, *Le roseau d'or*, toward that end. But unlike many other Catholic culture warriors, Maritain—perhaps owing to the influence of Raïssa, who was both a mystic and a poet—never forgot that good art has its own rules and that the work must first be well made before other considerations intrude. In a famous formula, he compared art and prudence: prudence is the right reason of what is to be done (*recta ratio agibilium*) and art is the right reason of what is to be made (*recta ratio factibilium*). These are large Thomistic ideas, but Maritain's astute treatments of actual artworks and specific poems show that he understood art in practice as well as in theory.

He also was engaged in politics, at first—though he had started out as vaguely socialist—in the monarchism of Action française. With Charles Maurras, he contributed his own money to found the movement's paper, *La Revue universelle*. But he left the movement when it was condemned by Rome in 1929. As totalitarian clouds began to gather in the 1930s, he turned more directly to social questions and political philosophy, most notably with *Humanisme intégral* (*Integral Humanism*; 1936), *Les Juifs parmi les nations* (The Jews among the Nations; 1938), *Scholasticism and Politics* (1940), *Le crépuscule de la civilization* (*The Twilight of Civilization*; 1941), *Les droits de l'homme et la loi naturelle* (*The Rights of Man and Natural Law*; 1942), *Christianisme et démocratie* (*Christianity and Democracy*; 1943), *Education at the Crossroads* (1943), and *La personne et le bien commun* (*The Person and the Common Good*; 1947), among many other titles. Maritain also gave a series of radio broadcasts to the French people from New York as part of the war effort of the Free French.

This melding of philosophical and political interests will probably remain Maritain's most lasting influence in both the theoretical and practical spheres. Maritain had an enormous influence in the development of Christian Democracy, both as an intellectual system and as a political party, in many parts of the world, but especially in Europe and Latin America. The marriage to Raïssa sensitized him to the Jewish question, and he influenced the recalibration of Catholic attitudes toward Jews at Vatican II.[24] His careful philosophical analysis of the human person—a being located between the twin modern distortions of individualism and collectivism—lent great weight to the larger Catholic project in the twentieth century of seeking to reconcile Church teaching with modern democracy. Maritain proposed a "true humanism" rooted in a rich appreciation both of the person, a term that took on a more precise notion in his work and in subsequent Catholic social reflection, and of society as "personalist and communitarian". This proper view of the person recognized an individual side to each of us that has to be respected by governments in protecting rights to religious liberty and free expression. But persons are not radically free-standing entities, as they are presented in many philosophical systems since Descartes. All individuals learn to speak and act in communities, and we can only flourish when we participate in communities—political, social, economic, cultural, religious—that nourish personhood. In this perspective, persons do not merely claim individual rights; they acknowledge fundamental duties to the common good as well. Clearly, this presented a program not only for the Christian democrat political parties, but for the later emphasis on persons and a proper understanding of democracy in Pope Paul VI, a friend of Maritain's, and in John Paul II.

This line of social thought had a great success in the twentieth century. The whole history of Europe and Latin America, especially after World War II, might have been different without it, and the eventual defeat of Communism, in part through the influence of John Paul II's social vision, owes something to Maritain's efforts. But

[24] See Robert Royal, ed., *Jacques Maritain and the Jews* (Notre Dame, Ind.: American Maritain Association, 1993).

since the demise of some of the movements that called it forth, particularly National Socialism and Communism, Maritain's tradition of true humanism—Christian humanism—has had few successors. Figures such as Michael Novak have sought to perpetuate the basic vision of *Man and the State* and to combine it with further reflections about the need for economic liberties, a position that influenced John Paul II's encyclical *Centesimus Annus*, which spoke of the need to help people participate in "the circle of production and exchange". But the humanism Maritain espoused also had its weak spots. As he himself observed, the nations of the world agreed to the Universal Declaration of Human Rights, and that was fine, just so long as you did not ask for the basis of agreement. And in fact, institutions like the United Nations and the European Union have strayed far from the original vision and have become some of the principal promoters of rights to abortion and gay marriage around the world, to take just two controversial issues. Thin agreement was bought at the price of a loss of human depth and a foundation in truth

Nevertheless, Maritain's *Man and the State*[25] is one of the strongest books on Catholic social theory to come out of the Thomist revival. Maritain begins by carefully examining the age-old distinction between community and society, the former more a work of nature and the latter more a work of reason and intention. He also seeks to clarify the meanings of terms such as body politic, political society, people, nation, common good, and natural law. He is particularly concerned that all these be distinguished from the state: "The *Body Politic* or the *Political Society* is the whole. The *State* is a part—the topmost part—of this whole."[26] The topmost part, but only a part and meant to serve the people as a whole. In fact, Maritain sees the reconfiguration of the modern state as a burning issue: "It is necessary that many functions now exercised by the State should be distributed among the various autonomous organs of a pluralistically structured body politic—either after a period of State capitalism or of State socialism, or, as is to be hoped, in the very process of the present evolution. It is also necessary that the people have the will, and the means, to assert their own control over the State."[27]

[25] Jacques Maritain, *Man and the State* (Washington, D.C.: Catholic University of America Press, 1998), is one of the best recent editions of the 1951 original.

[26] Ibid., 10.

[27] Ibid., 27.

Some of this may seem obscure unless we see the mistaken notions that Maritain is seeking to combat. In Nazism, for example, the people (*Volk*) were identified with the state, a community being made to do duty for a society, in Maritain's terminology, since a state must be a willed thing. Similarly, Fascism sought to identify the nation with the state in Mussolini's totalitarian system, and Marxism singled out a single class (the workers) and its representatives as the true constituents of the state. Besides rejecting all these confusions and the distortions they introduced into political life, Maritain makes a far more radical break with modern thought in his analysis of the notion of sovereignty, which for him seems to lie behind all these distortions. Quoting Abraham Lincoln, he says that government of, by, and for the people comes closest to what he is seeking to establish. But Maritain warns that even asserting the sovereignty of the people is a mistake, as recent political developments had shown. Sovereignty does not lie with the people, class, race, body politic, or any of the other entities he has been at such great pains to define: "In the eyes of a sound political philosophy there is no sovereignty, that is, no natural and inalienable right to *transcendent* or *separate* supreme power in political society. Neither the Prince nor the King nor the Emperor were really sovereign, though they bore the sword and the attributes of sovereignty. Nor is the State sovereign; nor are even the people sovereign. God alone is sovereign."[28] As a corrective to misguided political claims of various types in the twentieth century, this is a breathtaking assertion. But it also perhaps reveals a limitation in Maritain's overall picture, which goes on to address actual political mechanisms, rights, church-state relations, and the global political order. God may be the only true sovereign, but in pluralistic modern societies where significant segments of the population dispute or do not believe this particular notion of sovereignty, how can such a vision operate? Even more, how in concrete practice will God's sovereignty be exercised through what must, at every level, be human judgments about what that sovereignty requires? Maritain corrected many errors and added much toward a theory of Christian democracy, but given modern societies, he did not—and perhaps could not—offer solutions for the practical difficulties of modern governance, which Leo XIII had hoped Thomism might provide.

[28] Ibid., 24.

One of Maritain's students, Yves Simon (1903–1961), made some additional Thomist contributions to philosophy and political philosophy. Ever since the creation of philosophy in ancient Greece, philosophers have had a reputation for being impractical and unreliable in ordinary matters. The great early philosopher Thales, according to a well-known story, allegedly fell into a hole because he was paying so much attention to contemplating the stars that he did not watch where he was going. Thales had the last laugh when he used his knowledge of meteorology to predict a large bumper crop of olives and made a killing by monopolizing all the olive presses before the harvest came in. Still, the image of the philosopher as a dreamer continues, and most philosophers who have turned their attention to practical matters—especially politics—have not shown themselves to be anywhere near as capable as Thales.

Yves Simon was a notable modern exception to the rule. He was also one of the truly great theoretical minds of the twentieth century. Among his many books, it would be enough to look at *The Great Dialogue of Nature and Space*, *The Tradition of Natural Law*, *A General Theory of Authority*, and *Philosophy of Democratic Government*—the last a true gem, combining theory and practice—to be convinced of that fact. Simon was not the type of philosopher who elaborated theories and then demanded that the world conform to them. He saw it as a moral task to understand human reality, and he looked upon the disorders visible throughout the West in the twentieth century as political but, more importantly, philosophical matter to be examined. If one or more countries make political errors, the remedy may be found via the normal mechanisms of politics. When countries set off on evil pathways because of philosophical errors or vicious ideologies, then normal politics is not enough. We have to think through the principles behind the situation both to fix the immediate problem and to prevent it from growing into an even larger threat in the future.

The two most urgent international questions in Simon's time, of course, were the challenge of Communism at home and abroad and the aggression of Nazism and Fascism in several guises. In the first pages of *A Philosophy of Democratic Government*,[29] he asserts, as others

[29] Yves R. Simon, *Philosophy of Democratic Government* (Notre Dame, Ind.: University of Notre Dame Press, 1993).

have done, that the two ideologies are quite similar, though partisans of either are horrified at the comparison. He then goes on to show in depth and detail why that is the case and why both are deficient from a properly democratic stance in both theory and practice. Typically for Simon, he also explores questions of the nature of proper authority, a difficult problem in both democratic and totalitarian states.

One of Simon's strengths as a political observer is his ability to hold to principle without turning it into an ideology, while appraising various particularities. His practice parallels his own theoretical efforts to explain the mysterious ways in which virtuous character and moral principles are needed to reach the point of "command" at which action may be undertaken with confidence. In the battle over Nazism and Fascism, for instance, he is clear in his mind about the goal of liberty and political decency—and at the same time critical of various French Catholics and others who were willing, in Simon's view, to betray France to the Germans in order to settle old scores. Since the French Revolution, French Catholics had a justifiable suspicion about the ideals of the Republicans, who had slaughtered Catholics and, in the government of Émile Combes, suppressed religious institutions in the name of liberty, equality, and fraternity. That ancient division into the "two Frances" made many Catholics vulnerable to the Fascist propaganda that sought to portray quite vicious authoritarians as virtuous restorers of a properly hierarchical society and a resistance to the atheistic depredations of international Communism. The anti-Catholic atrocities of the Spanish Republicans, who had links to the Soviet Union, in the 1930s only seemed to confirm that judgment.

Simon deplored the French and Spanish Republican outrages as much as any Catholic and was not in the least sympathetic to the Communist cause anywhere, least of all in France. But he was also not under the delusion that Fascism promised any good in the world. It took real courage to say this openly because highly influential figures in France and Rome such as Réginald Garrigou-Lagrange were also strong supporters of right-wing forces. Action française, the French monarchist movement, had drawn the allegiance of many, including the young Maritain, who later repented of this confusion between Thomist principles and authoritarian politics. Though the movement was condemned for its atheism in 1926 and Catholics who continued to be members after early 1927 were barred from the sacraments, the condemnation was lifted by Pius XII in 1939, partly in response to the slaughter the Republicans had carried out in the Spanish Civil War.

Simon understood that the French tragedy, which led to its submission to Nazi Germany, was the result of many internal factors. The only solution he believed to have been available—alliance with the Soviets against Nazi aggression (as America had accepted) while resisting Communist ascendancy within France—was not one that the French were able to carry out owing to longstanding intellectual and historical circumstances. Perhaps this colossal failure also shows the effective limits of practical wisdom at times. It is not a "science" in the strong sense of the word, but even when deliberation and good judgment result in what appears a wise course to pursue, it is not always possible actually to take such a course. Simon allowed himself angry denunciations of the "fools" and "traitors" who prepared the downfall of France and the spread of Nazism by their inability to analyze the situation properly and their readiness to rationalize collaboration with Germany. England and America, by contrast, were able to ally themselves with the Soviets against the Nazis without much fuss, but they were not countries with France's history of a strong Communist presence.

Toward the end of his brilliant book about the downfall of France, *The Road to Vichy*,[30] Simon explicitly states a principle that was implicit throughout much of his other thinking about practical wisdom in public affairs: the need of an energizing *myth* to unite various, otherwise ineffectual, aspirations. It may seem odd for a philosopher to be recommending myth as a form of wisdom or practicality—something in dispute at least since the pre-Socratics. But one measure of the "practically practical wisdom" Simon spent much effort trying to identify was the ability to see that, in order to move groups of men, such entities as myth are necessary. A cool science will never do, either theoretically or practically, because the philosopher who is not merely going to withdraw from human affairs, as if they were beneath the notice of an Olympian rationality, is going to have to reckon with the perennial role of myth in human communities.

[30] Yves R. Simon, *The Road to Vichy, 1918–1938*, trans. James A. Corbett and George J. McMorrow (Lanham, Md.: University Press of America, 1988).

Indeed, with or without philosophers, myths—either good or bad—will move public opinion. Better, then, a myth of freedom that cannot entirely describe the future because the future will depend on the uses made of freedom. The myth of freedom can assert with passion, however, that the things the tyrants cannot offer, "neither truth nor freedom nor justice",[31] are precisely the goals sought by all who pursue what is right in every country. The international cooperation of various peoples—the Free French, the Free Poles, even the Free Germans—was "already converging to form one great vision which will be the victorious myth of the future: *the sublime vision of the liberation of the world*".[32] In the continuing confusion about the nature of practical wisdom and its uses in a now globalized world, Simon's work continues to offer a rich reflection, an extension of Maritain, on what international order may yet be and how a wise practicality may yet make it a reality.

Étienne Gilson

The other Thomist who had a high public profile, again even in secular academic circles, was Maritain's fellow Frenchman and almost exact contemporary, Étienne Gilson (1884–1978). Though his family was traditionally Catholic and he seems never to have strayed from that heritage, Gilson, like Maritain, came to his Thomism by an indirect and independent route. He studied philosophy at the Sorbonne, and his area of specialization—not surprising in France—was Descartes and post-Cartesian philosophy. At the suggestion of Lucien Lévy-Bruhl, his adviser, Gilson wrote his doctoral dissertation on Scholastic elements in Descartes.[33] Almost a century later, it seems unremarkable that someone might look into the medieval philosophical currents that might have influenced Descartes. But at the time, a certain historiography dominated philosophy; simply put, it was assumed by most philosophers that real philosophy died out with the Greeks and Romans. What passed for philosophy in Christian times

[31] Ibid., 203.
[32] Ibid., 202.
[33] Étienne Gilson, *La liberté chez Descartes et la théologie* (Paris: Alcan, 1913).

was really theology—theology based on revelation, at that. "Rational" philosophy, which revived with Descartes, simply had nothing in common with what had intervened for a millennium and more. Gilson discovered, however, that this mythical framework was simply false, and it gave him the bases for his penetrating studies in the history of medieval philosophy, which it would not be too strong to say revolutionized thinking about the subject. He also made important contributions to the hotly disputed notions of what a "Christian" philosophy might be said to mean.

For example, whatever the great seventeenth-century thinkers such as Descartes, Leibniz, and Spinoza (and those who have studied them) thought, Christianity had introduced new material into philosophical reflection. The kind of God we find in Descartes, in all essentials the traditional Christian God, was not present in Greek thinking. The infinite Creator who is self-subsisting and maintains all things in being was not in Plato or Aristotle or later Hellenistic thinkers. Similarly, the immortal soul and other human features as they appear in Descartes and his successors owe a great deal to medieval thought. The standard reaction to these discoveries at the time would have been to dismiss them as residues of discarded superstition that have no place in purely rational systems of thought. Gilson made precisely the opposite argument: just as Greek religious notions had shaped the rational systems of ancient philosophers, Christian concepts had shaped later philosophy and added to the ideas philosophy explored. In other words, the study of what Gilson insisted on calling "Christian philosophy" was as legitimate as studying Greek philosophy.

For Gilson, philosophy done within a Christian horizon was not thereby illegitimate. Many outsiders, for example, thought that Christian philosophy was basically a uniform rationalization for irrational truths. An astute historian and analyst, Gilson was able to show that actually philosophical systems varied widely in the Middle Ages—something now perceptible because of the groundbreaking work by him and other historians of medieval thought, such as Denifle, De Wulf, and van Steenberghen. Leo XIII had praised the common philosophy in the Middle Ages best exemplified in Saint Thomas. Gilson found there was no such common philosophy, if you looked closely, though there was a common "spirit of medieval philosophy", the title of one of his best-known books.[34] That spirit meant doing philosophy within a certain set of theological ideas, but that starting point made it no more illegitimate than, say, a modern philosophy that tries to think about the nature of God on the basis of the current givens of Big Bang cosmology. On the contrary, medieval Christian thinkers—like their Arab and Jewish counterparts—were aware of the respective claims of reason and revelation, and Saint Thomas Aquinas distinguished between the two with particular care.

As Gilson observed in his brief but masterful *Reason and Revelation in the Middle Ages*:

> To have faith is to assent to something because it is revealed by God. And now, what is it to have science? It is to assent to something that we perceive as true in the natural light of reason. The essential difference between these two distinct orders of assent should be carefully kept in mind by anybody dealing with the relations of Reason and Revelation. I know by reason that something is true because *I see* that it is true; but I believe that something is true because *God has said it.* In these two cases the cause of my assent is specifically different, consequently science and faith should be held as two specifically different kinds of assent.[35]

He takes great pains in this work and others to show that Aquinas, great reasoner that he was, even warned Christians against making it appear that revealed truths like the Trinity, Incarnation, and Redemption can be explained rationally. Thomas says, "And it is useful to consider this, lest anyone, presuming to demonstrate what is of faith, should bring forward reasons that are not cogent, so as to give occasion to unbelievers to laugh, thinking that on such grounds we believe things that are of faith" (*ST* I, q. 46, a. 2, 243).

This historical vision of philosophy through the ages and the relative roles of reason and revelation not only influenced Catholic institutions all over the world (Gilson was asked to help found the Pontifical Institute of Mediaeval Studies in Toronto in 1929), but was

[34] Étienne Gilson, *The Spirit of Medieval Philosophy*, trans. A. H. C. Downes, Gifford Lectures (New York: Charles Scribner's Sons, 1940).

[35] Étienne Gilson, *Reason and Revelation in the Middle Ages* (New York: C. Scribner's Sons, 1938), 72–3. "Science", here, is meant to indicate certain knowledge on the basis of true data and proper reasoning, not the various sciences as we use the word in ordinary language.

also much appreciated in the secular world. Like Maritain's, several of Gilson's books were given as prestigious lecture series: *The Spirit of Mediaeval Philosophy* started as the 1931–1932 Gifford Lectures at the University of Aberdeen in Scotland; *The Unity of Philosophical Experience* came from Gilson's William James lectures at Harvard (1936–1937); and *Reason and Revelation in the Middle Ages* collects the 1937 Richard Lectures at the University of Virginia. Gilson spoke to the growing interest in all things medieval that had begun in the nineteenth century with Romanticism, and the fact that he spoke and wrote from a Catholic perspective seems to have been outweighed at these eminent secular institutions by the freshness of his thinking and the formidable scope of his scholarship. He also spoke with great precision: people who heard both Maritain and Gilson lecture say that the former, in keeping with his whole life, roamed over vast realms and left the listeners to figure it all out afterward. By contrast, Gilson was very orderly in his presentations, often finishing seconds before the bell would ring to close the academic hour with an epigram that summed up everything he had just said.[36]

In addition to his labors to make the idea of Christian philosophy credible, Gilson is often described as the originator of existential Thomism, which means something different from what the two terms linked together might seem to suggest. The existence he emphasized was God's, the "I am who am" spoken to Moses. Several earlier modern interpreters had claimed that Thomas had emphasized the form or essence of God, but Gilson saw that the distinctive thing about God was that his act of pure existence *was his essence.* Great intervening philosophers such as Cardinal Cajetan and Francisco Suárez had misunderstood this, said Gilson. In Thomas *agere sequitur esse* ("action follows being"), and God, who is Pure Act, is also Pure Being. Humans and all other created things with which we are familiar in the world are radically different. All created things have both an "essence", what they are, and actual existence, communicated to them from the source of all existence, which is God. For Gilson, there is a "real distinction" between existence and essence—a concept to be much debated among Thomists—but both are present in each created being. Modern "existentialists", however, had mistakenly attributed being without essence

[36] I owe this characterization to Kenneth Schmitz in a private conversation.

to the human person, a radical separation from anything that would give human life a status and direction, which naturally resulted in anguish, nausea, absurdity, and despair when used by a figure like Jean-Paul Sartre. Gilson traces this out in fullest form in his *Being and Some Philosophers*.[37]

Gilson wrote as well on multiple less abstract subjects that lie out on the borders of philosophy, such as Dante, music, and painting. Though he clearly did not have quite the wingspan of a Maritain, his historical reach was far and wide. His studies of Augustine, Bonaventure, Duns Scotus, and Thomas Aquinas are penetrating and remain worth reading.[38] But he discerned a certain scheme within Christian philosophy that has had many critics, even among those who share Gilson's enthusiasm for Aquinas; and he himself could be bitingly critical of others—even Maritain—who did not see things his way. The controversies cannot be looked at very extensively here, but we may at least trace some of their general lines.

The largest controversy Gilson's work provoked involved his insistence on a strict historical reconstruction of the meaning of Thomas' texts. This exactness was proper to a historian of philosophy who lived during a period when it first became possible to appreciate fully the differences among medieval philosophers as well as the departures from the strict letter introduced by later interpreters. But Gilson pushed this view quite far in two ways. First, he attacked what he saw as the false and misleading interpretation of Thomas put forward in the often consulted commentaries by Cajetan and John of Saint Thomas (Jean Poinsot). Any interpretation, of course, will differ of necessity from an original by the mere fact that it is not identical with the text on which it comments. Gilson laid into two of the most respected guides to Saint Thomas, in effect rejecting the whole tradition of Thomistic interpretation in favor of an allegedly purer historical reconstruction of Thomas—something others criticized as itself a debatable interpretation. Gilson's belligerence about his own view—which grew sharper

[37] Étienne Gilson, *Being and Some Philosophers*, 2nd ed., rev. and enlarged (Toronto: Pontifical Institute of Mediaeval Studies, 1952). The remarks about Sartre and existentialism appear on page 152.

[38] Étienne Gilson, *The Christian Philosophy of Saint Augustine* (New York: Random House, 1960); *The Philosophy of St. Bonaventure*, trans. Dom Illtyd Trethowan and F.J. Sheed (New York: Sheed & Ward, 1938); *Jean Duns Scot: Introduction à ses positions fondamentales* (Paris: Vrin, 1952).

as he grew older—did not represent the best side even of his own achievements, which involved, in works such as *The Unity of Philosophical Experience* and *Being and Some Philosophers*, original insights into the meaning of the history of philosophy for philosophy itself and were not limited to mere Thomistic comment.

In addition to this historical controversy, Gilson let fly at contemporary efforts to do what Leo XIII had asked for in *Aeterni Patris*: the application of Thomas' philosophy to contemporary cultural and social questions. It might be argued that Gilson's approach observed the letter but disregarded the spirit of Saint Thomas, who was not at all reticent about thinking in original ways about problems that arose in his own day. Gilson's targets even included Maritain, who clearly was thinking creatively with the light of Thomistic philosophy. In the 1950s, Gilson had tried to get Maritain to join him in the attack on the great older Thomistic commentators, without much success, although Gilson claimed Maritain agreed with him. After Maritain's death, Gilson read his posthumous *Untrammeled Approaches* and wrote in a letter to Armand Maurer:

> I was naïvely maintaining that one cannot consider oneself a Thomist without first ascertaining the authentic meaning of Saint Thomas' doctrine, which only history can do; during all that time, he [Maritain] was considering himself a true disciple of Saint Thomas because he was *continuing* his thought. To strive to rediscover the meaning of the doctrine such as it had been in the mind of Thomas Aquinas was straight historicism. We had been talking at cross-purposes the whole time.[39]

Gilson is clearly confessing here a fixation on original meaning that is probably an impossibility to achieve and is not even the best way of characterizing his own original work. As with every great philosophical figure, there are various plausible interpretations of Saint Thomas, some that can be definitely discarded, but to demand a single and final determination of Thomas' thinking and to limit future Thomists to a

[39] Étienne Gilson and Jacques Maritain, *Deux approches de l'être: Correspondance 1923–1971*, ed. Géry Prouvost, Bibliothèque des textes philosophiques (Paris: Vrin, 1991), 275. On this and the broader relationship of the two philosophers, see Ralph McInerny, *The Very Rich Hours of Jacques Maritain: A Spiritual Life* (Notre Dame, Ind.: University of Notre Dame Press, 2003), 124–28.

mere reproduction of that seems to misconstrue the very nature of a large philosophical vision. A modern reader also cannot help wondering: Even if we could grasp that thought in its original form, what could it then mean for the Church and the world today?

Transcendental Thomism

Some Catholic philosophers involved in the Thomist revival took far more heterodox views of the use of Thomas than these relatively *en famille* disagreements. One current, transcendental Thomism, sought to engage several of the seeming foes of the whole Catholic project through a kind of intellectual jujitsu. Neo-Thomism generally recognized that since Descartes—and more recently in Hume and Kant—it had become difficult to argue from thoughts and images in the mind back to things in the world. Most neo-Thomists believed and would continue to believe that once the fatal Cartesian error was made of turning to the experience of the subject, there was no way out of the dead end of *subjectivism*. At the same time, the mechanistic view of nature had made it appear that man, too, was merely a machine. The enthusiasm for Bergson's *élan vital* and, as we saw earlier, for Maurice Blondel's philosophy of the dynamic subject was one symptom of the felt need of a different approach.

It was probably inevitable that someone would try to combine what seemed still living in Thomism with modern critical epistemologies (that is, theories of how we obtain knowledge) in the hope of responding to cultural challenges. One of the earliest leaders in this process was Pierre Rousselot (1878–1915), a Jesuit theologian.[40] He openly argued that certain portions of Thomas' philosophy and world view had been superseded by modern knowledge, but other elements—"architectonic theses"—could be saved along with "necessary absorptions" from modern thought. In his book *L'intellectualisme de Saint Thomas*, he argued that *intellectus* in Thomas should not be identified with the modern notion of *reason*. Intellect held within itself a living impulse toward life, love, and the Beatific Vision. It was not simply a device for assembling rationally coherent systems. In this

[40] On Rousselot, see McCool, *Neo-Thomists*, 97–116.

perspective, our limited concepts and mental images are not, despite Kant's proper warnings, shut out from the world; rather, they contain within them a drive toward affirmation of what is real, including ultimate reality. In a strong phrase, Rousselot likened this internal dynamism of the mind to "a natural drive to become an angel".[41] Though Rousselot died in combat early in the First World War, his work suggested pathways later traveled, to different destinations, by Joseph Maréchal, Karl Rahner, and Bernard Lonergan, all Jesuits.

Even in brief outline, it may be seen that this philosophical position obviously appeals to people who are already sympathetic to religion on other grounds. The modern Scottish philosopher John Haldane claims that transcendental Thomism's blend of Kant and Thomas, "though widespread in its influence among theologians, was never taken very seriously by philosophers".[42] The drive to become an angel may be a little too strong a spirit for more cool-headed philosophers; still, it may in fact contain various things worth considering. As odd as a rapprochement between Kant and Thomas may at first appear, Joseph Maréchal (1878–1944) followed Rousselot in believing that, though the proper objects of the human intellect were the essences of finite beings, the mind had a natural thrust toward Infinite Being.

Thomas, of course, also knew that the human mind could not grasp God, but he believed that we could arrive at some knowledge of him via an analogy of being derived from our knowledge of objects in the world. For example, when we use the terms "good" or "mighty" or "supreme" of God, we draw on our judgments of things we observe in the world and use them to hint at a reality that such terms can never express fully. By contrast, Kant believed that there were certain a prioris that made knowledge of a class of necessary truths possible (for example, $2 + 2 = 4$), but that we could never know things in themselves or God. Maréchal believed that a *rapprochement* of sorts between these two positions might be performed and therefore applied some of the procedures of Kant's "transcendental logic" to Thomas' categories in order to tease out similarities and differences. Both clearly allowed an active role for the mind in

[41] Quoted in ibid., 108.

[42] John Haldane, "Thomism", in *Routledge Encyclopedia of Philosophy* (London: Routledge, 1998), 3:384.

producing understanding of the object. As with everything involving Kant's theory of knowledge, these comparisons quickly head into deep waters, but it is worth looking at some of the features that emerged in Maréchal's five-volume study, aptly named *Le point de départ de la métaphysique*.[43]

Maréchal's contention was that the starting point for Saint Thomas' metaphysics was not an abstract idea of being, as earlier neo-Thomists had claimed, but instead presupposed an affirmation of God as Necessary Being prior to any judgment about contingent beings (that is, things in our world). Kant and Thomas disagreed on the possibility of metaphysical knowledge, according to Maréchal, but agreed on what such a knowledge would be: a clear intuition of Absolute Being. They agreed, at least in Maréchal's reading, that knowledge of beings in this world could not give us access to the Being that transcended this world. Yet Thomas believed we could discern Absolute Being by way of analogy. Was this just a result of Thomas' medieval beliefs, Maréchal asked, or did he notice something Kant had missed about the way the human mind construed phenomenal objects? Put slightly differently, were there conditions of the mind's activity besides those posited by Kant's transcendental logic (singular sensibles, universal categories of the understanding, the transcendental unity of apperception) that made not only knowledge of singular objects possible but the "appearance of any object of consciousness whatsoever"?[44]

Maréchal looked carefully at the similarities in their positions and pointed out a serious divergence: Thomas' assumption, following Aristotle, that the mind is also directed in its cognitive activity by a unified tendency toward its final end. Each individual act of knowing contingent objects led to further questions and knowledge, reflecting the insatiable mental attraction toward final causes, which Maréchal termed "the ontological affirmation". In this, Thomas was justified, in Maréchal's eyes, in regarding this drive as validating a kind of metaphysical realism. Despite Kant's affirmation of a saying emblematic of the whole Enlightenment—*Sapere aude* ("Dare to

[43] (Brussels: Éditions Universelles; Paris: Desclée de Brouwer, 1944–1949). The most extensive translation of excerpts from this work along with excellent commentary is Joseph Donceel, S.J., ed. and trans., *A Maréchal Reader* (New York: Herder and Herder, 1970).

[44] The language is McCool's, *Neo-Thomists*, 122.

know")—he had not noticed the overall significance of this dynamism of the mind. Aquinas had applied the transcendental method more thoroughly than Kant himself, said Maréchal, and had not neglected the fullness of our mental movement. Kant had partly recognized this lack in the *Critique of Pure Reason* by calling Absolute Being a "regulative ideal" as the mind goes about trying to unify more and more knowledge. But Kant famously denied that the mind, confined as it always is to phenomenal existence, can ever say anything about a transcendent God's existence.

Maréchal, applying the transcendental analysis to Kant himself, claimed that Kant failed to recognize that the intelligibility of the mind's move toward knowledge of all things depends on a final cause. And for Maréchal this meant that the complete and consistent application of the transcendental method ends in realism—and acceptance of God as infinite and necessary being. Otherwise, the appetite we discern as present in the dynamism of the intellect is directed toward nothing, which seems to be impossible by definition. For Maréchal, Kant's method led to Thomas' conclusions, a result that very few neo-Thomists or Kantians accepted or even believed was possible. In fact, it is fairly common to find highly critical remarks about Maréchal in the first- and second-rank Thomists of the first half of the twentieth century; they seemed to believe that any deviation from certain well-worn approaches to epistemology carried grave dangers. From the perspective of several decades later, however, whatever weaknesses may be attributed to Maréchal's efforts, it is clear that they were sincere and innovative and at least made a plausible case that what often seemed Kant's fatal move toward the subject and the consequent loss of the world in subjectivism was not necessarily the last word, even about Kant.

In the decade after Maréchal's final volume of *Le point de départ de la métaphysique*, another significant thinker was developing a different approach to securing philosophic truth and metaphysical propositions consonant with the Catholic faith. Bernard Lonergan (1904–1984), a Canadian Jesuit and professor of philosophy at the Gregorian University for many years, had a wide array of interests outside philosophy proper, including modern mathematics, science, and—not least—economics. His major contribution, *Insight: A Study of Human Understanding*, reflects that breadth of scope and has often been described as trying to accomplish the kind of synthesis of all knowledge in our time that Saint Thomas carried out in his, a modern *Summa* of sorts that proceeds by careful distinctions of its own.[45]

It is, in effect, two related books. Part I, "Insight as Activity", consists of more than three hundred densely argued pages that seek to show how a self-conscious recognition and analysis of our own understanding of the process of knowing in mathematics and the sciences and in the realms of common sense provide a unified field of knowledge and a grounding for a philosophy that can put forward a verifiable metaphysics:

> The beginning, then, not only is self-knowledge and self-appropriation but also a criterion of the real. If to convince oneself that knowing is understanding, one ascertains that knowing mathematics is understanding and knowing science is understanding and the knowledge of common sense is understanding, one ends up not only with a detailed account of understanding but also with a plan of what there is to be known. The many sciences lose their isolation from one another; the chasm between science and common sense is bridged; the structure of the universe proportionate to man's intellect is revealed; and as that revealed structure provides an object for a metaphysics, so the initial self-criticism provides a method for explaining how metaphysical and anti-metaphysical affirmations arise, for selecting those that are correct, and for eliminating those that patently spring from a lack of accurate self-knowledge.[46]

The quite ambitious goal here is both an understanding of various kinds of empirical knowledge and a way to adjudicate metaphysical claims, sorting truth from error—precisely what much modern philosophy, most notably in Kant's antinomies, denied was possible.

As is clear even from this brief description, although Lonergan, like many Catholic philosophers in the twentieth century, devoted a great deal of attention to epistemology and particularly to the question of how modern science and its new statistical side relate to more traditional questions of God and man, he did so starting from the more

[45] Bernard J. F. Lonergan, *Insight: A Study of Human Understanding* (New York: Philosophical Library, 1958).

[46] Ibid., xxix.

empirical tendencies of the English-speaking philosophical tradition. Even as he was in the process of setting up a very sophisticated and subtle argument for the need for "insight into insight" or the necessity of combating the flight from understanding in our time, he sounded a call to action: "The program, then, is both concrete and practical, and the motives for undertaking its execution reside, not in the realm of easy generalities, but in the difficult domain of matters of fact."[47] In this, he was trying a different approach to the common problems in the modern age: the slide into skepticism and relativism, often fueled by a mistaken understanding of the meaning of modern science.

Part 2, "Insight as Knowledge", therefore gathered together the wisdom gained by a thorough and supple understanding and demonstrated how a solid metaphysics can be developed on the basis of a personal investigation of our modes of knowing. In a sense, Lonergan was attempting something similar to what Husserl, at his best, and the stronger side of the phenomenological tradition were doing, though he set out from a non-Continental standpoint. He ascended from the understanding of what it means to have empirical knowledge, to what this signifies about the structure of the knower, to what the nature of the world must be to allow such knowing—in his own way restating the familiar progression from experience to understanding to judgment. Furthermore, Lonergan tried to account for the current resistance to this kind of knowledge in the biases and attachment to habits that mark much of modern civilization, which is built on an insubstantial pragmatism and error about the nature of reality. In this, he was responding in his own personal way to Leo XIII's desire in *Aeterni Patris* for a renewed philosophy to help renew the social order.

In a later work, *Method in Theology*, Lonergan would also explain how these hard-nosed analyses related to more traditional religious themes: "The facts of good and evil, of progress and decline, raise questions about the character of our universe. Such questions have been put in very many ways, and the answers given have been even more numerous. But behind this multiplicity there is a basic unity that comes to light in the exercise of the transcendental method. We can inquire into the possibility of fruitful inquiry. We can reflect on

[47] Ibid., xvii.

the nature of reflection. We can deliberate whether our deliberating is worth while. In each case, there arises the question of God."[48] A very serious labor of clarification and synthesis lay behind these apparently simple words. Lonergan's collected works are still being published and will eventually reach more than twenty volumes. At mid-century, his philosophical approach attracted a number of eminent disciples who wrote about him or produced important bodies of work in their own right, including Anthony Kenny, Bernard McGinn, Michael Novak, and David Tracy.[49] As often happens to a writer, after his death Lonergan's influence faded somewhat, perhaps because many other systems arose around the same time attempting to deal with the role of science and human understanding in the larger framework of human life. But he continues to have a strong influence within his own order and made a permanent contribution to the overall thinking of the Church as a whole in the modern world.

Against Dryness: Josef Pieper

As early as the 1930s, some writers were complaining about "the dreariness of Thomas-interpretation".[50] And it is not difficult to see why. Time has preserved the better and livelier works, but, as is the case in any field, those existed alongside much that was mediocre and dull—which may be passed over here in silence. One figure who was decidedly in the opposite category, however, was the German writer Josef Pieper (1904–1997). Pieper was a gifted expositor who brought life and freshness and original perspectives to everything he touched. This fluidity and vitality coexisted with a very exact and deeply internalized knowledge of both ancient and medieval philosophy, so that the personal and the traditional seemed to speak with one, unique voice in him, revealing truths that were far from commonplace. Pieper's writing is rarely technical in the bad sense of that term. Every page displays easy mastery of both the vocabulary and the substance of the philosophical material, but

[48] Bernard J. F. Lonergan, *Method in Theology* (New York: Herder and Herder, 1972), 101.

[49] In particular, see David Tracy, *The Achievement of Bernard Lonergan* (New York: Herder and Herder, 1970).

[50] Josef Pieper, *Guide to Thomas Aquinas* (San Francisco: Ignatius Press, 1991), 20.

his work also shows a constant concern to engage the reader and draw him into the subject by the most lucid and economical means. Unlike those of many other modern Thomists, Pieper's works are generally short, though not easy, in the sense of oversimplified. The great Swiss theologian Hans Urs von Balthasar said that Pieper wrote "thick little books".[51] The matter seems easy, but it needs to be meditated on to reach Pieper's own depth.

His lively little book *Guide to Thomas Aquinas* describes the basic qualities of the great Dominican: "In his first actions, I would say, there emerges the paradigmatic ... the assimilative powers which excluded nothing, omitted nothing, which insisted that everything that is, 'belongs'—for example, both the Bible and the metaphysics of Aristotle." A few pages later, he is explaining what makes Aquinas a great teacher:

> Teaching in the real sense takes place only when the hearer is reached—not by dint of some personal magnetism or verbal magic, but rather, when the truth of what is said reaches the hearer as truth. Real teaching takes place only when its ultimate result—which must be intended from the start—is achieved: when the hearer is "taught." And being taught is something else again from being carried away, and something else again from being dominated by another's intellect. Being taught means to perceive that what the teacher has said is true and valid, and to perceive why this is so. Teaching therefore presupposes that the hearer is sought out where he is to be found.[52]

As even these brief excerpts show, Pieper was no plodding or dreary expositor. He had a vivid sense of the enterprise of philosophy and what it means even when you are trying to explain Aquinas. Both points in the quotations above—about powers of assimilation and the gifts of true teaching—were prominent features of his lecturing and writing.

Pieper wrote on love, truth, and the virtue tradition. His book *The Four Cardinal Virtues*[53] is a brilliant modern recuperation of ancient ethical wisdom, a modern classic, which he supplemented with

[51] Josef Pieper, *An Anthology* (San Francisco: Ignatius Press, 1989), ix.

[52] Pieper, *Guide to Thomas Aquinas*, 22, 32.

[53] Josef Pieper, *The Four Cardinal Virtues* (Notre Dame, Ind.: University of Notre Dame Press, 1966).

equally illuminating volumes on the theological virtues. Reflecting the Platonic side of Catholic philosophy, *Enthusiasm and Divine Madness*, his commentary on Plato's *Phaedrus*, explores how we "stand outside ourselves" in ecstatic experiences such as love, illness, prophecy, and the perception of beauty. It is one of the richest little books to be produced in the entire twentieth century. But perhaps his best-known work is *Leisure, the Basis of Culture*, which first appeared in English with a preface by no less a figure than T. S. Eliot. Writing in the early 1950s, Eliot pointed out how much of modern philosophy had manifested an inferiority complex in the face of modern mathematics and science. Symbolic logic and even ethics early in the twentieth century, and logical positivism toward the middle, had tried to do philosophical imitations of their more intellectually respected scientific competitors. But as many complained, while this orientation might lead to small-scale precision, it did not produce great philosophers as that term had been understood in the past: noteworthy thinkers who offered *insight and wisdom*. Eliot rightly characterized Pieper's work as grounded in Plato, Aristotle, and the Scholastics and as offering precisely that kind of timeless dimension of philosophical greatness.

The reference to Plato was a shrewd perception. Twentieth-century Thomism had rediscovered the Platonic element in Thomas' thought. Cornelio Fabro and Louis-B. Geiger in particular had teased out how Thomas incorporated Platonic notions of participation,[54] and various scholars had unearthed Thomas' debt to the apophatic way of Pseudo-Dionysius. But adopting Platonic ideas formed only one part of Plato's influence on Pieper. Pieper did not write dialogues, as Plato did, but his brief, well-crafted essays were often in dialogue with one or more features of contemporary life. In that, he resembled Plato and Plato's Socrates even more than the way in which he made use of ideas he inherited from them. That intellectual tact and grace were and are something quite unique in the generally heavy-going Thomism of the twentieth century.

Leisure, the Basis of Culture begins with a quotation from Plato about festivities' being the gift of the gods and the line from Psalm

[54] Cornelio Fabro, *Participation et causalité selon S. Thomas d'Aquin* (Louvain: Publications universitaires de Louvain, 1961); and Louis-Bertrand Geiger, *La participation dans la philosophie de S. Thomas d'Aquin* (Paris: J. Vrin, 1953).

65: "Be still and know that I am God."[55] These both might seem rather abstract points of entry. But Pieper immediately turns to concrete applications. In those immediate postwar years, everyone was focused on rebuilding, an understandable emphasis. Is the reconstruction, however, going to be based on classic Western principles, Pieper asks? The great pagans and Christians saw civilization as resting on *schola*, leisure, or contemplation, not on practical action, no matter how valuable. By contrast, our civilization has difficulty even in understanding that, as Aristotle put it, "we work in order to have leisure." Our world has been tending toward regarding work itself as a kind of human end. "These great subterranean changes in our scale of values, and in the meaning of value, are never easy to detect and lay bare, and they can certainly not be seen at a glance", Pieper observes, and adds that we must therefore go deep to the root if we wish to understand and guide the present age properly.[56]

To do so, Pieper confronts Kant, but in a way that is different from that used by the Thomists who tried to respond primarily to Kant's epistemological strictures. The ancients, pagan and Christian, believed in pure intellectual contemplation. By contrast, says Pieper, Kant believes that such a thing is romantic emotionalism and that real knowledge is the fruit of intellectual work, *ratio* not *intellectus*. Reason is associated with strict and striving observation, while intellect partakes of a more ample and effortless vision. The ancients made room for reason, of course, as a power specific to human beings, but they also regarded *intellectus* as "already beyond the sphere allotted to man".[57] This notion is so foreign to us that it is difficult to understand, but to leave it out would be to "omit something essential".[58] To equate knowledge with our work is to assert that there is nothing intellectual that comes to us freely; we cannot be *inspired* or *receive* a gift of understanding. And Pieper sees this view of intellectual work as similar to Kant's view of morality as demanding duty rather than the effortlessness of perfected human virtues or of love. By contrast, Aquinas says that loving an enemy, usually thought of as very difficult,

[55] Another translation gives this verse a slightly different emphasis related to Pieper's title: "Have leisure and know that I am God."

[56] Josef Pieper, *Leisure, the Basis of Culture* (San Francisco: Ignatius Press, 2009), 23.

[57] Ibid., 28.

[58] Ibid., 30.

would be even more meritorious if it came with no effort because of perfect love (*Quaest. disp. de caritate* 8 ad 17). All this concludes in the observation that "the highest form of knowledge comes to man like a gift—the sudden illumination, a stroke of genius, true contemplation."[59] Contrary to Kant, in Pieper's understanding, Saint Thomas believes that "the end and the norm of discipline is happiness."[60]

Pieper shrewdly notices that there is a social dimension to all this as well. Intellectual "workers" wish to be justified in their existence by being seen as part of the socially useful world of work. But as understandable as the emphasis on practical results always is, given human need, civilization has always also recognized the need for the liberal arts, those studies that belong to man precisely because he is free to contemplate himself, nature, and God. A crucial dimension of what makes us human depends on recognizing this: "Is there a sphere of human activity, one might even say of human existence, that does not need to be justified by inclusion in a five-year plan and its technical organization?"[61] Pieper was already worried in the 1950s about the confusion between real education and practical training, both valuable attainments, but not at all the same thing.

As was typical of Pieper, he connects the inability to see this clearly with a modern vice, *acedia*. That Latin term means "sloth", and at first sight it seems contradictory to everything he has said for Pieper to call modern life slothful. But there is a deeper meaning of the term that he brings forward. Mere activity can be a refusal to face the questions that are specifically ours as free beings capable of understanding and facing choices about our eternal destiny, or, as Aquinas puts it, we fail to have "the peace of the mind in God" (*ST* II-II, q. 35, a. 3 ad 1).[62] Pieper has the uncanny ability to quote a line like this from Aquinas or the ancient Greeks precisely at a point when you might believe that, in his engagement with modern problems, he is most distant from their thinking.

And this is true whether he is addressing the orientation of an individual soul or a social question. As he points out in several works, we need institutions, particularly religious institutions, to

[59] Ibid., 34.
[60] Ibid., 35.
[61] Ibid., 38.
[62] Ibid., 45.

preserve the proper notion of leisure as a form of celebration. This is a major theme in his work. There is no real festivity without the gods, whether we are speaking about a marriage or a holiday. We can have periods in which we rest from labor—for the sake of returning to labor. But it is only in that foretaste of the eternal we sense during a true festivity that man touches on an essential feature of the world. Or, as Pieper sums up: "Cut off from the worship of the divine, leisure becomes laziness and work inhuman."[63] The Platonic academy specified sacrifices to the gods on special feasts—a philosophical anticipation of truths that the Christian world took up and preserved in its own holy days and special celebrations. Only that practice takes us out of our workaday world into the realm of the divine.

In addition to his other work, Pieper wrote two very fine books on Aquinas, both of which reflect his lively and original mind. His *Guide to Thomas Aquinas* belongs with Chesterton, Chenu, and Gilson's introductions—all monuments to the twentieth-century Thomist revival and as counters to the "dreariness of Thomas-interpretation". Pieper made clear, by situating Thomas in the historical context reconstructed by modern scholarship, how radical and capacious his mind truly was. He joined a mendicant order, the equivalent for a nobleman—as Pieper and Chesterton have both pointed out—of marrying a gypsy or running away with the circus. But at the same time, he embraced the most cutting-edge intellectual material available in his day: in the newly translated work of Aristotle, Pieper claimed that unlike lesser men, Thomas did not seek to create a closed system. The whole spirit behind each article of the *Summa* and the other works is a communal discovery of truth in which the objects themselves help lead further toward truth, which always, however, remains beyond our grasp in this life. In this, the true achievement of Thomas "is quite close to the Platonic dialogue".[64] In another insightful little book, *The Silence of St. Thomas*, Pieper quotes Aquinas: "This is what is ultimate in the human knowledge of God: to know that we do not know God."[65]

[63] Ibid., 68.

[64] Pieper, *Guide to Thomas Aquinas*, 81.

[65] Josef Pieper, *The Silence of St. Thomas*, trans. John Murray and Daniel O'Connor (New York: Pantheon, 1957), 64.

Behind this rather calm description lay an obvious dissatisfaction with the way the energetic and open Thomas was presented as a tired and closed system. Pieper denied that Thomas had written a systematic work, because at every point it shows its roots in the thinking of others with whom he disagreed and his response to those points of view (for example, the points and counterpoints in each article of the *Summa*). In this view, Thomas was not even Aristotelian, despite all his references to "the Philosopher", because he did not hesitate to disagree with his great Greek predecessor or to challenge what he thought were too-superficial rebuttals of Plato in Aristotle's works. Aristotle, of course, bulked large in his thought because at that moment in medieval history Aristotle's texts had been rediscovered and their wisdom was being absorbed and renewed.

In the end, however, Pieper seemed to be an advocate of what John Paul II called in *Fides et Ratio* "the method of Thomas", that is, the systematic pursuit of truth by building on earlier truth, rather than the common way of characterizing Saint Thomas as offering a theory of knowledge, an ontology, and a metaphysics, as those were presented in most textbooks and Catholic institutions.

Further Explorations

In the mid-1950s, a new hybrid began to emerge that would continue growing into the twenty-first century: analytic (or Wittgensteinian) Thomism. In a largely English-language phenomenon, figures like Elizabeth Anscombe and her husband Peter Geach started to expand the analysis of "ordinary language" and the rigorous but narrow subjects associated with Bertrand Russell and Ludwig Wittgenstein in the English philosophical tradition by looking to Aristotelian and medieval concepts such as intentionality. Both philosophers also explored virtue ethics.[66] On the surface, any attempt to join these two traditions, which look like nearly polar opposites, seems doomed

[66] See John Haldane, "Thomism and the Future of Catholic Philosophy", *New Blackfriars*, 80 (1999): 158–69; also Fergus Kerr, *After Aquinas: Versions of Thomism* (Malden, Mass.; Oxford: Blackwell, 2002), 29–30 and 115–16; G. E. M. Anscombe, *Intention* (Oxford: Blackwell, 1957); and Peter Geach, *Mental Acts, Their Contents and Their Objects* (London: Routledge and Paul, 1957).

to failure. But in truth, read from a certain angle, there are ways that Saint Thomas can be seen to be sorting out our "ordinary" language as well as extraordinary matters (again, almost any article of the *Summa* explicates the meaning of terms already widely in common use). His attention to and valuing of the particulars of Creation also offer some paths of mutual communication. For the most part, the traffic between these two traditions has been one-way, Thomists taking an interest in analytic philosophy, almost never philosophers becoming interested in Thomism. But some significant figures, such as the Scottish philosopher John Haldane, may broadly be described as analytic Thomists, and several books have appeared that suggest avenues for further development along this and other lines.[67]

As will become apparent in the next chapter, even though this half century of expansion of Thomist philosophy seemed to come to an end in the 1960s at Vatican II, that was not really the case. The perennial philosophy got its name because it has been able over the centuries to put out fresh shoots, even in periods like the last third of the twentieth century that offer very thin soil for philosophical growth of any kind. And there were surprises of several philosophical kinds in store once the turmoil of the postconciliar Church dissipated.

[67] In English, Craig Paterson and Matthew S. Pugh, eds., *Analytical Thomism: Traditions in Dialogue* (Burlington: Ashgate, 2006). Cf. Roger Pouivet, *Après Wittgenstein, saint Thomas* (Paris: PUF, 1997), trans. Michael S. Sherwin as *After Wittgenstein, St. Thomas* (South Bend, Ind.: St. Augustine's Press, 2008).

Chapter 2

Catholic Philosophy in a Time of Turmoil

During the night between November 10 and 11, 1691, a Frenchman in his twenties named René Descartes had a series of three powerful dreams or visions. He was then in the service of a foreign prince, but he was working feverishly on several complex mathematical problems. The dreams came to him as he slept, or tried to, in Neuburg an der Donau, a town about midway between Augsburg and Regensburg, the former the site of the famous 1530 Confession that described Lutheran belief, the latter a university town where Joseph Ratzinger, the future Pope Benedict XVI, would teach theology in the 1970s. Descartes was working on trying to combine mathematics and physics when his dreams came to him, and they seem to have revealed a solution that somehow also involved religion. In the first dream, he found himself in the midst of howling winds as he tried to get to the chapel at his old Jesuit college at La Flèche. And in the last, he was beset by evil spirits of some kind. In any event, he felt he had been given the key to his problem, and, sometime after, he therefore vowed to undertake a pilgrimage to the shrine of Our Lady of Loreto in Italy, which he later carried out.

So began one of the most momentous turns in modern philosophy: a mathematical description of physical phenomena and, in a further development, Descartes' inward turn to seek an absolute certainty in the fact of his own existence as a thinking being—the famous "Cogito ergo sum" (I think therefore I am). The science and mathematics have had a highly successful career. The philosophy is more in dispute. An early story, perhaps apocryphal, has a featherheaded young woman approaching the philosopher in a French salon and asking, "But Monsieur Descartes, what about me? I do not think, and I exist." More serious minds have asked what this proposition means, for instance, when we are sleeping or unconscious or otherwise unaware of ourselves. But for all the doubts that have arisen about the turn for certainty to the contents of the individual mind, Descartes has had an incalculable effect on how virtually every modern philosopher has thought about the human person and the world.

The Philosophy That Dare Not Speak Its Name

Another large current that must enter into our account of modern Catholic philosophy goes by a name that, some people joke, is so formidable that it is best not to mention it in public: phenomenology. This school is quite significant, not least because, for the last quarter of the twentieth century and beyond, the Church was led by a pope who was himself a significant figure in phenomenological thought. John Paul II may not have made great, original contributions to the larger phenomenological movement, but he illustrates one of the reasons why it appealed to many people disenchanted with the turn toward the subject from Descartes to Kant, on the one hand, or with some of the more arid practitioners of Neoscholasticism, on the other. Phenomenology seems by its very name to be a rather esoteric, heavily Teutonic enterprise removed from everyday life. But as in the case of Karol Wojtyła, the practice of phenomenology actually opens up the subject to the world again and adds to a tradition like Thomism that help make it more richly reflective of the whole of reality.

As is well known, the term *phenomenology* goes back at least to Hegel, but the modern version takes its origins essentially from Edmund Husserl (1859–1938). Whatever else may be said of phenomenology in Husserl's hands—and it is a complex and much contested topic—its effects on his students are well established. Many of the most distinguished figures—Adolf Reinach, Dietrich von Hildebrand, and Edith Stein prominent among them—became Christians, and others, like Max Scheler and Martin Heidegger, expressed views that, to a greater or lesser degree, were on the frontiers of faith. Stein was particularly important to Husserl's work when she served as his assistant (followed in that post by Heidegger), organizing his manuscripts—which were often produced haphazardly—into publishable books. In any event, the old master himself noted how many of his students were taking the plunge and returning to the faith, claiming he should be dubbed a Father of the Church. He became a Christian himself as he neared the end.

There was a reason why so many of his students began to think that faith was a possibility again. Husserl began by trying to reformulate a problem that has plagued all modern philosophy: If we begin with ideas in the mind, as in Descartes, how is it possible to know that anything else exists "outside" our thoughts, and what possible relationship is there between the world outside and what we find inside? In brief, modern philosophy has been suffering from a crisis in epistemology (the theory of knowledge) and from a very shaky connection to reality. Though Husserl's intentions have sometimes been misunderstood (and according to his students and later readers, he often seemed to be slipping back toward the old subjectivism), he attempted to remedy these problems by reframing the way we look at phenomena, the self-disclosure of a world that addresses itself to us. He did not begin with the isolated subject—a bit of an absurdity when we begin to think about it. How did Descartes learn to say "Cogito ergo sum" if not in Latin courses with the Jesuits at La Flèche, and why would he be in such a desperate search for epistemological foundations if those foundations had not crumbled in the culture of which he was a brilliant part?

By situating all such questions as "always already" within a concrete context, phenomenology rightly eliminates many of the modern philosophical conundrums that arose and still often arise from a faulty and one-sided view of who and what we are. Modern Thomism had also tried to solve the epistemological problem in Descartes, but it sometimes seems to proceed along lines—at least in modern conditions—that invite the very same dead ends as Cartesianism. In classic Thomism, "phantasms" are worked up into mental images by the agent intellect and impressed on the possible intellect. This formula seems to explain things but also seems to interject a kind of mysterious power as well as images or intermediaries of some sort between ourselves and the world. In its own way, the process, viewed from a certain angle, might also seem to divorce world and thought, though it was not used that way. Thomism is, of course, a sophisticated movement and has many ways of responding to such problems. But phenomenology at its best has some interesting starting points that amplify the basic Thomist thrust to make knowledge fully congruent with the way things are.

A key notion in phenomenology is *intentionality*, which is a technical term that means something quite different from what we usually mean by intention. Phenomenology accepts the everyday view we have that when we are conscious it is always consciousness *of something*. Sometimes we are conscious only of our own thoughts or perceptions, as in Descartes, but more typically we are aware of ourselves as being in a world in which things manifest themselves to us in a variety of ways that can be carefully spelled out. We are both in that world and a kind of being capable of receiving manifestations of the beings in that world, "datives of disclosure", as Father Robert Sokolowski puts it.[1] Manifestations, in this view, are not mere "appearances" as those have been conceptualized in much modern philosophy, particularly in Immanuel Kant's famous contention that we can only ever know *phenomena* (appearances in our minds), never the *noumena* (the things-in-themselves as they actually exist, assuming that they really do). Once we posit appearances as a kind of intermediary between the mind and things in the modern fashion or as a representation in the mind, the whole difficulty of getting back outside to the world arises again.

Phenomenology does not solve this dilemma, because it cannot be solved. It starts in a different place by saying that beings in the world "disclose" themselves to beings capable of receiving that disclosure. Disclosure simply is those beings in one way of their existing:

> Phenomenology recognizes the reality and truth of phenomena, the things that appear. It is not the case, as the Cartesian tradition would have us believe, that "being a picture" or "being a perceived object" or "being a symbol" is only in the mind. They are ways in which things can be. The way things appear is part of the being of things;

[1] Robert Sokolowski, *Introduction to Phenomenology* (New York: Cambridge University Press, 2000), is by common agreement one of the best guides to the subject. Father Sokolowski has taught for many years at the Catholic University of America and clearly has Catholic issues in mind—such as the relationship of phenomenology to Thomism—but for the most part presents phenomenology as a purely philosophical approach that puts us back in touch with the world and gives us a better notion of knowing, thereby alleviating many of the problems posed by philosophy since Descartes. This discussion of phenomenology is in many points indebted to his work and to several helpful conversations.

> things appear as they are, and they are as they appear. Things do not just exist; they also manifest themselves as what they are.[2]

The usual response to this type of assertion is that we make mistakes about what appears to us or that we sometimes have visual or auditory hallucinations of things that do not "really" exist and that such experiences should make us wary about the truth of appearances. Phenomenology does not deny that such problems arise, but it argues that we could not make such errors if we did not already have—and trust to some extent—the ordinary deliverances of our conscious knowledge of the world. Errors, hallucinations, and other misleading phenomena are themselves manifestations that can be examined. A hallucination, for example, can be identified as such even by the person who had it and then perhaps traced it out to a misperception or some physical or emotional condition that produced it. None of these difficulties, however, requires us to deny that we are recipients of widely different manifestations of many kinds of beings.

This may seem a small matter, but for anyone familiar with the difficulty many different schools of modern philosophy have in moving from ideas in the mind to the world—and the great damage this difficulty has done to public notions of truth as a common standard—it has explosive potential. Almost all the later elaborations of this one move pale by comparison. Once we admit that commonsense beliefs and knowledge have a truth value of their own in a normal mode of regarding things, all the rest—the philosophical reflection that uses, but does not replace, these "normal" modes of knowing—may be better or worse depending on the skills of the thinker and the sensitivity and skill of the individual phenomenologist in sorting out various levels and kinds of truths. In addition, the emphasis on the way things manifest themselves to us requires both careful observations at the normal level and careful inclusion of all of the many kinds of phenomena that come to us. Some of the very best phenomenologists, for example, will turn to a subtle novelist like Henry James or to poets for insights into the world and man.

[2] Ibid., 14.

This philosophy cannot rely solely on abstract deductions in the manner of idealism or rest content with crude realist notions of outside objects impinging on a kind of mental photographic film:

> For phenomenology, there are no "mere" appearances, and nothing is "just" an appearance. Appearances are real; they belong to being. Things do show up. Phenomenology allows us to recognize and to restore the world that seemed to have been lost when we were locked into our own internal world by philosophical confusions. Things that had been declared to be merely psychological are now found to be ontological, part of the being of things. Pictures, words, symbols, perceived objects, states of affairs, other minds, laws, and social conventions are all acknowledged as truly there, as sharing in being and as capable of appearing according to their own proper style.[3]

Serious philosophers will naturally wish to go on to use this corrective insight for further explorations in philosophy, and many have done so in a variety of ways.

One sign that phenomenology has tremendous power in opening up the closed space of modern philosophy, as noted earlier, is that many of Husserl's students, sometimes to his chagrin, became Christian believers, while others who started out as believers found additional support in the way the approach allowed them to look at the phenomena of belief. As mentioned before, one adherent of the phenomenological method was Karol Wojtyła, who both absorbed the tradition and contributed to it before he was carried off by other duties.

Though he comes later in these developments, Wojtyła's participation helps illuminate several features of the whole process. As we saw in the first chapter, Wojtyła had an experiential approach to intellectual questions. When he studied under Garrigou-Lagrange in Rome, he perforce assimilated a great deal of the central Thomist philosophy of the first half of the twentieth century, but in his doctoral thesis, he applied it to works of the great Carmelite mystic Saint John of the Cross. When Wojtyła later decided to do his second doctorate, he turned to the phenomenology of Max Scheler and later even wrote a dense treatise, *The Acting Person*, which takes up various

[3] Ibid., 15.

phenomenological themes. One of his most astute interpreters, however, claims that Karol Wojtyła showed an "eventual return to Thomas, which followed each of his meetings with modern philosophy. This return, upon which he meditated critically, was the means by which Wojtyła created an original philosophical construction."[4]

It is not surprising that Wojtyła turned to phenomenology. His interest in philosophy was never merely intellectual, but, rather, it meshed with his concern for others and his various pastoral roles. At its best, phenomenology, with its respect for natural modes of knowing and careful attention to all the ways beings disclose themselves to us, offers a fresh approach to philosophical questions, one that is perhaps richer than anything else in modern or even ancient philosophy. A great Thomist like Jacques Maritain, aware of the usual charges of rigidity and lack of imagination often directed at much modern Thomism, proposed the following in a well-known letter:

> The unfortunate thing about typical scholastic instruction, and above all manualism, has been the neglect in practice of that essential intuitive element, and replacing it from the start with a pseudo-dialectic of concepts and formulas. There is nothing to be done if the intellect has not *seen*—if the philosopher or apprentice philosopher has not had the intellectual intuition of being. One should note from this viewpoint the great pedagogical interest of a year of philosophical initiation entirely centered on the necessity of leading minds to the intuition of being and to the other fundamental intuitions by which Thomist philosophy lives.[5]

Wojtyła's first attraction to phenomenology seems to have been driven by a similar feeling and also by friendship with Roman Ingarden, one of Husserl's greatest students and a fellow Pole.

Ingarden himself took an enthusiastic but critical stance toward Husserl's work, believing that in his later texts Husserl had turned his back on the vital intuitions of the earlier work. Ingarden regarded

[4] Rocco Buttiglione, *Karol Wojtyła: The Thought of the Man Who Became Pope John Paul II*, trans. Paolo Guietti and Francesca Murphy (Grand Rapids, Mich.: Eerdmans, 1997), 44.

[5] Jacques Maritain, "Lettre sur la philosophie à l'heure du concile", in *Approches sans entraves*, in *Oeuvres complètes*, vol. 13 (Paris and Fribourg: Éditions Universitaires Fribourg Suisse, 1992), 540. Trans. Bernard Doering as *Untrammeled Approaches* (South Bend, Ind.: University of Notre Dame Press, 1997), 65.

phenomenology as a method that might enrich other philosophical schools, not as a complete philosophy in itself. He seems to have objected primarily to its lack of metaphysics and relatively undeveloped ethical concerns, at least prior to the middle of the century—two items of central interest to Wojtyła as well. No one has been able to determine precisely why Wojtyła chose to write on Max Scheler, a colorful but unstable figure among Husserl's immediate students, whose work emphasized in particular the phenomena of emotional reactions to things and experiences as opposed to abstract philosophical concepts. Perhaps both Ingarden, who was one of the members of Wojtyła's dissertation committee, and the future pope himself simply believed that Scheler was important enough in Polish circles to demand some response. After Scheler's death in 1928, no less a figure than the great Martin Heidegger had called him "the strongest force" in modern philosophy.

For Wojtyła, still moving between Thomist and phenomenological approaches, Scheler's critiques of Kant brought important material back into ethical inquiry. Kant's strict emphasis on duty against feeling left much out of ordinary human experience. As in many other modern intellectual constructs, the truths Kantianism contained—there is an element of duty in our lives—and the seeming clarity of his concepts were purchased at the price of much that was humanly valuable and rich. Scheler argued that value and disvalue, much like love and hate, are basic reactions to things in the world. Our initial reactions may be mistaken, but without recognizing our spontaneous emotions, we will not be able to identify value at all. He arranged values in a hierarchy and tried to show how wrong choices involve preferring a lower value like pleasure to a higher one like the noble, the true, the beautiful, or the holy. For all its potential difficulties, Scheler's approach at least had the virtue of permitting discussion of lived experience, which for Kant seems to be, at times, an irrelevancy and perhaps a distraction from categorical duty.

For a figure like Wojtyła, who all his life manifested a pastoral concern for encouraging the good, a literary sensitivity to the complexity of human motives, and a philosopher's desire to understand, there seems to have been a fascination with this mode of thought that almost got things right. At least it began with a kind of unified acceptance of all things human. But Wojtyła also seems to have drawn on his work in Thomism—though no one would call him a Thomist in a strong sense of the term. He argued that Scheler failed to see that values, though perhaps originating in emotion, can only be evaluated or ordered on the basis of something else, namely, judgments about the value of human action. Human action in Aristotle and Saint Thomas has a double value: it aims at a good to be realized and also perfects the person doing the action by developing within the rightly acting person potential powers traditionally called virtues. (In this Wojtyła represents a different tradition from Josef Pieper: he wishes to bring back an enriched view of human work that speaks, perhaps, about their dignity to the working classes of Europe, who were notorious for having abandoned the faith.) Kant had little use for virtue, because for him ethical action was the naked choice of the will in accord with moral law. Scheler had gone to the opposite extreme of trying to found the ethical on emotions that guide the will, which might lead to the mistaken belief—one that seems to have led to no little disorder in Scheler's own personal behavior—that the stronger emotions tell us most about our own moral perfection.

Whether Scheler's philosophy or Wojtyła's partial critique of it will stand the test of time remains to be seen. At the moment, it appears that neither will be remembered as making a major contribution to philosophy, strictly speaking. But the interest in recovering a fuller human life, including the emotional life, for philosophical and ethical reflection led Wojtyła and many of his contemporaries into new paths. In a sense, what Kant, Scheler, and Wojtyła himself, along with other modern philosophers, have been seeking to do is to preserve essential human things by beginning with the human person. The older Aristotelian-Thomistic tradition began, in most readings, with certain metaphysical ideas derived from the world. Ancient science with its geocentric cosmology seemed to provide a solid backdrop for their views of the human person. The replacement of that older cosmology by a modern one not only undermined philosophical and ethical positions rooted in ancient science, but complicated the very use of science for human matters. Modern physics presents a much more difficult system to integrate into a tolerable understanding of human and divine things.

Under the circumstances, the only two alternatives are chaos—which has clearly emerged in some of the more radical postmodern currents—or a recasting of the whole project starting with a strong emphasis on the philosophical meaning of the human person. How that project begins is quite important. In Descartes and Kant, the person operates within a clear and distinct, but also sterile and limited, horizon. Scheler, in reaction, tried to bring the human affections and the totality of experience back into view. Wojtyła, sensing the problem in all these approaches, turned to Aquinas and the Thomist tradition, where he found a deep notion of the human person, but one that is relatively undeveloped by contemporary standards. Wojtyła posited the deep remedy for this with a true "innovation" by taking goodness and ethics, rather than being, as a starting point that might help us recover the metaphysical dimension.[6] Rocco Buttiglione, a friend of Wojtyła's for many years and an authoritative interpreter, comments: "In the light of this, it becomes clear how important it is to ask whether the fundamental categories of Thomistic metaphysics can be regained on the basis of a reflection upon the moral experience of the person, as conducted with the phenomenological method."[7] Buttiglione says that the last of Thomas' famous Five Ways to prove the existence of God, usually called the argument from design, is dependent on human experience. Therefore, it offers a pathway from the person and the good to metaphysics proper—a metaphysics that does not, as Scheler feared, merely impose abstract truths on the person but rather makes the truth of personal experience a doorway into the order of being.

Perhaps the greatest importance of this study for Wojtyła's later vocation was the fresh ground it gave him for approaching sexual questions in works such as *Love and Responsibility* and, as pope, The Theology of the Body. In both these crucial works, he allows, as Scheler did not, for both the emotional component of ordinary human love and a normative element that derives from a phenomenology of the experience of love and the meaning of bodily acts.

Wojtyła's major contribution to phenomenology proper, however, was *The Acting Person.* The English translation of this text has been the source of great controversy, beginning with the title, which in the original Polish is more literally rendered "Person and Act".[8]

[6] Buttiglione, *Karol Wojtyła*, 73.

[7] Ibid., 73–74.

[8] For brief accounts of this, see Buttiglione, *Karol Wojtyła*, 117n1, and George Weigel, *Witness to Hope* (New York: Cliff Street Books, 1999), 174–75 (long footnote).

Published in 1969, it was clearly intended as a response to some of the antinomian tendencies let loose around the Second Vatican Council, which had sought to affirm the good in modern notions of human freedom but somehow became entangled with the global cultural upheavals of 1968. The future pope, who had been a progressive of a sort at the Council, introduced some crucial distinctions. In his preface, he announced that he would seek to answer a question located precisely at the intersection of two traditions: "What is the relationship between action as interpreted by the traditional ethic as *actus humanus* and action as an experience?" The answer is labyrinthine and couched in a near impenetrable language, but the ideal—uniting good ancient and modern insights—is clear. Wojtyła did not succeed in solving this problem, but he was not alone in the effort.

A Martyr for Truth

One person who labored along similar lines—and later was canonized by John Paul II as a martyr—was the German philosopher and contemplative Edith Stein. She will probably remain more important in the broader Catholic culture for the life path she followed—conversion from Judaism, entry into a Carmelite convent, death at Auschwitz—than for any major contribution to philosophy as such. (It should be remembered, however, that she was killed when she was only fifty, after years of evading Nazi persecution, and might have done much more.) But she was among a large group of talented young Germans in the first half of the twentieth century who were dissatisfied with what amounted to a neo-Kantian stranglehold on academic philosophy in their country. For them, Husserl offered a new starting point that opened up all sorts of possibilities. As Stein was to describe it later:

> All of us had the same question on our minds. The *Logische Untersuchungen* [*Logical Investigations* of Husserl] had caused a sensation primarily because it appeared to be a radical departure from critical idealism which had a Kantian and neo-Kantian stamp. It was considered a "new scholasticism".... Perception again appeared as reception, deriving its laws from objects not, as criticism has it, from

> determination which imposes its laws on the objects. All the young phenomenologists were confirmed realists. However the *Ideas* [also by Husserl] included some expressions which sounded very much as though their Master wished to return to idealism.[9]

Stein had initially intended to study psychology, which she seems to have believed would lead to wisdom in understanding the human soul (*psyche*). Husserl's demolition of a rather shallow rationalism in modern psychology helped draw students to him.

But the occasional backsliding by the master on the crucial thing that drew followers to him—his reframing the whole question of knowledge and world so as to open up old areas of experience again—led to consternation among them and then explorations in different directions. Adolf Reinach, one of Stein's friends, explored law as "public speech", from a phenomenological perspective, a matter intrinsically involving more than one mind in a common understanding. Stein herself set out to develop a theme that she had noticed existed in Husserl but that had only received brief mention: our feelings of empathy toward others. Anyone looking into Stein's development from the standpoint of her later death at Auschwitz and canonization by John Paul II may be tempted to think her study of empathy anticipated later saintliness. It may do that in some fashion, but it is also a rigorous attempt to understand something that would be difficult to explain in terms offered by several of the great modern philosophers, such as Descartes, Hume, and Kant: How do we know the internal feelings of others and enter into fellow feeling with them? In the "life world", it happens all the time. But empathy presents an even greater philosophical problem, in a way, than opening up the mind to the world because it involves at least two minds, two of those strange, isolated, interior regions, hard to bring into theoretical contact with a world—let alone each other—in much modern philosophy

Empathy was, therefore, a crucial question in several respects for the kind of phenomenology his followers thought most significant in Husserl. Edith Stein was only twenty-five when she submitted

[9] Edith Stein, *Life in a Jewish Family, 1891–1916*, trans. Josephine Koeppel, O.C.D., The Collected Works of Edith Stein, vol. 1 (Washington, D.C.: ICS Publications, Institute of Carmelite Studies, 1986), 250.

this dissertation, and in many ways it shows. But there is also a precociousness in the way she sorts through some of Husserl's categories, which convinced her examiners to pass her *summa cum laude* and Husserl to ask her to become his personal assistant. She consistently hewed to the realist side of Husserl's thought, an orientation that illuminates how empathy is not merely *my* understanding of the *other* through insight, but also the way in which our mutual understandings of one another are partly constitutive of our larger sense of ourselves in the world. The way *others* may sometimes have a better understanding of *me* than I have of myself is a commonly experienced part of this process.

As in other phenomenological categories, the fact that I or any other individual may be mistaken in reading someone does not invalidate a basic phenomenological intuition: the way another's bodily gestures and other signs present themselves to me makes present real elements of his own inner life—as mine do for him. Much has to be sorted out in the highways and byways of this disclosure and the corrections that may come to it by memory, analysis, contextualization, another's report, and much else. But what we have here is not two solitudes who can never truly know each other, but two dynamic agents of truth who are present to each other and mutually shape each other. And beyond the case of two such persons, insight and input from larger numbers of people help confirm or deny truths that present themselves in these empathic modes. All this reasoning is quite solid and, in several respects, revolutionary and showed great promise on a vital subject.

It is easy to see how opening up interpersonal pathways of this kind might also make it possible again for someone to entertain religious belief. Stein, who grew up in a traditional Jewish household, had stopped believing in her teens. But given her intellectual development and the emotional upset of World War I—several people around Husserl, including Adolf Reinach, died at the front—the way was open to religious development as well. And this despite Stein's clashes with the quite difficult Husserl, who eventually drove her to resign. Yet she showed quite good and empathic judgment about him: "One must keep reminding oneself that he himself suffers most because he has sacrificed his humanity to his science. That [work] is so overpowering and the amount of gratitude that we owe him for it is so incalculable that, in view of that, any kind of personal resentment should not even arise."[10] Perhaps resentment did not arise, but the need for self-preservation eventually did.

World War I had a profound effect on Stein as both a philosopher and a person, much as World War II (and the experience of Nazism and Communism) was later to affect Karol Wojtyła. Throughout her life to that point, Edith Stein had been a more or less instinctive supporter of the order and discipline associated with the Prussian element in Germany. Something in the way the war unfolded, however, or perhaps simple maturation, caused her to take a more skeptical view of state sovereignty and the self-righteousness of all political parties. In the summer of 1918, she wrote to her sister: "Good and evil, knowledge and ignorance are mixed on *all* sides, and each one sees only the positive of his own side and the negative of the others'. That holds for peoples as well as parties.... Life is much too complex for anyone to impose on it even the most clever plan for bettering the world."[11]

Like Maritain, she wrote some essays about the state and sovereignty, and when she decided to write her *Habilitationsschrift*, the second doctorate normally required to teach in European universities, she chose to write on a topic that involved phenomenological analysis of persons and communities. Its lumbering German title, *Beiträge zur philosophischen Begründung der Psychologie und der Geisteswissenschaften*, was wisely reduced by the English translators to *Philosophy of Psychology and the Humanities*.[12] Like the title, the text is not user-friendly. But it offers some highly original insights into individual psychology as it relates to philosophical reflection and participation in community. To begin with, Stein writes we are embodied creatures, and our physical condition, especially states like tiredness or energy, plays a significant role in how we perceive the world at any given moment. This alone is already an important phenomenological difference from the pure mind as it appears in Descartes or Kant.

[10] Edith Stein, *Self-Portait in Letters, 1916–1942*, trans. Josephine Koeppel, O.C.D., The Collected Works of Edith Stein, vol. 5 (Washington, D.C.: ICS Publications, Institute of Carmelite Studies, 1993), letter 32, p. 37.

[11] Ibid., letter 24, p. 27.

[12] Edith Stein, *Philosophy of Psychology and the Humanities*, trans. M.C. Basehart and M. Sawicki (Washington, D.C.: ICS Publications, Institute of Carmelite Studies, 2000).

Embodiedness, Stein had observed in her first dissertation, is one of the conditions for empathy. But it also plays a role in our sense of belonging or not belonging to a community. All sorts of outside factors shape our psyches for good or ill. We have to explore this structure of participation to understand what it means for an embodied psyche that necessarily must live in one or more communities. In what may be a borrowing from Scheler, whom she knew, Stein points out that *Gemütsakte*, the kind of emotional reactions to presentations to us from outside, involve our whole appraisal of value. Some objects in the world present themselves as of merely utilitarian value—technology, for instance. But others—persons, families, nations, other close associations—are very different phenomena that cannot be excluded from view.

She also attempts to sort out good and bad in persons and communities. The fundamental psyche of each of us, she argues, is an individual thing and different from one person to another. The habits that come to reside in us are the result both of our acts and of outside influences. We may try to direct our actions or change ourselves on the basis of insights, but given our natures, we are often unable to do so without outside help—help that is also beyond the network of our natural relationships. Those networks may also be affected when something from outside transforms them. So neither persons nor communities are simply an unfolding of natural forces; they are dynamically active and, at least in principle and intermittently, open to unforeseeable new energies.[13] Stein draws a variety of useful distinctions along the way in the best phenomenological tradition, even if these have to be mined from some dense verbiage.

The other way in which the war affected Stein was to bring her face-to-face with the reality of the Cross, and her reflections on embodiedness, community, and transformation may have had something to do with her conversion. Or perhaps the opposite is true, and her growing awareness of Christian truths affected her philosophical reflection. We have no good means of knowing which took precedence;

[13] "If a change enters into this sphere, then it's not the occurrence of a 'development,' but rather is to be regarded as a transformation through an 'otherworldly' power, that is, a power situated outside the person and outside of all of the natural connections in which she is entangled": ibid., 233.

and perhaps they both simply occurred simultaneously. The story of Stein's conversion is well known.[14] It first began in earnest when she visited with Adolf Reinach's wife right after news that he had been killed at the front. Instead of consoling the widow, who like her husband had become a committed Christian, Reinach's friends found themselves being consoled by her: "It was my first encounter with the Cross and the divine power that it bestows on those who carry it. For the first time, I was seeing with my very eyes the Church, born from her Redeemer's sufferings, triumphant over the sting of death. That was the moment my unbelief collapsed."[15] In addition to this collapse of unbelief, Stein also happened to pick up a copy of Saint Teresa of Avila's *Autobiography* in 1921 while staying at the home of her friend Hedwig Conrad-Martius. She read through the entire volume in a single night and put it down saying: "This is the truth." After some study, she was baptized on January 1, 1922.

A great deal might be said about this whole conversion process. For our present purposes, however, it had the effect of shifting some of her philosophical interests. Like Karol Wojtyła, Stein began to look at some of the phenomenological categories from a different perspective, notably those involving the ontology and metaphysics of Thomism. She studied Saint Thomas a little and even produced a German translation of the *Quaestiones Disputatae de Veritate*. Along the way, she had been accused by Thomists (of the strict observance) of introducing phenomenological concepts and language into a text that contained neither. Given her background, this was probably true, but she was also clearly interested in seeing how the two traditions might supplement one another.

In the very year the translation appeared, Husserl turned seventy, and Martin Heidegger organized a *Festschrift* in honor of the master. He invited Stein to write an essay, and she first sent a fictional dialogue between Aquinas and Husserl. Heidegger turned it down and asked her for another contribution. She wrote an essay arguing that faith was a kind of knowledge, and, in addition, it was the kind of

[14] For a good overview, see Waltraud Herbstrith, *Edith Stein: A Biography*, trans. Bernard Bonowitz, O.C.S.C. (San Francisco: Ignatius Press, 1992); or Robert Royal, *The Catholic Martyrs of the Twentieth Century: A Comprehensive World History* (New York: Crossroad, 2000), 167–91.

[15] Herbstrith, *Edith Stein*, 56.

knowledge that raises a problem with one way of conceptualizing reason. If reason, as modern philosophy uses the term, is allowed to define its own limits, a contradiction arises. Reason of that kind must know what is beyond or below it and, therefore, is implicitly relying on some knowledge it says it cannot have. As Alasdair MacIntyre has summarized Stein's argument: "If natural reason is able to demarcate its own boundaries and to say what lies within and what outside its territory, it must be able to view itself and its limitations from outside, that is, it must somehow or other transcend limits that, so it is claiming, cannot be transcended."[16]

To say that reason transcends a falsely limited notion, Stein adds, is not to say that it has or can ever have complete knowledge. In this, too, the traditional idea of God is useful, whether or not he exists, because only God as traditionally understood could have such knowledge. And in light of that idea, we can see more clearly that we do not. On this point, she invokes a significant name: "It is surely clear by now that from Saint Thomas's point of view this goal is unattainable."[17] Stein was not yet a very accomplished Thomist and was clearly working through some ideas about the ways in which ontology and metaphysics related to the real insights of phenomenology. In the two serious studies she would complete in later life, that would be a continuing goal.

Finite and Eternal Being *and After*

The Science of the Cross has affinities with some of Karol Wojtyła's work: the future pope had examined the Carmelite mystic Saint John of the Cross using the categories of Aquinas; Stein looked at Saint John through the lens of phenomenology. But Stein, by now Carmelite Sister Teresa Benedicta of the Cross, prepared this book for a celebration of an anniversary of John of the Cross in 1942. She wrote it at the Carmel in Echt, Holland, with no real prospect in view that such a work, written by a person of Jewish background, could be

[16] Alasdair MacIntyre, *Edith Stein: A Philosophical Prologue, 1913–1922* (Lanham, Md.: Rowman and Littlefield, 2006), 179.

[17] Ibid., 180.

published under Nazism. It is largely hagiographic and consists of a series of connected quotations with brief commentary, which many have tried to mine for philosophical purposes, but there is nothing in the book that is of substantial interest to philosophy.

Finite and Eternal Being (probably finished in 1937 but not published until 1950), on the other hand, is a very serious work, beyond all doubt her most important contribution to philosophy. In it, she does take some concrete steps in trying to integrate phenomenology and Thomism, which she had been studying for several years by this point. This shows up most notably in the way she conceptualizes the human person. To the traditional ideas of form and matter, she is careful to add a third element, essence, which in specific human individuals has specific characteristics.[18] The example she uses prominently is *joy*, which exists in various persons even though its specifics may be different in each case. Individuality—which here seems to stem from the careful phenomenological attention to particulars—gets special emphasis in her hands, a real plus over the usual Thomism, which tends to lose the concrete person in technical discussion.

Saint Teresa Benedicta also seeks to move in the direction of the metaphysics of Eternal Being, that is, God. The subtitle of *Finite and Eternal Being* is *An Attempt at an Ascent to the Meaning of Being*. She writes of Augustine as a predecessor who trod a similar path. But as she did in her dissertation on empathy, she emphasizes the role of the body. We are not pure minds, and our bodies affect our internal experience and moods. She traces out elements in experience that bring us close to Eternal Being.[19] All of this is interesting and carried out with great acumen, but it may be that the most striking feature of all in this text is one that was left out of published versions for some time: a long and very successful critique of one of the greatest modern philosophers, Martin Heidegger.[20]

This critique takes the form of summaries and then evaluations of several works: *Being and Time*, *Kant and the Problem of Metaphysics*, *The*

[18] There is a useful discussion of these questions in Sarah Bordon, *Edith Stein* (New York: Continuum, 2003), 103–16.

[19] See Mary Catherine Basehart, *Person in the World: Introduction to the Philosophy of Edith Stein* (Dordrecht, Boston, and London: Kluwer Academic Publishers, 1997), 110–12.

[20] Edith Stein, "Martin Heidegger's Existential Philosophy". This appendix appeared for the first time in the 2006 (Herder) edition of *Endliches und Ewiges Sein*; trans. Mette Lebech, *Maynooth Philosophical Papers*, no. 4 (2007): 55–98.

Essence of Reasons, and *What Is Metaphysics?* The most impressive aspect of the whole enterprise is the ease with which Saint Teresa Benedicta moves through Heidegger's dense and difficult work, exhibiting an understanding and nuance probably owing to their common interest in various themes that circulated among Husserl's students. These summaries are very much worth reading as a contribution to understanding how Heidegger looked early on to a very intelligent commentator formed in the very same intellectual milieu, especially since a kind of Heideggerian Catholic philosophy came into some prominence in the 1950s and after during the heyday of existentialism in the secular world.[21] In some ways, his work taps into Augustinian themes missing from modern Catholic philosophy and focuses on the experiences of life in this world absent God, which Augustine called the "realm of unlikeness". The brooding *Angst* that marks existentialism as a whole and Heidegger's sweeping dismissal of all philosophy since Plato as "forgetful of Being" made him seem powerful and deep as few other thinkers in the second half of the century.[22]

For instance, Stein, now writing from a partly Thomist perspective, notices that in *Being and Time* Heidegger claims that *Dasein* (his term for the human being as a "being-there") is the kind of being whose *essence* is *existence*: "That means nothing else than that something is claimed for human beings which according to the *philosophia perennis* is reserved for God" and that the human being "is conceived as a little god". At the same time, she sees a serious flaw in the way Heidegger presents *Dasein*: "That the human being has a body is not disputed, but nothing further is said about it."[23] She allows that Heidegger's exposition does not claim to be complete, but she asserts that ignoring the body has philosophical consequences for some of the central ideas of Heidegger's whole project: "The fundamental determinations of the human being—for example, state-of-mind, thrownness, and understanding—must be very undetermined abstractions, as they do not take account of the specificity of the psychosomatic being

[21] Among many influential works, see William J. Richardson, *Heidegger: Through Phenomonology to Thought*, 4th ed. (New York: Fordham University Press, 2003), the latest of several editions; and John Caputo, *Heidegger and Aquinas* (New York: Fordham University Press, 2003).

[22] James Collins, *The Existentialists: A Critical Study* (Chicago: Regnery, 1952), is a surefooted guide to the whole movement.

[23] Stein, "Martin Heidegger's Existential Philosophy", 69.

into consideration."[24] Stein's early interest in the role of the body for empathy and community here finds a serious gap.

For her as for many readers, Heidegger's distinction between an inauthentic "everyday" self and an "authentic" being was one of the most striking and persuasive parts of the analysis. The everyday self is shaped by the "they", while the authentic self alone and resolutely faces the truth of its "being toward death". Stein allows a certain truth to this way of putting things, but adds that the "they" are not only a force of inauthenticity. Given the kinds of beings we are, others nurture, protect, and direct us in our earliest development, and the authentic self is indebted to various communities for its very life and even for its subsequent ability to criticize such communities. Even the "being toward death" that lends so much *gravitas* to Heidegger's thought is incomplete if death is presented as something we can know nothing about: "Human beings have, since time immemorial, spontaneously met the experience of death with the question of the *destiny of the soul.*"[25]

In treating this question, Stein brings personal experience and phenomenological observation to bear:

> I refer to the fact that many a dead person lies there, after the fight, like a victor: in majestic calm and deep peace. So strong is the impression on the survivors that the pain over the loss fades in comparison to the importance of what has happened. Could the simple cessation of life, the transition from being to not being, bring forth such an impression? And could it be thought that the spirit, which has impressed this seal on the body, does not exist anymore?[26]

In this and many other passages,[27] Stein shows herself to be a better observer of many phenomena connected with *Dasein* than Heidegger

[24] Ibid., 70.

[25] Ibid., 77.

[26] Ibid., 78.

[27] "There is a dying in which something else happens: in which all signs of struggle and suffering disappear, even before bodily death sets in. Here the dying person is illumined by another life in a manner visible to all those who surround him.... Then, however, *Dasein*—as being towards death—is not being towards the end, but towards a new [kind of] being: even though it is reached through the bitterness of death, the violent sundering of natural existence" (ibid.).

himself, who seems more schematic and abstract by comparison. Of course, his system remains a massive achievement, but her unsystematic observations open up significant paths that were never explored fully. These observations on death are reflected in the text as a whole, in which she even disputes whether anxiety [*Angst*] may truly be said to mark authentic human existence. Our general experience of calm and security in the world may sometimes be the result of a turning to inauthenticity in forgetfulness of our mortality, but it may also reflect a "trust in being", a phenomenon that reveals something about our intuitive grasp of ultimate things.

Finite and Eternal Being was fairly traditional in its understanding of the way that created—contingent and non-necessary—beings receive existence from uncreated—and absolute and necessary—Being (that is, God). Part of Heidegger's ever-increasing influence involved his championing of Being over the scientific investigation of beings, things in the world, which in spite of his denials seemed to echo the older view. And in fact, Heidegger and his followers were an important school of criticism against technological and scientific reductionism. They also argued that in, say, metaphysicians like Aquinas, the "ontological difference" between Being and beings was not present. This seems absurd. At that altitude, many different philosophical schools converge on the absolute. Heidegger's philosophy had the additional effect, however, of encouraging poststructuralist and deconstructive destabilizing of meaning. It demolished the old Enlightenment transparency, which assumed things were easy to grasp. But instead of opening traditional spiritual possibilities, it at the same time introduced an uncanniness not exactly anchored in Being. Catholics, by and large, when they engaged Heidegger, tried to adopt the existential opening without the seemingly impassible *Angst* of the abyss.

One of the most brilliant attempts by a Catholic philosopher to go beyond Heidegger was Jean-Luc Marion's *God without Being*, which sought to reestablish the God-creature relation post-Heidegger by abolishing contingent-absolute being and beings-Being alike.[28] And all within a profound and sophisticated spirituality rooted in the

[28]Jean-Luc Marion, *God without Being: Hors-texte*, trans. Thomas A. Carlson (Chicago: University of Chicago Press, 1991).

Fathers of the Church and the mystical tradition. Marion was a student of the leader of the deconstructionist movement, Jacques Derrida, but he turned the seeming indeterminateness of that movement's insights away from its skeptical and relativist tendencies and toward a conception of all being as divinely gratuitous and a gift—and God conceived of as fundamentally Love rather than Being. In his hands, the indefensible assumptions of mastery over created beings in the past is a form of idolatry that must be let go. Though it is not easy to judge at such close proximity, Marion, despite his difficulty, may well be one of the lasting Catholic philosophical figures of the latter part of the century (he was elected to the Académie française in 2008).

The Turbulence of the 1960s

Though Thomism was still going strong when the Second Vatican Council began in 1962, existentialism of the Heideggerian and other kinds, to say nothing of other philosophical currents, was starting to rise. Those tended to become more dominant as the global social upheaval of the 1960s—everything represented by the year 1968—replaced all traditional certainties and norms with more experiential judgments. The impact of the Council was such that—it would be fair to say—it, too, disrupted many of the old traditions of inquiry, and for some time after, although there was much ferment on the surface, very little appeared that could be characterized as great and enduring Catholic philosophy. Pieper continued to write vigorously into his old age. In *The Peasant of the Garonne*, Maritain produced a trenchant response to some of the sillier things that arose after the Council. Paul VI's 1968 encyclical *Humanae Vitae* produced a firestorm of dissent as well as a trenchant philosophical defense from Elizabeth Anscombe.[29] And in 1975, Frederick Copleston, an English Jesuit, completed his *History of Philosophy*, a massive work begun in 1945 that became a standard reference even for many secular thinkers.

But it took some years and some shifts in perspective before really strong philosophical work of Catholic inspiration emerged. A new

[29] "Contraception & Chastity" (1970), reprinted in "Contraception and Chastity", new ed., CTS Explanations, EX. 14 (London: Catholic Truth Society, 2003).

version of natural law, combining post-Kantian and traditional elements, was developed by England's John Finnis, America's Germain Grisez, and Canada's Joseph Boyle.[30] It posited several "basic goods", rather than the traditional metaphysical order, as a ground for natural law ethics, thereby avoiding some treacherous philosophical ground by beginning from things that seemed more evident. The "new natural law" attracted many distinguished adherents, among them Robert P. George of Princeton and the Catholic ethicist William E. May—and some incisive critics.[31] It gave rise to a significant ferment in natural law thinking, and not only among Catholics, but its long-term prospects remain uncertain.

By contrast, one of the most powerful and seemingly lasting philosophical voices of the last quarter of the twentieth century—Catholic or not—was, significantly, a convert. Alasdair MacIntyre passed through several philosophical phases including Marxism before writing the book that began a truly fresh current in Catholic thought and became in fact one of the most influential philosophical projects of the second half of the twentieth century, even in secular circles.

In his 1981 *After Virtue*,[32] he argued that the Enlightenment project, as he termed it, of expecting to arrive at purely rational, unbiased moral principles had clearly failed, in no small part because it neglected the fact that human beings are time-bound creatures who emerge from a particular history and life story. Our philosophical traditions, too, have an inescapable and crucial historical dimension, he claimed. Within each of them, we can make progress and pass judgments grounded in something other than mere whim. Outside of them, we quickly reach the fragmented condition so clearly now a part of modern life. The neglect of particular history not only misrepresented what human life is like, it gave rise to an inability to recognize that traditions themselves sometimes go into crisis and become incapable of resolving problems from within themselves—which seems to be our state in late modernity or postmodernity.

Since we make decisions all the time, however, we have to make them on some basis, and MacIntyre argued that typically we find

[30] John Finnis, *Natural Law and Natural Rights* (New York: Oxford University Press, 1980).

[31] See in particular Russell Hittinger, *A Critique of the New Natural Law Theory* (Notre Dame, Ind.: University of Notre Dame Press, 1987).

[32] Alasdair MacIntyre, *After Virtue: A Study in Moral Theory*, 3rd ed. (Notre Dame, Ind.: University of Notre Dame Press, 2007).

ourselves "after" virtue, in the sense that we possess some fragments of older ethical systems that are not very convincing because they have only a limited meaning outside their original, fuller contexts. In fact, to some who have broken with all earlier traditions of understanding, all older moral prohibitions may seem rather like the odd taboos of some distant tribe. So we pick, rather arbitrarily, from these fragments on the basis of personal emotion. Emotivism, as he named this phenomenon, has become the standard, *faute de mieux,* and it is quite common to hear people claim that something is "right for me", while refusing even to consider other arguments. Clearly, this reveals a reliance on naked will in ethics and a lack of any common external standard in nature, society, or God. Representatives of the old Enlightenment rationality still cling to the idea of a pure unbiased reason, but with something of a bad conscience, since they know that no such undisputed position has resulted from the purely "rational" arguments of the past three hundred years. Nietzscheans and other critics of the Enlightenment have pointed to that clinging to the past as pursuing false idols and a covert will to power rather than an adherence to reason. In a sweeping characterization of the whole history of Western philosophy, MacIntyre claims that we are presented with the choice between these two incoherent systems or the need to create something else.

Three exemplary figures in modern societies confirm this analysis, he argues: the rich aesthete, the manager, and the therapist.[33] The first can do whatever he wishes because the material means are available. In a sense, this is the paradigmatic modern case of massive means without ends that are anything more than personal preferences. And the spread of wealth to large swaths of people makes this a position common among more than just the super wealthy. But the other two are important as well. Managers in public enterprises and therapists in private relations are regarded as experts who provide in their respective spheres means to arbitrarily chosen ends: in the first case, financial profit with no care for the common good; and, in the second case, personal freedom—presented as what feels good for the patient—usually without concern for larger commitments or moral standards. These expressions of pure will not only block any coherent

[33] Ibid., 62–79.

moral account, they render a coherent life story, as that was understood in pre-emotivist times, virtually impossible.

In some of the most original contributions of the book, MacIntyre recommends three potential remedies for our situation, which he derives from historical study: practices, narrative, and tradition. These are all part of his attempt at a retrieval of a kind of Aristotelianism, which MacIntyre would develop further into a Thomist-Aristotelian view of human flourishing in his subsequent book *Whose Justice? Which Rationality?*[34]. "Practices" in MacIntyre are all the modes of excellence in human activities that make high achievement possible. For instance, no musician or painter, athlete or architect can be an entirely self-made success (the ghost of the isolated Cartesian or Kantian self appears in the contrary assumptions, which are widespread). We all learn to speak in families, acquire the habits of work and self-discipline, but also need steady apprenticeship under good teachers or guides in any field to achieve anything truly great. In addition, there have to be institutional structures—schools, conservatories, hospitals, training facilities—for full human flourishing. The emotivist and individualist strains in our culture emphasize how merely conventional and stultifying institutions often are, while the Nietzscheans regard "socially constructed" norms as *ipso facto* arbitrary. But, both views are false and incomplete. The radical denial of the value of social norms at bottom simply destroys morality and solidarity. Corrupt institutions make all the more clear how dependent we are on good institutions to help bring out the best human practices.

MacIntyre links the development of good practices with virtue, which he defines as "an acquired human quality the possession and exercise of which tends to enable us to achieve those goods which are internal to practices and the lack of which effectively prevents us from achieving any such goods."[35] Though there are, of course, many human virtues, there are some that must guide any serious effort at excellent practice. We must be able to recognize those who possess expertise; we must be willing to work at achieving existing standards and possibly fail; and we have to accept proper criticism.

[34] Alasdair MacIntyre, *Whose Justice? Which Rationality?* (Notre Dame, Ind.: University of Notre Dame Press, 1988).

[35] MacIntyre, *After Virtue*, 191.

Put in different terms, we need justice, courage, and honesty to make the barest beginning in all endeavors, and many other virtues as well. And here a possible second meaning of MacIntyre's title appears: we are all *seeking after virtue*, many perhaps without knowing it.

Since virtues are stable habits that perfect our natural powers, they point toward a second human need in addition to practices: a narrative of a whole human life. Just as ethical principles became mere fragments outside of their original contexts, so too can human activities lacking an overall life story fall into mere episodic forays. MacIntyre makes a very bold move as a result of this insight. He argues for the value not only of personal inquiry but of whole traditions of philosophical thought—and in a clever way that does not simply turn our awareness of the concrete history of a given position into a relativizing historicism—one of the bugbears of the older Catholic metaphysical systems.

On the contrary, he says, the Enlightenment thought to give us timeless, traditionless, rational principles. Three centuries later, we can see two large things. First, that effort has not succeeded: we are as divided as ever not only about particular moral questions but also about the nature of rationality—perhaps even more divided than in the past. And, second, we can now see that the Enlightenment quest for a pure, self-transparent rationality was itself one such tradition of philosophical inquiry that has generated various problems that it does not seem able to solve from within its own resources. It is not the fact that we can now see the Enlightenment as just one more historical tradition that has weakened it. All serious philosophical inquiry depends on the work of various minds over an extended period. It was the Enlightenment's blindness about its own status as merely one moment in Western thought that made its decline into a self-induced crisis inevitable.

Part of the appeal and cleverness of MacIntyre's analysis is that he is able to combine this recognition of the time-bound nature of all forms of inquiry with arguments that ward off the impulse to think that because all views are time-bound, they are merely relative. We are creatures inescapably caught in time, and our philosophical reflection must take that into consideration, without falling into the absurd Hegelian belief that time is the unfolding of absolute spirit. We can both gain and lose ground philosophically. There is no automatic thesis-antithesis-synthesis mechanism at work because the theses are multiple, not single and progressive as in Hegel. Some get lost, others are dead ends, regressions occur. Human life and thought are much more complex than Hegelianism usually lets on. But at its best, philosophy that takes place within traditions can both make progress against new problems and transcend those traditions by incorporating others when a given tradition reaches an impasse.

Traditions inevitably imply communities of meaning as well. One of the most famous lines in MacIntyre's book appears at the very end of his last chapter, which is entitled: "After Virtue: Nietzsche *or* Aristotle, Trotsky *and* Saint Benedict". By this, he intends to express his conclusion that, with the failure of the Enlightenment hopes, our choice becomes either a radical skepticism or something like Aristotle's account of human nature, suitably revised. Despite the failure of Marxism (a product of the Enlightenment), such an account will mount a strong social and economic critique as well as create alternative communities of meaning:

> What matters at this stage is the construction of local forms of community within which civility and the intellectual and moral life can be sustained through the new dark ages which are already upon us. And if the tradition of the virtues was able to survive the horrors of the last dark ages, we are not entirely without grounds for hope. This time however the barbarians are not waiting beyond the frontiers; they have already been governing us for quite some time. And it is our lack of consciousness of this that constitutes part of our predicament. We are waiting not for a Godot, but for another—doubtless very different—St. Benedict.[36]

By the time MacIntyre delivered the 1988 Gifford Lectures, which were published two years later as *Three Rival Versions of Moral Enquiry: Encyclopaedia, Genealogy, and Tradition*, he was ready to announce his belief that Thomism was a valuable extension of Aristotle and a far more coherent and convincing philosophy than either the Enlightenment project or the radical rejection of rationality found in the kinds of nihilistic genealogies associated with Nietzsche. Traditional Thomists were intrigued but far from uniformly happy about this

[36] Ibid., 263.

turn. To begin with, MacIntyre's insistence that all philosophical positions are historically situated seems to contradict Thomas' own claims for truth. As one modern Thomist argued:

> For Aristotle and Aquinas there may indeed be a history of practices, a history of the means to ends, but the defining standards by which they may be judged have no history, they are universals absolutely, they are the natures or essences grasped by the definition of their goal. Hence MacIntyre, in asserting that standards are not immune from criticism, misunderstands how Aristotle and Aquinas define practices in terms of what they aim to achieve, their ends. A definition is not culture bound nor is it temporal. Both names and definitions which grasp the essence of a subject have no temporality.[37]

Thomism has often been criticized in the twentieth century, however, precisely for its lack of attention to the human importance—and sometimes even the sheer existence—of time and history. MacIntyre has replied to this and similar criticisms by Thomists that it is simply a fact that Aristotle and Thomas were aware of the history of various debates that preceded them. Part of the strength of both figures is their serious engagement with all the previous arguments of which they are aware. Aristotle knows his pre-Socratics, and Thomas is able successfully to integrate the thought of the ancients, the Church Fathers (especially Augustine and Christian Platonists), and the recent Arab and Jewish thinkers. Of course, he is ultimately after *truth*, as MacIntyre is himself, but the very structure of the individual articles in the *Summa Theologiae*, with its drawing up of the various opinions pro and con on each point and its attempt to reconcile them, both reflects a developing tradition and shows how those who come later can make further progress by entering into still fuller truth. Real truth is, patently, not historical. But how people come to learn those practices that lead to truth and how truths as discovered in one tradition are to be defended "against rival answers proposed from within the standpoint of some fundamentally different tradition" require some historical analysis.[38]

[37] Janet Coleman, "MacIntyre and Aquinas", in John Horton and Susan Mendus, eds. *After MacIntyre* (Notre Dame, Ind.: University of Notre Dame Press, 1994), 81.

[38] MacIntyre responds to Coleman in Horton and Mendus, *After MacIntyre*, 299–300.

It should be noted that in the subtitle of *Three Rival Versions of Moral Enquiry,* MacIntyre presents Thomism, as he reads it, from *Aeterni Patris*, as tradition itself, *the* practice of moral inquiry that coherently responds to the failures of other versions at the end of the twentieth century. Just prior to the beginning of the new millennium (1999) and, therefore, within the purview of the present work, MacIntyre takes these insights further in *Dependent Rational Animals: Why Human Beings Need the Virtues*.[39] Focusing less on history than on individual experience, somewhat like Edith Stein, he emphasizes the body as an integral part of our existence and the need for attention to this fact in order to understand full human flourishing. Other contemporary traditions, he states, overemphasize pure rational powers and individuality. By a careful examination of the kinds of understanding that exist in dolphins and other highly intelligent creatures, and by making use of recent science that demonstrates the social nature of animals, MacIntyre tries to show a similar relatedness of our own minds and social networks to our bodies and, as in his earlier work, the need for the right communities of nurture and practice to develop the virtues necessary to a rational and coherent human life.

The fact that we have a body and that bodily needs make us dependent on others in ways too numerous to explicate fully is the most powerful antidote to the radical autonomy assumed by many modern thinkers. That dependency does not end with our passage from childhood to maturity, either. MacIntyre calls this book a "work of correction"[40] of his own previous rejection in *After Virtue* of Aristotle's claim that the human good is related to our animal nature—we are "rational *animals*", after all. In it he seeks to add that concrete bodily dimension to the social context of practices and virtues, though with a properly updated version of Aristotle's teleological biology. He also highlights ways in which Aquinas corrects elements in Aristotle and in Greek culture more generally that overvalued the great-souled man who was independent of others and prided himself on being, as he thought, self-sufficient. MacIntyre is struck by a prayer of Saint Thomas' in which "he asks God to grant that he may happily share

[39] Alasdair MacIntyre, *Dependent Rational Animals: Why Human Beings Need the Virtues* (Chicago: Open Court Press, 1999).

[40] Ibid., x.

with those in need what he has, while humbly asking for what he needs from those who have",[41] a more rational acknowledgment of the true human situation.

MacIntyre sees this interdependence as showing up the short-sightedness of theories like "rational choice", wherein people are viewed as fundamentally individualistic and making moral decisions in a vacuum. In fact, we are all indebted and need to be grateful to parents, families, communities, teachers, coaches, pastors, and many others. Most of us make our choices in reality by recognizing the validity of those claims upon us. Deciding what to do and what not to do, as is clear in all theories of virtue, plays a major role in shaping who we *become* and, therefore, the kind of person who will make future decisions.[42] We do reason as individuals, of course, and have the responsibility to develop the capacity to think clearly and comprehensively. The usual way of understanding the individual dimension of man in modern culture is to see him as utilitarian in the public arena and emotivist in private. But there are three elements at play here: practical moral reasoning, dependence on and indebtedness to others, and communities that help or hinder us in flourishing with full respect for everything we are and can be.

Thomists and non-Thomists alike have hotly debated every step in MacIntyre's development. One particularly strong criticism of the place at which he has arrived is that in his proper critique of the patent failures of modern liberal societies, MacIntyre at least partly overlooks the gains in areas such as liberty and tolerance that they may also have brought over earlier social forms. Further, given that we exist today in societies with large minorities of Nietzscheans, it is difficult to say how the kinds of communities MacIntyre envisions could coexist peacefully. Modern societies show tendencies toward out-and-out war between parties with orientations as different as those between slave owners and slave emancipators prior to the American Civil War.[43]

[41] Ibid., xi.

[42] On this point, see Bruce W. Ballard, *Understanding MacIntyre* (New York: University Press of America, 2000), 86. Ballard's whole book is a very good short introduction to MacIntyre's thought.

[43] For a very sensitive review of *Dependent Rational Animals*, see Gilbert Meilaender, *First Things* 96 (October 1999): 47–55.

Sources of the Modern Self

It is interesting to view MacIntyre in comparison with a contemporary, the Canadian Catholic philosopher Charles Taylor. Taylor studied at McGill University in Montreal and then at Oxford, where his dissertation supervisors were Elizabeth Anscombe and Isaiah Berlin. From the former, he acquired some connection with the thought of Ludwig Wittgenstein and is sometimes spoken of as a type of analytic philosopher. But the kind of analytic philosophy he most typically carries out acknowledges, as did Wittgenstein himself, that there are presuppositions we bring to understanding the things we see around us and to human thought that are not immediately visible. In other words, each of us exists in a community and tradition—in many cases a quite complex one because of the multiple currents running through the modern world. In this, at least, Taylor has definite affinities with MacIntyre.

For most people, this simply means that you have your views and I have mine, and there is no further inquiry into where these views come from, what degree of validity they may contain, or how we might navigate among them in contemporary free societies. These considerations have immediate relevance to many questions. For instance, Taylor made a very useful contribution to debates about multiculturalism at a time when it seemed that the center could not hold—indeed, that there was no center—in an essay he wrote that presented an admirable balance between respect for differences and a recognition of some of the central historical "axes", as he sometimes called them, of our modern valuing of freedom, human dignity, and justice.[44] This balance has been a hallmark of his work: seeing what may be good in modernity and, at the same time, seeking to anchor it in a certain hope: "implicit in Judaeo-Christian theism (however terrible the record of its adherents in history), and in its central promise of a divine affirmation of the human, more total than humans can ever attain unaided."

That sentence is from the last page of Taylor's best-known work: *Sources of the Self: The Making of Modern Identity*.[45] In this *tour de force*,

[44] Charles Taylor, *The Ethics of Authenticity* (Cambridge, Mass.: Harvard University Press, 1992), and Taylor et al., *Multiculturalism: Examining the Politics of Recognition* (Princeton, N.J.: Princeton University Press, 1994).

[45] (Cambridge: Harvard University Press 1992), 521.

he traces the values implicit in the Homeric age, Plato and Aristotle, Augustine, Descartes, Locke, Rousseau, Kant, and the Radical Enlightenment. Many historians of philosophy have done the same, but Taylor's genius is to have noticed how they have all contributed, among other influences, to our modern sense of human *identity* and our choices of values. For example, many of us still hold to elements of the old view of a Creator God and a divine order in nature, even late into modernity or postmodernity. But those classical elements have now been combined with the kind of "inwardness" visible in Cartesian and Lockean thought, wherein the mind is severed from God and nature, and value comes to be created by the individual person. Indeed, the mind starts to look on itself, he says, as an object that can be understood and engineered like objects in the external world. And there are cross-currents to the old biblical views in Rousseau's vision of man as born good but corrupted by society and in the Kantian and Enlightenment views that a universal reason will give us infallible moral principles.

Taylor sees a problem in this quintessentially modern assumption that a universal morality will be marked by, say, a goodwill toward others, which is actually a concealed Christian value. There have been other formulations in history of highest goods, such as pleasure or utility or peace of mind, that do not easily fit with an ethic of an active benevolence. There are choices made about what things we value that reflect moral frameworks that are not immediately evident to the person doing the choosing or to society as a whole. "Liberty, equality, fraternity", for instance, was the battle cry of the French Revolution. These were hardly new values in Western civilization, though they clearly represented a new emphasis on things that had been given less emphasis previously. Today, we can see—or should see—that those goals for society and respect for persons have a quality that did not exist in the ancient Greco-Roman culture and, one might add, may not survive, at least in an identifiable form, in post-Christian societies.

In a 1996 lecture at the University of Dayton on the occasion of being given the Marianist Award, Taylor tackled directly the question of a Catholic modernity.[46] The emphasis, he begins by saying,

[46] Published with responses from several scholars as Charles Taylor, *A Catholic Modernity?* (New York: Oxford University Press, 1999). Taylor developed these themes at great length in *A Secular Age* (Cambridge, Mass.: Belknap Press, 2007).

should not be on a "modern Catholicism", as if what is to be sought is a uniformity of Catholicity within the modern age. In Taylor's view, the proper emphasis is rather on a wide and modern diversity within unity, the properly universal and catholic in our day, which acknowledges that the Trinity itself is a communion of difference within unity. To say this is not to give modern civilization some sort of precedence as the standard by which to gauge Catholicism because modernity is itself just "another of those great cultural forms that have come and gone in human history".[47] It might be best, even if it seems outlandish, to see our task as the same kind of thing the Jesuit missionary Matteo Ricci did "four centuries ago in China".

Taylor acknowledges two difficulties with this approach. First, modern civilization still has many Christians and Christian elements, so the role of pure outsider for Catholicism is not quite exact. And second, there are obviously movements in modern civilization that are non-Christian and, more importantly, that "strive to define Christian faith as the other, as what needs to be overcome and set firmly in the past"[48] in the name of promoting Enlightenment humanism. It may appear, he says, that we therefore have a good way of adjudicating what is and is not compatible with Christianity. But in fact, as *Sources of the Self* also argued, some modern developments—universal human rights, for instance—are both grounded in Christianity and had to develop outside of Christianity to take on their full scope. Christendom—an impossible yoking of Christianity and a society—could not, for instance, give proper rights to atheists, homosexuals, and others seen as having wrong belief or engaging in immoral practices.

There are dangers in the modern developments, in "exclusive humanism", of course, "which remain very underexplored".[49] We can see this in the large fact that the twentieth century produced, on the one hand, Hiroshima and Auschwitz and, on the other hand, Amnesty International and Doctors Without Borders, says Taylor. But more radically, modern forms of humanism tend to exclude the transcendent—less, Taylor believes, because of a convincing argument against the possibility that our lives go beyond this life than

[47] Ibid., 15.
[48] Ibid.
[49] Ibid., 19.

because many see, both rightly and wrongly, that the old metaphysical systems tended to block certain developments in the valuing of life in this world, particularly "everyday life". Paradoxically, however, the exclusion of the transcendent winds up diminishing this life, because it can see suffering and death only as diminishments of human flourishing, not as opportunities to witness to truths that go beyond and undergird our lives in the world. How might a modern dissident who risks his life for human rights, for instance, see the loss of his own life as an affirmation?

Taylor locates the struggles over these multiple, complex, and sometimes paradoxical truths as occurring among secular humanists, neo-Nietzscheans who affirm something beyond this life in the hardness of a kind of warrior ethic, and those who believe in transcendence—the last group further divided between those who want to return to an earlier order and others, including Taylor, who think that when a transcendent ethos dominates in a society it becomes stifling and that, therefore, we do better practically to posit no overarching system and to choose identifiable human goods. Taylor does not think this as simple or straightforward a process as may first appear. Those who profess human rights and global benevolence, for example, often come to embrace a kind of totalizing self-righteousness that echoes the older tyrannies—the global Green movement, he points out, has been known to manifest unbridled hatred toward opponents. But a Christian, knowing human nature, should not be surprised at such a thing: "It is perhaps not an accident that the history of the twentieth century can be read either in a perspective of progress or in one of mounting horror."[50]

As is clear from this far-too-brief account, Taylor, as compared with MacIntyre, is cautiously welcoming of modernity in its fragmentation. He seems quite content to take modern gains along with the uncertainty of the bases for them, while keeping a critical eye on the way that modern systems can themselves become stifling—a more genial postmodernism in its way than was found among the more ferocious postmodernists in France and, later, America. But difficulties arise quickly on the question of whether such a modernity can be *Catholic*. Catholicism, even when it allows for a proper

[50] Ibid., 37.

diversity, has been the religion par excellence that seeks for unity and universality in the perennial contemplation of the many and the one. Further, as has become clear even in the mild society of Taylor's Canada a decade after Taylor's analysis, modern secular governments can become quite aggressive toward and intolerant of communities within it, like the Church, that resist general trends.[51] Something within us ineluctably seeks transcendence, Taylor says. And, it might be added, we also seek some coherent unity, which our institutions will either impose well—because the bases for such a unity may be found—or impose out of willfulness.

In contrast to Taylor who accepts much of the modern situation as inevitable, Alasdair MacIntyre sometimes gives the impression that it might be possible to construct human communities that will enable us to perfect ourselves and our societies. Such utopian ideas have often led to unfortunate and bloody experiments in recent centuries, and these might have been avoided with a dose of Augustinian realism. Christian thinkers will no doubt continue to debate these and other of MacIntyre's powerful theses and to weigh whether his more aggressive stance or some form of accommodation along Taylor's lines is more realistic. But it is perhaps a fitting tribute to the vision of Leo XIII and John Paul II that, at the end of the second Christian millennium, two of the most prominent and ambitious philosophers—in the English-speaking world, no less—are working out how faith and reason can be reconciled in modernity, drawing on a variety of sources, ancient and modern, including among other luminaries the Angelic Doctor, not only as someone to help sort out the disorder bequeathed to us over the past few centuries, but also for guidance about how to understand man in the only way that permits real understanding: in his relationship to God.

[51] For a critique of Taylor's stance, see Matthew Rose, "Tayloring Christianity: Charles Taylor is a Theologian of the Secular Status Quo", *First Things*, Dec. 2014. "We would do well to listen to Taylor, but apprentice ourselves to MacIntyre."

Chapter 3

Theology and the Throes of Modernity

Christianity is not a private way of salvation and a guide to a pious life; it is a way of world salvation and a philosophy of total life. This makes it a sort of dynamite. So when you send missioners out to preach it, it is well to get ready for some explosions.

—Bishop James Edward Walsh, M.M.[1]

On June 29, 1972, at a Mass on the feast of Saints Peter and Paul, Pope Paul VI remarked during his homily that he felt "the sensation that through some fissure, the smoke of Satan has entered the temple of God. There is doubt, uncertainty, trouble, disquiet, dissatisfaction, confrontation. The Church is not trusted.... It was believed that after the [Second Vatican] Council there would be a day of sunshine for the history of the Church. What has come instead is a day of clouds, of darkness, of seeking, of uncertainty.... We believe that something preternatural (the devil) has come into the world to disturb, to suffocate the fruits of the Ecumenical Council and to prevent the Church from bursting into a hymn of joy for having regained full awareness of itself."[2] These were spontaneous remarks during a homily by a pope who had not at all been opposed to the theological renewal of the Council (1962–1965). Indeed, as even this passage shows, he had expected great things, and he had even pushed some reforms—the vernacular liturgy prominently among them—much

[1] Quoted in Raymond Kerrison, *Bishop Walsh of Maryknoll: A Biography* (New York: Putnam, 1962), 13.

[2] There has been some dispute about the exact words Paul VI used on this occasion since the homily has so far only been published on the Vatican website in the form of a report by someone present, who both summarizes and quotes the pope. But whatever uncertainty or imprecision may exist, no one in a position to know has denied the basic account.

farther than the Council Fathers had anticipated. The mention of the devil may put off secularists or even Catholic liberals embarrassed by such premodern notions of the origins of evil and confusion. But Paul was describing an indisputably serious theological as well as ecclesial development that persisted through the last third of the twentieth century. And he was not alone in his distress.

Many of the most innovative theologians who had prepared the ground that led to the Council, such as Yves Congar and Henri de Lubac, and several of the significant participants in the conciliar deliberations—two later popes (John Paul II and Benedict XVI) among them—were equally appalled at how their work had been interpreted and at the subsequent consequences. Prior to the Council, the Church occupied a seemingly strong position in the world—though she had been overly distrustful of modernity.[3] And her willingness to undertake self-analysis was intended to engage the modern world more effectively from the standpoint of a richer understanding of the Catholic tradition. After the Council, it was not a mere theoretical question in some quarters whether there was even an identifiable and authoritative tradition at all.

What had begun as a higher reevaluation of earthly life moved quickly to what seemed to many a radical abandonment of the properly religious for worldly and political categories. Karl Barth, perhaps the greatest Protestant theologian of the twentieth century, who had been invited to be an observer at the Council but was prevented from attending by ill health, remarked in its aftermath, "Is it so certain that dialogue with the world is to be placed ahead of proclamation to the world?"[4] The popular blueprint for Catholic social engagement, *Gaudium et Spes*, the "Pastoral Constitution on the Church in the Modern World", in particular struck Barth as not only overly

[3] The young Joseph Ratzinger remarked at the time that "the first real task of the Council was to overcome the indolent, euphoric feeling that all was well with the Church" and to deal with a kind of "anti-Modernist neurosis": Joseph Ratzinger, *Theological Highlights of Vatican II*, trans. Henry Traub, S.J., Gerard C. Thormann, and Werner Barzel (New York: Paulist Press, 1966), 83 and 11. This book is a compilation of four short reports Ratzinger wrote at the conclusion of each of the four sessions (1962 to 1965) of the Council.

[4] Quoted in Philip J. Rosato, S.J., "Ad Limina Apostolorum in Retrospect", in Stephen Sykes, ed., *Karl Barth: Centenary Essays* (Cambridge and New York: Cambridge University Press, 1989), 91.

optimistic but out of tune with the vision of the world to be found in the New Testament.[5]

Theology is usually regarded by non-theologians as an ethereal and abstract discipline, similar in its virginal purity to fundamental physics or mathematics. There is something to be said for this view with respect to certain dimensions of theology. But theology is also a human activity and as such is powerfully affected by the world in which it is carried out, even as it, in turn, affects that world—and not merely in "religious" ways. A tradition like Catholicism—which sees engagement with all things as part of its theological self-understanding—has much to say about marriage, education, the organization of society, economics, international affairs, care for the poor, war and peace, the ethics of bio-medical research, abortion, sexuality, and a host of other questions. And it was inevitable that Catholicism would be drawn into the heated disputes over such matters, which are difficult questions even in the best of times, because both the Church and the world faced multiple crises and radical challenges in the twentieth century. These problems were somewhat masked by the general improvements in material prosperity and human health that began to spread around the globe during the same period under the notion of "progress". Two world wars, the development of nuclear weapons, and worries about environmental threats shook the simple faith in progress somewhat, but progress as an overarching fact continues, despite all counter-indications, to shape modern and postmodern cultures.

As John Paul II noted in his 1991 encyclical *Centesimus Annus*, looking back over the previous one hundred years, there was much to be admired in modern social developments. But much also went wrong in the twentieth century, and it largely had to do with a mistaken and, therefore, harmful "anthropology". By this anthropology, he meant a view of man that was both stunted and distorted in a variety of ways. Nazism and Communism, of course, were the most obvious examples of a larger problem that Henri de Lubac examined with great theological and philosophical sophistication in his classic

[5] Quoted in Fergus Kerr, O.P., "French Theology: Yves Congar and Henri de Lubac", in David Ford, ed., *The Modern Theologians: An Introduction to Christian Theology in the Twentieth Century* (Cambridge, Mass.: Blackwell, 1997), 116.

book *The Drama of Atheist Humanism*.[6] In both cases, an exaggerated response in the direction of collectivism (in Nazism, the *Volk*; in Communism, the working class) to what many saw as excessive Western individualism and the ravages of capitalism ended in oppression and the destruction of millions of ordinary human beings (one hundred million and counting under Communism, forty million under Nazism). Ironically, these two large twentieth-century ideologies were advanced as a kind of alternative religion that promised to do for the poor and downtrodden what Christianity had not been able to do. John Paul II noted that a distorted anthropology could also be found in the developed and democratic nations. Although they did not (and do not) operate the death camps and gulags of the totalitarians, they do contain within them a "culture of death"[7] linked to a mistaken notion of personal freedom, most notably in the acceptance of abortion, which has killed several times more human beings since it was legalized in the West than Nazism and Communism combined. The culture of death also shows itself in a blitheness about experimentation on human embryos as well as to the creeping specters of eugenics (a Nazi specialty), the "right to die", and even outright, physician-assisted euthanasia.

De Lubac's analysis of how all this came about pointed, of course, to the modern intellectual errors, as he saw them, that had enabled such monstrosities to convince enough people to make them a public presence in an age that regarded itself as the culmination of various progressive currents. But in one of the most famous theological debates within Catholicism in the twentieth century, de Lubac and some of his fellow theologians also laid the blame partly at the feet of some deep elements in Catholic theology as well—particularly, in a way of conceiving nature and grace, after the Counter-Reformation, that permitted some to think of natural things as somehow existing almost autonomously, in their own right, without reference to God. This separation had been intended as a way to argue against Lutheran and Calvinist notions of grace,

[6] Henri de Lubac, S.J., *The Drama of Atheist Humanism*, trans. Edith M. Riley, Anne Englund Nash, and Mark Sebanc (San Francisco: Ignatius Press, 1995), from the 7th French ed., 1944.

[7] He first used this phrase in his 1995 encyclical *Evangelium Vitae*.

which seemed to some Catholic theologians in the sixteenth century and later virtually to obliterate nature, somewhat in the fashion of extreme Islamic thought. Matters of grace and nature are notoriously difficult, and the positions of the various parties remain contested. But de Lubac and his allies professed to see in the Catholic tradition a current derived in part from a mistaken interpretation of Aquinas for over almost a half a millennium in the Catholic Church that posited a nature existing apart from grace as creating an opening for an atheist naturalism.[8]

In that sense, de Lubac was part of the larger movement of renewed study of Aquinas and the Scholastics that we examined in previous chapters—though his views contradicted those of some of the most influential neo-Thomist theologians, and he was attacked and suffered under disciplinary limitations as a result. Further, in his view, a false way of conceiving nature and grace had distorted the proper understanding of the laity as the Body of Christ—making of them largely passive recipients of a grace distributed by the clergy. The theology that he and others proposed on the basis of historical studies that returned to the sources (*ressourcement*) in the Church Fathers and the tradition prior to Aquinas had multiple goals, among them, correcting the relationships of grace and nature, laity and religious, Church and world. He even cofounded a book series, *Sources chrétiennes*, to make key texts available. Paradoxically, this return to ancient sources, properly construed to be sure, was also thought at the time of the Council to be the basis for an updating (*aggiornamento*) along more pastoral and less rigidly Scholastic lines. The Scholastics, of course, objected, but when it became apparent after the Council that de Lubac's vision of a tradition rooted in the Church Fathers was itself a serious brake on dissent and experimentation, some accused him of having concocted a mythical unified tradition that passed over the voices of women and others.[9]

[8] His 1946 book *Surnaturel: Études historiques* was the foundation of this critique, which he and others continued in other works. Thomists of a more traditional stripe have variously debated his contentions. For a representative sampling, see Serge-Thomas Bonino, O.P., ed., *Surnaturel: A Controversy at the Heart of Twentieth-Century Thomistic Thought* (Naples, Fla.: Sapientia Press of Ave Maria University, 2009).

[9] See Robin Darling Young, "An Imagined Unity: Henri de Lubac the Ironies of Ressourcement", *Commonweal*, September 4, 2012.

Nuptial Mysticism

Another large and remarkable shift occurred during the twentieth century within Catholic theology. The Catholic faith is a complex thing—not merely a set of creedal propositions or a hierarchical authority or a worldwide diocesan system organized down to the local parish. It is all of those things, to be sure. But it also contains immense cultural riches, influences going back to the dawn of human history in Egypt, the Middle East, and Israel; the whole range of thought and practice of the Greco-Roman civilization and the areas it touched, from Britain to India; repeated infusions from new peoples who were catechized in Germany and the Slavic nations, Africa, the New World, and the Far East; and the modern age stretching from the birth of modern science through political revolution down to the postmodern and sometimes post-Christian currents in the contemporary world. There is nothing in the world quite like this entity that has gathered to itself the multiple wealth of all the nations. The great Swiss theologian Hans Urs von Balthasar summed it all up by saying that, in a proper Catholic perspective, "truth is symphonic."[10]

At the same time, Catholicism has been notable throughout its existence as a faith for an obvious and substantial coherence. By comparison, even the conflicting jurisdictions of Eastern Orthodoxy seem fragmented, to say nothing of the proliferating and fissiparous Protestant denominations that have sprouted in the West and continue to sprout around the world. In the twentieth century, however, something remarkable happened within Catholicism. It moved from a tightly disciplined and rigidly conceptualized philosophical and theological stance—most notably informed by the Neoscholastic revival that looked back to Saint Thomas Aquinas as a model for how to think about the truths of the faith—to a fluid, multifaceted, unsystematic way of reflecting on God and man. Some historians have characterized this new stance, which predated the Second Vatican Council in a quiet form, as "nuptial mysticism", in which the passionate love of God for his people is best expressed as an analogy: by the passionate love between a man and a woman.

[10] See Hans Urs von Balthasar, *Truth Is Symphonic: Aspects of Christian Pluralism*, trans. Graham Harrison (San Francisco: Ignatius Press, 1987).

That theme had long existed in the tradition, beginning with the Old Testament, most notably in the Song of Songs. It had taken on different characteristics in the New Testament in the view of the Church as the Bride of Christ. Saint Augustine, Saint Bernard of Clairvaux, Saint Francis of Assisi, Saint Thomas Aquinas, Dante Alighieri, Pascal, Saint Francis de Sales, Chateaubriand, Gerard Manley Hopkins, and many other great Catholic figures participated in this traditional emphasis on God's love. But even their combined presence was minor compared with the turn that began before the Second World War and came to dominate everywhere in Catholic philosophy and theology except for a very few pockets of Thomism and similar traditions. Henri de Lubac's *Catholicism*, written in 1938, began to exert wide influence in this direction immediately after World War II and was "the one indispensable text" for figures as influential in their own right as Karol Wojtyła (later John Paul II), Joseph Ratzinger (later Benedict XVI), and Hans Urs von Balthasar (by common agreement one of the greatest Catholic thinkers of the twentieth century). Balthasar's own key volume *Love Alone Is Credible*, published in 1963, expresses in its very title how Catholic thought had shifted. Of course, von Balthasar's title might be accepted by a Thomist or the adherent of some other highly developed school of cool reasoning, but that is not what happened. In great hands—von Balthasar, de Lubac, Wojtyła, Ratzinger—the new emphasis remained coherent, dynamic, and faithful to the tradition. Indeed, *Love Alone Is Credible* is remarkable because it demonstrates how love in the Christian sense leads, not to a faith defined by vague emotion, but into core dogmatic truths. But outside of the great figures, for the most part, the emphasis on God's love often enough led to what might fairly be called theological drift.

Still worse, just as both Catholic theology and popular culture were starting to emphasize that "all you need is love", the nuptial side of "nuptial mysticism" entered into a crisis, even among Catholics, from which it has not emerged. Older theologies and morals had viewed sexual passion with no little wariness—and rightly so, because the power of sex, as the stories even of the great kings of Israel David and Solomon show, has led to much heartache, violence (even murder), and the dissolution of marriage itself. The medieval poet Dante wrote his great *Divine Comedy* about "the Love that moves the Sun and other stars", but he also noted how the passionate adulterers Paolo and Francesca were murdered by a jealous husband and wound up in hell, blown about relentlessly by winds of passion. Starting in the 1960s, just as emphasis on love came to the fore, marriage in all the Western nations went into a crisis; divorce, adultery, and fornication became widespread. Illegitimacy mushroomed. There is nothing new under the sun, and these problems had always existed in the world of fallen humanity. But the scale was something new. For example, most societies in history have had illegitimacy rates of about six percent and have reacted to rises in that rate with vigorous moral crusades.[11] In America, at the start of the third Christian millennium, the illegitimacy rate had become about twenty-five percent for whites, seventy percent for blacks, and more than thirty percent overall. In 1960, there were about nine divorces for every one thousand marriages. By 2000, there were about twenty.

There is a correlation, but no certain cause and effect in either direction between the shifts in thought and the changes in practice, because these shifts also led to developments in practice that have reshaped the tradition. Catholics, too, divorced and sinned at essentially the same rates as their non-Catholic neighbors. Annulments, for instance, were little known in the Catholic Church prior to the second half of the twentieth century. Some quite credible priests say that perhaps it was the earlier low rate that was the mistake since many who marry are in fact not in a proper condition to do so. But there is no denying that annulment became a virtual equivalent to divorce for many Catholics in the period we are studying. And that sense of the impermanence of many marriages could not help but affect the reception and effectiveness of the quite orthodox presentations of matrimony and its relationship to nuptial mysticism by the great modern theologians and popes. John Paul II's Theology of the Body, for instance, is a notable effort to combat the widespread tendencies but has had little impact on the thought and behavior of most Catholics.[12]

In many ways, however, the new theology was a real improvement on the sometimes simplistic and defensive rigidities of the established

[11] See, for example, Gertrude Himmelfarb, *Marriage and Morals among the Victorians: Essays* (Chicago: I.R. Dee, 2001).

[12] John Paul II, *Man and Woman He Created Them: A Theology of the Body*, trans. Michael M. Waldstein (Boston: Pauline Books & Media, 2006).

Thomism. Réginald Garrigou-Lagrange, teacher of both Maritain and the young Karol Wojtyła, coined the term *la nouvelle théologie* for the new movements—and argued in a famous article that they were leading the Church to perdition.[13] At times over the twentieth century, it appeared as if Garrigou-Lagrange and his allies had not exaggerated the dangers. But any comprehensive account of the Catholic intellectual tradition over the past century has to assess all these phenomena, in their still unfinished roles, both positive and negative.

Thomism of the Strict Observance

What was the Thomistic system against which the new theology—and later some of the radical spinoffs of the Second Vatican Council—rebelled? It is difficult to assign it to any particular person. Garrigou-Lagrange seems to be on almost everyone's list. The Roman authors of Latin manuals of theology often appear in the indictment as well, especially Louis Billot, S.J. Whatever the justice of attributing a rather narrow and authoritarian Thomistic theology to any individual or to the movement as a whole, the newer theologians had significant historical and theological grounds for disputing questions of fundamental concepts, principles, and assumptions in the Thomism they encountered as the then-dominant framework for Catholic theological studies. As we saw in the previous chapters on philosophy, one of the strongest charges that could be made against this particular form of neo-Thomism was that in seeking to combat various notions about rationality, epistemology, and ethics rooted in what many people today see as a problematic hubris in the Enlightenment, the Catholic opponents themselves accepted a number of Enlightenment assumptions that made their Thomism different from Thomas' own—indeed, a kind of modern rationalism. This can be documented in several ways.

Perhaps the strongest evidence of a certain excessive reaction to modernist threats came from the Vatican itself. After Leo XIII's brilliance and openness to various modern currents, his successor quickly

[13] Réginald Garrigou-Lagrange, "La nouvelle théologie, où va-t-elle?", *Angelicum* 23 (1946): 126–45.

moved to a very different stance. Pius X, a sincere but much simpler man with strong pastoral concerns, just five years into his pontificate (1907) issued a Syllabus of Errors, *Lamentabili Sane Exitu*, followed shortly after by an encyclical, *Pascendi Dominici Gregis*, that sought to repel various "modernist" threats both within and outside the Church. In 1910, he instituted a loyalty oath for clerics, *Sacrorum Antistitum*, and in 1914 the Holy See promulgated the Twenty-four Theses in Thomistic philosophy that Catholic philosophers and theologians (who were to base their theological analysis on the philosophical grounding) were expected to hold.[14] "Modernism" was a real problem for the Church because various contemporary concepts in metaphysics, ethics, psychology, and other fields at the beginning of the twentieth century were difficult or impossible to reconcile with Catholicism. They were far from being ironclad certainties anyway, as subsequent postmodern thought has shown. Still, even to list the papal documents and their goals is to see, at least in retrospect, that the tools employed to face this very real problem may have had some utility with regard to Church discipline but were not really suitable for resolving the intellectual challenge.[15]

Lamentabili, for example, lays out sixty-five theses that are to be condemned. Most of these touch in one way or another on the growing problem in Scripture studies that, at that point, seemed to pit historical-critical analysis of the texts against the tradition and teaching of the Church. The historical-critical approach had and has its uses for Catholicism, but it also has limitations that in multiple ways actually can suggest the need for a believing community—as even scholars themselves better understood by the end of the century.[16] The naturalistic assumptions in such studies tended to undercut notions like divine revelation, inspiration, Christ's divinity, the divine establishment of the Church, and other premodern beliefs that, properly handled, are quite defensible. But *Lamentabili* cast its

[14] In theory, these were proposed, not imposed, but in practice they required adherence to a highly schematic philosophy, cast in an absolute manner far from Thomas' own open inquiry.

[15] "Pius X took drastic measures to suppress similar [i.e., liberal Protestant] developments within Catholic theology so as to prevent a similar impoverishing of the substance of faith, but this did not solve the problems": Ratzinger, *Theological Highlights*, 99.

[16] See chapter 6.

indictment mostly in the odd form of negative propositions such as this: "4. Even by dogmatic definitions the Church's magisterium cannot determine the genuine sense of the Sacred Scriptures." Such negative propositions were *not* to be held by loyal Catholics, a double negative that even many loyal philosophers—Étienne Gilson, hardly an anti-Thomist modernist, among them—and theologians found an odd approach merely on logical grounds. The document's basic perspective is summed up in the last of the condemned propositions: "65. Modern Catholicism can be reconciled with true science only if it is transformed into a non-dogmatic Christianity; that is to say, into a broad and liberal Protestantism."

A few months later, Pius X treated the problem at greater length in *Pascendi Dominici Gregis*. In that encyclical, he replies to the whole range of naturalist assumptions again. But he even takes on the idea that religion finds its origins in individual experience and sentiment. This, perhaps, was to become the crux of the dispute between the strict Thomists, defenders of a notion of scientific theology possessing certitude, and the newer theologians who looked to a natural desire for God, of one kind or another, and the love between persons in community as both an inescapable part of theology and the more normal path by which believers come to faith (Saint Thomas himself says in several places that few people have the ability, opportunity, or time to become philosophers and theologians in the strict sense). The Thomists were and are right that a faith without established and reliable truths is not much of a faith, and those truths cannot be limited a priori by assumptions that are themselves quite reductionist and questionable. But the whole text of the Bible suggests that, even when God himself is doing the writing, his usual procedure is not to proceed by way of theological and philosophical treatises. He appeals to the hearts and minds of his people. Both elements are necessary and well into the twenty-first century a workable balance still had not been found for most Catholics, members of a Church that has from the first prided herself on embracing both faith and reason.

Pascendi gives the impression of threats everywhere: modernists outside the Church, modernists within the Church, science, anthropology, and politics. The significance of the last category in Pius' overall thinking is difficult to assess in retrospect. In Germany, Bismarck's *Kulturkampf* ("culture war") against the Church was still fresh in memory. The French government under Émile Combes had just outlawed religious congregations and virtually submitted the entire French Church to state control. What happened in France at the time had serious repercussions throughout Europe and beyond. In Italy, the pope had been the "prisoner of the Vatican" since Vittorio Emanuele had invaded the Papal States (1870) and reduced the pope's political jurisdiction to what was to become known as the Leonine or Vatican City State, breaking up almost five hundred religious houses and dispersing over twelve thousand religious.[17] And it is clear that Pius X wanted to warn his bishops about a potential movement toward democracy in the Church herself: "Note here, Venerable Brethren, the appearance already of that most pernicious doctrine which would make of the laity a factor of progress in the Church" (27).

This is not an entirely wrong assessment about Catholic matters, however authoritarian or elitist it may appear in democratic nations. A great deal of sentimental nonsense about the "people of God" appeared after Vatican II, when it was clear that what often emerged from empowering an unprepared laity was hardly anything Catholics—or Protestants—in the past would have identified as Christian faith and morals. In addition, after Vatican II, dissenting clerics began to use the media as a public ally in pressuring Church authorities, something Pius X had also anticipated. Paul VI, of course, was the most conspicuous victim of a media campaign. The day after he issued his 1968 encyclical *Humanae Vitae*, which reaffirmed traditional Catholic (and at one time Protestant) prohibitions against contraception, a full-page ad appeared in the *New York Times* signed by scores of clerics. This tactic became so troublesome that in 1990, when the Vatican issued a document about the role of the theologian in the Church (*Donum Veritatis*), it contained a request that they refrain from using the media and accept, instead, a slower and quieter path of dialogue toward truth. The suggestion, of course, was met with angry outrage.

[17] Pius IX said in his Syllabus of Errors that among such was the idea that "The Roman Pontiff may and ought to reconcile himself to, and to agree with, progress, liberalism, and modern civilization." Under the circumstances, it seems that this sweeping condemnation was intended less as a general objection and more a response to the depredations of the new Italian state.

Pascendi's tone alone makes it difficult to like, whatever its hard truths and anticipation of problems. It is not entirely mistaken, for instance, when it says trenchantly that many of the critics of Catholicism did indeed proceed according to "a philosophy borrowed from the negation of God, and a criterion which consists of themselves" (34). But its rush to portray any personal experience of religion as subjectivist undermines a great deal of Catholicism's own piety and popular devotions. And its picture of depraved and devious dissenters who fail to heed the authority of the Roman pontiff does not read well a century later and could not have looked much better at the time it appeared. In addition, even when the "agnostic and immanentist" (34) elements are properly excluded, the encyclical seems to pit the whole Catholic Church against the idea, as John Henry Newman had brilliantly shown, that doctrines can be developed which is to say, elaborated in various ways without abandoning the original deposit of faith. *Pascendi* seems to see only danger in change or growth of any kind and, therefore, seems to propose a static Church that proudly ignores engagement with the modern world—that is, the world in which Catholics and the Church live.

But even more difficult to justify was the sequel a few years later, when loyalty oaths and mandatory philosophical positions were imposed by Rome. *Pascendi* took special pains to point out that the goals of the modernist "reformers" within the Church who would relegate Thomas to the past of philosophy in seminary formation and would change the hierarchical character of the Church are especially pernicious because they represent an enemy within. Even priestly celibacy would be abolished. To combat this Catholic fifth column, a network of informers known as the Sodalitium Pianum (or, in French, La Sapinière) arose, mostly in Italy and France, and continued in existence until the 1920s, with the goal of reporting unreliable clerics to Rome. When Pope Benedict XV was elected in 1914, he was surprised to discover that the Holy Office had a file even on him and worked to disband the Sodalitium. *Pascendi* repeated Leo XIII's words about the importance of Scholastic metaphysics and the proper study of science, but then moved on to order the appointment only of those loyal to such views—something Leo had never suggested—and the removal of those disloyal. "Modernist" books and periodicals were to be kept away from seminarians. These Leo had also warned about, but not with such sweeping orders. Censors to prevent the publication of unreliable religious books were given wide powers. And as if this were not enough, conferences of priests or laity who might address issues touching on the Church were to be kept to a minimum and "Diocesan Watch Committees" established. Bishops and heads of religious orders were instructed to report within one year on their implementation of these rules, and every three years thereafter.

The Anti-Modernist Oath promulgated in September 1910, which remained in place until 1967, therefore began: "I firmly embrace and accept each and every definition that has been set forth and declared by the unerring teaching authority of the Church" and continued, "*especially* [emphasis added] those principal truths which are directly opposed to the errors of this day". These truths were basically five: that God's existence could be known by the light of natural reason; that the divine signs—miracles and prophecies—were certain proof of Christianity's divine origins; that the Church and the authority of Peter were of divine institution; that dogmas constituting the divine deposit of the faith could not change their meaning; and that faith was not a sentiment welling up from the heart but "a genuine assent of the intellect to the truth received by hearing from an external source". There were and are good arguments for each of these points, though the last, interpreted too strictly, essentially would disbar almost the whole human race from possessing true faith. The first, for example, was commonly held by Aristotle, Saint Paul, and Thomas Aquinas—three very different figures, to be sure, but men whose ideas have not been simply exploded by modern anti-metaphysical philosophies. The rest of the oath essentially denies that modern historical-critical methods can justly introduce a division between historical truth and the text of Scripture, its interpretation in tradition, or the substance of the faith long ago established by the Fathers.

All of this, too, is quite true, properly understood, but the oath gave the impression of not even wanting to know how these methods might continue to be justified or propagated in a contemporary context:

> Therefore I most firmly retain the faith of the Fathers, and will retain it up to the last gasp of my life, regarding the unwavering charism of the truth, which exists, has existed, and will always exist in the

> succession of bishops from the apostles; not so that what is maintained is what may appear better or more suitably adapted to the culture of each age, but so that the absolute and unchangeable truth preached by the apostles from the beginning may never be believed or understood otherwise.
>
> All these things I pledge myself to keep faithfully, integrally, and sincerely, and to watch over them without fail, never moving away from them whether in teaching or in any way by word or in writing. Thus do I promise, thus do I swear, so help me God [and so on]. (Pius X, Motu Proprio *Sacrorum Antistitum*)

The goal of fidelity was the right one, but it would be difficult to say that the means proposed and the ways of formulating them were equally right, and the explicit disavowal of trying to speak in a way so as to be heard in contemporary culture prepared the way for an explosion. When at Vatican II, as shall be seen below, the Church decided to make a serious effort to engage modern culture, the result was an opposite extremism that made of that culture a stick with which to measure—and sometimes beat—Catholicism.

The problems with the fortress mentality become even clearer in the Twenty-four Thomistic Theses published by the Vatican in 1914. As we saw previously, there are many Thomisms, and some of them are quite creative and fertile, even well into the twenty-first century. Just as Aristotle and Plato will never be driven out of philosophy, the same can be said of Aquinas and Augustine in Catholic philosophy and theology. The Congregation of Studies "proposed" these theses as the proper ways to understand Saint Thomas, but others regarded the move as expressing principles that were to be "imposed", especially on seminarians doing preliminary preparation for the study of theology proper. Most of them are a kind of standard reading of Aristotelian and Thomistic principles, but it is difficult to know why these twenty-four were chosen. Securing the idea that there is an "ontological difference" between the Being of God and the created being of creatures may seem important to those who want to distinguish Thomas from Duns Scotus or Suárez or to head off pantheism and other metaphysical muddles, but they seem unnecessarily mixed into the battle with modernism. Thesis 22 plausibly argues that we know God, not by immediate intuition, but by a gradual sorting out of God's nature through something like Thomas' Five Ways. Thesis 15, however, seems to suggest that "ensoulment" does not occur until the fetus reaches a certain stage of development—faithful to Saint Thomas' medieval biology, but a problem for modern Catholic struggles against abortion. Étienne Gilson and others at the time who cannot be accused of modernism regarded the whole exercise as untrue to Saint Thomas.

In any event, this whole development under Pius X of seeking to combat modernism with Scholastic principles and restricting even those to debatable propositions forms the background both for the fruitful developments in Thomistic theology in the twentieth century and for *la nouvelle théologie*, a dismissive name given to the work of a whole group of theologians—Maurice Blondel, Marie-Dominique Chenu, Yves Congar, Jean Daniélou, and Henri de Lubac—by Réginald Garrigou-Lagrange.[18] They, along with the theological giant Hans Urs von Balthasar, returned the rancor; von Balthasar referred to the thin rationalist philosophy and theology he had studied in the seminary as "sawdust Thomism". Von Balthasar was a prominent exponent of the view that what was being studied was not the true Thomas Aquinas, but a defensive and overly rationalized Baroque Scholasticism rooted in Francisco Suárez's struggles against the Reformation: "when the feeling for the glory of God was lost—that glory which pervades the Revelation as a whole but which is not perceived by conceptual rationalism, or concerning which it remains silent, or which it wholly removes by means of method". And this mode of doing theology, he claimed, "annuls the experience of reality and encloses thought in a sphere which is characterised by bare, essential predications, by the play of the analysis and synthesis of concepts, and accordingly by the inner-subjective opposition of the act of thought (*noesis*) and the content of thought (*noema*)."[19] And yet not only von Balthasar but Chenu and de Lubac drew a great deal on Aquinas and sought to present his work in a fuller way that, after a fashion, might be considered part of the Thomist renewal Leo XIII had stimulated.

[18] Notably, in the article "La nouvelle théologie", 143. He answered his own question: "It is going back to Modernism."

[19] Hans Urs von Balthasar, *The Glory of the Lord: A Theological Aesthetics*, vol. 5: *The Realm of Metaphysics in the Modern Age*, trans. Oliver Davies et al. (San Francisco: Ignatius Press, 1991), 26–27.

At the time, *la nouvelle théologie* was partly confused with the kind of modernism that denied many things indispensable to the Catholic faith and sheer belief in God that had traditionally been understood in Judaism and Christianity. But in retrospect, this proved to be a false identification. The main figures cited above have proven to be crucial to an orthodox understanding of the Second Vatican Council—the "hermeneutic of continuity" of which Joseph Ratzinger (Benedict XVI) frequently spoke. A more radical group—Karl Rahner in certain moods, Hans Küng in most ways, and several others of varying degrees of heterodoxy—seem not to be destined to play as lasting a role in Catholic thought, although part of Rahner, once a giant figure who dominated thought and seminary study and had a great influence at Vatican II, may continue to have some significance. By contrast, the French figures who led the new theology may still be of importance as a better balanced reading of Vatican II takes hold.

One of the sub-themes in the conflict between strict Thomistic theology and the newer theological forms was the relationship between timeless truths and historical revelation. Thomists, of course, tended to be champions of a theology that was scientific and founded on the kinds of impersonal, timeless reflections in classical Greek metaphysics. The newer theologians, relying on the Church Fathers and other strands in the tradition, emphasized more strongly the work of God in history, as evidenced in the Bible and the life of the Church, and the need for the Church in every age to find a way to respond to questions put to her. The controversy may have been further complicated by the fact that liberal Protestants had for decades deplored the "Hellenization" of Christianity as unfaithful to the gospel, thus making the newer theologians appear to be treading a path that Protestants had taken with unhappy results, from a Catholic perspective. In his famous 2006 Regensburg Lecture, Benedict XVI—one of the prominent thinkers on the historical side of things when he was an academic theologian—deplored the three phases of "de-hellenization": by Luther, most famously in his rejection of reason; by Kant, in his postulating faith as outside reason; and by Harnack, in his claiming that Greek "additions" to the gospel were late and illegitimate. Perhaps looking back over the course of the twentieth century, Benedict—ironically, an Augustinian more than a Thomist—saw both the historical and the timeless as essential elements of a full Christianity that are always in need of further reconciliation as new questions present themselves.[20]

It is useful to look closely at what older Thomists thought the new theology was denying. In his trenchant essay "Where Is the New Theology Going?",[21] Garrigou-Lagrange makes several specific charges. He first addresses the contention, present in multiple writers, that theology must continually change to be current in order not to be a false theology. There are two ways to understand this claim. One he does not seem to see: that as new questions arise or old expressions may be misunderstood, theology has to find a mode of changing the presentation without shifting the substance. The other he pounces on: if, say, concepts such as nature, person, substance, accident, transubstantiation, Real Presence, sin, grace, and so forth, are not "fundamentally unchangeable" in the sense that they were developed in Saint Thomas, relying on Aristotelian categories, how can there be unchanging truths in Catholicism? And how can a famous theologian say, "The affirmation that is expressed in them remains"? This is a touchy point in later theology because, in announcing Vatican II, Pope John XXIII said explicitly that he was hoping that the age-old truths of the faith would remain but that by changing their manner of expression, they could be presented in a form more suitable to the modern age. Modern philosophers of language might impart support to Garrigou-Lagrange here because changes in language are not easily distinguishable from changes in thought.

Garrigou-Lagrange criticizes Maurice Blondel by name for proposing that truth should be sought in "conformity of mind and life" instead of in the "adequation of intellect and reality"—the old Scholastic formula. He continues, "It is very dangerous to say: 'Ideas change, the affirmation remains.' If even the idea of truth is changing, the affirmations do not remain true in the same way, nor according to the same meaning." Further, this change would alter the meaning of theology:

[20] Aquinas himself was not unaware of the historical dimension; Fergus Kerr, "French Theology", 185, points to *ST* I-II, q. 106, and other texts that might be brought to bear, as some of the newer theologians did.

[21] Garrigou-Lagrange, "Nouvelle théologie", 126–45. English trans. from www.traditionalcatholicmass.com/home-m109.html.

> *"Theology is no more than a spirituality or religious experience which found its intellectual expression."* And so follow assertions such as: "If theology can help us to understand spirituality, spirituality will, in the best of cases, cause our theological categories to burst, and we shall be obliged to formulate different types of theology.... For each great spirituality corresponded to a great theology." Does this mean that two theologies can be true, even if their main theses are contradictory and opposite? The answer will be no if one keeps to the traditional definition of truth. The answer will be yes if one adopts the new definition of truth, conceived not in relation to being and to immutable laws, but relative to different religious experiences. These definitions seek only to reconcile us to modernism.

This is not an easy assertion to assess. There obviously are and can be different types of theology that do not contradict primary truths of the faith: Aquinas and Bonaventure, Newman and Ratzinger, for example. But as subsequent developments were to show, there are theologies that quite quickly slip from one or two innovations into incoherence and heterodoxy. Garrigou-Lagrange castigates a recent writer for calling neo-Thomism and the deliverances of the Pontifical Biblical Commission "a guardrail but not an answer". The new theology, he counters, has put more than one practitioner "on the road of skepticism, fantasy and heresy".

There are important insights in this trenchant critique. Hell, for example, seems to be one of those concepts no longer "current" and, therefore, no longer true. Where multiple perspectives prevail, probabilities replace real truths. Several theologians have put in doubt an original Adam. Others have challenged the classical understanding of the Cross as redemption and replaced it, Hegel style, with a concept of a moment in world evolution toward a cosmic Christ; such a process allows Christian terms to be retained while changing their significance. The Real Presence and transubstantiation are redefined and are no longer real but symbolic. The upshot is this: "Thus to cease to defend the Traditional definition of Truth by permitting it to be illusory, it is then necessary to substitute the vitalist and evolutionary. This then leads to Complete Relativism and is a very serious error." Garrigon-Lagrange quotes Pius XII in conclusion: "If we were to accept such an opinion [that is, what the pope worried was the new theology], what would become of the unchangeable dogmas of the

Catholic Faith; and what would become of the unity and stability of that Faith?" There is much that Garrigou-Lagrange and Pius X had wrong about the new theology, and there was much in that theology that was valuable for addressing precisely some of the problems about which they worried. But it is also a matter of historical record that the "unity and stability" they sought to preserve were later undermined by people claiming the mantle of new theologies.

Appreciating Garrigou-Lagrange

The British Dominican Aidan Nichols has written a well balanced little book on what Garrigou-Lagrange, aside from theological controversy, has meant in terms of modern Catholic theology: "If one were looking for distinctively Roman Catholic theology of a kind that might be described as relatively representative in terms of content and form of the writing of Latin Christians in communion with the Holy See produced between Trent and the 1950s, the corpus of Garrigou's writings was certainly one possible contender."[22] This may seem faint praise to those who dismiss that whole period as an unfortunate detour. But Nichols adds that post-conciliar theology students can learn from Garrigou-Lagrange how to "reason with piety", which is never a small achievement in any theological tradition. Nichols is quite aware that this Thomist of the Strict Observance and many of his colleagues and successors were in truth less concerned with strict adherence to the historical Thomas, insofar as we can reconstruct him today from the historical sources (and Garrigou admits as much in his works). Instead, their strictness almost equally consisted in respect for the commentators of the Second Scholasticism (that is, the rebirth of Scholastic thought from the sixteenth to eighteenth centuries). And their main purpose was to use the metaphysical, epistemological, and moral resources available in the tradition as a means of opposing and refuting the anti-metaphysical, skeptical, and relativist currents to be found in Catholic modernism.

[22] Aidan Nichols, O.P., *Reason with Piety: Garrigou-Lagrange in the Service of Catholic Thought* (Washington, D.C.: Catholic University of America Press, 2009), viii.

Catholic modernism, at least according to its opponents, was poisoned at its root by a kind of interior religious sentiment that was the standard by which salvation history, dogma, Scripture, authority, and other such exterior manifestations of the faith were to be evaluated as more or less adequate. Against these, Thomist theology—with its support for papal authority and the Church magisterium—was thought to be the remedy. An authoritarian regime, laying this out in punitive regulations for the Church as an institution, gave a certain kind of Thomism a bad name in various quarters, but the abuse of legitimate concerns in this fashion did not entirely discredit the attempt to meet challenges with adequate philosophical and theological hardware.

Most modern philosophy and theology have moved away from rational arguments for the knowledge of God, for example. Saint Thomas' *Quinque viae* seem inconclusive as a matter of strict rationality, understood in a modern manner. But as Simone Weil once argued, such approaches are addressed, not solely to what passes for reason in any given age, but to love. Nonetheless, there is a defensible set of propositions on which natural theology has always been based, and Garrigou-Lagrange was one of their champions. Saint Thomas often remarked that we can know that God exists, but we can say more clearly what he is not than what he is. This may seem a small point in light of the whole Catholic faith, but it is a significant starting point for a "scientific" theology.

Much of the debate between the strict Thomists and the newer theologians may be said to revolve around the question of whether only a scientific theology is worthy of the name theology at all. Again, Thomas early in the *Summa Theologiae* takes great pains to show how a scientific theology may be erected on the foundations of revelation, a subordinate science that regards the facts of revelation in much the same way as physical science regards the facts of the physical world. But within the textual corpus of revealed truths, a corpus significantly not presented by divine inspiration through the scriptural authors in the form of a "scientific" treatise, are many other elements that a more supple theology may legitimately try to take into account. Garrigou certainly was not wrong to defend—and defend through Church institutions as well as intellectual argument—principles such as non-contradiction, substantiality, sufficient reason, causality and finality, and induction. All these help establish a substantial body of theological premises and the truths that may be said to flow from them. Further, they offer something most modern theologies and philosophies do not: a set of notions that take both religious truth and other human truths out of the dead end of mere subjectivism and into the light of significant objective truths about the world.

The serious question to be raised once that has been conceded is whether there are not other truths that need just as serious an exposition, but not in quite so small an orbit. It did not help matters that this sort of reasoning was also identified, particularly in France, with the reaction against the outrages of the secularists against Church property and freedom. Garrigou was a supporter, for instance, of Action française, over against the radical socialists, even when it was condemned by the pope in 1926. For a certain type of Catholic, caught in these political squabbles with very real practical consequences, the defense of truth and the denial of modern political liberty seemed elective affinities, since popular views could not be relied upon to reach essential principles. Since antiquity, it was a common theme in political philosophy that whole peoples could become corrupt. And the advent of modern democracies did not do away with an observation that seems merely to be an accurate description of human nature.

La nouvelle théologie might seem to present a similar problem to certain persons with a similar perspective. By the beginning of the twenty-first century, some of the very people who continue the work of the new theology also respected—even embraced—a strict Thomism properly contextualized. As Nichols observes in another context, for the newer thinkers, formed on historical studies that had emerged as part of Leo's Thomist renewal, "the true *nouvelle théologie* ... was the late Scholasticism defended *à l'outrance* by Garrigou.... This was the upstart theology alien not only to the Fathers but to the Golden Age of the thirteenth century itself. That was the point at issue with de Lubac's study of the relation between human nature and the vision of God in his *Surnaturel*."[23] But part of that context required appropriating a living faith that took scientific theology as one of its tools, not as a rational system that required all religious experience to be trimmed to fit a standard Procrustean bed.

[23] Aidan Nichols, O.P., "Thomism and the Nouvelle Théologie", *The Thomist* 64 (2000): 17.

Some quite orthodox Catholic thinkers had been moving in other directions even before the appearance of *la nouvelle théologie*. One theologian who illustrates various dimensions of the situation at the beginning of the twentieth century, for example, is the much loved Romano Guardini (1885–1968). Although his family name is obviously Italian and he was born in Verona, Guardini's parents moved within a year to Mainz in Germany, where he spent almost his entire childhood and adolescence except for regular trips back to Italy. Classifying thinkers by national background is perilous, but there was something in Guardini that reflected both the more intuitive and emotional side of Italy and, simultaneously, the analytic and objective element of Germany and thus provided a balance between the northern and southern elements in European Catholicism. Even as he wrote penetrating commentaries on a wide variety of subjects, he took a decidedly personalist approach. He started studying theology after a nominal interest in chemistry and economics. At about twenty, he passed through a period of depression that lifted after several spiritual experiences that also convinced him he was called to the priesthood. Though his thought was beyond question always orthodox, he was never much interested in the Neoscholasticism then common in seminaries. And it is no surprise that his 1922 doctoral dissertation was on Saint Bonaventure's doctrine of salvation (*Die Lehre des heiligen Bonaventura von der Erlösung*). His early work, therefore, belongs to both the conservative and liberal currents of the first half of the twentieth century, and his admirers included figures as different as Hans Urs von Balthasar, Joseph Ratzinger, Karl Rahner, and Karol Wojtyła.

Though Guardini was soft-spoken and shy, he seems to have had a personal warmth that attracted students and seekers. His first major book, *Vom Geist der Liturgie* (*On the Spirit of the Liturgy*) appeared in 1918, when he was only thirty-three, and attracted wide attention not only among Catholics but even among established non-Christians like Martin Buber (the Jewish philosopher and author of *I-Thou*), who subsequently invited Guardini to participate in a regular Jewish-Christian dialogue in Frankfurt. Buber's personalism deepened Guardini's own, and the two of them remained friends for the rest of their lives. Guardini's views on the need for a more participatory and interpersonal sense in the liturgy played a major role in the growing movement for liturgical reform up to the Second Vatican Council's Constitution on the Sacred Liturgy (*Sacrosanctum Concilium*) and beyond, even though he had deep reservations about many things the Council did.

The movement for a more participatory liturgy got its start in 1833, when Prosper Louis Pascal Guéranger, an ultramontane Benedictine monk, refounded the Abbey at Solesmes. From there, the initiative spread in several directions, including the Benedictine Abbey of Beuron, where Guardini first encountered it during a visit in 1906. Up until that time, he had been troubled by the fact that laypeople prayed the Rosary or performed other private devotions during the regular Latin Mass. A real liturgy, he argued, means a communal prayer of the Church, not a collection of individuals in personal conversations with God. The communal dimension is reflected in centuries of Christian experience in the way the Church has brought together various elements—vocal prayers, symbolic acts, sacramental eating and drinking—in a liturgy that involves our bodies, hearts, and minds in a comprehensive act centered on Christ. Though there are quiet moments in the liturgy in which each individual is more aware of God's presence, private devotions in general offer a different and more personal dimension of the Christian's relationship to God and are also necessary for a balanced prayer life. Each should be given its proper place in order to have its full spiritual effect.

To read Guardini on liturgy is to see how different from his vision was the reality that emerged after the Council. Though in his Masses for young people in Berlin Guardini early turned around the altar and put the students in a semi-circle, the intention was never to create community—still less to make the community the primary focus. The liturgical emphasis was always on Christ, though one dimension of that focus was to respond to the hyper-individualization of modern societies and of the Church herself, which often suffers from currents in the surrounding culture. One development about which Guardini was perhaps not sufficiently wary was what might be called a Protestantization, in a sense very familiar in all the advanced Western democracies. Local communities become more influenced by their immediate social ambience—usually one formed on grounds quite different from Catholicism. Such communities find themselves at odds not only with Rome but with different Catholic communities in other cultural circumstances. It was clear that one of Guardini's hopes for a really renewed liturgy was that it would move us beyond the limited circle of knowledge allowed by modern philosophy and ultimately bring us into the real presence of the living Word. In practice, it provided some resistance against Nazism in 1930s Germany but has had less success against the blandishments of postmodern affluence.

Guardini developed quite early a notion of what he called "oppositions" (*Gegensätze*), or tensions, as they were often called later, to capture the fullness of truth in matters where we find it hard to reconcile two truths. He applied it not only to liturgy but to a host of other situations. He distinguished such necessary oppositions from sheer contradictions (*Widersprüche*), which violate the law of noncontradiction. One way he put such notions to good use was in his 1927 *Briefe vom Comer See* (*Letters from Lake Como*), one of the earliest Catholic reflections on ecology, among other things. This work has its limitations, including some over-idealization of his Italian birthplace, but it also has at least one enduring insight. In visits back to Italy from Germany, he noticed the difference between the way nature was being roughly handled by German industrialization and the older Italian sense of building in harmony with the landscape. Guardini recognized the goods of industrialization, of course, and rejected Romantic notions that we should simply return to an undisturbed nature. We had to find a way to reconcile opposing interests, to incorporate respect for nature, including human nature, alongside our proper technological progress in order to prevent modern societies from becoming inhumanly one-sided.

Guardini belonged to the more Platonic side of the Catholic tradition and wrote books on the death of Socrates, Augustine's conversion, Dante, Montaigne, Pascal, Rilke, and Dostoyevsky, as well as further studies in the liturgy, prayer, and the love of God. His book *The Lord*[24] is a classic twentieth-century exposition of the life of Jesus, which also connects episodes in Christ's life with the beliefs

[24] Romano Guardini, *The Lord*, trans. Elinor Castendyk Briefs (Washington, D.C.: Regnery, Gateway Editions, 2000).

and practices of the Church; the shrewd American writer Flannery O'Connor was moved to say after reading the book: "There is nothing like [it] anywhere."[25] Some recent Scripture scholars have carped at Guardini's neglect of critical approaches to the Bible and declared his work out-of-date, but there is no possibility of that for the brilliant appeal to the heart he carries out. Appeals to the "heart" always appear in theology when mere analysis seems to have arrived at an impasse, and in Guardini this appeal is connected with his lifelong literary interests. He wrote on Dante's *Divine Comedy* and other classics, but he had an ongoing interest in what was happening in modern culture as well. His book on Rilke's *Duino Elegies* was controversial when it appeared because it combined a careful, objective reading of the poems in the manner of modern literary criticism with an evaluation of Rilke's vision from a Catholic perspective, which was unacceptable for scholars who wanted to be taken seriously in German academic circles. But he was not cowed by such criticism, and his reading of modern poets—not only Rilke, but Hölderlin, Mörike, and others—performed a very useful service, both in opening up a new perspective for the kind of Catholics who feared the modern world and for their opponents who tried to make modernity the measure of everything within the Church.

One of Guardini's most influential books in the world at large appeared in 1950: *Das Ende der Neuzeit* (*The End of the Modern World*).[26] Its several chapters may be thought of as falling into two large parts. In the first, Guardini provided a very rich reading of the entire history of the West—with interesting comments in passing on prehistoric and Eastern culture as well. He began by identifying the main elements that preceded the creation of the modern world before explaining, in the second half of the book, why he thought that modernity was now coming to an end and what that would mean.

The Greeks, despite their far-ranging speculations, regarded the world as a closed system, indeed, could not even think of anything beyond the world until revelation put that notion in front of classical civilization. There was a certain liberality of spirit in that system and

[25] Letter to Sally Fitzgerald, August 28, 1955, in *The Habit of Being: The Letters of Flannery O'Connor*, ed. Sally Fitzgerald (New York: Farrar, Straus & Giroux, 1979), 99.

[26] Romano Guardini, *The End of the Modern World*, trans. Joseph Theman and Herbert Burke (Chicago: Regnery, 1968).

a basic sense of the place of the human in the world's order—hence its creative but balanced achievements and its enduring interest for the several ages to come.

Christianity brought the Jewish notion of creation to that classical world: "This created universe is found only in the Bible. Elsewhere the origin of the universe was always thought to have been mythical; either some formless chaos had evolved into the world or some divine power had fashioned it from an equally formless chaos."[27] The Creator God requires trust and obedience, two notions that look oppressive from a modern standpoint, but in the ancient world: "A new freedom dawned in history for the human spirit. Sundered now from the world, man was able for the first time to face all things from a new plane, from a vantage point which depended neither upon intellectual superiority nor cultural attainment. Thereupon was wrought a transfiguration of being utterly impossible for the old pagan world."[28]

The Germanic element of the Middle Ages added something new to this mix, a "mobile and nervous soul"[29] that sought the transcendent in the farthest bounds of the universe and the deepest recesses of the human soul. And the conflicts that arose between Church and emperor therefore reveal a much deeper set of questions than the play of political influence. "From one point of view the Church bound and limited man by its authority; from another point of view the Church made it possible for man to surmount his world. She gave a vision which of itself was vast and liberating in scope."[30] But all men and societies need authority, says Guardini, and without true spiritual authority, the emergence of its earthly caricature is inevitable: force—a notion that would occupy him in the sequel to this volume.

As the West broke with this vision and began to concentrate on gaining power over nature rather than thinking about what nature means, three elements emerged quite plainly: nature, personality (man), and culture. Kant was able to formulate the concepts most powerfully in his three *Critiques*. First, there was the kind of nature described mathematically by modern science. In its very conception, such a nature can have no human value other than its utility. And

[27] Ibid., 24–25.
[28] Ibid., 25.
[29] Ibid., 26.
[30] Ibid., 30.

divinity was not indirectly present in nature as it had been earlier in Creation. At the beginning of the modern age, the discovery of nature's variousness and vast extent had provided a kind of religious awe for Giordano Bruno and the German Idealists but is most visible in Goethe. That feeling soon dispersed. Second, man had to be defined as something other than that impersonal nature, which left him without a "location" (a favorite word of Guardini) in the cosmos, alienated by definition from the world and in need of asserting freedom, immortality, and God as preconditions of practical reason. Finally, there was the realm of culture:

> The threefold result is evident. Insofar as modern man saw the world simply as "nature," he absorbed it into himself. Insofar as he understood himself as a "personality," he made himself the Lord of his being, and insofar as he conceived a will for "culture," he strove to make of existence the creation of his own hands.[31]

Revelation, which denies much of this, had to be regarded as "empty of meaning and hostile to life".[32]

The most striking part of his analysis concerned culture. For primitive man, said Guardini, culture helped provide security from both unimproved nature and the lack of orientation men feel before they have conceptualized their place in the cosmos. From the Enlightenment on, many people thought Western culture was identical with human culture and would provide both material well-being and humane relationships among all people and with the world. The Nazi horrors proved that this optimism was ill-founded, Guardini argued, and many in the postmodern age easily agree. But, he added, "The danger confronting man today arises from within culture itself."[33] The horrors of the twentieth century were not simply the result of a few men or ideas that had achieved power; they stemmed directly from a nature that had lost its true master and therefore been invaded by a false one, including demonic powers—a reality the modern world thought it had eliminated. In 1950, when *The End of the Modern World* first appeared, however, Guardini believed that not enough people

[31] Ibid., 59.
[32] Ibid., 55.
[33] Ibid., 109.

had understood the depths of the problem and that culture still presented "a vision of factories and barracks to the eyes of the mind".[34]

It is the human spirit that must respond to this challenge, and in doing so it must also come to grips with the new reality of power: "Man today holds power over things, but we can assert confidently that he does not yet have power over his own power."[35] And Guardini observed that there was no proper training ground among elites or masses to deal with this situation and that human culture would exist now on the brink of danger:

> The wildernesses of nature have long been under the control of man: nature as it exists round and about us obeys its master. Nature now, however, has emerged once again into history from within the very depths of culture itself. Nature is rising up in that very form which subdued the wilderness—in the form of power itself. All the abysses of primeval ages yawn before man, all the wild, choking growth of the long-dead forests presses forward from this second wilderness, all the monsters of the desert wastes, all the horrors of darkness are once more upon man. He stands again before chaos, a chaos more dreadful than the first because most men go their own complacent ways without seeing, because scientifically-educated gentlemen everywhere deliver their speeches as always, because the machines are running on schedule and because the authorities function as usual.[36]

For Guardini, this threat clearly went beyond nuclear and other weapons of mass destruction. It was the very nature of what he called "non-cultural culture".[37]

One old answer to this new situation was asceticism, a deep recognition that without self-mastery there would be no mastery of the very large public challenges. The modern world, Guardini said, was organized precisely to deny this and substitute the notion of individual autonomy for human perfection. Given how widespread this attitude had become, reversing it did not seem likely. We should not, however, engage in a false pessimism, he said, merely an accurate assessment of the truth. Part of that assessment was to correct the

[34] Ibid., 108.
[35] Ibid., 109.
[36] Ibid., 111–12.
[37] Ibid., 107.

Enlightenment's self-congratulatory but false history of itself as the discoverer of values, such as the person and liberty, precisely by liberating the human race from the limits conveyed by revelation. These values were extended in the eighteenth and nineteenth century, said Guardini, but once the person began to value himself outside God—the only true guarantor of personhood—the person himself became threatened by forces then unleashed from God's sovereignty: "As the benefits of Revelation disappear even more from the coming world, man will truly learn what it means to be cut off from Revelation.... Nietzsche has already warned us that the non-Christian of the modern world had no realization of what it truly meant to be without Christ. The last decades have suggested what life without Christ really is. The last decades were only a beginning."[38]

And for Guardini, the answers offered by the neo-pagans, the new age of Rilke, and French existentialism were all obviously too unsubstantial and Romantic to solve a problem that called for the most sophisticated and profound realism—the kind found in Christian revelation of a Savior "who knew what is in man". Given this situation, the usual charges against Christianity should take on a different light: "Men have often said that Christianity is a refuge from the realities of the modern world, and this charge contains a good measure of truth, not only because dogma fixes the thought of a Christian on an objective, timeless order and creates a life which survives the passing of the ages but also because the Church has preserved a full cultural tradition which would otherwise have died. The world to come will present less basis for objecting to Christianity as a refuge."[39]

Guardini predicted that this tradition would be threatened as civilization itself decayed, but that at least dogma would show itself to have a vitality and value in its very need to defend itself, and that an "illiberal stand" directed toward obedience to "Him Who is Unconditioned" would show itself, not as violence, but as an "act of freedom" "based in God Who really is".[40] Just as in the Old Testament, we would rediscover the living God who casts down the mighty from their thrones and overcomes the demonic powers and can deal with the modern problem of power: "It is a strange thing that we

[38] Ibid., 123–24.
[39] Ibid., 129.
[40] Ibid., 130–31.

should glimpse this holy way, this divine possibility, rising out of the very midst of universal power as it increases day by day."[41]

A half century after Guardini wrote all this, we can assess his powers as a prophet. Fortunately, he was wrong about a future world of factories and barracks. The human race gradually saw through totalitarian ideologies, which were withering even as he was writing. *The God That Failed*, the highly influential collection of essays by ex-Communists such as Arthur Koestler, Ignazio Silone, André Gide, and others appeared in the same year as Guardini's analysis. But it cannot be said that those ideologies were replaced by a resurgent Christian vision or even a more adequate humanistic one. Though the West championed "freedom" against Soviet tyranny during the Cold War and continues to defend several values derived from its Christian past, it has for the most part opposed evil with incoherence. Postmodernism—basically a denial of all foundations as the only way to prevent the evils of totalizing systems—was also dead by the end of the twentieth century, but only as a more or less organized disorganization.

Guardini was regarded by many as an inspiration and precursor of the Second Vatican Council. But the conciliar optimism about modern culture contrasts quite sharply with his realism. It was perhaps inevitable that Catholics of lesser gifts than his own would try to engage modern culture, as he did, but would wind up finding modernity a more potent brew than they were able to drink without getting drunk. After the Council, the very divisions of a free-standing nature, isolated personality, and Enlightenment culture that he saw as triply wanting got a temporary boost in the Church as those constructs began to play through Catholic institutions. Much of the chaos, disorder, unrest, heartache, and outright worldliness that ensued might have been avoided if Guardini had been better assimilated. But as he knew only too well, human reason and will, if not deeply rooted in revelation and the now long tradition given us by God, very quickly turn into what Newman called the "wild living intellect of man".

Yet it has to be said that Guardini's vision itself was perhaps a little one-sided in its reaction against the collapse of modernity. No one who reads his trenchant pages on what we have done, not only to nature, but to the very idea of nature, should ever forget them. They join hands

[41] Ibid., 131.

across decades with certain environmental currents that have arisen. But like those movements, they show a certain set of oppositions, to use Guardini's terms, that we have not yet reconciled sufficiently. In his beloved Middle Ages, some of the scientists and technologists regarded human inventions as means of partly repairing what had happened to nature in the Fall. Of course, Guardini is right that when we regard nature *solely* as something to be remade in our likeness, we have passed over into Promethean dreams. But his treatment tends to underestimate the very real human suffering that premodern and pretechnological humanity experienced—and the motivation it therefore had to seek dominion over nature. The key to resolving this problem is the one Guardini noted in his *Letters from Lake Como*: inserting the merely technical into a much richer human and divine context.

For that to happen, of course, we need a spiritual renewal. And Guardini—along with many figures who came after him, notably John Paul II and Benedict XVI (both admirers)—insisted that we will continue to get human things wrong unless they are rooted in God. In his 1991 encyclical *Centesimus Annus*, John Paul II reviews the whole history of the West since Leo XIII wrote *Rerum Novarum* exactly one hundred years earlier and sums up the problems that arose in the interim as stemming, as mentioned earlier, from a mistaken anthropology that left out God and therefore became murderous toward man. But it is not in better analysis alone that salvation will come, as Guardini well knew. It is precisely in a true appeal to the heart. And all his work, even the most technical, was a crucial and lasting contribution to Catholic theology precisely because it helped move the many people who read, heard, and loved him toward a different orientation toward the world. A German journalist, Walter Dirks, has said that "during the Nazi time, we lived spiritually out of [Guardini's book *The Lord*]." It is no exaggeration to say that many will continue to be kept afloat in bad times by Guardini's words and example.

Turning toward the Sources

One of the other significant figures who began the move away from an adherence to strict Thomism—at least among those who remained orthodox Catholics—was Marie-Dominique Chenu (1895–1990), a

Dominican who studied strict Thomism for seven years in Rome and wrote his dissertation under the direction of none other than Garrigou-Lagrange. Chenu's doctoral work seems to have been intended to direct the focus in contemplation away from concern with the individual soul and toward God himself, using conceptual tools partly to be found in Aquinas. He then returned to the Dominican House Le Saulchoir, the Belgian chateau to which the French Dominicans had fled when religious orders were expelled from France in 1903. There, the standard approach to Aquinas was a reading of his text, line-by-line, with little historical context or spiritual reflection. Chenu was not senior enough to teach Aquinas and instead lectured on Thomas' patristic sources—the Fathers of the Church being a common thread among all the writers of *la nouvelle théologie*. His main line of argument—quite conventional by the end of the twentieth century, by which time the plan of the *Summa Theologiae* as an account of the coming forth (*exitus*) from and return (*reditus*) to God was widely recognized—was that Thomas' greatest work was itself a kind of "Journey of the Mind to God", as Saint Bonaventure had titled one of his best-known treatises.

Despite established ways of doing things and doubts about the "historical" approach as potentially a slippery slope toward relativism and modernism, Chenu's work and his obvious personal gifts led to his being appointed regent of Le Saulchoir in 1937 at the relatively young age of forty-two. He also issued a biting critique of the old a-historical approach: *Une école de théologie: le Saulchoir*. It was brought to the attention of Rome, and Chenu was summoned to defend himself before a panel of examiners, including Garrigou-Lagrange. In the process, he was forced to sign a document affirming his acceptance of ten "propositions" not absurd on their face but simplistic and authoritarian.[42] Five years later, the book was placed on the Index, and Chenu was relieved of his duties. He transferred to the École des hautes études in Paris, a secular institution. At Vatican II, he was an adviser but not a central figure.

Chenu perhaps was the first to bring to a head a certain misunderstanding. Because many obvious modernists had used historical

[42] For further information on this episode, see Fergas Kerr, *Twentieth-Century Catholic Theologians* (Oxford: Blackwell, 2007), and the facsimile edition of *Une école de théologie: Le Saulchoir* (Paris: Cerf, 1985).

studies in an attempt to relativize Catholic teaching, a certain type of Thomist regarded all historical studies as of the same spirit. That was not true of Chenu. He used historical studies to try to open up the text of Thomas, as Thomas himself was open to examining various objections, and to give greater weight to biblical elements and the human side of the great thinker. He also sought to reconcile the intellectual giant with the spiritual master, as it has been put more recently.[43] Unlike the modernists, Chenu knew that the strict Thomists had a hold on a portion of the truth in defending timeless metaphysical principles, but these needed to be balanced with truths about God's action in history, persons, action, and "becoming". Protestants, modernists before Chenu, and Catholics after Vatican II have regarded such ideas as exploding the old Catholic emphasis on permanent truths, but their excessive focus on the particular and the historical does not mean that Chenu was wrong, merely that it is possible to lose your balance in multiple directions.

Indeed, Chenu was to write an introduction to the study of Aquinas[44] that showed how a different balance might be brought to the subject, one not without certain affinities from the theological side with philosophical Thomists such as Jacques Maritain, Étienne Gilson, and Josef Pieper. As we saw in a previous chapter, this approach recognized a certain dialogue in the working out of individual articles in the *Summa*. The reconciliation of different positions and voices was no little part of the theological process. In addition to enriching the "answers" thus achieved, it reveals that Thomas was not merely writing the kind of rationalist texts more properly the product of philosophy and theology grounded in the Enlightenment, with their aspirations to geometrical and logical certitude. Still less was he merely rationalizing in support of predetermined dogmas. He was a Christian looking to all available light in the thought with which he was familiar for a living presentation of the faith. The movement that came to be known as *ressourcement* sought to broaden Catholicity to include what Thomas had included in the study of Thomas himself and in reflection on Catholicism in general.

[43] See, for instance, Jean-Pierre Torrell, O.P., *Saint Thomas Aquinas*, vol. 2: *Spiritual Master*, trans. Robert Royal (Washington, D.C.: Catholic University of America Press, 2003).

[44] It appeared in French, after some scuffles with authorities in 1950, and in English: *Towards Understanding Saint Thomas*, trans. A.-M. Landry and D. Hughes (Chicago: Regnery, 1964).

At a minimum, that meant realizing that the historical action of God in the Bible and in his Church over the centuries was not merely material to be turned into a narrow set of rational statements. But in the twenty-first century, while much has come to be taken for granted, it must be said that many of the fears expressed by Garrigou-Lagrange and other opponents of Chenu and his fellows about *la nouvelle théologie* have come to pass. The embrace of new perspectives at Vatican II did not result in the kind of reattunement of two different sides of Catholic truth—the timeless and the timely—such as can be seen in Chenu's work on Thomas. Catholicism, despite two highly intellectual popes, John Paul II and Benedict XVI, has a difficult time defending long-established dogmas and morals. Though it was not their intention, the critics of the old system were better at stating what they were against than the limits that would stay in place once those overly stringent approaches were eliminated.[45] After the Council what are sometimes called the "acids of modernity" found no sufficiently resistant material to contain them. Individual theologians and bishops have emerged as leaders in the struggle, but the situation is far from sound—especially in Europe, but also in the whole developed world—and is likely to remain so for some time to come.

Congar: Church, Laity, Collegiality

Among those who prepared the way for Vatican II, perhaps no one was as influential as Yves Congar (1904–1995), another theologian who studied Thomist philosophy and theology but turned in several different directions. Congar entered the seminary in Paris and became a pupil of Jacques Maritain. But his experience in the military, especially five years in Nazi prisons, led him to emphasize the value of Christian unity and Church reform. Like Chenu, he got involved in the worker-priest movement in the 1950s, and he was removed from a teaching post in Le Saulchoir as a result. In fact, he was sent to England and forbidden by the Dominicans to teach. But John XXIII was enthusiastic about Congar's work and appointed him to the committees drafting texts for the Second Vatican Council. If

[45] See R. R. Reno, "Theology after the Revolution", *First Things*, May 2007.

Chenu wanted to recover a broader context for theology, Congar wished to do the same for several fields, especially the study of the Church: ecclesiology. And for similar reasons: in his view, in reaction to Reformation attacks, the Church had narrowed her own claims to a constricted and defensive position. Unity with most Protestants, he believed, was highly unlikely owing to deep divisions. But a healing of the rift between the Greek East and Latin West and at least an approach to the Anglicans seemed possible.

Congar was also largely responsible for the heightened sense of the role of the laity in the Church.[46] Though new in contrast with the emphasis on the hierarchy, it was not as radical as his opponents—and subsequent developments—made it seem. There are quite solidly Catholic arguments of the same general tenor in the great Cardinal Newman and even among orthodox lay movements such as Opus Dei. (Newman, asked whether the Church needed laypeople, responded tartly that she would look very foolish without them.) The fact that this is not better understood and that the Church, as in the Newman anecdote, is so often identified with the hierarchy has been attributed to an all-purpose villain: the defensiveness of the Church since the Reformation. Far better, Congar argued—and succeeded in getting on the agenda at Vatican II—to think of the Church as also the people of God, mystery, and other now-familiar notions.[47] He also was involved in the declaration on religious liberty and in the promotion of collegiality.

All of these notions are now familiar to Catholics. And Congar, though his importance has diminished as the reforms he sought have succeeded, has to be regarded as one of the most influential Catholic theologians of the twentieth century. John Paul II, much influenced by his work, made him a cardinal in 1994. But even Congar himself saw difficulties ahead. He feared for example the conciliar document on religious freedom, that would lead to people thinking all religions essentially the same; this has largely happened among many Catholics, with disastrous effects on the teaching of Catholic doctrine and the sense of Christianity as a missionary and evangelizing faith, as

[46] Especially through his book *Jalons pour une théologie du laïcat* (Paris: Cerf, 1953); in English, *Lay People in the Church: A Study for the Theology of the Laity*, trans. Donald Attwater, 2nd rev. ed. (Westminster, Md.: Newman Press, 1965).

commanded by its Founder. And it would not be an exaggeration to say that ideas about collegiality and laypeople in the Church were also distorted to such an extent after the Council that it often seemed as if the people and even some clergy were more anti-Catholic than the by-then friendly Protestants. Congar, like Chenu, brought much good into the Catholic Church in the twentieth century. But it seems that the cultural radicalism that affected the world as a whole in the 1960s took his work in many directions he did not desire.

Salvation: Personal and in Community

Though Congar and Chenu were among the most influential practitioners of *la nouvelle théologie* in the first half of the twentieth century, the figure often regarded as the most prominent of all was the Jesuit Henri de Lubac (1896–1991). De Lubac came from a noble French family, but studied mostly in England—where some French seminaries had fled after repression under the socialist Combes government in France. For diverse reasons, this meant that he was mostly self-taught, and he consequently became a highly productive and innovative theologian who made crucial contributions to Catholic theology on several fronts, but especially on the nature of the Church and on the vexed question of nature and grace. Though he was an admirer of Saint Thomas, his thought over the whole course of his long career was most influenced by the studies he made on his own of the Church Fathers. As a result of all these factors, he encountered no little resistance and outright hostility from the Scholastic establishment quite early on, though he was never asked to justify himself in Rome. Indeed, despite the suspicions about him in some quarters before the Second Vatican Council, his thought played a major role in developments at that pivotal event, and he was made a cardinal by John Paul II in 1983.

As noted earlier, de Lubac's first really significant book, *Catholicism*, was regarded by many of the twentieth century's key Catholic thinkers—Wojtyła, Ratzinger, von Balthasar—as the "one

[47] The American theologian Avery Dulles, S.J., gave influential expression to the ideas that started to circulate after the Council in his book *Models of the Church* (Garden City, N.Y.: Doubleday, 1974).

indispensable text". And with good reason.[48] After World War II, it revolutionized thinking about the Church for many people who were both orthodox and had a living sense of the need for a new form of ecclesial existence. The organizing thesis of de Lubac's *Catholicism* is that the early Church, patristic sources, and great figures such as Augustine and Aquinas all speak of salvation, not in the exclusively individual terms that sometimes marked Catholic piety in the first half of the twentieth century, but in social terms that recognized the Church as the Mystical Body of Christ on its way toward its promised end. Indeed, he characterizes the belief of the Fathers of the Church as all-inclusive: "For them, in fact, in a certain sense, the Church was nothing else than the human race itself, in all the phases of its history, in so far as it was to lead to Christ and be quickened by his Spirit."[49] And he comments in another context that "the Spirit of Christ once came down upon the Apostles not to unite them together in a closed group but to light within them the fire of universal charity" (110). These and many other passages present a clear and unequivocal vision of a Church both social and universal—and evangelizing by her very nature.

A careful reading of de Lubac shows that he is not at all trying to deny the properly individual side of the spiritual life, but merely to situate it and add to it—as it seems we must—in the larger life of the Church and salvation history. Pascal said in one of his letters that "whatever happens to the Church happens also to each individual soul" (206). And *mutatis mutandis*, the reverse is also true. De Lubac elaborates:

> The widespread speculations of antiquity on the subject of the microcosm and the macrocosm [the microcosm is the order of the world's macrocosm reflected in each man] become, by a double transposition, a doctrine both of social (historical) and of individual salvation. There is a correspondence between the spiritual growth of the world and

[48] It is curious that the book had different subtitles in French and English. The French edition's subtitle is *Les aspects sociaux du dogme* (Paris: Éditions du Cerf, 1947), while the English subtitle suggests something quite different: *Christ and the Common Destiny of Man*, trans. Lancelot C. Sheppard and Sr. Elizabeth Englund, O.C.D. (San Francisco: Ignatius Press, 1988). The first English edition appeared in 1950.

[49] Ibid., 191. References to pages in this 1988 edition will hereafter appear in the main text.

> that of the individual soul, for both are caused by the same divine light. The soul is the microcosm of that great universe, the Church, and all the stages traversed by the Church in her long pilgrimage are to be found in the vicissitudes of the spiritual life. (209)

Whatever qualifications a reader might want to introduce into some of de Lubac's ideas, there can be no doubt that careful attention to his text precludes classifying him as grossly neglectful of traditional spirituality.

But in *Catholicism,* de Lubac is not only concerned with correcting the historical record. On the very first pages, he makes it clear that an exclusive focus on individual piety has hampered the Church in two main ways. First, people outside the Church do not see her value for them in their particular circumstances or in the future of humanity: "'How', they ask in particular, 'can a religion which apparently is uninterested in our terrestrial future and in human fellowship offer an ideal which can still attract the men of today'?" (13–14). That was especially the danger in Europe, which, even at the beginning of the twenty-first century and after more than a hundred years of very rich Catholic social teaching, still seems to believe that Catholicism has nothing to add to the existing secular arrangements of the European Union.

For de Lubac, a second problem stems from the first, in that two categories of people have come into existence: those who have withdrawn from human interaction and focus exclusively on their personal relationship with God and those who have fully embraced the modern framework of the world and its scientific laws with no further concern about religious matters. Clearly, de Lubac sees these two stances as related to one another, and in other places he lays part of the blame for the emergence of a pure secularism at the feet of a view of faith that has one-sidedly emphasized individual piety. For de Lubac, Catholicism itself bears some of the blame for these developments because, in controversies with Lutherans and Calvinists about nature and grace, it overemphasized the idea of a self-existent "pure nature" to avoid their crushing overemphasis on grace as essentially abolishing nature. At the opposite extreme, where Catholic Renaissance figures sought a human nature divorced from God, Catholicism did not sufficiently engage the properly human but fled to "spirituality".[50] Nothing in any of these views touches on settled dogmatic questions. Indeed, de Lubac refers his readers to skillful expositions of that side of things in books like Karl Adam's *The Spirit of Catholicism*.[51] He sees his own task as restoring a fuller sense of the tradition with the aim of making Catholicism once again a spiritual energy that will revivify the world while remaining true to its own spirit.

He assembles a crowd of witnesses—one of the most enjoyable parts of the book is the appendix, which contains extensive quotations from the Church Fathers and more modern writers such as Cardinal Newman and Cardinal Faulhaber (a heroic leader of the Church in Germany in opposition to Hitler), as well as the poet Paul Claudel and Teilhard de Chardin, a friend from his days in the Jesuit seminary. The primary purpose for this documentation is to make clear what God was doing in becoming man:

> For Irenaeus again, as indeed for Origen, Gregory Nazianzen, Gregory of Nyssa, for Cyril of Alexandria, Maximus, Hilary and others, the lost sheep of the Gospel that the Good Shepherd brings back to the fold is no other than the whole of human nature; its sorry state so moves the Word of God that he leaves the great flock of angels, as it were to their own devices, in order to go to its help. The Fathers designated this nature by a series of equivalent expressions, all of a concrete nature, thus demonstrating that it was in their view a genuine reality. (25–26)

Sin itself in this view has its personal side, but the person is by nature set in a social network that shows how—in separating themselves from God—men have separated themselves from one another. De Lubac quotes a passage from Claudel that recounts how God's confusion of tongues at Babel in the Old Testament is repaired by the down rush of the Holy Spirit at Pentecost in the New Testament. In that sense, the Incarnation was not simply a mission *to* fallen peoples around the world; it *created a new people* (56).

[50] Henri de Lubac's late book on the Renaissance humanist Pico della Mirandola argues this point: *Pic de la Mirandole* (Paris: Aubier Montaigne, 1974).

[51] Adam was a priest and theologian who taught at the University of Tübingen. *The Spirit of Catholicism* first appeared in German in 1924 and has been translated into several languages, including more than ten English-language editions.

The Church, which is this new people, is also in a sense a continuation of the covenant God made with the Jews, but transfigured while remaining a concrete and living reality. The error of Protestantism was to reject that reality *in toto* because of some failures that had occurred in part. This meant more than a social division; it meant rejecting the this-worldly, concrete embodiment of God's saving action in favor of both a theory and a practice that quite quickly destroyed themselves: "The experience of Protestantism should serve us as sufficient warning. Having stripped it of all its mystical attributes, it acknowledged in the visible Church a mere secular institution; as a matter of course it abandoned it to the patronage of the state and sought a refuge for the spiritual life in an invisible Church, its concept of which had evaporated into an abstract ideal" (75–76).

In de Lubac's eyes, it was a Protestant error that forms no part of the thinking of great figures such as Saint Paul and Saint Augustine to believe that true Christianity, the pure faith, must be entirely distinct from everything human that had gone before or would come later:

> When the "reformers", not content with attacking abuses that were only too real, took it on themselves to expose on all sides what they called pagan infiltrations into the Roman Church, they were obliged in order to indicate their source to go back farther and farther to the very beginnings of Christianity. Scripture itself seemed contaminated.... Christianity transformed the old world by absorbing it. Can St. Paul's thought be imagined cut off from the numberless roots which bound it to Tarsus and Jerusalem, to Greek civilization, Eastern mysticism and the Roman Empire? These ties are necessary to it, the more so because of its profound transcendence. (284–85)

The desire to keep the Catholic faith as a kind of pure concept separated from the journey of Christ's people through time will end up by going down the same self-destructive path as that taken by the Protestant Reformers. It was to avoid various dangers of this sort that many in the tradition had warned that if we want to have God as our Father, we must have the Church as our Mother.

The way that the Church joins us to this family is by the living stream of grace in which we participate concretely in the sacraments, which thus also become channels of human unity, especially the Eucharist, *sacramentum unitatis ecclesiasticae*. Many people consider this a kind of added side benefit, but as its name implies, unity with God and with one another is the very definition of Holy Communion. Elsewhere, de Lubac uncovered in the tradition the way in which the original meaning of *corpus mysticum*—which signified the Eucharist—was later transferred to the concrete people who received the sacrament and thereby constituted the Church. In this perspective, the Church exists where the Eucharist exists. As Thomas Aquinas put it: "The Eucharist is the sacrament of the unity of the whole Church: and therefore in this sacrament, more than in the others, mention ought to be made of all that belongs to the salvation of the entire Church" (III, q. 83, a. 4 ad 3; 3:2519) (89).

So strong was the sense of solidarity among the early Fathers, says de Lubac, that a theological dispute arose over whether the saved who had died could enter into eternal life before the remaining faithful who were to come also did. It was a mistaken transposition of a temporal notion to the other world, but it shows how great was the sense of the total solidarity of the Church. This serves as a prelude to some considerations about the importance of history in Christianity and in the Judaism that preceded it. All other world religions (with the partial exception of Mazdaism) are systems of escape from the world. The Platonism of ancient Greece as well as the Hindu and Buddhist paths recognize the pain and illusion of life in this world and seek liberation from those evils in liberation from the world itself. By contrast, Christianity seeks not a liberation from the world, but a restoration of its original goodness and the redemption of the human race from its bondage to sin. Furthermore, this process inevitably gives real value to history—the history of Israel pointing toward Christ's Incarnation—because "if the salvation offered by God is in fact the salvation of the human race, since this human race lives and develops in time, any account of this salvation will naturally take a historical form—it will be the history of the penetration of humanity by Christ" (141). Universal and eternal principles, such as those developed in Thomist and Neoscholastic schools, still retain their proper importance, but Christian salvation is God's work in history.

The Bible itself must be seen, in this perspective, as a record of that historical process of salvation. On the level of understanding, the Bible both recounts concrete historical events and contains what Saint Paul and the Fathers called theories and allegories. Still, the

Scriptures give us an encounter with "a mystery which was to be fulfilled, to be *accomplished* historically and socially, though always in a spiritual manner: the mystery of Christ and his Church" (170). This is, therefore, not some "intellectual scheme" invented by gifted theologians or even the creative vision of genuine mystics. Rather, it is an account of how God has chosen to deal with and redeem his people, beginning with the covenant with the Jews, through the definitive entrance of God in the world with Jesus, and continuing into our own time and the future in the Church. That Church is also a concrete social body composed of saints and sinners, and potentially grace extends indirectly to the entire human race.

De Lubac anticipates that some will see this universal call as, in a way, eliminating the need for the Church, since every person is already enveloped in God's forgiveness and love. Christ's own directive to the apostles at the end of Matthew to preach the gospel to all nations would then seem unnecessary. In Pascal's day, the Jansenists warned that the Jesuits were teaching a similar, implicit Christianity that led to unbelief since it suggested salvation was possible outside the Church. (The influential Jesuit theologian Karl Rahner's "anonymous Christian", a much criticized notion, is analyzed here before the fact.) As can be seen in de Lubac's overall scheme, he is not himself suggesting any such thing. The Church is God's willed vehicle for the salvation that comes to us out of human history. But one of the least satisfactory parts of *Catholicism* is his attempt to deal with this difficulty. De Lubac is firm in seeing the Church—at least implicitly—as the only way of salvation for the human race. But at the same time, it is hard not to sense that even he fears there will be some diminution in missionary zeal if people come to believe that God's salvation extends to all anyway. This was a difficulty that would become pronounced once the Second Vatican Council made its well-known turn to recognizing the partial truth in other Christian bodies and the redemptive energies at work even in non-Christian religions. De Lubac wants to preserve the truth contained in the old saying *extra Ecclesiam nulla salus*, but without interpreting it in a narrow, triumphalist, and ultimately uncharitable way. All he can say about the obvious difficulty this truth presents for the practice of evangelization is that God, "desiring that all men should be saved, but not allowing in practice that all should be visibly in the Church, wills nevertheless that all those who answer his call should in the last resort be saved through his Church. *Sola Ecclesia gratia qua redimur*" (234).

De Lubac refers specifically to two central problems that arose in the Middle Ages: distorted uses of Aristotelian logic and Roman law. The latter sometimes led to a legalistic outlook in explaining elements of the Church that were clearly the mysteries of the faith. The former, in some cases, established rigorous philosophical categories for dealing with concepts, which were extremely useful for certain purposes but which set up almost a kind of philosophical equivalent of modern materialistic science that focused on discrete aspects of existence and put off the kind of organic approach that is needed when we deal with the great unsystemizable relationship between God and man. Taken together, these dimensions of the Catholic tradition, as de Lubac suggests here and elsewhere, left an opening for the splitting off of an abstract "nature" with its own laws from the more universal view of nature as creation interpenetrated at every point with mystery and grace. In a chapter on "The Present Situation", he adds that not only has the radically secular emerged from these imbalances in the Christian tradition, but the lack of the communal dimension has had disastrous consequences. He quotes Philippe de Régis, a spiritual writer with whom he obviously agrees: "Perhaps Marxism and Leninism would not have arisen and been propagated with such terrible results if the place that belongs to collectivity in the natural as well as in the supernatural order had always been given to it" (309).

Several of these distortions arose, de Lubac believed, in the confrontation with Protestantism. If Luther emphasized Christian liberty, the Catholics long had to deny it. The Reformers' errors were real, but a Church that overemphasizes her otherwise proper role as a corrector of errors to the detriment of her more positive, inspirational functions loses a great deal of her essential nature. In this light, the avoidance of error is a mere starting point for the spiritual life. Unfortunately, an embattled Church, he implies obliquely, became a "Protestantism turned inside out" and retreated from many social places into what she rightly believed was correct teaching but which was also an isolation from larger tasks that the Church must always renew from age to age in order to carry out her full mission. In withdrawing from certain disputes, the Church left the field open to the "confirmed secularists".

For de Lubac, the remedy was to "return to the sources", the *ressourcement* that would become much more widely known after the Second Vatican Council. Those sources included not only Aquinas (though it included him, too, in his full and proper teaching), but the Church Fathers and many others since the great medieval flowering of Christian thought. De Lubac argues that a return to the sources "will be the very opposite of an escape into a dead past" (322). By fully appreciating how the Church came to dominate the ancient world and to preserve herself by proper adaptations to circumstance over the two millennia of her existence, we would find a living stream of tradition that is faithful, effective, and perpetually fresh. Even theology must be engaged in this dynamic tradition: "For although dogma is essentially unchanging, the work of the theologian is never ended" (325). And he adds in a way reminiscent of Cardinal Newman's distinction between notional and real assent, "The idea of unity is not unity itself" (342).

Unfortunately, after the Second Vatican Council, many religious people misunderstood the new emphasis on the social dimension of the Church's mission. They embraced it—and often enough forgot that it was the *Church's* mission. Furthermore, some people began to scorn the old religious practices, particularly the necessary withdrawal from public view of certain religious functions. In the Catholic Church, there is as much need of the monks who went out into the Egyptian desert and their modern-day brothers and sisters in cloisters as there is of social activists. The Church is a synthesis of everything human. De Lubac makes a point of citing Joseph Maréchal's book on the psychology of mystics[52] to show that mysticism properly understood is itself a participation in the joys and sorrows of the Church in the world and that even the hidden life of those in cloisters is still a part of community. The world needs this integration of the life in God and the life in the world because otherwise it is subject to "that social humanism which is the present phase of man's hopeless endeavor to save himself by his own efforts" (355). De Lubac is unconcerned about how this will appear to those deluded by false solutions: "In examining this entirely secularized concept of society,

[52] Joseph Maréchal, *The Psychology of the Mystics*, trans. Algar Thorold, Dover Books on Western Philosophy (Mineola, N.Y.: Dover Books, 2004), is a convenient recent edition.

which at the present time dominates men's minds everywhere and only degrades what it has inherited of the historical and social character of our Faith, we must have the courage to show ourselves resolutely reactionary" (357), in the sense that certain elements in the Christian view cannot be discarded without tyrannies and totalitarian outbursts on the one side, and radical individualism and empty liberties on the other. De Lubac touches here on the deeper vision that will lie behind his masterly work *The Drama of Atheist Humanism*.[53] The Church—contrary to what many thought after the Council—does not have political or policy answers for every problem we face in the modern world. She does not offer, like modern ideologists of every stripe, utopias that delude and enslave, but she provides the indispensable background within which decisions can be made that will dignify rather than degrade the human race.

The most controversial side of de Lubac's thought for many theologians had to do with his relationship to the thought of Aquinas and, more particularly, his views on nature and grace. De Lubac enjoyed a close friendship with Étienne Gilson over several decades. Though they had their differences, they were united in a desire to correct what they both thought a misrepresentation of Catholicism as well as of Thomism. In a published letter to de Lubac in 1956, the philosopher complains: "People conjure up a Thomism after the manner of the Schools, a sort of dull rationalism which panders to the kind of deism that most of them, deep down, really prefer to teach."[54] De Lubac similarly protested in a letter to someone who accused him of being opposed to Saint Thomas that "my analyses hardly do more than put Saint Thomas into French."[55] This was true even of de Lubac's contention that it was a wrong interpretation of Thomas and of the Catholic view to posit a human nature entirely set off from God and his grace. Both he and Gilson cited Saint Thomas on this score: "Omnis intellectus naturaliter desiderat divinae substantiae visionem" (*Summa Contra Gentiles* I, 3, 57, 4). Clearly, this indicates that the human intellect is not, as in pure rationalist philosophy, closed in on itself in a naturalist way, but rather as a divine creation

[53] De Lubac, *Drama of Atheist Humanism*.

[54] *Letters of Étienne Gilson to Henri de Lubac*, trans. Mary Emily Hamilton (San Francisco: Ignatius Press, 1988), 23.

[55] Ibid., 35n7.

is always already open to the possibility of grace. And a second truth had to be coordinated with this one "quid vero sit (Deus), penitus manet incognitum", (*Contra Gentiles*, I, 3, 49, 7), which is to say that we are powerless to know anything of what God is without the assistance of divine grace.

The debate between de Lubac and his followers, on the one hand, and the Neo-Thomists of various stripes, on the other, about grace and nature has been one of the most interesting and profound theological conversations of the twentieth century. And it continues well into the twenty-first. Despite more than a half century of wrangling (de Lubac's *Surnaturel: Études historiques* appeared in 1946), the two camps have not resolved their differences, but the very engagement of one another has heightened some crucial issues that, even in the absence of agreement, have borne fruit.

The relationship of nature and grace has long been one of the most contested questions in theology, not least because it is not a problem but a mystery. And yet there are some common starting points in orthodox Christian theology. All orthodox believers accept that nature is created by God and therefore retains some essential relationship to him. At the same time, nature—or the creation—has a relative autonomy willed by God in the very act of Creation, and things in their individual natures and the order of the universe as a whole may be studied by science and understood in a certain perspective apart from theological considerations, which in the past have sometimes impeded a proper appraisal of the world God actually created as opposed to the one some theologians believed he had created. In the case of man, furthermore, because of our creation as rational creatures, we have a natural end like other created things and a supernatural end attainable only by grace, which is to say, a gift given freely by God. It is in this meeting in man of the natural and the supernatural that great theological difficulties arise.

The dispute between de Lubac and the Neo-Thomists hinges largely on what Saint Thomas himself called the *desiderium naturale visionis Dei*—the natural desire to see God. To put it simply,[56] we

[56] This very complex and subtle debate cannot be fully reproduced here. A good summary by a defender of de Lubac is Nicholas J. Healy, "Henri de Lubac on Nature and Grace: A Note on Some Recent Contributions to the Debate", *Communio* 35 (Winter 2008): 535–64.

seem to have a natural desire for something supernatural. In one way of reading Saint Thomas—the tradition that takes its beginnings from around the sixteenth century in the "second Scholasticism"—the idea of "pure nature" was put forward in a hypothetical way, then developed further so that, at least for de Lubac and his followers, the real Thomist view was lost. The Neo-Thomists' view is that natural desire must be able to find its fulfillment in what is "proportionate" to it in nature, as it is often expressed by Saint Thomas. Beyond the intellectual incoherence that de Lubac's view would seem to produce, their fear seems to be that if there is a "natural desire" for the Beatific Vision inherent in human nature, the free gift of supernatural happiness through grace is destroyed and man may even be said to have some kind of natural "right" to beatitude. In addition, such a view may weaken or even obscure the natural law principles necessary to an objective moral order and proper organization of human society.

According to de Lubac, this is a truncated reading of Thomas, one that helped produce the arid Neo-Thomism of recent times and facilitated the notion of a purely secular realm, which in the past five hundred years has degenerated into a disastrous secular humanism and even led the Church away from the mystery of the Incarnation: "What I have more than once regretted in highly regarded theologians, experienced guardians, was less, as others made it out, their lack of openness to the problems and currents of contemporary thought than their lack of a truly traditional mind (the two things are, moreover, connected)."[57] As has already been mentioned, his notion of tradition meant reading Thomas in continuity with the early Fathers and others who preceded him; de Lubac's critics tend to read Thomas in the light of the tradition of the commentary to which his work gave rise.[58] De Lubac points to

Among the strongest recent challenges to de Lubac are Lawrence Feingold, *The Natural Desire to See God according to St. Thomas Aquinas and His Interpreters* (Rome: Apollinare Studi, 2001); Stephen A. Long, "On the Loss, and Recovery, of Nature as a Theonomic Principle: Reflections on the Nature/Grace Controversy", *Nova et Vetera* 5 (2007): 133–83; and by the same author, "On the Possibility of a Purely Natural End for Man", *The Thomist* 64 (2000): 211–37. A good collection of essays sympathetic to de Lubac may be found in Bonino, *Surnaturel*.

[57] Henri de Lubac, *At the Service of the Church*, trans. Anne Englund Nash (San Francisco: Ignatius Press, 1993), 145.

[58] Healy, "Henri de Lubac", notes that Feingold especially takes this approach.

several places in Thomas' work where he says that human nature, made in the image of God, does have a natural desire for God, even if it cannot satisfy that desire on its own. For example, "In the very beginning of creation, human nature was ordained to beatitude, not as to an end proper to man by reason of his nature, but given him solely by divine liberality. Therefore, there is no need for the principles of nature to have sufficient power to achieve that end without the aid of special gifts with which God in his generosity supplements them" (*De Veritate* q. 14, a. 10 ad 2).

For de Lubac, this means that God has built into such a nature, not a supernatural power, but a certain receptive potentiality, which is to say, a capacity to recognize that what will truly make us happy is something we cannot attain or know or even fully anticipate on our own. From the Neo-Thomist perspective, this looks quite close to saying that we have a "natural" supernatural power (though some of the representatives of this tradition have conceded that there is a conflict of Thomistic texts not easily reconcilable.)[59] It is certainly a good thing to beware of implying anything of the sort; by and large, de Lubac was aware of and repudiated that way of construing his work. Still, the whole Christian tradition also contains affirmations such as this from the modern *Catechism of the Catholic Church*: "The desire for God is written in the human heart, because man is created by God and for God; and God never ceases to draw man to himself" (*CCC* 27). Several commentators have rightly added that, at least so far as human nature is concerned, this means that when God finally revealed himself in Christ, he also revealed the nature of nature. A human nature left, even hypothetically, as pure in itself would be difficult to understand as somehow also open to what transcends it.

De Lubac's work seems to point toward the truth that there are two gifts involved in human nature: the first is being itself, and of a kind that allows for the reception of the second gift, the grace of eternal life, as something in a way "natural", something unexpected that is paradoxically also expected, not just a bolt out of the blue. And yet: "The fact that the nature of spiritual being, as it actually

[59] See Long, "On the Loss", 137, and Henry Donneaud, "*Surnaturel* through the Fine-Tooth Comb of Traditional Thomism", in Bonino, *Surnaturel*, 41–57.

exists, is not conceived as an order destined to close in finally upon itself, but in a sense open to an inevitably supernatural end, does not mean that it already has in itself, or as part of its basis, the smallest positively supernatural element."[60] So even if there are two ends of human nature, one natural and the other supernatural, they may both find potentiality in human nature itself prior to the actual arrival of God's grace needed for the elevation of that nature to its otherwise unattainable beatitude.

Since the middle of the twentieth century, it has sometimes been believed that Pius XII's 1950 encyclical *Humani Generis* implicitly criticized de Lubac's whole project.[61] And there is evidence that this was so in that, after the encyclical appeared, de Lubac had his teaching curtailed and his books removed from libraries by the Jesuits. In his little book on de Lubac, Hans Urs von Balthasar reports that, at the very end of his life, de Lubac expressed his hope of writing a comprehensive theological work "that would have been less systematic than the manuals but more saturated with tradition, integrating the valid elements in the results of modern exegesis, of patristics, liturgy, history, philosophical reflection.... The lightning bolt of *Humani generis* killed the project."[62] But de Lubac himself later pointed out that Pius XII criticized in that encyclical those who "destroy the gratuity of grace" and place a necessity on God to order and call every intellectual creature to the Beatific Vision. He himself took no such views and characterized the encyclical as "very different from what some had anticipated: it even caused in them some disappointments.... It is not by chance that it avoids any mention of the famous 'pure nature' that a number of highly placed theologians were accusing me of misunderstanding and which they wanted to have canonized."[63] In the longer perspective, he seems to be right; certainly the dominant figures in later Catholic theology and de Lubac's high status with

[60] Henri de Lubac, S.J., *The Mystery of the Supernatural*, trans. Rosemary Sheed, Milestones in Catholic Theology (New York: Crossroad, 1998), 31.

[61] For an account of events before and after the encyclical appeared, see Aidan Nichols, O.P., "Thomism and the *nouvelle théologie*", *The Thomist* 64 (2000): 1–19.

[62] Hans Urs von Balthasar, *The Theology of Henri de Lubac: An Overview* (San Francisco: Ignatius Press, 1991), 10–11.

[63] Henri de Lubac, *Theology in History*, trans. Anne Englund Nash (San Francisco: Ignatius Press, 1996), 281.

several subsequent popes suggest that he did not lack for supporters (John Paul II named him a cardinal in 1983). But in the dozen years between *Humani Generis* and the first session of the Second Vatican Council, the future was far more uncertain.

Chapter 4

Critical Interlude: The Second Vatican Council

The Yes said wholeheartedly to the Council and to all its legitimate consequences must, in order to remain consistent and sincere, be coupled with a No that is just as resolute to a certain type of exploitation that is in fact a perversion of it.

—Henri de Lubac[1]

Catholic intellectual developments occur, as happens in other traditions, in response to new facts in the world or questions raised by contemporary culture. But they also arise in no small part from the way the Church's teaching authority seeks to preserve and to present revealed truths. One of the distinctive features of Catholicism from the very first has been the belief that God has revealed manifold truths about himself and human life that he asks to be preached to all nations (cf. Mt 28:18–20). For about the first two-thirds of the twentieth century, as we have seen, efforts by Church authorities to preserve revealed truths often took the form of nervous defensiveness toward much that was, and is, threatening to faith in the modern world. For the last third of the century, Catholic intellectual life—by then, for the most part, radically independent of Church authority—seemed to run to the opposite extreme, often embracing the world and modern ideas with uncertain relationships to the revealed truths of Catholicism. The single most important factor in that massive change—indeed, the hinge on which the whole turned—was, of course, the Second Vatican Council (1962–1965), which not a few people believe was the most important religious event in the

[1] *At the Service of the Church: Henri de Lubac Reflects on the Circumstances That Occasioned His Writings*, trans. Anne Elizabeth Englund (San Francisco: Ignatius Press, 1993), 118.

twentieth century. It calls for brief treatment here insofar as it had an impact on the Catholic intellectual tradition.[2]

Vatican II was unique among the more than twenty previous ecumenical councils both in being convened without any looming crisis or the intention of issuing new dogmatic definitions—the most typical reasons for a council—and, at the same time, in giving the impression of having radically altered everything. Proper understanding of the Council was not helped by the fact that it occurred just prior to the cultural revolution that swept through various nations around the globe in 1968. The changes introduced by the Council were, therefore, caught up in many quite radical public disputes that formed no part of its actual deliberations. Most notably, Vatican II has often been characterized as a battle royal between good liberals, led by the easygoing Italian Angelo Roncalli—Pope John XXIII—and evil conservatives, shadowy forces of reaction that, allegedly, resisted the promptings of the new outpouring of the "Spirit" of the Council.

It is not surprising that outside commentators saw things in the binary terms of political factions—and with a bias toward the faction that seemed most congenial to secular liberal perspectives (*Time* magazine named the pope 1962 "Man of the Year").[3] That is how things are generally viewed in the world of contemporary democratic politics and how they were reported by secular media at the time. But it is surprising that many *Catholics* came to accept the same politicized framework, which guaranteed that interpretation of the Council would be mired in what seemed to be mere partisan claims and power struggles, rather than focused on the perennial *religious* search for the One who is good, true, and beautiful. It did not have to be that way and could have unfolded differently—if the Church herself had been prepared to instruct her own people about the Council and implement it in an orderly way. But the Church in the 1960s was, for the most part, not so prepared. Once the earlier, rather rigid and

[2] See also chapter 6 for a discussion of Vatican II's Dogmatic Constitution on Divine Revelation *Dei Verbum*.

[3] A series of articles in the *New Yorker* during the Council by "Xavier Rynne" famously established this approach in the English-speaking world. The series (actually by the Redemptorist Father Francis X. Murphy) was later reprinted in book form as *Letters from Vatican City*, 4 vols. (London: Faber and Faber, 1963–1966). A less partisan account from roughly the same time is Ralph M. Wiltgen, *The Rhine Flows into the Tiber: The Unknown Council* (New York: Hawthorn Books, 1967).

authoritarian stance was relaxed, many Catholics assumed everything was up for grabs. And instead of the Council's fulfilling John XXIII's wish to make the Church a more effective instrument of evangelization in the modern world, that world—it might be said—in several ways evangelized the Church, sometimes for the good, but in many unfortunate ways, too.

Anyone familiar with what has been often *said* to be conciliar teaching, for instance, about the relationship of people, priests, theologians, bishops, and popes for the half century since the Council might be shocked by actually reading *Lumen Gentium*, the crucial Dogmatic Constitution on the Church. In a common telling, Vatican II put laypeople on the same plane as the institutional leadership—which it did, in the sense that the Council made clear, for the first time in the history of ecumenical councils, that all Christians participate in the Mystical Body of Christ, a notion that had already begun to be emphasized during the papacy of Pius XII.[4] But *mutatis mutandis*, this is a bit like saying that all Americans, from ordinary folk to the president, are equally citizens. It does not abolish the necessary and proper authority of executives, legislators, and judges, the kinds of structure needed for any human institution to function. To be sure, there were Catholic *theologians* who made such radical and utopian claims and both laypeople and religious who believed them. And this in itself became a large part of the problem of interpretation, the confused sense that theologians have a special authority, in certain matters greater than that of bishops and popes acting as successors to the apostles (or that theologians—a contentious lot—all agree and have settled difficult questions). But there is nothing whatever in any document approved by the Council Fathers that countenances such radical departures from a traditional Catholic understanding of the nature of Christ's Church as involving a creed and successors to the apostles (popes and bishops) who hold the keys to the kingdom and certain, if circumscribed, authority over faith and morals.

In many ways, *Lumen Gentium* was quite a traditional document—with, to be sure, some important new emphases on the Church as the people of God, the mission of laypeople, the universal call to holiness (for religious and laity alike), collegiality among the bishops, and the relationship of the Catholic Church to other Christian

[4] See Pius XII, *Mystici Corporis* (1943).

churches, non-Christian religions, and even sincere non-believers. In other documents, Catholics would even be encouraged to read the Bible on their own without much fear of the Protestant error known as "private interpretation". All this reflected John XXIII's desire to enter into a fruitful cultural dialogue rather than issue proclamations and condemnations, which many thought had been too large a part of Catholic practice in the recent past. And the more than 2,500 Council Fathers (bishops and others), their theological advisors (*periti*), along with lay participants and Protestant "observers" were by large majorities in agreement with him.

Still, the very first paragraph in *Lumen Gentium* proclaims that the Church: "desires now to unfold more fully to the faithful of the Church and to the whole world its own inner nature and universal mission. *This it intends to do following faithfully the teaching of previous councils*" (emphasis added). And it delivers on that promise, though the Council Fathers by their very manner of writing broke with the more authoritarian and legalistic manner of previous councils and clearly encouraged dialogue and persuasion over more confrontational models. Furthermore, the Council Fathers were echoing the very intention of "good" Pope John XXIII in calling the council, which he said in *Gaudet Mater Ecclesiae*, his opening address, was "*to transmit the doctrine, pure and integral, without any attenuation or distortion, which throughout twenty centuries, notwithstanding difficulties and contrasts, has become the common patrimony of men*" (emphasis added). He, of course, explained that modern conditions required new ways of presenting the timeless truths of the faith. That was his whole intention in calling together the bishops for such an event, which strictly speaking was, as he put it, "not necessary". And he made a special point of shifting away from the nervous opposition to the modern world: "Errors vanish as quickly as they arise, like fog before the sun. The Church has always opposed these errors. Frequently she has condemned them with the greatest severity. Nowadays, however, the spouse of Christ prefers to make use of the medicine of mercy rather than that of severity. She considers that she meets the needs of the present day by demonstrating the validity of her teaching rather than by condemnations."[5]

[5] A translation of *Gaudet Mater Ecclesia* is included in Walter M. Abbott, S.J., ed., *The Documents of Vatican II* (New York: America Press, 1966), 710–19.

This was a brave and confident stance, especially in view of the fact that such patient explanation, as the pope well knew, may be misinterpreted as weakness and that dialogue often fails to overcome real differences. In the aftermath of the Council, dialogue often led Catholics into situations in which they entered into much better relations with others but often lost a grip on their own tradition. The pope placed his confidence in the solidity of the two-thousand-year-old tradition; his declared intentions do not even mildly suggest he was opening the way to radical departure from Catholicism's self-understanding since the early centuries as a Church whose teachings develop in response to new questions and conditions, but always in living continuity with her own past. There was much, despite the confidence, that still needed to be contested. Indeed, it has often been overlooked that he immediately added, "Not, certainly, that there is a lack of fallacious teaching, opinions, and dangerous concepts to be guarded against and dissipated." But John generously added that even many in the secular world see the dangers in such aberrations (unlike the Council Fathers, he even noted the absence of bishops prevented mostly by Communist governments from attending the Council). His was meant to be a "predominantly pastoral", not a dogmatic, council, one that would seek more effective ways to carry out the perennial task of evangelizing an ever-changing world.

One sign that this fundamental orientation had been misunderstood would soon come to the fore. Some interpreters would put the above-mentioned "pastoral" needs above dogmatic ones, as if the care for Christ's flock could be opposed to the truths on which it had always been understood to be based—a bit like a doctor having a good bedside manner but little medical knowledge. Though many good things were to come, even in the short run, out of the Council a more heartfelt connection to the faith for many laypeople and religious and a Church now seen as a Mother who squarely engaged the public and private lives of ordinary modern people in a caring and elevated way that acknowledged their dignity and freedom—the consequences of this misunderstanding were many and grave. No one—let alone John XXIII or the Council Fathers—would have dreamed that their enthusiasm for a more open, self-assured, and evangelical Catholicism, within the framework of long-established truths, would lead within a few years to: mass exodus from the priesthood and various male and female religious orders; an ongoing crisis of vocations;

steep declines in Mass attendance in the wealthier countries; debates within the Church over married and female priests; "Catholic theologians" who offered themselves as "a parallel magisterium" equal to and even superior to popes and bishops in certain matters, who challenged longstanding Church teaching on contraception, abortion, divorce, gay "marriage", and even such theological mainstays as the Real Presence in the Eucharist, the divinity of Christ, his Resurrection—even Christ as the unique Savior—and all while enjoying official positions within Catholic institutions.

Participants in the Council and observers have recorded the great hopes and enthusiasms present at the outset, which anticipated a worldwide renewal. The new spirit was evident from the first in that the *schemata* (draft texts) prepared prior to the first session in 1962, some of which were couched in the heavy Scholastic and bureaucratic terminology of the past, were for the most part discarded by the bishops. They asked for new drafts of documents that better represented John XXIII's intention that a Church, confident in her teachings and practices, would engage the modern world without fear in a language the world could understand. As a young Joseph Ratzinger described the process:

> The Council's statements are not a body of purely intellectual teaching; still less are they simply a collection of technical and pragmatic directives. They are the product of a spiritual process. A process or movement can only be comprehended by participating in it, by gradual, step-by-step, obedient involvement in it. We would misunderstand the Council's teaching were we to take it as a sudden switchover, a sudden shift from "conservatism" to "progressivism" in the Church. Ultimately the Council sought simply to do at the present time what the Church's proclamation is supposed to do at all times: to lead the way on the journey of faith.[6]

That journey, he reminded readers, began when God called Abraham out of "Ur of the Chaldees" toward the land of promise. To apply terms like progressive or conservative to such a journey was simply not appropriate: "The measure of the renewal is Christ, as scripture

[6] From his preface to the English edition of *Theological Highlights of Vatican II* (New York: Paulist Press, 1966), 1.

witnesses him.... *Aggiornamento* [should be] an updating aimed at finding a pathway from our transitory today into the never-ending today of the Lord."[7]

At the same time, the sheer scope of the undertaking was vast, perhaps precisely because the Council was not convened to deal with a set of specific issues. The preparatory commissions had written seventy *schemata*, or about two thousand pages—more, according to Ratzinger, than all previous councils put together. The active participation of the bishops of the world in reviewing and, early in the Council, asking for substitute drafts of the various documents gave many observers the sense of the college of bishops as a true *governing* presence in the contemporary life of the Church. The body of bishops included members confronting Communism in the East and materialism in the West, those rooted in traditional societies of the developing world and in highly technological ones in the developed world. Their differing perspectives and concerns made agreement more complex, but they also—especially in the conversations that took place largely outside the more formal atmosphere of the official meetings in Saint Peter's—enriched the final results with a global universality that perhaps no other institution in the world at the time or since could match. And this dialogue only became stronger over the four sessions that took place each fall from 1962 to 1965.

As noted elsewhere in the present study, two ideas—*aggiornamento* and *ressourcement*—became the watchwords for the whole Council. *Aggiornamento* referred to the updating most participants in the deliberations saw as a legitimate need of "reading the signs of the times". *Ressourcement*, a term apparently coined by the French poet Charles Péguy, entailed a return to the ancient sources and was thought of, by de Lubac and many others, as the way to open the Church to a greater richness within her own authentic tradition by drawing on the sources from which Thomas himself drew. These two orientations are not as contradictory as they may seem on the surface. One of the ways that persons, groups, and even nations often discover the resources needed to meet present challenges is by a return to the origins, not in a spirit of antiquarianism, but as a way to reconnect with the living germ that may have been obscured by later growth.

[7] Ibid., 2.

At the same time, it is clear that authentic renewal is never merely a radical departure, a discontinuity with the originating spirit, but is, rather, a chance to bring forward new growth from the old trunk under changed conditions.

For essentially two decades after the close of the Council, all this was obscured in a swirl of contention, usually between one group that considered the Council's texts authoritative and another camp that thought the new, more open "spirit" that produced them should be given further scope. Paul VI set up a synod of bishops, as requested by the Council Fathers, to help with implementation. Already in 1967 (that is, only two years after the Council ended), the synod was concerned about theological developments in some places where "it is no longer a question of sound and fruitful investigation, or of legitimate efforts to adapt the expression of traditional doctrine to new needs, and to the ways of modern human culture, but rather of unwarranted innovations, false opinions, and even errors in the faith."[8] And this was before the firestorm of dissent set off the following year by Paul VI's encyclical *Humanae Vitae*, which reaffirmed traditional teaching on sexual matters, including contraception. Such battles over what once seemed—and indeed was—settled teaching on fundamental matters like God, Jesus, scriptural truth, and sin, unchanged by anything in the actual documents published by the Council, only seemed to grow and spread in the following decade, and not only in ethereal debates among scholars but in formation programs from Catholic grade schools and First Communion classes to universities and even to seminaries.

So much so that in 1985, early in the papacy of John Paul II, an extraordinary synod of bishops met to assess the reception of Vatican II almost twenty-five years after the Council had opened and to recommend ways to make better use of the Council. These bishops, who came together in Rome from all over the world, overwhelmingly agreed that the Council had been a great step forward, but they also reported various problems with its interpretation and implementation. As a young bishop, John Paul II had been an enthusiastic participant in the Council, especially in its openings to religious liberty, engagement with the modern world, and a more evangelical

[8] Report of the Synodal Commission, *The Furrow* vol. 19, no. 2 (Feb. 1968), 108.

than regulatory Church. Indeed, he kept his priests and laypeople in Kraków informed about events in Rome during the sessions and, after the Council ended, made sure they understood the documents by establishing the Synod of Kraków and a network of groups that met precisely to study and think through implementation.[9] These groups produced four hundred pages of documents of their own. Kraków was one of the few dioceses in the world where the new and old found a workable balance, avoiding the gross misunderstanding, ill-advised experimentation, and contentious spirit that marred the renewal in most places. In the first decades of the twenty-first century, dozens of such groups were still actively meeting in Kraków.

Kraków also benefited from having a bishop who had thought through many issues in confrontation with two of the nastiest inventions of the secular world in the twentieth century: Nazism and Communism. It was one of the themes of his thinking from the 1940s until the end of his papacy that a "mistaken anthropology" lay at the heart of these murderous ideologies—just as a different kind of error about man drove the increasingly materialist, if free, societies of the West. Wojtyła touted the "dignity of the human person", properly understood as including an opening to the transcendent, as the remedy for many modern aberrations. That dignity was also the basis for a larger and more active participation by laypeople in the Church; they would take on their own proper roles in the Church and the world, roles not identical with those of the clergy or hierarchy, but of crucial significance in their own right. Wojtyła worked these theories out in books he wrote before and after the Council (and covertly during some of the more boring sessions, as he later confessed).

Those principles had spectacular success, eventually, against Communism. But in terms of recalling the West to a saner understanding of its own foundations and of tempering some of the excesses let loose by the Council within the Church, the picture was more mixed. The "dignity of the human person" in the West usually leads to the postmodern assumption that such dignity entails a radically individual autonomy. In that view, nature and God are regarded, not as conditions of our very being, the guarantee of our liberty and

[9] For an account of this adaptation, see George Weigel, *Witness to Hope: The Biography of John Paul II* (New York: Cliff Street Books, 1999), 155–74.

dignity, but as external restraints to be accepted only if a particular person feels they should be. "Feels" is the *mot juste* here, as we saw in examining Alasdair MacIntyre, since it is assumed there are no conclusive arguments in favor of the traditional view of truth as forming one coherent and universal whole. Critics began calling Church members who embraced some of these views "cafeteria Catholics", meaning they chose only what they wanted from what was on offer from the Church. Though this was originally a term of deprecation, cafeteria Catholics later came to embrace the label as if it were perfectly compatible with being a Catholic, an idea never before seriously entertained in two thousand years of Church history.

That was a central reason why, outside of the Archdiocese of Kraków, even Catholics needed some better orientation in what their Church now did—and did not—teach. The 1985 extraordinary synod, clearly called by John Paul II as an effort to do for the universal Church what he had done in his own archdiocese, sought to provide clarity about what had changed and what always remains the same. Some have praised or blamed him for trying a "restoration", a fair description only if it means that he sought a fuller implementation of the Council.[10] Nothing in his papacy sought merely to go back to a preconciliar Church. The synod's final report[11] offered guidelines for the future, which the American theologian Avery Dulles, S.J., summed up under six headings:

1. Each passage and document of the council must be interpreted in the context of all the others, so that the integral meaning of the council may be rightly grasped.
2. The four constitutions of the council ... are the hermeneutical key to the other documents....
3. The pastoral import of the documents may not be separated from, or set in opposition to, their doctrinal content.
4. No opposition may be made between the spirit and the letter of Vatican II.
5. The council must be interpreted in continuity with the great tradition of the church, including earlier councils.

[10] See Paul Johnson, *Pope John Paul II and the Catholic Restoration* (New York: St. Martin's Press, 1981).

[11] "The Final Report: Synod of Bishops", *Origins* 15 (December 19, 1985): 444–50.

6. Vatican II should be accepted as illuminating the problems of our own day.[12]

It is not very difficult to read between the lines. With the exception of the very last point—presumably intended to stop conservatives and traditionalists from wholesale repudiation of the Council because of excesses—the guidelines implicitly underscore misuses of the Council by various parties.

The 1985 synod also clearly moved away from an overemphasis on terms like "people of God" in referring to the Church, which—though a much-needed corrective from earlier attitudes, especially among the bureaucratic Roman Curia—had led to massive confusion about the relationship of the hierarchy and the laity. The "people of God" is not synonymous in the documents with the laity but, rather, is constituted by laity, clergy, religious, and hierarchy alike. In the immediate aftermath of the Council, many thought that "mature" laypeople, now finally taking responsibility for their own spiritual lives, and Church authorities had been placed on an equal plane. Catholicism has always accepted that an unlettered holy person may be given access to great truths unseen by others. That is a common element in the lives of the saints. And such insights then deserve to be listened to and incorporated into the universal Church. In the nature of things, however, individuals with "prophetic" powers are few, and most untrained laypeople do not have significant insights into matters of faith and morals. The vast majority of Catholics, especially given the poor preparation of Catholic laity in Scripture and other subjects crucial to understanding the faith—long a complaint about the Church—were not especially suited to an advisory role. The easy assumption that all have prophetic gifts or at least opinions of equal worth to anyone else's essentially guaranteed that contemporary attitudes, popular primarily in wealthier countries, but untethered to

[12] Avery Dulles, S.J., "The Reception of Vatican II at the Extraordinary Synod of 1985", in Giuseppe Alberigo, Jean-Pierre Jossua, and Joseph A. Komonchak, eds., *The Reception of Vatican* II, trans. Matthew J. O'Connell (Washington, D.C.: The Catholic University of America Press, 1987), 350. Alberigo and Komonchak have also produced a five-volume *History of Vatican II* (Maryknoll, N.Y.: Orbis Books, 1995–2006), which is somewhat uneven but is the most exhaustive source in English. Herbert Vorgrimler, ed., *Commentary on the Documents of Vatican II* (New York: Herder and Herder, 1967–1969), though older, remains, at five volumes, another useful tool.

biblical understanding and often even opposed to it, would come forward as the voice of the "people of God". But as all the conciliar documents underscore, people and hierarchy are not opposed, "either-or" terms, but are mutually enriching and necessary—a "both-and" relationship typical of Catholic perspectives.

The 1985 synod also clarified, while still endorsing, ecumenism as a necessary Christian effort to achieve the unity Christ desires among his flock. That proper task cannot detract from another: the perennial need to evangelize the whole world, meaning to bring the world to the full truth, which Catholics believe exists in the Catholic Church. The synod even referred to the Cross—a theme almost totally absent at Vatican II—which some saw as a reminder that Catholics, like Christ himself, should expect clashes, not harmony and not even a benign neutrality, with the world.[13] Some of the properly progressive currents survived in the synod's final report—as did even militant elements like liberation theology. But all these formulations were far removed from the situation in the 1960s, with its easy assumptions of the rightness of radical experimentation and the opposition of a "people's church" to the actually existing Catholic Church. Avery Dulles summed up the new outlook; it affirmed what was legitimate in several new currents, but with proper cautions. The judicious Dulles strongly asserted: "If the Catholic Church has a will to survive—and all the evidence suggests that it does—it would do well to heed the prescriptions of the Synod."[14]

Of course, the fact that the bishops of the world meeting in a synod produced a corrective document did not and does not mean that theological confusion was dispelled. In fact, even one of the synod's concrete and highly successful proposals, the preparation of a *Catechism of the Catholic Church* based on Vatican II (which appeared seven

[13] One sign of the complexity of Vatican II is that the German bishops, who led the way on liturgy reform, scriptural interpretation, and collegiality of bishops with the pope—all usually thought of as progressive issues—resisted what they regarded as the overly optimistic view of the modern world in *Gaudium et Spes*. By contrast, Cardinal Ottaviani, one of the conservative leaders, wanted to declare nuclear weapons intrinsically immoral while the Germans thought they might be justified as a deterrent. And two thinkers usually thought of as polar opposites—Joseph Ratzinger and Karl Rahner—were in agreement in criticizing the optimism of the text of *Gaudium et Spes*, as was Karol Wojtyła. See John W. O'Malley, *What Happened at Vatican II* (Cambridge, Mass.: Harvard University Press, 2008), 258–59.

[14] Dulles, "Reception of Vatican II", 356.

years later in 1992), had only a limited effect, largely on those already inclined to respect Church authority and on potential converts. Indeed, it would be truer to say that by then, despite the efforts of John Paul II, a disjunctive view of the Council had become institutionalized at the highest academic levels—as a sort of parallel magisterium—and in catechetical and other Church training programs that depended on Catholic colleges and universities for intellectual guidance.

The Vatican seems to have recognized as much because it made three more attempts to rein in theologians who had come to view themselves as somehow operating with authority independent of the Church but with a right to speak to laypeople, who were put in the impossible position of having to decide, mostly in ignorance, whether the pope or the professors had the authority to speak:

1. In 1989 the Vatican required a profession of faith for all those who fill an office or teach in the name of the Church.
2. Also required was an oath of fidelity for those in official Catholic institutions. Both measures encountered stiff opposition. Many theologians took refuge in a legal technicality: since most Catholic universities and colleges had been converted to lay governance while retaining a nominal Catholic identity, faculty were not subject to the oath.
3. After eight years, the Vatican closed this loophole by reforming the relevant canons.

As with the fidelity oaths at the beginning of the twentieth century, these administrative moves did little to resolve fundamental problems, notably entrenched opinions in colleges, universities, seminaries, and even some chanceries, though what was requested here was not in any way as crude or sweeping—or unfair—as the earlier efforts against modernism.

Well into the twenty-first century, however, much of the institutional bureaucracy that had come into being as a result of progressive initiatives remained in place. Confusion and conflict at a fundamental level continued to make the transmission of the most basic truths about Catholic faith and morals a very difficult thing indeed. As late as 2010, Pope Benedict XVI remarked in an interview that it was puzzling how Catholics who had attended Catholic schools for a dozen years or more often seemed to emerge with a sympathy for Islam or a basic acquaintance with Buddhism, but not to have acquired much loyalty toward or knowledge of their own faith. Benedict did not speculate on the reasons for this phenomenon, but it is clear that they involve ongoing conflicts within Catholicism in the wake of Vatican II that make any straightforward presentation of even the simplest truths, paradoxically, in Catholic institutions themselves, quite difficult.

A Brief Tour of the Documents—and Controversies

The great English convert John Henry Newman—later made a cardinal and by general agreement among the most brilliant Englishmen of the nineteenth century—was asked in 1859 by Bishop Ullathorne of Birmingham "Who are the laity?" He replied, he said, though not exactly in these words: "The Church would look foolish without them."[15] It is an exaggeration to say that, prior to the Second Vatican Council, laypeople had been essentially discounted in the theology of the Church: there was appreciation of the lay vocation not only in Newman, but in earlier figures such as Saint Philip Neri, Saint Francis de Sales, and several others, and later even in a "conservative" group such as Opus Dei, founded in 1928—more than three decades before Vatican II. But as Newman's anecdote makes clear, there *was* a presumption among many members of the hierarchy, and not only among Roman curial insiders, that the Church was to be identified primarily with pope, bishops, and priests. Laypeople, when they were thought of at all, were expected to be largely passive recipients of sacraments and graces distributed by clergy.[16]

Perhaps the most far-reaching and urgently needed change brought about at Vatican II was a shift in the understanding of the Church, which gave much greater prominence to the laity—"empowering the laity", as it came to be said—though not in the ways often believed. A great irony in this shift was that, for some interpreters,

[15] Memorandum, May 22, 1859, *Letters and Diaries of John Henry Newman*, vol. 19 (London and New York: T. Nelson, 1969), 140–41.

[16] For a lively exploration of this subject, see Russell Shaw, *To Hunt, To Shoot, To Entertain: Clericalism and the Catholic Laity* (San Francisco: Ignatius Press, 1993).

the complaints about the over-clericalization of the Church meant that the laity should be "empowered" to perform *clerical* tasks. More people than it would previously have been thought possible began to cluster around the altar as lectors, music "ministers", and extraordinary ministers of the Eucharist. In addition, a vocal contingent of "lay" people consisted of laicized former priests and nuns who often did not cease from wanting a say in running the Church. Laypeople were also included, with greater fidelity to the Council, in advisory boards in parishes and dioceses.

Some of these changes did significant good or no harm, but the primary conciliar vision for the laity was something quite different. Chapter 4 of *Lumen Gentium*, the first extensive treatment of the lay vocation by the Council, declares:

> What specifically characterizes the laity is their *secular nature*. It is true that those in holy orders can at times be engaged in secular activities, and even have a secular profession. But they are by reason of their particular vocation especially and professedly ordained to the sacred ministry.... *The laity, by their very vocation, seek the kingdom of God by engaging in temporal affairs and by ordering them according to the plan of God.* They live in the world, that is, in each and in all of the secular professions and occupations. They live in the ordinary circumstances of family and social life, from which the very web of their existence is woven. They are called there by God that by exercising their proper function and led by the spirit of the Gospel they may work for the sanctification of the world from within as a leaven. (*LG* 31, emphasis added)

The basic orientation here is a Catholicism that does not rely solely on pope and bishops to exert influence on developments in the "world" from outside; laypeople "in all of the secular professions and occupations" would inspire society, culture, law, and politics with Christian values from within, and might even engage in evangelization, in the place where they had the greatest expertise.

This is very nearly the exact opposite of what began to happen. Earlier in the century, there had been varied attempts to create lay associations, everything from Catholic Action to Christian democrat parties to Christian labor unions to Catholic medical, legal, and professional societies to deal with the challenges for Catholicism in modern culture. Paradoxically, after a meeting of all the world's bishops, which commended precisely this kind of activity on an individual and group basis, many such institutions began to wither away—as did the distinctive Catholic perspective that gave them their reason for being. It was perhaps inevitable that inviting the laity, with their secular expertise, into the Church's conversation about herself would require the assimilation of much that had been fearfully excluded in the past. But the assimilation did not occur with any degree of real expansion of the lay Catholic vocation to carry the truth into the world. Pope John XXIII had opened the Council confident that no restatement of what "has repeatedly been taught" was necessary and that the basics of Catholicism could be "presumed to be well known and familiar to all". They were not. Instead, laypeople—from politicians to doctors to academics—with no special training in theology or pastoral work began to speak to the Church. They spoke sometimes with justice, about reforming institutions that needed to enter into dialogue with real modern achievements, but perhaps even more often in dissent about core Church matters about which laity knew very little, which set the whole Catholic system into a tailspin.

Lumen Gentium as such was, strictly speaking, not responsible for any of this. Each of its seven chapters was carefully crafted, and even the order in which they appear was thoroughly discussed by the Council Fathers in order to communicate precisely what was new, and not new, in these essential pages. The preparatory Neoscholastic *schema* (draft document) essentially repeating Vatican I was rejected early on in favor of a text—and a vision—more evangelical and less institutional and legalistic. But "less" does not mean that institutional elements and defined dogmas were ignored or eliminated; they were merely placed in a different context where the kind of authority exercised by the Roman pontiff and definite dogmas were shown to be in the service of—not abrogated by—the care of the flock and the command to evangelize all nations. The "light of the world" of which the title speaks is not the Church, but Christ himself, about whom Catholicism has elaborated many truths.

Chapter 1 accordingly treats "The Mystery of the Church", a mystery that proceeds from and finds its summit in the Eucharist, which is the Body of Christ and the force behind the creation of the

Mystical Body.[17] All men are called to union in that body—not, as was sometimes later asserted, irrespective of the beliefs they actually hold, but to union in the invisible Church by membership in the visible Church. *Lumen Gentium* would go on to make clear that there is value in other forms of belief, especially the Christian and Jewish communities with deep historic and theological connections to the Catholic Church. But all this supposes a dogmatic background for an understanding of the reason why the "mystery" matters or has anything important to say. Yves Congar, whom we have seen was one of the inspirations of the Council and a strong proponent of Christian ecumenism, criticized the way in which after the Council "people of God" was given some kind of vaguely democratic meaning independent of its connection with the idea of Church as a sacrament and as the body of Christ, "Only thus does it secure its adequate Christological reference."[18]

Chapter 2, "The People of God", was deliberately placed after the earlier exposition. There it becomes clear that God wills to save all wherever they are, even those who do not and perhaps cannot have known the one Mediator, Jesus. So the Church looks out to all with love and a kind of respect for those made in God's image, though with no loss of belief in the importance of actual conversion. And the chapter concludes:

> As the Son was sent by the Father, so He too sent the Apostles, saying: "Go, therefore, make disciples of all nations, baptizing them in the name of the Father and of the Son and of the Holy Spirit, teaching them to observe all things whatsoever I have commanded you. And behold I am with you all days even to the consummation of the world." The Church has received this solemn mandate of Christ to proclaim the saving truth from the apostles and must carry it out to the very ends of the earth.... For the Church is compelled by the Holy Spirit to do her part that God's plan may be fully realized, whereby He has constituted Christ as the source of salvation for

[17] It is probably not a coincidence that the first chapter of de Lubac's *The Splendor of the Church* (1956) had a similar title: "The Church as Mystery" (in the original French, "L'Église est un mystère": The Church is a mystery).

[18] Yves Congar, "The Church: The People of God", in Edward Schillebeeckx, ed., *The Church and Mankind* (Glen Rock, N.J.: Paulist Press, 1965), 37.

> the whole world.... Through her work, whatever good is in the minds and hearts of men, whatever good lies latent in the religious practices and cultures of diverse peoples, is not only saved from destruction but is also cleansed, raised up and perfected unto the glory of God, the confusion of the devil and the happiness of man. The obligation of spreading the faith is imposed on every disciple of Christ, according to his state.... In this way the Church both prays and labors in order that the entire world may become the People of God, the Body of the Lord and the Temple of the Holy Spirit, and that in Christ, the Head of all, all honor and glory may be rendered to the Creator and Father of the Universe. (*LG* 17)

It is only after this treatment of the mystery of the Church and the people of God that chapter 3, "On the Hierarchical Structure of the Church and in Particular on the Episcopate", appears. Some Council Fathers, Karol Wojtyła among them, thought that what became chapter 4, "The Laity", should have followed instead. But the Council decided to resolve first a question left over from Vatican I when Garibaldi's troops invaded Rome in 1870 and the participants in the earlier council dispersed. They had proclaimed papal infallibility in matters of faith and morals but had left the question of the status of bishops untreated. What came to be called "collegiality" was Vatican II's resolution of that unanswered question. In popular treatments, it is often suggested that the bishops were now given equal authority individually or as a body to the pope's, somewhat in the way that, say, a parliament or legislature exerts checks and balances over a chief executive. But this confuses political and theological categories. Bishops were recognized as proper successors to the apostles in their own dioceses when they teach in continuity with the apostles, the whole Church, and the Roman pontiff. This articulation of things is less a matter of separation of powers than a theological statement that the Church exists in individual dioceses theologically in her union with Christ, not as a mere franchise of the central corporate offices.

This way of viewing episcopal authority clearly did not please many in the Roman Curia or their supporters among the Council Fathers. They were wrong in principle, but partly right about dangers in practice. A lot of misreading went into trying to claim that the "collegiality" of the bishops in cooperation with the Holy Father was somehow a license for individual bishops to depart from the practices of the universal Church.[19] The Council did indeed emphasize the proper authority of the bishop in his own diocese, but nowhere does it suggest that this authority is exercised separately from the general authority Christ gave to the Church or from that of the pope. The traditional limits, however, are clearly repeated and were approved even by the progressives: "But the college or body of bishops has no authority unless it is understood together with the Roman Pontiff, the successor of Peter as its head. The pope's power of primacy over all, both pastors and faithful, remains whole and intact. In virtue of his office, that is as Vicar of Christ and pastor of the whole Church, the Roman Pontiff has full, supreme and universal power over the Church. And he is always free to exercise this power." Even councils themselves are subject to the Petrine powers: "The supreme power in the universal Church, which this college enjoys, is exercised in a solemn way in an ecumenical council. A council is never ecumenical unless it is confirmed or at least accepted as such by the successor of Peter" (*LG* 22). A reader coming fresh to such passages with no knowledge of what happened in the years after the Council would be justified in thinking that many of those who claimed that the documents authorized some sort of wild new spirit simply had not read them.

The Council Fathers perhaps anticipated that there might be some confusion, because they included a passage that would be repeated in later attempts to rein in dissident theologians and aberrant practices, though with little effect:

> In matters of faith and morals, the bishops speak in the name of Christ and the faithful are to accept their teaching and adhere to it with a religious assent. This religious submission of mind and will must be

[19] In Canada, for example, the national bishops' conference put out the Winnipeg Statement after the publication of *Humanae Vitae*, which, in somewhat confusing fashion, acknowledged the binding moral principles of the encyclical, but told Canadians who, in good conscience, had trouble with it that they "should not be considered, or consider themselves, shut off from the body of the faithful. But they should remember that their good faith will be dependent on a sincere self-examination to determine the true motives and grounds for such suspension of assent and on continued effort to understand and deepen their knowledge of the teaching of the Church." This position, encouraged by open dissidents, was later repudiated by the bishops, but it is a clear example of the way Catholic unity seemed to be breaking down under the aegis of collegiality.

> shown in a special way to the authentic magisterium of the Roman Pontiff, even when he is not speaking ex cathedra; that is, it must be shown in such a way that his supreme magisterium is acknowledged with reverence, the judgments made by him are sincerely adhered to, according to his manifest mind and will. His mind and will in the matter may be known either from the character of the documents, from his frequent repetition of the same doctrine, or from his manner of speaking. (*LG* 25)

This, even though just a few paragraphs later strong claims are made for the powers of bishops as well: "In virtue of this power, bishops have the sacred right and the duty before the Lord to make laws for their subjects, to pass judgment on them and to moderate everything pertaining to the ordering of worship and the apostolate" (*LG* 27). This is a large development. Bishops need no longer think of themselves as mere subordinates of curial officials. They are free to evangelize as they find best for their dioceses, but always in continuity with Catholicism.

There are two other larger developments in the expansive chapter 4—"The Laity"—and in chapter 5's universal call to holiness. Many scholars have noted that these two chapters seem deliberately placed *after* the general remarks on the Church and the hierarchical dimension. The laity have the prerogatives of all Christians, but their primary place of action is in the world. *Gaudium et Spes*, the later "Constitution on the Church in the Modern World", would treat this at greater length and sometimes with excessive optimism about a modern world allegedly "come of age". But here the emphasis is on bringing gospel values to the secular world. And the way the laity orient their whole lives and prepare themselves for action in the world is through the pursuit of holiness in the midst of the world. The chapter on the laity ends with the famous line from the Epistle to Diognetus: "Christians must be to the world what the soul is to the body" (*LG* 38).

The remainder of *Lumen Gentium* deals with ways within the Church to satisfy the universal call to holiness. Chapter 5 treats the religious life briefly, and chapter 6 deals with the pilgrimage of the Church through time. They were not meant to be comprehensive treatments, but the summary nature of both might be fairly taken to mean that the Council Fathers did not have much to say about either subject—and therefore that they did not see them as of much importance. This might be one source of the decline in religious vocations, but perhaps even more significant was chapter 6's emphasis on heaven to the neglect of hell, which is never mentioned except by circumlocutions. There is a legitimate theological debate about whether anyone is actually in hell, but hell as a real possibility cannot and should not be ignored for the simple reason that Jesus himself speaks about it quite a bit in the New Testament. John XXIII wanted a positive, not a negative, council, but it eviscerates the whole dynamic of Catholicism—to say nothing of Christ's death and Resurrection—if the eternal destiny of man is vaguely assumed to be heaven whatever he does on earth.

A world in which heaven is a guarantee is one in which striving for holiness seems far less urgent. Parallel to the misreading of many statements listed above, many of the older acts of piety and practices of asceticism were abandoned in the wake of the Council. This was not and, on reflection, could not have been the intention of the Council Fathers. Instead, in keeping with John XXIII's pastoral goals, the Fathers had tried to make participation in the Eucharist central and to make other devotions less a matter of rules and more a matter of a growing personal engagement with God himself. It was another generous intention, especially in a modern world planted thick with laws, rules, and bureaucracy. But it gave those with a will to deny the need for such asceticism a license to ignore the practices developed in the distant past that had proved so effective for centuries. For many people, the fact that abstaining from meat on Fridays was no longer required simply meant that penances and ascetic practices as such had been swept away.

The Constitution ends in the usual way of most Vatican documents with a section on Mary as the perfect example of the Christian life. There was great debate over whether to include the section on her here or to develop a separate document going over the importance of various dimensions of the Virgin Mary's life. In the closest vote over anything at the Council, 1,114 bishops voted *non placet* (no) to the idea of addressing her in another document, while 1,074 voted *placet* (yes). It might seem to a dispassionate observer that, so long as the essentials about Church teaching on the Blessed Virgin were expressed, either way of proceeding would have been satisfactory. In the event, she was included only as the concluding chapter in *Lumen Gentium*. Some Council Fathers objected that she had been "dethroned" by this mere mention at the end of an important document ... an exaggeration and perhaps a wrong interpretation. But in practical terms, the objectors had a point. Some Marian devotions were excessive, but such devotions were among the most ubiquitous expressions of popular piety prior to the Council. Afterward, they declined almost everywhere, in some places to the point of disappearance—an unintended effect of a Council intended partly to raise the status of the laity.

Gaudium et Spes

Most Church documents are written by committees and, in addition to the specialized and abstruse nature of much of their material, bear the stylistic drawbacks of such authorship.[20] The great modern Irish poet William Butler Yeats once argued that stylistic flatness indicated a lack of true belief: "'The Holy Spirit is an intellectual fountain', and did the Bishops believe that Holy Spirit would show itself in decoration and architecture, in daily manners and written style? What devout man can read the Pastorals of our Hierarchy without horror at a style rancid, coarse and vague, like that of the daily papers?"[21] It is a fair criticism, in a way, but not equally applicable to all production by the hierarchy. A notable exception from Vatican II, for instance, is the often energetic and perspicacious text on the Church in the Modern World, *Gaudium et Spes*.

Henri de Lubac played a role in the drafting of various conciliar documents, but it may be that his spirit is most evident in the ways that *Gaudium et Spes* envisions closer connections of a new kind between the Church and the world and engages a range of issues—not just family and morals, as in similar documents, but also atheism,

[20] Joseph Ratzinger also remarked on the conditions at Vatican II, where he was a young theological adviser, "it is difficult for an assembly of 2,500 men, each accustomed to having the last word [i.e., they are bishops and final authorities in their own dioceses], to get used to working together": *Theological Highlights of Vatican II*, 39.

[21] "To All Artists and Writers", reproduced in David Pierce, ed., *Irish Writing in the Twentieth Century: A Reader* (Cork, Ireland: Cork University Press, 2000), 291.

technology, economics, and the particular nature of modern globalizing culture. If *Lumen Gentium* in a way may be said to mark the end of the Counter-Reformation, *Gaudium et Spes* seeks to come to terms with several of the modern themes of freedom and human dignity that Catholics had largely opposed, partly because of the violence done to the Church after the French Revolution. All these developments seem to support de Lubac's contention that the separation of earthly and spiritual affairs characteristic of the modern world has its deepest roots in the theological separation of "pure nature" and grace, which de Lubac thought was a distorted reading of the Catholic tradition.

But it was not only the deep theological substance, it was also the openness and confidence of outlook, within renewed commitment to the truths of the faith, that most reflected de Lubac:

> The joys and the hopes, the griefs and the anxieties of the men of this age, especially those who are poor or in any way afflicted, these are the joys and hopes, the griefs and anxieties of the followers of Christ. Indeed, nothing genuinely human fails to raise an echo in their hearts. For theirs is a community composed of men. United in Christ, they are led by the Holy Spirit in their journey to the Kingdom of their Father and they have welcomed the news of salvation which is meant for every man. That is why this community realizes that it is truly linked with mankind and its history by the deepest of bonds. (*GS* 1)

These are the heartfelt and well-calibrated opening words of the text, and it would be difficult to find a better expression of the sense of a Catholicism—ever ancient, ever new—anywhere. Such large sentiments had many good effects and, in the ways that John Paul II and Benedict XVI labored to draw a more faithful version of the vision out of the turmoil that later ensued, still hold out great promise.

But against that potential, it also must be said that the combined influences of the energies let loose at the Council and the radical activism of the 1960s and 1970s inside and outside the Church, along with several other factors, led to quite mixed results. As often happens when a powerful corrective is applied to a longstanding problem—in this instance, the Church's fear of and sometimes absence from the modern world—the pendulum swung after the Council to the opposite extreme. It was no coincidence that not a few religious orders began to see their faith commitments as little different from those of social workers and political activists and regarded the problems of society as easily solvable if only goodwill were applied. (This despite the general discrediting of the optimistic view of "progress" after the horrors of World Wars I and II.) Much of the spiritual side of the faith and a more realistic appreciation for sin and the stubborn disorder of the world were lost across wide swaths of Catholicism in the years immediately following the Council.

The Church and Culture

One of the most controversial themes that emerged in the document *Gaudium et Spes* was the treatment of contemporary culture. In keeping with Pope John XXIII's general orientation, modern culture was spoken of almost everywhere in terms of praise and almost admiration, with just a few warnings that, for all its riches, it should not remain turned in on itself and, therefore, closed to God. But even more than in its judgments of political and social currents, *Gaudium et Spes* was quite optimistic that the Church would be able to draw productively on modern culture as she had on the ancient Greco-Roman culture that has since become a central element in Catholic self-understanding. As many critics pointed out, however, ancient culture was both open to God and pre-Christian. It could, therefore, be adapted and reoriented by a dynamic Christian faith. Modern culture, however, was largely developed under the assumption that culture could be autonomous with respect to theological considerations, which meant necessarily that its principles, being post-Christian, are also anti-Christian. Turning those principles to Christian use is not only quite difficult, it risks something that, in fact, came to pass: the reconfiguration of Christian ideas and practices to fit within the strictures of modern culture.[22]

Though the Council rightly wanted to engage modern culture and the world more generally as a long overdue way of evangelization, the approach it took could not help but quickly run into

[22] The analysis here is partly informed by Tracey Rowland, *Culture and the Thomist Tradition: After Vatican II* (New York: Routledge, 2003).

trouble. In the early 1960s, modern liberalism regarded itself and was often regarded by others as culturally neutral. It seemed to be a kind of open marketplace of ideas, in which all were free to make their case and convince others of its strength. If this had been true, a kind of dialogue between liberalism and Catholicism—dialogue being a much-used term in *Gaudium et Spes*—might have been possible. In fact, personal autonomy and rights as often conceived in modern liberalism were a radical departure from a Christian view. That was evident in the way that, say, the French Revolution had led to the repression of Catholicism and then to the exclusion of Catholicism and all other religious notions from public affairs, and largely from public culture as well. The result was that, at most, Catholicism would exert a claim on certain individuals, but the widespread ethos was one that recognized no divine claims on state or individual, and the political and personal rights thus fenced off were restricted only by liberal conceptions of what constituted harm to others. While Christian values still had a residual existence, this meant that practices like fornication, abortion, divorce, and so on, were practiced but looked down on. And larger justice claims associated with Christian solidarity had a shadowy existence.

But worse, with the radicalization that occurred during the late 1960s, it became clear that the old liberal tradition had nothing with which to oppose the Nietzschean self-assertion that later came to the fore.[23] Going forward, many of the traditional restraints on private or public behavior were looked upon as improper and unjustifiable "religious" impositions on radically autonomous people. In several countries, the zone of privacy—the protected area into which the state could not enter—grew enormously in sexual matters, while restrictions on economic activity and activities deemed harmful to the environment and health became increasingly onerous. Where the older rights seemed rooted in nature and nature's God—or, in the American context, in "the Creator"—the newer rights were a matter of pure will, and it was a difficult task for the state—and the Church no less—to argue that there was anything in the order of things that constituted an authoritative standard by which all men were to be measured.

[23] See James Hitchcock, *The Decline and Fall of Radical Catholicism* (New York: Herder and Herder, 1971).

As these cultural currents began to emerge, their advocates might understandably have seen passages in *Gaudium et Spes* as a kind of license to operate even within the Catholic Church. Section 59 of the Constitution seems moderate enough at first sight, but it opened up potentially large difficulties:

> For the above reasons, the Church recalls to the mind of all that culture is to be subordinated to the integral perfection of the human person, to the good of the community and of the whole society. Therefore it is necessary to develop the human faculties in such a way that there results a growth of the faculty of admiration, of intuition, of contemplation, of making personal judgment, of developing a religious, moral and social sense.
>
> Culture, because it flows immediately from the spiritual and social character of man, has constant need of a just liberty in order to develop; it needs also the legitimate possibility of exercising its autonomy according to its own principles. It therefore rightly demands respect and enjoys a certain inviolability within the limits of the common good, as long, of course, as it preserves the rights of the individual and the community, whether particular or universal.
>
> This Sacred Synod, therefore, recalling the teaching of the first Vatican Council, declares that there are "two orders of knowledge" which are distinct, namely faith and reason; and that the Church does not forbid that "the human arts and disciplines use their own principles and their proper method, each in its own domain"; therefore "acknowledging this just liberty," this Sacred Synod affirms the legitimate autonomy of human culture and especially of the sciences.
>
> All this supposes that, within the limits of morality and the common utility, man can freely search for the truth, express his opinion and publish it; that he can practice any art he chooses; that finally, he can avail himself of true information concerning events of a public nature.
>
> As for public authority, it is not its function to determine the character of the civilization, but rather to establish the conditions and to use the means which are capable of fostering the life of culture among all even within the minorities of a nation. It is necessary to do everything possible to prevent culture from being turned away from its proper end and made to serve as an instrument of political or economic power.

"The above reasons" at the head of this passage referred to the gospel of Christ in the preceding section, but these paragraphs gave a slightly nervous green light to a sort of autonomy that the Council Fathers seemed both to want to affirm and to qualify. The sciences they affirmed elsewhere were psychology and sociology—specifically, in practice, Freudianism and other psychological theories, on the one hand, and Marxism, on the other—which had disastrous effects within the Church on religious self-understanding and parts of Catholic social teaching, especially liberation theology.[24]

But the problem for a Catholic goes still deeper. If de Lubac was right that a wrong conceptualization of the relation of nature and grace amounted to an "extrinsicism" that left nature wholly divorced from God and, therefore, made possible what he called the "drama of atheist humanism", what might be said of a modern Church document that seemed to think there were various autonomous human activities? This is not simply a matter of making sure that, say, modern scientific discoveries are used for moral purposes—as important as that, of course, is. It has much to do with how many individual and social human questions are framed. There is no neutral "scientific" framework of religious belief or sexual mores or social practices, and this became clear even to postmodern secular thinkers within just a few years of the Council. What appeared neutral was, in fact, laden with values and interpretive canons, many of them anti-Christian. Further, as Catholics were jumping on the bandwagons of Freud and Jung, Marx and Dewey, within a short time secular thinkers who took the postmodern turn would deny that the old modernist "masters of suspicion" were objective and scientific analysts.

Lurking in the background of the document was a quasi-Kantian view of a human race at last "come of age" and reaching full "maturity", a highly doubtful proposition in light of the half century since, when the human race has shown itself to be pretty much at the same level it has always been. Nonetheless, the Council saw something else becoming possible:

> From day to day, in every group or nation, there is an increase in the number of men and women who are conscious that they themselves are the authors and the artisans of the culture of their community. Throughout the whole world there is a mounting increase in the sense

[24] "In pastoral care, sufficient use must be made not only of theological principles, but also of the findings of the secular sciences, especially of psychology and sociology, so that the faithful may be brought to a more adequate and mature life of faith" (*GS* 62).

> of autonomy as well as of responsibility. This is of paramount importance for the spiritual and moral maturity of the human race. This becomes more clear if we consider the unification of the world and the duty which is imposed upon us, that we build a better world based upon truth and justice. Thus we are witnesses of the birth of a new humanism, one in which man is defined first of all by this responsibility to his brothers and to history. (*GS* 55)

A humanism "defined first of all by this responsibility to his brothers and to history" is a far cry from what Jacques Maritain called "true humanism" and invites misunderstanding. On the surface, to affirm that people now living are the "authors" of culture ignores human continuity with and dependence upon the past. And it encourages in the modern context, again perhaps without intending to, a shallow notion of human dignity as consisting in autonomy and radically individualistic choice. Further, the Council seemed to want a universal culture to emerge and was simultaneously worried that such a culture would obliterate traditional—often religious—cultures, which in fact does occur to some extent when international bodies ride roughshod over local cultural practices. And on practical questions, there are passages that seem to have been written in great haste: "In the economic and social realms, too, the dignity and complete vocation of the human person and the welfare of society as a whole are to be respected and promoted. For man is the source, the center, and the purpose of all economic and social life" (*GS* 63). Man is the *source* of all economic and social life? Does God have no say in these and other allegedly autonomous realms? It is no wonder that Christians and Marxists seemed blurred in the minds of certain people in the decades to come.

Jacques Maritain, whose work in support of modern democracy and contemporary notions of human rights influenced the drafters of *Gaudium et Spes*, nevertheless had some sharp criticisms of the way many Christians interpreted the document under two large categories: the "temporalization of Christianity" and "kneeling before the world". By the first, he meant that people had confused, on the one hand, the proper recovery of the valuing of the world as God's creation, which reconnects us with Genesis and, on the other hand, the whole sweep of God's action in time, with abandonment of the transcendent destiny of the human race for worldly projects. Justice, liberty, the elimination of poverty, education, and other human goals are, of course, real goods, says Maritain, and Catholics are obliged to seek them and value this world, not shun it after the fashion of the Manichees. But somehow, in less than brilliant minds and hearts, social action became the primary and only goal and even mutated into a kind of *kneeling before the world.*

What Maritain meant by this second phrase was that Catholics, now unsure of their own Christian vision, began to defer to worldly values, as if those, at least, could not be disputed in modern culture. Ironically, he says, you do not see people in the world—scientists, "technicians, manufacturers, trade unionists, statesmen"—bowing to the "world"; you see them pursuing their own visions of the good. By contrast, even in pulpits (Maritain was writing in 1966), sin, fasting, transcendent ends, the other world, the Cross, and sanctity had virtually dropped out of Christian parlance.[25] The only remedy for this abandonment of the Church's mission was sanctity—and saints, he argued. We need to be rescued from the "insane mistake" of believing *there is no kingdom of God distinct from the world.* We seek to do right by this world, of course, but, in Christ's own words, "If anyone loves the world, the love of the Father is not in him."

That one of the figures who had helped shift Catholic attitudes in favor of democracy and a proper notion of human freedom had such a reaction, and so soon after the Council, should have been a warning that something was seriously awry. Some subsequent scholars have argued that it was partly Maritain's own optimism about modern culture and his talk about rights that helped lead to the debacle. And there is some truth in the charge: Maritain had helped draft the United Nations Universal Declaration of Human Rights, a highly useful document in its way, but also plagued by the fact, which Maritain himself recognized, that the underlying principles for its new rights differed among various groups—and soon led to conflicting interpretations of what those rights meant in practice. The principles of freedom and rights, for example, have been turned against the Church herself. And notwithstanding the several, somewhat weak,

[25]Jacques Maritain, *The Peasant of the Garonne*, trans. Michael Cuddihy and Elizabeth Hughes (New York: Holt, Rinehart, and Winston, 1968), 56–57. The section on *Gaudium et Spes* gives it a reading that was not the common one in the decades that followed.

places in *Gaudium et Spes* where the human projects were put in a proper theological perspective, even more radical was the way that some unguarded commendations of modern culture were used as a battering ram against *Lumen Gentium*.

As we have seen, the Constitution on the Church contained some developments on the laity and the view of the Church as the people of God. But the prerogatives of bishops and popes as the governors and necessary successors to the faith of the apostles were also reasserted in no uncertain terms. Some interpreters of the Council who were quite influential on the life of the Church in the years to come saw all that as the mere institutional survival of a past that needed to be discarded—outmoded notions that needed to be inserted into the developing documents to gain enough votes for passage. It was therefore no surprise that, contrary to *Lumen Gentium* and even parts of *Gaudium et Spes*, opinions that had never been part of historic Catholicism on authority, obedience, discipline, ordination of women, priestly celibacy, liturgy, the sacraments, and a host of institutional and moral matters were put forward as though taught by the Council. They were, in fact, taught by the interpretations of the Council that Maritain rightly stigmatized as the "temporalization of Christianity".

Sacrosanctum Concilium

Besides these technical debates about Church and culture—which at least at the beginning touched only a few thinkers—perhaps the most far-reaching theological development to come out of the Council was something most people would not consider theological at all: the radical changes in the Catholic liturgy. Reading *Sacrosanctum Concilium,* the Constitution on the Liturgy, is a melancholy exercise, because it shows precisely how the actual conciliar texts were engulfed by subsequent developments and how misconceived experiments about what was required to engage popular culture tended to take over. The longstanding joke among people who did not like the high-handedness of alleged liturgical experts in the late sixties and seventies was perhaps unfair, but—like all jokes—unfair in the general direction of the truth:

"What's the difference between a liturgist and a terrorist?"

"You can negotiate with a terrorist."

Sacrosanctum Concilium still envisions a central role for Latin and, even more, Gregorian chant, but it also—perhaps even more than *Gaudium et Spes*—leaves the door open to innovations of all kinds, many of them, as it turned out, a failure in the very terms the Council set out for changing the ancient liturgy: the active entering of the people into the mystery of Christ and the Church. The very first sentence describes this as "to adapt more suitably to the needs of our own times", a vague aspiration that envisions greater understanding of and participation in a reformed liturgy on the part of the laity. In places, this seems to mean training laity to understand what liturgy is and even to be able to sing Gregorian chant—in other words, educating and raising the cultural level of the people with regard to at least some aspects of the ancient rites. Seminarians, too, are supposed to be trained to a higher level so that, when they are in place in parish work, they will be prepared to forward the work of creative adaptation.

Driving in a different direction, however, are indications in the document that rites are to be simplified and adjusted to modern culture, similar to the way in which missionaries throughout history have taken elements of indigenous cultures and turned them to sacred use: "The art of our own days, coming from every race and region, shall also be given free scope in the Church" (*SC* 123). The problem with this approach, as we saw in the analysis of *Gaudium et Spes*, is that modern culture is deeply marked by elements that are not merely non-Christian, they are deliberately anti-Christian, and many of the new adaptations were not particularly sensitive to secularizing overtones or sheer superficiality in the adoption of modern forms. As a result, they lost the rich symbols and resonance of older forms without replacing them with anything remotely comparable from contemporary culture.

The theology of *Sacrosanctum Concilium* is sound enough,[26] and liturgy was important enough to be the first subject the Council Fathers addressed, adopting the document on December 4, 1963, with a nearly unanimous vote of 2,147 to 4. Perhaps it was thought that,

[26]See Pamela E.J. Jackson, "The Theology of the Liturgy", in Matthew L. Lamb and Matthew Levering, eds., *Vatican II: Renewal within Tradition* (New York: Oxford University Press, 2008), 101–28.

if the Church was strong enough and the adaptation clever enough, Catholics—large percentages of whom were then attending Sunday Mass—would be even more attracted by greater familiarity and accessibility and, it was hoped, depth of experience. What happened instead, largely, was a reduction of an elevated and dignified liturgy to a very low cultural level, which offered little of the numinous spirit associated throughout history with the rituals of the world's great religions. The laity may have understood much more in a matter-of-fact way because of the simple language of the vernacular—if they actually went into a church. But contrary to expectation, they went to the new Mass much less than to the old one, a remarkable shift in a Church that claimed, quite rightly, that the celebration of the Eucharist—"through which the work of our redemption is accomplished"[27] (*SC* 2)—had been the continuous sacrament of Christ's redemptive act of drawing people back to God since the very days of the apostles and Jesus himself.

Some of the defection no doubt had to do with the flat and uninspiring nature of the new liturgy, not least because both the reforms and misinterpretations of other elements in the conciliar teaching led many to believe that the Mass was simply not all that important any more.[28] It was unfortunate that the reform of the liturgy was hit by a perfect storm of unfavorable circumstances. A far more sober movement for liturgical renewal had been brewing for more than a century prior, starting at Solesmes and later including Vatican eminences Pius X, XI, and XII and some other figures of quite acute judgment, such as Romano Guardini and Joseph Ratzinger. The atmosphere of the late 1960s, however, a moment of global cultural revolution, encouraged all sorts of ill-advised experimentation, some of it quite radical. *Sacrosanctum Concilium* is careful to point to certain norms and to the oversight role of bishops in any adaptations, which should display "a

[27] That this quotation from the Roman Missal had also been quoted in Pius XII's 1947 document on the liturgy, *Mediator Dei*, suggests a deliberate decision to express a continuity with both theory and practice prior to the Council. Other references to *Mediator Dei* affirm the role of the priest and the Real Presence of Christ's Body in the Eucharistic elements as the center of the Christian religion.

[28] As was often the case, the document itself proclaimed the precise opposite: "The liturgy is the summit toward which the activity of the Church is directed; at the same time it is the font from which all her power flows. For the aim and object of apostolic works is that all who are made sons of God by faith and baptism should come together to praise God in the midst of His Church, to take part in the sacrifice, and to eat the Lord's supper" (*SC* 10).

noble simplicity" (*SC* 34). The simplicity came, but little nobility, and the document assumed that bishops would be able to stand up to or do something about radical departures from the past.[29] In the event, all sorts of experiments, often justified on the basis of highly speculative reconstructions of what scholars said were early liturgies, were simply imposed. Paul VI himself caught the spirit, and it was his influence more than that of any other single figure that led to the virtual extinction of the old liturgy.

This was an unfortunate step for many reasons, and not just because it led to felt banners and guitar Masses that were not good liturgical means at the time and soon became outmoded, even in terms of the "needs of our age". Joseph Ratzinger, a young theologian participating as a designated expert in the liturgical debates at the Council and enthusiastic about liturgical reform, noted that the question of liturgical language was the issue most debated, though no intention to utterly suppress Latin, something that subsequently occurred. Indeed, he remarked that the Council Fathers did not intend "a liturgical revolution". That may be so, but by any measure that is what they got. And anyone—ordinary layperson or theological expert—who believes Vatican II represented a radical break with the past could probably best make the case on the basis of what Catholics all over the world came to experience at Mass as a result of the Council. Indeed, from those days well into his papacy Ratzinger would lament repeatedly the rough imposition of Paul VI's missal and the suppression of the Tridentine Mass and would encourage a "hermeneutic of continuity" to counter what had been an overzealous effort to introduce the new by virtual abolition of the old—hardly a good strategy in an institution that embraces the principle of tradition.

But perhaps worst of all, as Ratzinger and many others have pointed out, the radical shift in the most common liturgical experience of the people turned the Mass from something held in common and taken for granted, something coming down from antiquity, into

[29] Section 40 of *Sacrosanctum Concilium* in the English translation speaks of cases where "more radical" adaptations may be "needed". This is curious because the Latin says simply *profundior*, meaning "deeper" adaptations, and the French translation says, quite faithfully, *plus profondement*. The "radical" translation in English remains official, as can be seen on the Vatican website.

a bone of contention. If the criterion for successful liturgy is to be the experience of the participants, especially where the priest is facing, not God, as in the old form, but the congregation,[30] the priest himself becomes a kind of entertainer and his "performance" the subject of a kind of theater criticism. Older notions such as the Communion of Saints and Mystical Body of Christ are mentioned but not communicated by what seems a far more mundane experience. The formalities thrown out as "medieval" may have required no little educating of the laity to make them intelligible, but at least they were not the product of a particular personality or local habit.[31] Further, over centuries, they had come to embody the kinds of acts that anthropologists recognize as a universal feature of ritual, which seeks to create and enter into sacred space and time, often by using cosmic symbolism and sacred language, thereby linking time and eternity. Instead of promoting deep recollection and participation in the mystery of Christ and his Redemption—the avowed goal of the reform—even the shallow rationality of the new vernacular was subjected to all sorts of improvisations and deviations drawn from modern anti-Christian culture and middle-class mores, hardly congruent with the ancient forms sought by scholars.

The constant state of agitation this introduced—and the breakdown of community, as different factions assumed they had a right of control over the now man-made celebrations—led even those who wanted a "reform of the reform", such as Ratzinger, not to attempt anything too radical: though in the early twenty-first century Benedict XVI would bring back a Latin liturgy as an extraordinary form, the existing vernacular "ordinary" forms were gently retouched to restore a bit more of the mystery and poetry of the past and a little less of the intellectualism and prose of the present, without putting the faithful through another revolution. Whether that will be a sufficient

[30] The Council said nothing at all about the direction of the altar celebration; and even those who wanted to reproduce what they believed corresponded to the Passover meal at which Jesus gave his apostles his body and blood knew that, at ancient feasts, people reclined and did not stand or sit looking at one another as if they were sitting around a modern dinner table.

[31] These alleged formalities and accretions go back a long way to early centuries and, as the history of the Eastern rites shows, are hardly due to medieval Latin Christianity. See Martin Mosebach, *The Heresy of Formlessness*, trans. Graham Harrison (San Francisco: Ignatius Press, 2006), 179–85.

remedy in response to the ongoing and militant desacralization of the modern world remains to be seen. But it is clear that the old stability that connected the Catholic worshipper to Christ—and through him to generations long dead and yet to come—as well as to the cosmic order of Creation, is largely gone. And the liturgy that replaced it provides little counterbalance to the chaos and disorientation that are the usual experience of man without God.

Religious Liberty, Ecumenism, and Non-Christian Religions

Some of the most positive aspects to come out of Vatican II were the documents on religious liberty and on the relationship to other Christian denominations and non-Christian religions. In light of the framework of change within continuity outlined in previous pages, which best represents the mind of the Council Fathers, it is regrettable that many people inside the Church and outside saw the embrace of religious liberty and outreach to non-Catholics as a kind of surrender to a modern Western understanding, as if the Church were admitting, on the one hand, that Catholicism is no more than one among many world religions and, on the other hand, that religious liberty means that Church authorities could not define doctrine and exercise discipline over Catholics, even on matters that seem confirmed by Christ's own words and the entire history of the Church.

In a way, this was simply a logical extension of another, more fundamental misreading of the Council, as if it had enacted a kind of radical Protestant assault on everything in between Christ and the modern believer. In that perspective, not only was the long tradition of the Church mistaken, but it confirmed that anything based on the tradition was, by that very fact, suspect. In biblical studies (as shall appear in chapter 6), this led to a Protestantism beyond Protestantism that disputed even the words found in the biblical texts themselves as already reflecting Catholic "developments" from some aboriginal reality apparently visible only to modern Scripture scholars, and even then only if they practiced the historical-critical methods in a certain way.

Dignitatis Humanae, the document on religious liberty, needed to address several issues, some not immediately apparent if religious liberty is taken to refer only to things the Catholic Church herself needed to change about her self-understanding. Very serious theological questions and church-state issues were involved that have been largely ignored but underpinned the approach to the more familiar questions. To begin with, already in the nineteenth century, the Church was seeking the separation of church and state to preserve her own religious liberty. Historically, popes had opposed separation of church and state in theory but also had to battle secular powers to secure the independence of the Church. In France, as is somewhat known but not appreciated, Gallicanism meant that the intervention of the state in the appointment of bishops and other leaders was a longstanding practice, with all the attendant dangers that, say, the running of the Chinese Patriotic Church by the Communist government shows in modern times. But other nations had their own forms of incursion in Church matters. The names of Josephitism (Austria), Riccism (Italy), and Febronianism (Germany) are less known, but the reality was equally stark.[32]

When the Church proclaimed universal papal governance with *Pastor Aeternus* at Vatican I, it was not only, as some dissidents have claimed, a power grab to centralize authority in Rome. It was perhaps even more an attempt to wrest control of local churches from the clutches of governments. Those governments knew what was happening: in retaliation, Austria canceled its Concordat with Rome and Bismarck's *Kulturkampf* in Germany threw the majority of Catholic bishops in jail. The Vatican protested the loss of the Papal States to Vittorio Emmanuele in the new unified Italian monarchy. Nonetheless, Vatican I had reasserted the independence of the Church from the state.

By the time Vatican II was convened, the situation was quite different. In 1904, France, under the presidency of the radical socialist and bigoted Freemason Émile Combes, had passed laws that confiscated much Church property, closed ten thousand religious schools, and curtailed activities by religious orders. As bad as this was, it was only a precursor of what was to come. Before the middle of the twentieth century, virulently anti-religious regimes would arise in

[32] See Russell Hittinger, "*Dignitatis Humanae*", in *The First Grace: Rediscovering the Natural Law in a Post-Christian World* (Wilmington, Del.: ISI Books, 2003), 215–42.

Mexico, Italy, Germany, Spain, and the Soviet Union and throughout the entire Communist bloc from Hungary to China. Compared with the totalitarian ideologies behind these regimes, the modern democratic states seemed far preferable. Leo XIII had encouraged a *Ralliement* to the French Republic before the Combes repression. Despite problems even in the democracies, several modern popes looked upon them as a kind of inevitable byproduct of modern conditions and began to accept them as the context in which the Church would have to operate in the modern world.

For that and other reasons, *Dignitatis Humanae* opens with the observation that "a sense of the dignity of the human person has been impressing itself more and more deeply on the consciousness of contemporary man" (*DH* 1). One immediately links this dignity with the kind of freedom that can only be realized under a constitutionally limited government. Further, it views "these desires" carefully to see how they accord with truth and justice and with legitimate developments within the Catholic tradition, from which new things may be drawn "that are in harmony with the things that are old". And the declaration states explicitly—and truly—that it is going to develop the teaching of "recent popes on the inviolable rights of the human person and the constitutional order of society". That person and those rights are not, however, the same as what they have come to mean in the twenty-first century, which is to say, a kind of zone immune to all claims of religion, law, and ethics. For the Council Fathers, rights and the rightly ordered community flow from human nature in its full sense as created by God.

With this move—later rather lost because of contrary claims of a secular cast—*Dignitatis Humanae* carefully assigns a special place to religious freedom: "Therefore the right to religious freedom has its foundation not in the subjective disposition of the person, but in his very nature. In consequence, the right to this immunity continues to exist even in those who do not live up to their obligation of seeking the truth and adhering to it and the exercise of this right is not to be impeded, provided that just order be observed" (*DH* 2). This is a clear repudiation of an earlier formula that "error has no rights." But as is already clear by this second section of the document, squaring this expansive view of the right to religious freedom with the true and the just will not be easy, to say the least. (Though an overwhelming majority of the Council Fathers believed that democratic freedoms were the best the modern world could offer, it is telling that *Dignitatis Humanae* wound up with the most negative votes of any text issued by the Council, probably because of the difficulties in finding the right theological justifications.) In most Western societies, the tendency has been to see the very intrusion of a particular religious opinion in the public square as a breach of a pluralistic social ethics.

Dignitatis Humanae takes pains to say that this is not nearly enough. Churches must be free *as institutions* to practice their religion in a public way and bring their truths into the general discourse; parents have rights in education, and states should not set up compulsory secular systems or rules that burden parents who want a religious education for their children. Even where particular historical circumstances have given one faith a dominant role in some society, other faiths must enjoy full civil protections and freedoms. In the perspective offered here, the kind of *laïcité* practiced in France, which shuts out religion from the public square, is inadequate. It is not enough for civil authorities to be neutral with regard to the claims of different faiths, or even neutral between belief and non-belief (in practice, this almost always leads to declaring non-belief to be "neutral"). No, civil authorities have a responsibility to foster the religious search and actual exercise of a responsible freedom—because this is the only way that they will achieve a mature liberty in civic life as well.

It does not take much probing beneath the surface of these general notions to see that there are differing values pulling in different directions here. *Dignitatis Humanae* was clearly meant to be a more practical "declaration", not a full-blown "constitution" requiring a more elaborate working out of fundamental principles. So even as it explains that there is no coercion in religion, that Jesus counseled (Mt 13:30) letting the wheat and tares grow together until harvest time, and that Jesus did not come as a political Messiah, there is an undercurrent that cuts in a different direction: that the Church claims freedom before all authority, that she will spare no effort in evangelizing the whole world, and that it is her duty "to give utterance to, and authoritatively to teach, that truth which is Christ Himself" (*DH* 14). The Fathers themselves seem to feel the tension here because, in the very same section (*DH* 12) in which they express that the gospel supports a proper religious liberty and the dignity of the human person, they concede that the Church has worked against freedom in the past: "In the life of the People of God, as it has made its pilgrim way through the vicissitudes of human history, there has at times appeared a way of acting that was hardly in accord with the spirit of the gospel or even opposed to it. Nevertheless, the doctrine of the Church that no one is to be coerced into faith has always stood firm."

Perhaps this was the most that could be achieved in a deliberately brief statement aimed at practical approaches: the Church aligned herself with a high view of responsible liberty and a textured notion of human dignity as the freedom, not to do whatever we want, but to do what we ought. Problems multiplied when the misreading of this position was combined with the decrees on ecumenism and the non-Christian religions. *Unitatis Redintegratio*, the decree on ecumenism, spoke to something dear to the heart of Yves Congar: Christian reunion. As we saw, Congar himself thought this, at best, a distant prospect once the relatively easier cases of Eastern Orthodoxy and, perhaps, Anglicanism were addressed. There was simply too much distance from the major Protestant groups (to say nothing of the distance among Protestants themselves) and, even more, from the many splintered smaller faith communities to expect anything like Christian unity even in the broadest sense to emerge. And the Council noted both the scandal this represented and the need to do something about it—a widespread feeling at the time.

So the "ecumenical" dialogues were given a boost by a universal council of the Catholic Church—a good thing in itself, but unfortunately, for many Catholics, yet another reason to believe that perhaps specifically "Catholic" Christianity was nothing more than someone's idea of what real Christianity ought to be. And the respect toward others seemed to suggest as well that maybe if you did not follow all the truths even in your own Church, it was not so bad because, after all, who is perfectly and fully Christian?

> Moreover, some and even very many of the most significant elements and endowments which together go to build up and give life to the Church itself, can exist outside the visible boundaries of the Catholic

> Church: the written word of God; the life of grace; faith, hope and charity, with the other interior gifts of the Holy Spirit, and visible elements, too. All of these, which come from Christ and lead back to Christ, belong by right to the one Church of Christ. (*UR* 3)

The generosity evident in passages like this was perhaps needed to overcome a certain longstanding Catholic exclusivity and arrogance. It did much good in encouraging respectful dialogue and, if the Church had retained a firm grip on her own teaching in subsequent decades, it might have done even more. But in fact, the ecumenical movement a half century later has achieved little, despite much enthusiasm, other than a generalized sense among Catholics that there is not much that differentiates them from Protestants and a sense, even among theologians, that perhaps theological distinctions do not mean much.

The more conservative members of the college of bishops at the Council had predicted as much. They were right, practically speaking. At the same time, the "triumphalism", or the militant assertion of the truth of Catholicism and the errors of all others, was a traditional stance with diminishing returns. Catholics were encouraged by the Council to read "the signs of the times" and adapt the message to the needs of a new moment. That was certainly the proper mean between two unhelpful extremes. But everything depended on the intelligence with which such signs were read and the wisdom employed in responding to them.

Confusion and uncertainty were not the teaching of the document on ecumenism, of course. It counseled that, even as Catholics refrained from unnecessary polemics, Catholic teaching be presented "in its entirety" and a "false irenicism" (desire for peace at any price) be avoided (*UR* 11). Indeed, it called for a mutual, ambitious investigation: "Thus the way will be opened by which through fraternal rivalry all will be stirred to a deeper understanding and a clearer presentation of the unfathomable riches of Christ" (*UR* 11). For a decade or two after the Council, dialogue ensued on multiple fronts. Earlier a great step forward had occurred in the closing days of the Council when the Orthodox Patriarch Athanagoras and Pope Paul VI issued a joint declaration, each lifting the excommunication of the other that had been in effect since the Great Schism of 1054 between the Eastern and Western Churches.

Further dialogue with the Orthodox proceeded slowly, however, as did similar conversations with Protestant groups. In fact, even though John Paul II announced the importance of ecumenism to his papacy and, in his 1995 encyclical *Ut Unum Sint* took the unprecedented step of inviting the other Christian faith groups to help him think through the "Petrine primacy", the intractable differences in theology and practice began to resurface. In several respects, this was inevitable, because divisions were real and significant. To believe otherwise is to think that all division is merely a matter of misunderstanding on peripheral issues, not a question of conscious and deliberate choices of irreconcilable paths on major issues such as authority, priesthood, apostolic succession, sacrament, tradition, Scripture, and so forth. Both Protestants and Catholics, for all the goodwill they brought to their search to understand one another's views more dispassionately and to find common foundations, acknowledge the existence of many such conscientiously held positions, which they, rightly or wrongly, view as involving their fidelity to Jesus Christ himself.[33]

If there were problems in the way Vatican II dealt with intra-Christian relations, its views on other religions presented still other difficulties. *Nostra Aetate* is commonly thought to be the text in which the Catholic Church definitively repudiated anti-Semitism—and it does so indeed, though there were already ample precedents in the tradition, not least in Pius XI's encyclical, *Mit Brennender Sorge*, written in 1939 as Nazism was reaching its zenith. But perhaps more importantly, even as it repeats the usual duty to proclaim Christ "the way, the truth, and the life" (*NA* 2), *Nostra Aetate* acknowledges the mystery of Israel. Christian figures from Saint Paul to Jacques Maritain have argued that, though the Jews rejected the Messiah when he came, God does not repent of his promises, and the covenant made with the Jewish people in the Old Testament, though now amplified by the addition of the New Testament, was not simply abolished.

[33] For a sympathetic reading of the ecumenical movement, as well as a survey of its successes and impasses to the mid-1980s, see René Girault, "The Reception of Ecumenism", in Alberigo, Jossua, and Komonchak, *Reception of Vatican II*, 137–67.

When Christ comes again at the end of time, in a way not clear to our sight, Israel will be reintegrated into the fullness of communion with the people of God.[34]

Now, it is clear that this emphasis was partly a response to the *Shoah*, the Nazi attempt at genocide against the Jewish people, but it also has solid roots in the tradition, despite the historic anti-Semitism practiced by some Catholics (notably the charge of deicide that was sometimes attributed to all Jews, even those living two thousand years after Christ's clash with some of the Jewish authorities of his day). The practical question arises, however: How then are Catholics to act toward Jews? Though proselytizing, that is, attempts to coerce into conversion are declared improper with regard to all faiths, does this mean Judaism in particular is now a parallel path to salvation? If so, why did Christ's followers, mostly Jews at first, realize they had to separate themselves from the synagogue? And even more urgently, if Christ is the only way, can Catholics in good conscience not preach the gospel even to God's Chosen People, something Christ himself did? Postconciliar relations with Jews were better than perhaps at any point in all of Christian history yet also remained touchy in the wake of the *Shoah*. For the rest of the century, there was no resolution of the question of how preaching the good news was to be done when it came to the Jewish people.

Nostra Aetate and *Ad Gentes Divinitus*, the document on missionary activity, are somewhat conflicted about approaching other religions as well. The Church has always taught that the "good pagan", as well as members of other faiths, may through a kind of "baptism of desire" come to salvation. But given modern sensibilities—and the repudiation of Western colonialism in the 1960s—it was only to be expected that the respect for people of other traditions—pagans, Hindus, Buddhists, even Muslims (long military foes of Christians)—would be taken by many people, looking to get along in pluralistic societies, as, in essence, a recognition that we are all after the same thing under different names. The traditional name for this much-deplored phenomenon is indifferentism, the belief that it does not

[34] Cf. Robert Royal, ed., *Jacques Maritain and the Jews* (Notre Dame, Ind.: American Maritain Association, 1994), and the select bibliography of Maritain's writings on Jews, Judaism, and anti-Semitism, pp. 273–75.

make much difference what religion you follow if you are a "good person", a problematic category in Catholicism, which holds that all are deeply distorted by original sin. There were even Catholic theologians who dared to suggest, contrary to Scripture, that it was not true that there was "no other name" than Christ's by which we might be saved. Missionary orders began to lose the confidence they had once had, and the overall process of evangelizing the whole world seemed a large embarrassment, however much it, too, has scriptural warrant.[35]

Anything less, of course, implies that the actual content of the great world religions is of no importance; paradoxically, a move meant to produce mutual respect winds up not just telling Christianity that it is not exclusively superior, but telling all religions that their beliefs, too, are of no consequence, especially in comparison with the modern liberal idea of social tolerance. *Lumen Gentium*, the Constitution on the Church, had heightened the "universal mission" that takes shape "visibly" in our world in the growth of the Church, because all men are called to union with Christ, and the Church has received "the mission to proclaim and to spread among all peoples the Kingdom of Christ and of God" (*LG* 5). These traditional themes were "front-loaded", so to speak, and provide a context for passages that come later—indeed, a context for the Council as a whole—which were often misconstrued. The respect expressed toward all persons of goodwill was, somehow in some quarters, regarded as the equivalent of the Church's saying that all the standard activities of teaching, evangelizing, and striving for truth had been abrogated. The Council Fathers explicitly denied that very attitude, since Christ's injunction to preach the gospel to all nations can never be revoked or ignored by those who intend to follow him. To put it in John XXIII's "pastoral" perspective, the Church was to treat all outside her borders with respect, without denying herself by pretending that the "dogmatic" side had simply been relegated to vestigial status.

Indeed, it is difficult to see how any institution that makes truth claims and sees God himself as having established sure means of

[35] "To seek to make converts is not proselytism, since the faith is offered freely in order to offer union with God, salvation in Jesus Christ, and participation in the blessings and tasks of God's kingdom—although it is also necessary that the 'motives for conversion should be examined' (*AG* 13)": Francis Cardinal George, O.M.I., "The Decree on the Church's Missionary Activity, *Ad Gentes*", in Lamb and Levering, *Vatican II: Renewal within Tradition*, 299.

salvation for his people could much indulge whatever happens to be the prevalent opinions of its members at any given moment, which will always and inevitably contain a great deal of theological ignorance and error. Despite the many attempts to portray the Council as some kind of transformation, shift to the subject, democratic turn, Copernican Revolution, or the privileging of the new over the old, of the contemporary over the timeless, Avery Dulles, S.J., named a cardinal late in life and perhaps the most noted scholar on the "models" of the Church, has remarked, "All of these generalizations, I maintain, are false."[36]

[36] Avery Cardinal Dulles, "Nature, Mission, and Structure of the Church", in Lamb and Levering, *Vatican II: Renewal within Tradition*, 25.

Chapter 5

A Renewed Theology and Modern Culture

The cult shapes the culture, as the sociologists of religion are fond of saying. But it is equally true that culture can determine what it is possible for a religious body to do, even one as large and—occasionally—influential as the Catholic Church, at any given moment. The last third of the twentieth century, the period following the Council, was not a fertile period for culture in general. The early twentieth century produced great names such as James Joyce, Thomas Mann, and Marcel Proust; Igor Stravinsky and Claude Debussy; William Butler Yeats and Rainer Maria Rilke; Picasso and Matisse; Einstein and Freud; and many other great figures in a variety of fields. After the 1960s, by contrast, the secular world had few great minds and creators of that caliber. But despite the appearance of chaos, the postconciliar period was also a period of considerable theological ferment in the Catholic Church.

The most influential theologians had received their initial formation in an earlier age, but they were also long-lived and survived to the 1980s and 1990s. No great new systems emerged, except for Hans Urs von Balthasar's massive trilogy, which began (1961) before the Council and did not reach completion (1987) until more than two decades after the Council ended. And it is not clear whether it is right to call what von Balthasar did a theological "system". But in its own particular ways, the postconciliar period resulted in some lasting theological developments. To make the varied mass of material a bit more manageable, it is necessary to limit the scope here to certain key figures and the currents to which they gave rise. We shall examine four of them in this chapter: Karl Rahner, Hans Urs von Balthasar, Karol Wojtyła, and Joseph Ratzinger.

Karl Rahner and the "True Church"

Karl Rahner (1904–1984) was probably the most influential figure in Catholic theology in the years immediately following the Council. The sheer brilliance of his two early books *Geist in Welt* (*Spirit in the World*; 1939) and *Hörer des Wortes* (*Hearers of the Word*; 1941) quickly brought him to global prominence and contributed directly to several directions taken by the Council, where he served as an adviser. But he loomed even larger in the 1970s and early 1980s in Catholic circles, especially in seminary formation, as Catholic institutions of higher learning tried to work out implications of the Council during a turbulent cultural period. The Church as a whole, however, did not continue down the paths he opened up and, in the papacies of John Paul II and Benedict XVI, began to turn away from older "existential" questions toward a different way of engaging the modern predicament.

Rahner was and is—sometimes fairly, sometimes unfairly—regarded as heterodox because on several of the neuralgic issues of the last half of the twentieth century—collegiality, women's ordination, contraception, liberation theology, and a more generally secularized and politicized notion of Christianity—he was openly and sometimes aggressively on the side of the "progressives". Indeed, it was Rahner who claimed that Vatican II had opened up a "third era" of the Church, a change comparable in its magnitude to the shift, first, from the early Jewish-Christian community to a Greco-Roman form and to the later change into a Constantinian alliance of church and state.[1] Still, Rahner's highly innovative and rigorous philosophy and wide-ranging theology are, carefully approached, far from unorthodox and even suggest potential methods for answering several modern questions about the faith.[2]

His usual approach is to assume the truth of basic teachings found in the creeds or the tradition as starting points and then to go on to try to understand them in fresh ways that take into account contemporary experience. Thus, he does not try to prove the existence of God or the Trinity, the divine institution of the Church and the sacraments, or the importance of the magisterium and authority. He

[1] Karl Rahner, S.J., "Towards a Fundamental Theological Interpretation of Vatican II", *Theological Studies* 40, no. 4 (1979): 716–27.

[2] Mark Lowery, "Retrieving Rahner for Orthodox Catholicism", *Faith & Reason* (Fall 1991), 251–72.

takes them for granted, to a large degree, but then tries to situate them in a context or explain their foundations or otherwise reformulate them so that they can stand up to modern criticism and the explosion of knowledge. Some scholars have argued that Rahner was the first Catholic theologian really to take that explosion into account and to realize that it introduced an era of "irreducible" complexity and pluralism into intellectual life that theologians must ponder.[3] Whether the situation is permanently or only temporarily "irreducible", or whether it is even irreducible at all, is of course a subject for theological debate and the passing of time. But read fairly, Rahner—successful or not—must be seen as, at bottom, sincerely engaged in exploring how to offer modern theological arguments for Christian truths.

Indeed, there have been efforts among indisputably orthodox theologians to save Rahner from the more heterodox interpretations of parts of his theology, taken in isolation. In several places, for example, Joseph Ratzinger has written in admiration of Rahner's immense scope in both philosophy and theology and concludes that he is "kein Häretiker" (no heretic)—rather someone who is fundamentally committed to the Church, whatever weaknesses or problems his theology may present. Over decades, the Vatican rebuked Rahner on a couple of occasions but never formally charged him with anything. Ratzinger, who worked with Rahner and came to know him at the Council, also pointed out during a Rahner Jubilee, "You have to understand Rahner in the fullness of his intention and thinking and simply recognize that it was not his aim to stand against the faith of the Church." Ratzinger continued that Rahner has to be taken as a whole and was anchored in the desire to show the dynamic that might further open up the faith: "But the whole is very complex, and Rahner ... in the end stood for love of the Church and the wish to be a Jesuit and the will to stand in the original sense of the word in the Society of Jesus, to live and think and so to serve the Church."[4] Some readers believe his spirit is best appreciated in his prayers and works on spirituality, particularly Ignatian spirituality.[5]

[3] See, for example, Karen Kilby, *Karl Rahner: A Brief Introduction* (New York: Crossroad, 2007), 75–78. Kilby's book presents Rahner's arguments fairly, but she also weighs their strengths, weaknesses, and plausibility, given Rahner's "apologetic" side.

[4] Joseph Ratzinger, radio interview with Stephanscom, March 3, 2004.

[5] Philip Endean, *Karl Rahner and Ignatian Spirituality* (New York: Oxford University Press, 2001).

Karl Rahner's earliest work, *Spirit in the World*, was rejected by his director as a doctoral dissertation in philosophy, but it was accepted in theology and later published—followed by another major work, *Hearers of the Word*. Both help explain his ongoing theological work. Whatever else may be said about it, *Spirit in the World* offers a brilliant and far-reaching interpretation of a single article in Aquinas' *Summa Theologiae* (I, q. 84, a. 7). Rahner reads Thomas through the lens of several insights he absorbed from Kant and Heidegger. (He had studied under Heidegger at Freiburg, though he claimed later on several occasions that it had not fundamentally marked his theology.) He also learned from predecessors in "transcendental" Thomism, such as Rousselot and Maréchal, yet sometimes resisted being classified with them. There is also in his vision something influenced by or akin to the dynamism of the human spirit in a figure like Blondel. This early, technical philosophical side of his work is of great intellectual interest, but he sometimes warned that "the lopsided work of my youth" was not necessarily to be thought of as underpinning his vast and unsystematic output in the *Theological Investigations*, short essays that he chose to publish over decades, in collected volumes, instead of large scholarly tomes, which fill twenty-three volumes in English translation.[6]

This whole approach has often been described as a Catholic "turn to the subject", but it is not *subjectivism*, as was thought by some Thomists. Some of his difficult technical vocabulary has to be summarized here. By analyzing the transcendental conditions of knowledge, Rahner developed an original view of man as simultaneously a being with a kind of "preapprehension" (*Vorgriff*) of all being as the horizon of existence, on the one hand, and, on the other hand, a knowledge of particular existents—"sensible singulars"—nearer by. This dynamic being (that is, man) is in its very constitution *related* to other beings, indeed to all being, and therefore not merely closed in on its own subjectivity. And in its intellectual reaching out to beings in the world and the horizon of ultimate Being as the matrix of its own being, it finds a way to understand what it is in itself. In highly simplified terms, man comes to know his self as a spirit in the world situated between inanimate beings, others persons, and God.

[6] Karl Rahner, S.J., *Theological Investigations* (New York: Crossroad, 1982–).

> God thus understood becomes essential to a full understanding of human nature: Whether he is consciously aware of it or not, whether he is open to this truth or suppresses it, man's whole spiritual and intellectual existence is orientated toward a holy mystery which is the basis of his being. This mystery is the inexplicit and unexpressed horizon which always encircles and upholds the small area of our everyday experience of knowing and acting, our knowledge of reality and our free action. It is our most fundamental, most natural condition, but for that very reason it is also the most hidden and least regarded reality, speaking to us by its silence, and even while appearing to be absent, revealing its presence, by making us take cognizance of our own limitations.[7]

The "horizon"—that is, God—cannot be grasped anywhere within the horizon and, so, remains forever a mystery that by its very nature eludes our every effort.

In his early work, Rahner formulates all this in far more complex terms in the tradition of contemporary German philosophy, and it is not always easy to grasp what he is saying or its significance. Indeed, it was one of the attractions of Rahner's whole method for scholars formed in the older ways that he seemed to allow for the continuation of the serious German theological tradition in the usual academic channels, while at the same time opening them up to the non-Catholic dimensions of the modern world.[8] For Rahner, therefore, the thorny theory described above is not merely a theory of knowledge, it is a kind of spiritual vision (an "epistemological metaphysics"). The spirits in the world that we ourselves are exist both in the mode of "being with" other things and also, somehow, in ways that allow us to objectify things by withdrawing back into ourselves and thereby becoming capable of observing and standing over against them. It is in the dynamic oscillation (*Schwebe*) between the "horizon of being" and particular existents in our world that the individual human being basically constitutes itself—and in the process unites many of the seemingly opposed polarities in the world.

This esoteric vision can at times have concrete application to contemporary questions. For instance, since so many people, even in the

[7] From *Theological Investigations* 9:122, quoted in Kilby, *Karl Rahner*, 6.
[8] See R. R. Reno, "Rahner the Restorationist", *First Things*, May 2013.

modern world, have still not even heard about Christ and we know that God desires all men to be saved, what can we say about their—and our—"ontological" status of them? Is there something that already exists in all persons by their very nature, even those clearly outside the visible bounds of the Church, that disposes them toward the fullness of truth? One of the key concepts that Rahner developed was the "supernatural existential", by which he meant something similar to what theologians of *la nouvelle théologie* were pursuing in opposing the Scholastic notion of "pure nature". As we have seen, de Lubac and others rejected that view as a kind of "extrinsicism", as implying that the created world could exist by itself and grace would come to it from outside. Though Rahner claimed his own ideas differed from the one proposed by *la nouvelle théologie*, the "supernatural existential" fits into a larger picture of man as a spirit existing in the world, but constituted by God's grace (existentially) to be able to hear the word of revelation, a revelation that by its nature exceeds the natural (hence supernatural). He presents this in an intellectual synthesis that is brilliant even though, as is the case with all human speech about God, it also raises many difficulties.

Every one of the elements in this overall system is, by nature, difficult both to state and to understand. More traditional Thomists argued over whether such a creative reading of Thomas in terms that were not really his own was legitimate. Even followers of Rahner have given different and sometimes opposed interpretations of what he meant by these ideas and many other things that flowed from them, including interpretations pointing in a non-theistic direction.[9] But his new emphasis on the dynamic nature of the human spirit and intellect, as well as the centrality of the human person—the "anthropological turn", as it was sometimes called—produced something of a revolution for many people at the Council and immediately after.

In one of its most immediate effects, it seemed to transform notions of grace and nature, already being debated in different terms by traditional Thomists and the practitioners of *la nouvelle théologie*.

[9] See Thomas Sheehan, "Rahner's Transcendental Project", in Declan Marmion and Mary E. Hines, eds., *The Cambridge Companion to Karl Rahner* (Cambridge and New York: Cambridge University Press, 2005), 29–42, particularly at 33.

Though these two movements had their own internal disputes, as we have seen, Thomists of the older persuasion tended to defend "pure nature" and the possibility of strictly natural fulfillments, while the newer theology saw human nature as, in some sense, always already open to supernatural ends. Rahner disagreed with both: he left open the notion of "pure nature", but only as what he called, at least at times, a "remainder concept" (*Restbegriff*). In Rahner, there appear to be three "graced" levels of creation, which follow.

1. The grace of creation: human beings are by nature dynamically open to all being, including the supernatural, though God does not owe us the supernatural fulfillment of his grace, and we in some way are also ordered to a kind of natural fulfillment;
2. The supernatural existential: a much debated term that seems to suggest a kind of grace that orders us beyond our natural dynamic to God but is not traditional "supernatural grace";
3. Uncreated grace: the traditional supernatural grace by which God communicates himself to us.[10]

Added to this complexity is one of Rahner's most controversial moves of all. In the standard treatment, "created" grace predisposes us to receive "uncreated" grace, the indwelling of the Holy Spirit in us. Rahner, though, says that uncreated grace abides with all of us fundamentally, at all times, in an unconscious form and that it is because of this primary gratuitousness that we can receive created grace. At the same time, the two appear to have a kind of alternating precedence that assures God is always with us, even within those of us who sin or have consciously turned away from him. Since all graces are given through the Incarnation, this is perhaps the deepest source of Rahner's later idea of the "anonymous Christian", which provoked much controversy because for many people it seemed to make Christ and formal Christianity all but superfluous and relativized. Indeed, Rahner argues that the historical revelation and its understanding within the Church was—only?, the critics asked—the coming to conscious confirmation of the deeper and constant presence of grace.

[10] See the discussion of these questions in Patrick Burke, *Reinterpreting Rahner: A Critical Study of His Major Themes* (New York: Fordham University Press, 2002), 47–72.

But that was only one side of what Rahner appeared to be doing. In other places, the Incarnation and presence of Christ in the world are characterized in the most absolute terms:

> The incarnate word is the absolute symbol of God in the world, filled as nothing else can be with what is symbolized. He is not merely the presence and revelation of what God is in himself. He is the expressive presence of what, or rather who, God wished to be, in free grace, to the world, in such a way that this divine attitude, once so expressed, can never be reversed, but is and remains final and unsurpassable.[11]

In a complex and innovative thinker like Rahner, it is never easy to gauge how much weight to give to any individual passage, but this seems to clinch the case that he saw Christ as a universal singularity. "Symbol" in this passage does not refer to some merely coincidental expression of God's truth; in Rahner, things themselves are by deep nature symbolic in that they all communicate themselves to one another.

Critics of the "anonymous Christian", a group that included some remarkable and by no means doctrinaire figures, tended to overlook passages like the above and to worry, instead, about what could easily turn into a sentimentalized view of everyone as Christian, regardless of actual conscious beliefs and behaviors. If this is the meaning of being a Christian, many observed, the concept is so broad that it loses all meaning. On a human level, the anonymous claim easily lends itself to all sorts of absurdities about people who are not only non-Christian but even anti-Christian "really" being part of the Church at some deep, transcendental level. This conundrum drove Hans Urs von Balthasar to an uncharacteristically nasty joke in *The Moment of Christian Witness*. In that work, a commissar observes to a proponent of this theory that perhaps he was really starting to think like an "anonymous atheist".[12] But Catholic "progressives" also disliked the idea at times, for quite different reasons: it might be read as saying, not that Christianity did not matter, but that all people, whatever their conscious religious on non-religious views, were

[11] Quoted in ibid., 97, from "Zur Theologie des Symbols", *Schriften* 4:293–94.

[12] Hans Urs von Balthasar, *The Moment of Christian Witness*, trans. Richard Beckley (San Francisco: Ignatius Press, 1994), 119ff.

"really" striving without knowing it to be Christian, a kind of theological imperialism that absorbed the Other without permission.

Viewed in its proper light, this notion may only be claiming that there is a real transcendental structure of the human person, that deep mysterious part of ourselves rooted in and directed toward God, which superficial events and even our everyday thoughts obscure to us. This is a bold vision that has some affinities with several of von Balthasar's own concerns. And while the later Rahner seems to have emphasized "uncreated grace" as in itself a universal inner revelation that was—again, only?—confirmed by outer revelation, there is no place at which he denies the need for the outer, explicit revelation and even, in the right conditions, open membership in the Church, for salvation.

At that deeper level, the anonymous Christian is no joke. If the *Vorgriff auf esse* (preapprehension of being) can be really said to exist, and some theologians sympathetic to Rahner's project have their doubts, it must also change our sense of our situation. But at the same time, many readers were puzzled. Rahner found it hard to say how explicit Christianity, which even Saint Thomas recognized is always a partial and weak expression of the great mystery, relates to those things that are by nature, in his system, beyond our grasp. The historically Catholic and orthodox explanation is that Church dogmas are a true articulation of Christian truths, though never a complete or final system because everything ends in the mystery we call God. Doctrines can "develop", in Newman's sense of that term, by remaining true, as they always have been, but also by becoming the occasion for further insight, newer truths, or a recognition of wider applications. A truth of the faith once achieved and recognized as such is, in the standard orthodox view, never simply abandoned or superseded. And the Church, as God's vehicle for his continuing action in time, is the guardian of the fullness of his truth as well.

Rahner famously proclaimed his desire to remain within the Church (and Cardinal Ratzinger in the interview cited above expressed his belief that Rahner was a sincere Churchman). And it is not difficult to find passages where he is defending the Church as the great Sacrament or the seven sacraments as the Church's definitive "development" of her understanding of revelation over time. But it is also not difficult to find passages in his work that give a very different impression. For instance, in his essay on the "Third Church", he writes:

> The various aspects and perspectives from which any Christian regards his personal life as it unfolds, or alternatively the totality of Christian doctrine from his own intellectual standpoint, vary very greatly. And this is quite as it should be. In this context, we may do something which is also done in other departments of human life with regard to the various areas of knowledge as they are presented to us, namely, we may, with full deliberation, go out of our way to avoid this or that theological question because we instinctively feel that we cannot cope with it in the concrete circumstances of our lives. It is also possible to bring a certain subjectivity to bear in selecting certain special and preferred truths of faith to live by, and in this to allow other truths, which are just as valid and important, to recede into the background when we notice that this "subjective attitude" is healing and liberating.[13]

Rahner is often not the clearest of writers; his brother Hugo once joked that if he, Hugo, had time, he would try to translate Karl into German. But this passage is clear enough and reflects exactly the sort of picking and choosing on the basis of one's own preferences and circumstances that are, from one angle, a textbook definition of heresy (*hairein* in Greek meaning "to choose").

Further, to imply that one's relationship to God is one among many "departments of life" would seem, even within Rahner's own account of the transcendental nature of the person—and perhaps even the Christian structure of all reality—precisely to characterize such choices as inauthentic, partial, and shortsighted—the exact opposite of the deep structure oriented toward the fullness of Christian truth of which he talks elsewhere. If the anonymous Christian is really what Rahner says he is, either he must be drawn toward the wholeness of truth and reality, or he is in pretty much the same boat whether Christianity exists or not.

Rahner tried to respond to such charges by claiming that Christianity is the end point for

> anyone who courageously accepts life—even a shortsighted, primitive positivist who apparently bears patiently with the poverty of the superficial—has really already accepted God. He has accepted God as he is in himself, as he wants to be in our regard in love and

[13] "Third Church?", *Theological Investigations* 17:38–39.

> freedom—in other words as the God of the eternal life of divine self-communication in which God himself is the center of man and in which man's form is that of the God-man himself. For anyone who really accepts "himself," accepts a mystery in the sense of the infinite emptiness which is man.... And if Christianity is nothing other than the clear expression of what man experiences indistinctly in his actual being ... what reason could I have then not to be a Christian?[14]

This was a point on which Joseph Ratzinger took sharp exception, departing from his usual appreciation of Rahner and saying on the concluding page of the lengthy and wide-ranging interview with him by Vittorio Messori published as *The Ratzinger Report*, "According to these theories the Christian's 'plus' is only that [the one who accepts himself] is *aware* of this grace, which inheres actually in all people, whether baptized or not. Hand in hand, then, with the weakening of the necessity of baptism, went the overemphasis on the values of the non-Christian religions, which many theologians saw not as *extraordinary* paths of salvations but precisely as *ordinary* ones."[15]

When as intelligent and basically appreciative a mind as Ratzinger's notes that something in this effort results in the weakening of the need for the sacraments, missionary work, and the Church—as subsequent developments in the Church confirmed—there is something awry, even if the theoretical position is better than its consequences. Ratzinger puts this very trenchantly in one passage:

> Is it true that Christianity adds nothing to the universal but merely makes it known? Is the Christian really just man as he is? Is that what he is supposed to be? Is not man as he is that which is insufficient, that which must be mastered and transcended? Does not the whole dynamism of history stem from the pressure to rise above man as he is? Is it not the main point of the faith of both Testaments that man is what he ought to be only by conversion, that is, when he ceases to be what he is? Does not Christianity become meaningless when it is reinstated in the universal, whereas what we really want is the new,

[14] Karl Rahner, *Thoughts on the Possibility of Belief Today*, trans. Karl-H. Kruger (Baltimore: Helicon, 1966), 7–8.

[15] Joseph Ratzinger with Vittorio Messori, *The Ratzinger Report: An Exclusive Interview on the State of the Church*, trans. Salvator Attanasio and Graham Harrison (San Francisco: Ignatius Press, 1985), 197.

> the other, the saving trans-formation [*Ver-änderung*]? Does not such a concept, which turns being into history but also history into being, result in a vast stagnation despite the talk of self-transcendence as the content of man's being? A Christianity that is no more than a reflected universality may be innocuous, but is it not also superfluous?[16]

This eloquently expresses the worry that many had at the time and have since seen grow into too great an emphasis on the universals of human experience. Yet von Balthasar and Rahner both approach, from different angles, a notion of universal salvation that raises difficulties for the whole mechanism of Christian conversion and salvation. *Lumen Gentium* 16, perhaps reflecting Rahner's influence, is the *locus classicus* for the understanding of the Church's views about the relationship with Jews, Muslims, and even those entirely outside the standard sacred history "who in shadows and images seek the unknown God". Rahner also countered that his view was better understood as the basis on which missionary activity proceeds, the assumption that there are already seeds present in all the peoples with whom missionaries come in contact that make the explicit preaching of the gospel fruitful.

Put into the right context, there may be solid defenses of Rahner's views. How those views were thought of and acted on, however, still remains disturbing, as, it must be said, was the case for several of the expressions of the Council. In the 1960s and 1970s, for reasons that are not entirely clear, almost any departure from the preconciliar conception of Church doctrine and discipline had a tendency to be carried by the revolutionary cultural currents of the time far beyond what new formulations like Rahner's explicitly stated.

Alongside anonymous Christianity, another Rahnerian concept had great influence for a while: the "fundamental option". Rahner proposed that our most basic decision, our Yes or No to God, is the horizon within which other moral decisions take their place. Of course, no Christian could deny this once it is pointed out. Indeed, it helps move Christian moral life from an avoidance of sin to a recognition of the obligation, under God, to do good toward others,

[16] Joseph Ratzinger, *Principles of Catholic Theology: Building Stones for a Fundamental Theology*, trans. Mary Frances McCarthy, S.N.D. (San Francisco: Ignatius Press, 1987), 166.

a recuperation in its way of Saint Thomas' statement of the natural law, "bonum est faciendum et prosequendum, et malum vitandum" (*ST* I-II, q. 94, a. 2). But there are elements in Rahner's way of presenting this large subject that can make it appear that specific moral decisions—the kinds of things that Catholics have traditionally mentioned in the confessional—are of less importance if the fundamental option remains firm. This obviously lends itself to all sorts of rationalization and confusion, both of which appeared abundantly in the decades after the Council. Rahner's dissent from the 1968 encyclical *Humanae Vitae*, though far more nuanced and respectful of Church authority than most such dissents,[17] was a clear break with the Church over a crucial moral definition and began to open a distance between the earlier Rahner, loyal to the Church if sometimes critical, and a later one often perceived as a dissenter.

Without mentioning Rahner's name, John Paul II seems to have thought it necessary when he issued *Veritatis Splendor* in 1993 to spell out what he thought valuable and what misleading in such speculations. He welcomed the fact that

> the heightened concern for freedom in our own day has led many students of the behavioral and the theological sciences to develop a more penetrating analysis of its nature and of its dynamics. It has been rightly pointed out that freedom is not only the choice for one or another particular action; it is also, within that choice, a *decision about oneself* and a setting of one's own life for or against the Good, for or against the Truth, and ultimately for or against God. Emphasis has rightly been placed on the importance of certain choices which "shape" a person's entire moral life, and which serve as bounds within which other particular everyday choices can be situated and allowed to develop. (*VS* 65)

But the playing down of individual acts, the point at which individual ethical or moral decisions must be made, he found to be slightly schizophrenic:

> A *distinction* thus comes to be introduced *between the fundamental option and deliberate choices of a concrete kind of behavior*. In some authors this

[17] See Avery Dulles, S.J., "Karl Rahner on *Humanae Vitae*", *America*, September 28, 1968.

> division tends to become a *separation,* when they expressly limit moral "good" and "evil" to the transcendental dimension proper to the fundamental option, and describe as "right" or "wrong" the choices of particular "innerworldly" kinds of behavior: those, in other words, concerning man's relationship with himself, with others and with the material world. There thus appears to be established within human acting a clear disjunction between two levels of morality: on the one hand the order of good and evil, which is dependent on the will, and on the other hand specific kinds of behavior, which are judged to be morally right or wrong only on the basis of a technical calculation of the proportion between the "premoral" or "physical" goods and evils which actually result from the action. This is pushed to the point where a concrete kind of behavior, even one freely chosen, comes to be considered as a merely physical process, and not according to the criteria proper to a human act. The conclusion to which this eventually leads is that the properly moral assessment of the person is reserved to his fundamental option, prescinding in whole or in part from his choice of particular actions, of concrete kinds of behavior. (*VS* 65)

Whether or not this was Rahner's position, it certainly was the attitude of many who claimed to be influenced by him. The pope went on to explain why traditional notions of mortal and venial sin were still crucial to moral and spiritual life.

Despite differences with Rome, Rahner remained a powerful presence within the Church, particularly in seminary training, until his death in the 1980s. But remarkably, his influence declined sharply thereafter and seems to need some reworking before it will return. Part of the reason for that decline is, no doubt, the combined effect of Wojtyła and Ratzinger on Catholic institutions. But part also seems the sheer result of the passage of time. Though Rahner makes indisputable theological contributions to a modern understanding of Catholicism, there are many ways in which those contributions are tied to a specific moment in the twentieth century. The admirers who cite him as providing means to speak about the faith to "the men and women of today" are often enough in fact referring to a certain segment of sophisticated opinion in the 1960s and 1970s, a project that looked dated after the revolutionary fevers of those decades died out in the 1990s, to say nothing of the new millennium. What Rahner argued *against*—a narrow and unimaginative official

Neoscholasticism—no longer exists. What Rahner argued *for*—an open and living existential encounter with the reality of God and his grace—has taken a different path from the one he was on in very different circumstances. And his work would now need to be recontextualized to address more recent concerns.

The very last lecture he delivered, just a few months before his death in 1984, gives some indication of why this is so. His "Experiences of a Catholic Theologian" emphasizes four main points, each of which displays both his lifelong concerns and how those have been overtaken by other considerations. He speaks first, for instance, about the analogical nature of all theological statements, even drawing on the work of Erich Przywara, who was also important, as we will see, for Hans Urs von Balthasar. But Rahner's reasons for emphasizing analogy are probably best summed up in this passage:

> In theology we talk about a great many things and, when we have finished, we think—although this goes against our basic convictions—that we have really reached the end and that we can draw things to a close. We think that the few affirmations we have made will quench every metaphysical and existential thirst, not realizing the challenge (as we really should) that after making all these affirmations we are destined finally to reach that *aporia* that, according to Saint Paul in 2 Corinthians 4:8 characterizes our human existence and that does not provide us with any answers.[18]

But by the 1980s, every undergraduate who took a course in literary theory was already being bombarded with *aporias*—and many were getting impatient to find a few simple answers, the kind that believers always drew from the Bible's parables and principles. Rahner's call for "a loving, trusting self-surrender to the unfathomable reign of God, to God's merciful judgment and sacred incomprehensibility"[19] possesses permanent value but is not the only and certainly not the dominant need of believers bewildered by the experience of the past quarter century.

[18] "Experiences of a Catholic Theologian", Marmion and Hines, *Cambridge Companion to Karl Rahner,* 297–310. The passage quoted here may be found at 300–301.

[19] Ibid., 299.

Rahner's second point in his summary of his experiences as a theologian repeats his belief in "God's radical self-communication",[20] both prior to any formal religiosity and specifically in what is "given in Jesus and in him alone".[21] The tension between the universal and particular here is always a part of the Christian vision, and Rahner takes pains to say that the universal message should not be confused with "an unbelievably modest humanism",[22] nor the particular with an "inflated" humanism.[23] He even confesses that sin and the forgiveness of sin perhaps play too small a role in his theology compared to the mystery of love. Rowan Williams, a gifted Anglican theologian later to be named archbishop of Canterbury, has said with both appreciation and studied understatement of Rahner: "He is by no means insensitive to the need for a theology of the Cross, though it is true that his system as a whole could not be so described."[24]

The absence of the Cross, sin, and the need for forgiveness are all, of course, hallmarks of weak, suburban Christianity at the turn of the new millennium. Rahner cannot be entirely blamed for these developments, as even this brief account shows. But he played a role in their emergence. And much of the ongoing labor of theology now is devoted to finding ways of reappropriating those notions, without which Christianity in all its forms is regarded by "the men and women of today" as an anodyne and bloated restatement of God's love and love of neighbor, that is, things they already know. By comparison, Rahner's third and fourth points in his summary—that we need to accept the helpfulness of different schools of theology flourishing side by side and that we need to keep working at knowing and integrating the other disciplines developed in the modern world—are minor warnings whose lessons have been learned and more than learned in the years since.

Practitioners of liberation theology like Gustavo Gutiérrez and of the *politische Theologie* like Johann Baptist Metz, who sought to use Rahner's joining of theory and religious experience with additions from Marxism and the Frankfurt School. They enjoyed some

[20] Ibid., 301.

[21] Ibid.

[22] Ibid., 302.

[23] Ibid., 304.

[24] Rowan Williams, *Wrestling with Angels: Conversations in Modern Theology* (Grand Rapids, Mich.: Eerdmans, 2007), 99.

influence, above all in the late 1970s and 1980s. (In addition to the side of Rahner's thought that was quite abstract, Rahner's increasing emphasis in later years on the religious experience of the person provided an opening for a theology "from below".) But the dialogue between his theology and politics frayed as the political partners in the dialogue showed themselves to be threadbare in practical terms. Worldwide Marxism received a serious blow with the collapse of the Soviet Union in 1989, partly because of the efforts of John Paul II. And the Frankfurt School showed itself to be more an intellectual fashion than a social analysis of real staying power. Liberation theology was to mutate into something less openly ideological with the end of the Cold War. These brands of political Christianity were curious developments that had found all sorts of seeming certainties ("the preferential option for the poor", for example, conceived along class struggle lines), which had earlier been seen as depending to a large degree on prudential judgment. And they de-emphasized historical theological and moral views as somehow merely an expression of "personal morality" and unincarnate spirituality. Rahner's role in all this is of course complicated and debatable, but at the same time it is clear that the debate has moved on.

No fair reader of Rahner, however, decades after the controversies that surrounded him have mostly subsided, can help being impressed with his boldness in engaging the modern world with a universal vision and his equally relentless embrace of the Christian mystery in the person of Jesus. As the future Benedict XVI said, there is much to debate and even criticize in how he carried out this massive task, but also a great deal to admire. Still, an admirer may wonder whether, at least for the foreseeable future, this work has not achieved what it set out to do. Another set of questions has now arisen that contemporary spirits as intrepid as Rahner's might feel obliged to address, though in a far different way, thereby pursuing goals similar to Rahner's: providing plausible explanations of the Catholic faith in the conditions of postmodernity.

Hans Urs von Balthasar: "God Is His Own Exegete"

By near unanimous recognition, the largest presence in late twentieth-century Catholic theology—both in terms of influence and sheer bulk of output—is Hans Urs von Balthasar (1905–1988). Karl Rahner, a figure von Balthasar both appreciated and sometimes sharply criticized, was perhaps the single most influential theologian just after Vatican II, but his influence waned rather quickly and does not seem likely to come back soon. By contrast, von Balthasar's stock continues to rise, most notably in quarters such as the group associated with the journal *Communio*. (That journal was founded by von Balthasar along with Joseph Ratzinger and other prominent theologians seeking a different path after the Council from the one promoted by the earlier, more progressive journal *Concilium*, with which several of them were initially affiliated.) One obstacle to understanding von Balthasar, besides the great range of his work, is his method: as von Balthasar himself put it in one of his books, truth is "symphonic"[25] and therefore cannot be reduced to a few systematic principles and elaborations after the manner of much academic writing.

As might be suspected from his impressive name, von Balthasar was the descendent of a patrician family with a long and distinguished history. He was born in 1905 in Lucerne, then one of the Catholic centers in Switzerland. During his early life, he was exposed to the heights of German, French, English, and other European literature, music, art, theology, and philosophy. Indeed, he was such a gifted musician that, had he not developed other interests, many believe he could have had a professional career in music. The ease he later showed in studies ranging over several languages and the whole of Western culture as he carried out his philosophical and theological work reflects the very roots of his upbringing. Henri de Lubac, himself a highly cultivated man of considerable critical acumen and a friend, once described von Balthasar as "perhaps the most cultivated [man] of his time".[26] In von Balthasar, high culture was combined with an immense capacity for work and a dazzling creativity. The output is so large and varied that it has given scholars difficulty just to classify it. Depending on how the works are broken down, von Balthasar wrote somewhere between sixty and a hundred books—most of considerable length—and several hundred articles before he

[25] *Truth Is Symphonic: Aspects of Christian Pluralism*, trans. Graham Harrison (San Francisco: Ignatius Press, 1987), originally published as *Die Wahrheit ist symphonisch* in 1972.

[26] Henri de Lubac, S.J., *The Church: Paradox and Mystery*, trans. James R. Dunne (Staten Island, N.Y.: Alba House, 1969), 105.

died in 1988, just two days before he was to be made a cardinal by John Paul II.

It is no easy task to trace even the large lines of so fertile a mind. And an additional difficulty arises from the fact that he was a very expansive writer (it did not help that for much of his life he was his own publisher as well, via Johannes Verlag, an operation he founded). A thought that occurs to him in the course of an argument can lead to digressions lasting dozens of pages before he picks up the main thread again. Fortunately, perhaps sensing the mountainous terrain he had produced, he provided readers with a short essay that is a true marvel of synthesis and concision, of which it seems he was capable when he wished to be: "A Résumé of My Thought".[27] These five pages are an indispensable guide to von Balthasar's central contribution to the Catholic intellectual tradition: his fifteen-volume trilogy, *The Glory of the Lord*, *Theo-Drama*, and *Theo-Logic*, which appeared from 1961 to 1987, came precisely during the period of the greatest ferment in the Church during the twentieth century. Each of the parts of the trilogy focuses on a particular "reflection on the situation of man".[28] The seven volumes of *The Glory of the Lord* are devoted, surprisingly to those unfamiliar with von Balthasar, to the aesthetic; the five volumes of *Theo-Drama* to the dramatic encounter between God and man; and the three volumes of *Theo-Logic* to the ways in which human reason is inescapably open to the transcendent, ways that, properly understood, lead us into the heart of Catholicity. Anyone who has studied philosophy may suspect that these divisions broadly echo, in a deliberate reverse order, Kant's three *Critiques*. While von Balthasar was largely a critic of Kant, it is clear that his aims in this masterwork are as ambitious as those of his great German predecessor.

As von Balthasar explains in his "Résumé", reflection must begin from our discovery of ourselves as contingent and finite beings in a contingent and finite world. Everything that exists in our world could just as easily not exist. Yet both we and the world are somehow also open to the infinite and eternal. The ancient philosophers intuited these truths but tried to resolve the tensions in erroneous

[27] In David L. Schindler, ed., *Hans Urs von Balthasar: His Life and Work* (Communio Books; San Francisco: Ignatius Press, 1991), 1–5.

[28] Ibid., 1.

ways. At one extreme, Parmenides declared that the real must be unchanging, rendering our ever-changing world an illusion, as in Buddhism and other world-denying mysticisms. At the other extreme, Heraclitus proclaimed that all things flow—but what then of the unchanging and eternal? Even the great Plato, facing the division, could only resolve this apparent dichotomy by arguing that the real truth must be elsewhere in an eternal realm of ideas, far removed from this world, which is merely an unstable and ever-changing copy of eternal things. Later Neoplatonists diverged in thinking the world itself a fall-off from the divine or a necessary emanation from an incomprehensible One. But these religiously shaped philosophies were not solutions for a duality that cannot be overcome within the Greek perspective, which has parallels in the rational reflections of other civilizations.

God himself is the only one who can give an answer to the question that involves the very being and essence of man:

> It is here that the substance of my thought inserts itself. Let us say above all that the traditional term "metaphysical" signified the act of transcending physics, which for the Greeks signified the totality of the cosmos, of which man was a part. For us physics is something else: the science of the material world. For us the cosmos perfects itself in man, who at the same time sums up the world and surpasses it. Thus our philosophy will be essentially a meta-anthropology, presupposing not only the cosmological sciences, but also the anthropological sciences, and surpassing them towards the question of the being and essence of man.[29]

This is a rather abstract way of putting something that von Balthasar also expresses in a more concrete fashion (and that helps explain the structural divisions within his massive trilogy). We all become conscious, he says, not by philosophical reflection, but in a personal encounter, concretely, with the smile of our mothers. According to von Balthasar, this primordial experience reveals to each person four things: "(1) that he is one in love with the mother, even in being other than his mother, therefore all being is one; (2) that that love is good, therefore all being is good; (3) that that love is true, therefore

[29] Ibid., 2–3.

all being is true; and (4) that that love evokes joy, therefore all being is beautiful."[30]

Undaunted by the usual criticism of such a view from Freudian or other schools of psychological reductionism, von Balthasar asserts that these early experiences display certain analogies with the classical exposition of the transcendentals: the one, the good, the true, and the beautiful. Furthermore, they remind us that "man exists only by interpersonal dialogue",[31] including the possible dialogue with God. In von Balthasar's trilogy, each of the three parts finds its inspiration in one of the transcendentals, but he conceptualizes these traditional categories in a fresh and highly original way. To begin with, the first part of the trilogy, *The Glory of the Lord*, is focused on beauty and aesthetical issues, the power of the beautiful to touch our hearts and take them beyond what we earlier believed was real. This is no plea for art and the sublimity of nature as a way of ordering and inspiring life in the vague way of Romanticism—a false subjectivism and irrationality that von Balthasar is well aware carries with it many dangers, as is evident in the history of the past two centuries. Rather, he seeks to connect "glory", in the deep Hebrew sense of *kabod*, with Jesus Christ, as the most beautiful "form" we perceive, and with other manifestations of beauty as they refract the fundamental beauty of existence presented to us in the events recounted in the Old and New Testaments.

"Seeing the form" is, to say the least, a daring place to begin such a vast theological enterprise, particularly in contrast to the hardheaded Aristotelian, Thomist, and Kantian currents in Catholic theology. These latter approaches looked to outmaneuver modern rationalism and scientific truth on their own terrain; von Balthasar, though quite aware of that part of the cultural tradition, looks to build on quite different ground. His appeal to the "heart"—and only subsequently to the head—has had precedents in other ages. Pascal, for instance, argued famously in the *Pensées* that the heart has its reasons of which reason knows nothing, a claim that seems to rise to prominence in periods when a narrow notion of reason is believed to threaten the special nature of the rational animals who

[30] Ibid., 30.
[31] Ibid.

have produced it. In that sense, von Balthasar's fundamental appeal to the totality of the human person initially runs the risk of being drowned in the high waters of modern subjectivism and relativism, but it takes the chance in order also to have the opportunity to irrigate the parched expanses of overly rationalist theology and philosophy. Von Balthasar liked to remind people that his only doctorate was in *Germanistik*, an interdisciplinary field that includes literature, philosophy, and culture. In Germany, it is often said that intellectuals must choose between the dry reason of Kant and the lush poetry of Goethe; von Balthasar was mainly in the latter camp with respect to his starting points, though he could be as rigorous as any modern thinker within his own chosen terrain.

This is clear enough even in the titles he gives to the seven volumes of *The Glory of the Lord*. He begins with "Seeing the Form", that is, the form of Christ and the whole sacred history that led up to his sacrifice as redemption of man and the subsequent Christian ages. Von Balthasar then traces the glory of this form over six volumes through three pairs of related witnesses: clerical and lay figures throughout Christian history (finishing with Charles Péguy, the French thinker and poet who died in 1914); ancient and modern metaphysics; and the Old and New Testaments. For von Balthasar, this tracing out of the glory is not only the way of emotion or a personal preference or one possible way of thinking about Christianity. It is the immediate way that truth reveals itself, that is, engages in a self-communication with us, since truth must choose to come to us in a mode of self-disclosure that could not take place in any other way. The echoes of phenomenology, which was examined in a previous chapter, are quite clear.

This approach also responds to a series of crises. First, the evaporation of the old cosmological approach that seemed to find in the order of the old geocentric universe of Ptolemy indications of the divine. Even before the Copernican Revolution, he says, that approach was on the way out and an anthropological perspective began to replace it. In this further perspective, the characteristically human things—reason, will, freedom, sentiment—took the place of the objective cosmic order as pointers toward God. Figures as diverse as Pascal, Luther, and even Kant shared this sense that the older reason could not reach to the heart of man, which was nonetheless rich with realities beyond the material. But this humanity beyond reason and the God who was supposed to appeal to it were vulnerable to charges of solipsism and the merely subjective. In rougher hands, such as Ludwig Feuerbach's, the anthropological perspective might be used as a privileging of human perspectives in order to judge dogmas that did not seem to meet human need, naturalistically understood: "Philosophy is in the end nothing other than anthropology."

Von Balthasar quotes this sentence from Feuerbach's *Principles of the Philosophy of the Future*, which had a strong influence on Marx and many other subsequent thinkers, in a brief and helpful volume that sets out the aims of the theological aesthetic, *Love Alone Is Credible*.[32] As he makes clear, love as understood in the fullness of the Christian tradition must now be the foundation, the Third Way that is the only way in our time that the great truths of the faith can be secured: "Neither religious philosophy nor existence can provide the criterion for the genuineness of Christianity. In philosophy, man discovers what is humanly knowable about the depths of being; in existence, man lives out what is humanly livable. But Christianity disappears the moment it allows itself to be dissolved into a transcendental precondition of human self-understanding in thinking or living, knowledge or deed."[33] We must encounter another in love, and encountering another means never having mastery over the other person or explaining away love within some system. For von Balthasar, an "aesthetic" perception is similar to, and makes up part of, this encounter with the other because "the aesthetic, just like the personal encounter, can serve at best as a sign of Christianity. But this sign is valid to the extent that, just as in mutual human love, where the other *as* other is encountered in a freedom that will never be brought under my control, so too in aesthetic perception it is impossible to reduce the appearing form [*Gestalt*] to my own power of imagination."[34]

The Christian revelation participates in this kind of dynamism and is not diminished by that fact. Instead, it shows it is related to the

[32] *Love Alone Is Credible*, trans. D.C. Schindler (San Francisco: Ignatius Press, 2004), 44; original German: *Glaubhaft ist nur Liebe* (1963). Many Balthasarians regard this little book as the best place to begin studying the great theologian.

[33] Ibid., 51.

[34] Ibid., 53.

other things we commonly call love but also that it is vastly superior to any such comparison: "The plausibility of God's love ... is illuminated only by the self-interpreting revelation-form of love itself. And this form is so majestic that we are led to adore it from a reverent distance whenever we perceive it, even if it does not explicitly command us to do so."[35]

Von Balthasar warns that without this root in love, theology itself risks a drift into atheism or agnosticism: *caritas forma revelationis* ("Love is the form of revelation"). Similarly, Church dogmas—necessary and true in themselves—without conspicuous love do not effectively occupy their proper place. All failures and corruptions of the Church have no weight where this essential feature is perceived. Love as the form of revelation can even survive the assaults of modern biblical scholarship, with which von Balthasar is quite familiar and values to a large degree. But he assigns the results of such scholarship to an ancillary function with respect to a larger truth. That truth goes beyond intellectual propositions to a recognition that the Christian faith is a drama in which God acts and men and women respond. It is not merely a set of propositions, though there is a proper role for well-articulated truths of faith. But those truths must be understood in the setting of a dramatic action, which forms the central theme of the second main section of von Balthasar's trilogy, *Theo-Drama: Theological Dramatic Theory*.

Theo-Drama: Theological Dramatic Theory

Like his theological aesthetic, the *Theo-Drama* can easily be misunderstood. For many people in the modern world, drama is associated with unreality, everything "theatrical", "staged", "play-acted", and so forth. Attitudes like these reflect a modern anxiety about a lack of authenticity in the playing of "roles" in society, which came to a head in the twentieth century in the work of Martin Heidegger, the German philosopher highly influential in many circles, including theology. Von Balthasar had studied Heidegger and absorbed certain influences from him, but this did not deter him from believing that

[35] Ibid., 56.

the Christian life is necessarily conceived of as a drama, first as the drama of Christ's Incarnation, death, and Resurrection, which provides the key to reading all the previous and subsequent dramas in the whole story of Creation, Fall, and Redemption. He even went so far as to say that Father, Son, and Holy Spirit function as playwright, actor, and director in this drama.

Why did von Balthasar place so much emphasis on the dramatic qualities of the Christian story? It is difficult to summarize this part of his work, and professional theologians differ in their assessments of its success or failure. Certainly, part of the emphasis reflects a personal sensitivity. Drama and dramatic poetry attracted von Balthasar's attention, so much so that he was the translator and main impresario behind the staging of several dramatic works, among them Paul Claudel's vast drama *The Satin Slipper* and Calderón's *Great Theater of the World*. When von Balthasar studied Kierkegaard under Romano Guardini in Munich, he was impressed by the great Dane, but it also put him off that so astute a Christian thinker rejected the aesthetic as the merely sensual, even in such obviously great artistic works as Mozart's *Don Giovanni*. For von Balthasar, drama seemed to express something better than other human modes of creativity. But what in particular persuaded him to use drama in a work that was, after all, primarily intended to contribute to Christian theology?

Von Balthasar wrote brilliantly about and became quite friendly with the greatest Protestant theologian of the twentieth century, Karl Barth. After initial studies with the Jesuits, von Balthasar was offered by his superiors either a professorship at the Gregorian University in Rome or a university chaplaincy in Basel. He chose the second. Barth was also living in Basel, and von Balthasar gave a series of lectures on his work, which Barth attended and which later became a book.[36] Working with some notions of the analogy of being (*analogia entis*) then in the process of development by Erich Przywara, von Balthasar demonstrated that Barth's main claim—that the Roman Catholic notion of analogy is an attempt to gain control over the idea of God—was the exact opposite of the truth. Since the decrees of the

[36] *The Theology of Karl Barth: Exposition and Interpretation*, trans. Edward T. Oakes, S.J. (Communio Books; San Francisco: Ignatius Press, 1992); German original: *Karl Barth: Darstellung und Deutung seiner Theologie*, 1951.

Fourth Lateran Council in 1215, it had been the received wisdom in the Church that "between Creator and creature no likeness can be discerned without a greater unlikeness having to be discerned as well." We have to glean some idea of the Creator from his creation, because the creation cannot misrepresent the Creator. It is all we know, but it tells us that nothing exactly like what we see within creation could have created it. Barth gradually moved in von Balthasar's direction in the course of their interactions. And von Balthasar spoke at times, perhaps partly in response to Barth's well-placed questions, of *cata-logy*, a movement from above downward, a contrast with analogy, by which God has chosen to disclose himself somehow in lesser things that may lead us back up to him.

Thus, Christians also have access to God by way of his revelation, not only through the Bible, but through the actual fact of God's entry into the world in the person of Jesus Christ. Von Balthasar refers to the life of Christ as the "singularity" (*Einmaligkeit*), the divine drama at the center of all creation in which all of us are supporting actors. This drama, though written, produced, and "starred in", so to speak, by the Trinity, allows for real if finite freedom within our horizons. Why do we need the dramatic perspective to understand that? Primarily because philosophical and theological approaches that tried to understand how finite freedom could exist given God's infinite freedom, power, and knowledge have historically wound up in contradictions. Either God knows and does everything via grace, and men are mere passive instruments of his grace (the saved) or the denial of grace (the damned), as in Calvinist double-predestination; or men have the limited but real power to incorporate the powers of limitless grace and therefore can save themselves, as in Pelagianism. For centuries Christian faith groups have clashed with one another over this insoluble problem, even within Catholicism. Witness the controversy in the sixteenth and seventeenth centuries between the Dominican followers of Domingo Báñez and the Jesuit supporters of Luis de Molina; the Jesuits accused the Dominicans of Calvinism for their emphasis on the omnipotence of grace, while the Dominicans accused the Jesuits of Pelagianism because of their emphasis on free will. Even Pope Pius VI could not resolve this conflict and was reduced merely to forbidding each side to attack the other.

One of the best interpreters of von Balthasar argues that this history led the great theologian to believe that we need something like a paradigm shift, which he found in *Theo-Drama*: "What he has done by foregrounding all of the theatrical and dramatic metaphors embedded in theology is to alter *in a stroke* the entire perspective out of which theologians consider this problem."[37] We might formulate the consequences as follows. When God himself becomes man in the Incarnation and enters into time, we are no longer involved in an abstract debate about grace; we have a fellow among us who communicates in a way we can understand, at least partly, and calls upon us for a response. In his book *A Theology of History*, von Balthasar explains: "The play does not exist in advance, but is conceived, produced, and acted all in one. The Incarnation is not the *n*th performance of a tragedy already lying in the archives of eternity. It is an event of total originality, as unique and untarnished as the eternally here-and-now birth of the Son from the Father."[38] And the purpose of rehearsing this truth is clearly stated by von Balthasar in *Theo-Drama*: "We need to keep ever before our eyes the way in which infinite freedom was pleased to appear in the midst of finitude, if we are not to be drawn aside into abstract (and hence falsely posed) speculative problems."[39]

Theo-Logic

Which brings us to *Theo-Logic* (the third portion of the trilogy). It deals in three volumes, in a more conceptual way, with a central problem stemming from this insight: How can human reason or intellect, created and limited as they necessarily must be, possibly take in the divine *logos*, which is by definition uncreated and infinite? In one sense, of course, we only receive the revelation of God as a mystery. But, says von Balthasar, in another way Jesus, as we see him in the Gospels, is the "exegete" of the Father and of himself, and the Holy

[37] Edward T. Oakes, *Pattern of Redemption: The Theology of Hans Urs von Balthasar* (New York: Continuum, 1997), 217.

[38] *A Theology of History* (Communio Books; San Francisco: Ignatius Press, 1994), 39–40; German original: *Theologie der Geschichte*, 1959.

[39] *Theo-Drama: Theological Dramatic Theory*, vol. 2: *The Dramatis Personae: Man In God*, trans. Graham Harrison (San Francisco: Ignatius Press, 1990), 250–51.

Spirit makes it possible for us to receive both what that means and what Christ says. In terms that are sometimes reminiscent of Heidegger, von Balthasar does not see this in the traditional way of the metaphysics of Absolute Being (though he is quite familiar with that approach and is more concerned with supplementing than discarding it). His view is more in keeping with the aesthetic and dramatic approaches he has developed as a kind of disclosure-concealment of Being. He pursues the "form" of that disclosure less in the abstract terms of Aquinas or Kant than in discerning how it has transpired in history. In this perspective, the dialogue between God and man benefits from the images that are available in the world, which are not simply themselves but retain mysterious roots in Being, while still offering themselves to us in a way we can grasp. So a kind of dialectic emerges from the immediate face of a being, a kind of icon through which we are led into another truth. We cannot lay hold of that mysterious being and truth because by its very nature it must choose to disclose itself to us. And so, it is neither the result of an intellectual effort on our part nor a merely subjective experience; rather, it is self-disclosure in love by the one who is beauty, goodness, and truth. And this self-disclosure is definitely a *theo*-logic; it depends specifically on the divine disclosure that is found in Christ.

Adrienne von Speyr and the Community of Saint John

One of the crucial ways that this was brought home concretely to von Balthasar was in his relationship with Adrienne Kaegi-von Speyr, quite a remarkable figure in her own right. She was a Swiss medical doctor from a distinguished family in Basel and a Reformed Protestant. She was received into the Catholic Church by von Balthasar in 1940, which caused no little stir among her former co-religionists. Remarkably, stories started to circulate about miracles in her medical office. The great Swiss theologian later claimed: "Her work and mine cannot be separated from one another either psychologically or theologically. They are two halves of one whole, with a single foundation at the center."[40] Von Balthasar left the Jesuits (though not

[40] Quoted by Peter Henrici, S.J., in his essay "Han Urs von Balthasar: A Sketch of His Life", in Schindler, *Han Urs von Balthasar*, 28.

the priesthood) a few years later to found with her the *Johannesgemeinschaft* (Community of Saint John) and Johannes Verlag, which published her and his many books. Since it is estimated that she wrote or dictated about sixty books to von Balthasar, some during her visions, and he produced nearly twice as many on his own, probably no one is in a position to describe the relationship and mutual influences fully. But some main lines can be identified.

Perhaps the single most important dimension of all involves a kind of Marian spirituality in which the primary theological orientation is receptivity to God's initiative. (Von Speyr had in the 1940s encouraged von Balthasar, amid all his other work, to found a journal—a suggestion that was followed only with the appearance of *Communio* in 1972, which took this Marian receptivity as a kind of central theological leitmotiv.) As he wrote in the "Program" for that journal: "*Agape*, however, is first of all a gift from above; only then can it tentatively be imitated by us. Consequently the horizontal interpersonal communion can never set the standard for the vertical established by God. Otherwise we should be back once again with a Church self-generated in a pharisaically interpreted Law. Or else in the Pelagian heresy (which is probably more dangerously prevalent than ever at the present time), according to which each Christian is capable of giving as much as he actually achieves."[41]

There was a personal instance of this in their relationship. As he instructed her in the faith, something unusual happened:

> When I showed her that our saying "Thy will be done" does not mean we offer God what we are able to do ourselves, but rather that we offer him our willingness to let what *he* does take over our lives and move us anywhere at will, it was as though I had inadvertently touched a light switch that at one flick turned on all the lights in the hall. Adrienne seemed to be freed from chains of restraint and was carried away on a flood of prayer as though a dam had burst.[42]

It also seems that this was the proximate origin of many visions and inspirations that she was to have over the next decades of her life. Among them, von Balthasar believed that the commentaries on

[41] Translated by W.J. O'Hara, reprinted in *Communio* 33 (Spring 2006): 166.

[42] Hans Urs von Balthasar, *First Glance at Adrienne von Speyr*, trans. Antje Lawry and Sr. Sergia Englund, O.C.D. (San Francisco: Ignatius Press, 1981), 31.

Scripture, especially those on the Gospel of John, the apostle of love, were the most important of anything he published.

But she also had regular visions on Good Friday, which led von Balthasar into one of his most controversial positions: a consideration of whether "we may hope" that all souls will eventually be saved.[43] To be clear, von Balthasar never says that they will, merely that we must remain faithful both to the scriptural warnings about the dangers of hell and to Scripture's witness that it is God's will that all be saved. In *Our Task*, a book that describes their common work, he notes:

> Adrienne unlocks a hitherto scarcely developed part of the theology of redemption. On Good Friday the Son's love renounces all sensible contact with the Father, so that he can experience in himself the sinner's distance from God. (No one can be more abandoned by the Father than the Son, because no one knows him and depends on him as much as the Son.) But then, after Good Friday, comes the final, the most paradoxical and most mysterious stage of this loving obedience: the descent into hell. In Adrienne's new experience and interpretation of hell, this means descent into that reality of sin which the Cross has separated from man and humanity, the thing God has eternally and finally cast out of the world, the thing in which God never, ever, can be. The Son has to go through this in order to return to the Father in the ultimate obedience of death.[44]

This view raised concerns not only about the denial of hell, but also over whether it is theologically sound to describe Christ's descent as involving a renunciation of "all sensible contact with the Father" and entry into the "reality of sin".[45]

Von Balthasar has sometimes been categorized by hasty readers as one more among the many figures who arose in the middle of the twentieth century who moved the Church away from her moorings in Thomism toward vague and sentimental positions. But this is to overlook the rigor in all his work, though, as has been seen, he begins

[43] See *Dare We Hope "That All Men Be Saved?"? With a Short Discourse on Hell*, trans. David Kipp and Rev. Lothar Krauth, 2nd ed. (San Francisco: Ignatius Press, 2014): German original: *Was dürfen wir hoffen?* (1986).

[44] Hans Urs von Balthasar, *Our Task*, trans. John Saward (Communio Books; San Francisco: Ignatius Press, 1994), 65.

[45] See the debate between Alyssa Lyra Pistick and Edward T. Oakes, S.J., on this question in *First Things*, December 2006.

in a different place from that of classical metaphysics. Since he was probably John Paul II's favorite theologian and seems to have had a somewhat similar status with Benedict XVI, he is likely to exert influence on the Church for some time to come. And von Balthasar cannot justly be accused of being some kind of covert modernist. Just as Vatican II, to which he was not invited, was coming to a close, von Balthasar wrote:

> The Church, they say, to appear credible, must be in tune with the times. If taken seriously, that would mean that Christ was in tune with the times when he carried out his mission and died on the Cross, a scandal to the Jews and folly to the Gentiles. Of course, the scandal took place in tune with the times—at the favorable time of the Father, in the fullness of time, just when Israel was ripe, like fruit ready to burst, and the Gentiles were ready to receive it on their open soil. Modern is something Christ never was, and, God willing, never will be.[46]

On October 6, 2005, the hundredth anniversary of von Balthasar's birth, Benedict XVI—himself an immensely cultivated and multi-talented man—recalled their mutual collaboration and witnessed to his intense personal search in literature, art, music, theology, and philosophy for "true life". And he commented on von Balthasar's sweeping tripartite exposition of the Paschal Mystery: "In Jesus' death and Resurrection, in fact, the mystery of God's Trinitarian love is revealed in all its fullness. The reality of faith finds here its matchless *beauty*. In the *drama* of the Paschal Mystery, God lives to the full his becoming man, but at the same time renders man's action significant and gives a content to the commitment of Christians in the world. Von Balthasar perceived in this the *logic* of revelation." Von Balthasar's example was for Joseph Ratzinger that of "a true theologian" who worked within the Church and sought to keep the strictly theological and the spiritual always together.

Karol Wojtyła (John Paul II)

Despite the speculative power of Rahner and von Balthasar, in several respects Catholic theology in the last twenty years of the twentieth

[46] Quote from *Wer ist ein Christ?* (Einsiedeln, Switz.: Benziger, 1965), 30, in Schindler, *Han Urs von Balthasar*, 36.

century was most significantly shaped by a figure who was not a professional theologian, so to speak, at all: Pope John Paul II (Karol Wojtyła). With the exception of Joseph Ratzinger, no theologian of the caliber of von Balthasar or Rahner arose during that period or the first decade of the third Christian millennium. Instead, it might be said, the pontificate of John Paul II stepped forward less with a new theological system than with a desire to affirm a reading of Vatican II that was both orthodox in terms of continuity with the two-thousand-year-old tradition and confident in facing new challenges from the kind of biblical, patristic, and pastoral perspectives most notable in the conciliar documents.

There *were* several innovations—most notably the "theology of the body", which in some form may yet prove to be a powerful current in the future of Catholicism—and, perhaps more significantly, in the way that Catholic social teaching and "the acting person" combine in John Paul II's thought. But Wojtyła's primary contribution to theology during these years was to find a steady tone and, at the same time, a powerful public presentation of a conciliar theology that seemed both sophisticated and also energetic enough to guide Catholic thought and practice into more authentic channels than had been the case between the years of the Council and the beginning of his papacy.

Given the pope's long experience of the sad politics in his Polish homeland during the twentieth century, it is not surprising that he sought to address Catholic social teaching extensively. Prior to his death in 1984, Karl Rahner had been a strong pillar of a kind of liberation theology. Despite the esoteric nature of Rahner's theological vision, it seemed to reinforce—in its contention for the "supernatural existential"—the notion that liberation "from below" and a Church "of the people" were legitimate. Since those "at the margins" and "the poor" were also directly graced by God as "spirits in the world" who were "hearers of the Word", they were thought to speak with an authentic and urgent voice. But given the tenor of the times, that voice from the margins often took on, seemingly inevitably, quite earthly Marxist overtones. The pope had responded to questions from reporters on the plane taking him to Mexico City in 1979, his first papal visit after his election: "Ah, liberation theology. But which liberation theology?" In his view, it should not be the Marxist-tinged, class-struggle version most typical of Latin American liberation theologians. That would only introduce yet another inhuman ideological aberration, whatever the intentions of its practitioners, into a world with no lack of them.

Instead, in the mid-1980s he worked with Cardinal Ratzinger on two crucial documents. The first, the 1984 *Instruction on Certain Aspects of the "Theology of Liberation"*, laid out the critical case. Mistaken views of man and the assumption that class struggle and violent revolution (instead of reconciliation and peace) were the necessary paths to freedom were rejected in the light of the fuller humanism and unity demanded by the Christian tradition. With the passage of time, these corrections now seem eminently sensible. But in the mid-1980s, during the dying years of the Cold War, the revolutionary path seemed to a significant minority of Catholics and other Christians to be the only effective way to respond to conditions of repression. The peaceful replacement of tyrannies in the Philippines, Nicaragua, and Chile, however, all carried out with the significant participation of Christian democrats, offered counter examples.

John Paul II was deeply convinced of the crucial importance for social doctrine of a correct view of man, human freedom, and the common good—all of which depended on the prior religious liberation that took place in Christ and made it possible for us to see what God had intended in creating the human race. The Church, then, was not exactly neutral in the political process or outside of it, except in the sense that she did not take partisan stances. Instead, she represented a comprehensive vision of what human life should and could be, leaving the working out of how that vision might be best realized in particular circumstances to the free action of a nation's citizens. A second document published in 1986, *Instruction on Christian Freedom and Liberation*, as its very title indicates, sought to present the positive vision, the natural complement to the criticism in the first document, which had political implications but was ultimately a theological exposition of a just social order.

These documents and the work in many fields to which they gave rise have had a fruitfulness and staying power that liberation theology has not. The primary explanation for this lies in the fact that they were really *theological*, that is, based in a Christian theology of man and society that emphasized four fundamental principles: human dignity, solidarity, subsidiarity, and the common good. These remained the heart of modern Catholic social teaching—especially a caution about the dangers of the modern state, which seeks to arrogate to itself all power and moral judgments. By contrast, the passage of time has made the classic texts in liberation theology, notably the Peruvian priest Gustavo Gutiérrez's *A Theology of Liberation*, look quite dated and limited to a particular moment.[47] The same might be said, generally, of the feminist and *tercermundista* theologies from roughly the same period. It was a good thing to seek the value of female perspectives and those of peoples in the developing world in a Church now more global than ever. But like liberation theology, these tended to be less a matter of indigenous and fresh perspectives than a mixture of secular ideologies and European theologies (Gutiérrez himself had done prolonged study in Europe) that have not worn well. John Paul II's 1988 apostolic letter *Mulieris Dignitatem* and multiple efforts to engage the churches of Latin America, Asia, and Africa tempered the more radical and non-Christian sides of those theologies while seeking to move some of their legitimate concerns into mainstream Catholic theology. And the collapse of the Soviet Union in 1989, partly because of the Catholic-inspired activity of Solidarity in the pope's native Poland, shook all Marxist and *marxisant* thought around the world.

All these efforts met with both partial success and resistance, of course. But the key texts to understanding John Paul II's theological vision are three: *Centesimus Annus*, *Veritatis Splendor*, and *Evangelium Vitae*—with *Fides et Ratio* as a kind of summation. As even their titles show, he was working along two main axes: social thought and moral-spiritual truth. In *Centesimus Annus*, he addressed the lessons of the hundred years since *Rerum Novarum* and the balance sheet between Communism and capitalism. The often quoted turning point of judgment comes after a review of the history culminating in the collapse of Communism in 1989:

> Returning now to the initial question: can it perhaps be said that, after the failure of Communism, capitalism is the victorious social system, and that capitalism should be the goal of the countries now making

[47] Gustavo Gutiérrez, *A Theology of Liberation: History, Politics, and Salvation*, trans. and ed. Sister Caridad Inda and John Eagleson (Maryknoll, N.Y.: Orbis Books, 1973). The Spanish original appeared in 1970.

efforts to rebuild their economy and society? Is this the model which ought to be proposed to the countries of the Third World which are searching for the path to true economic and civil progress?

The answer is obviously complex. If by "capitalism" is meant an economic system which recognizes the fundamental and positive role of business, the market, private property and the resulting responsibility for the means of production, as well as free human creativity in the economic sector, then the answer is certainly in the affirmative, even though it would perhaps be more appropriate to speak of a "business economy", "market economy" or simply "free economy". But if by "capitalism" is meant a system in which freedom in the economic sector is not circumscribed within a strong juridical framework which places it at the service of human freedom in its totality, and which sees it as a particular aspect of that freedom, the core of which is ethical and religious, then the reply is certainly negative. (*CA* 42)

So, in spite of very strong endorsements in many places in the text of the legitimacy of business and profits, private property and freedom, and even of "new" virtues such as business acumen and entrepreneurship (and warnings about the vices that welfare disincentives and intrusive government might produce), John Paul II comes out somewhere roughly at two cheers for capitalism. Its productivity and even its large congruence with a true view of the human person called for cheers; its relative weakness in the moral-cultural realm was reason for worry and perhaps even partial condemnation.[48]

The pope was quite aware of the Church's limitations in this sphere. He continues:

The Church has no models to present; models that are real and truly effective can only arise within the framework of different historical situations, through the efforts of all those who responsibly confront concrete problems in all their social, economic, political and cultural aspects, as these interact with one another. For such a task the Church offers her social teaching as an *indispensable and ideal orientation,* a teaching which, as already mentioned, recognizes the positive value of the market and of enterprise, but which at the same time points

[48] See George Weigel, ed., *A New Wordly Order: John Paul II and Human Freedom* (Washington, D.C.: Ethics and Public Policy Center, 1992), for a representative sample of early reactions pro and con.

> out that these need to be oriented towards the common good. This teaching also recognizes the legitimacy of workers' efforts to obtain full respect for their dignity and to gain broader areas of participation in the life of industrial enterprises so that, while cooperating with others and under the direction of others, they can in a certain sense "work for themselves" through the exercise of their intelligence and freedom. (*CA* 43)

But there is more than a balancing of owners and workers within the framework of the common good in his analysis. For the moral-cultural realm to play its part with effectiveness alongside political and economic forces, it has to have real truths and value to offer.[49]

To most Christians, this might seem obvious. The pope, however, astutely notes a contemporary phenomenon:

> Nowadays there is a tendency to claim that agnosticism and skeptical relativism are the philosophy and the basic attitude which correspond to democratic forms of political life. Those who are convinced that they know the truth and firmly adhere to it are considered unreliable from a democratic point of view, since they do not accept that truth is determined by the majority, or that it is subject to variation according to different political trends. It must be observed in this regard that if there is no ultimate truth to guide and direct political activity, then ideas and convictions can easily be manipulated for reasons of power. As history demonstrates, a democracy without values easily turns into open or thinly disguised totalitarianism. (*CA* 46)

Weimar Germany had had a legal system overly focused on legal positivism, and that had enabled Hitler to come to power through democratic means, of a sort. But there is no doubt that John Paul II also has in mind here forces within the principal democratic nations that regard "openness" and a kind of majoritarian pragmatism as all that is needed to guide societies. America's founders had not thought so and had even built republican structures precisely to prevent majority tyrannies from arising. John Paul II touched on a crucial point, one perhaps also relevant to disorders and dangers within the Church.

[49] A good guide to many of these issues by a friend of the pope's is Maciej Zieba, *Papal Economics: The Catholic Church on Democratic Capitalism, from* Rerum Novarum *to* Caritas in Veritate (Wilmington, Del.: ISI Books, 2013).

His response to the problem he identified was different from the one given in the past. Catholicism in the first half of the twentieth century had tried to reply with metaphysical arguments—useful and even essential as far as they go. The problem is that in practical terms metaphysics has a limited reach. In mid-century, arguments were often made on behalf of rights and freedoms that were taken to be evident to all modern democrats but showed their insubstantiality by morphing into all sorts of alleged "rights" in the second half of the century, including such problematic notions as a woman's "right" to control her own body through abortion, the "right" to medically assisted suicide, and the "right" of same-sex couples to "marry". Responding to all this, John Paul II insisted in two texts—*Veritatis Splendor* and *Evangelium Vitae*—that the dignity and freedom of the human person had to be understood in a Christian way or new forms of inhuman totalitarianism were inevitable.

Veritatis Splendor

Veritatis Splendor appeared in 1993, deliberately timed after the publication of the *Catechism of the Catholic Church*. It cleverly addresses a cleavage that had emerged after Vatican II: the various arguments that something that might be broadly called the "fundamental option"—that is, a basic commitment to God—could be maintained despite a departure in conscience from the moral norms that the Church believed God himself had communicated to the world. Theologians objected that the pope did not present their positions fairly or that they, individually, did not hold the positions some thought they did. (Karl Rahner had earlier, for example, allowed for something like a fundamental option combined with a limited dissent on contraception, but others had gone much farther.) To leave aside all speculations about who precisely fell within papal strictures, however, John Paul II makes a passionate and inspiring case for the unity of the human person and the need to see faith and morals as intimately connected in ways that many theological currents after the Council gave the impression, at least, of denying.

He opens, cleverly, with what might seem an instance that supports the opposite view: the story of the "rich young man"

(Mt 19:16) who asks Jesus what he must do to have eternal life. Christ first replies: follow the Commandments. But the young man already has since his earliest youth. Then, says Jesus, sell all you have, give it to the poor, and "come follow me." At least one way of reading this exchange might be that it is a kind of "fundamental option": the mere following of moral precepts is inadequate; what is far more fundamental is imitating Christ and being in communion with him. This perspective would be repeated by Benedict XVI and Pope Francis and drew on, even as it inspired, a strong modern current among Catholic ethicists.[50]

John Paul II affirms that, indeed, committing to Jesus is the crucial thing. But he then bends back to the question of what needs to be done, and the entire thrust of the text and the argument is that, hierarchy of truths notwithstanding, the spiritual orientation and moral life cannot be opposed, indeed, must be held together for the sake of the necessary unity of the human person: "To separate the fundamental option from concrete kinds of behavior means to contradict the substantial integrity or personal unity of the moral agent in his body and in his soul" (*VS* 67).

A brief digression here: John Paul II's famous "theology of the body" belongs to this set of reflections as well, though it was laid out a decade earlier, almost casually, in his Wednesday audiences from September 1979 to November 1984.[51] He was already insisting then on the unity of thought and behavior that leads to personal integrity. The essential point is easy enough to grasp: John Paul tries to connect the traditional Catholic views on sexuality, marriage and divorce, contraception, the love between a man and a woman, and related issues to a theological vision of the love between the Persons of the Trinity. In this perspective, human love is an "icon" of that divine love, and the latter offers a foundation for fidelity, fertility, and love within the family as all rooted in the very nature of God himself. Even in this brief summary, it is a powerful way of viewing things.

[50] A prominent example of this current is Servais Pinckaers, O.P., *The Sources of Christian Ethics* (Washington, D.C.: Catholic University of America Press, 1995).

[51] John Paul II, *Man and Woman He Created Them: A Theology of the Body*, trans. Michael M. Waldstein (Boston: Pauline Books & Media, 2006). This is a corrected and uniform translation that remedies some of the inconsistencies in the translations done individually by the Vatican as each audience was given.

Critics, of course, found its very power too idealistic and unrealistic for poor, fallen human beings. But many people, desperately seeking for guidance in a culture in headlong flight from age-old biblical truths, have found it a kind of lifesaver. The influence of the "theology of the body" has been limited, even within the Church. But where it has been embraced, it has been embraced with evangelical zeal. Only time will tell whether it can ultimately prevail against strong countervailing currents.

But let us return to *Veritatis Splendor*: The text pays special attention to the relationship of freedom and truth, recognizing that freedom and the role of consciences have become prominent in the modern world. Unlike most contemporary writers who addressed those subjects—even some writing in from Catholic perspective—John Paul II seeks, as he did in earlier philosophical work about the moral nature of the "acting person", to make clear that freedom and conscience always stand under eternal law and its embodiment in natural law. It is not, he argues, as if these were alien impositions from outside us. They are the very expression of what we must be to become who we were intended to be by our Creator. A "pastoral" approach to modern problems is never really pastoral when it gives the impression that the difficulty of certain moral stances somehow lessens the obligation to prefer the truth to everything. John Paul II invokes the example of the martyrs as showing the true Christian witness that, like Christ, is willing to stay faithful, not only in difficult conditions, but even to death. Such a commitment is not slavery but true freedom that transcends culture, history, and personal limitations.

Some specific philosophical and theological positions, of course, challenge such a view: "Today's widespread tendencies towards subjectivism, utilitarianism and relativism appear not merely as pragmatic attitudes or patterns of behavior, but rather as approaches having a basis in theory and claiming full cultural and social legitimacy" (*VS* 106). The pope systematically rejects and tries to refute a series of errors that seem to be both in the air and in modern theologians.

Subjectivism, for instance, gives the impression that only the person in the concrete circumstances can judge a given case—roughly equivalent to what has been called "situation ethics" in other contexts. This is a true perspective insofar as God has intended our freedom to be exercised by us in our own lives. But it cannot mean, says

John Paul, and has never meant in Christian history, that an individual is justifiably free to make judgments that contradict the whole moral tradition coming down to us from the Hebrew and Christian Scriptures or the principles of the natural law. Modern attitudes, especially toward sexual behavior, tend to suggest that such questions are fenced off not only from interference by the state but from God himself. The truth is quite the opposite: "Moral conscience does not close man within an insurmountable and impenetrable solitude, but opens him to the call, to the voice of God. In this, and not in anything else, lies the entire mystery and the dignity of the moral conscience: in being the place, the sacred place where God speaks to man" (*VS* 58). The pontiff worries that the opposite view has begun to influence Catholic theology, even seminary formation.

Veritatis Splendor therefore seeks to lay down some general orientations for Catholic thinkers, without dictating how they are to be handled in intellectual terms: "Certainly the Church's Magisterium does not intend to impose upon the faithful any particular theological system, still less a philosophical one. Nevertheless, in order to 'reverently preserve and faithfully expound' the word of God [as it was put in Vatican II's *Dei Verbum*], the Magisterium has the duty to state that some trends of theological thinking and certain philosophical affirmations are incompatible with revealed truth" (*VS* 29).

This leads him into various fields, the most important of which involve a denial of historicism—the view that basic moral truths change with time—though he invites a properly historical study of Scripture and tradition. The extreme historicist position that sees all moral views as time conditioned and the related view of morality as "socially constructed" would simply turn the very notion of moral universality into the common modern default position: relativism. There have been ethical questions that are peripheral to the great moral truths and may sometimes be regarded as derived from context. This is not the case, however, with the central principles. And there is a large and public price to be paid for rejecting universal principles in favor of historicism. It means that there is also no way to affirm universal rights and the ways people around the world should always be treated, irrespective of the time and place in which they find themselves.

The most technical (and disputed) parts of this analysis have to do with what he calls teleology and "teleologism". John Paul II is careful to say that some who may pursue a view of morality involving the weighing of various ends (*teloi*) ought to be equally careful in avoiding what seem to be bad consequences of their theories. He maintains that there are some views that simply cannot be rationally held, in particular consequentialism and proportionalism: "The former claims to draw the criteria of the rightness of a given way of acting solely from a calculation of foreseeable consequences deriving from a given choice. The latter, by weighing the various values and goods being sought, focuses rather on the proportion acknowledged between the good and bad effects of that choice, with a view to the 'greater good' or 'lesser evil' actually possible in a particular situation" (*VS* 75). Both of these approaches also reduce to a kind of utilitarianism in which we believe, usually wrongly, that we can predict that a greater good—or at least a lesser evil—can come from doing some evil.

Such theories have a certain plausibility in the modern world, John Paul II says, because they seem to parallel scientific and technological approaches to problems. But this has never been the way that moral thinking has been done in the Church. Further, mixed in with such calculations there is often a kind of sociological standard of what human behavior and human societies are like. There is no harm in surveying such phenomena, of course, but, since individuals and groups are marred by original sin, to set up what is often the case as a standard for what *should* be the case is to admit sin into the very calculation of what the human goods are. In all human societies, there is murder, rape, exploitation, and a host of other evils. And it would be absurd to think that these sociological facts or many others may be used either to support or to undermine moral standards. That is why the Church teaches that "there exist acts which *per se* and in themselves, independently of circumstances, are always seriously wrong by reason of their object" (*VS* 80).

The reason he has engaged in this whole exercise, he says to his fellow bishops, is that the "essential bond between Truth, the Good and Freedom has been largely lost sight of by present-day culture. As a result, helping man to rediscover it represents nowadays one of the specific requirements of the Church's mission, for the salvation of the world" (*VS* 84).

Whether he succeeded in this intellectual and spiritual exercise has been much debated, even within Catholicism, and especially by moral theologians themselves, whom John Paul called to understand their real service in relation to the Church. The magisterium proposes the large principles, and theologians provide the intellectual underpinnings.[52] Many have persisted in claiming that his insistence on disputed universal principles fails to help with the Church's pastoral responsibilities. But John Paul II anticipated such reactions and argued that it was hardly pastoral to call people to anything less than that to which God himself has called them. God's mercy, of course, is always available to repentant sinners, a theme he had sounded since his early encyclical *Dives in Misericordia* and even as a bishop prior to becoming pope.[53] He warned theologians against engaging in dissent on the secular model and reminded his fellow bishops of their responsibility to protect sound teaching of the faithful.[54] As has been noted earlier, his approach was more effective against the relatively coherent if murderous system of Communism than against the amorphous and multiple vices of the free world. Yet John Paul II reintroduced the true and the good into that free world, rich in practical matters but weak on principles and goals, in ways that may yet bear fruit.

[52] "While recognizing the possible limitations of the human arguments employed by the Magisterium, moral theologians are called to develop a deeper understanding of the reasons underlying its teachings and to expound the validity and obligatory nature of the precepts it proposes, demonstrating their connection with one another and their relation with man's ultimate end. Moral theologians are to set forth the Church's teaching and to give, in the exercise of their ministry, the example of a loyal assent, both internal and external, to the Magisterium's teaching in the areas of both dogma and morality. Working together in cooperation with the hierarchical Magisterium, theologians will be deeply concerned to clarify ever more fully the biblical foundations, the ethical significance and the anthropological concerns which underlie the moral doctrine and the vision of man set forth by the Church" (*VS* 110).

[53] "In fact, genuine understanding and compassion must mean love for the person, for his true good, for his authentic freedom. And this does not result, certainly, from concealing or weakening moral truth, but rather from proposing it in its most profound meaning as an outpouring of God's eternal Wisdom, which we have received in Christ, and as a service to man, to the growth of his freedom and to the attainment of his happiness" (*VS* 95).

[54] "*Dissent,* in the form of carefully orchestrated protests and polemics carried on in the media, *is opposed to ecclesial communion and to a correct understanding of the hierarchical constitution of the People of God.* Opposition to the teaching of the Church's Pastors cannot be seen as a legitimate expression either of Christian freedom or of the diversity of the Spirit's gifts. When this happens, the Church's Pastors have the duty to act in conformity with their apostolic mission, insisting that *the right of the faithful* to receive Catholic doctrine in its purity and integrity must always be respected. 'Never forgetting that he too is a member of the People of God, the theologian must be respectful of them, and be committed to offering them a teaching which in no way does harm to the doctrine of the faith' " (*VS* 113).

Evangelium Vitae

If *Centesimus Annus* summed up basic Christian anthropology, primarily as it related to public affairs, and *Veritatis Splendor* affirmed universal moral principles and the magisterium's duty to defend them, John Paul II clearly decided, partly at the prodding of the cardinals in a synod,[55] that he also needed to devote a substantial text to the "life issues" prominent in the developed world, such as abortion, euthanasia, eugenics, and assisted suicide. In accord with much of his thinking about problems in the modern world, he saw these phenomena as threats to the profound dignity of human life, which is to be valued because it is the gift of God. Taken together, such practices constitute, as he formulated it in a famous phrase, a "culture of death" (*EV* 12).

In fact, so worried did the pope seem about the cheapening of human life in modern democracies that, in theory, claimed to value each individual, that he added another category to these threats: capital punishment, which might still be accepted, but only in circumstances of "absolute necessity" that are "very rare, if not practically nonexistent" (*EV* 56). The pope argued that the death penalty should almost always be replaced, out of respect for life, with other methods of control and punishment now available in most developed societies, if those societies needed to defend themselves. The result of these concerns was the publication on March 25, 1995 (significantly, the Feast of the Annunciation), of his eleventh encyclical, *Evangelium Vitae* ("The Gospel of Life").

In many respects, of course, his arguments simply drew on a long tradition that forbids the deliberate intention to harm innocents (the sharp restrictions on capital punishment were a different matter and elicited controversies from various quarters). But as in several of the other documents dealing with social questions, John Paul II put the

[55] The summary of *Evangelium Vitae* issued by the Vatican the same day as it was published claimed not only serious authority for its teaching but *unanimity among the world's bishops:* "The encyclical is presented with great doctrinal authority: It is not only an expression, like every other encyclical, of the ordinary magisterium of the pope, but also of the episcopal collegiality which was manifested first in the extraordinary consistory of cardinals in April 1991 and subsequently in a consultation of all the bishops of the Catholic Church, who unanimously and firmly agree with the teaching imparted in it" (no. 5).

life issues in a social context. He ruled out the argument that, in a modern pluralistic democracy, states must remain neutral among differing moral views on questions like abortion. Instead, he asserted universal moral principles even against laws duly passed by democratic means: "Abortion and euthanasia are ... crimes which no human law can claim to legitimize. There is no obligation in conscience to obey such laws; instead there is *a grave and clear obligation to oppose them by conscientious objection*" (*EV* 73, emphasis added). He recognized that there might be times when a Catholic politician could not get an absolute prohibition of such practices, but he argued that there is always the obligation to minimize harm and to work toward a legal culture ("personally opposed" not being enough) that reflects a fundamental culture of life. This, of course, led to multiple disputes, especially in the United States, about the behavior of Catholics in legislatures.

But *Evangelium Vitae*, for all its tough talk on hot-button issues, had a better overall reception, even among theologians, than most of John Paul II's documents on controversial topics. His approach was firm, yet sensitive to complexities—where such sensitivity was warranted. For instance, he recognized that while abortion per se is the deliberate destruction of innocent human life and, therefore, prohibited by the moral law, medically there are cases when both mother and child will die unless something is done. And in line with the tradition of "double effect", he wrote that a mother's life may be saved even if the indirect consequence of that effort led in certain cases to the unavoidable death of the child. Similarly, though the willed death of the sick—euthanasia—is an evil in itself ("false mercy": *EV* 66), there is no obligation to continue any and all treatments of the terminally ill if such treatments merely prolonged suffering. And palliative pain treatment might be justified even if its indirect effect is to hasten death.

The distinction, of course, lay between allowing someone to die, as we all must, and easing the process of death, on the one hand, and, on the other hand, intending the death of a sick person. To many in the secular world, perhaps, it might seem a distinction without a difference. But *Evangelium Vitae* drew support from Christians and Jews and even some secular readers, who seemed to sense the slippery slope on which medicine was beginning to set foot.

To all those dealing with these new moral questions, John Paul issued a challenge to establish "a new culture of life".

Fides et Ratio

It was not merely symbolic that John Paul II's last great encyclical before the new millennium was the 1998 *Fides et Ratio*, an extensive examination of the relationship between faith and reason, which was published the same week that he canonized Edith Stein and celebrated his twentieth anniversary as pope. In many respects, *Fides et Ratio* also summed up Catholic thought during the whole long century and more since Leo XIII had called for a renewal of Thomism in *Aeterni Patris* (1879), which John Paul II presented as a "*diakonia* of the truth" (*FR* 2). Unlike Leo, John Paul did not point to Thomistic thought, whether in philosophy or in theology, as of unique importance for the future of the Church and the world (*FR* 45). He paid special homage to Thomas and his way of doing theology, which values both faith and reason. And he emphasized the need for a reason capable of "*genuinely metaphysical* range" [emphasis in original] in order to address any number of current questions (*FR* 83). But the pope repeated what he had said in *Veritatis Splendor*: the Church has no one official philosophy or theology, except for the ways that lead to Jesus Christ as the answer to the deepest human questions.

At the end of the twentieth century, John Paul II found himself in circumstances somewhat the reverse of those Leo had faced. In the late nineteenth century, a very narrow Enlightenment rationality was generally thought to be all that was necessary for human flourishing. By its nature, that rationality was based in naturalistic, empirical, and immanent categories. It was also supremely self-confident. By John Paul's day, Enlightenment rationality itself had been exploded in its self-understanding as the universal form of reason by postmodern currents. Reason in general—except for science and technology—had come to be viewed as weak, uncertain, partial, plural. The pope thought it had "wilted under the weight of so much knowledge and little by little [had] lost the capacity to lift its gaze to the heights, not daring to rise to the truth of being" (*FR* 5). A central reason why John Paul wrote was to encourage philosophers and theologians to rediscover the fuller power of reason—which begins, as in ancient times, in a sense of *wonder* at Being. And while he accepted the value and necessity of multiple approaches to truth, he warned against an "undifferentiated pluralism" that would simply leave individual persons and the human race as a whole morally and spiritually adrift: "With its enduring appeal to the search for truth, philosophy has the great responsibility of forming thought and culture; and now it must strive resolutely to recover its original vocation" (*FR* 6).

Once again, the pope set himself a difficult question that he began to answer by invoking a personalist approach. Though the encyclical is addressed to his fellow bishops, after a brief opening paragraph to them invoking faith and reason as the "two wings" on which the spirit rises to the contemplation of truth, he immediately invoked the ancient Greek saying, "Know thyself." This was not by accident. We all ask questions about our origins, the meaning of our lives, and our ultimate destination. Reflection on that journey is part of what it means to be fully human, because a human person is virtually by definition "*the one who seeks the truth*" (*FR* 28). And in the personalist view, the meaning of persons tells us something about the nature of things and of God as well. Limiting our questions to practical matters or a "technocratic logic" is not only insufficient, it has led to several of the horrors of recent times as people try to explain human life or satisfy themselves in ways that, in their narrowness, stunt humanity. This is just one manifestation of the disorder in the mind since the Fall that has led to reason's becoming "prisoner to itself" (*FR* 22).

Experience with the grotesque inhumanity that flows from atheistic humanism indicates the need for a transcendence even of ourselves. As we see in every great world culture, said the pope, there naturally arises an implicit philosophy, and the hunger we feel for such transcendence is a first sign that revelation—God's communication of things beyond human reason, but not contrary to reason—is not the mere creation of human reason or imagination but a reality that responds to our condition: "The truth made known to us by Revelation is neither the product nor the consummation of an argument devised by human reason. It appears instead as something gratuitous, which itself stirs thought and seeks acceptance as an expression of love" (*FR* 15).

Transcendence, however, does not abolish the need for reason. On the contrary, it is the stimulant for further—indeed, unending—rational investigation. For John Paul II, reason itself tells us that reason alone cannot save us. Something else is needed, and we find that it comes to us in the course of time, in sacred history, time being a reality that has special importance in the biblical perspective. The Cross—the expression of a love freely given that is stronger than death—is the answer that reason cannot give. But as we can see even from the history of philosophy, reason is involved in a temporal preparation for the reception of revelation. And even after revelation has occurred, reason plays a crucial role in understanding revelation and its relationship to natural truths.

Further, as we have seen in examining the work of Alasdair MacIntyre, naked reason or the reasoning of single individuals is in an inescapable relationship with traditions of inquiry that evoke a certain trust in what others have discovered and the frames of reference they have developed. In the realms of both faith and reason, even critical approaches begin first with a trust in those who introduce us to the great questions. The pagans prior to Christ knew that as well: "Reason too needs to be sustained in all its searching by trusting dialogue and sincere friendship. A climate of suspicion and distrust, which can beset speculative research, ignores the teaching of the ancient philosophers who proposed friendship as one of the most appropriate contexts for sound philosophical enquiry" (*FR* 33). The modern hermeneutic of suspicion, thus, is dependent on a prior "hermeneutic of trust".

In this perspective, both ancient philosophy and Christianity played a purifying role in eliminating religious superstition and in seeking universal truth. Christian revelation still contains many mysteries, of course, but these are of a kind that reason may defend. By contrast, many forms of modern "spirituality" are a return to the kind of esotericism that both reason and revelation contradict. Furthermore, as has often been noticed, a purely philosophic understanding of life is an elitist notion, one that does not sufficiently respect the implicit wisdom of the vast majority of men who cannot practice philosophy. At the same time, however, revelation encouraged classical reason to go farther than it had earlier thought possible, as we see in the great Greek Fathers of the Church. Both common people and the philosophers were caught up in the search for true wisdom.

For John Paul, both faith and reason have their own integrity but are at their best when they are distinct, yet related, as in Saint Thomas Aquinas. When they begin to diverge, faith becomes pietistic, and reason, unsteady in its powers and range, can become excessive in atheism and totalitarianism or defective in instrumentalized forms of relativism and skepticism: "Deprived of reason, faith has stressed feeling and experience, and so run the risk of no longer being a universal proposition. It is an illusion to think that faith, tied to weak reasoning, might be more penetrating; on the contrary, faith then runs the grave risk of withering into myth or superstition. By the same token, reason which is unrelated to an adult faith is not prompted to turn its gaze to the newness and radicality of being" (*FR* 48).

At the same time, the pope reserves the right of the Church to warn about forms of philosophy that seem incompatible with the truth. As mentioned above, rationalism and naturalism were often a problem in the past. Today, on the one hand, there is a widespread and more radical challenge: the distrust of reason that claims metaphysics is impossible, a view that has had an impact in theology as well. On the other hand, some react to that distrust with fideism or a biblical fundamentalism. Some methods of scriptural study—here, perhaps, an exclusive historical-critical approach may be intended—unfold as if they were the only way to understand revelation. Once again, however, he argues that faith is larger than all reason and stirs reason up to go beyond its partial views (*FR* 56).

John Paul II was a thoroughly modern man and an intellectual acquainted with various currents of thought. So it was only natural that he allows for the fact that social science, physical science, and other modern disciplines will play a role in Catholic thinking. But he maintains that these cannot be *normative* the way some have tried to make use of them. They provide information on which faith and reason must reflect in order to integrate them fully into a properly unified Christian world view, since Christians believe that there is only one truth. Similarly, our modern awareness of diverse cultures cannot set itself up as an argument for relativism or the imperialism of a single culture. All cultures contain truths mixed with errors, and it is one of the tasks of a properly understood reason to sift those cultures for what they can bring to the faith and what the faith can bring to them.

He concludes by laying out the tasks that philosophy and theology must now undertake for the sake of a truly human future, all of which might be subsumed under the need for a unification of knowledge: "This is one of the tasks which Christian thought will have to take up through the next millennium of the Christian era" (*FR* 85). As T.S. Eliot once put it, "Where is the knowledge we have lost in information?" John Paul II says we must recover the "sapiential dimension" of all our knowing to come again to a unity within ourselves and with one another. We cannot rest content with the hermeneutics of texts but must go beyond that to the reality and truth of the world. We must find a way to reassert that human knowledge is possible, that it can have a metaphysical range, if we hope to respond to our current crisis of truth and values, which are really a temptation to despair after the failures of the modern age, "and thus to correct certain mistaken modes of behavior now widespread in our society" (*FR* 83).

Paradoxically, many now believe that only postmodern skepticism can prevent the return of totalizing claims to truth, among which many might wish to classify Catholicism. John Paul II notes this worry and issues a challenge to theologians as well: "To believe it possible to know a universally valid truth is in no way to encourage intolerance; on the contrary, it is the essential condition for sincere and authentic dialogue between persons. On this basis alone is it possible to overcome divisions and to journey together towards full truth, walking those paths known only to the Spirit of the Risen Lord" (*FR* 92). And in accordance with his other great theological statements, he believes it is imperative to this dialogue that we explore universal questions in fundamental theology and moral theology as well.

John Paul II, of course, was writing primarily for an audience of believers, and mostly Catholic believers at that. His balanced appeal to both faith *and* reason is a leitmotiv of Catholic intellectual life that goes back, in differing forms, through the ages to the medieval and ancient periods. He encourages passion on both fronts: "The *parrhesia* of faith must be matched by the boldness of reason" (*FR* 48). At the same time, he is quite willing to point out what he calls the "exceptional philosophical density" (*FR* 80) of Sacred Scripture.

But in several respects his message may be even more vital for a world that has lost its faith in reason, often sees relationships solely in terms of a Nietzschean will to power, in many respects *fears* the truth and the demands it may make—and is deeply pessimistic as a result. He proposes as a touchstone to both philosophers and theologians "the authority of truth alone" (*FR* 79). It has sometimes been said that if Voltaire were to come back today, he would be shocked to find the greatest defenders of a robust reason sitting on the papal throne. But perhaps it is not so shocking in a century when it was the Church that tried, often unsuccessfully, to hold open the doors to dimensions of reality that the secular world denied even existed and suffered from losing as a result.

Karol Wojtyła was, famously, a poet, dramatist, and actor as a young man. In his old age, he combined that dramatic sensibility with a sense of historic responsibility. In 2003, less than two years before his death, he published *Roman Triptych*, a three-part series of poetic meditations on biblical themes.[56] Its aesthetic merit, so far as one might judge in translation, is modest, but there are moments when the meditations rise to great intensity. Not least among these is the conclusion of the central meditation, when for the first time in Church history, a sitting pope reflects in verse on what will happen at the Sistine Chapel conclave that will elect his successor:

> It is here, beneath this wondrous Sistine profusion of color that
> the Cardinals assemble—
> the community responsible for the legacy of the keys of the
> Kingdom.
>
> They come here, to this very place
> And once more Michelangelo wraps them in his vision.
> "In Him we live and move and have our being."
>
> Who is He?
> Behold, the creating hand of the Almighty, the Ancient One,
> reaching towards Adam. . . .
> In the beginning God created . . .
> He, who sees all things . . .

[56] John Paul II, *The Poetry of Pope John Paul II: Roman Triptych; Meditations*, trans. Jerzy Peterkiewicz (Washington, D.C.: USCCB Publishing, 2003).

The colors of the Sistine will then speak the word of the
  Lord:
Tu es Petrus—once heard by Simon, son of John.
"To you I will give the keys of the Kingdom."

Those entrusted with the legacy of the keys gather here,
  letting themselves be enfolded by the Sistine's colors,
by the vision left to us by Michelangelo—
so it was in August, and again in October, in the memorable
  year of the two Conclaves,
and so it will be once more, when the time comes,
after my death.
Michelangelo's vision must then speak to them.

"Con-clave": a shared concern for the legacy of the keys,
  the keys of the Kingdom.
Lo, they see themselves in the midst of the Beginning and
  the End,
between the Day of Creation and the Day of Judgment.
It is granted man once to die and thereafter, the judgment!

Final transparency and light.
The clarity of the events—
The clarity of consciences—
During the conclave, Michelangelo must teach them—
Do not forget: *Omnia nuda et aperta sunt ante oculos Eius.*
You who see all—point to him!
He will point him out.[57]

It was fitting that the dying pope included a classical aesthetic element in this forward-looking vision. In the event, it was Joseph Ratzinger that the cardinals, gathered under the colorful frescoes of Michelangelo, chose to become his successor as Benedict XVI. And he, in turn, remarked in a speech to the cardinals in the Sistine Chapel under those very same frescoes:

[57] Ibid., 24–25.

> I consider this a grace obtained for me by my venerated predecessor, John Paul II. It seems I can feel his strong hand squeezing mine; I seem to see his smiling eyes and listen to his words, addressed to me especially at this moment: "Do not be afraid!"
>
> The death of the Holy Father John Paul II, and the days which followed, were for the Church and for the entire world an extraordinary time of grace. The great pain for his death and the void that it left in all of us were tempered by the action of the Risen Christ, which showed itself during long days in the choral wave of faith, love and spiritual solidarity, culminating in his solemn funeral....
>
> How can one not feel sustained by this witness? How can one not feel the encouragement that comes from this event of grace?[58]

A torch had been passed.

Joseph Ratzinger (Benedict XVI)

The entire world now knows Joseph Ratzinger as Pope Benedict XVI. But few know that earlier he had made twin personal sacrifices—first, agreeing to Paul VI's request that he become archbishop of Munich and Freising (the historic see in his native Bavaria, established by Saint Bonaventure in 739) and, later, accepting John Paul II's invitation to become prefect of the Congregation for the Doctrine of the Faith in Rome—Ratzinger was a gifted theologian and a natural lover of the intellectual life. Even after years in demanding administrative posts in the Church, his lectures, speeches, and writings bear the unmistakable stamp of a powerful and wide-ranging mind. Though many have come to recognize this remarkable theologian only as his voluminous and wide-ranging writings have appeared since his election as pope, his place in the twentieth-century theological empyrean will only become clearer and more assured as time passes.

The theologian and future pope was born on April 16, 1927, and passed his early years steeped in the religious and popular culture of old Bavaria. He has written movingly of the religious festivals he

[58] "First Message of His Holiness Benedict XVI at the End of the Eucharistic Celebration with the Members of the College of Cardinals in the Sistine Chapel", April 20, 2005. From the Vatican Information Service official translation of the Latin original.

experienced as a child, connecting one of them with a line from a hymn by Aquinas, *Quantum potes, tantum aude* ("dare as much as you are able"):

> I can still smell those carpets of flowers and the freshness of the birch trees; I can see all the houses decorated, the banners, the singing; I can still hear the village band, which indeed sometimes dared more, on this occasion, than it was able! I remember the *joie de vivre* of the local lads, firing their gun salutes—which was their way of welcoming Christ as a head of state, as *the* Head of State, the Lord of the world, present on their streets and in their village. On this day people celebrated the perpetual presence of Christ as if it were a state visit in which not even the smallest village was neglected.[59]

For many people in those days, these popular religious practices would have just been taken for granted. They penetrated deeply into the future pope, however, and his attachment to the liturgy clearly stems from those early years: "Naturally, the child I then was did not grasp every aspect of this, but I started down the road of the liturgy, and this became a continuous process of growth into a grand reality transcending all particular individuals and generations, a reality that became an occasion for me of ever-new amazement and discovery."[60]

This relatively idyllic side of his youth was soon to be disrupted by the forces that began to creep into Bavaria with the rise of National Socialism. Ratzinger was drafted at sixteen and reluctantly served two years in the German army until he was captured by the invading Americans. He has said often since then that he learned a great deal from the Nazi takeover of Germany, not least the inability of liberal Christian theology to resist such onslaughts. He has described how a Nazi schoolteacher in his hometown once erected a Maypole

> as symbol of a life force perpetually renewing itself. The Maypole was supposed to bring back a portion of German religion and thus help gradually to expel Christianity, which was now denounced

[59]Joseph Ratzinger, "What Corpus Christi Means to Me: Three Meditations", in *The Feast of Faith*, trans. Graham Harrison (San Francisco: Ignatius Press, 1986), 127.

[60]Joseph Ratzinger, *Milestones: Memoirs 1927–1977*, trans. Erasmo Leiva-Merikakis (San Francisco: Ignatius Press, 1998), 20.

> as alienating Germans from their own great Germanic culture. He likewise organized midsummer sun festivals, again as a return to the sacredness of nature and to Germanic origins, to take the place of alien notions such as sin and redemption that had been imposed on us by foreign Jewish and Roman religion. When nowadays I hear how in many parts of the world Christianity is criticized as a destruction of individual cultural identity and an imposition of European values, I am amazed at how similar the types of argumentation are and at how familiar many a turn of phrase sounds.[61]

These early incidents left a mark on him that reveals his tremendous capacity for integrating thought and experience into a whole. In the seminary, he was drawn most strongly to the work of Romano Guardini, Josef Pieper, Theodor Häcker, and Peter Wust. He also remarks on the moral presence of Munich's Cardinal Faulhaber, one of the great churchmen who resisted Nazism. It was not only John Paul II whose philosophical and theological work was touched by the atrocities of the twentieth century.

Several threads appear early in Ratzinger's thinking. Theology done within the Church needs to keep historical and systematic theology together, to pursue careful examination of the historical record, especially a return to the Fathers. And he shows a strong inclination from the outset toward the Augustinian and personalist side of Catholic theology. As he put it some years later in 1969: "Augustine has kept me company for more than twenty years. I have developed my theology in a dialogue with Augustine, though naturally I have tried to conduct this dialogue as a man of today."[62] This was the basic line he pursued as a student and then teacher at Bonn, Münster, Tübingen, and Regensburg—and beyond.

It has often been said that Ratzinger started out as a liberal but, after the Second Vatican Council, became increasingly conservative. This frames his thought in the kind of political categories that are not particularly helpful in understanding such a fine mind and misrepresents the deep continuity in his thought as well as his basic nature. Far from being "God's Rottweiler" or *der Panzer-Kardinal*, as he has

[61] Ibid., 16.

[62] Quoted in Thomas P. Rausch, *Pope Benedict XVI: An Introduction to His Theological Vision* (New York: Paulist Press, 2009), 47.

sometimes been described by critics, Ratzinger almost everywhere manifested a very mild temper open to dialogue with other views, as even his most liberal university students have attested. He was enthusiastic about renewal before and during the Council because of his basic, lifelong sympathies with a more pastoral Catholicism rooted in the Bible and the Church Fathers rather than the sometimes rigid Thomism of the seminaries. But he grew disappointed with much—though not all—that emerged after Vatican II; this was a matter of his empirical judgments about what was happening in the Church, a quite different thing from a change in his theological positions. Indeed, as in his comment about his dialogue with Augustine quoted above, what is most remarkable in Ratzinger's work is its steady fidelity to certain theological currents and its clever application of them to contemporary questions and controversies.

Like many other innovative theologians in the first half of the twentieth century, Ratzinger emphasized the importance of doing theology within the living historical Christian reality, the Church, while also following modern developments in Scripture scholarship. He rejected early on the kind of approach he calls "a liberalism restricted by dogma",[63] following Guardini and other innovative thinkers long before the Council in trying to find in dogma itself a living, dynamic principle: "Dogma was conceived, not as an external shackle, but as the living source that made knowledge possible."[64]

His first book (1954) was *Volk und Haus Gottes in Augustus Lehre von der Kirche* (People and house of God in Augustine's doctrine of the Church), a title suggested by a professor, Gottlieb Söhngen, for an academic prize competition. Ratzinger responded eagerly to the topic. The emphasis on the divine institution of the Church shows that pitting an early "liberal" Ratzinger over against a later conservative does not do justice to the real substance of his preconciliar positions. He finds in the early Augustine a model of thinking within the common life of the Church as opposed to the speculations of some solitary mind about the modern world. In his view, humility and recognition of proper authority are two inescapable virtues of every true Christian,

[63] Ratzinger, *Milestones*, 52.

[64] Quoted in Peter Seewald, *Benedict XVI: An Intimate Portrait*, trans. Henry Taylor and Anne Englund Nash (San Francisco: Ignatius Press, 2008), 187.

both of which come to us in historical form, just as our earliest personal lives are shaped by the actualities of our individual families. In his reading of Augustine, Ratzinger sees the authoritative structures of the visible Church as one with the inner Spirit, as are people and clergy. Ratzinger the Bavarian here meets Ratzinger the brilliant thinker.

From the start, *caritas* (the subject of his first encyclical as pope) is held in strict relationship with ecclesial truth and brotherhood in Ratzinger's exposition of Augustine. Indeed, Ratzinger goes so far as to point out that we miss something if we see the early Christian centuries as merely a dialogue between the Bible and Greek culture. Rome, with its practical sense of organization and of the importance of common laws, has continuing *intellectual* significance as well. But *caritas* rules all.

This concern to keep the concrete historical nature of Christianity in direct contact with speculative theology continued in Ratzinger's next book, *The Theology of History in St. Bonaventure*,[65] which focuses on Bonaventure's lectures on the six days of creation (*Collationes in Hexaemeron*). Though he is trying to solve the intellectual problem of integrating salvation history and metaphysics, he is also prescient in seeing in Bonaventure's handling of the radical spirituality of the Franciscan followers of Joachim of Fiore a way of dealing with contemporary currents that would emerge only fully with the Second Vatican Council. The Joachimites famously believed that the Church and the world were entering a Third Age of the Holy Spirit, an entirely new kind of utopian existence that would signify a radical break with the past. Instead of merely rejecting these fellow Franciscans, Bonaventure would make the deft move of accepting that a new age of the Spirit had begun with Saints Francis and Dominic, but this represented a continuity, Bonaventure said, not a break with what had come before. Writing in 1959, Ratzinger describes a vision of what he finds in Bonaventure that would stand him in good stead throughout the conciliar period and long after:

> Scripture points to the future; but only he who has understood the past can grasp the interpretation of the future because the whole of

[65] Trans. Zachary Hayes (Chicago: Franciscan Herald Press, 1971). The German original was published in 1959.

> history develops in one unbroken line of meaning in which that which is to come may be grasped in the present on the basis of the past.... In this way, the exegesis of Scripture becomes a theology of history; the clarification of the past leads to prophecy concerning the future.[66]

And this emphasis on continuity is also united, in Ratzinger's reading, with an appreciation for Saint Francis in particular as the humble man of poverty who is more knowledgeable in divine things than the most learned doctors because of his great love of God. Ratzinger later expressed his admiration for Saint Thomas Aquinas, but it is clear that he was more personally attuned to Franciscan and Bonaventuran modes and welcomed the historical studies that recovered the Neoplatonic and Augustinian dimensions of all the Scholastic writers, including the Angelic Doctor. It would not be an exaggeration to say that Ratzinger was exploring the way of thinking *within* the Church that he thought was most needed. Thinking should be focused on Christ, rather than on philosophy and theology done in the usual modern mode of independent speculation, which then has somehow to be fitted to salvation history and the living reality of the Church.

Many of these themes came to a head in the Church at large at the Second Vatican Council, of course. Ratzinger was a *peritus*, a theological expert, invited to attend by Cardinal Josef Frings, archbishop of Cologne—even though he was only thirty-five when the Council opened. After each session, he wrote analytical essays that provide a window into his thought about what transpired, and of course he returned to the subject repeatedly in subsequent years. The first session he thought fittingly devoted to the liturgy, a central element in Ratzinger's thought as well, so much so that in 2008, when his complete works began to be published, the first volume deliberately collected various writings on liturgy. Way back in 1963, he had characterized liturgy as "the true life-spring of the Church and so the authentic starting-point of all renewal".[67] Though later he often expressed dismay over where liturgical "renewal" had ended up, he was initially enthusiastic about the overall approach, which seemed

[66] Ibid., 8–9.

[67] Joseph Ratzinger, *Die erste Sitzungsperiode des zweiten Vatikan Konzils: Ein Rückblick* (Cologne, 1963), trans. and quoted by Aidan Nichols in *The Thought of Pope Benedict XVI: An Introduction to the Theology of Joseph Ratzinger* (New York: Burns & Oates, 2005), 78.

less fixated on merely opposing "modernism" than had been the case earlier and more confident in seeking new ways of presenting old truths, sometimes even outside exclusive adherence to Latin in both liturgy and schooling.

He had a similar view of the discussion of revelation, another longstanding interest that led to his commentary[68] on the document *Dei Verbum* and most notably his 2007 *Jesus of Nazareth*. But in both places, he also appeared wary of the tendency to let optimism overtake the older, more realistic Catholic sense of the dark side of human existence. In several prescient remarks in the 1969 *Dei Verbum* commentary, he notes the absence of attention to the notion of the "anger" of God, a modern recasting of the whole of salvation history that makes it difficult to understand why Christ's Passion on the Cross needed to occur and shifts the whole human drama away from central truths of Christianity that have been present from the very beginning. He still thought the document quite valuable, but concluded that—as with the freelance theology we noted above—unless Scripture is read within the Church it will tend toward the extremes of literalism or, in the interminable scholarly disputes, an empty modernism.

And there was a fundamental problem, perhaps less with *Dei Verbum* than with the impression the Council somehow left that nothing should be taught "that was not expressly contained in Scripture":

> This new theory, in fact, meant that exegesis now had to become the highest authority in the Church; and since, by the very nature of human reason and historical work, no agreement among interpreters can be expected in the case of such difficult texts (since here acknowledged or unacknowledged prejudices are always at work), all of this meant that faith had to retreat into the region of the indeterminate and continually changing that characterizes historical or would-be historical hypotheses. In other words, believing now amounted to having opinions and was in need of continual revision.[69]

Ratzinger's natural moderation and sense of balance come through clearly in his comments on the second session of the Council, largely

[68] In *Lexikon für Theologie und Kirche*, vol. 13 (Freiburg im Breisgau: Herder, 1967).
[69] Ratzinger, *Milestones*, 125–26.

taken up with the Dogmatic Constitution on the Church, *Lumen Gentium*. He appreciates the role of the bishops, especially in communion with the bishop of Rome, and the importance of the latter in helping preserve the freedom of other bishops, especially when local or national conditions press on the Church—a phenomenon now familiar to us in both totalitarian and liberal democratic countries. Later sessions of the Council seem to have inspired him to a lesser degree, perhaps because some of the forces that would soon make for turmoil in the Church had begun to show themselves. Indeed, he complains of *Gaudium et Spes*, the document about the Church in the modern world, that it was vague to the point of being similar to just about any general reflection on ethics, "whereas what is proper to theology, discourse about Christ and his work, was left behind in a conceptual deep-freeze, and so allowed to appear, in contrast with the understandable part, even more unintelligible and antiquated".[70] Salvation, he continues, seems superfluous because, in such a presentation, men seem quite capable of living a full and happy life without bothering about such matters. Indeed, the document might leave the impression that doubt in matters of religion was to be expected while implying a kind of certainty about how to handle worldly affairs. This attitude could not help but diminish the old missionary zeal and make modern secular values a measure for true Christianity. Indeed, the fissure had already opened up by the end of the Council, pitting the preconciliar against the postconciliar Church. Ratzinger warned: "We must not forget that the Church remains the Church of all ages. In all generations, the way of the Gospel could be found in her, and was found."[71]

Even before the Council ended, however, Ratzinger began giving a series of lectures at Tübingen on the Creed, which eventually turned into *Einführung in das Christentum: Vorlesungen über das apostolische Glaubensbekenntnis* (*Introduction to Christianity*).[72] More than a mere exposition, the book is also a brilliant apologetic, cleverly presenting the modern arguments *against* specific articles of the Creed—and against any belief at all—and even more cleverly responding to them.

[70] Quoted in Nichols, *Thought of Pope Benedict XVI*, 100.

[71] Ibid., 102.

[72] Joseph Ratzinger, *Introduction to Christianity*, trans. J. R. Foster (Communio Books; San Francisco: Ignatius Press, 2004).

(It is only an "introduction" in the same exalted sense as Thomas Aquinas' *Summa Theologiae* is intended according to its author for "beginners".) He recognizes the scandal of "positivity" that Christianity presents compared with vague Eastern spiritualities (it is harder to defend something specific). And he notes the tendency, in the absence of confidence in salvation history, for what used to go by that name to become a this-worldly project, whether of a conservative or liberationist nature.

And in particular, he underscores that Christianity is not a set of doctrines but a communal—and Churchly—"way":

> The community with one's fellowmen is a reality that lies on a different plane from that of the mere "idea". If Platonism provides an *idea* of the truth, Christian belief offers truth as a *way*, and only by becoming a way has it become *man's* truth. Truth as mere perception, as mere idea, remains bereft of force; it only becomes man's truth as a way that makes a claim upon him, that he can and must tread.[73]

All of reality, including the Trinity, includes a relational element. At the same time, the transcendent Trinity, which many think outside our knowledge and concern, provides a way that is not a political project of any kind, indeed, stands in judgment above all political orders. Ratzinger asserts that we must exercise a necessary modesty in speaking of this mystery but also confidence that God the Father disclosed himself to us via revelation in ways that we could not have reached ourselves, a point that resembles similar claims, as we saw earlier, in von Balthasar. But that mode of disclosure—Jesus as both bearer of the message and the message itself—united, in his own person, history and faith. And the Holy Spirit remains present in the Church—however imperfect the Spirit may be in human terms—indeed, shows itself in the day-to-day existence of Christ's people rather than in grand ecclesial projects of reform and renewal.

It is not difficult to detect behind this position Ratzinger's dismay over developments around 1968 in the Church, the university, and the world. Some of his older differences with figures like Karl Rahner became sharper as Rahner himself moved from the theology of

[73] Ibid., 99–100.

Bultmann and the philosophy of Heidegger—the existentialist position of mid-century—to radical politics bordering on Marxism. Ratzinger complained of how many people retained their religious fervor but now directed it away from God and toward man's political activity:

> The blasphemous manner in which the Cross now came to be despised as a sign of sadomasochism, the hypocrisy with which some still passed themselves off as believers when this was useful, in order not to jeopardize the instruments that were to serve their own private ends: all of this could and should not be made to look harmless or regarded as just another academic quarrel.[74]

These are unusually harsh judgments from a man who most often sought the path of dialogue, but anyone who lived through the feverishness of opinion in those days, and not only in religious matters, will recognize the justness of the charges.

In 1972, Ratzinger was invited to join the International Theological Commission, where he, de Lubac, von Balthasar, Louis Bouyer, and others labored to resist the politicization of theology. Yves Congar tried to be a conciliator, but it was an impossible task that soon failed: "The debates over what we as theologians were bound to do in this critical hour were animated in the extreme, and they also required all the physical energy at one's disposal. [Karl] Rahner and Feiner, the Swiss ecumenist, finally left the Commission because, in their opinion, it was worthless since the majority of its members was not ready to subscribe to radical theses."[75] Happily, many from the group that remained founded *Communio*, a scholarly quarterly that is published in eighteen languages.

Sadly for Ratzinger, the Church's liturgy had earlier undergone a sudden and radical alteration with the 1969 publication of the Missal of Paul VI and the prohibition on using the previous missal. He regarded this, not as the usual process of liturgical reform, which had often occurred in the history of the Church, but as a rupture with the past that conveyed the wrong message. It brought some benefits over the Baroque Catholicism Ratzinger had long criticized, "but setting it as a new construction *over against* what had grown historically,

[74] Ratzinger, *Milestones*, 137–38.

[75] Ibid., 144.

forbidding the results of this historical growth, thereby makes the liturgy appear to be no longer a living development but the product of scholarly work and juridical authority; this has caused us enormous harm. For then the impression had to emerge that liturgy is something 'made', not something given in advance." And he continued: "I am convinced that the crisis in the Church that we are experiencing today is to a great extent due to the disintegration of the liturgy, which at times has even come to be conceived of *etsi Deus non daretur* [as if God did not exist], that it is a matter of indifference whether or not God exists and whether or not he speaks to us and hears us."[76]

That orientation, of course, signified in Ratzinger's view an overemphasis on the Church as the people of God, which in several modern modes of thought slipped easily enough into seeing the Church's primary task as political. But for Ratzinger this got things profoundly backward. As he wrote in *Feast of Faith*, "Only if man, every man, stands before the face of God and is answerable to him, can man be secure in his dignity as a human being. Concern for the proper form of worship, therefore, is not peripheral but central to our concern for man himself."[77] In phrases reminiscent of certain fundamental positions in von Balthasar, Ratzinger spoke of learning the language of liturgy from our Mother, the Church. And he followed Romano Guardini in saying that liturgy must always be a blend of the cosmological, historical, and mysterious. Making liturgies too popular has not only damaged dimensions of liturgy, like music—always of great concern for Ratzinger and his brother, Georg, a priest and Church musician—but has muted those deep, structural dimensions as well. Too much talk, the disappearance of kneeling, and the alleged slight of a priest "turning his back to the people"—in truth a sociological misreading of the age-old practice of having all participants in the Eucharist face toward the East as the image of the return of the Risen Lord—are the modes in which this false popularization has manifested itself. And the overall effect has been to trade the transcendent dimension of the person, which so many in the modern world seek, for a shallow sense of community.

Ratzinger was asked by Paul VI to become archbishop of Munich-Freising in 1977 and four years later was appointed by

[76] Seewald, *Benedict XVI*, 204–5.
[77] Ratzinger, *Feast of Faith*, 7.

John Paul II to be prefect of the Congregation for the Doctrine of the Faith—the Holy Office, as it was once called—with responsibility for institutional oversight of what falls within and outside of Catholic belief. This called for a great deal of tact on his part, but also applications of the very sophisticated ecclesiology he had been developing over the years, one that respected both a people-of-God dimension but also the indispensable roles of bishops in local churches and the global position of the pope in representing and teaching the truth of Christ. For instance, Ratzinger reminded people that *Lumen Gentium*, the first words of the conciliar Constitution on the Church, does not make the Church herself the light of the world, but Christ (*Lumen gentium cum sit Christus*). For that light to shine, we must see its historical origin but also allow for its development over time down to the present and into the future. It is not only doctrine but the living institution—bishops are bishops because they live and teach in continuity with those who have fulfilled the same role before them.

And though the Church will not be perfect and enter into the New Jerusalem until the end of time, she holds open possibilities that will not be realized in any earthly order, sacred or profane. It was this *theological* position, dating at least back to Augustine, that set Ratzinger the Prefect against liberation theologies in the 1980s. In one sense, he had earlier realized as much as a professor and university official in the 1960s: "I learned that it is impossible to discuss with terror and on terror, as there are no premises for a discussion—and such a discussion becomes collaboration with terror.... I think that in those years [1960s], I learned where discussion must stop because it is turning into a lie, and resistance must begin in order to maintain freedom", as he told the *New York Times Magazine* in 1985.[78] The age-old distinction between the things of Caesar and the things of God was also important because "where such duality is lacking, totality, that is, the totalitarian system is inevitable."[79]

Within the Church, the difficult balancing act is always to reflect the plurality of points of view—a plurality built into the New Testament by the four Gospels themselves as well as by the many interpretations

[78] November 24, 1985, quoted in Nichols, *Thought of Pope Benedict XVI*, 182n24.

[79] Joseph Ratzinger, *The Church, Ecumenism, and Politics: New Endeavors in Ecclesiology*, trans. Michael J. Miller et al. (San Francisco: Ignatius Press, 2008), 157.

advanced about them since the time of the Church Fathers—*and* the necessary unity willed by Christ. In addition, in modern circumstances, subjective and objective, historical and eternal, form various challenges that the Church must embrace without losing her missionary energy as the bearer of Christ's truth. For Ratzinger, in the aftermath of Vatican II, for example, the necessary relationship between *ressourcement* (a return to the sources in the Scriptures and Fathers) and *aggiornamento* (the restatement of the tradition for our particular time) was largely been severed in favor of the latter, with the result that the Church found herself present in the world, but with little to say that was not already part of the surrounding culture.

This came out quite clearly in *The Ratzinger Report*, a book-length interview with Vittorio Messori that had worldwide resonance in the 1980s. The then prefect of the Congregation for the Doctrine of the Faith spoke quite candidly about the many problems facing the Church, not least her own internal disarray and the need to "rediscover" Vatican II—that is, to read it more faithfully. Part and parcel of that rediscovery was the need also to reread many then-current notions about theology and ecclesiology that had led to disorder over authority, theological dogma, and basic Christian morality. He also had some sharp observations on feminism, liturgy, ecumenism, liberation theology, and the need to proclaim Christ once again. For those who appreciated Ratzinger, this was a breath of fresh air in a time of crisis. For those who disliked him, it confirmed what they believed was his turn from being a progressive to an authoritarian conservative.

But the latter charge was not entirely fair. In several subsequent books, sometimes assembled from lectures he was asked to give, he showed himself a wide-ranging and sensitive commentator on everything from ecology to the cultural crisis of the West.[80] Even a cursory look at these texts—which constitute an amazing output from a man then occupied with a demanding job in the Roman curial structure—shows that he is no conservative in the sense of merely

[80] Cf. Joseph Ratzinger, *In the Beginning . . . : A Catholic Understanding of the Story of Creation and the Fall*, trans. Boniface Ramsey, O.P. (Grand Rapids, Mich.: Eerdmans, 1995). On the cultural crisis: *Values in a Time of Upheaval*, trans. Brian McNeil (New York: Crossroad; San Francisco: Ignatius Press, 2006); *Truth and Tolerance: Christian Belief and World Religions*, trans. Henry Taylor (San Francisco: Ignatius Press, 2004), among others.

seeking to protect the status quo in the Church or the world. Indeed, his thinking is the polar opposite of the kind of nostalgia for the past some Catholic conservatives manifest. Ratzinger was truly trying to think through what an evangelical Catholicism should mean in the conditions of modernity and postmodernity. In dialogues with lay intellectuals like Jürgen Habermas and Marcello Pera,[81] Ratzinger showed himself to be the equal of any serious European intellectual of his day. He possessed of a mind trying to think, not backward, but forward to a new religious and cultural flourishing.

When he became pope, this stance became even more pronounced. Just prior to his election, he gave a homily to the cardinals assembled for the conclave in which he summed up much of what he had been saying over the previous twenty years. It was most noticed for a single phrase: "the dictatorship of relativism".[82] In 2005, a few days before John Paul II died, Ratzinger had given a lecture at the Benedictine monastery in Subiaco in which he had been quite expansive about many things besides the obvious modern inability to be confident about truth and moral judgments. In fact, he began by describing the present moment as "a time of great dangers and great opportunities for man and the world".[83] By this, he meant that science and technology have given us great powers, both for good and for evil. And further, the way mere technical knowledge has come to dominate everything else is itself cause for concern: "Thus, the splendor of being an image of God no longer shines over man, which is what confers on him his dignity and inviolability, and he is left only to the power of his own human capacities. He is no more than the image of man—of what man?"[84] There is a "new moralism" that speaks of freedom and dignity, but in concrete practice it not infrequently leads to states' riding roughshod over persons:

[81] Cf. Jürgen Habermas and Joseph Ratzinger, *The Dialectics of Secularization: On Reason and Religion*, trans. Brian McNeil, C.R.V. (San Francisco: Ignatius Press, 2006); and Joseph Ratzinger and Marcello Pera, *Without Roots: The West, Relativism, Christianity, Islam*, trans. Michael F. Moore (New York: Basic Books, 2006).

[82] Mass "Pro Eligendo Romano Pontifice", April 18, 2005, http://www.vatican.va/gpII/documents/homily-pro-eligendo-pontifice_20050418_en.html.

[83] "Cardinal Ratzinger on Europe's Crisis of Culture (Part 1)", Zenit, July 26, 2005, http://www.zenit.org/en/articles/cardinal-ratzinger-on-europe-s-crisis-of-culture-part-1.

[84] Ibid.

> Political moralism, as we have lived it and are still living it, does not open the way to regeneration, and even more, also blocks it. The same is true, consequently, also for a Christianity and a theology that reduces the heart of Jesus' message, the "kingdom of God," to the "values of the kingdom," identifying these values with the great key words of political moralism, and proclaiming them, at the same time, as a synthesis of the religions.
>
> Nonetheless, God is neglected in this way, notwithstanding the fact that it is precisely he who is the subject and cause of the kingdom of God. In his stead, great words (and values) remain, which lend themselves to all kinds of abuse.[85]

The root of this problem, according to Benedict, is the dominance of a kind of rationality that is irrational in that it regards the modern scientific method as the only mode of truth: "As morality belongs to an altogether different sphere, it disappears as a category unto itself and must be identified in another way, in as much as it must be admitted, in any case, that morality is essential."[86]

The exclusion of religion from European culture—and by extension from all cultures that make Enlightenment reason the standard—seems like an opening to a neutral and universal culture. But in fact it tolerates and includes other ways of thinking and reason only insofar as they submit themselves to Enlightenment criteria—which postmodern thinkers as well as Ratzinger know is neither neutral nor universal, but the product of European culture at a particular moment. There are universal elements in that Enlightenment culture, as there are in all human cultures, but they often stem from premodern views of the world and the person. They do not seem to flow naturally from the rather narrow rationality of modern science and technology:

> By stating this, one does not deny all that is positive and important of this philosophy, but one affirms rather its need to complete itself, its profound deficiency. And so we must again address the two controversial points of the Preamble of the European Constitution. The banishment of Christian roots does not reveal itself as the expression of a higher tolerance, which respects all cultures in the same way, not

[85] Ibid.

[86] Ibid.

> wishing to privilege any, but rather as the absolutizing of a pattern of thought and of life that are radically opposed, among other things, to the other historical cultures of humanity.[87]

This is the context in which the dictatorship of relativism emerges. Ratzinger's goal is a higher "rationalism": "Is this a simple rejection of the Enlightenment and of modernity? Absolutely not. From the beginning, Christianity has understood itself as the religion of the 'Logos,' as the religion according to reason.... It was and is the merit of the Enlightenment to have again proposed these original values of Christianity and of having given back to reason its own voice."[88] And even more deeply, this raises a question with which the modern world has a hard time coming to grips: "whether the world comes from the irrational, and reason is not, therefore, other than a 'sub-product,' on occasion even harmful of its development, or whether the world comes from reason, and is, as a consequence, its criterion and goal".[89] He minces no words about what this signifies, even if few see it: "A reason that springs from the irrational, and that is, in the final analysis, itself irrational, does not constitute a solution for our problems. Only creative reason, which in the crucified God is manifested as love, can really show us the way. In the so necessary dialogue between secularists and Catholics, we Christians must be very careful to remain faithful to this fundamental line: to live a faith that comes from the 'Logos,' from creative reason, and that, because of this, is also open to all that is truly rational."[90]

He closes with a final appeal. Immanuel Kant wanted to establish a morality from reason that would be an expression of what is right *etsi Deus non daretur*: "even if God did not exist". Ratzinger makes a somewhat different proposal:

> The attempt, carried to the extreme, to manage human affairs disdaining God completely leads us increasingly to the edge of the abyss, to man's ever greater isolation from reality. We must reverse the axiom of the Enlightenment and say: Even one who does not succeed in

[87] Ibid., pt. 3, July 28, 2005.
[88] Ibid., pt. 4, July 29, 2005.
[89] Ibid.
[90] Ibid.

> finding the way of accepting God, should, nevertheless, seek to live and to direct his life "veluti si Deus daretur," as if God existed. This is the advice Pascal gave to his friends who did not believe. In this way, no one is limited in his freedom, but all our affairs find the support and criterion of which they are in urgent need.[91]

When Ratzinger became Benedict XVI, he continued to sound this theme, though he also introduced, via his first encyclicals, a greater sense of urgency about the need for *caritas*, charity in the theological sense, to inform all human life from interpersonal relations to the particulars of economic life. In several respects, this reflected a more robust sense of solidarity, often interpreted as statism in the tradition of Catholic social doctrine, a fact that irritated no small number of Catholic conservatives. But Benedict's recommendation of public solidarity had not forgotten some of the lessons gleaned from the experience of Communism and the openings John Paul II had given to market-based economics. He seemed mostly to want to see human affairs at national and international levels more informed by a fuller sense of reason, a reason rooted in the *Logos* that is also *Caritas*.

In that sense, his controversial 2006 lecture at the University of Regensburg—where he had taught decades earlier as a young professor—caps off much of the theological debate of the last part of the twentieth century.[92] Benedict made a passing reference to Manuel II Palaeologus, a medieval Byzantine emperor who, in conversation with "an educated Persian" (a unnamed Muslim counterpart in the history), had argued that religion is a matter of reason and not force. In the fragile Christian-Muslim relations that existed after September 11, 2001, this was taken as an insult against Islam by many who also seemed to want to use an admittedly provocative example to attack the pope more generally. But his main point in the lecture was not about Islam—or at least not Islam alone—but about what happens when religion and reason are separated. It was about the de-Hellenization of Christianity, which had led to its divorce of faith from reason—and the ways in which, as he said at Subiaco, Western civilization was suffering from a narrow version

[91] Ibid.

[92] For an insightful commentary, with full text, see James V. Schall, *The Regensburg Lecture* (South Bend, Ind.: St. Augustine's Press, 2007).

of reason, not the fuller one that stemmed from embrace of the original, creative *Logos*.

The de-Hellenization, in his view, took place in three phases. First, there was Luther's emphasis on *sola Scriptura*, which had some justification as a reaction to an overblown Scholasticism—but went too far. Then there was Adolf Harnack and the rationalist school of theology in the nineteenth century that declared the Greek influence a later accretion and wanted to return to a "simple Jesus", who was actually recast in the form of nineteenth-century "rationality". That left out a lot of historic Christianity. Finally, there is the modern view that the early inculturation in Greece was just one form—many others are equally valid—of the primordial gospel message. Benedict is firm in rejecting all of these as mistaken intellectually and as disregarding God's providential plan in having Christianity emerge in the form it did:

> And so I come to my conclusion. This attempt, painted with broad strokes, at a critique of modern reason from within has nothing to do with putting the clock back to the time before the Enlightenment and rejecting the insights of the modern age. The positive aspects of modernity are to be acknowledged unreservedly: we are all grateful for the marvelous possibilities that it has opened up for mankind and for the progress in humanity that has been granted to us. The scientific ethos, moreover, is ... the will to be obedient to the truth, and, as such, it embodies an attitude which belongs to the essential decisions of the Christian spirit. The intention here is not one of retrenchment or negative criticism, but of broadening our concept of reason and its application. While we rejoice in the new possibilities open to humanity, we also see the dangers arising from these possibilities and we must ask ourselves how we can overcome them. We will succeed in doing so only if reason and faith come together in a new way, if we overcome the self-imposed limitation of reason to the empirically falsifiable, and if we once more disclose its vast horizons. In this sense theology rightly belongs in the university and within the wide-ranging dialogue of sciences, not merely as a historical discipline and one of the human sciences, but precisely as theology, as inquiry into the rationality of faith. Only thus do we become capable of that genuine dialogue of cultures and religions so urgently needed today.[93]

[93] Lecture of Pope Benedict XVI, University of Regensburg, September 12, 2006.

His very last words in the lecture confirm the kind of pursuit of reason he sees as both a secular and a religious task: "It is to this great *logos*, to this breadth of reason, that we invite our partners in the dialogue of cultures."[94] Combined with his studies in the Christian tradition and, in particular, his later books on the New Testament (which will be examined in the following chapter), Benedict has provided a kind of *summa* of modern Catholic thought and given theology a set of tasks in the realms of both faith and reason that cannot help but be a driving force, not only within the Catholic Church but in the now-global dialogue of religions and cultures.

[94] Ibid. On this point, see Tracey Rowland, *Ratzinger's Faith: The Theology of Pope Benedict XVI* (New York, Oxford University Press, 2008), 84–104.

Chapter 6

The Three Ages of Scripture Studies

A theology which denies the historicity of nearly everything in the Gospels to which Christian life and affections and thought have been fastened for nearly two millennia—which either denies the miraculous altogether or, more strangely, after swallowing the camel of the Resurrection strains at such gnats as the feeding of the multitudes—if offered to the uneducated man can produce only one or other of two effects. It will make him a Roman Catholic or an atheist. What you offer him he will not recognize as Christianity. If he holds to what he calls Christianity he will leave a Church in which it is no longer taught and look for one where it is.

—C. S. Lewis, "Modern Theology and Biblical Criticism"

C. S. Lewis gave the lecture from which the passage above is taken at Westcott House, Cambridge, in 1959, which is to say, just a few years before the Second Vatican Council and the blurring of the clear alternatives he offered between atheism and Catholicism.[1] His characterization of modern Scripture scholarship is also a bit one-sided. But the main questions he raised continue to present a formidable pastoral question for Church leaders. As we saw Joseph Ratzinger asking in the previous chapter, even in the best case, can the uncertain and contradictory reconstructions of scholars be combined with the practice of a faith that, clearly, in the very form of its embodiment in the Bible, is intended not for professors, but ordinary people? In addition, Lewis casts quite strong doubts on the very possibility of scholars' reliably determining origins, authorship, and early audiences—the mainstays of the modern academic approach to Scripture, even among

[1] It has been reprinted several times, among them: in Walter Hooper, ed., *Christian Reflections* (Grand Rapids, Mich.: Eerdmans, 1994), 152–66; and as "Fern Seed and Elephants", in a collection with that name, ed. Walter Hooper (London: Fount, 1998).

Roman Catholics, in the second half of the twentieth century. And he does so not out of mere rejection of the results, but out of personal experience—as a literary scholar and author himself—of the absurdities sometimes concocted by contemporary critics about the genesis and meaning of modern texts.

Modern critics writing about modern writers, of course, have vast advantages over modern scholars working on the Sacred Scriptures. They are not trying to figure out writings over two thousand years old that appeared in cultures quite alien from their own. They share the general atmosphere of our time and culture and, usually, immediate knowledge of many subtle linguistic nuances as native speakers of the author's language. And still, their reconstructions, says Lewis, of how his books or those of his colleagues and friends like J. R. R. Tolkien and Roger Lancelyn Green came to be are way off target, even about the simplest matters of fact and interpretation. (Several scholars, for instance, thought the "ring of power" in Tolkien's *Lord of the Rings* must be a symbol for the atom bomb, which it simply could not be, since Tolkien started to write that story before the bomb's invention.) Anyone who has read modern historical-critical studies of the New Testament will feel at times something similar and more portentous happening in efforts to reconstruct what the long dead scriptural author's intention *must* have been and what the long-past community he *must* have been addressing *must* have been like.

But Lewis does not stop even there. Questions of composition and dating aside, he says, the way many biblical scholars read the texts as we have them raises another problem: "I distrust them as critics",[2] says one of the most gifted of Christian writers and literary critics of our time. And it is not just the pedestrian practitioners (who necessarily make up the bulk of any profession) that come in for sharp comment. He fingers Rudolf Bultmann, by any account one of the most influential Scripture scholars in the twentieth century, as particularly tone deaf about the very figure of Jesus and, therefore, unreliable on a great deal else. Bultmann says no clear picture of Jesus' personality emerges from the Gospels; Lewis replies that one way he knows that some of the Gnostic "Gospels" are forgeries is that

[2] Lewis, "Modern Theology", in *Christian Reflections*, 154.

Jesus—who combines peasant shrewdness with both great severity and great gentleness—"didn't talk like that".

Even one of Bultmann's primary assertions—that the preaching of the Second Coming precedes the later developments about the Passion—gets serious demolition by Lewis in a brief but masterly examination of the "Get behind me" episode (Mt 16:21–23). Bultmann thought the abrupt turn from Jesus' praise of Peter for recognizing him as "the Christ, the Son of the Living God" to his sharp rejection of Peter's thinking like a man in seeking to avoid Christ's crucifixion—"Get behind me, Satan") shows a literary inconsistency reflecting a later interpolation of a Passion story into the more basic *Parousia* stories. Lewis, a sharp-eyed reader, claims to see no such thing, but rather a skillful juxtaposition of two fundamental truths.

Lewis sums up his skepticism about the approaches to the New Testament that claim to be the only valid literary analyses and have dominated academic studies for many decades: "I have learned in other fields of study how transitory the 'assured results of modern scholarship' may be, how soon scholarship ceases to be modern."[3] And he is far from being alone in this agnosticism. Ernst Käsemann, a student of Bultmann's and a formidable Protestant Scripture scholar in his own right, has given a similar picture of alleged scholarly unanimity: "I should certainly *not* say: 'We can venture on [this road] with confidence, nor need we fear that we are embarking on a perilous, fruitless adventure.' Can we for a single moment forget that we are dealing every day with a flood of dubious and even abstruse attacks on the exegetical, historical and theological fields and that our study is gradually degenerating into a worldwide guerilla warfare?"[4] To observe a problem is not necessarily to solve it, of course, but Käsemann rightly suggests that the answers to such questions will not be found along purely scholarly lines. A "Church" is needed for the kind of message (*kerygma*) the Bible is meant to convey, a Church that both listens to the Word and—not solely in the hierarchy, but among all believers—remains faithful and professes that Word.

[3] Ibid., 162.

[4] Ernst Käsemann, *New Testament Questions of Today*, trans. W.J. Montague and Wilfred F. Bunge (Philadelphia: Fortress Press, 1969), 29.

Unlike fundamentalism and some of the forms of modern scholarship that Lewis criticizes, the Catholic Church has never tried to read the Scriptures through a single, simple perspective. In the first Christian centuries, there were already different emphases at ancient Antioch (a more literal approach) and Alexandria (allegorical methods). The Church as a whole has contained complex and mutually enriching modes of biblical interpretation that, in their varying ways, reflect the multiple dimensions of the New Testament itself. A fair person today who looks through the Scripture commentaries of the ancient Church Fathers[5] (Clement of Alexandria believed at least five senses—historical, doctrinal, prophetic, philosophical, and mystical—were always present) or some of the better practitioners of the four senses of Scripture (literal, moral, allegorical, anagogical) developed in the Middle Ages[6] may find much that is eccentric or no longer valid. But he will also be impressed by the constant awareness in these allegedly naïve, "precritical" commentators that the text requires careful attention to its diverse modes and literary registers.

During the course of the twentieth century, both Catholic and Protestant Scripture scholars would come to appreciate and, in some cases, to recuperate and develop parts of that multiform tradition, which had fallen into neglect in the search for simple "proof texts" for Christian teachings, even in the Catholic Church. For almost the first half of the century, of course, Catholic authorities had largely prevented Church scholars from participating in the highly influential historical-critical approaches pioneered primarily in Protestant Germany in the nineteenth and twentieth centuries. And those restrictions held back several generations of Catholics from doing the kind of work necessary to develop a Catholic reading of the Bible in light of modern knowledge. In several cases, the Church wrongly

[5]Johannes Quasten, *Patrology* (Westminster, Md.: Newman Press, 1950–1986), 4 vols.; Frank Sadowski, *The Church Fathers on the Bible: Selected Readings* (New York: Alba House, 1987); Manlio Simonetti, *Biblical Interpretation in the Early Church: An Historical Introduction to Patristic Exegesis*, trans. John A. Hughes (Edinburgh: T. & T. Clark, 1994).

[6]See Henri de Lubac, S.J., *Medieval Exegesis: The Four Senses of Scripture*, trans. Mark Sebanc (Grand Rapids, Mich.: Eerdmans, 1998–2009); original French ed., 1959–1964); also Beryl Smalley, *The Study of the Bible in the Middle Ages*, 2nd ed. (Oxford: Blackwell, 1952).

dismissed scholars who, authorities thought, were taking dangerous paths. Some were; most were not. Catholic authorities worried that the harsher forms of historical-critical studies would lead to modernism, which had certainly happened in mainstream Protestant denominations. Ironically, however, some of the most common academic methods thought to offer "the assured results of modern scholarship" entered into considerable crisis on their own in the latter half of the twentieth century.

Scripture has always occupied a complicated place in Catholic thought, and, in several respects, modern Catholic scriptural scholarship is more difficult to pin down intellectually than are Catholic philosophy and theology. Disputes in those latter fields go on, and rightly, but do not much touch the practicing Catholic. But the basic framework of modern Scripture study typically pits the "historical Jesus" against the "Christ of faith". Joseph Ratzinger has noted that the "theological canon", that is, the reading of the text within the tradition and the Church, "is indeed precisely what modern exegesis set out to overcome".[7] Within this overall dynamic, therefore, quintessential Catholic principles are almost automatically suspect among scholars. That is not the whole story, of course. Since God works through history and entered time in the Incarnation, historical study is a necessity of the Catholic faith. But despite efforts to purify historical-critical methodologies from biased presuppositions, much Catholic biblical study in the academy stands, to put it mildly, in no little tension with the Church—and with ordinary believers who try to read the Bible.

The New Testament presents particular difficulties to scholars who seek to understand it in purely historical terms because it does not treat of merely historical material. Instead, it claims to be an account of a mysterious and unique phenomenon: that in the fullness of time, God actually entered into history and became man. In addition, the early Church decided—actually, the network of local churches that constituted the Christian diaspora almost universally accepted—that, even

[7]Joseph Ratzinger, "Biblical Interpretation in Conflict: On the Foundations and the Itinerary of Exegesis Today", in José Granados, Carlos Granados, and Luis Sánchez-Navarro, eds., *Opening Up the Scriptures: Joseph Ratzinger and the Foundations of Biblical Interpretation* (Grand Rapids, Mich.: Eerdmans, 2008), 6. Ratzinger's essay goes back to a New York conference held in 1988.

though they vary a good deal among themselves, four accounts of Christ's life had authoritative status: the three Synoptic Gospels (Matthew, Mark, Luke) and John. Even the three Synoptics, which receive their name (Greek: syn-optic—that is, to see together) because they seem to contain many similar elements, differ quite a bit from one another in their details, structures, and aims. Various modern theories have been proposed to account for both the similarities and the differences.[8] All of them, to one degree or another, acknowledge that there must have been some common source or sources, written or oral, going back even beyond Mark, which most scholars have accepted as the earliest Gospel (though a sizeable minority of equally well trained professionals dispute even that judgment). Since simple dates and mutual influences are in dispute, with no real hope of ever definitively resolving the questions, historical guesswork about the process that led to the composition of the NT writings, to say nothing of purely academic assessments of their reliability as historical accounts, are by their very nature speculative, provisional, fragmentary, and contested, even by scholars using the same modern "scientific" methods.

As a result of progress in historical knowledge, there have been real gains in understanding the early Church and both the Jewish and Greek contexts in which Christians first lived. But there also have been unwise and certainly overconfident reconstructions of the "historical" Jesus and the role—often assumed to be nefarious—of the early Church in producing the NT texts. One sign that these reconstructions go too far is that they produce conflicting and even contradictory accounts of who Christ "must" have been. The earliest efforts at reconstructing the "historical" Jesus in the modern sense began among the English Deists, Spinoza, the Continental *philosophes*, and odd American figures like Thomas Paine and Thomas Jefferson. (Jefferson famously produced his own "Bible" by cutting what he regarded as superstition or things unworthy of the real Jesus

[8] The early Church herself was not unaware of the apparent discrepancies. Thus, in the second century, heretics like Marcion wanted to keep only an altered version of Luke; Tatian, a more orthodox student of Justin Martyr's, produced the *Diatessaron*, a weaving together of the four Gospels into a single account that reconciled apparent discrepancies as he thought fit; and more than two centuries later, Augustine felt it was still necessary to make a similar effort in his *De Consensu Evangelistarum* (*On the Harmony of the Gospels*). Ancient opponents of Christianity, of course, thought these discrepancies showed the Gospels to be quite unreliable.

and said—with the combination of arrogance and naïveté typical of many of his contemporaries—that it is as easy to tell Jesus' real sayings from the false ones as to tell "diamonds in a dunghill".[9]) They are all very similar in that the Jesus this diverse group discovers behind what they regard as later distortions is really a simple ethical teacher—charismatic and perhaps even charming—but not a divine figure and more interested in a kindly society and liberal politics than in revealing a demanding God. In short, a person like themselves.

Various theories were put forward to explain how the "superstitions" and miracle accounts were added to this allegedly rational and simple figure of Jesus, who survived this treatment but only as a man no better than any other Enlightenment moralist. And that has remained a kind of background music to most subsequent scholarly attempts to parse out the history behind the NT texts. In 1906, for example, the year he was expelled from the Jesuits, the English Catholic convert George Tyrrell, his own "modernist" tendencies notwithstanding, complained of the great modern Protestant scholar Adolf von Harnack (1851–1930) and, by implication, the many others who shared his basic assumptions that the Bible *had* to point toward a view of the world and God typical of certain contemporary currents: "The Christ that Harnack sees, looking back through nineteen centuries of Catholic darkness, is only the reflection of a liberal Protestant face, seen at the bottom of a deep well."[10]

Recasting a first-century Jew as an eighteenth-century *philosophe* or a nineteenth-century liberal Protestant was already a stretch. But the liberal Protestant Jesus would soon give way, partly owing to similar impulses to claim him for contemporary causes, to the existentialist Jesus of Rudolf Bultmann, the countercultural Jesus of the 1960s, the feminist Jesus, the liberationist Jesus, and beyond, with no end to these variations in sight. The Jesus of classic Christian theology, who has endured through many fads and the collapse of whole civilizations, did not go away, either, to be sure. Of course, Christ may be

[9] *Jefferson's Extracts from the Gospels: "The Philosophy of Jesus" and "The Life and Morals of Jesus"* (Princeton: Princeton University Press, 1983), 352.

[10] George Tyrrell, *Christianity at the Cross-Roads* (London: Longmans, Green, 1909), 44. So harsh was Catholic discipline against modernism at the time that Tyrrell was denied a Christian burial and Henri Brémond, a friend, was reprimanded for merely making a sign of the cross at the grave.

said to contain, after a fashion, every human aspiration to the good. Elements of even the modernist versions of Christ may be detected in the ancient record. But the ways that these alleged historical reconstructions contradict and undercut one another—for example, Christ logically cannot be both a nineteenth-century liberal and a twentieth-century Che Guevara—have had the cumulative effect of revealing just how "constructed" such accounts really are. And further calls into question the methodological presuppositions and limitations, in many respects, of the historical-critical approaches on which they draw.

The Catholic Church was largely absent from these modern developments, partly from a settled belief, not wholly unjustified, that they would prove to be beside the main point, but also largely out of fear that all these "modernist" currents would lead to Protestantism and worse, which, in no small number of cases during the twentieth century, they certainly did.

Twentieth-Century Catholic Developments in the Theology of Scripture

In broad outline, during the twentieth century, Catholic Scripture studies passed through three large phases:

1. At the beginning of the century, the Church was very wary of modern scholarly developments, which were mostly a German Protestant preserve, when they were not actually aimed at debunking Christian beliefs or discrediting the Bible as true history. There were no Catholic scholars at the same level of sophistication as well-known nineteenth-century Protestant figures such as Baur, Wellhausen, Strauss, Schleiermacher, Feuerbach—and, in the twentieth century, Schweitzer and Bultmann. Catholic Scripture study remained well within traditional categories of interpretation that were useful in themselves and faithful to Church teaching but did not much engage modern archaeological discoveries, historical dissection of texts, new hermeneutical approaches, and other such developments.

2. Beginning with Leo XIII's *Providentissimus Deus* (1893), and in a series of slow changes culminating in Pius XII's *Divino Afflante Spiritu* (1943) and Vatican II's *Dei Verbum* (1965), the Church hierarchy gradually came to accept that the historical-critical method, as several

different approaches to the reading of Scripture were called, could be used to help illuminate the text and its history without necessarily presenting a problem for Catholic teaching and tradition. Once these methods were permitted, Catholics began to use them with scholarly acumen equal to others in the academy, though no Catholic exegete appeared who might be considered a world-class figure equal to the earlier Protestants.

3. In the closing decades of the twentieth century, Catholic Scripture scholars—who had eagerly embraced modern methodologies when Church authorities belatedly allowed them—began to realize the multiple limits of those very methods. Questions also arose about what relationship the results of scholarship in the academy had to belief and practice in the Church. Everyone agreed that academic scholarship has its role and its own criteria and methods, which need to be followed in order to be faithful to its own way of searching for truth. But the Bible presents an obvious difference from other texts. Scholars may read Homer or Dante or Shakespeare in an effort to reconstruct exactly what they meant and with little concern for what importance they have to contemporary life. The Bible, at least as Catholics (and many other Christians) believe, has a relevance not only for the time it was written or the time when it is now being read, but for all times and places. And even further, for believers the Bible is, in the words of Saint Jerome, "the Word of God in the words of men", a troublesome case of dual authorship. How the academic reading of Scripture was to serve—as it must in the Christian perspective—the ecclesial reading remained (and remains) a problem that many now recognize, but without as yet being able to offer an entirely satisfactory solution.[11]

It is important to recognize, however, that these were not merely intellectual shifts. They reflected a series of *theological* developments—necessarily so because one of the foundational principles of all Catholic scriptural study is that the writing, reading, and formal study of the Bible occur *within* the context of God's

[11] Joseph Ratzinger, later Benedict XVI, an astute scholar even as a young man, who helped develop *Dei Verbum* at Vatican II, has remarked on several occasions that it will take at least another generation to carry out the task. Cf. Ratzinger, "Biblical Interpretation in Conflict", 8—among other such expressions.

self-revelation to the human race. Without faith in that revelation, the Bible remains a closed book. Revelation, in this view, is not identical with the Bible, and the Bible is not, in any case, merely an owner's manual with all the answers. There are, among other dimensions of revelation, the actual events that took place in the history of the people of Israel, the life of Christ, his impact on his apostles and other disciples, and the ongoing understanding of revelation in the life of the people of God in the Church under the guidance of the Holy Spirit. (At times within the tradition, nature itself—which is to say, creation—is spoken of as a second book of revelation.) The written texts of Scripture are a central feature of this whole reality, normative for Christian life, because they witness to and are, in turn, explained by the totality of revealed truth about the relationship between God and men.

Precisely because of this complex significance, the Catholic Church has been careful about how Scripture is approached and used. It was one of the unfortunate results of Reformation disputes that the Church tended to discourage reading of the Bible at the very time that printing made books more widely available, because, it was said, it might result in "private interpretation", unfaithful to the tradition or partial in its emphases. In Catholic institutions, excerpts from the Bible, along with some citations from the tradition, were long used in textbooks as proof texts for specific dogmas. This meant that the Bible itself was largely regarded as already interpreted material, not a source of renewed—and perhaps even simply new—outpourings of the Holy Spirit. Biblical history was studied in outline, and of course the Gospels and other New Testament texts were familiar from Mass readings. But along with the growing theological recognition in the twentieth century that the Church is the people of God in pilgrimage through time, the desire for a more personal encounter with the Scriptures began to dissolve the old wariness. Later, it even began to reshape the evaluation of modern scriptural studies.

Though it falls a few years beyond the scope of the present book, the post-synodal apostolic exhortation *Verbum Domini* (2010) presents an overall perspective, informed by decades of experience, by which to appreciate how the various elements eventually came to coalesce in a Catholic approach to Scripture. As Benedict XVI writes there, borrowing from Hans Urs von Balthasar, such an approach must be "polyphonic", because we can see in Scripture itself multiple meanings of the Word that has been communicated to us (see *VD* 7).

1. The *logos* that was there in the beginning as we read in the first line of John's Gospel.
2. The Word that became flesh and dwelt among us in Jesus Christ.
3. The book of nature (*liber naturae*), as it is known in the tradition, which communicates God's loving wishes in creation.
4. Salvation history, which includes the story of Israel, the voices of the prophets, and Christ's Passion, death, and Resurrection.
5. The Word by which Christ commanded the apostles to go and preach to all nations.
6. The Church's living tradition that stems from that command.
7. And, "finally", the Old and New Testaments.

Benedict adds that, thus, though the Church venerates the Bible, Catholicism is not—as is often said—a "religion of the book" but a religion of the *Word* of God in each and every sense. And Catholics must be helped to understand these multiple and analogical meanings without losing the sense of the unity of God's plan, which encompasses them all.

As even this brief summary suggests, Scripture studies are part of a larger reception of the Word. That reception has intellectual elements but must also be seen, by a Christian, as an encounter between Creator and rational creatures. Indeed, as some modern scholars themselves came to understand, the purely formal studies will get many things wrong if they do not see themselves as fundamentally based on that relationship. Even the most probing historical-critical analyses, which must be carried out on their own terms in a first phase, will fall short of a proper understanding unless they are somehow later integrated into a larger synthesis that takes into account what the writers and editors of the sacred texts believed they were doing: talking about *God*. For *Verbum Domini*, the stakes are high: "In the light of the revelation made by God's Word, the enigma of the human condition is definitively clarified" (*VD* 6).

In light of the importance of modern scriptural scholarship to this task, it will be useful to go over its history briefly here, because the history helps illuminate both later conflicts and successes in Catholic biblical scholarship in the twentieth century.

The Eighteenth-Century Background

The deep background to the historical-critical method—the mainstream academic approach to Scripture outside of the Catholic Church for the past two hundred years—involves a set of assumptions intimately connected to European intellectual history. In its broadest terms, it reflects two intuitions difficult to reconcile: (1) the Enlightenment view of a universal Reason valid in all times and places (limited by certain presuppositions about what counts as "rational"), and (2) a Romantic reaction to that rationalist straitjacket, one which highly valued particular persons and cultures as unique and irreplaceable parts of the richness of the world (*Volksgeist* and *Volk* come to play a prominent role because of this flight from abstract and narrow rationality). Sometimes the two large and competing elements have even been identified with specific cultures: the universalism claimed by the French Revolution and the particularity of the Germans in a first phase, or *Zivilisation* as opposed to *Kultur*, as it was put in Germany. Later, of course, advocates of universal civilization appeared in Germany, just as Romantics (touting *peuple* and *culture*) appeared in France. But however this binary division is characterized, it affected a great deal of the Scripture scholarship that followed.

A true crisis arose when a kind of Enlightenment rationalism was applied to Scripture. In the standard Protestant histories, this begins with Hermann Samuel Reimarus (1694–1768). Albert Schweitzer's highly influential survey of this history, *The Quest of the Historical Jesus*, bore the German title *Von Reimarus zu Wrede* (From Reimarus to Wrede; 1906). Wrede was one of Schweitzer's contemporaries; he concluded that, from the texts we have, Christ is basically unknowable. Reimarus applied some of the modern textual analysis developed to study classical texts during the Renaissance by figures like Petrarch and Erasmus to the study of the Bible, a procedure also championed by Spinoza. Reimarus found the Bible wanting in consistency by such standards. Or rather, that was his public stance. Privately, as fragments published posthumously by Gotthold Lessing showed, he had already decided that Christianity was a pernicious falsehood and needed to be debunked. And he employed a set of assumptions drawn from the English Deists, philosophical naturalism, and secular skepticism in analyzing the Gospels, though in truth he did not really do much that a modern scholar would even recognize as analysis. Instead, he operated with a set of a prioris that seemed undeniably rational to many influential thinkers in the seventeenth and eighteenth centuries.[12] He rejected the possibility of miracles—and even the supernatural—in favor of what later became known as the search for the historical Jesus, who, Reimarus believed (despite his claim that we could not know much about him), was more of a political revolutionary than an otherworldly religious figure.

Many of these assumptions continue in various guises to influence contemporary scriptural scholarship, even among avowed Protestants and Catholics. It was long understood that there were three successive phases in the writing of the Bible and that these gave rise in modern scholarship to formal "diachronic" study: (1) there are the events and words spoken of in the Bible that, in the Old Testament, involve the history of the Jewish people and, in the New Testament, the actual life of Jesus; (2) in their wake, fragmentary oral and written accounts circulate and develop; (3) the texts receive a final shape by the human author or an editor ("redactor", in technical terminology).[13] Reimarus' distinction between the "historical" Jesus and the Jesus as understood by religious traditions remains a kind of baseline. To put this in slightly different terms, which have become starker as modern study has gone on, most modern scholars move uneasily back and forth between a focus, on the one hand, on the reliability or status of passages in the NT from an academic point of view tied to the presuppositions of modern universities and, on the other hand, on their meaning for the life of faith, where such a life exists, which is to say, not in the institutions of higher learning, but in the churches

[12] For a good and readable account of the history of the search, see Charlotte Allen, *The Human Christ: The Search for the Historical Jesus* (New York: Free Press, 1998).

[13] This is the main arc of composition, but even this simplifies somewhat because, as we know from the Dead Sea Scrolls and other archaeological discoveries, the "final" form of the text can remain quite fluid for a long time, and it is only when certain authorities, Jewish or Christian, have established a definitive canon that we know which books are included in the Bible and which forms of those books, though even this is subject to much labor and controversy with respect to differing manuscripts and readings.

and the belief and behavior of ordinary Christians, the vast majority of whom are not and will never be academics.

In one way, the historical-critical approach could be viewed as a kind of über-Protestantism, and there were Protestants of several stripes who saw it in those terms. From that perspective, the writing and canonizing of NT texts were too much influenced by the early "Catholic" Church, an influence that had to be eliminated to get back to the real, "historical" Jesus. This clearly reflects—if in a radical form—the old Lutheran idea of *sola Scriptura*, that only the Bible is reliable, not later traditions. It also recognizes that the Bible is the product of the early Church; those who had radical doubts about the Church could not even rely on the texts we have if they wanted undistorted access to Christ. But that was not the only way the new learning might be used. The first modern figure to apply these methods to the Bible was Richard Simon (1638–1712), a French Catholic priest who accepted miracles, the supernatural, and the authority of the Church, but believed in close readings, in part as a way to *rebut* Protestant overemphasis on *sola Scriptura*. Naturally, in the late seventeenth and early eighteenth centuries, Simon himself fell afoul of ecclesiastical authorities, in his case, the formidable Bishop Bossuet. It is interesting to speculate what might have happened had a Catholic engagement with modern textual criticism developed, with a place for tradition and a view of the Bible as inevitably related to ecclesial life. It might have offered a counterweight to what, given the Protestant commitment to the simple truth of Scripture, could only tend toward a division between a strict fundamentalism, on the one hand, and, on the other, a radically liberalized Christianity, rejecting the historically uncertain Gospels as contaminated by the Church and thereby heading, as C. S. Lewis feared, toward outright unbelief.

One early response to the Deist and Enlightenment application of an allegedly universal rational standard to the Bible was the Romantic reaction that viewed the Bible as inspired poetry. Typical of that reaction is a highly influential figure: Johann Gottfried Herder (1744–1803). Herder recognized that the various texts grouped together in the Bible could be construed as various "*moments*" (a word with complex meanings in German) in the history of the Jewish people, though particular literary geniuses had to be taken into account as well. So far, so good. Everyone can acknowledge that this is part of the truth. But then how is it that the Hebrew Scriptures may be said to have more importance than any other ancient literature or that Christianity can be regarded as a universal religion, a position that Herder wished to defend? Universal Reason, in the Enlightenment sense, seemed to undercut the value of the particular, and the irreducibly particular seemed to make the universal merely a matter of words. Herder's answer to this dilemma was to see in Christian particularity itself a unique aspiration: "the religion of the human race, the spur to love, and the bond of all nations",[14] as he put it at one point (he would make other efforts). Yet carried farther, this way of seeing Christianity seemed to dissolve back into those general principles—God, immortality, morality, and judgment in the afterlife—that Deism had preserved, without particularly needing Christianity to do so. This was a first sign of an insoluble problem given the tools that were available within Enlightenment assumptions about reason.

Among many other difficulties, this whole approach made the biblical text unique and fixed in the past and also asserted that an allegedly rationalist religion, which had never existed anywhere in prior history, was the "real" meaning of the particular religions and the true meaning of Christianity with nothing credible in between—church, theologians, spiritual experts, even simple Christian readers—an odd way to approach a text produced by and for ongoing historic communities, the Jewish people in the case of the Hebrew Scriptures and the Christian church in the case of the Old and New Testaments. Nor, in this perspective, is there the possibility that the texts may bear meanings other than those originally intended by their human authors. Here, as in many places in academic approaches to Scriptures, a kind of radical Lutheranism believes in a return to the origins without any intermediaries as the only possible way of reading or of being faithful. But can such an analysis be undertaken with any certainty, even from a secular perspective? As a modern hermeneutics of reading and semiotics might ask: Can we unequivocally know, can any reader be in a position to receive, the "original" text outside of all later interpretation, social

[14] Quoted in Nicholas Boyle, *Sacred and Secular Scriptures: A Catholic Approach to Literature* (Notre Dame, Ind.: University of Notre Dame Press, 2005), 19. My analysis of the German background to modern Scripture scholarship is indebted to Boyle's with some differences and additions.

context, personal perspective, or philosophical presuppositions?[15] And can such an "original" text even be said unequivocally to exist as some simply fixed object? To answer "yes" to this question will lead to more and more radical and—in truth—speculative interpretations of the history behind the text. To answer "no" to this question seems, by the lights of a certain kind of Enlightenment reason, to surrender to arbitrary and impure "tradition" and interpretation.

The Papacy of Scholarship

Of course, seeing the choice as between an empty historicism and universal principles is not the only way texts and human existence itself may be construed. Friedrich Schleiermacher (1768–1834), another highly influential figure, took stabs at the hermeneutical task that unfortunately did not succeed in overturning the usual historicist-rationalist oppositions, which are really two sides of the same coin. Schleiermacher stuck close to the literal interpretation of texts, a helpful procedure in several senses, not least in that it revealed what was later called the "hermeneutic circle"—we can only understand individual words and phrases and books (*moments*) from their contexts in languages and cultures, and we can only understand languages and cultures from an examination of the words, texts, and other artifacts they have produced. This is not as self-defeatingly circular as it sounds at first, since we all begin, even in our native language and culture, with a partial understanding that, with study and effort, we gradually enlarge, though it is never complete. Another complication of the biblical text, however, if we take it in the way it was written, is that the ultimate goal is not to understand the writing of Isaiah or Luke or Paul. The goal is to understand God, whom the tradition says speaks in special fashion in particular texts: the voice of God in human words.[16] How we can know this or how we react to it, of course, has been a much vexed question since the nineteenth

[15] Cf. Rudolf Bultmann, "Is Exegesis without Presuppositions Possible?", in *Existence and Faith: Shorter Writings of Rudolf Bultmann*, trans. Schubert M. Ogden (New York: Meridian Books, 1960), 289-96.

[16] "For the words of God, expressed in human language, have been made like human discourse, just as the word of the eternal Father, when He took to Himself the flesh of human weakness, was in every way made like men": Second Vatican Council, *Dei Verbum*, 13.

century, especially in academic circles where the assumption that God can speak to us is, to say the least, not widespread.

For all that, Schleiermacher wanted to preserve Christianity from destructive rationalism and historicism, and he proposed a kind of universal religious feeling—a move Rousseau had already made as well with his kindly Deist Vicar of Savoy in *Émile*—as preceding all efforts at hermeneutics. That feeling conveyed to us both the existence of God and our dependence on him. Faith comes to individuals through the church, because they can only hear about God that way, but—in another return of radical Lutheranism—the church can provide nothing reliable in terms of understanding faith. At least by implication, however, this means that the Bible—which had by now been subjected to various historical queries and carved up into pieces assigned to various periods by methods more and less defensible—had lost its old status within Protestantism as well. In Schleiermacher, the church may not be authoritative, but the academic priesthood operating on the text of the Bible takes its place. Indeed, at one point, he claims that hermeneutics is "understanding an utterance firstly as well as, and then better than, its author".[17]

With our greater consciousness of the inevitability of some kind of hermeneutics of reading, we might say today, by contrast, that a text intended to be read offers itself to an "implied reader" capable of grasping its meaning because that reader is already part of a certain tradition and community, with practices and beliefs that make the communication possible. Rational criticism internal to those communities and the attempt to reconcile texts within the tradition leave room for reason, but not as a kind of independent oracle that renders texts, traditions, and communities unnecessary and even rationally indefensible. Indeed, Schleiermacher's (and not only his) single reader sitting alone and analyzing a text, thinking he can understand it better than the author or than a tradition of interpretation, may strike us as a modern naïveté of a sort. For us, "reason" itself comes in several forms and may mean different things in different historical periods.

The large figure of Hegel lies behind this shift because, however inadequately, in the last analysis, he recognized that the root of the problem lay in the historicist-rationalist statement of the problem

[17] Quoted in Boyle, *Sacred and Secular Scriptures*, 43.

at the outset. Hegel famously—and, in a heated academic rivalry with Schleiermacher, passionately—historicized reason in the sense of recognizing that a reader will always bring his own spirit to the encounter with the historical movement of the Absolute Spirit that has revealed itself to us. Our suppositions and questions thus become visible and inescapable, as they had not in much previous historical scholarship, which assumed itself to be absolutely rational and scientific without further need to question. Nineteenth-century writers like David Friedrich Strauss and Ernest Renan produced very popular and influential "lives" of Jesus that differed in many details but agreed in those large assumptions (though they are not taken very seriously by informed readers anymore). For all that might be said against his project, Hegel explicitly states a lesson that has to be learned over and over: biblical commentaries inevitably reflect their own time, even as they seek to understand some historical past, which we can never grasp with scientific completeness or certitude because the subject matter, by its very nature, cannot be so known.

Further, Hegel wanted to overcome the split between the particular and the universal by integrating them in the flow of time. In biblical interpretation, this means that the church becomes a necessary outgrowth of an originating moment that is irretrievably in the past but has its importance because of a continuing spirit. Hegel parts with Reformation disputes about Scripture versus tradition at least insofar as he sees both as inspired by a single spirit. Indeed, he asserts that the church is necessarily different from Jesus, just as the interpretation of Scripture is necessarily different from Scripture. But all this is a necessary recognition of the passage of spirit through time. Hegel seems to have little use for the Old Testament in this scheme, except as something to be superseded, and his view of Jesus as an origin that cannot truly be retrieved virtually separates him from all that follows. Nevertheless, though even Hegelian approaches to the Scriptures have their shortcomings, Hegel was at least right in seeing that the historicist-rationalist split was the product of certain assumptions and had to be overcome before the Bible could become religiously fruitful again rather than mere poetry or inanimate matter for academic analysis.

That split was not overcome during the nineteenth and twentieth centuries, and it is no surprise that the Catholic Church was very skeptical of this Enlightenment or hyper-Reformation approach to Scripture. Indeed, until fairly late in the twentieth century, the Church severely restricted use of this academicized way of reading the Bible. In retrospect, though the caution stunted Catholic biblical studies for decades, it bore within it a deep insight. By the end of the twentieth century, even many Protestant scholars would come to recognize that it makes no sense—even in the interpretation and historical analysis of the Bible—to separate it so radically from the ongoing community that wrote it and continued to read and value it. Secular hermeneutics of various kinds further exploded the assumption that "objective" scholars standing outside the tradition were always better judges of Scripture texts and what they meant than those inside. By the twentieth century, some Protestant exegetes would even speak of their wish "to preserve the Christian laity from the *papacy of scholarship*".[18] The Church had resisted modern scholarship out of a kind of sane and severe prejudice, though she would have to pass through a period of absorbing, digesting, and going beyond the dominant historical-critical conventions to arrive at an intellectually respectable but religiously fertile way of reading the sacred texts—a process still very much unfinished even in the twenty-first century.

First Steps toward New Things

Given the history we have just summarized, it was inevitable that some of the first Catholics to venture out seriously into critical approaches to the Bible would run afoul of Church authorities. The most prominent among the modernists went so far, once they had crossed the approved boundaries, that they simply veered off into views that it would be difficult to reconcile with any real form of Catholicism. For example, Alfred Loisy (1857–1940), one of those prominent modernists,[19] rejected all the tenets of the Nicene Creed except that Christ was crucified. He had studied at the Institut Catholique in

[18] The phrase is Carl Braaten's, from his introduction to Martin Kähler's *The So-Called Historical Jesus and the Historic Biblical Christ*, trans. Carl E. Braaten (Philadelphia: Fortress Press, 1964), 26.

[19] Cf. John Ratté, *Three Modernists: Alfred Loisy, George Tyrrell, William L. Sullivan* (New York: Sheed & Ward, 1967).

Paris, where he was understandably appalled at some of the strained intellectual contortions in which his professors engaged in order to preserve what was then thought of as the literal sense of the Bible. He later taught at the Institut, but he was removed in 1893 and excommunicated in 1908.

His witty and infamous remark that Jesus announced the Kingdom but what came was the Church ("Jésus annonçait le Royaume et c'est l'Église qui est venue") sounds quite radical and was intended as a criticism of the more stiffly bureaucratic side of the institution. And in many obvious respects, Loisy took a wrecking ball to Catholic beliefs. Yet he claimed with some justice that his work had affinities with Cardinal Newman's. He believed that the development of the Church as an institution carrying on the work of Christ was necessary and that the indications that the Church had already "gone beyond" Jesus in the way the New Testament was put together only showed that even the earliest Catholic communities had an internal life that resulted in growth, as God had intended. In a sense, that could be read as saying that the modern Catholic Church had the authority to continue the mission, quite independently of the Bible. But the pope and the bishops refused the grounds on which Loisy's offer was made. They viewed his approach as, ironically, giving the Church authority by evacuating the text of Scripture of all permanent meaning and essentially leaving it behind as an outmoded stage in the institution's evolution.[20]

Loisy's book *The Gospel and the Church* (*L'Évangile et l'Église*, 1902) is usually considered his most controversial. It puts forward an odd thesis, however. Against liberal Protestants like Adolf von Harnack, who in his highly influential *What is Christianity?* (*Das Wesen*

[20] The full context of Loisy's comment on the coming of the Church is enlightening: "Jesus foretold the kingdom, and it was the Church that came; she came, enlarging the form of the gospel, which it was impossible to preserve as it was, as soon as the Passion closed the ministry of Jesus. There is no institution on the earth or in history whose status and value may not be questioned if the principle is established that nothing may exist except in its original form. Such a principle is contrary to the law of life, which is movement and a continual effort of adaptation to conditions always new and perpetually changing": Alfred Loisy, *The Gospel and the Church*, trans. Christopher Home (New York: Scribner, 1909), 166. Newman said, of course, that change is one of the proofs of life, but his idea of "development" meant change within organic continuity. Loisy's church is almost invented from whole cloth since the Passion "closed" Christ's ministry.

des Christentums, 1901) isolates a kind of Ur-Christianity associated with Jesus from which all ecclesial development is merely a falling off, Loisy sees all history as necessarily change and any attempt to identify an immutable essence of Christianity as an impossibility. Loisy admitted that the text of the New Testament was "static", but he could accept neither the Catholic claim for direct continuity with the truths expressed there nor the liberal Protestant watering down of Christian claims to the point that all that was left was Harnack's rather weak belief in the way Jesus reveals the individual soul's immediate relationship with God. Modernism, in Loisy's hands, amounted to a far-reaching historicizing of both text and Church.[21]

In England, George Tyrrell, who had been born in Ireland and became a convert to Catholicism and a Jesuit until his expulsion from the order, also raised fears of modernism, though on different grounds. Tyrrell's problems stemmed, it seems, primarily from his difficulties with Catholic authority, which he found narrow and, as he put it, individualistic in the concentration of infallible authority in the hands of one man: the pope. Church authorities regarded this, rightly or wrongly, as heading down the path whose terminus would be, yet again, the kind of private judgment they associated with Protestantism. In the heated atmosphere in which he found himself, Tyrrell seemed to go farther and farther beyond the boundaries of Catholicism, and even sympathetic commentators point to the ways in which his last books, *Through Scylla and Charybdis*[22] and *Christianity at the Cross-Roads*,[23] take an exaggerated view of religion as a mere assemblage of symbolic truths, breaking the connection not only to the events recorded in Scripture but to the whole Christian tradition.[24]

Loisy and Tyrrell figure large in the histories of the modernist crisis[25] that led to sharp Vatican reaction. But many other Catholic exegetes who were neither dissenters nor revolutionaries, fell victim

[21] Robert Bruce Robinson, *Roman Catholic Exegesis since Divino Afflante Spiritu: Hermeneutical Implications* (Atlanta: Scholars Press, 1988), 12–17.

[22] London: Longmans, Green, 1907.

[23] London: Longmans, Green, 1909.

[24] Fergus Kerr, *Twentieth-Century Catholic Theologians* (Oxford: Blackwell, 2007), 7.

[25] See Marvin O'Connell, *Critics on Trial: An Introduction to the Catholic Modernist Crisis* (Washington, D.C.: Catholic University of America Press, 1994).

to Roman repression in the twentieth century; Rome seemed to fear that any departure from traditional interpretation and understanding would inevitably lead to the most radical results.

Marie-Joseph Lagrange, O.P.

The first substantial and lasting effort among Catholics to come to grips with modern biblical scholarship was undertaken by Marie-Joseph Lagrange, O.P.[26] (1855–1938), an energetic scholar and leader who earned a doctorate in law before deciding to become a Dominican priest. In 1890, at the Dominican Monastery of Saint Stephen in Jerusalem, he founded a school, the École pratique d'études bibliques, for biblical study which in 1920 became the École biblique et archéologique française de Jérusalem and has remained a mainstay of Catholic scriptural studies ever since. (When the Dead Sea Scrolls were discovered at Qumran in 1947, for example, Roland de Vaux, a Catholic priest and scholar at the École was appointed to lead the team of researchers studying them.) In 1892, Lagrange started, with Pierre Battifol, what would become the *Revue biblique*, the most important Catholic publication in the field at the time. Lagrange himself came, at times, under suspicion, especially when in 1902 he began to lecture on the "historical method". He remained under something of a cloud until the 1930s and was even forbidden at one point to publish his commentary on Genesis. Yet he was the transitional figure whose work helped bring about conditions that made something of a breakthrough possible in 1943 with the encyclical *Divino Afflante Spiritu*.

Lagrange introduced several changes of perspective that lessened the tension between what seemed to be the unbridgeable gap between modern historical approaches to the Bible and ideas of inerrancy going back to at least the Council of Trent by way of more recent Church documents.[27] Lagrange calmed the fears of authorities both by allowing for the role of the Church in interpretation and by claiming that there was little in modern scholarship

[26] Bernard Montagnes, *The Story of Father Marie-Joseph Lagrange: Founder of Modern Catholic Bible Study*, trans. Benedict Viviano (New York: Paulist Press, 2006). French original (Paris: Editions du Cerf, 1995).

[27] The discussion here is indebted to Robinson, *Roman Catholic Exegesis*, 19–27.

that necessarily came into conflict with Church dogma. Leo XIII's *Providentissimus Deus* (1893) had asserted that inerrancy extended to historical particulars, but as those might, at least arguably, have appeared to authors or people at the time. Lagrange focused on this second point and drew from it a solid and useful principle: authorial intention, what the writers of Scripture were inspired to teach us, was inerrant. But did the writers intend to teach us about a variety of historical matters that historical criticism and archaeological discoveries put in doubt? About these, a distinction might be drawn: "It is very simple. A proposition is true or false, but here there is no proposition."[28]

Lagrange developed three large notions from this basic insight:

1. Scientific and historical matters often might lie outside authorial intention in the sense specified here.
2. The Bible teaches things "necessary for our salvation" without error, but other incidental matters may form no part of that aim.
3. The genre or form of specific sections of the Scriptures was essential to understanding what the author intended and, therefore, their meanings.

Pius XII would specifically recommend this latter kind of "form criticism" and would also emphasize authorial intention in *Divino Afflante Spiritu* (1943), largely it seems because this gave exegetes room to maneuver in handling troublesome passages that seemed historically inaccurate or places in the Scriptures that appeared inconsistent with each other.

That was the opening that permitted other approaches to be used as well, though figures deemed too adventurous could still be censored by Rome. At the same time, the refinements Lagrange helped put in place were not panaceas. Serious questions remained that were not easy to resolve. If a human author could be mistaken about nonessential historical matters or details, how was the old Catholic principle of Scripture as having "God as its author" to be understood in tandem with the human limitations? Similarly, if individual texts

[28] M.-J. Lagrange, *La méthode historique* (Paris: Librairie Victor Lecoffre, 1904), 105.

were given a certain form or edited ("redacted" in the technical terminology) in order to communicate a certain theological perspective or reach a certain community, how much did that affect the strict reliability and historicity of the versions of the texts we now have? In secular hermeneutics, for example, identifying "authorial intention" is a much vexed question. The influential secular literary movement known as the New Criticism basically dismissed it as the "intentional fallacy". It is also clear that attempting to reconstruct ancient communities—even from the best textual analysis and archaeological evidence—is a very difficult process and fraught with many uncertainties, as we have seen earlier from C. S. Lewis' barbed challenges. Catholic exegetes would soon be exploring these issues vigorously but, like their Protestant predecessors, would not arrive at entirely satisfactory or universally accepted solutions either to the scientific questions or to questions about how these results might serve communities of faith.[29]

Several of these questions had been in play in Catholic circles since the nineteenth century. The First Vatican Council (1869–1870) is most remembered for its declaration that the pope is infallible in matters of faith and morals. In scriptural matters, Vatican I remained rather conservative, of course, hewing close to the position of the Council of Trent, three centuries earlier. A key passage in the Council's Constitution *Dei Filius* from chapter 2, "On Revelation", put the matter rather starkly:

> These books of the Old and New Testaments are to be received as sacred and canonical in their integrity, with all their parts, as they are enumerated in the decree of the said council [Trent] and are contained in the ancient Latin edition of the Vulgate. These the Church holds to be sacred and canonical, not because, having been carefully

[29] In his bibliography to the second volume of *Jesus of Nazareth* (San Francisco: Ignatius Press, 2011), 296, Benedict XVI praised the American Catholic scholar John P. Meier's careful four-volume historical study *A Marginal Jew: Rethinking the Historical Jesus* (New York: Doubleday, 1991–2009): "in many respects a model of historical-critical exegesis, in which the significance *and the limits* [emphasis added] of the method emerge clearly". Meier's work essentially tries to establish things about Jesus that Catholics, Protestants, Jews, and even nonbelievers can accept as supported by the best recent historical scholarship. Clearly, such an approach, useful as it is, leaves out, by its own methodological choices, much of what makes Jesus important to later ages.

> composed by mere human industry, they were afterward approved by her authority, . . . but because, *having been written by the inspiration of the Holy Spirit, they have God for their author and have been delivered as such to the Church herself.* [Emphasis added.][30]

Of course, even trying to restrict readings of the text to the ancient Latin when many discoveries were starting to be made in archaeology and advances were occurring in decoding the previously indecipherable languages of the ancient Middle East and Mediterranean was perhaps a prudent move in an age of scholarly riot. But it was clear that the Church would have to meet the challenge of this new knowledge sooner or later.

Leo XIII's 1893 encyclical *Providentissimus Deus*, for example, in line with his other efforts at Catholic intellectual renewal, encouraged a more vigorous engagement with the sacred texts by scholars and professors at Catholic institutions, including the study of Near Eastern languages, which was revolutionizing understanding about the place of the Jewish Scriptures in their time. The Pontifical Biblical Commission, which came into existence in 1902, was one of the instruments Leo created as a way to promote an authentically Catholic understanding of Scripture and to defend it from critics. Still, he saw how new literary methodologies could be useful and even how private studies of contested questions might lead to useful discoveries, so long as it was always kept in mind that the results of scholarship could not contradict the dogmatic teachings of the Church.

Leo even acknowledged the role of "the human author" in the genesis of the texts, a factor that would be given added weight as the twentieth century progressed, but he argued that divine inspiration protected against error of any kind in Scripture:

> Hence, because the Holy Ghost employed men as His instruments, we cannot therefore say that it was these inspired instruments who perchance have fallen into error, and not the primary author. For, by supernatural power, He so moved and impelled them to write—He was so present to them—that the things which He ordered, and those

[30] Heinrich Denzinger, *Compendium of Creeds, Definitions, and Declarations on Matters of Faith and Morals*, ed. Peter Hünermann, English trans. ed. Robert Fastiggi and Anne Englund Nash, 43rd ed. (San Francisco: Ignatius Press, 2012), no. 3006, p. 602.

> only, they, first, rightly understood, then willed faithfully to write down, and finally expressed in apt words and with infallible truth. Otherwise, it could not be said that He was the Author of the entire Scripture. Such has always been the persuasion of the Fathers. (*PD* 20)

This way of putting things, however, essentially reduces the human author to the role of a mere scribe, not a true author. And the historical claim about "the Fathers" is itself not entirely accurate, since they noted discrepancies and took a more nuanced view of scriptural truth, allowing for some variations in details or even contradictions, as will appear below.

Still, in Leo and even in his strict successors, Pius X and Benedict XV, there also existed real encouragement of modern critical methods—so long as their conclusions accorded with Church teaching. In his 1920 encyclical *Spiritus Paraclitus*, Benedict "warmly commend[ed]" (*SP* 18) those methods, but rejected the notion that any distinction can be made between primary and secondary elements in Scripture or between absolute and relative truths (the latter, mostly questions of historical detail). Indeed, he even warned about the distinction, which gained strength after the Second Vatican Council, between a Greek or positivist conception of history and a Hebrew or biblical one and cautioned that biblical authors were not intending to affirm profane or historical facts. All of this was a restatement and condensation of similar points made in Pius X's earlier *Pascendi Dominici Gregis* (1907), aimed at refuting the Catholic modernists, as we saw in chapter 3.

But Pius X had muddied the waters in his encyclical *Lamentabili Sane Exitu*, which listed sixty-five negative propositions that, somewhat confusingly, Catholics are *not* supposed to hold. The problem with this list, as we saw earlier, is more than the double negative. Anyone who reads it will find that, depending on what is meant, he may agree or disagree. For instance, Pius X condemned the view that: "2. The Church's interpretation of the Sacred Books is by no means to be rejected; nevertheless, it is subject to the more accurate judgment and correction of the exegetes." Everything depends, here, on what we take to be covered by "interpretation". If it is a matter of indisputable dogmatic truths such as Creation, Trinity, Incarnation, Resurrection, and so forth, it is most certainly true. But does the same standard apply in quite the same way to, say, the passages (Mk 10:25,

Mt 19:24) where Christ speaks about "a camel" passing through the eye of a needle (or, if the text has been corrupted or misunderstood at this point), a modern exegete might say "a rope"?

And this is true of more consequential distinctions as well. Pius X also says Catholics should reject the following view: "5. Since the deposit of Faith contains only revealed truths, the Church has no right to pass judgment on the assertions of the human sciences." True, if those "sciences" try to say, beyond their own competencies, that the Creation never occurred, that nothing exists but matter and energy, or that miracles are impossible. But it would be quite false—to the Catholic tradition as much as to anything else—to say that human reason does not have a proper use of its own in determining truths in no way contradictory to the faith. That was, in part, what was in dispute when the Church condemned Galileo for the theory of heliocentrism. An Augustine or a Thomas Aquinas would have robustly defended the counter-proposition—and a properly conceived role for reason.

There are many more such claims, but they are all basically governed by the goal of retaining the right of Church authorities to judge of truth and to defend the faithful, in a strong sense, from every implication of the proposition that, "11. Divine inspiration does not extend to all of Sacred Scriptures so that it renders its parts, each and every one, free from every error." Pope Benedict XV, too, would seek to banish every hint of error from the sacred texts; he takes a very strong view of inspiration in *Spiritus Paraclitus* thirteen years later, even as he considers the role of human authors. He feels the need to defend Leo's position from those he thinks are distorting it:

> So far is it from being the case that error can be compatible with inspiration, that, on the contrary, it not only of its very nature precludes the presence of error, but as necessarily excludes it and forbids it as God, the Supreme Truth, necessarily cannot be the Author of error.
>
> 17. Then, after giving the definitions of the Councils of Florence and Trent, confirmed by the Council of the Vatican, Pope Leo continues: "Consequently it is not to the point to suggest that the Holy Spirit used men as His instruments for writing, and that therefore, while no error is referable to the primary Author, it may well be due to the inspired authors themselves. For by supernatural power the Holy Spirit so stirred them and moved them to write, so assisted them

as they wrote, that their minds could rightly conceive only those and all those things which He himself bade them conceive; only such things could they faithfully commit to writing and aptly express with unerring truth; else God would not be the Author of the entirety of Sacred Scripture." (SP 16–17)

In most accounts of the history of the Church's view on Scripture, a significant turning point arrived with the 1943 encyclical *Divino Afflante Spiritu* (*DAS*) of Pius XII. This involved more than the question of strict inerrancy, but that question is a prelude to others. By the time *DAS* appeared, there had clearly been a growth in the recognition of the human factor in the Scriptures, and Pius XII, along with his advisers, accepted a kind of form criticism or redaction criticism in the sense that they recognized the importance of the intention of the human author, who clearly constructed individual passages (pericopes) in order to convey something to a particular audience, both by the literary form adopted and by the way literary devices were deployed to create a certain effect. The literal sense as the sense intended by the author became a central hermeneutical emphasis. And the opening to literary forms also opened up the question of which texts in the Bible were intended to be historical and which might bear a different mark.

Divino Afflante Spiritu also refined and developed ideas offered fifty years earlier in *Providentissimus Deus*. (It was published to commemorate the anniversary.) Since the Council of Trent, the Latin Vulgate had been declared the standard text to be used. Pius XII now allowed original Hebrew and Greek texts to be studied and analyzed, while retaining the respect for the Vulgate as a marker of authoritative tradition. What is more, now that the original languages were better known and more widely studied, the Church could also make use of archaeology, history, and other disciplines. Most striking of all, however, is Pius' reminder, contrary to Benedict XV's certainties, that many points in Scripture are obscure and have eluded interpreters for centuries.

Furthermore, the Church has actually not pronounced on the meaning of many Scripture passages, and the consensus of the Fathers is of a more limited relevance than some previous claims suggested. So modern scholars should be granted some understanding:

> Let all the other sons of the Church bear in mind that the efforts of these resolute laborers in the vineyard of the Lord should be judged not only with equity and justice, but also with the greatest charity; all moreover should abhor that intemperate zeal which imagines that whatever is new should for that very reason be opposed or suspected. Let them bear in mind above all that in the rules and laws promulgated by the Church there is question of doctrine regarding faith and morals; and that in the immense matter contained in the Sacred Books—legislative, historical, sapiential and prophetical—there are but few texts whose sense has been defined by the authority of the Church, nor are those more numerous about which the teaching of the Holy Fathers is unanimous. There remain therefore many things, and of the greatest importance, in the discussion and exposition of which the skill and genius of Catholic commentators may and ought to be freely exercised, so that each may contribute his part to the advantage of all, to the continued progress of the sacred doctrine and to the defense and honor of the Church. (*DAS* 47)

It is hard to miss the generous spirit and tone here that was rightly interpreted as inviting a less confrontational engagement with the best elements in modern scholarship.

But in the same year that *DAS* was published, two professors of Scripture were censured and dismissed from Roman universities. And there must have been some nervousness after publication because when *Humani Generis* appeared in 1950, Pius was warning again about the kinds of scholars who professed the usual "wrong" ways of interpreting the Scriptures, particularly the restriction of their strict truth only to matters of faith and morals.[31] Instead of the earlier emphasis on what might be good in what was new and an appreciation of the labors of modern scholars, the pope seemed to fix his aim once again on a whole class of exegetes and presented his view as indistinguishable from those of a half century earlier:

> 23. Further, according to their fictitious opinions, the literal sense of Holy Scripture and its explanation, carefully worked out under the

[31] Some scholars dispute the "Golden Legend", as they call it, about Roman liberalization, arguing instead that there was no change in the teaching prior to Vatican II. Cf. Brian W. Harrison, O.S., "On Rewriting the Bible: Catholic Biblical Studies in the '60s", *Christian Order*, March 2002, accessed online at www.christianorder.com/features/features_2002/features_mar02.html.

Church's vigilance by so many great exegetes, should yield now to a new exegesis, which they are pleased to call symbolic or spiritual. By means of this new exegesis of the Old Testament, which today in the Church is a sealed book, would finally be thrown open to all the faithful. By this method, they say, all difficulties vanish, difficulties which hinder only those who adhere to the literal meaning of the Scriptures.

24. Everyone sees how foreign all this is to the principles and norms of interpretation rightly fixed by our predecessors of happy memory, Leo XIII in his Encyclical *Providentissimus Deus*, and Benedict XV in the Encyclical *Spiritus Paraclitus*, as also by Ourselves in the Encyclical *Divino Afflante Spiritu*. (*HG*)

The official view of Catholic Scripture studies in the decades before the Second Vatican Council, then, seemed to hover between a militant and defensive assertion of the total truth of Scripture, on the one hand, and a faithful, but more nuanced view of the substantial truth of Scripture, perhaps not including every historical particular, on the other. "Modernist" readings—which is to say, substantial departures from the settled truths of the Church—were not widespread or very influential, even among those figures under "suspicion". In the aftermath of the Council, however, things were quite different. Every position put forward by the most radical of the modernists appeared in—and sometimes held sway over—Catholic universities and even seminaries, though it is not clear that such developments should be attributed to the Council rather than to interpretations by particular scholars.

The Second Vatican Council

Vatican II did two things that might, at first view, seem mutually contradictory. On the one hand, it encouraged ordinary Catholics to read the Bible in a personal way, in line with the Council's general thrust toward a more relational religion of the heart and less a Church of rules. On the other hand, it authorized—or at least many thought it authorized—the application of sophisticated and exacting scholarly methods, developed for the most part by Protestant Germans over the previous two centuries, to the interpretation of the Bible. It is not difficult to see that what was given to the laity with one hand seemed to be taken away with the other hand—and restricted to "experts". But *Dei Verbum*, the Council's Dogmatic Constitution on Divine Revelation, ventured into an effort to combine the two. And it added the role of the tradition in guiding, integrating, and—at least at its best—stabilizing biblical hermeneutics so that the reading of the Bible by Catholics did not turn into a cacophony of conflicting personal spiritualities or rival academic schools.

The three elements here—individual believer, scholar, Church—are all necessary and valuable in the overall Catholic approach to Scripture. Ultimately, of course, the whole purpose of the Bible, as of all Christian revelation, is the salvation of souls in the widest sense, which is to say, individually and communally. Everything that serves that end can find a place within Catholic biblical reading, including the various intellectual developments that help enrich understanding of the various dimensions and inexhaustible depth of the sacred writings. The earlier problem, in both the ecclesial *and* the academic spheres, was that ideas of what could legitimately be said about Scripture were unnecessarily limited by certain presuppositions.

On the academic side, there is no denying that a strict approach to what the texts are and say may be quite valuable. To begin with, until fairly recent times, we did not even have really reliable or standard texts of the Bible. Even more surprising: both Old Testament and New Testament authors at times quote from versions of biblical books that do not seem to be the best attested. The startling discovery in the 1940s and 1950s of 972 texts called the Dead Sea Scrolls showed that, despite large-scale agreement in Scripture texts over centuries, there may not even have been what a modern reader might think of as standard OT texts until Jewish authorities, expelled from Israel, started to define their canon around A.D. 100. But why should we expect anything else in the centuries prior to the invention of printing, which made books more widely available and, by spreading literacy, made the desire for authoritative texts, not just the preserve of a few specialists, but a popular one? The result, of course, is not perfect even from a positivist scientific point of view, because we can eliminate many copyists' errors, omissions, supplements, and other such corruptions by comparing manuscripts. But which manuscripts are more authoritative and which readings are to be preferred—not just the most common or oldest in the records we have—are questions that lie partly outside pure textual criticism.

Something similar might be said about the whole group of historical-critical methodologies that, rather presumptuously, called itself the Higher Criticism in the nineteenth century. Careful reflection on the text of the New Testament, for example, led scholars to understand that a whole, and largely invisible, process took place to produce the texts we now regard as part of the Bible. Jesus, of course, lived and taught—all arguments to the contrary, his life is better attested to in surviving literature than are the lives of almost all the Roman emperors or other prominent ancient figures. This means that a process—a literary process—occurred by which the consolidation of reminiscences about him took place in two later phases. First, oral and written stories and lists of sayings (a putative Q document [Q for the German *Quelle* = source]) circulated in the early Christian community. Then, at differing times, these were incorporated and shaped into the NT texts that we now have, which were accepted as canonical by the Church. In fact, there were several such processes that gave us Paul's and other NT letters, the four evangelists (who display both similarities and differences), and other texts like Acts and Revelation. This complex historical evolution is beyond question, even for anyone who takes a very strict view of the "inspiration" of the sacred texts.

But the texts were composed in diverse ways for different uses of various communities already one in the faith, not strictly to convey information like a physics textbook. They were meant to remind and repeatedly *convert*, something no mere compilation of information ever does. During the Reformation, the Council of Trent affirmed both Scripture and tradition against the Protestant contention of *sola Scriptura*. That affirmation was sometimes understood in ways that were too narrow in the intervening years, which was doubly unfortunate, because the Church lost some of the "polyphonic" approaches inherited from the ancients and medievals. And she also, therefore, missed the chance to explain, early on, that modern historical-critical methods might equally be used to show that Scripture itself is also part of the tradition, an authoritative and central tradition to be sure, but a tradition of responding to Christ under the inspiration of the Holy Spirit.

It is a telling fact that after the Second Vatican Council allowed Catholic scholars to use these methods, they did so with very mixed results. Radical interpreters struck out on wild lines. More moderate exegetes were often able to find a way to reconcile historical studies with Church teachings, but they were less noticed as a result. Soon secular scholarship itself began to notice the limited range of questions addressed by the historical-critical method, and new approaches like reader-response criticism and narrative criticism[32] began to point toward the inescapable importance of the reader's *participation in* the whole of the writer-reader complex. This movement started to become so strong that a distinguished Catholic scholar, Raymond Brown, in his 1981 address as president of the Catholic Biblical Association of America, urged members to stick with the old historical-critical methods. But the tide was not to be stopped.[33] Yet neither was everything settled. As Cardinal Ratzinger observed, if hermeneutics is not simply going to be my personal creation, it has to be rooted in the reality of the text and the events to which the texts witness.

The Catholic view of Scripture differs from fundamentalist Protestant readings in several significant respects.[34] That Protestant reading has certain affinities with the Muslim view that God wrote the Qur'an by simply moving Mohammed to set down the words on paper (or, rather, to dictate them, since Mohammed was

[32] A clear account of these developments can be found in Terence J. Keegan, O.P., *Interpreting the Bible: A Popular Introduction to Biblical Hermeneutics* (New York: Paulist Press, 1985).

[33] Indeed, Raymond Brown's own approach underwent some changes. In the mid-1950s, he wrote his doctoral dissertation on the *sensus plenior*, an expression referring to the "fuller sense" of Scripture intended by God but not necessarily by the biblical authors. Though he was always a priest and scholar in service to the Church, some of his earlier books produced strong controversy. *The Birth of the Messiah: A Commentary on the Infancy Narratives in the Gospels of Matthew and Luke* (Garden City, N.Y.: Doubleday, 1977), for example, seemed to some Catholics trained in the old fashion to call into question whether the Virgin Birth could be proved historically. Some scholars might answer that it might not be provable historically and still be true. Fr. Brown stated several times that he thought the preponderance of evidence pointed to, but could not prove, the Virgin Birth. But such disavowals were widely viewed as undermining a key tenet of the Catholic faith going back to the ancient creeds ("born of the Virgin Mary"). A later work, however, Brown's *The Death of the Messiah: From Gethsemane to the Grave, A Commentary on the Passion Narratives in the Four Gospels* (New York: Doubleday, 1994), was almost universally regarded as a model of historical-critical rigor combined with settled Church teaching on Christ's Passion, death, and Resurrection.

[34] The fundamentalist movement was a reaction in the early twentieth century, primarily in America and Britain, against liberal Christianity. The leaders of various conservative denominations agreed to accept a brief list of "fundamentals" as essential to a common Christianity. See George M. Marsden, *Fundamentalism and American Culture* (New York: Oxford University Press, 1980), for an overview.

illiterate—*Qur'an* means "the recitation" in Arabic). For Catholics, the human author has a more important role than that—indeed, the authors are "true authors", but divinely inspired. At the same time, the text of Scripture itself seems to contain inconsistencies and outright historical errors. In the book of Tobit, for example, the king Sennacherib is described as the son of Shalmaneser (1:15) though his father was Sargon II, who was unrelated to Shalmaneser. The human author seems simply to have been misinformed about the royal line. And ancient as well as modern Scripture scholars have noted various similar difficulties in the biblical text, not least in placing the date of even such well-attested events as the Last Supper.[35] So does the Holy Spirit fail at times in his inspiration, or does the fact of such errors invalidate the whole idea of inspiration, or is there some way to put together divine inspiration and human limitation that still preserves the truth of Scripture?

At Vatican II, the Dogmatic Constitution on Divine Revelation, *Dei Verbum*, famously puts the matter in a carefully nuanced formula: "Since everything asserted by the inspired authors or sacred writers must be held to be asserted by the Holy Spirit, it follows that the books of Scripture must be acknowledged as teaching solidly, faithfully and without error that truth which God wanted put into sacred writings *for the sake of salvation*" (*DV* 11, emphasis added). The traditional case for the "inerrancy" of Scripture even in historical matters (*in qualibet re religiosa vel profana*), a position defended by some Council Fathers, does not seem sustainable in light of many historical and factual difficulties, which were recognized even in the early Christian centuries. But is it the case that sacred authors—let alone the Holy Spirit—always "assert" such details?

Would the author of Tobit, for example, be surprised to learn that he had mistaken the royal line in Persia (he was probably writing in the second century B.C. about events five hundred years earlier)? Or should later readers regard him as thereby discredited? The book of Tobit seems to be "asserting" a message of righteousness, mercy, and faithfulness through a story told by a real human being inspired to write, but—as all human beings are—limited in his historical

[35] Pope Benedict XVI faces this particular difficulty squarely in the second volume of his *Jesus of Nazareth* and, after reviewing the scholarly literature, is content to leave it unresolved.

knowledge. In addition, given what seems to be the fictional genre of the book, it is not clear that such a text is even affirming that the principal characters actually existed as historical figures. The text is one of many kinds of scriptural books more concerned with moral and theological matters than strict history.

Of course, other texts—the Gospels prominently among them—make larger and more properly "historical" affirmations. To recognize this is simply to see the different kinds of books that, together, make up the overall narrative of the Bible. The Church in the twentieth century began to move away from a narrow and defensive position on "inerrancy" to a stance that not only gave a better *theological* account of the Bible and its composition, but, perhaps surprisingly to some, was actually well attested in the Catholic tradition as well. For secular historians of a positivist bent, of course, the "truth" of any piece of writing is its alleged correspondence with a past reality. But the Bible is not a book—not only a book, at least—chronicling the past. It tells a story, based on past events, that lives on in the present and looks into the future—indeed, into eternity—a story that encompasses all men and all of creation. By its very nature, such a subject can be approached only partly with positivist historical tools. Those tools may be helpful for a variety of purposes, but a positivist approach that rules out a priori "unverifiable" issues like the ability of a Creator to speak in and to his creation and creatures has little to do with the overall intention and purpose of the Bible.

A believer, therefore, comes to the Bible with a different perspective from that of a pure historian or textual critic—a theological and faith perspective that can make use of scientific disciplines but cannot be reduced to or defined by them. Neither can theology, however, *dictate* to those disciplines, which must proceed by their own standards and principles. We may know by reliable human means that Sennacherib was not the son of Shalmaneser, whatever the text of the Bible may say. But we can also say that every page of the Sacred Scriptures is directed toward an overarching vision of God and creation that must be studied and interpreted by its own standards and principles, which should include a proper role for scientific disciplines but not be limited to them. Long before modern science, good ancient readers, for instance, were already aware that the world was not created in seven literal, twenty-four-hour "days", as Genesis calls them, if for no other reason than that the sun was not created until day four. And in every age, good reading of the sacred texts has consisted of a sophisticated mix of literal and figurative dimensions.

In the modern doctrinal developments within the Church, however, there was always great concern to make sure that the proper relationship between words and deeds did not lead to a split between, on the one hand, matters of faith and morals and, on the other hand, historical or literal meanings. The relationship is complicated, however, because "historical" and "literal" are not at all the same thing. The Church and the Jewish tradition on which it is based affirm certain things as historical, indeed, that the story of the Old Testament reflects a God who is not merely an abstract being or principle—as in some other religions or philosophy—but a God who acts in history. In the New Testament, of course, the figure of Jesus and his many deeds and words, however much read with nuance and careful comparison of different versions of the same events, have a literal meaning (what the words on the page say) and also a historical referent (the original events that can no longer be entirely captured by historical research and may include some variants according to what the authors of the Gospels wished to convey to their readers). The *intention* of the authors, which inevitably had a theological purpose, thus began to grow in importance as a way of reconciling historical and literal dimensions.

The fact that the "historical" elements are not precisely the same in the intended literal meaning of each author is no surprise if it is acknowledged, as it should be, that they were writing of a subject that exceeds the powers of human speech in the normal sense of the term. It is in the theological dimension that everything is affirmed that is needed *nostrae salutis causa* ("for the sake of our salvation"). This formulation leaves a bit of ambiguity over whether every historical detail falls within the purview of things necessary to salvation. As a classic essay on the subject put it: "God has revealed himself through a true *history*, the history of salvation. But the facts recounted in the Bible are not there to instruct us in the profane history of the ancient East."[36] Even so, as Pius XII said in *Divino Afflante Spiritu*, the

[36] Ignace de la Potterie, S.J., "La verité de la Sainte Écriture et l'Histoire du salut d'après la Constitution dogmatique *Dei verbum*", *Nouvelle Revue Théologique* 88 (1966): 149–69.

Bible is a much more reliable guide to history than anything in the surrounding cultures of its day. The facts in the Bible are at times just that and at other times intended to point to some truth needed for salvation according to the intention of the author. And this has long been recognized in the Catholic tradition.

Saint Paul (2 Tim 3:15) was already emphasizing that the Scriptures are "useful" in that they "are able to instruct you for *salvation*" (emphasis added). Saint Augustine was careful to say in his *De Genesi ad Litteram* that the Bible does not intend to instruct us in things other than the ones that lead to salvation. In another work, he observes, somewhat tartly, that Jesus did *not* say: " 'I am sending you the Paraclete who will teach you how the sun and moon turn.' He wanted to form Christians, not mathematicians."[37] Aquinas makes similar observations, commenting on Augustine in *De Veritate* (XII, 2). And, of course, Galileo echoed similar sentiments in defense of his new scientific ideas: "I would say here something that was heard from an ecclesiastic [Cardinal Baronius] of the most eminent degree: 'That the intention of the Holy Ghost is to teach us how one goes to heaven, not how heaven goes.' "[38]

Talk of the "inerrancy" of the Bible, ambitiously extended to all matters historical and scientific, is something of a modern invention that clearly sought to respond to the challenges coming from the Enlightenment model of truth as restricted only to positivistic science. In that sense, it was something of a departure from the Catholic tradition, which began to return in its fullness as the twentieth century approached. Even Vatican I already spoke of the Scriptures as canonical because they "contain *revelation* without error", not simply inerrancy in all respects. And this basically Augustinian perspective would emerge with greater and greater sophistication as the twentieth century unfolded.[39]

During the conciliar debate on Scripture, the Melkite Catholic archbishop of Edessa, Néophytos Edelby, rebuked his Western brethren for their *timiditas* in accepting historical results—saying it

[37] Augustine, *Against Felix the Manichee*, bk. 1, chap. 10.

[38] Quoted in James C. Swindal and Harry J. Gensler, eds., *The Sheed and Ward Anthology of Catholic Philosophy* (Lanham, Md.: Rowman and Littlefield, 2005), 243.

[39] Cf. R. F. Collins, "Augustine of Hippo, Precursor of Modern Biblical Scholarship", *Louvain Studies* 12 (1987): 131–51.

was necessary to "put an end to this obsession in order that we may once more enter into the totality of the mystery of the Church." On October 2, 1964, Cardinal König of Vienna made a landmark intervention in which he cited several passages that modern studies seemed to show at variance with historical fact. For instance, Mark 2:26 says that David ate the bread of the Presence under the high priest Abiathar. 1 Samuel 21ff., however, says it was Abimelech, Abiathar's father. Similarly, Matthew 27:9 refers to Judas' death as fulfilling a prophecy in Jeremiah, when in fact the passage Matthew cites is from Zechariah. And several other passages have shown faulty historical dates. Nothing in these cases or in other seeming conflicts in the New Testament, however, seems to detract in the slightest from the *revelation* God had presumably been making. And Cardinal Meyer of Chicago argued for a different mode of understanding inerrancy that would take into account the "human weaknesses and limitations in the human instrument", the sacred writers whom the Church did not regard as mere conduits but "true authors".

Indeed, some Council Fathers thought it *pericolosum* (dangerous) not to admit openly the problematic passages. It might even give rise to scandal to understand inerrancy as somehow dictating results a priori to the ongoing and valuable work of archaeologists and scholars in matters where reason and evidence were sufficient. To put the great good news on a virtual equal footing with minor matters of fact might discredit the former for very little reason. Only a very few Council Fathers retained the older view, hoping apparent errors and contradictions might someday be resolved. In any event, the entire matter had been acquiring significant textual nuances as each new draft of the *schema* on revelation was presented for review by the bishops at Vatican II.

Dei Verbum

All these things and many more were in play as the Fathers of the Second Vatican Council began the deliberations that resulted in *Dei Verbum*, the Dogmatic Constitution on Divine Revelation. The first *schema*, or preliminary draft, presented to them was based on an older Scholastic approach, which was quickly discarded by the Fathers, who sought something more pastoral and modern. At the very beginning of his well-known commentary on that document, Joseph Ratzinger sharply remarks that the preface's "barely concealed illogicalities ... betray the confusion from which it [the document] has emerged."[40] Since he was one of the group of *periti* who helped develop the new text, his view carries considerable weight, though he was a relatively young scholar at the time. He goes on to explain that though the opening line puts the proper emphasis on the Word itself, the preface, reflecting the text, falls into incoherence in two main ways.

First, it quotes from the First Letter of John: "We announce to you the eternal life which dwelt with the Father and was made visible to us. What we have seen and heard we announce to you, so that you may have fellowship with us and our common fellowship be with the Father and His Son Jesus Christ" (1 Jn 1:2–3). This is all well and good, says Ratzinger, but he objects that it puts a passage declaring the substance of the Christian faith [i.e., Jesus himself] at the head of a document intended to explicate the theological categories under which faith is now approached—basically revelation, tradition, and inspiration. For the young Ratzinger, the ambiguous attitude of the Council as a whole toward dogmatic truth, on the one hand, and pastoral concerns, on the other, remains glaringly unresolved here.

Another potential source of confusion, he says, is a later phrase in the preface: "Therefore, following in the footsteps of the Council of Trent and of the First Vatican Council" (*Propterea, Conciliorum Tridentini et Vaticani I inhaerens vestigiis* ...). This was obviously included to lay conservative fears to rest—as well as to assert what is always the case in Catholicism, that development is a combination of the new in continuity with the old. But for some it gave the impression that *Dei Verbum* itself was going merely to repeat those earlier positions, which was far from being the case, as shall soon appear (and this in a "dogmatic" constitution of a universal council). Ratzinger quotes the great Protestant theologian Karl Barth, who was prevented by ill health from being present as an observer at the Council, who said that the phrase might be better translated: "moving forward from the

[40] Joseph Ratzinger, "Dogmatic Constitution on Divine Revelation: Origin and Background", in H. Vorgrimler, ed., *Commentary on the Documents of Vatican II* (New York: Herder and Herder, 1969), 3:167.

footsteps of those councils". Ratzinger explicitly sees something akin to Newman's "development of doctrine" at work here, which allows for fidelity to the original revelation and for room for a dynamic tradition that includes "a constantly renewed appropriation" of the living faith.

The overall appropriation that Vatican II carried out, and not only in *Dei Verbum*, was a shift from a more abstract, intellectual approach to the faith, which laid heavy emphasis—along Scholastic lines—on definitions, to a more personalist one involving the relationship of the whole person to God: "Instead of the legalistic view that sees Revelation largely as the issuing of divine decrees, we have a sacramental view, which sees law and grace, word and deed, message and sign, the person and his utterance within the one comprehensive unity of mystery."[41] In fact, in the Latin text, Vatican II borrowed from Vatican I's formulation about divine revelation: "aeterna voluntatis suae decreta humano generi revelare", but changed the emphasis on "eternal decrees" to "mystery": "sacramentum voluntatis suae" (the sacrament of his will). Of course, this perspective on the mystery of love between God and his people as opposed to a God who is just an eternal lawgiver is precisely what many people most value about the Council. Multiple problems would emerge, however, when the overemphasis on decrees was abandoned to such a extent that it sometimes seemed there was nothing left as content in the revelation by way of traditional faith and morals except for the personal relationship to God.

This is a subtle balance to maintain. There are, of course, fixed truths of faith and morals and, at the same time, a historical process wherein each generation participates anew in the drama of salvation. In a drama, things are not determined in advance and may turn out one way or another on the basis of choices made. While many have praised the Council's assertion of the importance of God's promise of redemption despite the Fall, Ratzinger—only two years after the close of the Council—wonders aloud "whether the Council did not start from an over-optimistic view in its account of revelation and salvation history, losing sight of the fact that divine salvation comes essentially as a justification of the *sinner*." It is precisely here that Law

[41] Ibid., 3:171.

and Gospel needed to be integrated, since Scripture itself attests to the "mystery of the anger of God",[42] which the conciliar text largely passes over and, thereby resulting in only partial fidelity to the Bible.

Still, there is great benefit that accrues from the fact that the Scriptures were presented by the Council Fathers as not primarily information and rules, but unity and "transformation". By revelation, we learn who we are—the human person is of infinite value, far more than secular humanism suspects—because he is centered in Christ, the one who unites God and man. That had been implicit in the old intellectual formulas, of course, but now those were presented in an appealing way as part of the larger whole of personal life in God. The intellectual labors and the necessary authority of Rome served that ongoing revelation; revelation was no longer to be regarded as solely a kind of prop for certain propositions and practices of the Church.

All of this also had an impact on the idea of tradition. In the past, there had been a rather neat division between Scripture, things written down, and tradition, unwritten things part of the authentic Church begun by Christ (this is sometimes called the *partim-partim* view, partly one and partly the other). That both existed, no one can really doubt. Many habits and attitudes taken for granted are part of the normal operation of every human group, from the family to the nation-state. From the outside, no one could definitively account for why it is that, say, families eat certain foods or do certain things on certain holidays other than by a general appeal to expectations of family members and past practices, which may never be explicitly spelled out. And those unstated assumptions help explain things people in such families say, as well, and help in understanding things that might otherwise seem puzzling or uncertain.

But the relationship between Scripture and tradition called for some clarification at the Council. It was not simply that certain portions of tradition were unwritten but that tradition itself develops as people appropriate, live, and therefore understand more deeply and fully what the tradition means. To certain Protestants, of course, this is merely a corrupting of the original, allegedly simple Church. All parties can agree that the Church is always in need of reform (*Ecclesia semper reformanda*), but modern historical-critical studies complicated

[42] Ibid., 173–74.

the relationship between Scripture and tradition. Catholics had a hard time maintaining scriptural warrant, for example, of dogmas like the Immaculate Conception and the Assumption, which can only be developed from hints in the Scriptures amplified by the living experiences of the Church. But Protestants, too, found challenges to the vision of a simple beginning because historical-critical studies showed beyond all doubt that Scripture itself was a kind of tradition, an important and authoritative one, to be sure, but itself the result of developments going on in the Church before any words were written down. And, as Ratzinger would later say, it is an assumption—and probably a seriously erroneous one in the historical-critical mode—to think that the arrival of the greatest religious expression in the history of the human race is simple and only what comes later is complex. Saint Paul, one of the earliest NT writers, is hardly simpler than Clement of Rome, and the Pastoral Letters are much richer and more complex than the *Didache*.[43]

These new considerations raised several issues never entirely resolved at the Council. There had been talk of *traditions* (plural) at Trent but of tradition (singular) at Vatican II, for the most part. Even Protestants had been retreating some from the *sola Scriptura* argument because functioning churches need more than is explicitly spelled out in the New Testament as such, even in such a crucial matter as worship, which descends from the past. There is even a scriptural warrant for that view. "So then, brethren, stand firm and hold the traditions [*paradoseis*] which you were taught by us, either by word of mouth or by letter" (2 Thess 2:15) as well as the conclusion of John's Gospel, which leaves a door wide open: "There are also many other things which Jesus did; were every one of them to be written, I suppose that the world itself could not contain the books that would be written" (Jn 21:25).

At the same time, there must be a way to be *critical of traditions* in order for reform to be possible. The only way to remain faithful to the whole of revelation is to see it as involving Scripture and tradition in mutual relation. Since this is a living relationship that participates in the whole of God's action in history, it is difficult to give it any precise form other than to say that both must be operative

[43] Ratzinger, "Biblical Interpretation in Conflict", 13.

in the life of the Church. Some radical readers of these deliberations tried to make it appear as if unwelcome definitions in faith and morals, even those testified to in Scripture itself, might be ignored through interpretative cleverness or appeal to other texts, such as the Gnostic Gospels,[44] that had been excluded from the NT canon—by Church authorities. This was a problem that would persist.

The final text of *Dei Verbum* is quite brief, however, a mere twenty-six paragraphs. But is one of the richest produced by the Council. In addition to the points mentioned previously, it emphasizes that revelation includes both deeds and words (*DV* 2) and, with a balance that was not always later observed, that "through divine revelation, God chose to show forth and communicate Himself and the eternal decisions of His will *regarding the salvation of men*" (*DV* 6, emphasis added). Not only is the more modern personal element affirmed here, but so is the older concern for formal decrees, though that is nuanced essentially by the same qualification used of inspiration in general: that it is for the sake of salvation.

Furthermore, it acknowledges the transmission of the gospel truths by the apostles and other men as involving the spoken word, example, and institutions: "The comission was fulfilled, too, by those Apostles and apostolic men who under the inspiration of the same Holy Spirit committed the message of salvation to writing" (*DV* 7). Bishops, of course, were needed to make sure the teaching remained faithful, the Constitution says, but it is not difficult to detect here the affirmation of a prior process of composition that embraces both the possibility of historical-critical study and a role for tradition. The tradition, as presented here, is dynamic, not static. Believers come to know it more fully over time, and that concrete reality led to the formation of the canon (*DV* 8). But unlike some of the formulations of the past, Scripture and tradition in this view "in a certain way

[44] The so-called Gnostic Gospels are various ancient texts, most discovered in 1945 at Nag Hammadi in Egypt, though others came to light both earlier and later. They present a kind of Christianity combined with esoteric teachings that often seem to make an authoritative Church unnecessary. Champions of these "alternative" or "lost" Christianities, of course, draw lessons from them about current Church authority and teachings on faith and morals, which they allege are a narrowing of a rich diversity of beliefs in the ancient world. Elaine Pagels' *The Gnostic Gospels* (New York: Random House, 1979) has been highly influential, as has more recently Bart D. Ehrman's *Lost Christianities* (New York: Oxford University Press, 2003).

merge into a unity and tend toward the same end" (*DV* 9). The magisterium has a role as well: "The teaching office is not above to the word of God, but serves it" (*DV* 10).

We have already seen how the Constitution speaks of inerrancy (*DV* 11) in those things "for the sake of salvation" and of the possible nuances that may introduce. The same chapter lists, among the factors needed for proper interpretation, understanding the human words of the writer, attention to literary forms and expressions, the situation, time and culture, speech and narrative modes in the period, and conventions among people at the time (*DV* 12). All these factors offer an opening to historical, form, redaction, reader-response, and narrative criticism, among other approaches. But unlike the purely academic approaches that often leave out much that has always been essential in reading the Bible, the Council Fathers add three criteria for using such methods that guarantee the overall result will accord with the overall intention of all the biblical writers:

1. The divine authorship must be kept in mind;
2. the content and unity of the whole must also be considered;
3. and this necessarily involves the Church tradition and the *analogia fidei* (analogy of faith).[45]

All this helps understand what Saint Jerome once called the Word of God in the words of men.

The Constitution briefly affirms the importance of the Old Testament as a prelude to the New but also its value in itself. About the New Testament, it concedes (*DV* 19) that the authors selected, synthesized, and explained with an eye to the situation of the churches, while still preserving the truth of eyewitnesses, which is yet another tacit recognition of what might be good in historical studies. But it goes on to explain that these studies must be used in the life of the Church because "like the Christian religion itself, all the preaching of the Church must be nourished and regulated by Sacred Scripture" (*DV* 21). "Easy access to Sacred Scripture should be provided for all the Christian faithful" (*DV* 22), which means undertaking translation

[45] The 1997 *Catechism of the Catholic Church* (2nd ed.) further explicates these three principles in paragraphs 112–14.

perhaps even in collaboration with "the separated brethren". At the intellectual level, the "study of the sacred page is, as it were, the soul of sacred theology" (*DV* 24).

The Fathers conclude that all this is of the most vital importance because, as Saint Jerome said, "Ignorance of the Scriptures is ignorance of Christ" (*DV* 25). And just as frequent Communion advances life in God, so "we may hope for a new stimulus for the life of the Spirit from a growing reverence for the word of God, which 'lasts forever'" (*DV* 26).

Chapter 7

Scripture Study after the Council

The spur all this gave to Catholics in biblical studies would be difficult to exaggerate. Catholics entered with a vengeance into the scholarly debates formerly occupied almost exclusively by non-Catholics. Some of that work produced real contributions to a better Catholic formulation of scriptural interpretation. No small part of it also went quite far afield, and it was not uncommon in the ensuing decades to see wild—and, even from a scholarly point of view, quite unfounded—claims that scholars had "settled" some question by "showing" that the original texts in fact did not support or even contradicted established Catholic faith and morals. The Virgin Birth, miracles, the Eucharist, Christ's atonement for sin on the Cross, the Resurrection, as all these had been long understood, were not infrequently denied or sometimes distorted out of all recognition.

One former Catholic seminary professor claimed that not only did Jesus not rise bodily from the dead, but his body had probably been left on the Cross and eaten by scavenging birds or been thrown in a common pit and devoured by dogs.[1] There was no evidence of any such thing, of course, and much that denied it, but historical studies had "shown" that this was a common practice for criminals crucified by the Roman Empire, so it must be presumed to have occurred in the case of Jesus. Naturally, such shocking "scholarship" received wide media coverage, which sowed doubt among ordinary Catholics. Similarly, theologians who were not Scripture specialists, such as Father Hans Küng in his bestseller *On Being a Christian*,[2] discovered, they believed, in modern scholarship yet another historical Jesus who seems to have been anti-authoritarian—and just in time

[1] John Dominic Crossan, *The Birth of Christianity* (New York: HarperOne, 1999), 481–526. Crossan was already saying such things as early as the 1970s.

[2] Garden City, N.Y.: Doubleday, 1976.

to fit in with the wave of global cultural revolution of the 1960s and 1970s. Some Catholic feminists argued that to believe that God sacrificed his only Son in a horrible death on the Cross in order to forgive sins was a perverted scriptural interpretation that had historically been an encouragement to abuse women and children. Thomas Sheehan, a lapsed Catholic, argued with some scholarly acumen what others, less intellectually adept, were thinking: that the historical-critical study of the Bible had both exploded traditional belief and overwhelmed most officially Catholic institutions. (Sheehan himself taught at Loyola University in Chicago.) Despite his skepticism about the reliability of the Gospels, Sheehan, like many a critic before him, nonetheless arrived at a rock solid conclusion about Jesus: that he had come to abolish religion.[3]

An indication of how even more serious modern critical study of the Bible could go awry can be seen in the work of Edward Schillebeeckx, O.P. (1914–2009). Schillebeeckx was trained as a theologian in his native Belgium and France and studied Aquinas in the way that most students did in the first part of the twentieth century, which is to say, he spent years reading manuals and predigested accounts of the great Dominican before he was actually introduced to the texts themselves. Like many others as well, he found the a-historical approach unsatisfactory and—at several institutions under teachers like Congar, Chenu, and Gilson—he began to adopt the more personalist approach to Thomas that we examined in the first chapters of the present work, combined with phenomenological interests. A staunch liberal, he was arguing for optional priestly celibacy even prior to the Second Vatican Council and influenced the Council and its subsequent implementation, especially in Holland, though he was blocked from serving as a *peritus* to the Dutch bishops by opponents in Rome.

After the Council, Schillebeeckx turned to biblical studies—in which he had no formal training—because he believed that Christology on the old model of creeds, councils, and dogmas needed to be refashioned in more personal and experiential terms. Always a formidable and industrious scholar, he undertook an immense program

[3] Cf. Thomas Sheehan, "Revolution in the Church", *New York Review of Books*, June 14, 1984: 35–38.

of research into modern historical-critical methods and produced three noteworthy volumes in the 1970s, especially his highly influential, and highly controversial, *Jesus: An Experiment in Christology*,[4] which raised deep questions among not only conservatives but moderately liberal theologians as well. Two subsequent volumes, *Christ: The Experience of Jesus as Lord* and *Church: The Human Story of God*,[5] retreated somewhat from the radicalism of the first book—or put it into a broader context, as Schillebeeckx himself might have argued. But the impression that he had radically upended belief in historical events like the Incarnation and Resurrection remained, though it is not clear—the author himself denied it—that this is what he had done. Schillebeeckx was questioned several times by the Congregation for the Doctrine of the Faith, though—perhaps because of the complexity and ambiguity in his work—never formally censured.

There is something tragicomic in Schillebeeckx' story. Though he grappled mightily with modern biblical scholarship and seemed to have produced his own original synthesis intended to bolster modern belief on the basis of experience, it is not difficult to see him as part of a well-worn trajectory that came to a dead end in the twentieth century. Like other scholars, he took Mark as the earliest and, therefore, the most fundamental expression of the historical truths known to the early Christian community. And the Mark he accepted in this role ends with the women finding the empty tomb, not the "long ending" that includes post-Resurrection appearances of Christ. So the real history begins for him, as does Mark, with Jesus coming forward to be baptized by John and ends with the enigma presented by the empty tomb. In sum, Jesus' life was much like any other except for the extraordinary charisma he displayed in attracting followers and moving people.

But it is precisely after this general framework that things get complicated. In Schillebeeckx' telling, the "experience" of the disciples some time after Jesus' death and his "exaltation" led them to understand that he came uniquely from God (Jesus had had his own "Abba

[4] Edward Schillebeeckx, *Jesus: An Experiment in Christology*, trans. Hubert Hoskins (New York: Seabury Press, 1979).

[5] Edward Schillebeeckx, *Christ: The Experience of Jesus as Lord*, trans. John Bowden (New York: Seabury Press, 1980); *Church: The Human Story of God*, trans. John Bowden (New York: Crossroad, 1990).

experience") and carried out some singular task in dying and then being present to his disciples. To be sure, this later experience did not mean that the Annunciation and Virgin Birth, as traditionally understood, occurred at the beginning of Christ's life, or that his death and physical Resurrection, also as commonly understood, took place. As had been suggested in the work of many other modern biblical scholars, these tenets of the early creeds—which had been precisely included to exclude Gnostic and other "spiritualist" interpretation that played down Jesus' actual existence as a flesh and blood human being—were later accretions.

In Schillebeeckx, however, a complex hermeneutical theory seemed to suggest that Christ's connection to God as Father and his Resurrection were real, but not historical or physical. (He even cites the old tag from Aquinas, "Quidquid recipitur ad modum recipientis recipitur", to reinforce the notion that the first disciples' experience and reception of that experience had to be limited by their own capacity to take in the new revelation.) It has often been said that he turned Bultmann on his head and held that the later faith of the disciples was not independent of the historical truth (*sola fide*) but somehow revealed that truth after the fact, though there was, for example, no physical event that a camera might have recorded at the Resurrection.

Though the two later books on Christ and the Church put this theory into a context that connected it with other Catholic principles, it is difficult to see how such an esoteric reading can be reconciled with longstanding Catholic belief. Indeed, such a reading seems to follow the usual modern exegetical arc of regarding the miraculous reports in the NT—which were clearly understood to be something out of the ordinary by the writers and early readers themselves as an embarrassment in the modern, scientific world. A man of deep faith, as by all reports Schillebeeckx seems to have been, who accepts such limits on the story told in the Gospels therefore has to find some way to reconcile what appears impossible with a desire to find some meaning in the impossibilities that can be made plausible.

The tragicomedy in Schillebeeckx is that the whole project feels like a massively Teutonic undertaking to salvage a slender faith from a world view that leaves it little purchase on the world. But like many such projects, for all its scholarship, it really has no more certain foundation than dozens of others that reach very different conclusions. The Congregation for the Doctrine of the Faith may have been uncertain enough about the final significance of the project to refrain from condemning Schillebeeckx. But bad blood swirled around him—and around his case—for many years. As early as 1968, Karl Rahner, who was designated by the Vatican to defend Schillebeeckx privately from early accusations, broke a confidentiality oath he had sworn with the excuse of having made a "mental reservation" and sent Schillebeeckx the dossier against him.[6] This sort of freelance crusading—and after a sworn oath—further exacerbated existing tensions.

Schillebeeckx' later interviews with the CDF in the 1980s stopped short of condemnation, and his work continued to exert wide, if destabilizing, influence for the rest of the twentieth century. It became quite common in many Catholic institutions to get into elaborate arguments about Christ's "glorified body" having arisen, as though his body, as that would be understood by an average person, had ... well, what happened to that body would be hard to say. As Raymond Brown, a liberal bogeyman for some conservatives, once thought it necessary to say of theories like this one or Crossan's: "Let me state boldly: there is no evidence whatsoever that any in the NT who considered themselves Christians thought that Jesus' body could still be moldering in the grave."[7]

In the same book where he makes that statement, Brown also defends the historical-critical method from both its liberal and conservative distorters (conservatives tend to be "ultraconservatives" in that text). But there is an asymmetry in their effects in both theory and practice. The conservative or ultraconservative distorters offer an untenable defense of how some Catholic doctrines are related to the biblical revelation in light of developments in knowledge, but at least they preserve the faith expressed in the creeds. The liberal

[6] This episode is recounted in Edward Schillebeeckx, *I Am a Happy Theologian: Conversations with Francesco Strazzari* (New York: Crossroad, 1994), 32–34. More broadly, cf. Ted Schoof, ed., *The Schillebeeckx Case: Official Exchange of Letters and Documents in the Investigation of Fr. Edward Schillebeeckx, O.P., by the Sacred Congregation for the Doctrine of the Faith, 1976–1980* (New York: Paulist Press, 1984).

[7] Raymond E. Brown, *Biblical Exegesis and Church Doctrine* (New York: Paulist Press, 1985), 38n29.

distorters, in this at least agreeing with the conservatives, often seem to believe that, if doctrines are not directly rooted in clear biblical passages, they—like Protestants before them—are justified in regarding them as unsupported and, therefore, reformable in the direction of modern liberalism.

Brown, as a self-proclaimed centrist Catholic scholar (a description others would dispute), says that he and his fellows deplore that view and see it as falsely failing to appreciate the "trajectories" that lead out of the Bible. Though there may not be *textual* evidence in the NT or historical evidence elsewhere for defined dogmas, this is not always an obstacle to belief in *the Church's ability to discern and define*—after the limited perspective of first-century writers—truths belonging to the faith, even on central questions like the Virgin Mary and the authority of Peter.[8] This is true and it is one way of explaining things, though it comes dangerously close to the views of George Tyrrell. But beyond this theoretical point, *in wide practice*, approaches like Brown's have led to dissent and uncertainty among the ordinary faithful. These effects are, as Brown rightly says, not the fault of the scholars, whose work is being misused. But at the same time, a pastoral problem arose, perhaps stemming from earlier Protestant *and* Catholic views of Scripture as a kind of founding text, rather than a central reference point that is, however, itself part of the tradition. Brown himself, for example, has argued that the words of Eucharistic institution ("This is my Body.... This is ... my Blood"), a central point in the liturgical experience of every Catholic, would be thought of by most exegetes as a later development, not the actual words of Jesus (even though they first appear in 1 Corinthians, one of the earliest of NT texts). The "moderate" exegetes claim that such words may be unhistorical yet a true expression of the early faith of the Church; but this moderation has the practical effect on most believers of suggesting that they are not real at all, as C. S. Lewis warned.

[8] Brown edited two volumes that make the case on precisely these two subjects: *Mary in the New Testament* (Philadelphia: Fortress Press, 1978); and *Peter in the New Testament* (Minneapolis: Augsburg, 1973), both the result of ecumenical conferences. Brown's and other such works called forth conservative rejoinders. René Laurentin, a French biblical scholar, wrote numerous works on the Blessed Virgin. And George Kelly, an American sociologist by training, produced a passionate, global rejection of the whole historical-critical method in *The New Biblical Theorists: Raymond E. Brown and Beyond* (Ann Arbor: Servant Books, 1983).

Schillebeeckx himself occupies an ambiguous position in this perspective, precisely because of his involvement in liberal causes somewhat unrelated to his work in Scripture. After the initial enthusiasm, his name waned in prominence, and scholars moved on to other concerns, though the whole form of the issues he raised remained. And the most crucial point of all persists: whether a faith in the uniqueness of Christ and his Passion, death, and Resurrection can survive reformulation as based on a "Paschal experience" rather than, as in orthodox Christianity, a belief in actual events—in a simpler, though not naïve understanding—that actually took place in our world and changed the conception of that world and the world to come forever.

Debating the "Jesus Seminar"

One of the most notorious public presences of twentieth-century scriptural scholarship was the so-called "Jesus Seminar", founded in 1985 by a small group of radical scholars, Catholic and Protestant, who garnered a great deal of media attention by representing themselves as *the* voice of modern scholarship. In fact, not all of them were scholars—one was a movie producer—and the "scholars" were generally not very eminent. But among their media gimmicks was to hold votes on sayings of Jesus, using different colored beads to indicate whether they were likely or not likely to be authentic, that is, originating from Christ himself. (Only about twenty percent of Christ's recorded words, they claimed, are very likely to be his.) Real scholars have done a creditable job of criticizing both the form and the matter of this PR circus. But despite the unseriousness of the Jesus Seminar—except in the sense that the modern media serves as a megaphone for everything that looks lurid and confrontational, and therefore might attract an audience—it does serve as a rather colorful example of several quite serious questions about much contemporary scriptural studies.

Luke Timothy Johnson, a Catholic Scripture scholar and one of the best-balanced practitioners of modern biblical criticism, has identified three pairs of perceptions that lie behind much of the clash over the meaning of Scripture. Very briefly summarized, the assumptions behind the approaches might be presented like this:

I. Differing Perceptions of the Christian Religion
   A. as based on and enlivened by God's self-disclosure, or revelation
   B. as just another of the world's religions, which are human constructions of symbolic worlds
II. Different Understandings of the Church
   A. as an institution measured by fidelity to the sources that provide her identity
   B. as a social organization to be judged by the criteria of contemporary society
III. Different Understandings of the New Testament, especially the Gospels
   A. as reliable guides for apprehension of the true Jesus in the ongoing experience of believers and the Church
   B. as ancient texts that must be purified of any faith perspective, perhaps even deconstructed to get to the reality behind the texts.[9]

Johnson immediately adds that what appear to be neat intellectual divisions between a faith approach and a rationalist approach, however, are not equally neat social separations between the Church and the academy. One of the most vexed features of modern Christianity is less the traditional Catholic-Protestant division (though that remains nettlesome) than the confusion *within the churches themselves* about how the Scriptures should guide the lives of believers.

To a certain extent, of course, this division continues to reflect an older split between Enlightenment and pre-Enlightenment modes of thought, which we encountered earlier. We need to be careful about making this distinction, however, since many modern people assume it is a question of faith as opposed to reason. In fact, faith makes use of reason all the time—and has throughout history. The question, therefore, is not whether Christianity will rationally examine the texts it has always taken to be authoritative. The real question is what is regarded as rational. Is reason to be solely identified with the naturalistic premises of certain kinds of thinking that became a potent cultural

[9] Summarized from Luke Timothy Johnson, *The Real Jesus: The Misguided Quest for the Historical Jesus and the Truth of the Traditional Gospels* (New York: Harper Collins, 1997), 57–58.

force in the Western world in the eighteenth century and since. Or are there forms of reason that precede and follow the Enlightenment version that have their own validity? In the former view, as Johnson rightly says, it is assumed that the human mind—and the human mind operating within a rather crude and limited theory of the world and knowledge, as postmodern critics would later show—is the measure of reality, not God or revelation. The gap between the two views may ultimately be unbridgeable. It is clear, for instance, that the tools applied to reach the "historical Jesus" can never discover the person in whom Christians believe or, it ought to be added, any similar spiritual being, since all such are essentially ruled out in advance by the assumptions of the supposedly neutral historians.

Still, almost all the Christian churches that are not merely dismissive of modern thought in its entirety have absorbed some of the real achievements and procedures of the Enlightenment. And for most Christians who are committed to the pursuit of all truth as a reflection of God, this has been a necessary, if sometimes disconcerting, process. The problem in all faith groups, including the Catholic Church, is twofold. First, how much does accepting certain approaches automatically dictate results that cannot help contradicting the living faith of the Church? And second, what other culturally effective approaches to interpreting Scripture might then be brought forward in fuller fidelity to the truths that more rationalist approaches are, by nature, unable to appreciate properly—truths that are crucial to the very survival of Christianity? Johnson points out that this is especially crucial for seminaries where future priests are being trained and that resistance to the model of academic freedom as practiced in the academy should not be viewed merely as authoritarian blindness.[10]

But the challenge is a larger one engaging the Church as a whole, since any Church that does not make a forceful and convincing presentation of a way of life different from that of the surrounding culture has very little claim on people's attention except on ceremonial occasions. And this explains a great deal about the decline of

[10] "Indeed, it might be argued that the Jerry Falwells and the Cardinal Ratzingers of this age have a sharper intellectual grasp of the cultural consequences of such seminary training than do their liberal counterparts who appeal simply to the ideal of academic freedom" (ibid., 62).

liberal mainline Protestant churches as well as the rise of fundamentalism. The Catholic Church, viewed in a sociological perspective, has looked at the Bible from a position somewhere between the liberalism of the Protestant mainline and the conservatism of the fundamentalists. And that has given rise to endless haggling about what are settled and unchangeable scriptural truths and what merely culturally conditioned expressions intended for some community in the past but inapplicable now (or, worse still, some early Church invention). The very way this argument is framed accounts for some of the acrimony visible in Catholicism since the Second Vatican Council, even after four decades and two popes—John Paul II and Benedict XVI—who took a very sophisticated approach to engaging modernity. As early as the 1970s, no less a figure than Karl Rahner warned, "The Church cannot be a debating society: it must be able to make decisions binding on all within it. Such a demand cannot be *a priori* contrary to man's dignity if . . . he is indeed a social being. And then a supreme point at which all reflections and democratic discussions are turned into universally binding decisions cannot be without meaning."[11]

The search for the historical Jesus (deliberately not capitalized here to mean the ongoing historical research, not just the results of a certain period) has real intellectual validity. There is nothing wrong—and a good deal right—with using whatever tools we have at hand to try to understand better the man who is the most influential figure in all of human history. But ironically, there has been a certain naïveté and even simplemindedness in the search as it has been practiced by scholars. To begin with, when we are dealing with a highly influential public figure, even when we have far greater documentation than we do for Christ, there is no escaping certain complexities that, in the nature of things, cannot be eliminated. Abraham Lincoln, for example, is revered by many people as a man who became a near religious icon in the progressive deepening of his mind as he tried to grapple both with preserving the Union and with the meaning of the struggle for both sides in the Civil War. To this day, however, there are, on the one hand, many people who see in him a new birth of freedom and, on the other hand, many who see him as a fanatical authoritarian

[11] Karl Rahner, S.J., *The Shape of the Church to Come* (New York: Seabury, 1974), 54.

figure who started a war that led to the death of hundreds of thousands of people when less drastic means were available to achieve the same goals. All great historical figures lend themselves to different interpretations. And Jesus Christ—as we can see from the history of Christianity and the post-Christian world—is not an exception, in a purely natural perspective.

Good historians are well aware of such difficulties, which are compounded when the documentary evidence becomes slender. Modern scriptural scholars by and large have abandoned the notion that the history of the Church as it appears in the Acts of the Apostles is unreliable. That may or may not be so, but the question that immediately presents itself is this: If we abandon that story, which had to make its way between A.D. 70 and 100, which is to say, at a time closer to the original events than we are, and therefore would have had to stand up to scrutiny by many people who knew the apostles and their followers, what standard will we set up in its place to help us understand Christ's life? In a similar development, it was once thought that the Gospel of John, with its cosmic perspective starting with "In the Beginning was the Word", was "pure theology", as it was sometimes put. Then it was noticed that, among the evangelists, John seemed to have the most accurate knowledge of ancient Palestine as well as a detailed account of Jesus' life—and this from the Gospel that was supposed to be the latest and therefore the least factually reliable.

There is an initial question in all such studies about dating (it used to be that scholars pushed dates farther and farther into the second century A.D. to account for "developments" after the eyewitnesses and those who knew them were dead; now the consensus seems to be that the Gospels were all written within the first century, making the time for additional "development" correspondingly less). If we had Lincoln's Gettysburg Address without the famous opening "Four score and seven years ago", and the text began instead with the second sentence, "Now we are engaged in a great civil war", how would we date it? Some historians would read "Now" as meaning that Lincoln must have been speaking at the very beginning of the conflict, when his hearers had to be reminded that they are at war "now". Others might be more skeptical. But anyone who looked at that brief speech without the precise reference at the beginning, even today when we know the history of the Civil War in great detail, would have a hard time without external evidence knowing when Lincoln might have said such a thing.

A great deal of the results of the historical-critical method, though far from all, find themselves in this profound difficulty and others as well. One of the early hypotheses of modern scholarship was that a collection of Jesus' sayings (*logia*), which German scholars designated as the Q document, circulated independently. The Gospel writers must have inserted these sayings into different contexts for differing motives, scholars hypothesize, because Jesus' words do not always appear in the same context in all the Gospels. But even this sometimes helpful hypothesis immediately reveals various difficulties. To begin with, why just sayings and not a collection of stories? Most human beings, let alone a figure who makes a number of public pronouncements in different places where there were no modern means of communication, repeat themselves. I may sometimes tell a story in one context for one purpose and in another context for another. One of the most fundamental suppositions of modern scholarship, then, though by no means entirely invalidated, shows serious flaws both in its conceptualization and in its use.

Furthermore, if those sayings were a contextless collection as theorized, any later attempt to assign them a historical context would be essentially doomed, as would be the dating of a contextless Gettysburg Address. Many things would simply mislead us. For instance, we know the Qumran community read a wide variety of texts; was it the case that each of the Gospels was directed to or read by only one Christian community—in other words, is the *Sitz-im-Leben* simple or compound? The attempt to hypothesize how each of the highly uncertain elements in the whole relate to another would simply multiply misunderstandings as one guess was piled on top of another on top of another, and so forth. There are no criteria by which to make judgments except for ones introduced from outside both the New Testament as we already have it and the supposedly circulating collection of quotations, the Q document. Any results that may be achieved can have a certain interest for scholars trying to come to grips with the complex texts we have. And they may lead us to look in directions that may help us explain certain things. But they are not scientific scholarship in any real sense of the term.

And even further, what kinds of criteria are to be employed—since there must be some way to organize the alleged fragments. By and large, scholars tend to dismiss the evidence provided by interested religious observers such as Saint Luke in the Acts. Indeed, believers in Jesus, especially orthodox believers, come in for the greatest suspicion of all. One sign of the nature of this rejection is that other religious texts—the Qumran documents, the Nag Hammadi Library, especially documents like the so-called Gospel of Thomas—with even less reliability than the Gospels by any sane assessment, are often taken as of equal or even greater value than the "approved" texts. It is hard not to conclude from all this that the otherwise laudable effort to try various hypotheses to see if they help us understand early Christianity better displays, at its heart, a bias against the classical and best-attested tradition surrounding Jesus. There has arisen a commitment to interpretive *autonomy* rather than *accuracy*, which considers its main threat as coming from religious belief and Church authority.[12]

In any event, large numbers of priests and bishops in the Church during the twentieth century had been taught either to reject or ardently to welcome the new developments, meaning that clashes between people who had been trained to one view or another in different times and places would be inevitable.

Seeking Balance

The reckless and sometimes overtly iconoclastic nature of much scriptural work was obvious to more sober scholars, but it had no little influence over Catholic institutions and many Catholic faithful. As one historian has noted, even the best work has had the effect of cutting off the Church from her roots:

> The great founders of the Church together with its most influential theologians based their theological reflection on interpretations of the Scriptures, both Old and New Testaments, which modern scholars would consider invalid. One need only think of the many New

[12] R. R. Reno, "Whither Historical Criticism?" *First Things*, March 2, 2009, online at www.firstthings.com/web-exclusives/2009/03/whither-historical-criticism.

> Testament sayings which have traditionally been interpreted as words of Jesus but which modern scholarship ascribes to the early Church to see the problem in all its force.

And, he continues, this has had an impact not only on the simple believers in the pews, bewildered by claims and counterclaims; it has paralyzed sophisticated theologians who would like to turn to the Bible for moral, spiritual, and pastoral foundations:

> Some tentativeness is acceptable in theology as a check against dogmatism. But the situation that has developed in historical criticism goes far beyond this necessary check. Very few historical reconstructions of more than the most trivial details have managed to win an enduring consensus among scholars. The absence of consensus on the situation has extended to absence of consensus on the meaning of the text which is dependent on that situation. Without even a relatively firm base in the text, theological reflection has been postponed. Too often the postponement is indefinite. Theological reflection is adjourned *sine die.*[13]

Even before these symptoms manifested themselves, the Vatican was worried about what might emerge from the new opening. During the Council itself, while the Fathers were debating the document on Scripture, the Pontifical Biblical Commission issued an "Instruction on the Historical Truth of the Gospels" (in Latin, *Sancta Mater Ecclesia*), which laid out six dangers for Catholic exegetes to avoid:

1. denial of a supernatural order
2. denial of God's intervention in the world in strict revelation
3. denial of the possibility and existence of miracles
4. incompatibility of faith with historical truth
5. an almost a priori denial of the historical value and nature of the documents of revelation
6. a disdain for apostolic testimony and undue emphasis on the creative community of the early Church

[13] Robinson, *Roman Catholic Exegesis*, 2 and 151.

The Instruction went on to assert that discrepancies should not call into question the essential trustworthiness of the text: "For the truth of the story (or narrative, if one insists) is not affected by the fact that the evangelists relate the words and deeds of the Lord in a different order and express his sayings not literally, but differently, while preserving [their] sense."[14] Needless to say, such warnings and the careful efforts in *Dei Verbum* to foster both scholarship and a personal engagement with Scripture did not have the intended effects.

"The Interpretation of the Bible in the Church"

Not surprisingly, Rome made several other attempts to shore up confidence in the Scriptures. In 1993 the Pontifical Biblical Commission convened to prepare a wide-ranging and well-balanced document on "The Interpretation of the Bible in the Church".[15] As we have noticed, the commission had been created in the first years of the twentieth century following Leo XIII's lead in *Providentissimus Deus*—another institution that expressed his practical goals of intellectual renewal. Until Vatican II, it was an official and authoritative source of biblical interpretation and provided academic training for exegetes, even granting them pontifical degrees. In 1971, however, it was restructured by Paul VI and made a merely consultative body to the Congregation for the Doctrine of the Faith, composed of a variety of scholars from all over the world. When they met in 1993 on the hundredth anniversary of *Providentissimus Deus* to prepare some guidelines about the interpretation of the Bible within the Church, its members were themselves skilled practitioners of various modern methods of exegesis, and the document they produced strikes a reasonable balance between the needs of academic scholarship and the uses of that scholarship in the Catholic Church.

[14] See Joseph A. Fitzmyer, *The Interpretation of Scripture: In Defense of the Historical-Critical Method* (New York: Paulist Press, 2008), 44.

[15] Cf. Joseph A. Fitzmyer, *The Biblical Commission's Document "The Interpretation of the Bible in the Church": Text and Commentary* (Rome: Pontificio Istituto Biblico, 1995), and Peter S. Williamson, *Catholic Principles for Interpreting Scripture: A Study of the Pontifical Biblical Commission's The Interpretation of the Bible in the Church* (Rome: Pontificio Istituto Biblico, 2001).

Balance in and of itself is not a very exciting quality, and it can tend to smooth over outright crises. At times, the commission's text can appear far too bland to respond adequately to the vast intellectual disorder and pastoral turmoil it is addressing. But every paragraph also offers solid insights into the various exegetical methods—and their uses and misuses in the almost thirty years that had elapsed since the Council issued *Dei Verbum*. No method in existence—even the thornier forms presented by liberationist and feminist approaches—is wholly ruled out. Every method is surveyed and apprized from its strengths and its common weaknesses. The commission even recognizes that "some value this plurality of methods and approaches as an indication of richness, but to others it gives the impression of much confusion."[16] Without recommending any particular interpretations or anathematizing any approach, however, the text presents a sound and open way of reading the Scriptures—a way that properly values the contributions of the scholar and the needs of the ordinary believer and the universal Church.

Perhaps the overarching principle of the whole, therefore, is a concern to preserve both an objective investigation into the past and a living faith in the present: "what it meant then, and what it means now". As then Cardinal Ratzinger put it in a prefatory note: "The biblical word comes from a real past. It comes not only from the past, however, but at the same time from the eternity of God and it leads us into God's eternity, but again along the way through time, to which the past, the present and the future belong."[17] The incarnational nature of Christianity demands the investigation into human history, the document itself says, but it also warns scholars not to fall into the same errors as the lawyers criticized in Scripture for having taken away the key of knowledge from others and not entering in themselves (Mt 23:13).

Ratzinger asserts, "Everything that shrinks our horizon and hinders us from seeing and hearing beyond that which is merely human must be opened up. Thus the emergence of the historical-critical

[16] Pontifical Biblical Commission, *The Interpretation of the Bible in the Church*, April 15, 1993, introduction; Eng. trans. (Mar 18, 1994) provided by EWTN online: www.EWTN.com/library/curia/pbcinter.htm.

[17] Ibid., preface.

method set in motion at the same time a struggle over its scope and its proper configuration which is by no means finished as yet."[18] As the document begins to examine the various methods, for example, it shows how in the otherwise valuable "documentary hypothesis" for the Old Testament (which says four sources—Yahwist, Elohist, Deuteronomist, and Priestly—contributed to the Pentateuch) the final form and meaning of the OT are sometimes lost amid the complex theories. Something similar happens with the "two-source hypothesis" in the New Testament (Mark + an unknown Q document lie behind Matthew and Luke).

This is a common complaint against the several modern approaches. For instance, only after redaction criticism came into its own (a redactor means a final editor or group of editors who give us the final form we have, a form that is presumably inspired) could it be seen that the editing process, the form of any particular text, and the communities for which they were intended did not constitute extraneous factors qualifying the truthfulness of the final text (as sometimes appeared in prominent exegetes like Martin Dibelius and Rudolf Bultmann). To the contrary, these methods showed the various processes by which the believing community was informed by and acknowledged the validity of the texts we now have. For a Catholic or other Christian who recognizes the indispensability of that community—which is to say, the Church—in the whole development, indeed, that the Church was intended by God as part of the process of salvation, the modern methods point in a very different direction from what they do when guided by positivist principles alone. The commission observes of the historical method as a whole: "It is a method which, when used in an objective manner, implies of itself no a priori. If its use is accompanied by a priori principles, that is not something pertaining to the method itself, but to certain hermeneutical choices which govern the interpretation and can be tendentious."[19] Happily, the method has been separated from those assumptions, and exegetes now have a fuller notion of how various approaches may be used legitimately and recognize that no one method is adequate to the entirety of the task.

[18] Ibid.

[19] Ibid., IA4.

Literary Methods

Indeed, the commission surveys some methods—rhetorical, narrative, and semiotic analysis—that were prominent in the latter part of the twentieth century in secular literary studies and that help broaden approaches to the biblical text. Each of these, though in different ways, makes it clear that a literary text is not merely a thing for objective analysis, like a specimen in a test tube. By its very nature as a literary text, it seeks to elicit a certain response from the reader—not merely to convey neutral information. To many of the stricter historical-critical advocates, this seems to introduce subjectivism into the reading of Scripture, which even the older, traditional exegesis had worried about. But there is a difference between, on the one hand, saying that someone uses a certain rhetoric or tells a story in a certain way or employs particular signs to evoke a response in a subject and, on the other hand, a thorough-going *subjectivism*, with its unfortunate offspring relativism and skepticism. It is clearly not impossible to study the objective side of the text and also take into consideration how those objective materials were intended to have a personal effect on an audience. It has often been said that the historical method serves as a kind of "window" onto the past, while the literary methods hold up a kind of "mirror". The way members of a community receive the text is no guarantee that they have properly interpreted it, which calls for theological criteria. But in the case of tradition, it offers some explanation of how audiences from the early days of Christianity may have reacted.

Tradition-Based Approaches

The commission takes up, in fact, what it calls a whole group of approaches "based in tradition". The most prominent of these at the time was "canonical criticism", pioneered by the American Protestant Brevard S. Childs and his students at Yale University. They proposed various hypotheses about why the particular texts were formally accepted by the believing community as part of the "canon" or rule by which Christianity was defined. James A. Sanders, another American Protestant whom the commission examines, took a novel approach to the question of "form" by arguing that acceptance into the canon is also a validation of the final form of the Scriptures as we now have them. Both of these methods are in substantial harmony with one of the central Catholic interpretive principles expressed in *Dei Verbum*: that individual parts of the Bible take their full meaning only when their significance is seen in light of the whole. Clearly, this also involves a sensitive and sophisticated understanding of the Christian dependence, historically as well as spiritually, on the Jewish texts.[20]

In this same large grouping, the commission also devotes special attention to the approach via the history of the influence of the text, *Wirkungsgeschichte*, as it is called in German. This raises, of course, all sorts of historical questions about the validity or lack thereof in developments within the Church at different periods. But it also brings into focus the fact that, in large degree, readers of the text are not—as both positivists and fundamentalists sometimes think—isolated individuals who come to the text with no presuppositions. Most reading of the Scriptures occurs within already existing traditions of some kind, which need to be considered. An individual reader may accept or partly reject such traditions and, in rare instances, come to a new understanding that is valid but has long lain unrealized in the texts. But even that individual component has a history over two millennia that now needs to be incorporated into interpretive efforts.

New Scientific Dimensions

The knowledge explosion of the past two centuries has provided biblical exegetes with interesting new archaeological and documentary material—the Qumran ("Dead Sea") Scrolls being probably the most striking in terms of information about Palestine around the time of Christ. But there are other modern sciences that influence interpretation as well: sociology, cultural anthropology, and psychology (including psychoanalysis). These have obviously been used with a

[20] In 2001, just beyond the years dealt with in the present work, the Pontifical Biblical Commission issued a study entitled *The Jewish People and Their Sacred Scriptures in the Christian Bible*, which seeks to establish the value of the OT both in itself and in its relationship to and fulfillment in the NT.

certain naïve confidence in the first rush of enthusiasm after their development. But they have more defensible uses as well. Sociological analysis, for instance, is often a kind of form criticism looking at the *Sitz-im-Leben* of writers and readers in community. Problems with this approach often come from its overemphasis on economic, social, and political factors and relative neglect of "religious and personal dimensions". Clearly, there are similar cautions to be applied to cultural anthropology and psychology. Since they were developed in decidedly secular contexts thousands of years after the texts they study, they can help—but also distract.[21]

The most controversial approaches that the commission examines, however, are the liberationist and feminist schools, which it characterizes as "contextual". Liberation theology, which has roots both in Europe and in the developing world, seeks the social liberation of peoples now alive and does not necessarily require belief in any particular political or economic theory. In practice, however, especially in places like Latin America and Africa, it has tended to adopt dubious Marxist notions, such as exploitation, dependency, and the class struggle—and those not only within individual nations but at an international level.[22] The Marxist element receded somewhat with the collapse of the Soviet Union in 1989, however, obviously a method that focuses so passionately on immediate social questions opens up some dimensions of the Bible but tends to read them in ideological ways. The commission observes that liberation theology is still developing and that "for its further development and fruitfulness within the church, a decisive factor will be the clarification of its hermeneutical presuppositions, its methods and its coherence with the faith and the tradition of the church as a whole."[23]

[21] Joseph Ratzinger takes a more jaundiced view regarding the enthusiasm for such examples of "reading the Scripture against its own intentions" as "the most dramatic sign of the state of emergency in which exegesis and theology find themselves": "Biblical Interpretation in Conflict", 5.

[22] Two of the classic liberationist texts are Gustavo Gutiérrez, *A Theology of Liberation: History, Politics, and Salvation*, trans. Caridad Inda and John Eagleson (Maryknoll, N.Y.: Orbis, 1973), and Jon Sobrino, *Jesus the Liberator: A Historical-Theological Reading of Jesus of Nazareth*, trans. Paul Burns and Francis McDonagh (Maryknoll, N.Y.: Orbis, 1993). A useful collection of texts is Alfred T. Hennelly, *Liberation Theology: A Documentary History* (Maryknoll, N.Y.: Orbis, 1990).

[23] Pontifical Biblical Commission, *Interpretation of the Bible*, IE1.

No method has been more controversial within the Church, however, than feminist approaches.[24] In fact, in one of only three footnotes, the commission records that out of nineteen scholars who voted on this particular section, eleven were in favor, four opposed, and four abstained—and the four opponents requested and were granted a note explaining their reactions. Feminist approaches involve questions of women's roles within the Church and, as such, are even more widely felt than liberation theologies. At the same time, the commission warns that using critical or sociological principles to dismiss biblical texts as merely culturally conditioned—the famous "hermeneutic of suspicion"—often proceeds by way of radical a priori assumptions and runs the risk of "interpreting the biblical texts in a tendentious manner. To establish its positions, it must often, for want of something better, have recourse to arguments *ex silentio* [that is, from silence]." The commission continues:

> Feminist exegesis often raises questions of power within the church, questions which, as is obvious, are matters of discussion and even of confrontation. In this area, feminist exegesis can be useful to the church only to the degree that it does not fall into the very traps it denounces and that it does not lose sight of the evangelical teaching concerning power as service, a teaching addressed by Jesus to all disciples, men and women.[25]

Fundamentalism

If the commission is cautiously critical of certain ways of using "progressive" analyses, it simply rejects fundamentalism. It dismisses any "naïvely literalist" approach, which, however well intentioned and passionate, and however understandable as a reaction against what Protestant fundamentalists saw as a deliberate debunking of Scripture truths, is simply unfaithful to the Bible:

[24] Among the many works in this field, cf. Elisabeth Schüssler-Fiorenza, *In Memory of Her: A Feminist Theological Reconstruction of Christian Origins* (New York: Crossroad, 1983). Of more radical bent are the many influential books of Mary Daly, particularly *Beyond God the Father: Toward a Philosophy of Women's Liberation* (Boston: Beacon Press, 1973), *Gyn/ecology: The Metaethics of Radical Feminism* (Boston: Beacon Press, 1978), and others.

[25] Pontifical Biblical Commission, *Interpretation of the Bible*, IE2.

> Its way of presenting these truths is rooted in an ideology which is not biblical, whatever the proponents of this approach might say. For it demands an unshakable adherence to rigid doctrinal points of view and imposes, as the only source of teaching for Christian life and salvation, a reading of the Bible which rejects all questioning and any kind of critical research.
>
> The basic problem with fundamentalist interpretation of this kind is that, refusing to take into account the historical character of biblical revelation, it makes itself incapable of accepting the full truth of the incarnation itself. As regards relationships with God, fundamentalism seeks to escape any closeness of the divine and the human. It refuses to admit that the inspired word of God has been expressed in human language and that this word has been expressed, under divine inspiration, by human authors possessed of limited capacities and resources. For this reason, it tends to treat the biblical text as if it had been dictated word for word by the Spirit. It fails to recognize that the word of God has been formulated in language and expression conditioned by various periods. It pays no attention to the literary forms and to the human ways of thinking to be found in the biblical texts, many of which are the result of a process extending over long periods of time and bearing the mark of very diverse historical situations.[26]

Specifically, fundamentalists have such a strict understanding on inerrancy that they read texts as historical that were not meant to be so and, partly as a result, fail to understand how the first Christian communities wrote and received the Bible—which involved creeds, doctrines, and liturgy. In its desire to be faithful, it destroys Christian thought: "Without saying as much in so many words, fundamentalism actually invites people to a kind of intellectual suicide. It injects into life a false certitude, for it unwittingly confuses the divine substance of the biblical message with what are in fact its human limitations."[27]

Hermeneutical Questions

Cardinal Ratzinger said around the time, and truly, that it would take a whole generation to work out the necessary "criticism of the

[26] Ibid., IF.
[27] Ibid.

criticism" from within the critical tradition itself, because, at a deep philosophical level, the "theological canon" that had formerly shaped interpretation "is indeed precisely what modern exegesis set out to overcome".[28] The pontifical commission was clearly aware of this difficulty because it devoted the whole second half of its reflections to hermeneutics.

Hermeneutics is the science of interpretation—of any text—and although the language and tone can seem obscure, it does explain several things. The great modern theorists in the field such as Schleiermacher, Dilthey, and the highly influential early Heidegger provide the secular background for the labors of many Scripture scholars. Rudolf Bultmann set the tone for many subsequent hermeneutical approaches by rightly pointing out that, as Heidegger argued, we can only have interpretation where there is already a pre-understanding (*Vorverständnis*) about various matters and a life-relationship (*Lebensverhältnis*) to what is being interpreted. The problem in Bultmann and many others is that these necessary relations were reduced, as in Heidegger, to what "people of today" could believe. For Bultmann, modern science had simply destroyed an earlier world view, or, as he put it notoriously in *Kerygma and Myth*: "It is impossible to use electric light and the wireless [radio] and to avail ourselves of modern medical and surgical discoveries, and at the same time to believe in the New Testament world of spirits and miracles."[29] For Heidegger, this led to an existential understanding on an intricate model he developed in various obscure works. It does not take much reflection to see, however, that the normative "existential" reader was a passing construct of a certain moment in philosophy that reached its peak from roughly the 1930s to 1960s. By the early twenty-first century, Heidegger was still regarded as a very powerful thinker, but his kind of existentialism was hardly without challengers and his approach merely one of several possible sets of philosophical presuppositions.

Other thinkers, like Hans-Georg Gadamer and Paul Ricoeur, had, in the meantime, come forward with hermeneutical systems more

[28] Ratzinger, "Biblical Interpretation in Conflict", 6. Ratzinger's essay goes back to a New York conference held in 1988.

[29] Hans Werner Bartsch and Rudolf Bultmann, *Kerygma and Myth: A Theological Debate*, vol. 1, trans. Reginald H. Fuller (London: SPCK, 1953), 5. This useful volume contains Bultmann's original 1941 essay and several commentaries on it.

congenial to the Bible's own self-understanding.[30] As the commission observes, even though hermeneutical approaches help by moving our understanding away from the exclusive and one-sided "objective" stance of the critical methods:

> We must frankly accept that certain hermeneutical theories are inadequate for interpreting Scripture. For example, Bultmann's existentialist interpretation tends to enclose the Christian message within the constraints of a particular philosophy. Moreover, by virtue of the presuppositions insisted upon in this hermeneutic, the religious message of the Bible is for the most part emptied of its objective reality (by means of an excessive "demythologization") and tends to be reduced to an anthropological message only. Philosophy becomes the norm of interpretation, rather than an instrument for understanding the central object of all interpretation: the person of Jesus Christ and the saving events accomplished in human history. An authentic interpretation of Scripture, then, involves in the first place a welcoming of the meaning that is given in the events and, in a supreme way, in the person of Jesus Christ.[31]

Joseph Ratzinger put this in a more trenchant formulation: earlier efforts had enacted a *reductio historiae in philosophiam*, "a reduction of history to and by philosophy", a glaring error that it is difficult to believe was not much noted in the past.[32]

Reason alone could not have fully anticipated what appears in the Bible, and that was quite well understood by "precritical" thinkers like Gregory of Nyssa, Augustine, and Aquinas, followed by Newman and many other careful Catholic exegetes. But a properly disposed reason can show why it is not unreasonable to think that a Creator God can communicate unusual truths to us. And hermeneutical methods applied to the Bible have to be able to account for those possibilities—and not just in subjective experience, but in the normative terms of the text, the believing community that writes and

[30] Paul Ricoeur, *Essays on Biblical Interpretation*, ed. Lewis S. Mudge (Philadelphia: Fortress, 1980); and Hans-Georg Gadamer, *Truth and Method* (New York: Continuum, 1975).

[31] Pontifical Biblical Commission, *Interpretation of the Bible*, IIA2.

[32] "Biblical Interpretation in Conflict", 19. See also Vincent A. McCarthy, *Quest for a Philosophical Jesus: Christianity and Philosophy in Rousseau, Kant, Hegel, and Schelling* (Macon, Ga.: Mercer University Press, 1986).

reads those texts, and finally the spiritual realities of which all this claims to be aware.

The commission recommends a sophisticated reappropriation of the fact that there are literal and spiritual senses to Scripture as well as the *sensus plenior.* For instance, is even the literal always reducible to only one thing? It does not quote Saint Thomas, but Aquinas long ago recognized an interesting fact: "Since the literal sense is that which the author intends, and since the author of Holy Writ is God, Who by one act comprehends all things by His intellect, it is not unfitting, as Augustine says (*Confess.* xii), if, even according to the literal sense, one word in Holy Writ should have several senses" (*ST* I, q. 1, a. 10).[33] Even literary texts seem to be capable of projecting more than one "literal" sense without thereby falling into a simple indeterminacy that allows readers to attribute to them any meaning at all. And a literal sense—say a description of Christ and the Paschal Mystery—may be both literal and spiritual, since in the biblical optic everything has a spiritual dimension. Similarly, the "fuller sense" is something that the author may not have intended but, owing to divine inspiration, may become clear in further reflection on the whole of Scripture. The commission cites the "young woman" in Isaiah (7:14) who becomes a "virgin" bearing the Savior in Matthew (1:28).

Catholic Characteristics

Catholics may clearly make use of all available approaches, but there are some specific Catholic principles of interpretation that situate it amid all these complexities:

> What characterizes Catholic exegesis is that it deliberately places itself within the living tradition of the church, whose first concern is fidelity to the revelation attested by the Bible. Modern hermeneutics has made clear, as we have noted, the impossibility of interpreting a text without starting from a "pre-understanding" of one type or another.
>
> Catholic exegetes approach the biblical text with a pre-understanding which holds closely together modern scientific culture

[33] See John F. Boyle, "St. Thomas Aquinas and Sacred Scripture", *Pro Ecclesia* 4 (1995): 92–104.

> and the religious tradition emanating from Israel and from the early Christian community. Their interpretation stands thereby in continuity with a dynamic pattern of interpretation that is found within the Bible itself and continues in the life of the church. This dynamic pattern corresponds to the requirement that there be a lived affinity between the interpreter and the object, an affinity which constitutes, in fact, one of the conditions that makes the entire exegetical enterprise possible.
>
> All pre-understanding, however, brings dangers with it. As regards Catholic exegesis, the risk is that of attributing to biblical texts a meaning which they do not contain but which is the product of a later development within the tradition. The exegete must beware of such a danger.[34]

The final caution applies to the otherwise useful attempts to recuperate patristic, medieval, academic, traditional, and personal readings within the Church. And the commission concludes with rich reflections on how all this may be carried out with special attention to liturgy, *lectio divina*, pastoral ministry, and ecumenism, always keeping in mind the ultimate goal:

> Through fidelity to the great tradition, of which the Bible itself is a witness, Catholic exegesis should avoid as much as possible this kind of professional bias and maintain its identity as a *theological discipline*, the principal aim of which is the deepening of faith. This does not mean a lesser involvement in scholarly research of the most rigorous kind, nor should it provide excuse for abuse of methodology out of apologetic concern. Each sector of research (textual criticism, linguistic study, literary analysis, etc.) has its own proper rules, which it ought follow with full autonomy. But no one of these specializations is an end in itself. In the organization of the exegetical task as a whole, the orientation toward the principal goal should remain paramount and thereby serve to obviate any waste of energy. Catholic exegesis does not have the right to become lost, like a stream of water, in the sands of a hypercritical analysis. Its task is to fulfill, in the church and in the world, a vital function, that of contributing to an ever more authentic transmission of the content of the inspired Scriptures.[35]

[34] Pontifical Biblical Commission, *Interpretation of the Bible*, III.
[35] Ibid., conclusion.

Benedict XVI

Benedict XVI's *Jesus of Nazareth*, volume 1 (2007), attempts to grapple with various issues raised by modern Scripture scholarship and integrate them into a faithful reading of the Gospels, without in any way wishing to diminish, let alone dismiss, the historical-critical method.[36] As several readers of the book pointed out, it often addresses disputes that go back to quite a bit earlier than its publication date, primarily among German scholars. But for our present purposes, that makes this "personal search 'for the face of the Lord'"[37] all the more useful in that it represents a kind of retrospective evaluation of Catholic Scripture scholarship in the twentieth century as well. Benedict begins by outlining several serious problems. The method that was supposed to take us back behind the inconsistent later accretions to the basic story itself has produced widely diverging interpretations of Jesus as an anti-Roman revolutionary or a "meek moral teacher who ... comes to grief".[38] But even worse than this apparent inability of allegedly scientific analysis to reach a consistent portrait is the cumulative effect of this kind of inconclusive study: "If you read a number of these reconstructions one after the other, you see at once that far from uncovering an icon that has become obscured over time, they are much more like photographs of their authors and the ideals they hold. Since then there has been growing skepticism about these portrayals of Jesus, but the figure of Jesus himself has for that very reason receded even further into the distance."[39]

And the effect has gone even farther among scholars and ordinary believers alike:

> All these attempts have produced a common result: the impression that we have very little certain knowledge of Jesus and that only at a later stage did faith in his divinity shape the image we have of him. This impression has by now penetrated deeply into the minds of the Christian people at large. This is a dramatic situation for faith, because

[36] *Jesus of Nazareth: From the Baptism in the Jordan to the Transfiguration*, trans. Adrian J. Walker (New York et al.: Doubleday, 2007).

[37] Ibid., xxiii.

[38] Ibid., xii.

[39] Ibid.

> its point of reference is being placed in doubt: Intimate friendship with Jesus, on which everything depends, is in danger of clutching at thin air.[40]

Two points in particular are crucial in the Christian understanding, says Benedict: Christ's divinity in his relationship to the Father and his actual historical existence. Clearly, Trinitarian theology and the whole Judaeo-Christian belief in a God operative in history, first in the Jewish people and then in the Church, are inescapably mixed into the scholarly conflicts and confusions, as are the impenetrable mysteries of a being who is both God and man.

Benedict cites Rudolf Schnackenburg, "probably the most prominent Catholic exegete writing in German during the second half of the twentieth century",[41] as aware of the gulf that had opened between scholarship and faith and, by the end of his life, seeking to overcome it in several synthesizing works. Benedict proposes to do something similar himself, basing his analysis on *The Interpretation of the Bible in the Church* (1993) and *The Jewish People and Their Sacred Scriptures in the Christian Bible* (2001). But he emphasizes that the historical-critical method has to be, as it has been for more than a half century, a serious part of the conversation within the Church because the very fact of the Incarnation requires us to think through, not myths or stories or "symbolizing suprahistorical truths",[42] but the concrete human and historical foundation of the Christian faith: the earthly existence of Jesus, true God and also true man. Without the commitment to the real history of a real human person, we would be practicing a different faith.

But to say that the historical-critical method is indispensable to traditional Christian belief does not mean it is exhaustive or always a reliable guide. In Benedict's formulation, historical study by its very nature is limited to investigating things that are in the past or attitudes, such as those of the NT writers and their intentions in producing the Gospels, Acts, letters, and other texts in our NT canon. Even if the historical-critical method seeks to draw parallels with the present, it does not, if it remains true to itself, get involved in trying to see what

[40] Ibid.

[41] Ibid., xii–xiii.

[42] Ibid., xv.

about the past is living in the present. To say that the method has limits is not to say it is wrong; its limits, like those of any science properly undertaken, define an area in which it makes its most precise and valuable contributions. In this particular case, history will not venture into the spiritual or theological. Its specific object is "the human word as human".[43] A noble perspective on the method by Benedict, but a nobility more honored in the breach than in the observance.

Even so simple a thing for the Church as the unity of all the books included in the Bible is something that historical studies either cannot reach or have a hard time justifying, though in actual fact those texts have been joined for many years. But in this very lack, says Benedict, the method shows it needs other methods; it looks to complementary studies to try to answer questions it cannot. Like the commission, he cites Brevard Childs of Yale University and a whole school of exegetes who grew up around him and virtually invented the discipline known as canonical criticism, which takes as its starting point the books of the Bible already assembled and interrelated. From this quite different point of departure, it can look at the reciprocal ways in which the texts contribute to the formation or reading of one another, since many of the human authors understood themselves to be writing precisely in such relationships with other texts. The unity of Scripture, says Benedict, is a *theological datum*, but nonetheless it is not merely imposed from the outside. It has an organic, living existence in the historical developments by which texts are rereceived, reread, reinterpreted in light of new circumstances. Yet there is reason, "historical reason", in this process.

The pope also points to a complex reality familiar to many scholars in literary studies but usually less so among Scripture scholars. All human utterances contain elements that go beyond what the human authors intend. Although Benedict does not use the term, some literary scholars consider it an "intentional fallacy", as we noted earlier, to think that the meaning of a work is solely what the author says he meant or some critic claims the author meant. Even merely human statements contain more than the author may be aware of. And when the author is engaged in writing something that is divinely inspired—something history as such can neither confirm nor deny—the old

[43] Ibid., xvii.

question in scriptural studies of authorial intention reveals itself to be a real but highly circumscribed area, and the contours of what inspiration might mean become better delineated.

Modern hermeneutics help a great deal here. Benedict accurately describes how the Scriptures are not mere disparate texts written by isolated individuals. They consist in writings that emerge from "the heart of a living subject—the pilgrim People of God".[44] As such, there are three "subjects" involved in their production. First, a human writer who is part of this community that draws out ever new living meaning from previous texts; second, the people of God provide a certain context, particularly because, third, they are "of God". But being "of God" also implies a certain self-transcendence in identity in a community that allows itself to be "ordered, guided, and led by him".[45]

For Benedict, this leads to a basic trust in the Jesus as portrayed in the Gospels. All attempts to reduce him to something more naturalistic, more manageable within the categories of secular history or academic settings fail to account for the remarkable effects he had on his immediate followers and subsequent history. Those facts, too, need to be registered in a scientific, critical assessment. And Benedict finds it unpersuasive to assume that the Christology that was already in place a mere twenty years after Christ's death was the creation of the anonymous community:

> How could these unknown groups be so creative? How were they so persuasive and how did they manage to prevail? Isn't it more logical, even historically speaking, to assume that the greatness came at the beginning, and that the figure of Jesus really did explode all existing categories and could only be understood in the light of the mystery of God?... Though the New Testament writings display a many-layered struggle to come to grips with the figure of Jesus, they exhibit a deep harmony despite all their differences.[46]

That, of course, has been the main bone of contention between the strict historians with their fragmentary reconstructions, on the one

[44] Ibid., xx.
[45] Ibid., xxi.
[46] Ibid., xxii–xxiii.

hand, and, on the other hand, all those who still find the NT texts as we have them—with their general agreement on the ministry, Passion, crucifixion, and Resurrection, as well as their importance for all the human race—to be the most reliable framework for understanding Jesus.

Conclusion: The Three Generations

Luke Timothy Johnson cleverly compares the stages of Catholic biblical scholarship in the twentieth century with the experience of immigrants in America. We can see, he says, that there are three periods in the scholarship: (1) a mostly precritical period up to *Divino Afflante Spiritu*; then, (2) a fervent embrace of historical-critical approaches, once they were permitted, which ran through the Council and on for the next quarter century or more; and (3) finally, a critical turn about the historical-critical method itself by Catholic scholars fully at home in the new methodologies but increasingly aware of their limitations, especially their distance from the needs of the Church and the life of faith. These are similar, Johnson argues, to the experience of immigrant families in that the old generation was like someone who came to America fully formed in European roots but able to live in the alien atmosphere of a new culture with minimal adaptation; the second generation, the children of those immigrants, often wanted nothing to do with the old ways and wished to become fully American; and finally, the third generation takes Americanness for granted and would like to know Grandma's recipe for *ossobuco*.[47]

More than just a clever image, however, this comparison captures some real questions that need to be put to Scripture scholarship. The "scientific" study of texts, for example, has a limited but real value in helping us toward understanding the historical setting in which Jesus lived and the possible history of composition of the biblical texts as we have them. But anyone of any degree of historical sophistication

[47] See his chapter, "What's Catholic about Catholic Biblical Scholarship?" in Luke Timothy Johnson and William S. Kurz, S.C., *The Future of Catholic Biblical Scholarship: A Constructive Conversation* (Grand Rapids, Mich.: Eerdmans, 2002), 3–34.

will understand that these reconstructions are by their very nature speculative, not scientific. Since we do not have the Q document, for example, which various scholars have posited with some plausibility as one source of Jesus' sayings, we do not know whether it really existed or whether some other theory, yet to be proposed, might better explain the commonalities among the Gospels or their order of composition. By the time we get whole volumes being written—indeed an "International Q Project" was created in the 1980s—with great assurance about the "three layers" that must have existed in a document we are not even sure existed, something has gone terribly wrong even with the scientific study of the texts.[48] It would not be entirely wrong to say that much of nineteenth-century scholarship, primarily as done in Germany under certain assumptions, has now fallen by the wayside. And much scholarship in the twentieth century that was based on those assumptions—even when it departed from earlier conclusions—is in an equally precarious state as scholars have begun to ask different questions.

Another point that Johnson and many others with different views from his have emphasized is that the academic study of the Bible is, crucially, divorced from the Christian community. In fact, the German scholarship that largely shaped modern critical methods looked with suspicion on what it regarded as developments from some Ur-Gospel—additions that appeared to some Protestants as "Catholic" accretions on Jesus' pure message. Though the scholars themselves could not agree on what that prior message was, somehow they regarded any acceptance of the communal tradition as necessarily tainted with institutionalization of authority and the "routinization of charisma". But a Catholic, even a Catholic critically aware of such developments, might argue that whatever additions may have occurred might also be seen as legitimate enrichments or attempts within the early Church to sift what was widely recognized as authentic from what was not. The multiple attestations we have, for example, to basic agreement on the authoritative NT texts might lead an unbiased observer to conclude that even among the differing churches around the Mediterranean basin in the first Christian centuries, there was broad agreement on certain basic lines.

[48] Cf. Allen, *The Human Christ*, 269–71.

In addition to these difficulties within modern scriptural scholarship, there is a problem about the cultural location of such scholarship outside of the churches. Since academic etiquette frowns on connections with particular communities of believers as by nature biases rather than, like the academic community itself, a helpful tradition of understanding and application, modern biblical scholarship, which largely takes place at secular institutions, finds itself in the unhappy position of claiming authority over a text with little significance divorced from its importance to Christian believers. If Christianity as traditionally understood in the life of many of those believers is really illegitimate or unfounded or actually to be opposed, it would be difficult to see why state monies should be spent on the study of the Bible rather than, say, Babylonian or Egyptian studies.

It is unlikely that even the third-generation scholars, Catholic or Protestant, will make much headway against this academic guild, since the promotion and tenure process tends to perpetuate existing practices, much as happens in the creation of bishops or cardinals in the Catholic Church. In the latter case, however, there is a self-conscious rationale operative: the Church seeks to hand down a tradition (that is what tradition is) that is both faithful to an originating experience and adaptable to new conditions. It is precisely here that a different kind of third-generation scholarship may be useful if fully trained Scripture scholars who understand both the uses and limits of the historical methods, but are faithful to the Catholic tradition, carefully go about an attempt to reconnect with their great forebears without losing what is good in current scholarship.

This of course is no easy undertaking, and for the moment it is difficult to say how this new synthesis of the historical-critical and the tradition might become possible even within Catholic institutions. There seems still to exist a sense, held over from conciliar times, sometimes by people trained by people who suffered under preconciliar narrowness, that any effort to reconnect with precritical Catholic exegesis will lead to the old refusal to engage modern thought. Anything is possible in human affairs, but the opposite danger seems far more likely at the beginning of the twenty-first century—that the dismissal of almost two millennia of Christian self-understanding by a historical criticism all too confident that it represents a neutral scientific study of biblical texts will simply result in an unbridged gap between scholars and ordinary believers. This is not a healthy or happy situation, even for scholars who feel answerable only to their fellows within self-enclosed guilds, much less for a Church committed to seeing all truth, from whatever source, as coming ultimately from God.

Part Two

CREED AND CULTURE

Chapter 8

The Emergence of Culture as Protagonist

There is a small terrace on the Capitoline Hill in Rome that overlooks the Forum and thousands of years of pagan and Christian history. On that spot, you can still drink water from the Aqua Marcia, the longest of the ancient aqueducts that brought water down from the hills east of Rome. Immediately below are the Umbilicus Urbis Romae, the "navel" from which all distances were measured in the Roman Empire, and the Rostrum, where Cicero's head and hands were nailed after he was executed during the Roman Revolution. Tucked into the hillside is the Mamertine Prison, where Saints Peter and Paul were held at different times before being executed in places outside the old city. A copy of the Equestrian Statue of the emperor-philosopher Marcus Aurelius stands in the piazza nearby, and at the foot of the hill a monument to the fiery fourteenth-century Roman revolutionary Cola di Rienzo. In short, from that spot, an informed visitor can take in much of Rome's pagan and Christian culture in a single glance. Though that long history was only rediscovered, piecemeal, beginning in the Renaissance, a rediscovery that is still ongoing today, enough was still visible that it stimulated the young Edward Gibbon to write: "It was at Rome, on the fifteenth of October 1764, as I sat musing amidst the ruins of the Capitol, while the barefooted fryars were singing Vespers in the temple of Jupiter, that the idea of writing the decline and fall of the City first started to my mind."[1] The result was *The Decline and Fall of the Roman Empire.*

On Easter Day 1909, a nineteen-year-old Englishman sat on the same spot. He felt moved by something he later described as a kind of mystical experience to undertake an equally ambitious project, in several respects a rebuttal of Gibbon's account of the decay of pagan

[1] *The Autobiographies of Edward Gibbon*, ed. John Murray, 2nd ed. (London: John Murray, 1897), 137.

Roman virtue through the corrupting influence of Christianity: an ambitious history of human culture, including quite emphatically the importance of Christian culture to understanding and restoring the modern world. In a later journal entry, he described his plan as, in fact, "a vow made at Easter in the Ara Coeli" and added that, since the initial inspiration, he had received "great light on the way it may be carried out. However unfit I may be, I believe it is God's will I should attempt it."[2] Whatever is to be made of this story—Rome often bewitches Romantic temperaments—the sequel, though slow in developing, was quite impressive and was to have widespread influence on both Catholic historical self-understanding and the view of its relation to modern culture, both inside and outside the Church.

After almost two decades, including fourteen years of quiet but intense reading and preparation, the author finally published his first book, *The Age of the Gods: A Study in the Origins of Culture in Prehistoric Europe and the Ancient Near East* (1928), which was intended as the first of a comprehensive, global, five-volume history of culture. He followed the first with two other volumes in the series: *Progress and Religion* (1929) and *The Making of Europe* (1931), but never finished the final two. Nonetheless, he was immediately recognized as a major cultural voice. T. S. Eliot thought him "the most powerful intellectual influence in England"[3] and invited him to become a regular contributor to his journal, *The Criterion*, as did the editors of other prestigious publications. By the time his 1948–1949 Gifford Lectures at the University of Edinburgh were published under the title of *Religion and the Rise of Western Culture*, the praise was universal. *The Saturday Review* called the author "the most exciting writer of our day" and "unequaled as a historian of culture". *The New York Times* characterized him as having few rivals "for breadth of knowledge and lucidity of style". In England, the reaction was, if anything, even more effusive. *The Spectator* called *Religion and the Rise of Western Culture* "one of the most noteworthy books produced in this generation". The author's old tutor at Oxford, the eminent professor of classical political philosophy Sir Ernest Barker, referred

[2] Quoted in Christina Scott, *A Historian and His World: A Life of Christopher Dawson, 1889–1970* (New York: Sheed & Ward, 1984), 49.

[3] Ibid., 210.

to him as "a man and a scholar of the same sort of quality as Acton and von Hügel".[4]

These accolades make it all the odder that today hardly anyone even knows the name of one of the twentieth century's greatest historians and cultural commentators: Christopher Dawson. Several factors may help account for this. First, Dawson converted to Catholicism after his Roman experience, in part because he believed that Catholic culture was a central and overlooked feature in the West, and he was greatly concerned about the future of Western civilization. For Dawson, real existing Catholicism came, primarily, not out of ancient or medieval Christianity—periods he admired but thought were being overemphasized by certain modern Catholic apologists—but from more recent centuries of Christian humanism, which is the true core of Western culture. And therefore the best path to a revitalization of the spiritual underpinnings of the West lay, in his view, in the study of Christian culture. He even outlined a program of studies for Catholic colleges and universities for this very purpose,[5] and a few Catholic institutions created programs along the lines he suggested.

Christian culture as a specific subject offers many advantages, not least that it can be clearly identified and approached in much the same way that we can study Meso-American or classical Greco-Roman culture. Christian humanism arises in the late Middle Ages and the Renaissance and underpins the recovery of classical antiquity, the new growth of art, and the development of early modern science. To overlook that Christian humanism—and the role it has played in shaping Western culture, even in its now mostly post-Christian form—would be to misconceive the modern world and to leave it both culturally and spiritually rootless. And any living thing cut off from the sources of its life is living on borrowed time.

It was on this crucial point that Dawson challenged not only Gibbon but a whole English and European tradition that believed that for humanism to emerge, Christianity had to recede. These are deep historical and spiritual matters and difficult to frame clearly. But it is

[4] Ibid., 110.

[5] See Christopher Dawson, *The Crisis of Western Education*, with a new introduction by Glenn W. Olsen (Washington, D.C.: Catholic University of America Press, 2010), a reprint of the 1961 original.

evident that Dawson's approach is far more wide-ranging and sympathetic to the large contours of human history than that of most historians who concern themselves with such matters. He praised Gibbon, for example, for having labored to carry out a careful and factual study of the past, as opposed to French figures like Voltaire and Bayle and Leclerc who were content to make large philosophical statements without much exact historical knowledge. Yet Gibbon shared some of their narrowness in philosophic sympathies. As Dawson wrote in an essay on Gibbon in the 1930s, "The leaders of eighteenth-century thought often show a positive contempt and hatred for the past. Or else they write as though they had transcended the limitations of time by an effort of pure reason so that they could look down on history from the summit of their philosophy with an Olympian detachment and calm."[6] As a result, they (including Gibbon) typically regarded only four periods as worthy of study: classical Greece, Augustan Rome, Renaissance Italy, and the France of Louis XIV.

To a man like Dawson, whose first book was on the Stone Age and whose thought ranged widely over cultures from the Americas to the whole of European history to the Far East, this was a stunted view of the human. And it stemmed primarily from the fact that specifically religious values were an "unknown dimension" to minds like Gibbon's. Evelyn Waugh was to satirize this blindness, while pointing out Gibbon's literary gifts, in his novel *Helena*. There, an ancient historian says:

> "Suppose that in years to come, when the church's troubles seem to be over, there should come an apostate of my own trade, a false historian, with the mind of Cicero or Tacitus and the soul of an animal," and he nodded toward the gibbon who fretted his golden chain and chattered for fruit. "A man like that might make it his business to write down the martyrs and excuse the persecutors. He might be refuted again and again but what he wrote would remain in people's minds when the refutations were quite forgotten. That is what style does—it has the Egyptian secret of the embalmers. It is not to be despised."[7]

[6] Christopher Dawson, "Edward Gibbon and the Fall of Rome", in *The Dynamics of World History*, ed. John J. Mulloy (Wilmington, Del.: ISI Books, 2002), 341.

[7] Evelyn Waugh, *Helena: A Novel* (Boston: Little Brown, 1950), 116.

Dawson himself was too scrupulously fair a man to put things quite this sharply, but in his own way he not only offered another refutation of Gibbon's historiography—many modern historians have done that as well—but, by the charm of his own thought, imagination, and style, sought to shift our global understanding of Christianity's importance to a true humanism.

This has been a major bone of contention in the modern world. As we have seen in previous chapters, it revolves around the question of whether the properly and fully human can be understood apart from God. One current in Western thought certainly believes that the answer is yes and that bowing to a being above the human and the world has only given risen to tyranny and limited human freedom. The disasters of the twentieth century—Marxism, Nazism, Fascism—which arose from a "humanistic" perspective, have raised many questions about the "human, all too human" (in Nietzsche's phrase) absent God. Dostoyevsky, of course, predicted before these movements ever got going that "if God does not exist, all things are permissible." The slaughters of the twentieth century destroyed a certain type of optimism, but in other quarters—now more liberal, democratic, and postmodern—the dream of a free humanity in control of its own destiny has taken new forms. Despite Nietzsche's contention that it is an impossibility, there are strenuous efforts to preserve some of the old Christian morals in the absence of the Christian faith.[8]

Culture, of course, is a more nebulous reality than philosophy or ethics or theology. And in several respects, it is more important precisely because it insinuates itself into individuals and societies, almost beyond the control of any person or group. The influential Italian Marxist Antonio Gramsci was fond of arguing that Communists should take a lesson from the Jesuits who had been in the forefront of the battle against the Protestants in the Catholic Counter-Reformation. Through their teaching and broad cultural influence, they had established a *cultura capillare*, a "capillary culture" that had infused the farthest nooks and crannies of Europe. Not only had it carried the day by explicit argument, but its general presence was such that it was

[8] Luc Ferry, *A Brief History of Thought: A Philosophical Guide to Living*, trans. Theo Cuffe (New York: Harper Perennial, 2011), is a serious effort along these lines, though ultimately a failure.

difficult to dislodge via any single frontal attack. That sort of religious culture, which Gramsci hoped could be imitated by Marxists in the twentieth century, dominates almost passively and persists out of its own resources and life scattered over many millions of lives.

In the modern world, as Popes John Paul II and Benedict XVI have argued brilliantly, a different culture has been diffused that makes it hard for the religious argument to get a hearing. This shift has occurred quite rapidly. For almost his whole adult life (he died in 1970), it seemed that Christopher Dawson had caused a major shift in cultural and historical thinking, not only within Catholicism but outside of it, to no small degree, as well. But that perspective seems to have evaporated by the last third of the twentieth century. In the mid-1950s, Harvard's Dean Douglas Horton recruited Dawson as the first Chauncey Stillman Professor of Roman Catholic Studies, telling Dawson that the invitation was "the most important I have ever had the honor of carrying". Like Maritain's in philosophy, Dawson's multidisciplinary forays into anthropology, sociology, ethnology, history, religion, and culture—which in addition to his own individual genius were also inspired by a more general modern rebirth of Catholic intellectual life—gained recognition in the very highest academic circles. Dawson taught at Harvard from 1958 to 1962, the key years just prior to the Second Vatican Council. And he might have stayed in the New World's Cambridge if ill health had not forced him to return to England. Since then, however, Dawson's belief in religion as a central explanatory factor in the human record—from the Stone Age practices in the "age of the gods" down to the post-Enlightenment forms of religion in the developed world—and as the cult that inspires the culture has receded in academic life, at Harvard and very often in Catholic institutions of higher learning as well.

Instead of believing in the historical importance of religion and the kind of culture to which it gives rise, we tend to believe that race, gender, and class or large economic and political forces are what make the world move, and then we are surprised when we find that people are willing to commit suicide, blow up the World Trade Center towers or each other, or suffer torture and death over religious belief. After the great cultural revolution of the 1960s, which Dawson already sensed to be coming as early as the 1920s, an implicit materialism became the great explanatory key. As Dawson remarked in one of his early essays: "Only the most robust optimist can deny that a new barbarism, manifold and incoherent, is threatening not only the material order which was the work of the last [that is, nineteenth] century, but the whole intellectual tradition on which Western culture has been based."[9] The immediate threats were Fascism, Nazism, and Communism, but Dawson knew that the drive for power, not freedom and spiritual balance, had eaten deeply into the Western democratic heritage as well.

And this was reflected in large-scale institutional shifts: "In the modern state the mind of the average citizen is moulded by the government school and the popular press, and these afford no genuine substitute for the more profound spiritual guidance that was provided by the teaching of the old religious traditions."[10] By the time he died, both the Catholic Church and the world had left behind his legacy and much of the Catholic intellectual revival of which he was such a prominent leader. This was a serious loss. As the English Dominican Aidan Nichols has rightly observed, the whole of Dawson's work constitutes a kind of latter-day *City of God*. And like Augustine's work by that name, Dawson's elaborated a compelling Christian account of human history and on a far vaster scale than was possible in Augustine's day, given its limited knowledge about distant cultures.

Dawson's historical thinking was enriched and, in a sense, stabilized by his study of Catholic philosophy and theology. Much recent historical, sociological, and anthropological work—as he pointed out—has swung between two extremes, two reductive visions that seemed to exclude one another. In a figure like Oswald Spengler or Marx, the material side of human existence dominates and gives rise to a doctrinaire materialism that simply leaves out much of the specifically human. In the early modern sociologists, Dawson pointed out, the importance of biology (today it would be genetic inheritance), place, and economy were properly brought into view. Human beings have not only material being but a material inheritance that has to be looked at both in the sociological snapshot of immediate analysis as well as in historical perspective

[9] "Civilisation and Order", *Order*, vol. 1, no. 2 (August 1928): 42.

[10] Christopher Dawson, *Enquiries into Religion and Culture*, with an introduction by Robert Royal (Washington, D.C.: Catholic University of America Press, 2009), 49.

across time (diachronically, in the technical jargon). But this way of seeing things leaves out the crucial human difference: the intellectual or spiritual dimension—notably apparent in the fact of language—that strongly marks out *Homo sapiens*, the human animal, who differs from all the other animals on earth.

It was partly in reaction to the overemphasis on material factors that idealism—and especially the Hegelian notion of history as the passage of Absolute Spirit through time—exerted a strong influence on historical theory for a considerable period. Dawson, of course, believed in God who is the Absolute Spirit, but he saw Hegelianism as a different reductionism and regarded it as a "spiritual" oversimplification to posit the system of thesis-antithesis-synthesis as a full account of spirit in the world. Such high-level abstraction falsified the historical record—history shows many steps backward as well as forward, and many historical particulars have to be stretched or ignored to fit into the Procrustean bed of the System. There is no automatic process of greater and greater truth and progress in a species that, individually and in communal groups, is capable of sudden bursts of self-defeating violence and returns to mindless savagery, as became clear to many thinkers during the twentieth century's global wars.

But Dawson did not stop there. He noted that even though the elaborate Hegelian system, a typical product of Continental philosophizing, had been largely abandoned by his day, related notions remained among less systematic thinkers of the liberal school. Liberalism incorporates some of the deeper Western ideas drawn from the millennia of Judaeo-Christian tradition and therefore has managed to survive down to the present, but Dawson saw in it both strengths and a fatal flaw:

> The Liberal movement, with its humanitarian idealism and its beliefs in the law of nature and the rights of man, owes its origin to an irregular union between the humanist tradition and a religious ideal that was inspired by Christian moral values, though not by Christian faith.... The whole development of liberalism and humanitarianism, which has been of such immense importance in the history of the modern world, derived its spiritual impetus from the Christian tradition that it attempted to replace, and when that tradition disappears this spiritual

> impetus is lost, and liberalism in its turn is replaced by the crudity and amoral ideology of the totalitarian state.[11]

That was written in an essay on "The Eclipse of Europe" in 1951. More than half a century later, the process Dawson described has spread to such an extent that it is much farther advanced and much more easily seen. And it has spread so that, virtually everywhere, "European" influence and values—other than science and technology—are rapidly disappearing and being replaced by other values quite foreign to the Western tradition. As he put it in *Progress and Religion*, one of his most powerful books, "Even when he [the average modern man] had lost his faith in Reason, he still believed in science, and in the final character of the new scientific culture."[12]

"Belief" is the operative term here, because a new faith had emerged that made it hard to preserve the old human things, no matter how much proponents of the new scientific "culture" professed humane aims—which are difficult to justify under a regime of strict materialism. As Vladimir Soloviev once remarked, it is quite a stretch to say: "Man is descended from monkeys; therefore let us love one another." In Dawson's view, only a full notion of the human person—one significantly shaped in Dawson's own case by the Aristotelian-Thomistic sense of man as a composite being of body and spirit—enables us to do justice to ourselves and to the historical record. To say this is not to deny that, at a given historical moment, some almost purely material or purely spiritual or intellectual factor may explain developments. Neither does Dawson's acceptance of the philosophical and theological truths of the Christian tradition lead him to treat history itself as unimportant compared with eternity or to solve concrete historical questions by means of large, non-historical principles. Indeed, one of his most obvious strengths is his encyclopedic learning and the attention he gives to historical detail.

In this fuller historical approach, he was working somewhat in parallel to some of the practitioners of *la nouvelle théologie* we encountered

[11] Dawson, *Dynamics of World History*, 424.

[12] Christopher Dawson, *Progress and Religion*, with a foreword by Christina Scott and an introduction by Mary Douglas (Washington, D.C.: Catholic University of America Press, 2001), 29.

in earlier chapters, who appreciated Aquinas but wanted to situate his work in the larger sweep of Christian thought and life. As Dawson argued, a Christian view of history does not stem from the Greek sources but from the Jewish sense of a God active in time—and engaged with men for his own purposes. That is the story told in the Old Testament and, in the culminating moment of the Incarnation, in the New Testament as well. For Dawson, this meant that a Christian view of history "is not a secondary element derived by philosophical reflection from the study of history. It lies at the very heart of Christianity and forms an integral part of the Christian faith."[13]

To posit a God who is always and everywhere active in human history makes the historian see the past in a different light. Unlike the sociologists and anthropologists of his day, who often studied early people as a now-superseded form of human existence, Dawson saw fundamental continuities in all cultures. In particular, he argued that "primitive religion" was not a fanciful superstructure built on the material existence of early peoples or a "deification" of the community, as Emile Durkheim had famously argued. Dawson carefully demonstrated from the historical and anthropological materials available to him that the spiritual dimension was a sense of the transcendent that always accompanied primitive peoples' sense of the physical world.

For similar reasons, Dawson was also critical of historians of culture like Arnold Toynbee, who in their large-scale assertions generally classified elements like simple village life as superseded by large cultural and civilizational forms. In this, his own personal history—most of his life was spent in private study in the family home in the lush English countryside—contributed to his more strictly intellectual effort. For Dawson, the full range of humanity is always in play, and even in the moments when a one-sided or narrow expression of social life is evident—or an extraneous force like a plague or invasion produces unpredicted effects—they are best appraised by the historian from the standpoint of a richer and more detailed anthropology.

He often used a phrase that might be easily misunderstood: "the organic nature of society", which might make it appear as if historical causes and influences cannot be clearly identified. That is far from

[13] Christopher Dawson, "The Christian View of History", in *Christianity and European Culture: Selections from the Work of Christopher Dawson*, ed. Gerald J. Russello (Washington, D.C.: Catholic University of America Press, 1998), 214.

being the case. He used the term only to point out that a culture has to be a living thing—or it is a dead or dying thing. He had good reason to address this question because it was clear to anyone with eyes to see in the first half of the twentieth century that Western civilization was in a profound crisis—still dominant materially, but largely cut off from its cultural, historical, and spiritual roots. It continued on because of the accumulated sap it had absorbed from the past, but there was—and still is—a large question as to how long it can continue to do so without the spiritual element that is the living energy of every culture.

Considerations like these led Dawson to make some preliminary studies toward a kind of world history that would do justice to individual civilizations while recognizing not only that the world—and therefore human life—was becoming unified via modern technologies, but that the time was approaching when some sort of account would have to be given of the human past in order to help light the way toward the future. This would have to be carried out, as Dawson admitted, even though no one as yet could count on careful enough studies of the various cultures, civilizations, regions, and historical periods to be able to do so with any great degree of confidence. But that did not lessen the urgency of finding some way to envision the totality of human life on earth.

The older periodization of Western civilization—ancient, medieval, Renaissance, modern—was inadequate for this task. Dawson thought these divisions inadequate even to give an account of Western history. For example, the Renaissance has often been regarded in the usual historiography as a turn from religion and faith toward reason and science. As such, it would be a precursor of the modern. But Dawson and others—Wallace K. Ferguson, Hans Boersma, and many more recent scholars—looked closely at the record and saw that "Renaissance man" was a thoroughly Christian being despite efforts since the Enlightenment to claim him for modernity and skepticism—or outright atheism. Further, if any age may be said to have been marked by a vigorous use of reason, it was the high Middle Ages. The early Renaissance figures fled that hyper-rational Scholasticism because they wished to focus more on morality, aesthetics, and civic life—they became more humanist because less abstractly rational.

Dawson situated the whole of European development within a different scheme. First, there was a global movement from the primitive cultures in which human beings were still close to the earth and animal being but already possessed large, if unarticulated, intuitions about the things the human mind perceives beyond mere physical existence. Those intuitions received an articulation in the great archaic cultures, Dawson's second phase of world history—an important phase that has left many traces on human life, not least the traditions of great cities. The great world religions introduced yet another watershed, Jaspers' "Axial Age", which saw the rise of the Greek philosophers and the Hebrew prophets, Buddha, and Confucius. Finally, for Dawson, there was the fourth age, the rise of science and technology, which he saw, contrary to many other analysts, as indebted in its modern and highly influential form to the Christian view of God, man, and nature.

One of the distinctive features on which Dawson insisted was the constant presence of religion across these ages and a certain continuity as well. The world religions do not entirely dispense with the primordial intuitions of the primitive age. And even our own day, whether it knows it or not, takes its impulse toward knowing creation and seeking to make it more human from a religious vision of the world. Furthermore, that vision is Christian. It is because the *Logos* lies behind the creation that the logical deductions of science can reach truth, for these are rooted in the prior belief in an ordered and partly intelligible universe. A religion that believed that the world is an illusion or that God acts capriciously as he wills could not arrive at a view of the creation as a reasonable, rational realm with its own discoverable laws and secondary causes. And as Benedict XVI argued repeatedly, this makes all the difference to how we look at ourselves as well: Are our minds simply a bubble of intelligence thrown up by forces of chaos and, therefore, freeing us to do whatever we want? Or is our thinking itself a product of that originating *Logos*, a participation in an ordered truth and a reality to which we owe our being and our allegiance?

For Dawson, the West has entered into a crisis because it has retained some of the older Christian values without the foundations on which they rest. Such a situation is by nature unstable, and developments since his day have shown it to be such. Human rights, for example, are an offshoot of the older Christian notion of the sacredness of the human person. Only man, the composite of body and rational soul, could be the bearer of rights because only man has both the intelligence and will to choose good or evil and the freedom that makes such a choice possible. That is one reason why men and their consciences have been given certain protections in the West.

But without the religious framework in which such notions operate, dangers immediately come to the surface. Modern science and technology, it is now clear, even to many who do not consider themselves religious, have disenchanted the world to such an extent that they threaten both the environment on which we depend and the human ecology that enables us to flourish as full human beings. Even human rights can quickly degenerate into a dangerous set of ideas if one believes there is no truth—only the deliverances of individual human wills—or that, as in widespread abortion, one human being may take the life of another for reasons of self-interest. Such contradictions become inevitable once a culture tries to make material or technological advances a substitute for religion and a fully human culture, which are ruled out in advance by a materialist ideology.

Christopher Dawson understood this large-scale crisis in the West quite early and knew that the only remedy is for the culture to rediscover its roots in the Christian religion. As he was already saying in his 1933 book *Enquiries into Religion and Culture*:

> It is no more possible for society to live by bread alone than it is for the individual. Technology and material organisation are not enough. If our civilisation is to recover its vitality, or even to survive, it must cease to neglect its spiritual roots and must realise that religion is not a matter of personal sentiment which has nothing to do with the objective realities of society, but is, on the contrary, the very heart of social life and the root of every living culture. The desecularisation of modern civilisation is no easy matter; at first sight it may seem a hopeless task. But we can at least prepare the way for it by desecularising our intellectual outlook and opening our eyes to the existence of the spiritual forces that create and transform civilisation.[14]

One of the ways that "desecularization" has gotten a significant foothold in modern Western culture is via Christian art—particularly Christian literature. In the following chapters, we will look at some of the most eminent modern writers in the Catholic tradition, all

[14] Dawson, *Enquiries into Religion and Culture*, xxi–xxii.

of whom show a vigorous engagement with the modern world. Some—Belloc and Chesterton most notably—take a rather militant approach to contemporary culture, even if they do so with great wit and charm. Others examine the struggle between good and evil in individual human hearts and how that struggle impacts the wider world. In every case, we see in these figures concrete examples of how a Christian culture has found a way to express itself even in a society that denies many of its starting points and modes of expression. The result—varied, creative, charismatic—gives witness that a Catholic culture can exist and continue to put out fresh shoots even where mere abstract analysis might think it all but impossible.

Chapter 9

Freshness Deep Down Things: The Catholic Literary Revival

Christopher Dawson identified the large cultural-historical context facing Catholicism in the modern world. But there was a more personal dimension to that context that many Catholic writers began to explore in response—and often enough an urgent personal dimension. In Muriel Spark's novel *The Girls of Slender Means*, for example, one of the characters—bewildered by modern life as many people were in the twentieth century—confesses that things had come to such a critical pass that he could "never make up his mind between suicide and an equally drastic course of action known as Father D'Arcy."[1] Martin D'Arcy, S.J., was a real-life priest at London's Farm Street Church who guided a number of eminent Britons, including Evelyn Waugh, into the Church. Not all of them were quite so desperate. But Spark—herself a convert—had noted something in the secularized society of modern England, right on the verge of the cultural revolution of the 1960s, that we have also seen at the very beginning of the present volume in the mutual suicide pact of Jacques and Raïssa Maritain: with the disappearance of God, at least some of the more sensitive hearts and minds, even in solid, well-off, middle-class nations, sensed that the starkest of alternatives had emerged amidst all the wealth and leisure and "culture"—for anyone who wanted to live a genuine and meaningful life.

In England, a Catholic literary revival began long before World War I, which is to say, it was well underway prior to the first of the two major cataclysms that shook the dominant Western faith in progress and Enlightenment rationality in the twentieth century. England had had an early start toward this revival with truly world-class figures

[1] Muriel Spark, *The Girls of Slender Means* (New York: Knopf, 1963), 63.

such as John Henry Newman and one of his students, the great poet Gerard Manley Hopkins (Hopkins died in 1889; his poems were written before, but not published until after, the First World War and became a landmark in twentieth-century English poetry). Matthew Arnold, perhaps the greatest non-Christian commentator on culture in nineteenth-century England, famously wrote in his poem "Dover Beach" (1867) that he thought he heard the "withdrawing roar" of the sea of faith. And in several respects, of course, that proved to be the case. But at the very same time, that withdrawal also created a countercurrent over the next century, a veritable tidal wave of great Catholic literature and other Catholic cultural artifacts in English: a broad arc composed mostly of converts stretching from Newman and Hopkins through Oscar Wilde, Robert Hugh Benson (son of an archbishop of Canterbury), E. I. Watkin, Ronald Knox, Maurice Baring, and G. K. Chesterton to another generation in Graham Greene, Evelyn Waugh, Alec Guinness, Muriel Spark, Siegfried Sassoon, Edith Sitwell, Malcolm Muggeridge, and the most globally influential of all: J. R. R. Tolkien.

What were the characteristics of the nineteenth century that turned many distinguished minds in Britain toward the Catholic Church? It was not poverty or political oppression. Wealth began to grow for all at an unprecedented pace, and liberal democratic participation started to spread. The various revolutionary movements clustered around Marx—who wrote *Das Kapital* in London—were wrong in believing that they had scientifically demonstrated that capitalism and bourgeois democracy would dispossess the poor and marginalized. Everywhere the poor started to enjoy greater wealth and freedom, with obvious shortcomings and social disruptions as well. The workhouses and urban blight of Dickens were transitory phenomena. But anyone of a spiritual cast of mind might have predicted—and many did during the nineteenth century—that such wealth and freedom were profoundly empty and could not ultimately satisfy the human heart. Indeed, one of Marxism's attractions well into the twentieth century was that, over and above its materialist presuppositions and despite its colossal historical crimes and failures, it provided a seeming substitute for the meaning and enthusiasm formerly associated with religious faith.

The failure, as people at the time saw and later popes would emphasize, was a failure of anthropology, in the sense that a social ideal that saw only material prosperity and personal liberty as an end posited a truncated idea of man. By the naturalistic standards of the nineteenth century, people in that age and in the years since should have become more and more fulfilled, more and more *human*, owing to material and social conditions better suited to human nature. Robert Hugh Benson's dystopian novel *Lord of the World* (1907) brilliantly predicted the ways that materialism and psychology would leave people in a grimly "humanist" world. And that was before the two world wars, the atomic bomb, the *Shoah*, and the ongoing restlessness of people in the most prosperous and freest nations known to history put an end to that illusion for all with eyes to see. But the more personal side of the problem was already clear to Matthew Arnold, who had written in "Dover Beach":

> Ah, love, let us be true
> To one another! for the world, which seems
> To lie before us like a land of dreams,
> So various, so beautiful, so new,
> Hath really neither joy, nor love, nor light,
> Nor certitude, nor peace, nor help for pain;
> And we are here as on a darkling plain
> Swept with confused alarms of struggle and flight,
> Where ignorant armies clash by night.

This was to place a heavy burden on love between man and woman—a burden that often proved unbearable, especially as culture itself started to thin out into a world with flattened dimensions. Arnold also famously argued in *Culture and Anarchy* (1869) that culture could function as a substitute for religion. But in a materialistic age, that proved no more durable or reliable than romantic love. In the twenty-first century, multiple forms of naturalism still hold out ultimate happiness based on material and social goods, but they have to make a more indirect case. The direct claims of the past about "progress"—a future of peace and plenty and secular humanist solidarity—are only useful today for beauty pageant contestants and politicians with very simple-minded constituents.

Still, why turn away from this wasteland toward Catholicism? In nineteenth-century England, Newman was indisputably a writer of the highest rank in his prose and, occasionally, came close to that level even in his verse ("The Pillar of the Cloud" and excerpts from his "Dream of Gerontius" regularly show up in secular anthologies of Victorian poetry—and the English Catholic composer Edward Elgar turned "Gerontius" into a much-admired choral work). Newman and the Oxford Movement within Anglicanism had, on good historical grounds, argued, as he famously put it, that "to be deep in history is to cease to be Protestant." He was to have a large influence on the intellectual profile of the Church in English-speaking countries and beyond. But Newman also laid out a particularly English stance toward both the decline in faith and the attenuation of the content of Christianity. As he expressed in his "Biglietto Speech" upon being made a cardinal:

> For thirty, forty, fifty years I have resisted to the best of my powers the spirit of Liberalism in religion. Never did Holy Church need champions against it more sorely than now, when, alas! it is an error overspreading, as a snare, the whole earth; and on this great occasion, when it is natural for one who is in my place to look out upon the world, and upon Holy Church as in it, and upon her future, it will not, I hope, be considered out of place, if I renew the protest against it which I have made so often.
>
> Liberalism in religion is the doctrine that there is no positive truth in religion, but that one creed is as good as another, and this is the teaching which is gaining substance and force daily. It is inconsistent with any recognition of any religion, as *true*. It teaches that all are to be tolerated, for all are matters of opinion. Revealed religion is not a truth, but a sentiment and a taste; not an objective fact, not miraculous; and it is the right of each individual to make it say just what strikes his fancy. Devotion is not necessarily founded on faith. Men may go to Protestant Churches and to Catholic, may get good from both and belong to neither. They may fraternise together in spiritual thoughts and feelings, without having any views at all of doctrines in common, or seeing the need of them. Since, then, religion is so personal a peculiarity and so private a possession, we must of necessity ignore it in the intercourse of man with man. If a man puts on a new religion every morning, what is that to you? It is as impertinent to think about a man's religion as about his sources of income or his management of his family. Religion is in no sense the bond of society.[2]

[2] Quoted in Wilfrid Ward, *The Life of John Henry Cardinal Newman* (New York et al.: Longmans, Green, 1912), 2:460.

Ronald Knox, a convert (who also went from Anglican clergyman to Catholic priest and, after being helped to the Church by reading Chesterton, helped Chesterton in his final steps toward the Church), wrote brilliantly of his conversion in his *A Spiritual Aeneid*. But his essential insight, like that of many other like-minded English converts, can be glimpsed in a few satirical verses from his poem about Anglican wishy-washiness, "Absolute and Abitofhell".

> When, on his Throne at Lambeth, Solomon
> Uneasy murmur'd, " Something must be done,"
> When suave Politeness, temp'ring bigot Zeal,
> Corrected, " I believe," to " One does feel."

That English reticence and vagueness about religious matters drove many to the then still clear doctrinal certainties of Rome.

Yet the Catholic revival in England was not conspicuously linked to the renaissance of Thomism or any other strict intellectual current in Catholicism. England produced distinguished Thomists such as Vincent McNabb, Victor White, Gerald Vann, Thomas Gilby, Kenelm Foster, Aidan Nichols, and many others. And the English Dominicans, especially at Blackfriars, performed a valuable service in publishing an annotated translation of Aquinas. But perhaps owing to the British pragmatic tendency to put practice above theory—as well as Newman's preference for the early Church Fathers over Aquinas—conversions and Catholic influence came less through purely intellectual channels and more by way of a general cultural approach. The two figures who dominate—in quite different ways—the earliest years of the twentieth century in English Catholic culture (and continue to exert great influence well into the twenty-first) are Hilaire Belloc and G.K. Chesterton. Though in strictly literary terms, they probably fall just short of the first rank for various reasons, both carried out rollicking apologetics in many books that are still read a century later. They both show great humor, high spirits, and multiple talents in prose and verse. Indeed, their humorous verses may be the very best things (from a purely literary standpoint) either ever did. But the fame of the Chesterbelloc—a term coined by George Bernard Shaw, a friend despite sharp disagreements with both Catholic figures, in just appreciation of the fact that they were joined in common purposes—rests on their power and cleverness in Christian apologetics and broad cultural commentary.

The Catholic Dr. Johnson

Hilaire Belloc (1870–1953) was the older of the two and a cradle Catholic, not a convert. He was born (appropriately, during a thunderstorm and as Vatican I was declaring the pope infallible in matters of faith and morals) at La Celle-Saint-Cloud just outside Paris to an English mother and French father.[3] His mother quickly nicknamed him "Old Thunder". Both parents had forebears distinguished in cultural fields including literature and painting. Belloc's mother was also the great-granddaughter of the chemist Joseph Priestley and moved in exalted Victorian literary circles. Belloc was educated in England (at the Edgbaston Oratory School, founded by Newman), where quite early he showed signs of rare literary gifts. But he spent summers in France, traveled back and forth across the Channel, and was fluent in both French and English. One of the conspicuous strengths he brought to Catholicism in England—besides being one of the greatest *talkers* of any age—was a concrete familiarity with Catholic culture and everyday life on the Continent. A vigorous man both physically and intellectually, he had to support himself by producing a steady stream of lively volumes on varied subjects—history, culture, warfare, religion—after, as he believed, he was denied a professorship at Oxford (where he had studied history) because of his Catholicism. He began working on some of the same historical problems that Christopher Dawson would later treat with equal power. But by temperament and choice, Belloc adopted a clever if pugnacious attitude toward Protestantism and its monopoly over English thought, which badly needed to be opened up beyond its standard cultural assumptions. Indeed, it might be said that Belloc's efforts to correct British insularity through his familiarity with continental Europe's deep historical links to the Church is a common feature among many of the great British figures in the modern Catholic literary revival.

[3] His father died young. Robert Speaight observes that if that had not happened, Belloc would have been "a Frenchman with an English mother instead of being an Englishman with a French father", with significant effects on the English Catholic literary revival. *The Life of Hilaire Belloc* (New York: Books for Library Press, 1970), 10.

Father Martin D'Arcy once characterized Belloc's stature quite justly, calling him the "Catholic Dr. Johnson",[4] an opinion echoed by the London *Times* at Belloc's death. Like Johnson, Belloc was not only a great writer but one of the period's most impressive personalities, as multiple witnesses have confirmed. From his days debating at the Oxford Union until a creeping senility began to rob him of his powers, he was a lively voice and presence in any company. But he was a *Catholic* Dr. Johnson and unapologetic about his faith, even in the midst of strong Protestant prejudice. In a notorious episode, during a political rally when he was standing for Parliament to represent South Salford, he was heckled for being a "papist". Belloc took out his rosary and replied, characteristically: "As far as possible I kneel down and tell these beads every day. If you reject me on account of my religion, I shall thank God that He has spared me the indignity of being your representative."[5] The crowd loved it, and Belloc won the seat.

But Belloc could be casually cantankerous in Catholic settings as well. In another well-known instance, he was once kneeling, in the French manner, during Mass at London's most magnificent Catholic church, Westminster Cathedral. A cathedral sacristan approached him:

"Excuse me, sir, we stand here."
"Go to hell."
"I'm sorry, sir, I didn't know you were a Catholic."[6]

And this was far from being the only instance in which piety and a certain brusqueness showed themselves, simultaneously, during Belloc's life. It might even be said that he thought the brusqueness one of the necessary elements of a real Catholic piety worthy of the name in the smug England of his time.

Yet his earliest books, and some of his very best, are volumes of light and clever children's poetry, particularly *The Bad Child's Book of Beasts, More Beasts for Worse Children*, and *Cautionary Verses*.[7] The last begins with an invocation to the young reader, which concludes:

[4] Quoted in Joseph Pearce, *Old Thunder: A Life of Hilaire Belloc* (San Francisco: Ignatius Press, 2002), 284.

[5] Ibid., 104.

[6] Quoted in Joseph Pearce, *Wisdom and Innocence: A Life of G. K. Chesterton* (San Francisco: Ignatius Press, 1997), 58.

[7] A comprehensive collection of these and other such books has been published under the title *Hilaire Belloc's Cautionary Verses* (New York: Knopf, 1981).

And when your prayers complete the day,
Darling, your little tiny hands
Were also made, I think, to pray
For men that lose their fairylands.

Both Belloc and Chesterton wrote brilliantly of this kind of childhood whimsy joined to more serious purposes. Both men expressed their deep veneration for innocence. And in a sense Chesterton, more than almost any twentieth-century writer, preserved over the course of his whole life a kind of extended child's delight in the world as the true stance of a Christian toward the creation. His poem "A Second Childhood" is a fair representation of the attitude of both men:

When all my days are ending
And I have no song to sing,
I think I shall not be too old
To stare at everything;
As I stared once at a nursery door
Or a tall tree and a swing.

Wherein God's ponderous mercy hangs
On all my sins and me,
Because He does not take away
The terror from the tree
And stones still shine along the road
That are and cannot be.

Men grow too old for love, my love,
Men grow too old for wine,
But I shall not grow too old to see
Unearthly daylight shine,
Changing my chamber's dust to snow
Till I doubt if it be mine.

Behold, the crowning mercies melt,
The first surprises stay;
And in my dross is dropped a gift
For which I dare not pray:
That a man grow used to grief and joy
But not to night and day.

Men grow too old for love, my love,
Men grow too old for lies;
But I shall not grow too old to see
Enormous night arise,
A cloud that is larger than the world
And a monster made of eyes.

Nor am I worthy to unloose
The latchet of my shoe;
Or shake the dust from off my feet
Or the staff that bears me through
On ground that is too good to last,
Too solid to be true.

Men grow too old to woo, my love,
Men grow too old to wed;
But I shall not grow too old to see
Hung crazily overhead
Incredible rafters when I wake
And I find I am not dead.

A thrill of thunder in my hair:
Though blackening clouds be plain,
Still I am stung and startled
By the first drop of the rain:
Romance and pride and passion pass
And these are what remain.

Strange crawling carpets of the grass,
Wide windows of the sky:
So in this perilous grace of God
With all my sins go I:
And things grow new though I grow old,
Though I grow old and die.[8]

Belloc's verses for children work along these same lines at times, but he also points to some clever morals. The first of Belloc's *Cautionary Tales* (some editions are entitled *Cautionary Verses*) is titled, "Jim,

[8] From *The Collected Works of G. K. Chesterton*, vol. 10: *Collected Poetry*, pt. 1, ed. Aidan Mackey (San Francisco: Ignatius Press, 1994), 250–51.

Who ran away from his Nurse, and was eaten by a Lion", and teaches the following lesson:

His Father, who was self-controlled,
Bade all the children round attend
To James' miserable end,
And always keep a-hold of Nurse
For fear of finding something worse.

Amid much inspired nonsense, holding on to the right authority recurs again and again until Belloc's *Ladies and Gentlemen* pronounces a religious variation on the following theme: "The moral is (it is indeed!), / You musn't monkey with the Creed."

Cardinal Manning of London, who had impressed Belloc's mother so much that she had become a Catholic, also exerted great influence on Belloc, as he did on the whole English Church of his day. Belloc met with him many times and always remembered a remark that the cardinal once made to him personally: "*All human conflict is ultimately theological.*"[9] This seed bore much fruit in Belloc's relentlessly militant reading of English and European history. Like Christopher Dawson, he brought a Catholic perspective to historical events that, often enough, illuminated various things left out of the standard Protestant histories—especially about England. For instance, he pointed out, again and again, that the British aristocracy got its great wealth from the plundering of the lands of the monasteries and the Church during the Reformation. And in his telling (not entirely accurate, as will appear below), it was upon this first injustice—more than the philandering of Henry VIII and the theological disputes with the Calvinists (though he denounced those, too)—that later social injustices were based. His perspective on the French Revolution in particular—especially that it took a wrong and unnecessary turn when it set Church and democracy against one another—is a position Belloc shared with Péguy. And he persuaded many in the English-speaking world who might otherwise have been inclined toward Edmund Burke's sharp critique of that foreign conflagration, not least Chesterton. Further, Belloc brought back into prominence a more general notion of religion as a crucial public, not merely a private, force in understanding past and present.

[9] Ian Turnbull Ker, *The Catholic Revival in English Literature, 1845–1961* (Leominster: Gracewing, 2003), 57–58.

Belloc's writing is always vigorous—a feat in itself because he had to turn out many books in a hurry to make a living (which may also have contributed some to his tendency toward sweeping "Catholic" explanations of complex historical questions). His first and perhaps most lasting book for adults, however, was *The Path to Rome*. The title is a literal one. As a cradle Catholic, Belloc did not need to write about a conversion—which the title might otherwise suggest to a modern reader. It recounts a pilgrimage he made on foot—"for my sins"—from Toul in Alsace, where he did his military service for a year in the French Army, over the Alps into Italy and down to Rome to be present on the Feast of Saints Peter and Paul. It is not exactly clear what provoked him to make that journey, though Belloc hints it had something to do with a painting of the Virgin Mary in his French birthplace. But whatever its religious origins, and for all its minor faults, the book is a classic: a marvelous account of an amazing solitary journey on foot over a remarkable landscape matched only by Belloc's great literary verve. And with an additional grace: like Chesterton, Belloc had gifts for drawing, and he illustrates with pencil sketches a terrain that, in places, would have killed many other men and very nearly killed him.

The whole work is permeated with a rare sense of independence and freedom—an almost primordial energy and simplicity. Belloc plays with an imaginary "Lector" for several pages at the beginning before getting down to business. This is unfortunate because it gives the wrong impression that the whole book will be aimless frivolity. That has no doubt kept a few readers from getting to the many memorable pages to come that recount adventures walking this demanding route and minute observations of people and nature rarely told with such power. (Two of Belloc's other volumes—*The Four Men*, a "farrago" about a hike across his native Sussex, and *The Cruise of the Nona*, the *Nona* being Belloc's own beloved boat—share a similar masculine energy.) To all these intriguing elements, Belloc adds another defining dimension: the presence of the old Catholic culture of Europe as the real backbone of concrete daily life, far from the trains and other accommodations of modern civilization. The whole forms a kind of fresh Catholic immediacy in the world that bears some affinities with Gerard Manley Hopkins' much more rarefied efforts to achieve face-to-face contact with God's original creation.

When he cannot keep to this arduous program, Belloc feels himself diminished. Indeed, after he fails in attempting to climb over the greatest barrier between Switzerland and Italy—the Gries Pass—he complains, "The Alps defeated me", and speaks of the road others have already taken with disdain:

> I re-entered "The Bear" [an inn], silent and angered, and not accepting the humiliation of that failure. Then, having eaten, I determined in equal silence to take the road like any other fool; to cross the Furka by a fine highroad, like any tourist, and to cross the St. Gothard by another fine highroad, as millions had done before me, and not to look heaven in the face again till I was back after my long detour, on the straight road again for Rome.... Not till Como should I feel a man again.[10]

When Belloc is high up in those mountains off the beaten track, however, he confronts and records things as few others could have: "Let me put it thus: that from the height of Weissenstein I saw, as it were, my religion. I mean, humility, the fear of death, the terror of height and of distance, the glory of God, the infinite potentiality of reception whence springs that divine thirst of the soul; my aspiration also towards completion, and my confidence in the dual destiny. For I know that we laughers have a gross cousinship with the most high, and it is this contrast and perpetual quarrel which feeds a spring of merriment in the soul of a sane man."[11] This "sane" man is a common theme of the Chesterbelloc, a sanity that has its echoes and roots in sanctity.

The Path to Rome is also a record of everyday life discovered along the way with large quantities of wine, food, song, and poetry. One of Belloc's most famous poems was written, he says, as he passed through Undervelier ("they cook worse at Undervelier than any place I was ever in, with the possible exception of Omaha, Neb.").[12] He asked a peasant for coffee, and when the latter refused, "I took him to be a heretic." Then Belloc composes a song along the road:

[10] Hilaire Belloc, *The Path to Rome* (1901; Chicago: Regnery, 1954), 248–49. Belloc was a great walker as well as a great talker. When he was courting Elodie, his future wife, in California, he walked most of the way from the Midwest to her home in Napa!

[11] Ibid., 180–81.

[12] Ibid., 163.

Heretics all, whoever you be,
In Tarbes or Nîmes, or over the sea,
You never shall have good words from me.
Caritas non conturbat me.

But Catholic men that live upon wine
Are deep in the water, and frank, and fine;
Wherever I travel I find it so,
Benedicamus Domino.

On childing women that are forlorn,
And men that sweat in nothing but scorn:
That is on all that ever were born,
Miserere Domine.

To my poor self on my deathbed,
And all my dear companions dead,
Because of the love that I bore them,
Dona Eis Requiem.[13]

Great fun, but also unfair—heretics are not all stingy, and not all Catholics are cheerful wine drinkers. Belloc liked to affect this blunt Catholicism that denied any good in the world and all real civilization (a living reality not to be identified with the material comforts that most people think is civilization) to anything not explicitly within the Church. He even claimed that a Catholic has a special mode of understanding history and the story of Western civilization. As he put it famously in another notable book, *Europe and the Faith*: "A Catholic as he reads that story does not grope at it from without, he understands it from within. He cannot understand it altogether, because he is a finite being; but he is also that which he has to understand. The Faith is Europe and Europe is the Faith."[14]

Only the last line of this passage is usually quoted, and standing alone it seems to beg many questions. But within a few pages Belloc explains further:

[13] Ibid., 164–66.

[14] Hilaire Belloc, *Europe and the Faith: "Sine auctoritate nulla vita"* (New York: Paulist Press, 1921), viii.

> The Catholic understands the soil in which that plant of the Faith arose. In a way that no other man can, he understands the Roman military effort; why that effort clashed with the gross Asiatic and merchant empire of Carthage; what we derived from the light of Athens; what food we found in the Irish and the British, the Gallic tribes, their dim but awful memories of immortality; what cousinship we claim with the ritual of false but profound religions, and even how ancient Israel (the little violent people, before they got poisoned, while they were yet National in the mountains of Judea) was, in the old dispensation at least, central and (as we Catholics say) sacred: devoted to a peculiar mission.
>
> For the Catholic the whole perspective falls into its proper order. The picture is normal. Nothing is distorted to him. The procession of our great story is easy, natural, and full. It is also final.[15]

All this is true, though pushed a little too far; otherwise, Catholics would have an obvious eminence in European historical studies, which unfortunately has not been the case. But Belloc is certainly right that there is an identifiable Western culture heavily indebted to Catholicism that is best grasped from the inside.

This sort of approach breaks down, however, when Belloc seeks to use it for large-scale explanations that do not really explain. For example, he believes that the then Prussian portion of German lands was insufficiently catechized when the Church was expanding in Europe—an arguable point. But then he goes on to blame the eruption of World War I on this fact:

> Why did Prussia arise? Because the imperfect Byzantine evangelization of the Eastern Slavonic Plains just failed to meet, there in Prussia, the western flood of living tradition welling up from Rome. Prussia was an hiatus. In that small neglected area neither half cultivated from the Byzantine East nor fully from the Roman West rose a strong garden of weeds. And weeds sow themselves. Prussia, that is, this patch of weeds, could not extend until the West weakened through schism. It had to wait till the battle of the Reformation died down. But it waited. And at last, when there was opportunity, it grew prodigiously. The weed patch overran first Poland and the Germanies, then half Europe. When it challenged all civilization at last it was master of a hundred and fifty million souls.[16]

[15] Ibid., ix.

[16] Ibid., xiii.

This strains belief. European nations have gone to war against one another since they arose—Catholics against Catholics as well as Catholics against Protestants. If incomplete evangelization is the explanatory key, then, given fallen human nature, the war of all against all is inevitable.[17]

Belloc was on surer footing when he made clear that the balance in civilization offered by Catholicism, with its institutional separation from the state but influence on behavior, is a necessary condition for freedom. As he says of Saint Thomas Becket's notorious clash with the English king over the prerogatives of the Church:

> A Catholic sees, as he reads the story, that St. Thomas was obviously and necessarily to lose, in the long run, every concrete point on which he had stood out, and yet he saved throughout Europe the ideal thing for which he was standing out. A Catholic perceives clearly why the enthusiasm of the populace rose: the guarantee of the plain man's healthy and moral existence against the threat of the wealthy, and the power of the State—the self-government of the general Church, had been defended by a champion up to the point of death. For the morals enforced by the Church are the guarantee of freedom.[18]

A Catholic *does* understand this, as, say, the American Founding Fathers understood it because the personal discipline formed in the faith is a spur to the kind of liberty that prevents the state from swallowing up everything.

In this regard, Belloc was right to oppose a tradition from the Enlightenment, and in England specifically from Gibbon, that Christianity only became the religion of Rome in her decline. He counters: "The Faith is that which Rome accepted in her maturity; nor was the Faith the cause of her decline, but rather the conservator of all that could be conserved."[19] That was a real corrective to an old anti-Catholic historiography, and subsequent historical studies broadly confirm it. The same might be said of Belloc's view of the "Dark" Ages and the Middle Ages: they were not as dark as the Renaissance

[17] The argument is vigorous, but wrong: "So much for the example of the war. It is explicable as a challenge to the tradition of Europe. It is inexplicable on any other ground. The Catholic alone is in possession of the tradition of Europe: he alone can see and judge in this matter": ibid., xv.

[18] Ibid., xix.

[19] Ibid., xxi–xxii.

and Enlightenment believed, and the Church was not a cause of darkness but a preserver of such light as could be maintained in changed social conditions. Against the myth of Teutonic tribes' bringing democratic impulses to Europe, Belloc maintained that monastic habits of voting, for instance, more typically lay behind later democratic practices. And the Church, far from preventing learning, supported schools and created universities because of a genuine appreciation for knowledge, which she had shown since her entry into the ancient world. This, too, has been confirmed by further scholarship.

At many points, it becomes clear that Belloc's central target was the false sense of history that had found its way into British textbooks. The multiplicity within unity of the Old Roman Empire and Old Roman Church had been distorted for the sake of a flattering national myth. The Church, as he often argued, was a concrete institution with definite principles, not a vague mood or almost contentless "faith". That is what permitted her to survive and flourish against forces that might otherwise have easily overwhelmed her. And Christians understood this instinctively:

> They were attached to the conception of a thing: of an organized body instituted for a definite end, disciplined in a definite way, and remarkable for the possession of definite and concrete doctrine. One can talk, in speaking of the first three centuries, of stoic*ism*, or epicurean*ism*, or neoplaton*ism*; but one cannot talk of "Christian*ism*" or "Christ*ism*". Indeed, no one has been so ignorant or unhistorical as to attempt those phrases. But the current phrase "Christianity", used by moderns as identical with the Christian body in the third century, is intellectually the equivalent of "Christianism" or "Christism"; and, I repeat, it connotes a grossly unhistorical idea; it connotes something historically false; something that never existed.[20]

Similarly, Belloc exploded—rightly—the myth that vigorous "barbarian tribes" had overthrown a corrupt empire. In fact, figures like Alaric were Romans by birth, if Germanic by family origin, and trained as Roman military officers before allegedly "invading" the softened Mediterranean peoples. In this, he resembled many previous generals involved in civil turmoil *within* the Roman lands. He took

[20] Ibid., 34–35.

over Roman territory when it seemed expedient to him. Belloc was far ahead of much of the British scholarship of his day in these matters, which historians now generally accept as he understood them. He was right to characterize the alleged fall and conquest of the empire thus: "There was no such conquest. All that happened was an internal transformation of Roman society, in which the chief functions of local government fell to the heads of local auxiliary forces in the Roman Army. As these auxiliary forces were now mainly barbaric, so were the personalities of the new local governors."[21] This fact changes our view of the "Dark" Ages as well because, even though the empire as a whole was now fragmented, the local governors preserved much of the basic earlier ethos, and some of them evolved into kings who began to rule kingdoms that turned into the modern nations. All of this is intended to lead up to a different understanding of modern Britain, which Belloc shows was part of the same civilization, contrary to recent national myth making.

Belloc clearly had a large bet on this different story line. As he says of the national myths, "They not only render an Englishman ignorant of his own nation and therefore of himself, they also render all men ignorant of Europe: for a knowledge of Britain in the period 500–700 as in the period 1530–1630 is the test of European history: and if you are wrong on these two points you are wrong on the whole."[22] England, he argues, has not become free and exceptional because of alleged Teutonic or Viking invasions in the Dark Ages and the freeing of itself from Rome in the Renaissance. Belloc has no trouble demolishing the unfounded historical arguments for the northern invasion and dominance. But at the same time a reader cannot help but feel that in rejecting one gross misunderstanding he is ignoring some realities—realities that did not entirely sever Britain from the general Christian civilization of the West, of course, but gave it some distinctive and even perhaps improved features not common to the Continent.

Ultimately, Belloc seems to blame the Reformation on the devil. And as he approaches more modern times, he can only say that the Church would have eventually humanized modern developments, but

[21] Ibid., 81.
[22] Ibid., 118.

they came too fast and overwhelmed her in a moment of weakness. One of the most pernicious results was economic exploitation and the breakdown of the spiritual balance of Western societies; another was the monstrous growth of an all-consuming modern state that no longer had an institutional counterweight in the Church:

> Men might and did rebel against a particular government, but it was only to set up something equally absolute in its place. Not the form, but the fact of government was adored.
>
> I will not waste the reader's time in any discussion upon the causes of that astonishing political fever. It must suffice to say that for a moment it hypnotized the whole world. It would have been incomprehensible to the Middle Ages. It was incomprehensible to the nineteenth century. It wholly occupied the sixteenth. If we understand it, we largely understand what made the success of the Reformation possible.[23]

And it was the final loss of Britain in particular that cemented the permanent division of Christianity in Europe: "What we call 'the Reformation' was essentially the reaction of the barbaric, the ill-tutored and the isolated places external to the old and deep-rooted Roman civilization, against the influences of that civilization."[24]

Belloc and Chesterton both embraced this quite different historiography, with its apologetic for Catholicism as the real basis of both earthly civilization and heavenly salvation—in stark contrast to the usual cultural assumptions. But for them it was not an abstract intellectual point. It had immediate, concrete embodiment in the world. In their experience, it could lead to some amusing juxtapositions. Chesterton tells a story in his *Autobiography* about how Henry James, the highly refined American novelist, was visiting Chesterton's home once when Belloc burst into the garden "shouting for bacon and beer":

> Henry James had a name for being subtle; but I think that situation was too subtle for him. I doubt to this day whether he, of all men, did not miss the irony of the best comedy in which he ever played a part. He left America because he loved Europe, and all that was meant by England or France; the gentry, the gallantry, the traditions of lineage and locality, the life that had been lived beneath old portraits in

[23] Ibid., 219.
[24] Ibid., 229.

> oak-panelled rooms. And there, on the other side of the tea-table, was Europe, was the old thing that made France and England, the posterity of the English squires and the French soldiers; ragged, unshaven, shouting for beer, shameless above all shades of poverty and wealth; sprawling, indifferent, secure. And what looked across at it was still the Puritan refinement of Boston; and the space it looked across was wider than the Atlantic.[25]

Viewed in its fullness, the whole set of attitudes is more nuanced and challenging than it might at first seem. Though Belloc's sweeping rejection of modern politics and economics as a departure from what he regarded as the saner arrangements of the Middle Ages and Catholic nations is not wholly right, he has a grip on several key points. It is good to keep in mind that Belloc showed harshness toward Protestants (and Puritanical Catholics—a contradiction in terms for him) because this also partly explains—though only partly—some of the things he has to say about Jews, which in a post-*Shoah* world have led some to paint Belloc as a crude anti-Semite. This is quite false. Belloc went through periods of admiration for Fascism and a figure like Mussolini—mostly, it seems, because of what they had that Britain lacked. But he dismissed as pernicious nonsense the kind of anti-Semitism directed at Jews as such. He had several close Jewish friends who understood what he was about. Still, he could use what may seem to us quite "anti-Semitic" language when he was speaking of Jews as participants in modern capitalism, a virtual devil term for Belloc.[26] This was by no means everything we could ask from a modern Catholic. But like Charles Péguy in France, his was a voice that essentially proceeded from and labored in defense of the old popular ways that had grown out of a Catholic people and were even then quickly disappearing through the spread of modern technologies and economies.

That the old ways were disappearing was clear. That the Middle Ages were "the happiest periods of our past history",[27] as Belloc argues in *The Servile State*, another of his memorable books, is quite another matter. Catholicism flourished in the Middle Ages, of course,

[25] G.K. Chesterton, *Autobiography* (London: Hutchinson, 1937), 221–22.

[26] Cf. Michael Coren, *Gilbert: The Man Who Was Chesterton* (New York: Paragon House, 1990), especially 214–17.

[27] Hilaire Belloc, *The Servile State*, 3rd ed. (1912; London: Constable, 1950), 106.

and there is no question that Christianity helped turn the ancient Greco-Roman society based on slavery into a feudal one in which the peasantry had some share in the land. But the exact connection between the two is not very clear. Even Belloc admits the surviving records do not tell us much. Somehow slaves turned into serfs, but we do not see much outright Christian teaching against slavery per se until the Age of Discovery, well past the high point of the Middle Ages. Belloc argues further that the modern plight of the workingman owes less to industrialization than to the worship of Mammon under Calvinist impulses and a monstrous exploitation of workers and economic inequality, which spread from England to the rest of the world. Despite all our talk of democracy and free markets, the West itself was headed for the servile state, Belloc predicted, just as surely as Marx had.

Belloc convinced Chesterton that this was the true history suppressed by official histories, and they both remained basically faithful to this large-scale reading of the past and present. But the records we do have could be and have been read in very different ways from the story Belloc tries to make them tell. Guilds, for example, restrained economic competition and, therefore, in a sense kept inequality from developing within certain professions. But this was not an unmixed blessing. Competition within markets reduces costs of goods and services. And guilds and other means of allegedly preventing inequality also restrict membership and slow invention and innovation. (Even Belloc admits elsewhere that they came to protect "privilege" in their "corruption".) Further, in simple historical terms, the shift from medieval distribution of land to modern capitalism does not clearly follow the growth of Protestantism, either. Belloc is right that the British aristocracy became wealthy because English noblemen appropriated land from the monasteries and other Church properties. But that aristocracy was something quite different from the modern economic and industrial order, which did not grow out of expropriation of the Church. And a telling instance is that France took basically the same path as England without a strong Protestant influence.

The social program of Belloc and Chesterton was called "distributism", an effort to restore a wider distribution of productive property that would escape the twin evils of collectivism and a radical individualism (identified by them as with many others in the Church as equivalent to an unbridled capitalism). In this historiography,

Protestantism leads directly to social evils, never to any human goods. Pre-Reformation Europe seems never to have experienced any of the problems we see in Post-Reformation society. So we now have, as he sums it up in *Europe and the Faith*:

> The abomination of industrialism; the loss of land and capital by the people in great districts of Europe; the failure of modern discovery to serve the end of man; the series of larger and still larger wars following in a rapidly rising scale of severity and destruction—till the dead are now counted in tens of millions; the increasing chaos and misfortune of society—all these attach one to the other, each falls into its place and a hundred smaller phenomena as well, when we appreciate, as today we can, the nature and the magnitude of that fundamental catastrophe.[28]

There is some truth in every one of these claims, of course, less so in how they "attach one to the other".

Belloc and Chesterton identified a past that appeals to many people in the modern world: a village life of face-to-face community, a closeness to nature, and a traditional sense of God as active in these cozy human and natural worlds—what J. R. R. Tolkien would immortalize in *Lord of the Rings* as the Shire. Indeed, some passages in Belloc that recount his travels seem to anticipate the dialogues among the characters in *Lord of the Rings*. But we know beyond all reasonable dispute now that the historical record does not confirm the idealized portrait of what they thought once existed. And even the Shire needed a much larger political and military order to ward off evil. Distributism, however appealing in its humane aims, is not really a practical solution to modern political and economic problems and could never have produced the prosperity and, more importantly, the independence they sought.[29] Effective solutions to several modern social problems still remain to be worked out.

[28] Belloc, *Europe and the Faith*, 207.

[29] Cf. Thomas E. Woods, Jr., *Beyond Distributism*, Christian Social Thought Series, no. 13 (Grand Rapids, Mich.: Acton Institute, 2012). Woods is a relentless defender of markets and capitalism from a libertarian perspective, but the evidence he assembles from numerous sources of varying ideological orientations about economic and political history—studies that have only appeared in the decades after Belloc and Chesterton wrote—make a strong case that the twin founders of distributism simply had little knowledge of what they claimed about the past. In addition, neither was the sort of practical man who understands business or politics as a living practice.

Belloc predicted that capitalism was unstable and would inevitably produce socialism and servility, or distributism and liberty. In fact, of course, many problems arose within capitalist societies and continue to exist, but these stark alternatives were overdrawn. For the most part, capital and labor in the course of the stormy twentieth century took the less radical path described by Leo XIII in *Rerum Novarum*. They were not opposed to one another in principle, said Leo, but were each important elements in a social whole, with their respective rights and responsibilities. That was the kind of society that emerged in England, France, and America, irrespective of their religious histories, and took over in Germany and Italy and Spain after their Fascist periods. Workers in all those nations are far better off than many monarchs and nobles were in the Middle Ages, even if modern democracies do lumber along—like every society known to history—with numerous political and economic inequities and uncertainties—and now confront the deep cultural problems associated with wealth and a consumerist mentality. By the 1980s, Marxists could be heard to complain that by enriching the workers, capitalism had drained them of their revolutionary fervor.

Nevertheless, Belloc's vision appealed to a large segment of modern readers, all those who looked back to the greater simplicity and agrarian nature of medieval times with nostalgia—and a sense of something missing in modern life that technology and prosperity did not satisfy. The popularity of J.R.R. Tolkien's *Lord of the Rings* trilogy and C.S. Lewis' *Chronicles of Narnia* later in the twentieth century attests to the fact that the burst of medievalism that began in the early nineteenth century with Romanticism had a long life that has continued even into the third Christian millennium. Tolkien was a Catholic and Lewis a traditional Anglican, and large numbers of their readers were themselves serious Christians. But the readership and the sympathies for medievalism were even wider than that, with varying views of the role of the Catholic Church in that long-ago age. In terms of solving modern social problems, agrarianism and medievalism do not get very far. They point to a recovery of a different relationship to nature, God, and other men—and perhaps most importantly to a decentralization of property, which has become a crying need in modern politics and economics—but it is not clear how they could support and promote the flourishing of the billions in the modern world. No society anywhere has tried that solution.

If parts of Belloc's history and his social therapies were debatable, he had a sound theological insight. As he put it in *Europe and the Faith*, "Europe will return to the Faith, or she will perish."[30] He did not mean, of course, that every human being would disappear from the European continent unless Catholicism returned. He did mean that the deep values on which Europe had been built—its inheritance from Judaism and Christianity even more than from Greece and Rome—would evaporate in the absence of the central institution by which they were kept alive. And he believed all this though he was admittedly in his own nature something of a skeptic, as he wrote in a letter to Chesterton, just two days after the latter was received into the Church:

> The Catholic Church is the exponent of *Reality*. It is true. Its doctrines in matters large and small are statements of what is. This it is which the ultimate act of the intelligence accepts. This it is which the will deliberately confirms. And that is why Faith through an act of Will is Moral. If the ordnance map tells me that it is 11 miles to Wookey Hole then, [in] my mood of lassitude as I walk through the rain at night making it *feel* like 30, I use the Will and say: 'No. My intelligence has been convinced and I compel myself to use it against my mood. It is *11* and though I feel in the depth of my being to have gone 20 miles and more, I *know* it is not yet 11 I have gone'.
>
> I am by all my nature of mind sceptical, by all my nature of body exceedingly sensual. So sensual that the virtues restrictive of sense are but phrases to me. But I accept these phrases as true and act upon them as well as a struggling man can. And as to the doubt of the soul, I discover it to be false: a mood: not a conclusion. My conclusion—and that of all men who have ever once *seen* it—is the Faith. Corporate, organised, a personality, teaching. A thing, not a theory. It.[31]

G. K. Chesterton: Dickensian Catholic

The need for Christian renewal to save the world was put forward in even more remarkable and uproarious fashion by Belloc's comrade in arms, G. K. Chesterton, one of the most gifted humorists of the

[30] Belloc, *Europe and the Faith*, 261.
[31] Quoted in Pearce, *Wisdom and Innocence*, 271.

twentieth century. Where Belloc for the most part argues the Catholic "thing" as a straightforward corrective to various errors, Chesterton often sees Catholicity as consisting of a series of paradoxes: not least in the fact that, because God created the world, set human beings among its marvels, and became man himself to show us the way back to the true life, ordinary everyday life became a delightful, unpredictable, universal adventure. Chesterton did not convert to Catholicism until 1922, but from his very first work, he was already speaking in large terms about Catholicity as joining together two seemingly unrelated things: sanity and sanctity.

That realization had its roots in his own life. He showed considerable artistic gifts quite early and studied art at London's Slade School (later Belloc would ask him to illustrate his books, which Chesterton did, tossing off drawings to match Belloc's words almost as a lark). In art school, he claimed, he and the other students loitered with a ferocity that was astonishing even to him. And, with great consequence for Catholic apologetics in the twentieth century, the atmosphere he found there almost literally turned him into a "lunatic" (a term with theological meaning for GKC). Art students, then as now, were steeped in a chic skepticism, the usual aimlessness, and moral anarchy.

This deep and morbid experience—paradoxically—was to drive Chesterton in the opposite direction: to delight in the world's existence, pyrotechnic humor and wordplay, and Christian apologetics unequalled in his time. As he describes the experience in his *Autobiography*:

> What surprises me in looking back on youth, and even on boyhood, is the extreme rapidity with which it can think its way back to fundamental things; and even to the denial of fundamental things. At a very early age I had thought my way back to thought itself. It is a very dreadful thing to do; for it may lead to thinking that there is nothing but thought. At this time I did not very clearly distinguish between dreaming and waking; not only as a mood but as a metaphysical doubt, I felt as if everything might be a dream. It was as if I had myself projected the universe from within, with its trees and stars; and that is so near to the notion of being God that it is manifestly even nearer to going mad. Yet I was not mad, in any medical or physical sense; I was simply carrying the scepticism of my time as far as it would go. And I

> soon found it would go a great deal further than most of the sceptics went. While dull atheists came and explained to me that there was nothing but matter, I listened with a sort of calm horror of detachment, suspecting that there was nothing but mind. I have always felt that there was something thin and third-rate about materialists and materialism ever since. The atheist told me so pompously that he did not believe there was any God; and there were moments when I did not even believe there was any atheist.
>
> And as with mental, so with moral extremes. There is something truly menacing in the thought of how quickly I could imagine the maddest, when I had never committed the mildest crime.[32]

It was through wrestling with and finally overcoming this intolerable lunacy that he came to his lifelong passion for trying to explain the nature of "sanity". As all the world was later to learn, for him, this meant finding the remedy for the solipsism and skepticism he had experienced within himself—and in the multifarious cultural forms of these twin diseases that he encountered as a prolific journalist and public debater—in the most certain guarantee of things outside us: God.

Even though he wrote mostly as a secular journalist and for secular publications, Chesterton's thousands of brief essays, both those published in newspapers and magazines as well as those collected into books, all to a greater or lesser degree revolve around such themes. In 1905, he published his first great book, *Heretics* (soon to be followed by *Orthodoxy*). Though he would not formally enter the Church for more than fifteen years, a kind of Catholicity is present here in the very titles. In the first book, Chesterton wanted to show that his "heretics", celebrated figures like George Bernard Shaw, H. G. Wells, Rudyard Kipling, and others, expect to be able to preserve sanity and joy in this life without believing that they are rooted in a metaphysical reality—God himself. This, for Chesterton, is to ask for an impossibility. Because of his own experience of radical doubt, he understood in a radical way that inescapable and defining philosophical issues lie beneath the false ideals of the Superman, progressive scientism, rugged nationalism, and the other positions represented by the figures he examines in *Heretics*.

[32] Chesterton, *Autobiography*, 92.

He deliberately adds the—to many—bewildering charge of heresy to his analysis of philosophical shortcomings because a new heresy chic had emerged, as he notes in the introductory remarks to *Heretics*:

> Nothing more strangely indicates an enormous and silent evil of modern society than the extraordinary use which is made nowadays of the word "orthodox." In former days the heretic was proud of not being a heretic. It was the kingdoms of the world and the police and the judges who were heretics. He was orthodox.... The man was proud of being orthodox, was proud of being right. If he stood alone in a howling wilderness he was more than a man; he was a church. He was the centre of the universe; it was round him that the stars swung. All the tortures torn out of forgotten hells could not make him admit that he was heretical. But a few modern phrases have made him boast of it. He says, with a conscious laugh, "I suppose I am very heretical," and looks round for applause. The word "heresy" not only means no longer being wrong; it practically means being clear-headed and courageous. The word "orthodoxy" not only no longer means being right; it practically means being wrong. All this can mean one thing, and one thing only. It means that people care less for whether they are philosophically right. For obviously a man ought to confess himself crazy before he confesses himself heretical. The Bohemian, with a red tie, ought to pique himself on his orthodoxy. The dynamiter, laying a bomb, ought to feel that, whatever else he is, at least he is orthodox.[33]

As a recovering lunatic himself, Chesterton displays a certain geniality toward these actual persons who, as he once had, have been taken captive by various secular and religious absurdities. As a result, he does greater justice to the partial truths of each of his "heretics" than Belloc usually manages in his frontal assaults.

For example, in a famous chapter, he praises George Bernard Shaw (who, despite great differences in views, was to become a lifelong friend) for his consistency and defends him from the charge that he turns the way people regard things upside down. Chesterton was not himself so sure they were right side up. Shaw's problem, Chesterton argues, is not that he has an unusual and unusually unified system, but that his system is wrong. And this is most clearly seen in his embrace

[33] G.K. Chesterton, *Heretics*, in *Collected Works*, vol. 1, ed. David Dooley (San Francisco: Ignatius Press, 1986), 39. (Originally published 1905.)

of Nietzsche's Superman. For Chesterton, the desire to go beyond human beings as we find them can entail great spiritual dangers. He says of Shaw:

> Having come to doubt whether humanity can be combined with progress, most people, easily pleased, would have elected to abandon progress and remain with humanity.... If man, as we know him, is incapable of the philosophy of progress, Mr. Shaw asks, not for a new kind of philosophy, but for a new kind of man.... Mr. Shaw cannot understand that the thing which is valuable and lovable in our eyes is man—the old beer-drinking, creed-making, fighting, failing, sensual, respectable man. And the things that have been founded on this creature immortally remain; the things that have been founded on the fancy of the Superman have died with the dying civilizations which alone have given them birth. When Christ at a symbolic moment was establishing His great society, He chose for its cornerstone neither the brilliant Paul nor the mystic John, but a shuffler, a snob, a coward—in a word, a man. And upon this rock He has built His Church, and the gates of Hell have not prevailed against it. All the empires and the kingdoms have failed, because of this inherent and continual weakness, that they were founded by strong men and upon strong men. But this one thing, the historic Christian Church, was founded on a weak man, and for that reason it is indestructible. For no chain is stronger than its weakest link.[34]

These sorts of verbal fireworks and conceptual paradoxes became Chesterton's stock in trade. He is constantly turning up surprises; for instance, this about Auguste Comte's religion of humanity: "It is surely unreasonable to attack the doctrine of the Trinity as a piece of bewildering mysticism, and then to ask men to worship a being who is ninety million persons in one God, neither confounding the persons nor dividing the substance."[35] And Chesterton is preternaturally clear-eyed even in the less exalted realms of human affairs. Belloc had been a member of the House of Commons and was, quite rightly, often merciless in excoriating other members—the elite House of Lords in particular. Chesterton, who always saw close resemblances between Christianity and democracy, however, recognized an

[34] Ibid., 69–70.

[35] Ibid., 86–87.

unnoticed truth about the relationship between the hereditary peers and the talented and dynamic men who, like Belloc, had to work to win their seats: "The House of Lords, in its full and proper strength, consists of stupid men. It really would be a plausible defence of that otherwise indefensible body to point out that the clever men in the [House of] Commons, who owed their power to cleverness, ought in the last resort to be checked by the average man in the Lords, who owed their power to accident."[36]

The temptation for someone trying to characterize Chesterton's works is to go on quoting lines like these, because once you start, it is almost impossible to stop. Indeed, several volumes of such quotations have been collected.[37] And they are far from exhausting the sheer number of gems he came up with, many on short deadlines while writing for the popular press. They come in a flurry:

> It is quite as certain as it ever was that life is a gift of God immensely valuable and immensely valued; and anybody can prove it by putting a pistol to the head of a pessimist.[38]
>
> The Catholic Church is much too universal to be called international, for she is older than all the nations.[39]
>
> The way to love anything is to realize that it might be lost.[40]
>
> As for Reason, our [Catholic] monopoly is practically admitted in the modern world. Except for one or two dingy old atheists in Fleet Street (for whom I have great sympathy), nothing except Rome now defends the reliability of Reason.[41]
>
> Mysticism keeps men sane. As long as you have mystery you have health; when you destroy mystery you create morbidity. The ordinary

[36] Ibid., 188.

[37] See George J. Marlin, Richard P. Rabatin, John L. Swan, eds., *The Quotable Chesterton* (New York: Image Books, 1986), among several others.

[38] G.K. Chesterton, *Why I Am a Catholic*, in *Collected Works*, vol. 3 (San Francisco: Ignatius Press, 1990), 177.

[39] G.K. Chesterton, "The Challenge of the Curé d'Ars", in Henri Ghéon, *The Secret of the Curé d'Ars*, trans. F.J. Sheed (London: Sheed & Ward, 1929).

[40] G.K. Chesterton, *Tremendous Trifles* (New York: Cosimo, 2007), 23.

[41] G.K. Chesterton, *The Well and the Shadows*, in *Collected Works* 3:373.

man has always been sane because the ordinary man has always been a mystic. He has permitted the twilight. He has always had one foot in earth and the other in fairyland. He has always left himself free to doubt his gods; but (unlike the agnostic of to-day) free also to believe in them. He has always cared more for truth than for consistency. If he saw two truths that seemed to contradict each other, he would take the two truths and the contradiction along with them. His spiritual sight is stereoscopic, like his physical sight: he sees two different pictures at once and yet sees all the better for that.[42]

If you argue with a madman, it is extremely probable that you will get the worst of it; for in many ways his mind moves all the quicker for not being delayed by the things that go with good judgment.... The madman is not the man who has lost his reason. The madman is the man who has lost everything except his reason.[43]

These passages, taken almost at random, show how Chesterton's paradoxes reverse the usual categories of thought. The last two come from *Orthodoxy*, his positive statement following the negative criticisms in *Heretics*. But behind all the verbal fireworks and the multifaceted insights, there remains the simple intuition of the young lunatic at the Slade Art School, who threw off the prison of a narrow rationality for the wider rationality of God and humanity. He concludes *Heretics* with this bold flourish:

Truths turn into dogmas the instant that they are disputed. Thus every man who utters a doubt defines a religion. And the scepticism of our time does not really destroy the beliefs, rather it creates them; gives them their limits and their plain and defiant shape. We who are Liberals once held Liberalism lightly as a truism. Now it has been disputed, and we hold it fiercely as a faith. We who believe in patriotism once thought patriotism to be reasonable, and thought little more about it. Now we know it to be unreasonable, and know it to be right. We who are Christians never knew the great philosophic common sense which inheres in that mystery until the anti-Christian writers pointed it out to us. The great march of mental destruction will go on. Everything will be denied. Everything will become a creed. It is a reasonable

[42] G.K. Chesterton, *Orthodoxy*, in *Collected Works* 1:230.
[43] Ibid., 221–22.

> position to deny the stones in the street; it will be a religious dogma to assert them. It is a rational thesis that we are all in a dream; it will be a mystical sanity to say that we are all awake. Fires will be kindled to testify that two and two make four. Swords will be drawn to prove that leaves are green in summer. We shall be left defending, not only the incredible virtues and sanities of human life, but something more incredible still, this huge impossible universe which stares us in the face. We shall fight for visible prodigies as if they were invisible. We shall look on the impossible grass and the skies with a strange courage. We shall be of those who have seen and yet have believed.[44]

This literary brilliance, attached to an orthodox Christian view of God, man, and the world, sounded a unique note in twentieth-century literature. And no Christian apologist—with the possible exception of the Protestant C. S. Lewis—came close to matching it.

Chesterton wrote hundreds of essays and scores of books about such philosophical "paradoxes". But he was an effective writer in many other genres as well—novels, poems, short stories, a couple of plays—precisely because he could bring the exhilaration and humor he found in discovering the marvels of a real world to any subject to which he turned. Like Belloc, for instance, he had a gift for writing humorous verses in the long English tradition perfected by Lewis Carroll and Edward Clerihew Bentley. "Wine and Water" is his Christian defense of the fruit of the vine as opposed to the Puritanical impulse within Christianity and the inhuman asceticism of the Higher Thinkers of his day:

> Old Noah he had an ostrich farm and fowls on the largest scale,
> He ate his egg with a ladle in an egg-cup big as a pail,
> And the soup he took was Elephant Soup and the fish he took was Whale,
> But they all were small to the cellar he took when he set out to sail,
> And Noah he often said to his wife when he sat down to dine,
> "I don't care where the water goes if it doesn't get into the wine."

[44] Chesterton, *Heretics*, 1:206–7.

The cataract of the cliff of heaven fell blinding off the brink
As if it would wash the stars away as suds go down a sink,
The seven heavens came roaring down for the throats of hell
to drink,
And Noah he cocked his eye and said, "It looks like rain, I
think,
The water has drowned the Matterhorn as deep as a Mendip
mine,
But I don't care where the water goes if it doesn't get into the
wine."

But Noah he sinned, and we have sinned; on tipsy feet we trod,
Till a great big black teetotaller was sent to us for a rod,
And you can't get wine at a P.S.A. or chapel or Eisteddfod,
For the Curse of Water has come again because of the wrath
of God,
And water is on the Bishop's board and the Higher Thinker's
shrine,
But I don't care where the water goes if it doesn't get into the
wine.[45]

The Higher Thinkers here include not just the health fanatics, but the pacifists, vegetarians, socialists, internationalists, and other odd figures who in the London of Chesterton's time seem to have had a significant presence. As a daily newspaper columnist—and later as editor of his own magazine, *G. K.'s Weekly*—he could not help but notice the departures from the "sanity" of the older traditions of the English people and of the Christian appreciation of God's creation by these various eccentrics. That, too, resulted in a brilliant poem, "The Song of the Strange Ascetic":

If I had been a Heathen,
I'd have praised the purple vine,
My slaves should dig the vineyards,
And I would drink the wine.
But Higgins is a Heathen,

[45] Chesterton, *Collected Poetry*, pt. 1, 490–91.

And his slaves grow lean and grey,
That he may drink some tepid milk
Exactly twice a day.

And so on for several stanzas before Chesterton reaches the clincher:

Now who that runs can read it,
The riddle that I write,
Of why this poor old sinner,
Should sin without delight—
But I, I cannot read it
(Although I run and run),
Of them that do not have the faith,
And will not have the fun.[46]

Chesterton could also write beautifully in a more conventionally serious vein, "serious" being, as he once remarked, not the opposite of funny. As the poems above show, he could be quite serious and funny at the same time. The opposite of funny, he argued, was "not-funny", and some self-styled "serious" thinkers and writers were all the funnier in that they did not realize the self-undermining nature of their "seriousness". Dedicated Chestertonians have their favorites among the more serious literary works: usually the two long poems "The Ballad of the White Horse" (1912) and "Lepanto" (1915). But these have their drawbacks even for dedicated fans. The wit of the shorter pieces is not absent, but neither does the writing reach the sustained high level needed for most readers to retain interest through to the end. And the subjects—the exploits against the Danes of King Alfred the Great in the first long poem and, in the second, the decisive 1571 naval battle in which a Christian fleet defeated the Muslim fleet at Lepanto off the coast of Greece—though handled in ways that show their spiritual importance, have long arid stretches.

Tolkien and others deal with similarly heroic material with greater authenticity and literary merit. Still, with these two poems Chesterton achieved great success of which other writers can only dream.

[46] Ibid., 523.

Verses from "The Ballad of the White Horse" were sung with gusto by English soldiers in the First and Second World Wars alike. And when the London *Times* wanted to send off men to the second conflict with strong but encouraging words, it included two stanzas of "The Ballad of the White Horse" in an editorial, and words of the Blessed Virgin Mary to old King Alfred at that:

> I tell you naught for your comfort,
> Yea, naught for your desire,
> Save that the sky grows darker yet
> And the sea rises higher.
>
> Night shall be thrice night over you,
> And heaven an iron cope.
> Do you have joy without a cause,
> Yes, faith without a hope?
> Book I, 254–61

Few poets in any age could be quoted at such a moment in the hope of raising the spirit of their people. In the twentieth century, only Chesterton in England and Péguy in France received that rare honor.

Just prior to the passage quoted above, the Virgin appears and is described briefly:

> She stood and stroked the tall live grass
> As a man strokes his steed.
> Her face was like an open word
> When brave men speak and choose,
> The very colours of her coat
> Were better than good news.

And Mary appears at other crucial points in the tale to remind Christians that they need to fight boldly for their faith because it is always being assailed, sometimes by forces of barbarism, sometimes by a barbarism in the guise of civilization. At a poignant moment of battle, Chesterton connects the struggle to what he had treated differently in "The Song of the Strange Ascetic". Alfred himself sings a song that ends:

Therefore your end is on you,
Is on you and your kings,
Not for a fire in Ely fen,
Not that your gods are nine or ten,
But because it is only Christian men
Guard even heathen things.
Book III, 367–72

Christian claims to superiority no longer sit well with some people, especially in the half century during which the Catholic Church herself has encouraged dialogue among religions. "Lepanto" takes a very negative view of Islam as a kind of slavery compared with Christian freedom (the Christian slaves rowing in the Muslim ships are concrete images of this perspective). The form here, too, is odd, especially for a writer who clearly has such a sense of flow and form in other works. There is a way in which perhaps the militaristic side of Chesterton—as well as of Belloc, who correctly predicted the return of Islamic warfare against the West—simply does not find adequate form because there is no adequate form for the battles of the day. When he is treating historical subjects in verse, Chesterton strains to make it all work.

By contrast, Chesterton is quite in his element and the magical words just flow when he treats of the humble side of Christianity, as in "The Donkey":

When fishes flew and forests walked
   And figs grew upon thorn
Some moment when the moon was blood
   Then surely I was born.

With monstrous head and sickening cry
   And ears like errant wings
The devil's walking parody
   On all four-footed things.

The tattered outlaw of the earth
   Of ancient crooked will
Starve, scourge, deride me; I am dumb,
   I keep my secret still.

Fools! For I also had my hour,
 One far fierce hour and sweet
There was a shout about my ears
 And palms before my feet.[47]

The touching close of this poem, when Christ rides a donkey into Jerusalem to popular acclaim, shows a tender side of Chesterton that is often overlooked amidst the humor and paradox.

Chesterton's vast output—studies of Francis of Assisi, Thomas Aquinas, Dickens, Shaw, the Victorians, Cobbett, America (two books), Ireland, Jerusalem, Rome, and other subjects—along with the steady output of books assembled from his stray essays and daily journalism must be thoroughly browsed to get a sense of the truly extraordinary range of his genius.[48] His was such a universal mind that he appreciated other minds of his caliber, almost without having read them. A case in point: Étienne Gilson said of his book on Saint Thomas Aquinas:

> I consider it being without possible comparison the best book ever written on St. Thomas. Nothing short of genius can account for such an achievement. Everybody will no doubt admit that it is a "clever" book, but the few readers who have spent twenty or thirty years in studying St. Thomas Aquinas, and who, perhaps, have themselves published two or three volumes on the subject, can not fail to perceive that the so-called "wit" of Chesterton has put their scholarship to shame. He has guessed all that which they had tried to demonstrate, and he has said all that which they were more or less clumsily attempting to express in academic formulas.[49]

We know from Chesterton's secretary Dorothy Collins that Chesterton did borrow a few books by and about Aquinas but that he had only skimmed them before dictating daily chunks of his work on "Tommy". What he seems to have intuited from the relatively little

[47] Ibid., 134.

[48] No complete edition yet exists. But in addition to individual works available from many sources, several dozen volumes (some containing multiple works) have appeared in the still ongoing *G. K. Chesterton: The Collected Works*, ed. George J. Marlin, Richard P. Rabatin, and John L. Swan (San Francisco: Ignatius Press, 1986–).

[49] Quoted in ibid., vol. 2 (San Francisco: Ignatius Press, 1986), 8.

reading he did was Aquinas' own steady sense of the ordinary world, but an ordinary world kept sane through constant and dynamic contact with the highest and deepest realities.

This almost preternatural ability to grasp other great minds appeared early in Chesterton. He was a voracious reader from his youth and seemed wholly to absorb writers he had read. But unlike most "scholarly" readers, he took the authors he loved very much to heart and seemed instantly able to relate them to a timeless wisdom. His *Charles Dickens*, written when Chesterton was barely thirty, displays an encyclopedic grasp of the vast output of the great novelist, but also a capacity to rise beyond the thousands of pages and characters to moments of insight so remarkable that it seems a wonder that no one ever thought of them before:

> His power, then, lay in the fact that he expressed with an energy and brilliancy quite uncommon the things close to the common mind. But with this mere phrase, the common mind, we collide with a current error. Commonness and the common mind are now generally spoken of as meaning in some manner inferiority and the inferior mind; the mind of the mere mob. But the common mind means the mind of all the artists and heroes; or else it would not be common. Plato had the common mind; Dante had the common mind; or that mind was not common. Commonness means the quality common to the saint and the sinner, to the philosopher and the fool; and it was this that Dickens grasped and developed. In everybody there is a certain thing that loves babies, that fears death, that likes sunlight: that thing enjoys Dickens.[50]

To be able to write like that argues participation by Chesterton himself in that "common mind". The secret, related to the joyful discovery that there is a created world that is real and wildly interesting beyond our own creating, is one he applies to Dickens: "Unlearn that sinister learning that you think so clear; deny the deadly knowledge that you think you know. Surrender the very flower of your culture; give up the very jewel of your pride. Abandon hopelessness all ye who enter here."[51]

[50] G. K. Chesteron, *Charles Dickens: The Last of the Great Men* (London: Dodd Mead, 1906), reprinted (New York: Readers Club, 1942), 79.

[51] Ibid., 18.

Chesterton's own fiction aspires to the qualities he ascribes to Dickens. His earliest novel, *The Napoleon of Notting Hill*, is about a well-known area of London, not far from where Chesterton grew up, revolting against the tyranny of the city's central government, seceding from the city, and defending its ancient liberties in medieval fashion by force of arms against London's other boroughs. It is mostly humorous and not to be taken too seriously in its portrayal of violent battle between citizens of different neighborhoods, but it is to be taken seriously insofar as Chesterton, like Belloc, was working toward a belief that small face-to-face communities were necessary to preserve the deepest human things from a large-scale invasion by modern economic, political, and social forces.

Despite their colorful plots and verbal fireworks, Chesterton's fiction—which includes his immensely successful *Father Brown* series of stories about a priest-detective, some of which were also turned into films (starring the convert Alec Guinness)—display two general shortcomings. First, as was the case with Belloc, he always writes with an obvious thesis. In *Notting Hill*, for instance, it is narrowly local community and patriotism expressed through a kind of medieval pageantry. Despite modern theories to the contrary, there is nothing wrong with a work of art having a didactic purpose, so long as it is, first, a great work of art. To say anything different would be to dismiss three-quarters of the literature of the world, from Homer to Virgil, Dante to Shakespeare to Dickens. The problem arises when the overriding or didactic purpose mars the artistic form. Something like that often happens in Chesterton. Most of his fictional situations are deliberately improbable, and the paradoxical working out of various situations, which appears to good effect in his popular essays, is not as well suited to many of the fictional works, which often contain plots that would make operas look realistic. The conversations among characters, for example, often seem more disguises for some dramatized thesis than true fictional exchanges.[52]

And a second factor follows from this first one. In *The Napoleon of Notting Hill*, to stay with that example, it is great fun to imagine London breaking up into rival neighborhoods that bring back real community and chivalry. But it is not great fun to think of this

[52] The most comprehensive study of Chesterton's fiction is Ian Boyd, *The Novels of G. K. Chesterton* (New York: Barnes & Noble, 1975).

rebirth as dependent on urban warfare in the streets of London. In the right kind of book, the reader might suspend judgment because it is all meant as fun or fantasy. But in Chesterton, it is partly meant to be instructive, too. And that, combined with what are clearly sometimes immature jokes, lessens the literary quality. It is easy to imagine Chesterton rejecting such an airy thing as "literary quality". But when you are writing literature—as he is in the novels, poems, plays, and stories—you have entered one of those realms, beloved by Chesterton, that has its own age-old standards.

The one exception to this judgment might be the novel *The Man Who Was Thursday*, a work that cut a wide swath. It has been read with appreciation by diverse audiences around the globe and has influenced other writers as different as Kingsley Amis, Jorge Luis Borges, and Graham Greene. It is easy to see why. First, like everything by Chesterton, it has—page-by-page—unflagging strokes of genius. But in larger terms, it is difficult to say what the "purpose" of *Thursday* ended up being, and Chesterton himself may not have known, because it seems, in the end, to have escaped his own control and opened out into a religious mystery.

It starts in mystery as well. Scotland Yard recruits Gabriel Syme to help fight a band of anarchists. He goes underground and infiltrates one of the anarchist "councils". The members take cover names after the days of the week. Syme is Thursday—that is, the "Man Who Was Thursday". Another member of the council describes the anarchist creed: "The silly sentimentalists of the French Revolution talked of the Rights of Man! We hate Rights as we hate Wrongs. We have abolished Right and Wrong."[53] That, of course, is a fundamental Chestertonian paradox: many modern ideas seem progressive in that they go beyond the past under the impression that this will lead to human liberation. But there are some things you go beyond only by falling below. A human being without right and wrong is not more—a Superman—but less than a human being.

In an odd twist, however, after various adventures, the council members are all revealed to be police agents. Each thought he was fighting nihilists but is really only conducting surveillance over the

[53] G.K. Chesterton, *The Man Who Was Thursday: A Nightmare* (San Francisco: Ignatius Press, 1999), 54.

false pretenses of one another. They have all been manipulated by the president of the anarchist council, Sunday. And that is not all. This funhouse reflection of mutual suspicions and misjudgments gets a further turn when, late in the story, Sunday reveals he was the original Scotland Yard recruiting officer, seems to metamorphize from a man into something difficult to characterize—God, nature, Christ?—and leads them all on a wild chase. Multiple symbolic and allegorical elements arise in the course of that chase which can only be appreciated by reading the whole thing, but they come to a head, after the trail has been lost, in Syme's description of his first encounter with Sunday:

> "When I first saw Sunday," said Syme slowly, "I only saw his back; and when I saw his back, I knew he was the worst man in the world. His neck and shoulders were brutal, like those of some apish god. His head had a stoop that was hardly human, like the stoop of an ox. In fact, I had at once the revolting fancy that this was not a man at all, but a beast dressed up in men's clothes."[54]

But when Syme came around to the front, Sunday's face frightened him "because it was so beautiful, because it was so good".

> It was like the face of some ancient archangel, judging justly after heroic wars. There was laughter in the eyes, and in the mouth honour and sorrow. There was the same white hair, the same great, grey-clad shoulders that I had seen from behind. But when I saw him from behind I was certain he was an animal, and when I saw him in front I knew he was a god.[55]

Who is this being that, depending on how you look at him, can seem the embodiment of good or evil?

No clear answer is forthcoming. The six other "days" are invited to a meeting with Sunday and are given clothes to put on that reveal them to be six different kinds of philosophers. Then Syme understands also that they were put through their trials so that they could come to a fuller understanding of the world and be able to reply to

[54] Ibid., 245.
[55] Ibid., 246.

Satan's claims about God's indifference to suffering. And in the way of great visions, Syme ultimately finds himself, he knows not how, back in the ordinary world:

> Dawn was breaking over everything in colours at once clear and timid; as if Nature made a first attempt at yellow and a first attempt at rose. A breeze blew so clean and sweet, that one could not think that it blew from the sky; it blew rather through some hole in the sky. Syme felt a simple surprise when he saw rising all round him on both sides of the road the red, irregular buildings of Saffron Park.... There he saw the sister of Gregory, the girl with the gold-red hair, cutting lilac before breakfast, with the great unconscious gravity of a girl.[56]

There is much in this gentle, if inconclusive, ending that seems perfectly right and yet right in a way that Chesterton had not planned—a breakthrough that for once gives his inventiveness in local effects a framework that does not merely marshal them for a rather obvious purpose. *Thursday* was an unsettling if fascinating story, even, it turned out, for Chesterton.

Perhaps his greatest book of any type, however, is *The Everlasting Man* (1925)—which fascinated Evelyn Waugh, Graham Greene, and many others when it appeared and for long after. In it, Chesterton makes brilliant forays into some of the most difficult arguments of all: In what way is Christianity not just another religion in the general survey of world religions, and how does Christ (THE everlasting man) make a difference in the world? Actually, there are two "everlasting" men traced out in the book. Besides Jesus, there is the everlasting man whom we have already encountered in Chesterton's rejoinder to Shaw's Superman: "the old beer-drinking, creed-making, fighting, failing, sensual, respectable man". And it is this man, who has always had jumbled religious intuitions, from the first appearance of the human species down to the present day, who discredits simple progressivist visions like those of H. G. Wells' *Outline of History*. For Wells and many modern thinkers, religious man is simply a child, a primitive who during the childhood of the race made up fairy tales to explain natural phenomena for which he did not yet have scientific explanations. Against this denigration

[56] Ibid., 264–65.

of earlier human periods as somehow less than our own, Chesterton lays out a vision of man constant across the ages that also points toward the culmination of many vague and conflicting hints and guesses in the coming of the true God into the world.

The single greatest strength he brings to this subject is his own appreciation and experience of the imagination as an instrument of truth. Modern scholarship, as we have seen in the case of Scripture studies, seems divided between the kinds of scientific approach that, properly used, may lead to certain knowledge, but in the wrong hands rules everything out of bounds that cannot be empirically verified or logically demonstrated. It has long been clear that to make that initial move in religious matters is essentially to rule out what Christians consider to be their religion. By contrast, those who have pursued a more intuitive or emotional side of religion tend to lose themselves in what might almost appear pure fairy tales. Chesterton appreciated the truth value of fairy tales as well as their imaginative playfulness. But more importantly, his recovery from lunacy as a young art student here reaches its culmination in a brilliant synthesis of what is merely rational and practical, on the one hand, and what constitutes the various forms of true religious intuition and religious imagination, on the other.

If we recall his experience of the nightmare of solipsism and rationalism, which Chesterton detects scattered in various guises in modern culture as a whole, the picture he is trying to sketch becomes quite clear. His arguments are not exactly theological in the usual sense of strict rational analysis of Christian material; his whole approach can leave readers very much at sea. There is plenty of clear argument in *The Everlasting Man*, but it is contextualized in what probably should be called a literary anthropology. For example, Chesterton sees art as the dividing line between man and everything else we know of in creation. Animals make simple practical inferences, and some of them even use tools. There are even primitive "languages" detectable in whales, elephants, dolphins, the higher primates. But none of these animal traits is really comparable with the symbol-making and language abilities of the human species. Chesterton is aware of scientific explanations that would deny this fact, but he grasps human creativity in its fullness in a way that makes the great divide—and its importance for understanding human prehistory and history—difficult to deny.

Similarly, a keen literary sense enables him to see elements within the religious traditions of man that pure scholars often overlook. Long before the "history of religions" school was taken apart by scholars themselves, for example, Chesterton knew that the whole business was a "category mistake", something quite visible in once-influential books like Frazer's *The Golden Bough*. There are common elements across cultural traditions, he admits, especially in Judaism, Christianity, and Islam, which share some history. But things that have been classified as "religions" are not all the same thing. The gods and goddesses in Greek and Roman mythology, for example, do not seem to have really been the "religion" of those nations. From Plato to Virgil to Marcus Aurelius, there seems to have been an older monotheism, undeveloped and possibly a vestige of an older order, that coexisted with the much less serious—and Chesterton is right to see—sometimes merely playful stories about the gods (this playful element, which also exists in Native American stories of tricksters, coyotes, and so on, is still a relatively neglected element in religious scholarship). He may have been the first to put forward the clear idea that, since earlier human cultures contained people just as smart as we are, it was not only the occasional genius like Socrates who knew that ribald or frivolous stories about the gods were unworthy of religion. But Chesterton goes Socrates even one better by understanding that the myths may be both playful and yet worthy of serious attention of a kind.

When you start to move out to other cultures, he rightly notes, the idea of world "religions" becomes even harder to define. Confucianism, for instance, which is in many ways an ethical agnosticism, has very little in common with, say, ancient Middle Eastern or Meso-American cults that practiced human sacrifice and something like the dark arts. In a place like India, does Hinduism, with its thousands of gods and goddesses, belong in the same category with Buddhism, which has an austere asceticism and, in its way, a kind of liberation through self-annihilation? Confusions among all these arose, he argues, primarily because, at a certain moment in Western history, people wanted to use the similarities to deny the uniqueness of Christianity—in other words, the parallels seem true to people who are part way out of Christianity but not far enough, says Chesterton, to see it whole and for the unique thing, in crucial respects, that it truly is: "It is really the collapse of comparative religion that there is no comparison between God and the gods."[57]

So to make that uniqueness clear, he stimulates the imagination—"imaginative does not mean imaginary"[58]—more than he makes the usual philosophical or theological arguments. Quite apart from the proper work of philosophy and theology, these imaginative elements suggest correspondences in the world that "seem really to correspond to something in the soul".[59] And that must play a large role in how the later analytic efforts should understand themselves because "he who has no sympathy with myths has no sympathy with men."[60] In this large and imaginative view of the religious echoes of mankind, two large elements must eventually be reconciled: "The rivers of mythology and philosophy run parallel and do not mingle till they meet in the sea of Christendom."[61] It is only there that the searches of both the imaginative and the rational coalesce into a "complete and complex truth".[62]

Something such a truth makes evident is that men are more complex than usually thought and are not primarily or mostly motivated by economic and material factors, as most modern theories assume. There are real material necessities, of course, but necessities hardly exhaust a human life. Indeed, a *human* life is something entirely different from what the vision of *Homo economicus* or *Homo politicus* is able to capture. Or, as Chesterton says, "Economic history would not even be history."[63] It is an odd feature of much modern writing about history that the *internal* human story, the part all of us know from experience is our own real response to the world, is almost wholly left out. (Since Chesterton wrote, there has been a lot of emphasis on history written "from below" about ordinary life, but that has too often employed Marxist or other ideological lenses that missed the ultimate human things: "We want to know the real sentiment that was the social bond of many common men, as sane and as

[57] G.K. Chesterton, *The Everlasting Man*, in *Collected Works*, 2:231.
[58] Ibid., 237.
[59] Ibid.
[60] Ibid., 241.
[61] Ibid., 243.
[62] Ibid., 256.
[63] Ibid., 270.

selfish as we are."[64] Many things, perhaps most things, are undertaken with far different motives and goals:

> It will be hard to maintain that the Crusaders went from their homes into a howling wilderness because cows go from a wilderness to a more comfortable grazing-ground. It will be hard to maintain that the Arctic explorers went north with the same material motive that made the swallows go south. And if you leave things like all the religious wars and all the merely adventurous explorations out of the human story, it will not only cease to be human at all but cease to be a story at all. The outline of history is made of these decisive curves and angles determined by the will of man. Economic history would not even be history.
>
> But there is a deeper fallacy besides this obvious fact; that men need not live for food merely because they cannot live without food. The truth is that the thing most present to the mind of man is not the economic machinery necessary to his existence; but rather that existence itself; the world which he sees when he wakes every morning and the nature of his general position in it. There is something that is nearer to him than livelihood, and that is life. For once he remembers exactly what work produces his wages and exactly what wages produce his meals, he reflects ten times that it is a fine day or it is a queer world, or wonders whether life is worth living, or wonders whether marriage is a failure, or is pleased and puzzled with his own children, or remembers his own youth, or in any such fashion vaguely reviews the mysterious lot of man.[65]

This may appear to be special pleading, but Chesterton argues that it reflects hardheaded facts better than the monocausal approaches: "So long as we neglect this subjective side of history, which may more simply be called the inside of history, there will always be a certain limitation on that science which can be better transcended by art. So long as the historian cannot do that, fiction will be truer than fact. There will be more reality in a novel; yes, even in a historical novel."[66]

Chesterton does not mean this in some abstract sense. He points quite correctly to the fact that people fight wars—the actual soldiers,

[64] Ibid., 271.
[65] Ibid., 269–70.
[66] Ibid., 271.

that is, whatever the politicians may intend—because of their ultimate view of things, which is to say, their religion. They do not fight to secure warm-water ports or natural resources; rather, they do so in order to defend a homeland—or choose not to do so because they believe something is more important even than that or whatever politicians have chosen to tell them. People who do not believe in acting for such ultimate goals do so because their own ultimate view of things is that God is unreal, and they regard all high sentiment, chivalry, patriotism, and other ideals as therefore unreal. But for most men they are quite real, in fact, the most real things of all. And therefore any account of the human things that leaves out religion as a primary motivation is on its face an incomplete account. And crucial among these ultimate values is the family: "Only men to whom the family is sacred will ever have a standard or a status by which to criticise the state."[67]

Having established the centrality of theism, Chesterton turns to the specific claims of Christianity. It will not do, he argues, to say with the rationalists that it is improbable that God became Man. Christianity itself has always regarded it as more than improbable, in fact, a divine miracle. In this it was from the start stating openly what others have claimed only recently to have found out. And while this story has similarities to mythological stories, it differs from them—again, ever since the story began to be told—in that the tellers claimed it to be more than a story and actually true. We can see this in the fact that Jesus' birth is like that of any other child, from a human mother. Jesus' life, however, moves far outside all our usual categories of understanding.

Chesterton tries the difficult experiment of reading the Gospels as if he had never heard of them before. By that measure, he says, Jesus is quite extraordinary. He is not at all a man of his time, as historical criticism often claims, and his rejection in his time proves it. Further, he is not the gentle pacifist of the modern platitudinous approach to the Gospels. There is a fierceness at unexpected moments in the accounts of our Lord that argues some logic that attracts but exceeds us, Chesterton says. But perhaps the most striking thing about the Gospels is a kind of literary genius that cannot come solely from

[67] Ibid., 275.

literary geniuses. In a passage of genius in its own right, Chesterton gives an example:

> There is perhaps nothing so perfect in all language or literature as the use of these three degrees in the parable of the lilies of the field; in which he seems first to take one small flower in his hand and note its simplicity and even its impotence; then suddenly expands it in flamboyant colours into all the palaces and pavilions full of a great name in national legend and national glory; and then, by yet a third overturn, shrivels it to nothing once more with a gesture as if flinging it away '... and if God so clothes the grass that today is and tomorrow is cast into the oven—how much more....' It is like the building of a good Babel tower by white magic in a moment and in the movement of a hand; a tower heaved suddenly up to heaven on the top of which can be seen afar off, higher than we had fancied possible, the figure of man; lifted by three infinities above all other things, on a starry ladder of light logic and swift imagination. Merely in a literary sense it would be more of a masterpiece than most of the masterpieces in the libraries; yet it seems to have been uttered almost at random while a man might pull a flower.[68]

And Chesterton makes another claim for the uniqueness of Christianity. Of no other faith has it been said that its adherents confused the founder with God. Moses was not taken for Jehovah, nor Mohammed for Allah. Christ's claim in the Gospels, "Before Abraham was, I am", is so odd according to the usual "history of religions" approach—which sees all religions, despite clear factual differences, as essentially the same thing—that the sheer oddity of Christianity on this score must at least be noted. It is also odd from the point of view of first-century Judaism and the kind of mentality the apostles were likely to have had. And yet there it is, as remarkable now as it was then.

Father Ian Ker, an Oratorian priest and Newman scholar, has perceptively argued that Chesterton practiced what he calls "Dickensian Catholicism". Chesterton's early rejection of the nightmare of materialist reason and vigorous embrace of gratitude for the mere existence of the universe led him to an exuberance over common things closely akin to that of the great nineteenth-century novelist.

[68] Ibid., 332–33.

In Dickens, Chesterton discovered one of those writers who, like himself, held together the inevitable pessimism we feel at the evil in the world and our optimism at its beauty and sheer existence: they "do not approve of the universe; they do not even admire the universe. They fall in love with it. They embrace life too close to criticize or even to see it. Existence to such men has the wild beauty of a woman, and those love her with most intensity who love her with least cause."[69]

Chesterton, of course, views this in the context of Christian dogma: the dogmas of the goodness of God's creation and the evils introduced by the Fall. But this raises a further paradox—and perhaps a problem. Dickens not only rejected, he scorned the medieval Catholicism that both Chesterton and Belloc saw as the origin of such human exuberance. You can only be truly joyful if the universe itself, at the end of all things, is joyful. Chesterton wrote a book about Chaucer in which he made the connection quite closely. But what of Dickens? How did he come by the Catholic sentiment without Catholic belief? Chesterton himself had gotten to a similar point in his early life, before his rather late conversion to Catholicism. It is possible to argue that some great souls, owing to God's inexplicable grace, arrive at that Catholic life that, as we saw above, Belloc, too, touted: "But Catholic men that live upon wine / Are deep in the water, and frank, and fine."[70] That realization, however, undercuts the overly strict link both Chesterton and Belloc draw between Catholic beliefs and social sanity. And the fact that most Catholics do not seem to share in the spiritual exuberance of Dickens, Belloc, and Chesterton further complicates any simple picture.

What Chesterton sees *in* Dickens is brilliant and solid; what he argues *from* Dickens is helpful but less certain. This would not matter very much if it did not claim to be in a certain sense a *normative* description of "Catholic" literature. Certainly, the everyday heartiness about the world and delight in all God's children is one kind of Catholic literature, whether it appears in a Catholic like Chaucer or a non-Catholic like Dickens. Chesterton and Belloc work very much

[69] G. K. Chesterton, *Chesterton on Dickens*, in *The Collected Works of G. K. Chesterton*, vol. 15 (San Francisco: Ignatius Press, 1989), 62. Quoted in Ker, *Catholic Revival*, 82.

[70] Belloc, *Path to Rome*, 165.

in this line themselves (though Belloc is, to say the least, not equally delighted by all of God's children). But what are we to say about a work like Dante's *Divine Comedy*, the greatest Catholic poem ever written, fully two-thirds of which details terrifying sinfulness (*Inferno*) and excruciating purgation of sin (*Purgatorio*). Even the *Paradiso* presents the approach to the Beatific Vision as an often painful growth of human sight. And while there is little comedy, as Chesterton usually understands it, in the *Comedy*, Dante considered his work a comedy because it ends happily for the pilgrim.

Cardinal Newman addressed this difficulty directly in *The Idea of a University* when he said that literature, given the fallen state of man, will not be simply Christian in the sense of purely edifying and uplifting. Like the Bible itself, literature will show the dark and light in the human condition. Obviously, some genres of literature—children's poetry or light comedy, among others—need not reflect the sin and error that any Christian adult knows passes through the world and his own heart. But when we look at literature as a whole, alongside the Dickensian and Chestertonian exuberance and love of creation, we should expect to find much else besides, and that not always immediately subsumed by the theological awareness that we are participants in a divine comedy. And in fact, some of the greatest Catholic literature contemporaneous with or a little after Chesterton—Hopkins, Graham Greene, Waugh, among the British, and Mauriac, Undset, Flannery O'Connor, among many others elsewhere—provides empirical confirmation of this analysis. We shall turn to several of these in what follows.

Gerard Manley Hopkins

Carrion Comfort

Not, I'll not, carrion comfort, Despair, not feast on thee;
Not untwist—slack they may be—these last strands of man
In me or, most weary, cry *I can no more.* I can;
Can something, hope, wish day come, not choose not to be.

But ah, but O thou terrible, why wouldst thou rude on me
Thy wring-world right foot rock? lay a lionlimb against me?
scan

With darksome devouring eyes my bruisèd bones? and fan,
O in turns of tempest, me heaped there; me frantic to avoid
thee and flee?

Why? That my chaff might fly; my grain lie, sheer and clear.
Nay in all that toil, that coil, since (seems) I kissed the rod,
Hand rather, my heart lo! lapped strength, stole joy, would
laugh, cheer.

Cheer whom though? the hero whose heaven-handling flung
me, foot trod
Me? or me that fought him? O which one? is it each one?
That night, that year
Of now done darkness I wretch lay wrestling with (my God!)
my God.[71]

Although Gerard Manley Hopkins lived and died in the nineteenth century (1844–1889), his work was not published until Robert Bridges, a friend from Hopkins' Oxford days and later English poet laureate, brought them out in stages from 1889 to 1916. Hopkins' *literary* life was a twentieth-century phenomenon. He was a convert and much influenced by Newman, who at one point saw that he got a teaching post in a school run by the Oratorians. He later became a Jesuit. Hopkins was also one of the earliest English poets to experiment with new verse forms that seem, after several readings, to be intimately linked to the internal trials he underwent. "Carrion Comfort", one of the so-called "terrible sonnets" that he composed during a period of isolation in Ireland, shows quite clearly both the struggle and the frank admission that, like Jacob wrestling with the angel, Hopkins is wrestling with God himself.

Of course, this is a common theme in Catholic literature and the Bible. Unlike what is seen in the Chesterton and Belloc current in English Catholic literature, the sense of overwhelming suffering is never far away in Hopkins. Indeed, he tells God directly at times that he does not know how he could have been treated worse if God had been his enemy, though he knows God is just. The end of

[71] Gerard Manley Hopkins, *The Major Works*, ed. Catherine Phillips (New York: Oxford University Press, 2009), 168. All references to Hopkins' work in the text are to the versions that appear in this volume.

the following sonnet is one of the most poignant—and terrible—in modern poetry:

Justus quidem tu es, Domine,

si disputem tecum; verumtamen justa loquar ad te:
quare via impiorum properatur? etc. (Jerem. xii I.)

Thou art indeed just, Lord, if I contend
With thee; but, sir, so what I plead is just.
Why do sinners' ways prosper? and why must
Disappointment all I endeavour end?

Wert thou my enemy, O thou my friend,
How wouldst thou worse, I wonder, than thou dost
Defeat, thwart me? Oh, the sots and thralls of lust
Do in spare hours more thrive than I that spend,

Sir, life upon thy cause. See, banks and brakes
Now, leavèd how thick! lacèd they are again
With fretty chervil, look, and fresh wind shakes

Them; birds build—but not I build; no, but strain,
Time's eunuch, and not breed one work that wakes.
Mine, O thou lord of life, send my roots rain.[72]

Literary critics have often given into a temptation, in line with much in modern culture that is non-Catholic, to emphasize the psychopathology, perhaps even the homoerotic struggles, in Hopkins (there is conflicting evidence on this latter subject since Hopkins' works show indisputable attractions to women, less certain emotions toward men). It is clear that he went through dark nights of the soul that were quite stormy.

It is also clear that he had experiences that he called "inscape", a term for which he was indebted to his interest in the medieval thinker Duns Scotus, by which he was transported by nature or God. Perhaps the most successful of his poetic efforts to capture such an experience is the following:

[72] Ibid., 183.

The Windhover:
to Christ our Lord

I caught this morning morning's minion, king-
dom of daylight's dauphin, dapple-dáwn-drawn Falcon, in
his riding
Of the rólling level úndernéath him steady áir, and stríding
High there, how he rung upon the rein of a wimpling wing
In his ecstasy! then off, off forth on swing,
As a skate's heel sweeps smooth on a bow-bend: the hurl
and gliding
Rebuffed the big wind. My heart in hiding
Stirred for a bird,—the achieve of, the mastery of the thing!

Brute beauty and valour and act, oh, air, pride, plume, here
Buckle! AND the fire that breaks from thee then, a billion
Times told lovelier, more dangerous, O my chevalier!

No wónder of it: shéer plód makes plóugh down síllion
Shine, and blue-bleak embers, ah my dear,
Fall, gáll themsélves, and gásh góld-vermílion.[73]

The odd accenting in this poem and the previous ones is meant to be a help in understanding the rhythm of the lines. Hopkins often composed on long walks, and he tried to indicate by these typographic devices some of the sound effects he may have heard in his mind. In this instance, the originality of the rhythm and of the inscape combine to produce a powerful literary experience, indeed. And it was not just Catholics who noticed. Hopkins became the first major Catholic poet since Alexander Pope in the eighteenth century to enter the canon of English poetry.

Pope was only nominally Catholic, Hopkins substantially so. And it is another measure of his greatness that he made his way in the English literary world despite significant religious obstacles. Before the fact, it would have seemed absurd in the extreme to predict that an English convert who became a Jesuit, and who was formed by Ignatian spirituality and Duns Scotus, would become a major modern

[73] Ibid., 132.

English poet. But in another way, the sheer difference of Hopkins' sensibility when compared with that of poets in his time and well into the twentieth century provides him with something distinctive with which to work. And then his obvious verbal gifts, which strain to reach after unfamiliar insights into the world and life, and which were not part of the literary world of his time, joined together to produce something extraordinary and fresh, even if the work also contained elements both traditional and terrifying.

Readers encountering Hopkins in anthologies will usually see only the work that displays these particularities. It is useful, however, to note that in the earlier part of his life Hopkins could write poetry that was quite conventional in both matter and form. "The Habit of Perfection", for instance, seems to be about the typical themes of a withdrawn religious vocation and represents those in verses that are accomplished and well balanced, but without the spiritual and verbal fireworks he set off later: "Elected Silence, sing to me / And beat upon my whorlèd ear / Pipe me to pastures still and be / The music that I care to hear." And so on for six more well-crafted stanzas.[74] It might be easy to make fun of this sort of "Catholic" poetry if Hopkins had produced nothing else. Even these early poems have their charms, though, and—if nothing else—make it absolutely clear that Hopkins could write such formally correct but relatively uninspired work when he wanted to. Certain things simply came together in his life that took him out into deep spiritual and literary waters.

We know from various sources that Hopkins felt a certain tension between his priestly vocation and his poetic vocation, a tension that at times led him to cease writing or even to burn manuscripts. In December 1875, five nuns who had been expelled from Germany during Bismarck's *Kulturkampf* against Catholicism died when the *Deutschland*, a German passenger ship, sank in a storm at the mouth of the Thames. Hopkins' Jesuit superior asked him to write a poem on the event, which he agreed to do. "The Wreck of the Deutschland" was the result, and while it is not a poem universally prized, there is no question that it shows a new convergence of the religious and poetic in a way that gave freshness to both. In most editions of Hopkins' poetry, there are fewer than seventy-five pages

[74] Ibid., 80.

from the first line of "The Wreck of the Deutschland" to the last lines he wrote. But those few pages contain all the poetry on which Hopkins' reputation as a major English poet is based.

The opening stanza of "The Wreck of the Deutschland" immediately speaks in a new voice, a voice containing the taut rhythms and extraordinary word combinations of Hopkins at his highest pitch:

Thou mastering me
God! giver of breath and bread;
World's strand, sway of the sea;
Lord of living and dead;
Thou hast bound bones and veins in me, fastened me flesh,
And after it álmost únmade, what with dread,
Thy doing: and dost thou touch me afresh?
Over again I feel thy finger and find theé.[75]

In this unusual poetic invocation, Hopkins here departs from the standard nineteenth-century prosody he had for the most part used to this point for something he was to describe as "sprung rhythm", a set series of variable feet and verse patterns, not—as they are often mistakenly described—free verse, but experimental forms that also employ types of alliteration found in old Anglo-Saxon and Welsh poetry. Hopkins thought through these technical questions in several texts.[76] It may seem that these craft issues have little to do with the Catholicity of Hopkins, but in fact a Catholic *poetry* has to find its way to the highest aesthetic interest. Without first-rate literary qualities, it would be difficult to see why anyone would be interested in Catholic literature at all, since we can already go to philosophy, theology, and prayer books for doctrinal or devotional material.

The g reat genius of Hopkins that emerges in these lines is his ability to create unusual rhythms while maintaining strict stanzas and rhymes and, at the same time, finding verbal formulas ("giver of breath and bread, / World's strand, sway of the sea"; "fastened me flesh") that present the traditional Christian God in a vital and

[75] Ibid., 110.

[76] Cf., e.g., ibid., 106–9, "Author's Preface".

immediate fashion. As Hopkins says of God in stanza five, "though he is under the world's splendour and wonder, / His mystery must be instressed, stressed."[77] In more traditional Catholic writers such as Belloc and Chesterton, there is an invitation to see this age-old truth. In a modern inventive Catholic writer like Hopkins, the very form of the poetry incarnates the beauty that Saint Augustine famously described as *tam antique et tam nova.* The newness of Hopkins' work lies in this effort to grapple toward a sense of that beauty by way of a highly original kind of literature—one less concerned with Catholic apologetics than with a kind of verbal creation that deliberately stays close to the highs and lows of God's creation.

There is a kind of theological meaning in such efforts that can be observed in retrospect. As mentioned earlier, Hopkins felt a close kinship with the medieval Franciscan theologian Duns Scotus ("who of all men most sways my spirits to peace", line 11 of "Duns Scotus's Oxford").[78] What Hopkins seems to have sensed in Scotus was a Franciscan appreciation of the God-created particularity (*haeccitas*) of each thing in the universe. A theologian or philosopher might be tempted to try to parse out this intuition in terms of universals and nominalism, but that would perhaps unnecessarily transfer the concreteness of Hopkins' "inscape" into an abstract register where the originating experience is lost, whatever a later reflection might wish to do with it. In Hopkins' best poems, we see an inscape about the world, finding a unique form for its expression, which then provides further matter for analysis.

We might take as a prime example Hopkins' poem "Pied Beauty", in which, perhaps alone among the greatest poets of the world, he points to the particular beauties of imperfect rather than perfect things:

> Glory be to God for dappled things—
> For skies of couple-colour as a brinded cow,
> For rose-moles all in stipple upon trout that swim;
> Fresh-firecoal chestnut-falls, finches' wings;
> Landscape plotted and pieced—fold, fallow and plough,
> And áll trades, their gear and tackle and trim.

[77] Ibid., 111.
[78] Ibid., 142.

All things counter, original, spáre, strange;
Whatever is fickle, frecklèd (who knows how?)
With swíft, slów; sweet, sóur; adázzle, dím;
He fathers-forth whose beauty is pást change;
Práise hím.[79]

We get a sense here that in their very particular imperfections and, therefore, resistance to being reduced to general, universal statements, each thing both expresses something of him who "fathers-forth" and leads backs to the One whose "beauty is past change".

In a sense, all great poets find this way of using the particular to keep us from falling into a facile abstraction, even when they are making large conceptual statements. Hopkins is quite capable of doing that as well. Another of his most famous poems, "God's Grandeur", takes one of the oldest Christian themes of all, the glory of God (as we read in Psalms 8, 19, and elsewhere) as manifest in his creation. But to prevent the reader from merely slipping into a received "religious" attitude, Hopkins makes the whole idea new by a new song:

The world is charged with the grandeur of God.
It will flame out, like shining from shook foil;
It gathers to a greatness, like the ooze of oil
Crushed. Why do men then now not reck his rod?
Generations have trod, have trod, have trod;
And all is seared with trade; bleared, smeared with toil;
And wears man's smudge and shares man's smell: the soil
Is bare now, nor can foot feel, being shod.

And for all this, nature is never spent;
There lives the dearest freshness deep down things;
And though the last lights off the black West went
Oh, morning, at the brown brink eastward, springs—
Because the Holy Ghost over the bent
World broods with warm breast and with ah! bright
wings.[80]

[79] Ibid., 132–33.
[80] Ibid., 128.

There is much going on in the virtuosity of this sonnet. Not only is there the unusual flashing forth of foil and the gushing of crushed oil—two quite original images for the unexpected appearance of God—but we get a nature distanced from us by our own activity, yet which nevertheless dawns anew every day because of the light of the Holy Spirit.

There is a tendency in modern literature to regard all such experimentation as per se valuable. In fact, we often think the wilder the experiment, the more authentic and individual the artistic inspiration. This is a doubtful proposition, and Hopkins' most successful experimental poems combine both tradition and innovation. There are places in which his own innovations come so thick that the poem is a kind of singularity, in a bad sense, akin to some of the "concrete" poetry that came to be written later in the twentieth century. It speaks almost a private language, and the themes become impenetrable to such an extent that it is hard to say whether they are related to something in the world or out of it. (The curious reader can have a go at "Spelt from Sibyl's Leaves".)

Hopkins has sometimes been called the first truly modern poet in English. Such characterizations are probably not worth very much, but in large terms there is no Catholic poet in the twentieth century quite as distinctive. At his best—in the handful of poems for which he is best known—he speaks in a voice unique not only to literature but to the Catholic intellectual world of the twentieth century. Perhaps only Paul Claudel possesses the same strictly literary stature among modern Catholic poets. Attempts have been made to find some explanation for this creative burst in Hopkins' conversion and in his experience of both the stripped-down liturgies of English Catholicism (compared with the grandiosity of the Anglican tradition) and the humble working folk whom he served as a priest. Most of this in speculative and unconvincing. God seems to bestow his literary gifts, like the rain in the Gospel verse, on the just and the unjust, with a decided preference for the more numerous unjust, it would seem.

A better way of understanding his particular achievement as a poet is to see a kind of Scotist convergence between the particularities of the world and poetic language, on the one hand, and the individual things of the world that simultaneously "body forth" the Christ on the other:

As kingfishers catch fire, dragonflies dráw fláme;
As tumbled over rim in roundy wells
Stones ring; like each tucked string tells, each hung bell's
Bow swung finds tongue to fling out broad its name;
Each mortal thing does one thing and the same:
Deals out that being indoors each one dwells;
Selves—goes itself; *myself* it speaks and spells,
Crying *Whát I dó is me: for that I came.*

Í say móre: the just man justices;
Kéeps gráce: thát keeps all his goings graces;
Acts in God's eye what in God's eye he is—
Chríst—for Christ plays in ten thousand places,
Lovely in limbs, and lovely in eyes not his
To the Father through the features of men's faces.[81]

A Scandinavian Contribution: Sigrid Undset

In northern Europe during this period, beyond the great names, there are many other writers worth reading, but few likely to stand the test of time. A contemporary Catholic writer whose work does seem to have some staying power is Sigrid Undset (1882–1949). Undset was born in Denmark but grew up mostly in Norway. Her father was an archaeologist, and she early absorbed an interest in medieval Norse legends and literature. Like Tolkien, she was able to use this material—both the pagan and Christian elements that were for the most part wholesome or colorful—in writing novels that appealed to a wide readership, especially in her trilogy, *Kristin Lavransdatter.* But she did not simply romanticize the Middle Ages, and, indeed, the story of Kristin Lavransdatter explicates passion, betrayal, repentance, and forgiveness, as those were lived out in a setting very different from the modern world but identifiable as universal human experiences. Her Middle Ages contain elements of Catholicism, to which she converted in 1924, though in no way are the novels reducible to predictably pious lessons. Though her

[81] Ibid., 129.

conversion was a scandal that brought her much criticism in the militantly secularist and Lutheran circles that dominated Norwegian intellectual and cultural life, her obvious gifts led to her being awarded the Nobel Prize in Literature in 1928.

Kristin Lavransdatter follows the character in the title from her earliest years until her death. Her father and mother are people who are more than normally pious (unlike Undset's own secularist parents) and decent in their dealings with other people. One day when she is out in the woods with her father and a hunting party, she has an unusual experience. Just after casting a glance at her reflection in a pond and—Narcissus-like—coming to admire her own features, "all at once she was aware of a face amid the leaves—there stood a lady, pale, with waving, flaxen hair—the great, light-grey eyes and wide, pink nostrils were like Guldsveinen's [her father's horse]. She was clad in something light, leaf-green, and branches and twigs hid her up to the broad breasts, which were covered over with brooches and sparkling chains. The little girl gazed upon the figure, and as she gazed the lady raised a hand and showed her a wreath of golden flowers—she beckoned with it."[82] Kristin flees, but the "bridal wreath", which gives the title to the first volume of the trilogy, has been offered to her, and it will mean for her a turning from others and a fatal preoccupation with the fair attractions to her own powerful will.

It might be too coldly analytic to call this a literary device, since Undset no doubt set out to tell a story that came to her in the lively unfolding of the characters (the first volume of the trilogy was turned into a good film in 1995 by Liv Ullmann). But like the Ring of Power in Tolkien, this medieval and pagan temptation allows Undset to present a range of subjects that, in a modern setting, might put readers off. In the nineteenth and twentieth centuries, the widespread attraction to medieval simplicity and color—qualities very different from modern societies'—did not exactly make stories set in the Middle Ages a "vehicle", which would have required a kind of calculation that almost always kills literary work. Rather, various authors intuited that a simpler setting also brought out elementary human matters in ways that would be hard to produce as

[82] Sigrid Undset, *The Bridal Wreath*, vol. 1 of *Kristin Lavransdatter*, trans. Charles Archer and J.S. Scott (New York: Vintage, 1987), 17.

effectively in modern settings. Undset was and remains powerful because of her ability to combine rather lively and accurate portrayals of medieval Norway with lively and accurate portrayals of perennial human themes.

The result by any measure is impressive. *Kristin Lavransdatter* has been compared—and sometimes judged greater—than novels like *Anna Karenina* and *Madame Bovary*, but it is difficult to say how the medieval story should be estimated alongside those two quintessentially modern stories about tragically romantic women (Undset's earlier, preconversion novels are more in that genre). Kristin has also been called a kind of Nordic *Iliad*. But this, too, seems a bit wide of the mark because the story develops almost entirely in the private terms of Kristin's life, which is to say, of a medieval woman barred from many activities, not in terms of a heroic saga. Indeed, Norwegian feminists criticized her work because it seemed to make women dependent, but Undset replied that she saw women as having naturally different roles from men, though she herself shared their desire for greater female freedom. At the same time, her sharp eye for truth began to lead her to see that none of us—male or female—very much do what we ought to and therefore find ourselves fettered by sin. That was one of the insights that gradually led her to Rome and gave her a critical perspective on then highly influential intellectual currents like Nietzscheanism, Freudianism, and Darwinism.[83]

Perhaps *Kristin Lavransdatter* is best understood as a kind of modern-day *Divine Comedy*, though one that unfolds wholly on earth, not in Dante's journeys through earth, the mountain of purgatory, and the heavens. And maybe it has greater contemporary power for that very reason. As we follow the arc of Kristin's life—from her early discovery of her willfulness to her efforts as an older woman to recover a pure heart—we traverse the whole Christian journey of the soul to God. Each man makes that voyage in his own particular way, of course, and if it is presented in too schematic or overly pious a manner, it becomes a mere illustration of an abstract idea. Undset's power as a writer stems from the fact that she has a gift for telling a gripping story—any sympathetic reader who enters Kristen's world will be

[83] Cf. Theodore P. Fraser, *The Modern Catholic Novel in Europe* (New York: Twayne, 1994), 50–57.

fascinated and constantly eager to know what happens next, one of the sure signs that an authentically living character has been created. And Kristin is not only interesting but constantly surprising.

Though we see her early on as a highly intelligent and good-hearted girl, soon after she meets and becomes friends with Edvin, a good man and a holy monk, she realizes: "As Brother Edvin said: had a man but faith enough, his faith might work miracles. But she had no mind to have that faith herself. She did not love God and His Mother and the Saints *so* much, did not even wish to love them so—she loved the world and longed for the world."[84] This admission is all the more realistic and remarkable because Edvin has also been showing her the great artistic work being done in the building of a medieval cathedral, something that touches Kristin deeply—but leaves portions of her will unchanged. Kristin's father, Lavrans Björgulfsön, is not only the best man she knows, he is commonly regarded by all those with whom he comes into contact as a holy, good, and compassionate man, in addition to being a natural leader. So it is no small thing that, after falling in love with Erlend Nikulaussön, a man of bad reputation who has run off with another man's wife and had two sons with her, Kristin says, "Well I know that never can I give up Erlend now—not if I should tread my own father underfoot."[85] This, of course, sets her on the path that we might call the *Inferno* of this *Divine Comedy*.

Undset's novel even has a three-part structure like the *Comedy*. In *The Bridal Wreath,* the first part, as in Dante, we feel sympathy for the errant lovers and their sins, even though their path toward marriage causes great pain to others. A kind of *Purgatory* follows in *The Mistress of Husaby*, the second volume, inside and outside their marriage. They become somewhat hardened toward one another. Yet we also discover a greater goodness in Erlend and a greater coldness in Kristin than at first appeared. Erlend and Kristin's father reach a kind of reconciliation before the latter's death, and by the time of the birth of her first child, Kristin undertakes a kind of repentance. In the last volume, *The Cross*, Erlend emerges as a heroic figure, defending Norway from Swedish domination and dying in an attack by a

[84] Undset, *Bridal Wreath*, 62.

[85] Ibid., 214.

mob at home. Kristin, now severed from him irrevocably, embraces the religious life and, after hard but successful spiritual struggles, dies while nursing victims of the Black Death. She expresses her own version of Dante's "love that moves the sun and other stars": "God had held her fast in a covenant made for her without her knowledge by a love poured out upon her richly—and in despite of her self-will, in despite of her heavy earthbound spirit, somewhat of this love had become *part* of her, had wrought in her like sunlight in the earth, had brought forth increase which not even the hottest flames of fleshly love nor its wildest bursts of wrath could lay waste wholly."[86]

In the wrong context, this might be only a conventionally pious sentiment. After the accurate portrayal of Kristin's tumultuous and checkered life in a vividly told story, however, it is an affirmation that few authors, perhaps only Dostoyevsky among the moderns, have earned the right to say convincingly. But others among Catholic authors would try as well, on this and other subjects.

[86] Sigrid Undset, *The Cross*, vol. 3 of *Kristin Lavransdatter*, trans. Charles Archer (New York: Vintage, 1987), 401.

Chapter 10

The Two Frances

The usual historiography presents France as turning into a secular state (with periodic falls back into monarchy) during the nineteenth century—a political liberalization and secularization accompanying cultural ones as well. But this is in fact quite misleading. Like England in the same period, nineteenth-century France also experienced a vigorous spiritual flowering—and a kind of rebirth of Catholic culture. The revival stemmed from multiple and sometimes paradoxical causes, but it was strong in its way, nonetheless. Almost any attempt to explain large cultural factors in France has to look back to the French Revolution of 1789, which gave rise to what has often been called "the two Frances", one secular and militantly anti-Church, the other more traditionally Catholic with an occasional nostalgia for the French kings. Though this division weakened somewhat in the closing years of the twentieth century, it still helps to explain a lot even well into the twenty-first century. For instance, the violent persecution of the Church during the Terror and the attempt to paint the Church as a repressive force called forth counter-arguments, most notably Chateaubriand's *The Genius of Christianity* (1802), which pointed to all the art, poetry, painting, and architecture, to say nothing of the exalted religious feeling, produced by Catholicism. Chateaubriand's approach was Romantic and would be repudiated even by some Catholics as tastes changed. But his book was very influential and, coming so early after the Revolution, pointed to the fact that Christianity was not as moribund as its enemies assumed.

Indeed the nineteenth century, which saw little in the way of great Catholic thought in France displayed significant moments of new Catholic devotions and apparitions in Lourdes, La Salette, Rue de Bac, Paray-le-Monial, Lisieux, and several other places. And there was also a Catholic literary undercurrent. Charles Baudelaire, the notorious author of the collection of poems entitled *The Flowers of Evil* (first published in 1857, but added to in several subsequent editions), was the first of the great modern French poets. He was not a Catholic when he wrote those poems, but he became one later, and, in retrospect, we can see that religious themes were present throughout his work. In the opening poem, "Au Lecteur", of *Les fleurs du mal*, for instance, sin and the devil are a central occupation:

To the Reader

Folly and error, avarice and vice,
Employ our souls and waste our bodies' force.
As mangey beggars incubate their lice,
We nourish our innocuous remorse.

Our sins are stubborn, craven our repentance.
For our weak vows we ask excessive prices.
Trusting our tears will wash away the sentence,
We sneak off where the muddy road entices.

Cradled in evil, that Thrice-Great Magician,
The Devil, rocks our souls, that can't resist;
And the rich metal of our own volition
Is vaporised by that sage alchemist.

The Devil pulls the strings by which we're worked:
By all revolting objects lured, we slink
Hellwards; each day down one more step we're jerked
Feeling no horror, through the shades that stink.

Just as a lustful pauper bites and kisses
The scarred and shrivelled breast of an old whore,
We steal, along the roadside, furtive blisses,
Squeezing them, like stale oranges, for more.

Packed tight, like hives of maggots, thickly seething
Within our brains a host of demons surges.
Deep down into our lungs at every breathing,
Death flows, an unseen river, moaning dirges.

If rape or arson, poison, or the knife
Has wove no pleasing patterns in the stuff
Of this drab canvas we accept as life—
It is because we are not bold enough!

Amongst the jackals, leopards, mongrels, apes,
Snakes, scorpions, vultures, that with hellish din,
Squeal, roar, writhe, gambol, crawl, with monstrous shapes,
In each man's foul menagerie of sin—

There's one more damned than all. He never gambols,
Nor crawls, nor roars, but, from the rest withdrawn,
Gladly of this whole earth would make a shambles
And swallow up existence with a yawn ...

Boredom! He smokes his hookah, while he dreams
Of gibbets, weeping tears he cannot smother.
You know this dainty monster, too, it seems—
Hypocrite reader!—You!—My twin!—My brother![1]

The recognition of sin and folly in the poem (the translation here is by the English poet and convert Roy Campbell) is, of course, not yet a fully Catholic vision. But as other great nineteenth-century French writers and thinkers—Verlaine, Huysmans, even Rimbaud—reflected on the human condition, the Catholic view began to seem more realistic than the naturalistic or materialistic one. And they, like Baudelaire, ended up inside the Church, or very close, anyway.

This phenomenon is most clearly visible in the reaction to a highly important cultural figure in nineteenth-century France, Ernest Renan. Renan is believed to have left the seminary within days of Newman's conversion in England—a coincidence, but one with startling significance. Renan would become the great advocate of a secular and scientific view of the world, notably in his 1890 book *L'avenir de la science* (*The Future of Science*), which took the rather standard view at the time that religion was a fable concocted in the infancy of the human race that would now be superseded by the hard, factual knowledge of modern scientific research. In itself, of course, such a view is utterly inhuman; it leaves no room for the most human of things, including love,

[1] Charles Baudelaire, "To the Reader", in *Baudelaire in English*, ed. Carol Clark and Robert Sykes (London and New York: Penguin, 1997), 4–5.

beauty, devotion, and the spirit. And while Renan was very influential within one part of French culture, he produced a reaction in another. In fact, he produced a reaction in his own family. Ernest Psichari, his grandson, revolted and became a Catholic mystical writer and friend of Charles Péguy and Jacques Maritain, though his life was cut tragically short by his death in the early days of World War I. Maritain himself was the grandson of Jules Favre, one of the leaders of the anti-Catholic Republican faction. And the Maritains and Péguy were early admirers of Henri Bergson, whose whole philosophical effort was devoted to rejecting the merely mechanical understanding of the world (Bergson, who was Jewish by blood, only held back from becoming a Catholic in the 1940s out of solidarity with the Jewish people, then being persecuted in Nazi-occupied France). But the reaction to a strict materialism was, of course, much wider than these family differences.

The Pilgrim of the Absolute

The literary side of the French Catholic intellectual tradition in the twentieth century consisted, as artistic movements always do, of various eccentric people and works, but none odder than Léon Bloy. Bloy was so singular that it is difficult even to say what he and his writings were. He wrote what might loosely be called a couple of novels, *Le désespéré* and *La femme pauvre*, both of which appeared before 1900. They have their defenders, usually on extra-literary grounds. But it is clear that Bloy was one of those figures whose influence is of a more personal—we might say prophetic—rather than literary nature. Like the major prophets, he seemed at times to border on madness (no other word will do), involving wild speculations in which his analysis of men and society seems to be a blur of true religion and psychopathology, serious social criticism and disturbing self-absorption. He embraced poverty, fine in itself, but not so good for the father of a family. Two of his children may have died from their father's impecuniousness. Bloy denounced those who did not support him or his ideas, but he rashly alienated many who might have and showed signs of the kind of personality that, for reasons not entirely clear, almost seems poised to turn on people the minute they start to show sympathy and agreement.

How did such an irascible figure exert an influence in early twentieth-century France? That is difficult to say. In 1906, he was godfather for Jacques and Raïssa Maritain at their entry into the Catholic Church. By that step, the Maritains achieved their aim of finding a meaningful way of life in a world that modern science seemed to have pronounced absurd. So their closeness to such a man—someone who thundered like an Old Testament prophet against materialist France and emphasized the message of La Salette that God's avenging hand would not be stayed—may have had something to do with the emotionalism at the time of "two twenty-year-old children", as Maritain later put it. But they remained convinced, despite all evidence to the contrary—evidence that has only grown with time—that he was a "pilgrim of the absolute", a special figure who in the strange ways of God was a prophetic voice in pre–World War I France.

Part of that prophetic stance was, of course, to denounce the atheist socialism ascendant in the early years of the century in France, including the government of Émile Combes, which dispossessed the Church. But Bloy, and the Maritains, also looked askance at the Catholic Church, including much of the clergy and hierarchy, because of her lingering alliances with the *ancien régime*, the bourgeoisie, and the military over against the poor and what the Maritains, at least, regarded as humane social and intellectual developments. Bloy's personal vehemence about what Maritain called "the Gospels' improprieties" was needed, Maritain thought, to wake up those who were so dead to the Gospels that more measured and reasoned tones would not reach them. Bloy's violence, however, probably drove many away as well. But he exerted a fascination also for the revolutionary Catholic painter Georges Rouault and other cultural figures, despite—or perhaps because of—his apocalyptic messages that an "unheard-of Drama" was about to overtake France. Two world wars followed in a half century, but Bloy seemed to have had something even more cosmic and earth-shattering in mind.

To the eye, Maritain admitted, Bloy's flinty nature was like "a charred and blackened cathedral" with the whiteness within—the very opposite of a "whited sepulcher". Or he was a "cathedral gargoyle". Maritain admired his solidarity with the poor, especially "the poor among the nations: the Jews".[2] Nonetheless, Bloy's

[2] On this and earlier points, see Jean-Luc Barré, *Jacques and Raïssa Maritain: Beggars for Heaven*, trans. Bernard E. Doering (Notre Dame, Ind.: University of Notre Dame Press, 2005), especially 62–76.

book *Le salut par les Juifs* (Salvation through the Jews) today seems bizarre, allowing the Jews a special place in history, but special in that they themselves are always historically crucifying "money", which is the blood of the poor, and also somehow Jesus. The irrational sliding of images and metaphors from one conceptual register to another makes all his books frustrating reading. In another notorious instance, Bloy identified the female genitalia with paradise and the Cross with the male phallus, understandably raising cries of outrage from Catholics.[3]

Yet it was the personal appeal and the occasional sentence of sharp spiritual insight that, for a few readers and acquaintances, gave him convincing power as the "pilgrim of the absolute", a phrase that might have drawn jeers from most people. Graham Greene, for example, put one of Bloy's sentences as an epigraph to *The End of the Affair*: "Man has places in his heart which do not yet exist, and into them enters suffering, that they may have existence." And he anticipated several generations of Catholics to come: "Today we need apostles, not conference attendees; witnesses, not word-spinners." His most quoted line has become a modern Catholic proverb: "There is only one tragedy: not to have been a saint."

A man who could write like that, even if only in short bursts amid much that is less illuminating, had a real spiritual life. Even the admiring Jacques Maritain concedes that in his search for absolute justice, Bloy was sometimes unjust to individuals, whom he almost automatically transformed into symbols of his religious preoccupations,[4] a harsh procedure that had its practitioners among secular ideologues in the twentieth century as well, with quite bloody results. Fortunately, there were others almost as vehement as Bloy about the lack

[3] Conor Cruise O'Brien, writing under the assumed name Donat O'Donnell, gives an interesting account of Bloy in his *Maria Cross: Imaginative Patterns in a Group of Modern Catholic Writers* (London: Chatto & Windus, 1954), 201–22. In a footnote, he cites the original statement, in Latin (Bloy knew better than to put it in French), from *Le Mendiant ingrat* that brought Bloy much criticism: *Membrum virile symbolice Crucis effigies ab antiquitate videtur. Christus moriens in patibulo emisit Spiritum. Vir coïtans et hoc modo cruciatus in muliere anhelans emittit semen.* Just another instance of Bloy's rather loose relation to historical fact and capacity to allow symbols to run far beyond reason.

[4] See Jacques Maritain, "Quelques pages sur Léon Bloy", in Jacques et Raïssa Maritain, *Oeuvres complètes*, vol. 3 (Paris: Éd. Saint-Paul, 1985), 997. The whole essay is worth reading for a personal portrait of a difficult man by someone of no small power of observation and analysis.

of charity in the modern world but who were also artful enough to be able to capture the attention of a much wider audience.

"Not Since Dostoyevsky . . ."

Perhaps the most significant Catholic cultural and literary figure at the beginning of the twentieth century was the French Catholic, turned socialist (of a unique kind), turned—by a kind of "deepening"—Catholic socialist (of an even more unusual kind), Charles Péguy (1873–1914). Some in English-speaking countries might think G.K. Chesterton merits that position. The two shared several characteristics, as will appear below, but there are ways in which Péguy possessed a larger intellectual and spiritual scope. For example, both were converts, in a sense, but Chesterton regarded Catholicism as primarily sanity—the antidote to the madness and disorder of radical skepticism as he found it, mostly, in England. By contrast, Péguy regarded Christianity as the extension of temporal solidarity into eternity itself. He was not much concerned about skepticism, which weighed little for him in light of the need for solidarity. As he once tersely summed up the modern defenses of the faith: "It is not arguments that are wanting. It is charity. . . . All the pseudo-scientific arguments would be as nothing, would weigh nothing, if there were an ounce of charity."[5] His life and his work form a unified witness to integrity and catholicity, in all senses of the word. He resolved, after a fashion, the split between the "two Frances", the Republican and the Catholic. Even more remarkably, he presented a vision that draws together life in this world and the next, something without parallel in modern Catholic culture.

Péguy was, like Chesterton, astonishingly prolific and at the same time a great undisciplined genius. And, like Chesterton, by purely literary standards he may stand slightly lower in the literature of the period than, say, great Catholic poets like Paul Claudel or great novelists like François Mauriac. But in terms of spiritual depth and original intuitions, he has no rival. Like many other pre–Vatican II figures,

[5] Charles Péguy, *Temporal and Eternal,* trans. Alexander Dru with a foreword by Pierre Manent (Indianapolis: Liberty Fund, 2001), 56. This volume contains large portions of two of Péguy's most important essays: *Notre jeunesse* and *Clio I.* The quotation here is from *Notre jeunesse.*

he is negleced by current secular culture for complicated religious and political reasons, though older French cultural leaders were hypnotized by him and some contemporary French intellectuals have rediscovered his insight into modern matters as prophetic, if hard to grasp within modernity itself.[6] Gifted minds in their own right as different as the French philosopher Gabriel Marcel, the Swiss theologian Hans Urs von Balthasar, and the British poet Geoffrey Hill have tried to put various audiences into contact with his great spirit.[7] In fact, Péguy's life is a strong witness to the fact that a great spirit and heart outweigh even sheer genius. When cultural conditions change, Péguy may one day be recognized as a figure on the order of Kierkegaard or Newman, and perhaps something more besides. Alain-Fournier, the author of the classic French novel *Le grand Meaulnes*, who died in combat almost on the same day as Péguy in the First World War, expressed what many of his contemporaries felt: "I say, knowing what I am saying, that not since Dostoievsky has there been a man who was so clearly a man of God."[8]

Paying the Price

Péguy was killed by a bullet through the head at the Battle of the Marne in 1914. He was barely forty and had anticipated his death in a passage in his epic-length poem *Eve*, which later established itself as a popular item in anthologies of French poetry:

> Blessèd are those whom a great battle leaves
> Stretched out on the ground in front of God's face,
> Blessèd the lives that just wars erase,
> Blessèd the ripe wheat, the wheat gathered in sheaves.

It was a dramatic end to a heroic life.

[6] Cf. Alain Finkielkraut, *Le mécontemporain: Péguy, lecteur du monde moderne* (Paris: Gallimard, 1991).

[7] Marcel in *Creative Fidelity*; von Balthasar in his *The Glory of the Lord: A Theological Aesthetics*; and Hill in his poem "The Mystery of the Charity of Charles Péguy".

[8] Quoted in Marjorie Villiers, *Charles Péguy: A Study in Integrity* (Westport, Conn.: Greenwood Press, 1975), 236. Villiers is still the best biography of Péguy in English. In French, Robert Burac, *Charles Péguy: La révolution et la grâce* (Paris: R. Laffont, 1994).

Péguy was never a mere writer—the kind of thinker he sometimes called a "clever abstractionist" or an "intellectual"—that is, someone who stands outside life as some sort of superior observer. He even dismissed Dante's great poem *The Divine Comedy* because he believed—wrongly, students of Dante would argue—that Dante went through Hell, Purgatory, and Paradise as a kind of *tourist*, personally uninvolved in the fates of the souls he encountered in the afterlife and unaware of his solidarity with them. Though this judgment was mistaken, Péguy risked himself, his wife and children, and "the first of treasures ... peace of heart" for the truth, and truth not just as a concept, but as a living engagement with reality. In this, he was developing some truths out of his own experience and from notions he had encountered attending Bergson's famous lectures at the Sorbonne in the opening years of the twentieth century.

As we saw in the opening chapter of the present work, Jacques and Raïssa Maritain attended those same lectures in flight from a materialistic understanding of the world that led to despair. In contrast, Péguy felt less threatened by a materialist ideology perhaps because he had a natural affinity for Bergson's sense of the dynamic nature of existence as opposed to the static abstractions of concepts. It was clearly more a matter of kindred spirits than mere intellectual agreement. Bergson once said of him: "He had a marvelous gift for stepping beyond the materiality of beings, going beyond it and penetrating to the soul. Thus it is that he knew my most secret thought, such as I have never expressed it, such as I would have wished to express it."[9]

Péguy did not learn from Bergson a set of ideas that might be analyzed and debated, or "put into practice". All that was what Jacques Maritain would address—and generally find wanting—about the great master's philosophical work. Instead, in Péguy's hands, Bergson's central intuitions blossomed out into a life commitment. For example, once when Georges Sorel was making a point in the shop where Péguy produced his journal *Cahiers de la quinzaine*, Péguy interrupted: "You are right, but one has no right to be right unless one is willing personally to pay the price of demonstrating the rightness of the

[9] Quoted by Julien Green in Péguy, *Basic Verities*, trans. Julien and Anne Green (New York: Pantheon Books, 1950), 9.

truth."[10] In other words (and in ways that even go a bit beyond Cardinal Newman's well-known distinction between "notional" and "real" truth), truth required personal commitment—and action. When you read Péguy, you do not merely follow a string of words with your eyes or follow a chain of reasoning, you enter a passionate current of life.

He was born in 1873 near Orléans and grew up with a mother and grandmother who were basically illiterate (his father died during his first year). They earned a bare living recaning chairs sixteen hours a day, seven days a week. Péguy learned the trade and also helped out, well into his teens, with the annual harvests in the region. He followed a typical trajectory at first: he lost his faith in his teenage years in favor of a kind of utopian socialism. Though he showed great gifts from the moment he entered school, Péguy was as close to a peasant as any major literary or intellectual figure who ever lived. Part of his genius lay in the way he held on to simple human truths even as he moved into the complexities of faith and reason and a host of questions arising from the whole modern world. Sheer brainpower would take him to the École normale supérieure and the Sorbonne, the summits of the French educational system. But except for some activity in political causes, he would live a largely uneventful life—at least in the way most people conceive of events. His activity consisted in a wide-ranging attempt to retrieve an authentic temporal and spiritual life from the various incrustations that were making it difficult to find in the modern world, even for simple people. Despite the constant simplicity of his words, they have a brilliance and authority that seem to revitalize politics, mysticism, war, peace, love, honor, and death. In him, the timeless depths of the classical and Christian past suddenly find a new voice that is also a prophetic and urgent message to the present.

As a young man in Orléans, Péguy gravitated toward simple workers and peasants who were interested in freedom and learning, even if they had to pursue them in the evening after long hours at work: "I consider it a personal blessing to have known, in my earliest youth, some of those old republicans; admirable men; hard on themselves; and good for events; I learned through them what it means to have a whole and upright conscience."[11] Several sober intellectuals have disputed

[10] Quoted in Villiers, *Charles Péguy*, 211.

[11] Charles Péguy, *Oeuvres complètes*, vol. 2 (Paris: Nouvelle revue française, 1920), 164.

whether his exuberant portrait of the old France is accurate. Péguy is as skeptical as anyone of romantic fantasies, but he is there to witness that such people once existed and not all that long ago.

In a remarkable passage written near the end of his life, Péguy describes a world he claims to have known personally. He seems to have divined something profound about the shift from traditional France to modern France, and his way of presenting it is unforgettable:

> We have known, we have touched the bygone France and we have known her intact. We have been her children.—
>
> We will try if we can to present this.—The world has changed less since Jesus Christ than it has in the last thirty years [Péguy is writing in 1913]. There was the age of antiquity (and of the Bible). There was the Christian age. There is the modern age. Even after the war [1870, Franco-Prussian War], a farm in the Beauce country resembled a farm of the Gallo-Roman age infinitely more than this same farm resembles itself today. Or rather, this farm was like its Gallo-Roman self, as far as customs, regulations, seriousness, gravity, in structure itself, in institution and in dignity. (And even, at bottom, it was close to a farm in the time of Xenophon.) We will try to explain this. We have known a time when, if a simple woman spoke a word, it was her race itself, her being, her people, that spoke, which came out. And when a workman lit his cigarette, what he was about to tell you was not what a journalist had said in that morning's paper. The freethinkers of that time were more Christian than our devout people of today. An average parish of that time was infinitely closer to a fifteenth-century parish, or one of the fourth century—or let us say one of the fifth or eighth centuries—than to one of our present-day parishes....
>
> We will never know the true extent of the decency and truthfulness of the soul of this people. Such delicacy, such deep culture will never more be found. Nor such a delicacy and cautiousness of speech. The people of those days would have blushed for our best tone of today, which is the bourgeois tone. And today, everyone is bourgeois.[12]

Many people today blithely invoke "the people" and civil society as a counterweight to much that is wrong in the modern world. Péguy would agree, but he does not speak of the people in the

[12] From the 1913 *Cahiers de la quinzaine* entitled *L'argent*. Translation from *Basic Verities*, 77–79, with alterations by the present writer.

careless and superficial way of the modern media. For him, the older popular virtues—when there are truly such—have concrete connection to the high points of both classical and Christian culture, the two poles many think divide modern France. Péguy has a very different perspective. In a remarkable essay, *Les suppliants parallèles* (The parallel suppliants), for instance, he shows the noble parallels between the petitions the Russian workers presented as Christian subjects to the czar in 1905 and choruses from *Oedipus Rex*, the ancient Greek tragedy by Sophocles.[13] Without *fidelity*—a key term in Péguy's vocabulary—to the human nobility that may exist in all social classes, even the peasants and workers will become corrupt.[14] Indeed, it was one of his central preoccupations that the French people themselves were becoming corrupted. And it is the "intellectuals", in the sense of a cultural and intellectual elite that believes in nothing higher than its own superiority and material comfort, who have helped bring about that corruption of the French people.

It is typical of Péguy that he does not place the cause of this corruption where others typically would, in the standard large-scale political or economic upheavals. For him, the French Revolution, once it settled into classical Republican principles, is not as opposed to the Old France or Christianity as many think. The *mystiques*, roughly the ideal inspiration of each, is close to each other. But the *politiques*, political formations that have hardened around each *mystique*, can become blind and bitter foes. All *mystiques* develop a temporal side in their *politiques*, but there comes a point, among Christians or Republicans, when a partisan spirit takes over: "The whole point (what matters), the essential thing, is that *in each order, in each system*, THE MYSTIQUE SHOULD NOT BE DEVOURED BY THE POLITIQUE TO WHICH IT GAVE BIRTH."[15] When that happens, the deep humanity common to all the great *mystiques* is lost, and the politicians and intellectuals—who are not organically connected to the

[13] Charles Péguy, *Les suppliants parallèles*, in *Oeuvres en prose, 1898–1908*, Bibliothèque de la Pléiade 140 (Paris: Gallimard, 1959), 869–935.

[14] "I believe that it is in Péguy, and Péguy alone, that we can find certain elements of a metaphysics of fidelity": Gabriel Marcel, *Creative Fidelity*, trans. Robert Rosthal (New York: Farrar, Straus, 1964), 153.

[15] From *Notre jeunesse*, in the excerpted translation by Alexander Dru, in Péguy, *Temporal and Eternal*, 17.

people, the true source of greatness—predominate. That division has become the bane of France.

He has an instructive—and humorous—view of the division:

> Our good masters at the primary school told us, in effect, that, up to the first of January 1789 (Paris time), our poor old France was an abyss of darkness and ignorance, of horrifying miseries, of crude barbarity (in fact, they did their job, taught their lesson), and so well you could hardly believe it: on the first of January 1789, electric light was installed everywhere. Our good adversaries in the [Catholic] School opposite told us, roughly speaking, that up to the first of January 1789, nature's sun was shining; since the first of January 1789, we have only got electric light.[16]

In the heated ideological atmosphere of the "two Frances", he appeals to a common ideal:

> The argument is not between an *ancien régime*, an old France, that supposedly ended in 1789, and a new France, supposedly beginning in 1789. The fight goes much deeper. It is between the whole of the old France, pagan France (the Renaissance, the humanities, culture, ancient and modern letters, Greek and Latin and French), Christian France, traditional and revolutionary, monarchist, royalist and republican—and on the other hand, and on the other side, in opposition, the dominion of a certain form of elementary, primary thought, which became established about 1881, which is not the Republic though calling itself the Republic, which is a parasite on the Republic and is properly speaking the domination of the intellectual party.
>
> The contest is not between heroes and saints; the fight is against the intellectuals, those who despise heroes and saints equally.
>
> The argument is not between two orders of greatness. The fight is between those who hate greatness itself, who hate the one and the other equally, who have made themselves the official upholders of all that is base, small minded and vile.[17]

By around 1881, he argues, the old pride in hard work, productivity, and craftsmanship was beginning to pass even in farms and workshops. Though Péguy was an activist for workers, he deplores

[16] Ibid., 19–20.
[17] Ibid., 20.

the new practice among formal labor groups of demanding the largest compensation for the least work and even, something unthinkable in the old system, of destroying tools and machinery during strikes. Both the Church and the Republic, he claims, have contributed to this social disaster in their mistaken attacks on one another and by their intellectualism instead of real solidarity. For Péguy, the true Catholic and true Republican virtues are parallel achievements, producing saints, on the one hand, and heroes, on the other. The decline of Christianity, he warns, was part of the same evil spirit leading to the decline of the Republic, of education, of work, and of the French people themselves.

In 1900, Péguy founded a journal, the *Cahiers de la quinzaine*, as a forum for freely expressing truth, because, as he explains, "the man who doesn't bawl out the truth when he knows the truth becomes the accomplice of liars and frauds."[18] For Péguy, the root of any *mystique* consists in remaining *fidèle* (faithful) to truth and justice despite party commitments. He would refuse to impose an orthodoxy even on writers for the *Cahiers de la quinzaine*, which as a *journal vrai* practiced freedom of opinion by allowing contributors to express views that were not his own: "A review only continues to have life in it so long as each issue annoys at least a fifth of its subscribers. Justice lies in seeing that this fifth is not every time the same one."[19] And even as a youthful socialist, he rebelled when a socialist congress demanded that publications refrain from putting out material that might harm the party. Without support from either right or left in a sharply ideological France, his fidelity led to persecution, a Christ-like passion, and gradual economic strangulation of himself and his wife and children by established powers.

Hans Urs von Balthasar devotes the concluding 120 pages of the third volume of his *Theological Aesthetics* to Péguy, suggesting that Péguy's "way" of bringing together the temporal and the eternal, the carnal and the spiritual, clerical and anti-clerical, Catholic and Republican, *politique* and *mystique*, and several other pairs of seeming opposites is crucial to the authentic recovery of an incarnational Christianity in the modern world. In von Balthasar's view, Péguy is able to achieve such unity because he operates at a great spiritual

[18] Ibid., 133.
[19] From the *Cahiers* entitled *L'argent* quoted in Villiers, *Charles Péguy*, 311.

depth, far beneath all superficial oppositions, where fundamental convergence becomes possible. This is more than the common modernist description of complementary truths as "in tension", more even than Chesterton's "Christian paradoxes". It leads into a realm that can at least suggest God's primordial oneness behind the multiplicity of the created world.

In addition, von Balthasar discerns in Péguy one of his own deepest preoccupations: the restoration of hope as a theological virtue that may even suggest the possibility of universal salvation—a *cité harmonieuse* that extends across the whole of the natural and the supernatural with no one excluded, however great a sinner.[20] A major stumbling block about Christianity for the young Péguy is the doctrine about hell, which clearly goes back to Jesus himself and cannot be lightly or seriously dismissed. Péguy becomes one of the several main Catholic figures in the twentieth century who comes to express the hope that hell, with its eternal punishments, though a possible fate, might in fact be unpopulated through God's mercy.

Péguy is not modest in his claims about his importance in French religious history. As he writes to a friend after the "deepening" that led to his explicit embrace of Christianity again: "Mine is no ordinary life. My life is a wager. *At the deepest level, there is a Catholic renaissance coming to fulfillment through me* [emphasis added]. One must see this for what it is and stand one's ground. I am a sinner. I am not a saint. You can recognize a saint at first glance. I'm a good sinner. A witness. A Christian in the parish, a sinner, but one possessed of the treasures of grace."[21] There were others who contributed to this French renaissance. But in modern times, it is only Péguy who, both in his life and in his work, really offers a chance to bring back together the "two Frances", Republican and Catholic.

One sign of this power is that he has been claimed in the twentieth century by both the French political Left and the Right. He might even be said to have overcome in important ways (or at least to have pointed to possible solutions for) the rupture between France's past and present, which in his vision represents a parallel crisis to the

[20] Hans Urs von Balthasar, *The Glory of the Lord: A Theological Aesthetics*, vol. 3: *Studies in Theological Style: Lay Styles*, trans. Andrew Louth, John Saward, Martin Simon, and Rowan Williams, ed. John Riches (San Francisco: Ignatius Press, 1986), 400–517.

[21] Charles Péguy, *Lettres et entretiens* (Paris: L'Artisan du livre, 1927), 158.

ruptures within the modern Republican tradition and within Christianity itself. He spoke of the Dreyfus Affair, for instance, as a case that revealed a crisis or rupture in three *mystiques*: Judaism, Christianity, and France. When Catholics vehemently accused Dreyfus because they were anti-Semitic at the time, they betrayed the Catholic *mystique*, which in reality is rooted in Judaism. Similarly, when the Socialist government of Émile Combes (a bitter and bigoted ex-seminarian) oppressed religious orders, confiscated property, and made it difficult for Catholic schools to operate, as it did after 1905, it was betraying its own Republican *mystique*.

This fundamental fairness and honesty helps to account for his broad appeal beyond the usual party boundaries, something very nearly unique in a country like France. In the 1940s, when Jacques Maritain was broadcasting radio messages to Nazi-occupied France from New York, he invoked Péguy's name. Maritain had worked for Péguy as a young man in Paris. He spoke both from personal acquaintance and from a just appraisal of Péguy's heroic spirit when he addressed France as "ancient land of Joan of Arc and Péguy" and the French as "companions of Joinville and Péguy, people of Joan of Arc". In London, Charles de Gaulle made similar appeals and begins and ends his memoirs with quotations from Péguy. The French lionizing of Péguy in such a critical moment helped carry his name to the rest of Europe and beyond. In America, Julien Green's selections and translations from Péguy—*Basic Verities* and *Men and Saints*—appeared right after the war. Green did a brilliant introductory job (and rightly kept Péguy's incomparable French on the pages facing the translations), but his work can also foster certain misimpressions.

The brief passages Green chose can give the impression that Péguy is an aphoristic writer like Chesterton:

> The social revolution will be moral, or it will not be.[22]

> Tyranny is always better organized than freedom.[23]

> There is only one Lady in the world who has caused more wars than injustice: and that is justice.[24]

[22] Péguy, *Basic Verities*, 119.
[23] Ibid., 153.
[24] Ibid., 167.

All of us stand on the breach today. We are all stationed at the frontier. The frontier is everywhere.[25]

The sinner lies at the very heart of Christianity.[26]

Homer is new this morning and perhaps nothing is as old as today's newspaper.[27]

Everything begins in mysticism and ends in politics.[28]

This is all well and good, and many of these sayings have become well known even among people who have never read Péguy. But he also needs to be read in longer stretches to see the sheer power and trajectory of his genius. Indeed, his work is all characterized—from the earliest essays to the final poems and books—by a hypnotic, incantatory quality only occasionally studded with pithy sayings.

The Aesthetics of Incantation

There is a rationale to the repetition. Instead of linear argument, which for Péguy would only reflect a shallow rationalism, he draws the reader into a kind of participation in the developing work. From his earliest days, his texts are like the rushes woven by his mother and grandmother in recaning chairs, the cumulative result of small repetitive acts. Even in his more straightforward expository essays and in the literary texts, Péguy is always an incantatory writer, almost hypnotizing in his repetition of words and phrases as a way to involve the reader in the dynamic rather than merely abstractly describing something. André Gide once wrote brilliantly of this procedure after reading one of Péguy's *mystères* that "Péguy doesn't explain a thing, he represents." And Gide continued:

Twelve sentences would have sufficed me for summing up these 250 pages. But the repetitions ... are intrinsic and a part of the whole.... Péguy's style is like that of very old litanies ... like Arab songs, like the

[25] Ibid., 177.
[26] Ibid., 179.
[27] Ibid., 127.
[28] Ibid., 109.

> monotonous songs of the Landes; one could compare it to a desert; a desert of alfalfa, of sand, or of pebbles.... Each looks like the other, but is just a little different, and this difference corrects, relinquishes, repeats, or appears to repeat, accentuates, affirms, and always more certainly one advances.... Like a believer [saying] the same prayer during all the time in which he is praying, or at least, almost the same prayer ... almost without his noticing it, almost in spite of himself, [beginning] over again.[29]

To read Péguy is, as with no other mere writer, to become part of that demand for a blessing.

What Gide was referring to is something like the poetic texture as it can be seen and felt in passages like this excerpt from the third of the mysteries Péguy wrote, *The Mystery of the Holy Innocents*:

> I am their father, God says. *Our Father which art in Heaven.* My Son told them often enough that I am their father.
> I am their judge. My Son said it to them. I am also their father.
> I am above all their father.
> In short I am their father. Whoever is a father is above all a father. *Our Father which art in Heaven.* He who has once been a father can never cease to be a father.
> They are my Son's brothers; they are my children; I am their father.
> *Our Father which art in Heaven*, my Son taught them that prayer. *Sic ergo vos orabitis. Therefore you shall pray thus.*
> *Our Father which art in Heaven*, that day he knew very well what he was doing, my Son who loved them so much.
> Who lived among them, who was like one of them.
> Who went about like them, who spoke like them, who lived like them.
> Who suffered.
> Who suffered like them, who died like them.
> And who loves them so much, having known them.
> Who has brought back to Heaven, a kind of flavour of man, a kind of flavour of earth.
> My Son who loved them so much, who loves them eternally in Heaven.

[29] Villiers, *Charles Péguy*, 247–48.

He knew very well what he was doing on that day, my Son who loves them so much.
When he put that barrier between them and me, *Our Father which art in Heaven*, those three or four words.
That barrier which my anger and perhaps my justice will never pass.
Happy is he who sleeps under the protection of the vanguard of those three or four words.
Those words which go before every prayer as the hands of a supplicant before his face.
As the two hands of a supplicant advance joined together before his face and the tears on his face.
Those three or four words which conquer me, me the unconquerable,
And which they send in front of their misery like two invincible hands joined together.
Those three or four words which advance like a strong prow in front of a weak ship,
And which cleave the wave of my anger.
And when the prow has passed, the ship passes and all the fleet behind it.
Nowadays, God says, that is how I see them; And during my eternity, eternally, God says, By the contrivance of my Son, it is thus that I must eternally see them.
(And that I must judge them. How would you have me judge them, at present
After that)?
Our Father which art in Heaven. My Son knew just how to set about it,
To bind the arms of my justice and to loose the arms of my mercy.
(I do not speak of my anger which has never been anything but my justice,
And sometimes my charity).
And nowadays I must judge them like a father,
In so far as a father can judge.[30]

[30] Charles Péguy, *The Mystery of the Holy Innocents*, trans. Pansy Parkenham (New York: Harper, 1956); available online through the Catholic Information Network (www.centropeguy.org/cachepeguy7.htm).

This incantatory repetition, along with the note of tenderness, forms a central thread even in work prior to Péguy's conversion. One of his earliest texts, *La cité harmonieuse*, presents a perfected earthly city—via similar blocks of repetition—that is in some respects the young socialist's alternative to Augustine's *City of God*. It excluded none and, in particular, left no one without sufficient material welfare to live—and to live a decent human life. This initial focus on a just earthly realm remains the foundation for Péguy's spiritual realm when he finds himself a Catholic again. Like Christ, the Christian vision has to unite the human and the divine in a common life. Therefore—at least in his own mind—Péguy does not become a Catholic again by a conversion in the sense of a turning back. He claims that it is by continuing more deeply into the way of human solidarity, by *un approfondissement*, a new hope that all might also be redeemed in the coming City of God, that he comes to integrate the temporal and eternal, usually thought of as separated in French cultural politics, into a unified whole again.

He describes this process in characteristic style:

> We have constantly followed, we have constantly held to the same straight way, and it is the same straight way that has led us to where we are. It was not at all an evolution, as one says a little foolishly, employing without consideration, through an incessant abuse itself, one of the words of modern language that has become itself the most lax, it was a deepening.... It is by a constant deepening of our heart along the same way, it is in no way through an evolution. It is in no way through a turning back that we have found the way of Christianity. We have not found it in coming back. We found it at the end.... We may have been sinners. We have certainly greatly been so. *Pro nobis peccatoribus*. But we have never ceased to be in the good way.[31]

This is an unusual way of "conversion", and perhaps not as perfectly self-aware as it seems to be, since in the two-thousand-year-old tradition of the Church, not even the greatest of saints has ever claimed that he was already on the righteous path prior to conversion or even that a turning back was simply unnecessary because he came to discover that his own virtuous life included Catholicism.

[31] Charles Péguy, "Un nouveau théologien: M. Fernand Laudet", in *Oeuvres en prose, 1909–1914*, Bibliothèque de la Pléiade 122 (Paris: Gallimard, 1957), 998–99.

Conversion is usually an upheaval and a reorientation, even if it results in great peace. There is a fair amount of evidence that this was the case for Péguy, too, both in his interior life and in his relations with the people around him.[32] But even if Péguy's turn to the Church is questionable in the precise terms he uses, it was emblematic of something quite significant in modern conditions.

Writing "Mysteries"

There is a definite arc in Péguy's work that leads from simplicity to the major creations of his maturity. His first major literary effort, *Jeanne d'Arc*, published in 1897 when he was only twenty-four, is a long and rambling play in which, despite the basically socialist point of view, the religious dimension is already present although undeveloped (there clearly must have been some intuition on his part that this figure, so prominent in the religious and the political history of France, was both a precursor and a goal to which one should aspire).

Péguy literally "deepened" his view and presentation of this legendary French figure as he became a Catholic. He wrote many noteworthy essays over the next few years, but it was not until 1910, after his deepening into the faith, that he wrote another play, though "play" stretches the term. It is really a kind of long poetic reflection involving the voices of several characters. This one, too, is about Joan of Arc, but now the temporal and eternal dimensions are fully present in a very lyrical and evocative poetic text. The title of the entirely different work is significant: *Le mystère de la charité de Jeanne d'Arc* (*The Mystery of the Charity of Joan of Arc*). He planned on producing twelve to fifteen of such "mysteries" but was able to complete only two more—*The Porch of the Mystery of the Second Virtue* (a poem about hope) and *The Mystery of the Holy Innocents*—before he died.

In all these "mysteries", a term related to his notions of *mystique* and *politique*, the goal is never just to *present* some action or idea, but to draw the reader into a living relationship with the deep spirituality,

[32] For a comprehensive account of the conversion by people who knew him intimately at the time, see *Péguy au porche de l'Église: Correspondance inédite Jacques Maritain—Dom Louis Baillet*, ed. René Mougel and Robert Burac (Paris: Éditions du Cerf, 1997).

the *mystique* still living as a simple peasant girl in her little village of Domrémy. In other words, this is the evocation of the reality that preceded and enabled the public, world-changing career she would later have. In several respects, it is Péguy's story as well. Péguy decidedly criticizes the abstract spirituality of a certain kind of Catholicism as the failure of *mystique*, even as *the* modern heresy that has lost the people of France by failing to speak to them and remain in solidarity with them *in the everyday world of work*. This theme appears most fully and clearly in two of his long essays: *Notre jeunesse* and *Véronique, ou dialogue de l'histoire et de l'âme charnelle*.[33]

Notre jeunesse relates how the Jewish, Catholic, and French Republican interests that often clashed in the infamous Dreyfus Affair actually revealed the relationship of *mystiques* and *politiques* in the modern world. On the surface, the unjust trial and conviction of Captain Dreyfus, a Jewish army officer, seemed merely to show the sordid anti-Semitism and desire to find a scapegoat characteristic of many Catholics in France. But for Péguy, the Dreyfusards quickly declined from their exalted and just cause and showed themselves equally capable of pettiness and partisanship. In fact, Dreyfus himself proved to be a rather unattractive and shallow man—in Péguy's eyes an actual help to real Dreyfusism because Dreyfus' clear unsuitability as some sort of hero made the Dreyfusard cause all the purer in that it was supported by no quality of Dreyfus himself, only the disinterested commitment to achieve justice and, thereby, defend the honor of France.

As a man who valued discipline, courage, and the right use of military power in just causes, Péguy particularly detested what he saw as an anti-French, anti-military, near traitorous element among some Dreyfusards:

> The people want to insult and abuse the army, because today this is a good line.... In fact, at all political demonstrations it is a necessary theme. If one didn't take that line one would not look sufficiently progressive ... and it will never be known what acts of cowardice have been motivated by the fear of not looking sufficiently progressive.[34]

[33] *Oeuvres en prose, 1909–1914*, 307–498. A large portion of this dialogue may be found in a translation by Alexander Dru in *Temporal and Eternal*.

[34] From *Notre Patrie*, quoted in Villiers, *Charles Péguy*, 194.

Somewhere along this path of betrayal by the socialists and Dreyfusards, Péguy returned to Catholicism, though he was blocked from returning to the sacraments because of his marriage outside the Church and remained a critic of the Church's false social and political position as the Church primarily of the rich. A friend, Joseph Lotte, who was a university professor, stopped in to see Péguy when he was sick in bed at home. After a long conversation, Péguy merely remarked as the friend was leaving, "I've not told you everything ... I've recovered my faith. I am a Catholic." No great explanations were later forthcoming. Lotte was surprised—and surprised to realize that he himself was on the verge of conversion, which soon followed.[35]

But Péguy did not find that the Catholic parties—to say nothing of the Church as such—were doing much better than the others in keeping their *politique* from overwhelming their *mystique*. The Catholic Church seemed to have betrayed her *mystique* by becoming a temporal party in France and elsewhere. Péguy is rare among modern Catholic figures in that he faces squarely the de-Christianization of Europe without blaming it on external forces. He is quite aware of the philosophical arguments as we have seen, and the rise of modern science presents some obstacles. But the active de-Christianization of the people, the passing from a nearly unified Catholic sensibility to indifference, he thought a massive *internal* failure of the Church. Clerics who pointed to the external factors, he believed, were showing themselves to be modernists and intellectuals in the sense that they really believed a thin rationalism could disrupt deep spirituality. But because they did not possess a deep spirituality or charity, they placed undue emphasis on intellectual arguments.

Péguy was not warmly embraced by Catholics while he was still alive, perhaps partly because of this militancy toward the modern clergy. The Church had become a church of the rich and lost the working class. And that was partly owing to her venality and desire for comfort. But he went farther. Péguy made blanket claims about monasticism and withdrawal from the world that have a point—but a point taken much too far. It is true, as he says, that when God himself chose to become incarnate, he was not exactly withdrawing from the world. In a way, the Incarnation was the greatest imaginable form of

[35] Ibid., 219.

entering the world to save and transform it. As he jokes, if God had wanted to remain apart from the world—and wanted us to do likewise—he simply could not have come. But he did because that was the only proper way to save us. The Church, meaning bishops and clergy, had to enter the secular order where ordinary people—and their families—needed nourishing by the Christian *mystique*. Instead, they were holding themselves aloof from this "hostile" modern world, the exact opposite of what needed to be done. Obviously, in this, Péguy anticipated later theological development and the general orientation of the Second Vatican Council.

That vision lies behind Péguy's best-known literary work, his poetic play *The Mystery of the Charity of Joan of Arc*.[36] It opens on a hillside in Joan's small village of Domrémy, where she is tending sheep and saying her prayers. And then she talks more directly to God, touching on several themes in a long prayer (from which the following is a series of excerpts):

> God, if we could only see the beginning of your kingdom. If we could only see the sun of your kingdom rise. But there is nothing, there is never anything. You have sent us your son whom you loved so dearly, your son came, who suffered so much, and died. And now, nothing.... Fourteen centuries (but were they Christian centuries?), fourteen centuries since the redemption of our souls. And nothing, nothing, ever, the reign of the earth is nothing but the reign of perdition.... It is worse than ever. Only, if we could only see the sun of your justice rise. But it looks as if, God, God, forgive me, it looks as if your reign were passing away.... Perhaps something else is needed, Lord, you know everything. You know what we lack. Perhaps we need something new, something no one has ever seen. Something no one has ever done. But who would dare say, Lord, that there could be anything new after fourteen centuries of Christianity, after so many saints, men and women, after all your martyrs, after the passion and death of your son.
>
> (*She sits down and resumes her spinning.*)
>
> What we need, God, what we finally need, is a woman who would also be a saint ... and who would succeed.[37]

[36] The standard translation in English is by Julien Green (New York: Pantheon Books, 1950), which is the translation followed here.

[37] Ibid., 11–14.

Péguy then brings in Hauviette, Joan's ten-year-old friend, who is an average French peasant girl; she says her prayers but does not expect things to be other than the everyday prayer, work, and Sunday rest of village life. Hauviette is aware, however, that Joan is something else. All the other girls learn their catechism, but Joan is a good Péguyan: "You don't know these things, you see them, and your prayers, you don't say them, you don't say them only, you see them."[38] Joan claims to be only a parishioner like everyone else, which is true in a way, but that is not the whole story, and Hauviette is not deceived. She knows Joan is unhappy, not only over the seeming failure of Christendom, but over the simple hunger of the poor and homeless in the village.

Joan does not see things quite so simply, and in fact, after giving her food for the day to some orphans (whose parents were massacred by the Burgundians, that is, other Frenchmen, not the English), she has a terrible vision:

> The poor wretches who grow weary of misfortune and at the same time of consolation itself; they are sooner weary of being comforted than we are of comforting them; as if there were a hollow place in the heart of consolation; as if worms were at it; and when we are still ready to give, they are no longer ready to receive;... they no longer want to receive anything; how is one to give to him who no longer wants to receive; you would have to have saints; you would have to have new saints who would invent new kinds of consolation.[39]

This reflects, of course, a kind of general hopelessness among the destitute. But at the same time, Joan sees clearly that the sword and other social ills strike people down faster than any charity can lift them up, while no one, not even Jesus, has been able to "kill war", which walks the world. Hauviette jokes about the paradox that in order to kill war you have to make war. The clear implication is that this is a paradox Joan will have to embrace later in life when she becomes both a warrior for France and a martyr for her visions. In the meantime, the destruction and disorder are upsetting earthly and spiritual life, and one of the terrible results is as true of the twentieth as of the fifteenth century: "He who is too much in lack of daily

[38] Ibid., 17.
[39] Ibid., 24.

bread no longer has any desire for bread everlasting, the bread of Jesus Christ."[40]

At this point Hauviette withdraws, and "Madame Gervaise", a twenty-five-year-old nun especially called by Joan's father to help her with her difficulties, appears and launches on a long poetic evocation of the present crisis and the sweep of Christian history that goes on for over a hundred pages with only a few lines of interruption by Joan. In these poetic and evocative pages, Péguy presents his view of history as really rooted in the private life that precedes the public one, as the thirty years of Christ's life as a good workman living at home preceded those mere three years of his public ministry. Madame Gervaise knows that this is not a consolation for Joan because the younger woman is tormented that Christ came, died, rose, redeemed the world, and still nothing—it would appear—has changed. She has seen that the people in her village, her own beloved mother and father, are cowardly and can do nothing to change the way things are: "Accomplice, accomplice, it's like author. We are accomplices in this, we are the authors of this.... And when you allow the crime to be committed, you have the same crime, and cowardice to boot.... An accomplice, an accomplice, that is worse than being the author, infinitely worse."[41]

Joan would give up her own soul to perdition if it would prevent all the others from falling into hell, an old theme with Péguy, as von Balthasar was to notice. But Madame Gervaise, speaking like the Church, calls this foolishness. By definition, hell is a place where suffering for the redemption of others no longer applies. This, too, torments Joan. All Gervaise can do is to evoke the history of Israel and of Jesus' life, his singular life lived, however, for the most part like other humble people throughout history in a poor village:

> Until the day when he had begun disorder.
> Introduced disorder.
> The greatest disorder in the world.
> The greatest disorder there ever was in the world.
> The greatest order there had been in the world.
> The only order.
> There had ever been in the world.[42]

[40] Ibid., 28–29.
[41] Ibid., 75.
[42] Ibid., 115.

Péguy—through Madame Gervaise—extracts a certain gallows humor from Christ's life. The fact that everyone went against him, even groups who normally hate and oppose one another, such as the politicians and the people, shows that he had done something great: he had saved the world. From an earthly perspective, "He hadn't done that much harm",[43] and could not have because he did not have that much time. Only three years. But everyone, from the politicians to the learned to the people, intuitively sensed the revolution he was carrying out.

Still, Joan and Madame Gervaise do not entirely agree, and the play does not end with the two of them parting on good terms. Despite the way Madame Gervaise has evoked the story of Christ, Joan is adamant that the people in her own day would not have abandoned Christ; they would have fought for him. They are not cowards—though earlier she conceded that they were. Not only the modern saints like Saint Francis and Saint Louis, but even the townspeople, she now claims, are not afraid of suffering for doing what is right. And there are the "French knights", even the English knights (whom she does not like), who would do the same. Gervaise sees this as Christians living in Christendom when the faith is easier criticizing the first Christians, who not only bore their trials unprepared by previous training but unassisted by Christian history. The dispute grows as insistent on Gervaise's side as it is stubborn on Joan's and ends on a line that seems to be the beginning of a poem:

Orléans, qui êtes au pays du Loire.

But with this last, mysterious utterance by Joan—"Orleans, who are in the country of the Loire"[44]—the play ends, obviously pointing toward a sequel.

The next play is also a "mystery", but Péguy did not continue the story of the mystery of Joan of Arc's charity. This time he wrote about another of the three theological virtues in *Le porche du mystère de la deuxième vertu*,[45] one of the greatest and most unjustly neglected poems of the twentieth century. Hope is the virtue, we find, that

[43] Ibid., 127.

[44] Ibid., 216.

[45] The best complete translation of this work is *The Portal of the Mystery of Hope*, trans. David L. Schindler, Jr. (Grand Rapids: Eerdmans, 1996).

even most Christians have forgotten. And this time, instead of writing an indirect drama about how charity is formed in private, in obscure places, away from the gaze of the world, Péguy opens his poem with "God speaks":

> The faith that I love the best, says God, is hope.
>
> Faith doesn't surprise me.
> It's not surprising.
> I am so resplendent in my creation....
>
> That in order really not to see me these poor people would have to be blind.
>
> Charity, says God, that doesn't surprise me.
> It's not surprising.
> These poor creatures are so miserable that unless they had a heart of stone, how could they not have love for each other.
> How could they not love their brothers.
> How could they not take the bread from their own mouth, their daily bread, in order to give it to the unhappy children who pass by.
> And my son had such love for them....
>
> But hope, says God, that is something that surprises me.
> Even me.
> That is surprising.
> That these poor children see how things are going and believe that tomorrow things will go better.
> That they see how things are going today and believe that they will go better tomorrow morning.
> That is surprising and it's by far the greatest marvel of our grace.
> And I'm surprised by it myself.
> And my grace must indeed be an incredible force.[46]

In the entire history of Christian literature, and perhaps of literature of all kinds, this may be the only instance in which God pronounces himself surprised by anything, and even further surprised and almost

[46] Ibid., 3–6.

puzzled that his own grace could have such marvelous effects. There is a certain joking peasant tone in Péguy's Deity, and it would have been easy to overdo it. But Péguy carries off beautifully this direct, striking, and amusing poem about the hope that keeps the world alive and moving forward.

There is a pronounced and constant feminine element in much of what Péguy writes: Joan of Arc, Madame Gervaise, and, in later poems, Eve and Sainte Geneviève. And in this, he shows affinities with what will later become von Balthasar's emphasis on the need for a Marian receptivity prior to engaging in the more masculine virtues of action. Péguy even conceives of hope as a young girl leading her big sisters ahead:

> Faith is a loyal Wife.
> Charity is a Mother.
> An ardent mother, noble-hearted.
> Or an older sister who is like a mother.
> Hope is a little girl, nothing at all.
> Who came into the world on Christmas day just this past year.
> Who is still playing with her snowman....
> And yet it's this little girl who will endure worlds.
> This little girl, nothing at all.
> She alone, carrying the others, who will cross worlds past.[47]

Once he embraced them fully, fidelity, hope, and abandonment to the divine will started to become a full-time job. Péguy's son Marcel fell seriously ill around the time he was writing *The Porch*. He turned the son over to the protection of the Virgin and "walked away", promising that if Marcel recovered, Péguy would make a walking pilgrimage between Notre Dame in Paris and Notre Dame in Chartres, a good sixty miles. Marcel recovered, and Péguy kept his vow. He would later repeat the pilgrimage for other causes. In the interwar years, as the cult of Péguy grew in France, thousands of people reenacted this concrete devotion yearly. Even today, when hardly anyone reads Péguy anymore and many ancient devotional practices have all but disappeared, large groups of *fidèles* make the trek.

[47] Ibid., 7–8.

For Péguy, fidelity and hope are not static habits or concepts, but dynamic, living forces. It was a Bergsonian insight. Mere abstract doctrines of fidelity or hope may themselves become obstacles to the spirit. By contrast, real hope is the forward thrust of life; someone who is in despair, literally without hope, cannot merely be argued into another emotional state. Hope can only be received from God; it reconnects the hopeless person "to the source, to a reawakening in him of the child".

Passion and Fidelity

In God's Providence, Péguy found himself subject to new trials of passion and fidelity and hope around 1910, when—without any previous warning—he fell deeply in love. Madame Geneviève Favre, Jacques Maritain's mother, was close to Péguy at the time and has left a lengthy record of the "terrible hurricane" that struck him. For many years, the identity of the woman was kept confidential because of the various actors still living, including Péguy's wife. We now know that she was Blanche Raphael, a young Jewish friend of Péguy's since his university days and a collaborator in several projects. Once that passion ignited, it became, like everything else in Péguy's life, as much an eternal as a personal question.

Unlike many men who undergo similar experiences, Péguy remained perfectly *fidèle*—to everyone—and therefore suffered immensely. He wanted to respect all elements of the reality that had been presented to him. He could not think of being unfaithful or breaking with his wife, even though he might have gotten an annulment because, as young secular militants, they had been married outside the Church. But neither would he simply ignore his feelings for Blanche, which he regarded as a reality to be acknowledged. For the four years until his death, therefore, even after Blanche's marriage to another man, Péguy would struggle with himself and with God.

As he remarked, most Catholics repeat "Thy will be done" every day without noticing what they are saying: Péguy learned the true cost of such prayers.

Some of his finest poetry appeared during this period. To understand a poem like the one he wrote to the Virgin of Chartres under the title "Prayer of Confidence", though, it is necessary to know the other female figure behind the one he is openly addressing. That poem concludes:

> When we sit down at the cross formed by two ways
> And must choose regret along with remorse
> And dual fate forces us to pick one course
> And the keystone of two arches fixes our gaze,
>
> You alone, mistress of the secret, attest
> To the downward slope where one road goes.
> You know the other path that our steps chose,
> As one chooses the cedar for a chest.
>
> And not for virtue, which we don't possess.
> And not for duty, which we do not love.
> But, as carpenters find the center of
> The wood, to seek the center of wretchedness.
>
> And to approach the axis of distress,
> And for the dumb need to feel the whole curse,
> And to do what's harder and to suffer worse,
> And to take the blow in all its fullness.
>
> Through that sleight-of-hand, that very artfulness,
> Which will never make us happy anymore,
> Let us, O Queen, preserve at least our honor,
> And along with it our simple tenderness.[48]

Suffering, honor, tenderness: Péguy seems to have come to an understanding through this experience that pain and even a vulnerability to sinfulness often are the only ways to open up channels by which real grace can reach us, particularly those of us who think our faith and morals are already enough. Indeed, in his work, grace, too, becomes a dynamic element like hope and charity, a living force that cannot be tamed by theological formulae and that finds its ways into our lives, even through the most unlikely of channels.

[48] The translation is mine, from Péguy's "Prière de confidence" in *Les Tapisseries* (Paris: Gallimard, 1968), 132.

In this and a hundred other passages, Péguy shows that unique ability to reach normally inaccessible depths that overcome superficial divisions. When day and night, life and death are brought into a single unity, the ordinary clashes between left and right, secular and sacred, and many other features of daily life are, by comparison, child's play. Like C. S. Lewis, G. K. Chesterton, and a very few others in the twentieth century, Péguy was one of the most *converted* of men once his "deepening" occurred. It is characteristic of this profound, Catholic Péguy—and says something about his interior life that he, perhaps, was never willing to talk about openly—that when he was visiting the cathedral at Gisors just months before he died, a friend asked him whether he really believed, literally, in the resurrection of the dead. Péguy not only said yes; he "took me by the shoulders and shook me, saying: 'One day you will come and tell me.' "[49]

The French Cyclone

Hopkins and Péguy brought unique Catholic energies to poetry, but perhaps an even more purely *inspired* Catholic poet and dramatist of the early twentieth century—a figure verging on being a force of nature—was Paul Claudel. His literary gifts drew attention quite early in his life even from eminent non-Catholics. Stéphane Mallarmé, Paris' literary high priest in Claudel's youth, took the younger poet under his wing. André Gide, who helped found and run the highly influential *La Nouvelle Revue française*, lionized Claudel as "un cyclone figé" (a frozen cyclone),[50] though what was frozen in such a mobile, versatile, and fertile writer would be hard to say. Gide's admiration survived Claudel's sometimes crude attempts to convert him and Claudel's criticism of Gide as forever oscillating between yes and no because of lack of belief. Claudel leveled much the same criticisms at Marcel Proust, but Proust, too, remained a quiet admirer. Claudel was to go on to become part of the French diplomatic corps and even gloried in doing with bureaucratic professionalism the kinds of practical work that purer *litterateurs* might have regarded as *infra dig*

[49] Reported by Simone Casimir-Périer and quoted in Villiers, *Charles Péguy*, 385.
[50] Paul Claudel and André Gide, *Correspondance: 1899–1926* (Paris: Gallimard, 1949), 54.

for a serious artist. But he succeeded in both vocations—a rare combination of practical sense and inspiration in a poet, perhaps matched in the twentieth century only by Wallace Stevens, the American insurance executive (and deathbed convert). When Claudel was appointed French ambassador to Washington in 1926, he was already a celebrated figure. And his picture appeared the following year on the cover of *Time* magazine for both his literary and political eminence.

Like Péguy, Claudel was born in rural France, though to better-off parents. But Claudel's work rarely conveys much of a sense of ancient France or even of modern France. Daniel Halévy has argued that, in terms of their Christian attitudes, Péguy is a tranquil pre-Reformation and Claudel a fiercely post-Reformation Catholic. Like all such generalizations, this one is partly true and partly false. In the few instances where he treats of the older France, in plays such as *L'annonce faite à Marie* and *Jeanne au bûcher*, Claudel gives quite modernist stage directions that suggest it is better if the audience understands that, in a way, certain theatrical clichés are being adopted consciously and, perhaps, even with deliberate irony. By nature and perhaps owing to his wide travels in the world, Claudel is a fully modern figure and quite experimental in both his poetry and plays.

As a Catholic, he shared Péguy's reaction against the narrow scientific materialism and rationalism represented in late-nineteenth-century France, most notably by Ernest Renan (from whose very hands Claudel received a school prize in his youth). And he, too, emphasized the spontaneous inspiration and untrammeled creativity the poet receives from God himself (as will become clear below, this was both a strength and a weakness). A character who is a poet explains in *La ville* (*The City*), one of Claudel's plays:

> O Besme, to know what I am and what I say,
> You need a another science,
> And for its acquisition, forgetting an impious logic, it suffices
> to open your eyes to that which is.[51]

"That which is", of course, echoes a singular moment in scripture: when God tells Moses his name is "I AM WHO AM" (Ex 3:14). But it

[51] Paul Claudel, *The City: A Play* (New Haven: Yale University Press, 1920), 19.

also designates the poet's subject as all that is. Claudel wrote out of a complex mix of realities. He is Catholic, royalist, and international, in addition to being expansive, modern, and French. The way these diverse currents are woven into his work may account for why it has been so attractive, both in his native country and around the world.

In the same play (*La ville*) in which his character recommends a different kind of science, he also says, "Toute parole est une explication de l'amour" (Each word is an interpretation of love).[52] This is a golden thread that runs through Claudel's whole life. Like many young people in his day, Claudel lost his faith in his teenage years, but not for long. At eighteen, on Christmas Day 1886, he was standing before the well-known statue of the pregnant Virgin Mary in Notre Dame de Paris during vespers when a sudden burst of belief broke over him. Claudel attributed his conversion in part to a reading of Arthur Rimbaud, the wild modernist child poet who, in his life and work, fled every religious, social, and moral convention for the life of a bohemian poetic seer, but who came near in the end to Catholicism (if, indeed, as some relatives claim, he did not revert to the faith).

Claudel opens a later essay on Rimbaud with the claim that he was "un mystique à l'état sauvage, une source perdue qui ressort d'un sol saturé" (a mystic in the savage state, a lost stream that rises again out of a saturated soil).[53] It was a daring and highly personal reading of a disturbingly original poet, but Claudel identified Rimbaud's primitive spirit with the Holy Spirit and rejected the kinds of things that impeded this free inspiration, including some nonessential religious customs. He was fond of quoting Ecclesiasticus (Sirach) 32: "Speak, you who are older, for it is fitting that you should, but with accurate knowledge, and do not interrupt the music", or as in the direct Latin Vulgate formulation: "Non impediam musicam" (Do not impede the music).

Though this call not to get in the way of what seems to be a divine, natural music might be taken in the usual countercultural sense, Claudel's life developed as the virtual polar opposite of Rimbaud's. He was highly disciplined when he wanted to be and successful in his studies, entered the French diplomatic service, and moved through a series of important posts in the United States, Europe,

[52] Ibid., 21.

[53] Claudel, *Oeuvres en prose* (Paris: Gallimard, 1965), 514.

Brazil, China, Japan, and other nations. His duties, which he performed impeccably, at first left him only an hour a day to write, but he did not rebel against this limitation. In fact, he adopted a certain spiritual and writerly discipline of not revising very much as he went along and accepting what he was inspired to produce each day. For him, it was a remarkably successful regimen that led to a large body of first-order literary work. He did Catholic intellectual labors as well. Early in his career, in China, he "read and annotated" (in small daily doses) both of Aquinas' *Summas*; his output for the last twenty years of his life consisted solely of commentaries on Scripture. Critics have sometimes raised the question of whether there can be such a thing as a Thomistic Rimbaud. If the answer is yes, Claudel is the proof.

Not only was he a diplomat, but he had strong conservative and even royalist leanings, which he had to be careful about expressing as a *bon fonctionnaire de la République française*. Nonetheless, they found their way into a dramatic trilogy (1910–1920) beginning with Napoleon's imprisonment of the pope and the history of the fictional Coûfontaine family: *L'ôtage*, *Le pain dur*, *Le père humilié*. None of this seems to represent what most people who know Rimbaud associate with the influence of that poet. And yet, Claudel drew on Rimbaud and the revolutionary modern French poetic tradition throughout his life (Claudel believed in Providence, not coincidence, and the fact that he died at age eighty-seven on Ash Wednesday 1955 while reading a book on Rimbaud may confirm his belief). It was the Rimbaud of the mystical *Illuminations* that perhaps had the greatest influence, the *voyant* for whom the world appears in a perpetual revelatory freshness.

Behind both Rimbaud and Claudel, there was also Baudelaire, particularly his sonnet "Correspondances", which shows an even earlier poetic search to see each thing in the world as related to some ultimate spiritual meaning, a dimension left out of the world as interpreted by a nineteenth-century science, which had cut it up for purposes of a rather superficial rational analysis:

> Nature is a temple, whose living pillars
> Let escape, now and then, some confused words.
> Man passes through densely symbolic woods
> That observe him with familiar stares.

As long, distant echoes mix together
In a shadowy and deep unity,
Vast as the night, clear as the light of day,
Smells, colors, and sounds speak to each other.

There are smells fresh as young children's flesh,
Gentle as oboes, green as prairie springs,
—And others, rich, triumphant, and vicious
Expanding out to infinite things,

Like amber, musk, Benjamin, and incense
That sing the transports of spirit and of sense.[54]

For Baudelaire and others who preceded and followed him in the modern French poetic tradition, nature was not a simple machine but a mysterious temple.

Claudel's work echoes this sort of sensibility and sharpens it by moving in a Catholic direction. In this, he was also following Baudelaire, Rimbaud, and Verlaine—the first and last became openly Catholic, and Rimbaud, as we have said, seems to have taken a similar turn on his deathbed.[55] Claudel's foreign experience, for example, professionally quite conventional, provided his furiously creative imagination with raw materials that he often turned to very good use. Indeed, he seems to say at several points that it is the vocation of a Catholic to strive to "enlarge the world" and embrace it in its totality. In his massive dramatic trilogy *Le soulier de satin* (*The Satin Slipper*), Don Rodrigo, the main character—a figure who goes out and sets in order Latin America and other lands conquered by Spain—makes a point of explaining this phrase in French terms: "The Frenchman living in France, for instance, it is too little, he chokes! He has Spain underfoot, and England overhead, and at his sides Germany and Switzerland and Italy; fancy moving free with that!"[56]

[54] Author's translation.

[55] See, for example, Enid Starkie, *Arthur Rimbaud* (New York: New Directions, 1961), 415–32.

[56] Paul Claudel, *The Satin Slipper: or, The Worst Is Not the Surest*, trans. John O'Connor, with the collaboration of the author (New Haven: Yale University Press, 1931), 280. Despite Claudel's role in this translation, it shows many eccentricities. As the standard translation, it will be followed here.

Claudel has been sometimes branded—mistakenly—as a right-wing Fascist sympathizer because of that conservative expansiveness and more particularly because of a poem he wrote addressed to Marshal Pétain after the fall of the Third Republic and the creation of Vichy. That poem ("Paroles au Maréchal"), however, is less an embrace of collaborationism than a hope that France would survive the Nazi aggression. He was beyond all question conservative in political and social terms, while experimental in his creations. But he was the kind of Catholic who abhorred the three most influential modern ideologies: Communism, Nazism, and materialism—all of them quite diametrically opposed to the Catholic vision of God, man, and the universe. When the Nazis started to pass the racist Nuremberg laws against Jews, Claudel was quite vocal in denouncing them publicly and writing to French Jewish leaders in support of the Jews receiving unjust treatment in Germany. Despite all this, a certain view still persists in France that conservative Catholicism in the 1930s had to be anti-Semitic and, therefore, welcoming of the Fascist dominance of that nation after years of persecution of the Church by socialist governments. It is a false judgment in Claudel's and many other cases, but it has often led to a rejection or ignoring of his work—which is otherwise quite clearly extraordinary in its literary qualities—on political grounds.[57]

The literary qualities are remarkable, if sometimes obscured by Claudel's unsystematic system of writing. He set down what he felt inspired to do without much prior planning or later revision (a generic weakness he shares with Péguy). Some critics have claimed that Claudel is among the very greatest poets of the twentieth century, and that is certainly defensible, though his poetic output, like T. S. Eliot's, was relatively small. Others also claim he was the greatest French dramatist since Racine, but here the case is harder to make because Claudel's experimental work for the theater is often difficult to mount (*The Satin Slipper* takes about seven hours to perform), already a serious flaw, and even harder for an audience to take in,

[57] A famous instance of this ambivalence about Claudel occurred in W. H. Auden's great poem "In Memory of W. B. Yeats". In the original version, Auden wrote: "Time that is intolerant / Of the brave innocent / And that tires in a week / Of a beautiful physique / Loves all language and forgives / All of those by whom it lives." He then added: "Time that with this strange excuse / Pardoned Kipling and his views, / And will pardon Paul Claudel, / Pardons him for writing well." In a subsequent version, these lines were cut, in all likelihood because, as many have noted, Auden had mistakenly attributed objectionable views to both Kipling and Claudel.

which comes close to being fatal. And then there are cosmic themes. As an astute reader has observed: "To realize the enormous poetic vitality of Claudel means to accept the opulence of his language, his verbal incontinence, and his habit of recruiting dramatic characters among saints, angels, and stars."[58]

But experiment and grand ambition can be quite successful in the poetry. In one of his earliest great poems, "Les muses", the first in what later were to become his *Cinq grandes odes*, he writes furiously of divine inspiration. The Muses in this case are figured on a sarcophagus discovered in Italy near Ostia, later moved to the Louvre Museum. Claudel describes each one of them, the daughters of Memory, who herself is characterized as "poised in an ineffable manner / On the very pulse of Being". This might be thought falsely sententious in another writer, but there is a convincing cosmic impulse in Claudel that keeps such words from flying off beyond what the reader senses is authentic vision. For instance, he says explicitly that he will not follow the great Dante in presenting a well-reasoned and orderly vision of the world:

> O my soul, we must not devise any plan! O my savage soul, we must keep ourselves free and ready,
> Like the immense, fragile flocks of swallows when, without a voice, the autumnal call sounds!

It is probably not a coincidence that he calls his soul here *sauvage*, the same word he used to describe the quality of Rimbaud's mysticism.

This impulse toward poetic freedom takes its place in Claudel's view of artistic creation as something not merely alongside the universe, but participating in the very free act that God himself carried out in the Creation:

> Thus, a poem is not like a sack of words, it is not only
> Those things that it signifies, but it is itself a sign, an act of imagination, creating
> The time necessary for its resolution
> In imitation of human action studied in its strengths and weight.

[58] Wallace Fowlie, *Paul Claudel* (London: Bowes & Bowes, 1957), 74.

There is an Adamic quality in this poetry in the sense that it gives man a chance to name the world fresh again. As Claudel puts it:

> But your song, O Muse of the poet,
> Is not the drone of the avette, the brook that babbles, the bird of paradise in the clove-trees!
> But as the holy God invented each thing, your joy is in the possession of its name,
> And as He said in silence, "*Let it be!*", it's thus that, filled with love, you repeat, according to the way he called it,
> Like a tiny infant, who spells out, "*What it is.*"
> O servant of God, full of grace![59]

The poem bears the dates Paris 1900—Foutchéou 1904. So we are dealing with a major statement by Claudel when he is in his early thirties and coming into his mature vision. The reference to grace in the last quoted line also anticipates a poem that continues this theme, three years later, the fourth of the *Five Great Odes*, "The Muse Who Is Grace".

In this context of how Claudel viewed inspiration and the creative position of the poet, it is also worth noting his verse form, because it bears more than aesthetic meaning. As with Péguy, Claudel was quite capable of writing formal French alexandrines in what must be regarded as his lesser works. But his main poetic line, usually called the *verset claudélien*, which he used in both his poetry proper and his poetic dramas, displays a certain similarity to Bible verses, which is to say, he seems to follow a kind of psychological or even spiritual rhythm instead of a strict metrical one. Each idea is expressed in a bloc of words, which rise and fall and then give way to another inspiration, and so in series until the "act of imagination" reaches its fullness. As with the biblical verses, this means that the writing is neither prose nor verse, in the usual meanings of those terms, but something that partakes of both. For English readers, perhaps the closest comparison would be with the kind of poetry to be found in Walt Whitman's *Leaves of Grass*.

[59] The passages cited here are from the Edward Lucie-Smith translation with some modifications. *Five Great Odes* (Chester Springs, Penn.: Dufour Editions, 1967).

Like many Catholic writers at the time, and not only them, Claudel abhorred the modern mechanistic world view and the industrialized society coming to dominate human existence globally. He allowed that the strict regularities of the alexandrines of French classical verse could be used when a poet was working with the proper material. As for himself, however, "It is from the toll of bells and the melopoeia of vespers that I have drawn the meaning of that prosody borrowed from the Psalms, which so greatly exasperates the champions of our beautiful alexandrine."[60] Besides the avoidance of mechanical repetition, Claudel thought the effect his system produced to be similar to the "great Catholic voice of the Psalms". And the Psalms he meant were the Latin versions of Saint Jerome, which he claimed to consider, despite his admiration for Virgil, as close to the greatest work in the Latin language. He even defended himself on that basis: "All the criticisms that you direct toward me, incoherence of ideas, disorder, violence to grammar, obscurity, could also be as much and more directed" at the Psalms.[61] Claudel seems to have found a similar order in disorder in the ancient Greek dramas, of which he translated a number.

When we turn to his plays proper, it becomes clear—among many things that are deliberately not clear—that part of their force consists in the interplay between various unruly energies, not least between the sacred love of God and the profane love of men and women. This theme entered into Claudel's work relatively early because of a serious sinful episode. In the fall of 1900, he made a retreat at the monastery of Ligugé, with the intention of becoming a Benedictine monk. For various reasons, he was refused by the novice masters and later even stated that he had heard a definite "No" to his vocation from God himself. Despondent, he returned to the French diplomatic corps and a year later was on the ship *Ernest Simons* en route to China when he met and had an adulterous affair with Rosalie Vetch. Claudel was not married yet, but she was, and a tremendous struggle ensued that involved the birth of a daughter. Rosalie left Claudel

[60] Paul Claudel, "Mon pays", in *Contacts et circonstances* (Paris: Gallimard, 1947). For helpful further reflections on these questions, see Elfrieda Dubois, "'... la prosodie me fut enseignée par les psaumes ...' Some Reflections on Claudel's *verset*", in Richard Griffiths, ed., *Claudel: A Reappraisal* (London: Rapp & Whiting, 1968), 112–30.

[61] Ibid., 113.

behind in China in August 1904. But even decades later, long after Claudel was married and settled down with several children, this episode flooded him with guilt and, as he admitted, also seems to have left some gaping void that he was unable to fill. (He even made sure the illegitimate daughter was taken care of by assigning her some of his royalties.) For all that, it did add, however, to his literary efforts because he saw the sinfulness of the adulterous love as somehow opening him up to and helping him toward a fuller understanding of God's love and forgiveness.

One of his earliest successful plays, *Partage de midi* (*Break of Noon*), is a dramatic representation of the shipboard incident, but not in any realist or easily intelligible style. Claudel was always a symbolic and suggestive writer, and the drama here seems to draw in forces of nature as significant actors: the sun overhead in the Indian Ocean, pouring down some kind of illumination in the first act, while the ship and its passengers float on a vast, fluctuating element; the moon, earth, and stars weaving a mysterious backdrop in the second act; and the death of the lovers, already separated, and the child, in the third. There are large, puzzling gaps—intentional, of course—between the episodes, and the ultimately irresolvable question of why God had chosen to bring Ysé, the female lead, and Mesa, the male, together precisely at high noon in the vast expanse of the sea. The picture is further complicated by Mesa's inability to give himself totally and Ysé's involvement with a third man. Naturally, Claudel is not suggesting that God wills them to sin, but there are obscure signs that Mesa, closed in on himself, even in wanting to offer himself to God as a priest, had to be really opened up to others, which unfortunately came about through his sinful liaison. A play like this is deliberately multifaceted; as many critics have pointed out, even the name *Partage* is ambivalent, suggesting a "sharing" at the illuminated moment of high noon at the beginning of the play, but also a "division", which the Wallace Fowlie translation rightly captures as "Break of Noon", an odd expression in English as well as French.[62] This material was so personal that, though a version of the play was finished in 1905, Claudel did not allow it to be performed until 1948.

[62] Paul Claudel, *Break of Noon (Partage de midi): A Drama*, trans. Wallace Fowlie (Chicago: Regnery, 1960).

The tensions between human and divine love have long been a theme in Christian thought, and Claudel returned to that theme with a truly gargantuan production in *Le soulier de satin* (*The Satin Slipper*, 1919–1924). This "play" is divided into four "days", each virtually a play in itself. It has probably never been performed precisely as written. The famous French director Jean-Louis Barrault, whom Claudel allowed to do the first performance of *Break of Noon*, staged *The Satin Slipper* over two days in a little under nine hours, and a carefully edited production in New York City in the 1990s ran about seven hours. Claudel here presents another divided couple: Rodrigo, a Spanish nobleman, who is in love with Prouhèze, a Spanish beauty married to an elderly husband. In this instance, however, their passion for one another is not consummated. Instead, it is controlled and then sublimated into a vast epic that involves the Spanish—and Catholic—reach toward Africa, the Americas, China, and Japan. Claudel gives very clear stage directions from the outset that the fiction of the play is not to be maintained, that stage props and stage hands shifting scenery should be transparently evident as the action goes on, suggesting to the audience that there is not a sharp divide between actors and spectators. And in addition, he added two epigraphs to this massive work: "God writes straight with crooked lines", and Saint Augustine's remark *Etiam peccata* ("Even sins [serve God]").

Claudel was not embarrassed about the role that the Church had played in colonizing the world. In fact, he thought it part of the Catholic impulse to wish to evangelize the entire cosmos, and anything less would be a defection of a sort. (In a late play, *The Diary of Christopher Columbus*, with music by Claudel's friend Arthur Honegger, this theme is presented in another epic format.) Woven together with this, however, is the way in which a kind of crucifixion of earthly happiness is a necessary condition of the heroic and saintly. Rodrigo is a great success in taming the Americas and Japan (where he is maimed, losing a limb in battle). But he is a broken and humiliated—indeed, self-humiliated—figure by the end of the story. Claudel ties all sorts of humorous and grotesque incidents and secondary plots to this basic plot. One wonders what audience Claudel thought could sit through it. But many passages reveal the Claudelian magic, and many who have faithfully followed it to the end come away with the impression of something massive, both in subject and execution at the very limits of human aspiration—a goal Claudel openly set for the Catholic writer. Perhaps it is this ambition, along with his obvious lyrical gifts, that have made him a modern author impossible to ignore.

Not all his work was so difficult, or so indirectly Catholic. (*Partage de midi* is implicitly so, but proceeds via a kind of symbolist dreaminess; *Le soulier de satin* is openly Catholic, but proceeds by global and deliberately unexpected developments. Absent external knowledge of Claudel's Catholicism, a viewer might see faith as only incidental to either play.) One of his most popular and accessible dramas, *The Tidings Brought to Mary* (*L'annonce faite à Marie*)[63] has often been described as a kind of medieval mystery play, and as such it possesses many charmingly simple elements in addition to Claudel's usual gifts. Contrary to what the title might suggest, it is not a story about the Virgin Mary but is set in rural France at the time of Charles VII and Joan of Arc. The central character is a peasant girl, Violaine, a blonde with a deep simplicity and innocence. In an early scene, she is attacked by Pierre de Craon, a mason and builder of cathedrals, in a momentary fit of sexual passion. He repents right away and turns his life more purely toward praising God in his work. Meanwhile, Violaine's sister, Mara, dark-haired and devious (and an obvious counter-image to Violaine), contends with her for Jacques Hury, a young man in the village. The story turns on the fact that Pierre shows Violaine that he has a spot of leprosy. She kisses him in tenderness, but Mara regards this as full-blown infidelity, which seems even more probable when Violaine herself develops leprosy. Pierre is miraculously cured, Violaine is banished, and Mara and Jacques marry.

It would not be idle to see here another of Claudel's sexual dramas: the religious artist Pierre tempted by innocent beauty, the double nature of the two sisters. But Claudel does not leave the story there. Eight years later, during which time Violaine has been isolated in a leper colony, Mara comes to her with a baby—on Christmas Eve—dead by some accident. Mara begs Violaine to bring it back to life, which the evil sister believes the good sister can somehow do. In fact, Violaine takes the baby to her breast and suckles it, and it does revive

[63] Paul Claudel, *The Tidings Brought to Mary (L'annonce faite à Marie): A Drama*, trans. Wallace Fowlie (Chicago: Regnery, 1965).

miraculously, with eyes changed now to Violaine's own blue color. This rebirth occurring at Christmas has clear resonances. And it leads to a kind of healing. Violaine, who has blamed no one until now, in a kind of echo of Mary's story to Joseph, tells Jacques that if he had believed her, he might have healed her leprosy. Mara, infuriated by the rapprochement between the two, kills Violaine in what looks like an accident. But by rich Claudelian means, she later confesses her guilt and seems cleansed by Violaine's charity toward the dead child. And indeed, it seems as if the two sisters are somehow necessary to one another and to the emergence of holiness.

Though all this transpires in a delightful medieval village setting, and Claudel heightens the effects like a master medieval landscape painter, we are left with the knowledge that externals mean little; the same human tensions of love, jealousy, betrayal, and forgiveness must play out in human hearts. Nature, even the idealized nature of portraits of medieval life, contains forces that have to be overcome by supernatural forces, by the intervention of grace. But there is a co-relation between the tensions that nature and human nature produce and the resolution by divine action far beyond them. The one supplies the need for the other. And in the end, as Claudel was fond of saying of this play (quoting Lacordaire), "il n'y a pas deux amours," there are not two loves, only one, working its way through the lights and shadows of life.

Digression: Some Theological Reflections on Art

Great as Péguy and Claudel are, they share a common limitation that seems tied particularly to the French cultural milieu of the early twentieth century. There are passages in either writer that are equal to anything in the greatest modern French poets—whether Baudelaire, Rimbaud, Verlaine, Hugo, or Mallarmé. But where Claudel and Péguy both are weak is in *overall construction.* This fault seems to stem from a theological conviction. Because both believed that the scientific reductionism of figures like Renan and the mechanical civilization emerging in Europe and America were alike opposed to the spirit and to the spontaneity produced by grace in the soul, they relied a great deal on direct literary inspiration, not only for the spirit but for the *form* of their work. Belief in inspiration is a good thing, but in the entire history of literature it has never produced a supreme work for the simple reason that even if the inspiration is God's, the handwriting is man's. And the human hand does not steadily follow the movements of the spirit without hard labor and many successive approximations.

Further, while Claudel and Péguy were quite intelligent—one might almost say fiercely intellectual—they drew a line at using the rational intelligence to plan out a work. Péguy and Claudel alike went so far as to say that they not only did not have a plan, they should not have had one. But this mistaken "Thou shalt not" led to some of the *longueurs* in the "mysteries" that might have been eliminated if Péguy had gone back and fitted his materials better to his general purposes. Similarly, his *Ève* was potentially a truly great poem, perhaps even a definitive modern epic. His capacity to follow the strict rules of French prosody in the writing of the quatrains that make up the almost twenty thousand lines of the poem show that Péguy was quite capable of pouring his inspiration into something other than the kind of biblical *verset* that he and Claudel more usually employed. Yet in overall construction, he failed, and the quatrains tumbled out in large numbers, repeating themes endlessly beyond human capacity to enjoy, and no amount of readers' admiration for Péguy's work overall can make up for this artistic lapse.

Péguy and Claudel both admired Dante as a great predecessor, but they seemed to balk at one of the factors that made *The Divine Comedy* so great: its orderly and exhaustive structure, which adds to the poem. Claudel's essay "Introduction à un poème sur Dante" makes clear that he thought three things were needed for a great poet: inspiration, intelligence, and catholicity (in the sense of both universality and something approaching the faith itself). On the second point, he explained that "most often the poet only receives through inspiration an incomplete vision, an enigmatic and unformed call or a word, and becomes capable, through a bold and diligent research, through a severe interrogation of his materials, through the abnegation of every preconceived idea prior to the goal, to constitute a completed spectacle, a certain world interior to itself of which all the parts are governed by organic connections and indissoluble proportions."[64] This

[64] Claudel, *Oeuvres en prose*, 423.

is precisely true. But even an admiring reader will feel that in a great work such as *Cinq grandes odes*, the poet did not fully follow his own ideal. Too many utterly stunning passages are swallowed up amid material that could have been reworked or pruned with no loss and much advantage if the poet's idea of his art had included a balanced sense of inspiration and rational ordering, of grace and nature, faith and reason.

Catholics and other Christians produced some important reflections about aesthetics in the twentieth century, perhaps in reaction to an overemphasis on rational theology and a certain moralism—both of which provide a focus on the Good and the True, but neglect the Beautiful. As we have seen in earlier chapters, Hans Urs von Balthasar's theological aesthetics puts the beauty or glory of the Lord at the very center of the theological enterprise, to say nothing of the Christian life. Even within standard Thomist circles, there is Maritain's *Art and Scholasticism* and *Creative Intuition in Art and Poetry*; and Ralph McInerny's *Art and Prudence*, all characteristically brilliant works by distinguished thinkers. These Scholastic systems of aesthetics seem to draw inspiration indirectly from James Joyce, a lapsed Catholic who nonetheless worked out for his *Portrait of the Artist as a Young Man* (1914) some principles drawn from Thomism, most importantly the distinction between prudence as *recta ratio agibilium* (right reason for things to be done) and art as *recta ratio factibilium* (right reason for things to be made).[65]

The distinction may seem obvious and necessary enough, but many Catholic theologians and moralists who enter into literary matters attempt to make religious or moral questions the primary criteria

[65] Saint Thomas' clearest statement on the difference between art and prudence, and the difference between a good artist and a good man, appears in *Summa Theologiae* I-II, q. 57, a. 3: "Bonum artis consideratur non in ipso artifice, sed magis in ipso artificiato, cum ars sit ratio recta factibilium; factio enim in exteriorem materiam transiens, non est perfectio facientis, sed facti, sicut motus est actus mobilis. Ars autem circa factibilia est. Sed prudentiae bonum attenditur in ipso agente, cujus perfectio est ipsum agere; est enim prudentia recta ratio agibilium, ut dictum est. Et ideo ad artem non requiritur quod artifex bene operetur, sed quod bonum opus faciat. Requireretur autem magis quod ipsum artificiatum bene operaretur, sicut quod cultellus bene incideret, vel serra bene secaret (si proprie horum esset agere, et non magis agi, quia non habent dominium sui actus). Et ideo ars non est necessaria ad bene vivendum ipsi artifici, sed solum ad faciendum artificiatum bonum, et ad conservandum ipsum. Prudentia autem est necessaria homini ad bene vivendum, non solum ad hoc quod fiat bonus."

for works of art. Theological and ethical considerations—*pace* the modern artists and theorists—do have a role to play in judgments of art and of artists. But by definition, truly creative work will not merely follow already established patterns. Absent the properly *artistic* necessities, all we have are treatises disguised as stories or poems or commentaries on the often unedifying lives of artists, even Catholic artists. As the American writer Flannery O'Connor once put the point, memorably: "The Catholic novelist doesn't have to be a saint, he doesn't even have to be a Catholic; he does, unfortunately, have to be a novelist."[66]

Joyce cited Aquinas as specifying that the work of art will manifest beauty, and "ad pulchritudinem tria requiruntur: integritas, consonantia, claritas"[67] (three things are required for beauty: integrity, consonance, clarity). All three terms are difficult to translate, but the first two at least suggest a certain wholeness and harmony among the parts, while the last—as Joyce's protagonist Stephen Dedalus argues—does not mean clarity so much as a kind of "radiance" shining forth from within the work. These criteria form a bridge to a more Augustinian reading of art as well. Dorothy Sayers—a great modern novelist, playwright, mystery writer, and Dante translator, among multiple other achievements—perhaps owing to her Anglican roots, has brilliantly suggested ways in which Augustine's notions about the *vestigia* of the Creator in the creation may also be said to apply to works of art. Taking quite literally the idea of man as *imago Dei*, she puts forward a Trinitarian aesthetic that enriches the *recta ratio factibilium* argument:

> ... every work [*or act*] of creation is threefold, an earthly trinity to match the heavenly.
>
> First, [*not in time, but merely in order of enumeration*] there is the Creative Idea, passionless, timeless, beholding the whole work complete at once, the end in the beginning: and this is the image of the Father.
>
> Second, there is the Creative Energy [*or Activity*] begotten of that idea, working in time from the beginning to the end, with sweat and

[66] Flannery O'Connor, "Catholic Novelists and Their Readers", in *Mystery and Manners: Occasional Prose*, selected and edited by Sally and Robert Fitzgerald (New York: Farrar, Straus & Giroux, 1969), 172.

[67] Joyce's condensation of *ST* I, q. 39, a. 8c.

> passion, being incarnate in the bonds of matter: and this is the image of the Word.
>
> Third, there is the Creative Power, the meaning of the work and its response in the lively soul: and this is the image of the indwelling Spirit.
>
> And these three are one, each equally in itself the whole work, whereof none can exist without other: and this is the image of the Trinity.[68]

From one angle, this formulation may seem to reproduce the old Romantic myth that the creative artist is like a god. There have been plenty of bad examples of that presumption in the past few centuries. But from another angle, it ties the human artist to his origins in the Creator—a Trinitarian Creator—and makes the artist a kind of co-creator, as John Paul II would say of other kinds of human work. Yet however much, from a human perspective, the artist may seem to be an original, his originality is bound to the very order of the creation. There are no absolutely free artists in Christian aesthetics except those who are bound to the truth.

Creative work is not like other kinds of work. When a carpenter sets out to make a table, he pretty much knows what he will turn out. In fact, if the result is not close to entirely predictable, he may soon go out of business. An artist, by contrast, cannot—and should not—have such a goal. Creativity by its very nature has to do something we could not have anticipated, that the artist himself could not have predicted, to be worthy of our attention. The whole problem with, say, writing a satirical novel or sonnet sequence today after centuries of literary history is that we already know what to expect in both and, even when they are reasonably well made, all too often we find it. If man as made in the image of God be taken in an ampler sense than usual, we should not be surprised that what we really value in the truly new work is something that, however distantly, reminds us of that primordial Word of creative origin and makes even our daily surroundings momentarily look new. Something like this was present in Maritain: "If creative intuition is

[68] This passage is the concluding speech of Saint Michael in Sayers' play *The Zeal of Thy House* and is reprinted with further elucidation in her *The Mind of the Maker* (San Francisco: Harper and Row, 1979), 37.

lacking, a work can be perfectly made, and it is nothing; the artist has nothing to say."[69] Péguy and Claudel were clearly concerned not to let the mechanical side of modern life snuff out that intuition. But that very aim may have led them to a relative neglect of shrewd, calculated craftsmanship.

A clear example of what this meant in practice for Claudel emerges in a reading of one of his *Five Great Odes*, namely, "The Muse Who Is Grace". It begins with the poet describing how a "sea" comes in search of him again, and like a tied-up boat or horse he bounces and jumps at the stimulus: "Again, the departure, again communication established, again the door that opens!" These are all Rimbaudian echoes, something like "Le bateau ivre" ("The Drunken Boat") modulated into a classical and Christian key:

> Ah, I am drunk, ah, I am delivered over to the god! I hear a voice within me and the measure that speeds up, the movement of joy,
> The commotion of the Olympian cohort, the divinely tempered step!
> What do men mean to me now! It is not for them that I am made, but for the
> Transport of this sacred measure!

At the same time that he asserts this divine inspiration, he emphasizes that it will proceed with humble earthly means:

> The words that I use
> Are everyday words, and yet they are not the same!
> You will find no rhymes in my verse nor any trickery! These are your own phrases. None of your phrases that I do not know how to put to use!
> These flowers are your flowers, and you say that you do not recognize them.
> These feet are your feet, but behold how I walk on the sea and how I trample the waters of the sea in triumph!

[69] Jacques Maritain, *Creative Intuition in Art and Poetry*, Bollingen xxxv.1 (Princeton: Princeton University Press, 1992), 60.

With these heady preliminaries, Claudel then introduces a series of strophes and antistrophes reminiscent of Greek poetry, but in this case they present alternating statements by the poet to the Muse and the Muse to the poet. The poet wishes to remain faithful to the earth, and the Muse seeks to make him drunk and carry him away:

> And I want to encompass a great poem clearer than the moon that shines with serenity on the countryside in harvest time.
> And to trace a grand triumphal Way across the earth. . . .
> Let me sing the works of men and that each person will discover in my verses the things known to him,
> As from above one is pleased to recognize his house, and the station, and the town hall, and that good man with his straw hat, but the space around oneself is immense! . . .
> The great poem of man finally beyond secondary causes and reconciled to eternal forces,
> The great triumphal Way across the earth reconciled for man, removed from chance, as he advances![70]

Claudel continues on in this gorgeous mode with less repetition and padding than Péguy and greater range, but his very fertility starts to become cloying as this "inspired" dialogue proceeds and starts to undermine the loftiness of the inspiration by its expansive and disorderly invention. The Muse says she is a woman and inaccessible to reason, but even allowing for the great beauties and brisk motion of the whole, a reader starts to feel the absence of what reason in fact can do, even at these heights. In spite of stunning passages, a kind of necessity and inevitability of the final form—which is one of the sure marks of the greatest artistic work—seems wanting because of some imbalance of reason and artistic intuition. In this poem in particular, Claudel chose to enter into a dialogue with a being who tells him, "You call me Muse and my other name is grace." Yet there is something not quite in harmony in this relation, as evidenced by the artistic form, that seems to reflect a deeper problem of reason and faith.

[70] Claudel, *Five Great Odes*, 57.

In fairness to Claudel, there were similar artistic impulses in other French writers at the time. Saint-John Perse, an acquaintance, wrote in a similar fashion, though about secular matters. The French surrealists—André Breton, Louis Aragon, Paul Éluard, Philippe Soupault—taking depth psychology as a point of departure, deliberately suppressed reasoning and practiced "automatic writing" as a way to reach material inaccessible to a shallow Enlightenment rationalism. And other writers like Guillaume Apollinaire, Max Jacob, René Char, and Pierre Reverdy had similar aims. There was something in early twentieth-century France, unlike England and America, that pitted reason more bluntly against artistic intuition. Yet even in English literature, a figure like Joyce in *Ulysses* and *Finnegan's Wake* goes beyond reasonable bounds at times in search of some quasi-idolatrous absolute verbal creation. All, like Claudel, have their defenders and champions, but something common to them all also suggests an incompleteness that did not find its proper form in their age. The pull between earth and heaven in Claudel is noted and comes near to a point of balance, but perhaps because of Enlightenment hangovers that blocked a more vigorous relationship between intuitions of faith and reason among the artists (the philosophers and theologians did better), this was the best he or any artist could do in the first half of the twentieth century.

The Patron Saint of Imbeciles: Georges Bernanos

> The Catholic novel is not the novel which only nourishes us with nice sentiments; it is the novel where the life of faith is at grips with the passions. Everything possible must be done to make the reader feel the tragic mystery of salvation.[71]

The novel is an art form more forgiving than poetry of formal irregularities almost by design. It allows for the incorporation of all sorts of material in unexpected ways without harm to its basic story. France produced some amazing novelists in the twentieth century: not only

[71] Georges Bernanos, *Le crépuscule des vieux* (Paris: Gallimard, 1956), 82–84, as trans. and quoted in Tony Pipolo, *Robert Bresson: A Passion for Film* (Oxford, N.Y.: Oxford University Press, 2010), 211.

on the margins of Catholicism, as was the Proust of *Remembrance of Things Past*, but robust writers who were robust believers as well. One of the most artful and powerful was Georges Bernanos. His first novel, *Sous le soleil de Satan* (*Under the Sun of Satan*), opens with the story of Mouchette, a restless sixteen-year-old girl in staid rural France who, in the very first chapter alone, has steamy sexual episodes with two lovers, murders one with a shotgun, tries to get the other (a doctor) to perform an abortion on her, and goes mad temporarily—causing a stillbirth of her illegitimate child—primarily because of her increasing manipulation of and outright wickedness in relations with other people (who are to a greater or lesser extent also corrupt). This series of sins eventually leads to other things. But in almost every one of Bernanos' eight novels, similar sins form the bulk of the story, including sexual abuse of children, lesbianism, homosexuality, suicide (at least one in each novel), alcoholism, drug addiction, despair, and even unfaithful, unbelieving, and sacrilegious priests. Presented as isolated descriptions of his work, these elements would lead almost anyone to assume that Bernanos was a writer of melodrama or of novels with plots similar to those of the more implausible opera *libretti*. And that would not be entirely off the mark, except for the fact that Bernanos also made his characters quite believable, and he convinced the reader that this is the dark post-Enlightenment, post-Christian world of the twentieth century, which is only occasionally illuminated by brief flashes of grace.

While the omnipresence of evil is a constant Bernanosian theme, so is a sympathy for almost all his sinful characters and more than a hint of the possibility of universal salvation, which may be one reason why Hans Urs von Balthasar decided to write a massive study of Bernanos.[72] Robert Speaight has astutely observed of Bernanos that "he is not a moralist, but a metaphysician; his universe is a battlefield of good and evil, not of right and wrong."[73] Like several other of the great French Catholic writers, Bernanos is fascinated by the notion that we do not know ourselves or the world—an idea already present in the *poète maudit* Arthur Rimbaud, under the deliberately

[72] Hans Urs von Balthasar, *Bernanos: An Ecclesial Existence*, trans. Erasmo Leiva-Merikakis (Communio Books; San Francisco: Ignatius Press, 1996). This translation is 617 pages long, and even so it does not include all of the material in the original German text.

[73] Robert Speaight, *George Bernanos: A Study of the Man and the Writer* (London: Collins and Harvill Press, 1973), 16.

ungrammatical formula "Je est un'autre" ("I is another"). This mystery of the human person leads us out into the realization that only God knows us and our hearts and that our impotence—a frequent word in Bernanos—at the deepest level is, therefore, not necessarily a sign of failure. It often is the precondition for understanding "God's sweet mercy" and universal love, even amid the murders, adulteries, suicides, madness, hatred, and boredom that make up the world.

This was not always well understood at the time, even by friendly and intelligent readers like Jacques Maritain, who, as one of the founders of Le roseau d'or—a Catholic-leaning imprint of the prestigious publisher Plon—asked for and got a number of changes in Bernanos' manuscript of *Sous le soleil de Satan* before it was published. *Le roseau d'or* aimed basically at joining Catholicism to creative literary and intellectual currents and also published works by François Nikolai Mauriac, Julien Green, Berdyaev, and Graham Greene as well as non-Catholics. With Bernanos' first novel, *Le roseau d'or* not only got a runaway best seller, it showcased a writer who seemed a kind of French Dostoyevsky. Some of the greatest writing by any Catholic in the twentieth century comes in the long middle section of *Sous le soleil de Satan*, when the main character, Father Donissan, receives the gift of reading souls, a more frightening power than most people think who come upon that notion in more conventionally pious contexts. There is sheer literary genius in Bernanos' depiction of how this all comes about, not least because Father Donissan receives that gift, which will later make him famous and earn him the reputation of being a modern saint, after a personal encounter with Satan.

Donissan is introduced by way of a conversation between two older priests (one of them, Father Menou-Segrais, is Donissan's superior in a rural parish). They speak about his physical and spiritual clumsiness and sheer human oddities. He did not retain much from his seminary studies, either. Yet Father Menou-Segrais detects something special in his young curate, whom Bernanos has modeled, though in a clever re-creation rather than a mere reproduction, after Saint Jean Vianney, the celebrated Curé of Ars. Despite all his clumsiness, when the younger priest steps into the confessional, people awaken after years of merely formal religious observances. His rough, halting homilies—drawn from his soul rather than from the usual pious phrases—capture the attention of the whole parish.

The curate is also perfectly obedient to his pastor, welcomes his spiritual direction, and willingly accepts assigned tasks. He still feels an utter failure. And for all his self-reproach and prayer, he finds himself led imperceptibly by diabolical cunning into a direct confrontation with the devil. Donissan would say in later years, "When I was young ... I did not know evil. I only learned to know it from sinners themselves."[74] But his temptation is not to commit the ordinary sins of his flock, terrible as those might be. He has without noticing it entered into a personal struggle with Absolute Evil, a combat he felt he had to undertake. He enters into it, however, not relying on grace but rather looking for strength within himself: "The life of this strange man—a relentless struggle culminating in a bitter death—might have been very different if at this time he had foiled the tempter by trusting himself, unrestrainedly, to the mercy of God, if he had called for help!"[75] Instead, though he does many great things and even performs miracles, he winds up thinking himself defeated by his own inability to triumph in God's name over Satan.

His encounter with the devil comes after a long night of severe self-flagellation (also similar to stories of the Curé of Ars). Father Donissan sets out to help two priests who are offering a mission at a nearby church by hearing confessions. Here, Bernanos' spiritual as well as literary genius shows itself at its full power for the first time. The priest becomes lost in the unfamiliar countryside as the sun starts to go down. A thin mist rises, and he loses a sense of the road that he is on. Being lost in a dark wood as an image for the disorientation produced by sin and temptation goes back to Dante and beyond, but Bernanos draws true supernatural horror from the nightmarish feeling of both being lost and, strangely, returning to the same point of disorientation from which he set out no matter what path or direction the young priest takes. Then, with a smoothness that produces no sharp reaction, a strange person claiming to be a traveling horse-trader who "does not live anywhere" is walking along with him.

The stranger soothes him and even counsels patience, but the young priest soon senses himself somehow falling into a frightening pit and only escapes by holding on to the mysterious stranger,

[74] Georges Bernanos, *The Star of Satan*, trans. Pamela Morris (New York: Macmillan, 1940), 111.

[75] Ibid., 119.

who says, "We shall always be together now!" The scene unfolds with unclear images melting into one another until the horse-trader reveals his identity:

> Shall I tell you how it is? I kiss the whole lot of you, asleep or awake, alive or dead. That's the plain truth. I just love being with you, you little god-men, you funny, funny little brutes! To tell you the truth, I don't often leave you. You carry me in your murky flesh, me, whose very essence was light—in the folds of your guts—me, Lucifer! . . . I number you. None of you ever gets away from me. I know every one of my little flock by its stink![76]

This is only the beginning of ever more ominous interactions that, like the conversations in dreams, are not entirely logical in their development but seem to have a hidden meaning all the same—and all the more frightening for that.

But then things take an abrupt turn. Father Donissan finds within himself *pity* toward the devil: "I can see you, as far as it's possible for human eyes. I see you crushed down by your own agony, to the very point of annihilation—which will never be granted, poor tortured being!" which draws from the devil a "piercing lamentable scream": "Enough! Enough! You consecrated dog! Whoever taught you that pity is what we fear most of all? You anointed beast!" The young priest has found prayer again in the midst of this experience, and that gives him the power to extort from the devil the truth that he has been allowed to "put Donissan to the test" and will do so "from this day on until you die".[77] Suddenly, the devil morphs into Donissan's mirror image. The priest can see into its very depths, but he rejects the vision saying, "Get thee behind me, Satan!"[78] And in fact, the devil is infuriated by this rejection because God gives devils no final power over men. Still, the devil goes on over many pages showing how subtle he and his band are, and persistent, lurking at every corner, and predicts the priest will see their power very soon.

One last revelation awaits Father Donissan. The devil departs; a real human being finds him and guides him back home. Along the

[76] Ibid., 156.
[77] Ibid., 162–63.
[78] Ibid., 164.

way, the young curate acquires in an instant the power for which he was to become famous later in life as "the saint of Lumbres", the power to read souls:

> He saw. With his mortal eyes he could see that thing which still eludes the sharpest scrutiny—the subtlest intuition, the most careful upbringing: a human consciousness. Certainly our own nature is partly given to us; no doubt we know ourselves a little more clearly than others know us; but each must descend into himself, and as he descends the darkness thickens till he touches the dark core, the profound ego where the shades of ancestors come to life again, where instinct roars like a subterranean torrent. And now—now this poor priest found himself suddenly transported into the innermost secrecy of another, doubtless to the very point towards which the eyes of judgment turn.... He was ready, in the sincerity of his humble thought, to accuse himself of having by his own imperfections retarded this initiation, of never having loved human souls sufficiently, since he had not known them as they are.[79]

But this power is not without its dark side. In Bernanos' most famous novel, *Diary of a Country Priest*, the young curate also has a brief intuition of the knotted relationship of heredity, environment, mind, body, spirit, and community—all the factors that go to make up an individual soul and that no one in the normal state of things can ever fully know. The vision moves both priests to deep mercy for souls unconsciously as well as consciously trapped by personal sins and original sin. Father Donissan's first use of the new gift comes in a chance encounter with the wayward sixteen-year-old Mouchette, the young sexual adventuress and murderer. With his new gift, he recounts her whole sordid past to her and explains what she is and is not responsible for in this cosmic network of evil. They part with Donissan's offer of forgiveness and a new life. But in a strange testimony to evil's deep power, at home Mouchette takes a razor, cuts her own throat, and asks to be carried to the church to die—her death which Father Donissan, called to the scene, witnesses. Evil has been exposed but not conquered.

Father Donissan has a similar failure late in the novel. Now a revered figure, he is called to the bedside of a child who has just

[79] Ibid., 174–75.

died. Instead of refusing to attempt to raise the dead, which is here a temptation—he almost resuscitates the dead boy—he tries and fails because, after so many years of confronting the Evil One, he wants to see if he can make God really triumph in the world. The failure sends him back to his own sense of impotence, which should lead to greater humility before God. In the meantime, a prominent man of letters—clearly modeled after Anatole France, a figure Bernanos mocked in real life as a popular, merely "literary" charlatan—comes in his own despair to see the saint of Lumbres. Bernanos masterfully presents the old man's self-deceptions and vanities, even in the face of death. The priest is nowhere to be found, and the writer slowly begins to see himself as perhaps making a late conversion and coming to live in this modest village—with of course articles and photographs about the change to be published in Parisian newspapers and magazines. Impatiently, he steps into what he thinks is the empty confession box where Father Donissan made his reputation—and finds the priest dead there with a gaping mouth.

Bernanos concludes this bleak view of the power of evil, even in the life of a great saint, with a description of what Father Donissan seemed to be saying, along with the long line of real saints through the ages, at the very end:

> We are not those rosy-cheeked saints with golden beards whom pious folk behold in pictures, whose eloquence and perfect health even philosophers would envy. Our task is not as the world imagines it. Compared to it, even the urge of genius is a frivolous game. Lord, every life finely lived bears witness to You. But the witness which is borne by saints must be torn with irons out of their bodies.[80]

It is no wonder that this powerful novel convinced the literary world of France in the 1920s that here was an authentic Catholic voice capable of touching on all the traditional themes of the Church without the usual pious formulas and of staring straight into the worldly and otherworldly suffering, the "sun of Satan", under which the human race lives and from which it is liberated only by great effort—and grace.

But for all his power of spiritual insight, Bernanos did not have the great literary imagination of a Balzac or a Zola. All of his novels tend

[80] Ibid., 348.

to circle around similar themes of evil with a not-very-wide circumference as to treatment. But he did have an intensity and spiritual focus almost without equal in all of French literature. Though he valued his work and was a careful writer, he did not think literature as such very important except, as he put it, for the few souls that God had ordained might be reached by this humble human product. Indeed, it may be precisely because of his belief that spiritual matters were far more important than literary ones that his fiction achieved such power.

Bernanos' work was not driven solely, however, by a fixation on evil, much as that made his novels more substantial than those of his great contemporaries, such as Proust (who he thought opened up possibilities for faith) and Gide (whose ambivalence Bernanos regarded as Satanic). He had great insight into human nature and action, yet he tended to organize those insights around some simple and powerful ideas. For example, a baby comes into the world all innocence and smiles:

> Who is it then,—who, I ask you—that works away inside it with so sinister a care and clairvoyance, with the precision of a surgeon who knows where to put his scissors and forceps in order to reach the most delicate nerves, day by day and hour by hour, until twenty or thirty years later you find this radiant little creature transformed into an anxious and solitary animal—envious, jealous, or avaricious—eaten up alive by the absurd hatred of itself, and choosing the terrible and sterile pleasure that destroys it in preference to joy and freedom and all the good things of earth?[81]

Whatever advances psychology may have made in tracing environmental factors, especially families, in such developments, this question clearly transcends anything that can be answered by psychology conceived along strictly empirical lines. And as many readers have observed, this theme of the *enfant humilié* is a constant in Bernanos—as is a complex notion that the innocence of childhood faith is the condition toward which we must strive to return in a world where everything seems to militate against it.

That is one of the themes that also emerges powerfully in Bernanos' best-known work, *Journal d'un curé de campagne* (*Diary of a*

[81] Bernanos, *Le crépuscule des vieux*, 43–44; as trans. and quoted in Pipolo, *Bresson*, 212, and completed by the author.

Country Priest). The novel was even successful in the 1951 film version by the noted French movie director Robert Bresson, who may have been attracted to its bleak vision because of his own struggles with belief and unbelief. Again, the priest protagonist is not a conventionally pious figure. Rather, he is a man who confronts various modern problems in his parish and in himself. The parish, he tells us on the first page, is "eaten up by boredom", that very same *ennui* that Baudelaire had explained in the first poem of his *Fleurs du mal* is the modern monster that is "uglier, more wicked, more foul" (*plus laid, plus méchant, plus immonde*) than all our other vices. The curate has a stomach ailment and the usual self-doubts. But Bernanos also takes him through a series of encounters with the local aristocracy, their children—one an honorable soldier back from duty abroad—and the usual adulteries, resentments, despair, and occasional moments of grace they experience. This curé of Ambricourt, though not a Dostoyevskian character like Father Donissan, receives special moments of insight and eloquence when he confronts his troubled and sinful parishioners and can actually speak Christian truths to them *from the heart*, not from dogmatic formulas. Sometimes this leads to a catharsis that wipes clean the grime of a lifetime.

He also has a good friend in the older curé de Torcy, a robust, down-to-earth figure, who speaks in concrete terms of how to work with people. This curé is perhaps the one character in all of Bernanos' *oeuvre* who speaks in accents similar to the author's own. And it is therefore highly significant when de Torcy permits himself a certain flight of eloquence about the Virgin Mary:

> She is Our Mother, the mother of all flesh, a new Eve. But she is also our daughter. The ancient world of sorrow, the world before the access of grace, cradled her to its very heart for many centuries, dimly awaiting a *virgo genetrix*. For centuries and centuries those ancient hands, so full of sin, cherished the wondrous girl-child whose name even was unknown. A little girl, the queen of the Angels! And she's *still* a little girl, remember!... The simplicity of God, that terrible simplicity which damned the pride of the angels.... Our Lady knew neither triumph nor miracle. Her Son preserved her from the least tip-touch of the savage wing of human glory. No one has ever lived, suffered, died in such simplicity, in such deep ignorance of her own dignity.... For she was *born* without sin—in what amazing isolation!

> A pool so clear, so pure, that even her own image—created only for the sacred joy of the Father—was not to be reflected. The Virgin was Innocence.... The eyes of Our Lady are the only real child-eyes that have ever been raised to our shame and sorrow.... They are not indulgent—for there is no indulgence without something of bitter experience—they are eyes of gentle pity, wondering sadness, and with something more in them, never yet known or expressed, something which makes her younger than sin, younger than the race from which she sprang, and though a mother, by grace, Mother of all grace, our little youngest sister.[82]

This element in us, which is "*younger than sin*", is one of Bernanos' great discoveries and a constant subterranean current in his work. He and the curé de Torcy have little use even for the Church hierarchy, which has stiffened into a settled old age. Like Péguy, they have little use for the intellectuals of the Church who are too rigidly attached to and proud of their own thinking to understand that genius, too, needs redemption. But they both have some intuition of the childlike wellsprings of faith and purity that flow in a thin stream somewhere deep within us in spite of the load of sin in the world. Something like that wellspring persists in the curé d'Ambricourt, as well amid his people, in his path toward death from stomach cancer by the end of the novel, and in his often-quoted pronouncement: "Everything is grace" (actually, a quotation from Saint Thérèse of Lisieux).[83]

Despite the fact that Bernanos had other literary and financial successes, his seeming ability to run through large amounts of money despite a simple life-style nearly bankrupted the family on several occasions. At a low point, he wrote a detective story, *Un crime*, precisely because he needed money and his publishers believed he could produce something that would earn some, which turned out not to work very well. He would have to leave France, first for Mallorca and later Brazil, to economize, this despite the fact that his middle

[82] George Bernanos, *The Diary of a Country Priest*, trans. Pamela Morris, 2nd ed. (New York: Carroll & Graf, 2002), 211–12.

[83] Hans Urs von Balthasar applies an interesting insight to Bernanos himself: "This rough man in his depths housed a loving child who stood defenseless and disconcerted before every love, above all the love of God in Christ. Because he loved, he had a feel for the truth, including the truth of the times; and, because he felt, he had reactions that were interiorly more delicate and exteriorly harsher and fiercer than our own": Von Balthasar, *Bernanos*, 18.

novels such as *L'imposture* and *La joie*, which continue Bernanos' exploration of spiritual struggles, even in the lives of priests, sold well. *La joie* also won the Prix Fémina, and its author was offered membership in the Légion d'honneur, which he refused then and several times later.

In 1931, Bernanos began another large work, *Monsieur Ouine*, a book he himself called his "great novel". But it had an ill-starred history of delays, lost pages, and multiple attempts to bring it to completion. It was published only much later in 1943. Taken in the order in which it was begun, it shows a new dimension for Bernanos. To begin with, the odd suggestive discontinuities of the encounter with Satan and village people that crop up in the earlier work become the steady narrative method of this whole book about a certain M. Oui-ne, French for "Mr. Yes-no". Ouine, whom some see as a stand-in for André Gide, the great literary potentate at the time, is a retired professor of modern languages with an openly nihilistic character. He seems to abuse a boy sexually at the beginning of the story—like much else in the novel, even that is uncertain—and a young cowherd is murdered. At the end of the book, the murder still remains unresolved. All this uncertainty was clearly intended by Bernanos. Robert Speaight, a sensitive reader, has said of this book that it is puzzling because "the point of the novel is the disquieting depth of the questions which it poses. It represents the abdication of the omniscient narrator. There were more things in this hell upon earth 'than are dreamt of in your philosophy', and Bernanos does not trust in philosophy to find them out."[84]

It may be something of an exaggeration to classify Bernanos with the modern and postmodern non-omniscient narrators such as Robbe-Grillet and Nathalie Sarraute, not least because in spite of all the *aporia* in *Monsieur Ouine*, there remains a definite frame of reference. Speaight himself admits that the devil is still present in the later novel, as in *Sous le soleil de Satan*, but with this difference: "In the one case he [Satan] was a formidable substance; in the other a fascinating vacancy."[85] Bernanos, purposely or not, had attempted a theological investigation "to get to the bottom of something which had no base, to circumscribe something which had no contours, and

[84] Speaight, *George Bernanos*, 217.
[85] Ibid., 219.

to seize something which had no substance".[86] As a priest tells his "dead parish" (the original title of the novel) at a funeral, even the devil has withdrawn from them: "For the devil, you see, is a friend who never stays with us to the end."[87] *Monsieur Ouine* has its champions, and in William Bush's translation makes a better impression than in an earlier, imperfect one. But it has not aged well despite the postmodern elements some detect in it, perhaps because its absent devil is a step too far, even for postmodern irony. The two earlier novels about priests and a more traditional creation like Bernanos' script for *Dialogue of the Carmelites*, the story of a convent of nuns sent to the guillotine during the French Revolution, later turned into an opera with music by Francis Poulenc, have stayed far more popular.

The preoccupation with the evil of the modern world in the novels might give the impression that Bernanos was a dour writer and thinker. Whatever asperities of character and sheer combativeness Bernanos had—and they seem to have been many[88]—he also had a strong sense of humor. He was a man who sought holiness, but once remarked that he hoped to be canonized so that imbeciles, too, would have as a patron saint one of their own.[89] This side of his work comes out quite strongly in his nonfictional writing, particularly his commentaries on social questions. For instance, when he was deploring the tendency of people in modern societies to be submissive and to swallow the official optimism of increasingly dictatorial "democratic" authorities, he observed: "Optimism approves of everything, submits to everything, believes everything; it is the virtue above all of the taxpayer. After the public treasury has taken everything away from him, even his shirt, the taxpayer subscribes to a nudist magazine, declares that he's going around that way for reasons of health and never felt better."[90] The reduction of the free Christian *citoyen*

[86] Ibid., 215.

[87] Bernanos, *Monsieur Ouine*, trans. William S. Bush (Lincoln and London: University of Nebraska Press, 2000), 171.

[88] When Bernanos was fighting in a cavalry regiment during World War I, he decided that, if he died, he wanted revenge, even posthumously, with an epitaph, "Here lies a man who fought and died for his personal satisfaction and to enrage those who did not fight and die", as quoted by Roland N. Stromberg in *Redemption by War: The Intellectuals and 1914* (Lawrence, Kans.: Regents Press of Kansas, 1982), 152.

[89] William Bush, *Georges Bernanos* (New York: Twayne, 1969), 111.

[90] Georges Bernanos, "France before the World of Tomorrow", in *Last Essays*, trans. Joan and Barry Ulanov (Chicago: Regnery, 1955), 4.

to taxpayer and consumer seemed to him to sum up the whole failed materialist anthropology of the modern state.

Bernanos' views on society formed early and stayed steady. He was a monarchist and as a young man had been one of the *camelots du roi*, the street hawkers who sold papers for Action française, a classical and royalist movement led by Charles Maurras, who tried to appeal to Catholics, but was not a believer himself until the very end of his life. The *camelots* sometimes engaged in violent demonstrations, which has led some to see in them a precursor of later Fascist gangs. Bernanos himself participated in some of this public activity and was even arrested in 1908 with a group of *camelots* at the Montparnasse cemetery for trying to disrupt a memorial service for a political opponent. Action française unfortunately also contained anti-Semitic elements, and Bernanos took those a bit farther into the anti-Semitism of Édouard Drumont's paper *La libre parole* and his vile book *La France juive*, which Bernanos tries to explicate in his own *La grande peur des bien-pensants* (a title hard to translate, but something like "The Great Fear of Right-Thinking People"). It has to be said clearly that some of Bernanos' opinions about Jews were deeply prejudiced, but not all. He could never bring himself to admit the innocence of Dreyfus, despite his love for the Dreyfusard Péguy. All the same, when the Nazis started persecuting Jews, Bernanos denounced the racial violence, viewing it as just one more instance of "the divinized technological state", as he put it in *La grande peur des bien-pensants*.

In an odd and not entirely defensible way, all this, including the anti-Semitism, was for Bernanos an assertion of freedom against the modernist dictators, who for him included Marxists and Fascists, but also those who were leading to the monopoly of monopolies by a slightly different route, the capitalists. The last group, as in Belloc and Chesterton, was sometimes associated with the Jews. Jews were far from alone, however, in being targeted. Bernanos had been to school with the Jesuits, but he denounced them and other elements in the Church, including members of the hierarchy, who, he believed, tried to educate him and others into submission to a conservative bourgeois order that betrayed the poor and therefore also betrayed Christ. As noted above, he had little use as well for the modern Catholic intellectuals. Unlike the Maritains, who saw a proper restoration of reason as essential to the resurgence of the faith, Bernanos and a good deal of the royalist faction among the Catholics regarded reason applied to religious mysteries almost with the same degree of contempt as Martin Luther had. Indeed, Bernanos wrote a sympathetic essay on Luther, though he ultimately regarded the German as having pushed some true insights too far.[91] Bernanos combined all these elements into a certain belligerence and pride in himself as "le dernier des hommes libres" (the last of the free men).

He placed a great deal of emphasis on the importance of freedom for a Christian because only if we are free do we have the possibility of being saved or damned in God's plan. In a somewhat unrealistic reading of history, he believed freedom was better preserved under a monarchy than in allegedly free democracies and markets. The whole modern world, in this perspective, was not a civilization, but an "anti-civilization", which even after the Allied victory in World War II had resulted in "the greatest crisis history has even known"—a fall from the spiritualized Europe of premodern times to the nuclear nightmare that threatened the whole world. Europe and, for Bernanos, most tragically even France had been betrayed by its elites into allowing the invasion of "civilization" by machines, the idolatrous work of human hands, resulting in "sacrificing all the superior forms of the mind's activity, almost without a struggle, to practical intelligence and brutal efficiency, to a monstrously overdeveloped practical intelligence".[92] Especially after Nagasaki and Hiroshima, he predicted disaster if the world were not respiritualized in Christian terms. France was the historical bearer of civilization, in this vision, though in a very different way from what was typically asserted of her *mission civilitrice*. For Bernanos, France had to rediscover her political, economic, military, and ultimately spiritual leadership of the world, which he insisted she had possessed in the past. And that spirit was the reason, he claimed, why she was the beacon of freedom all over the world. France had to take the lead against Anglo-American market capitalism. France once had had the greatest military force in

[91] "Frère Martin" originally published in 1951 in the journal *Esprit*. An English translation, "Brother Martin", may be found in *Georges Bernanos and the Saints: Saint Dominic; Joan, Relapsed and Saint; Brother Martin; The Life of Jesus; with Selections from A Diary of My Times and We Frenchmen*, trans. Josephine S. Stewart and Paul Stewart (New York: Peter Lang, 1996).

[92] Georges Bernanos, "Revolution and Liberty", in *Last Essays*, 122.

the world—says Bernanos, in the teeth of much contrary evidence during the twentieth century—but had been weakened by the bourgeois values its elites had embraced, particularly the desire for security over liberty. France could be the leader of the world once again, if it returned to its intellectual tradition, which had been the model and ideal of the world—a tradition forged in the furnace of Christianity.

This vision of the world contains some sharp insights, but also a great deal that seems mere wishful thinking. Bernanos performs on French history the same sort of idealized purification that ecclesiologists sometimes do, with greater justification, on the Church: the real France (or Church) is a stainless part of the Body of Christ, whatever the sins and errors of individual Frenchmen (or Christians) in actual historical existence. As such, his vision was never a realistic political program—a weakness of many Catholic thinkers in both France and England at the time. Bernanos was sometimes called the "Ezekiel of Action française", and there is something of the Old Testament prophet in his nonfictional work. But his vision was too singular and literary to become part of any actual political formation. And in fact he always kept a certain distance from Action française during its various ups and downs, not least in its relations with the Holy See. His admiration for Charles Maurras, the gifted polemicist and leader of Action française, was based—while it lasted—in literary images more than politics. In 1913, for example, Bernanos discerned in Maurras

> the clear imagery of our poets, the method of our philosophers, the policy of our kings, the religion which has formed our consciences. Behind him, with the heroes who have built and defended our nationhood, I see the soil of our fatherland, the hills harmonious against the clear and light blue sky, our towns and villages that an imbecile régime would hand over to the defiling grasp of the conqueror. This armed and vigilant thinking has served them better than our guns.[93]

But Bernanos thought better of this stance and broke with Maurras before the Second World War because of the latter's weaknesses toward Fascist elements from abroad. Bernanos was living in Majorca

[93] Quoted in Speaight, *Georges Bernanos*, 47.

when the Spanish Civil War broke out and in his passionate book *Les grands cimetières sous la lune* (The great cemeteries under the moon) witnessed to the atrocities of both sides. But he was especially outraged by what he regarded as the shameful murders of Republicans by the Nationalists, aided and abetted by some Church figures, despite his opposition both to democracy and to the revolutionary socialism and Marxism that inspired many on the Republican side.[94] (Jacques Maritain and François Mauriac supported the Republican cause because of their belief in democracy.) Bernanos was repelled by political murder.

Clearly, "the soil of the fatherland, the hills harmonious against the clear and light blue sky" were not sufficient to prevent people from falling into murderous alliances. He denounced Maurras, even Charles de Gaulle, Robert Schuman, and the "Christian Democrats" for their compromises with the world that had emerged. France a half century after his death shows that he was right about its continuing de-spiritualization in spite of material progress. But Bernanos never himself undertook the hard practical thinking that was needed to create a tolerably Christian order within the inevitable imperfections of temporal life. As such, his social criticism is thought provoking and powerful as prophecy, but powerless—in the usual sense of the term—for the task of actually reforming a world badly in need of it. His more permanent contribution will always be the novels.

"The Pascal of Novelists"

When the well-known Belgian novelist J.K. Huysmans returned to Catholicism toward the end of the nineteenth century, he pointed in retrospect to a deep flaw, both aesthetic and theological, in the

[94] Simone Weil, a Republican sympathizer, read Bernanos' book, was much impressed by his honesty, and wrote him to say that she had left Spain, after going there to fight: "I no longer felt any inner compulsion to participate in a war which, instead of being what it had appeared when it began—a war of famished peasants against landed proprietors and their clerical suppporters—had become a war between Russia on the one hand and Germany and Italy on the other": 1938 letter of Simone Weil to Georges Bernanos, in *Simone Weil Reader*, ed. George A. Panichas, trans. Richard Rees (New York: David McKay, 1977), 75.

literary humanism of his time: "Naturalism was then at full tide; but that school, which was destined to perform the never-to-be-forgotten good service of showing real personages in accurate surroundings, was condemned to go on repeating itself, marking time for ever in the same spot."[95] He meant by this that naturalism had a restricted and rather superficial view not only of the human good, a fair enough judgment given the rarity of true goodness in the world, but naturalism also had a rather narrow view of human evil: "It was confined to the territories of the Seven Deadly Sins, and even of these seven, one only, that against the Sixth Commandment, was fairly accessible." Flaubert, the brothers Goncourt, and Zola were the great literary figures who dominated this kingdom. But there came after them others—contrary to *idées reçues*, notably Catholics—who saw the world as possessing much greater highs and lows than were dreamt of by these literary naturalists.

As we have seen, Bernanos offers one example of what might come from that Catholic anthropology in the creation of fiction. François Mauriac (1885–1970), winner of the 1952 Nobel Prize in Literature, presents a somewhat different case. Like Bernanos, Mauriac portrays some truly awful lives, usually provincial figures in his native Bordeaux. But unlike the robust Bernanos, Mauriac, who has been described as looking like "a bored greyhound", wrote in a consistently austere, classical style. And despite all the terribleness in the novels—particularly the way in which people victimize one another through emotional or financial or sexual manipulation, or even through "religious" pretenses—like Bernanos, Mauriac saw beneath these adult evils the thwarted loves of the child. He made a point of saying the following in his Nobel acceptance speech:

> To be obsessed by evil is also to be obsessed by purity and childhood. It makes me sad that the too hasty critics and readers have not realized the place which the child occupies in my stories. *A child dreams at the heart of all my books*; they contain the loves of children, first kisses and first solitude, all the things that I have cherished in the music of Mozart. The serpents in my books have been noticed, but not the doves that have made their nests in more than one chapter; for in my

[95] J. K. Huysmans, "Preface, Written Twenty Years after the Novel", in *Against the Grain* (À rebours) (New York: Dover, 1969), xxxiii.

books childhood is the lost paradise, and it introduces the mystery of evil. (Emphasis added)[96]

In Mauriac's fictional world, the Church mostly serves to reinforce some of the worst sides of the provincial *bourgeoisie*. At one point, Mauriac planned a story called *La paroisse morte* (The dead parish), the very same name Bernanos initially wished to give to his novel *Monsieur Ouine*. But while Bernanos was the ultimate outsider, refusing honors, accepting poverty, and critical of all parties, Mauriac was very much a social insider. He was elected to the Académie française in 1933 at the relatively young age of forty-eight and enjoyed steady and quite lucrative arrangements with highly prestigious publishers and periodicals. Mauriac moved in exalted literary circles, counting among friends Maurice Barrès, Marcel Proust, Jacques Rivière, Paul Valéry, André Gide, and many others. Several of Mauriac's books still sell very well, primarily, it seems, because they have been adopted as school texts by the French educational system. For some, the mainstream appeal diminishes his work. But Mauriac earned his place in literary history. Indeed, an argument could be made that he is the greatest French novelist of the twentieth century after Proust.[97]

Graham Greene once called Mauriac the "Pascal of novelists". It is an astute observation in several respects, not least because Greene himself shows several similar traits. There is a Jansenist element in Mauriac owing to the kind of upbringing he had, both at home and at school. His mother was a strict provincial Catholic, which at the time meant a Catholicism almost entirely occupied with a certain moralism, especially in sexual matters. She dominated his life because Mauriac's father—a freethinking Republican—died when he was only two years old. The school he went to at twelve, the Collège Grand-Lebrun, was run by kindly Marianite priests, but, unlike other Catholic establishments run by orders like the Jesuits and Dominicans, it did not encourage intellectual adventurousness or even much study of Catholic theology. As a result, Mauriac was to remain quite unsophisticated about theological matters until adulthood, though he

[96] See www.nobelprize.org/nobel_prizes/literature/laureates/1952/mauriac-speech.html.
[97] Cf. Henri Peyre, *The Contemporary French Novel* (New York: Oxford University Press, 1955).

conceived a passion for Pascal as a teenager and kept the classic Brunschvicg edition near to hand his whole life.

By then, his emotional makeup was largely formed—and bound to a moral strictness that he both adhered to and rebelled against. Ronald Knox once joked that many modern novels run through the conjugation *amo, amas, amat.* The *bon mot* applies well to Mauriac. When he wrote *Souffrances du chrétien* (Sufferings of the Christian) in 1928 for *La Nouvelle Revue française*, he opened with "Christianity makes no provision for the flesh; it suppresses it." And Pascal, he continued, said we must give God *everything*. Partly true, of course, but in some hands this way of putting things can tend toward an almost heretical notion that the body itself is evil. And there are traces of that tendency in Mauriac. He wrote a kind of recantation later as *Bonheur du chrétien* (Happiness of the Christian) and allowed there that Pascal was wrong in his dispute with the Jesuits. But it is a curious fact that sexual passion and religious passion always stand in stark conflict in Mauriac, and human love never broadens out into a larger love whether in marriage or in the kind of religious eroticism recorded in the Song of Songs. The stark tension between human and divine love informs both the manner and the matter of his very best novels.

Mauriac wrote a great deal, though his earlier and late novels generate little interest today. (The earlier ones are too focused on his own adolescent psyche, but the late stories are unjustly overshadowed by the four or five great titles[98] of his maturity.) His very first book was a poetry collection that gained him the support of Maurice Barrès and a whole network of literary figures. Late in life, he wrote several moderately successful plays. But it was the great novels, beginning in 1922 with *Le baiser aux lépreux,* that gained him wide notice. Two of his most powerful books—*Le désert de l'amour* (1925) and *Le noeud de vipères* (1932)—appeared in the middle years, one on either side of a personal turning point. It is often said that Mauriac underwent a "conversion" in 1928; however, this is not entirely accurate. He went through a spiritual and emotional *crise de quarante ans*—a period that included an affair with a young woman—during which, he says, "I

[98] Most readers would name *Le baiser aux lépreux, Génitrix, Le désert de l'amour, Le noeud de vipères*, and *La Pharisienne* in this category, along with Mauriac's stories about Thérèse Desqueyroux. *Le sagouin*, which is partly the story of a schoolboy, is often read in French schools.

wandered about Paris like a lost dog, like a collarless dog."[99] Yet he never lost his faith.[100] Rather, he emerged from this period of turmoil determined to live better and be more careful about the effects his work—often titillating for its time—had on readers.

A great deal of what Mauriac contributed to Catholic literature in the twentieth century can be gleaned from a look at *Le désert de l'amour* and *Le noeud de vipères*. Mauriac said that "the desert of love" (that is, human love) could well be the title of all his novels. *Vipers' Tangle* (more literally "knot of vipers") was his first novel after the "conversion". It is probably his most successful "Catholic" novel, a very powerful story involving the very often neglected sin of greed, and at the same time a sort of conversion and redemption. Not only do these stories show the internal conflicts in Mauriac and his characters, the reaction to them among both Catholics and others reveals a great deal about why Mauriac became such a powerful presence. Like Bernanos, Mauriac presents the Pascalian misery of man without God, which had become the typical case in the false dawn of humanism and may be operationally true even among many nominal believers. For him, there was an "essential difference between the sinful Christian who resists grace and the nonbeliever who gives in to his corrupted nature. The latter thinks he can make his peace with the corruption, assign limits to it, and integrate it into what the world calls a normal and honorable life."[101] This, of course, is a dangerous Rousseauian illusion.

It is quite easy to summarize the plot of *The Desert of Love*, and quite misleading, because it seems like a conventional melodrama. Old Dr. Courrèges and his son, Raymond, are both in love with a "kept woman", Maria Cross. (The "cross"—the woman who is both an earthly torment and potential path to redemption—is a

[99] François Mauriac, *Oeuvres autobiographiques* (Paris: Gallimard, 1990), 616; English trans. by Wallace Fowlie in *What I Believe*, Classic Reprint Series (London: Forgotten Books, 2012), 118.

[100] To the contrary, Mauriac claimed in the very same passage where he speaks of wandering about Paris like a dog, "I have often thought that You were never closer to me than [during] those days of endless suffering when I could easily at any moment have plunged into death": ibid.

[101] François Mauriac, *God and Mammon*, trans. Raymond N. MacKenzie (Lanham, Md.: Rowman & Littlefield, 2003), 44.

figure that recurs in Mauriac and in many French writers of the same period.)[102] Her husband, an army officer, was killed after just a few years of marriage. And she, lazy by nature and with a young child, first becomes secretary to a Victor Larousselle and then his mistress. But the identity of each of these persons is far more complex than might be assumed from the stock love triangle. Dr. Courrèges is universally regarded as a saint who has sacrificed himself tirelessly to his patients and his medical research—and finds himself quietly desperate because of the lack of love in any of his relationships. He feels great passion for Maria but is prevented from ever speaking to her about it because of the image he has in the community. His son, Raymond, is a cynical ne'er-do-well—his vices largely stem, like those of many of Mauriac's characters, from a damaged view of himself, which began even in childhood, as unlovable. Maria mistakenly regards him as the innocent and pious son of a saintly father. And Maria, whose life was shattered by her husband's death and, later, the death of her young son, rationalizes that all her actions were taken from the highest motives. She deludes herself, even about her attraction to teen-aged Raymond, whom she views both as a substitute child and as a sexual partner. In all three, the desert that is love (of the title) not only takes a singular shape but continues to deform their lives ever after, even though they have lost touch with one another for years.

There is surprisingly little explicit religious content in this story. Mauriac was often criticized by Catholics for that lack. Only in the very last pages, following a chance meeting by both father and son with Maria after seventeen years, does the author allow himself a Pascalian comment on the ways passion works itself out in all three: "There could be no hope for either of them, for father or for son, unless, before they died, He should reveal Himself, who, unknown to them, had drawn and summoned from the depths of their beings this burning, bitter tide."[103] The sexual passion they, and virtually all human creatures, experience at one time or another is much greater than can

[102] "Donat O'Donnell," a pseudonym for Conor Cruise O'Brien, used Maria's name in his previously cited study *Maria Cross* to help explain a common theme. His last chapter, "Maria Cross" (pp. 225–59), is especially insightful and synthesizes the image of the woman/cross in several modern Catholic writers.

[103] François Mauriac, *The Desert of Love*, trans. Gerard Hopkins (New York: Carroll & Graf, 1989), 213.

be satisfied by its human object. For that reason, human love is both nearly irresistible and a torment. As Pascal put it in *Pensées* (471), "It is not right for anyone to attach himself to me.... I would deceive those in whom I should awaken desire, for I am no one's end."

Mauriac quotes these words in a brilliant essay on Pascal,[104] in the course of which the novelist does homage to the mathematician's profound understanding of human nature. Pascal once wrote to an acquaintance, for example, that "it is useless to hide, one loves always." He possessed a deep insight into the fact that love is a tyrant, a truth, says Mauriac, that a novelist has to be careful to express indirectly. Of course, in every age, sexual passion and the love that is charity are mixed together in ways that only the greatest minds—and saints—are able to sort out. And sometimes, as in Dante and many lesser known cases, the passion leads on to true charity. Mauriac does not explain this reality very much in the novel. Instead, he merely depicts the disturbance that love of all kinds introduces into human existence—a disturbance that modern humanistic views cannot fully measure. Far from being "romantic", this is the clearest realism. Mauriac noticed the simple truth that Pascal's understanding of both the greatness and misery of man, which ultimately hinge on love, reflects the truth: "How far we are here from the middle ground, the moderation and the balance recommended by humanism. To be truthful, which one, Molière or Pascal, is the victim of a myth? Does temperate nature exist? And is not every man the prey of fearful forces that no one in the world has followed with impunity?"[105]

In the novel, all the characters except for the old doctor are oblivious to this truth about themselves and others: "[Dr. Courrèges] who had been made party to so many shameful secrets often said to himself: We always think that the happenings tucked away in newspaper paragraphs don't concern us, the murders, suicides, and scandals are what come to other people, while, all the time...."[106] It is because of his experience that the doctor understands Maria's situation to be the result of weakness rather than of wickedness, as many of the moralists in town imagine. Those same moralists think him a saint,

[104] François Mauriac, *Men I Hold Great* (*Mes Grands Hommes*, trans. Elsie Pell) (New York: Philosophical Library, 1951), 9.

[105] Mauriac, *Men I Hold Great*, 14.

[106] Mauriac, *Desert of Love*, 37.

not suspecting the passionate agony and temptations he quietly suffers. Work is his distraction from that suffering. Maria is tormented both by her social ostracism and her boredom at being alone, the very inability to remain quiet in a room that Pascal identified as the root of our troubles.[107] It was her fantasy of Raymond as possessing "angelic purity"—part motherly desire for a substitute for her own dead son, part unconscious sexual urge—which she concocted about the doctor's son in her loneliness, that drives him later in life to sexual promiscuity in a vain attempt to get revenge on women. At the same time, Mauriac comments that Raymond, who had lost his faith while still at a Catholic school, had nonetheless imbibed a "theological" caricature about "bad women" that kept him from seeing the truth about Maria.[108] As his father tells him of her, "You think me a fool, but of the two of us, it is you who are the innocent. If you think only ill of people, you'll never get to know them."[109]

After a fall in which she bangs her head, Maria becomes a kind of prophetess in her slightly incoherent ravings and speaks the fullest truth in the story:

> "No, not passions, but one single passion. It goes on inside us, and from a casual meeting, from the eyes and lips of some perfect stranger, we build up something we think corresponds with it.... We choose the one path open to us, but it was never designed to lead us to our hearts' desire.... And yet it *is* the only thing that makes us forget the object of our search, forget so far that it actually becomes that object. Stupefy yourself... that's easier said than done." How curious it was, thought the doctor, that she should speak of sexual pleasure precisely as Pascal had spoken of faith.

And Maria herself returns to her ravings in a way that confirms this insight, "Someone with whom we might make contact, someone

[107] "A nameless devil whispered in her ear, 'You may be dying [from passion], but at least you are not bored!'" Later, Maria's passion subsides, but she feels as a result "the threat of nothingness", which becomes "a temptation to lose herself in it, to feel herself dissolved and atomized, till the inner desert of her heart should become one with the emptiness of space, till the silence within her should in no way differ from the silence of the spheres": ibid., 142, 145, and 158. It is part of Mauriac's genius that he can suggest that even this temptation to suicide is a skewed spiritual aspiration.

[108] Ibid., 138–39.

[109] Ibid., 113.

we might possess—but not in the flesh—by whom we might be possessed." Anyone superficially familiar with Freud might read all this as confirming the psychoanalyst's belief in religion as sublimated Eros. But Mauriac convincingly turns the argument in the other direction: since physical passion seems by nature incapable of providing the real fulfillment it seeks, the full human nature of the persons in the story leads them toward something that seems to exceed any merely human object.

Mauriac's great novel after the "conversion" and perhaps his greatest novel period, *Le noeud de vipères*, takes up many of his usual themes but places another large one right in the middle of all the others: Mammon. He makes a point of also putting an epigraph from Saint Teresa of Avila before anything else: "Lord, consider that we do not understand ourselves and that we do not know what we would, and that we go infinitely far astray from that which we desire." So the Catholic element and the repudiation of greed are properly highlighted at the outset and, indeed, shape the whole. The story unfolds in a series of diary entries by sixty-eight-year-old Louis, a wealthy bourgeois lawyer in Bordeaux. He writes that he has just assured his heirs that he has left them his securities, but in fact he has secretly planned to disinherit them all out of a desire for revenge: "It seemed to me that even the most frightful pangs of death could not spoil that pleasure for me. Yes, I was a man capable of calculating like that. How was I brought to it—a man like myself, who was no monster?"[110]

The story, of course, answers this question. Louis is the only son of a family that has amassed a quite significant fortune by sheer hard work, frugality, and clever management of its affairs. Other than financial austerities at home, however, he is well cared for and loved by his mother, who sends him to good schools. He becomes a nationally and internationally known lawyer. But one of the constants in Mauriac's work is that love is the mainspring of every human life. Like Raymond Courrèges, Louis harbors doubts about himself and a kind of self-loathing for reasons that are not entirely clear, and his life, like Raymond's, will become a search for revenge. Mauriac seems to suggest that self-loathing may, in fact, just be an inescapable part of every human existence. When it comes time to marry, Louis

[110] François Mauriac, *Vipers' Tangle*, trans. Warre B. Wells (Garden City, N.Y.: Image, 1957), 12.

wins the hand of Isa, a beautiful young woman of the prestigious Fondaudèges family. But his apparent romantic success leads to all the misfortune and heartache to come.

Mauriac mercilessly dissects the cold calculation of provincial Bordeaux families when it comes to marriage and money. The Fondaudèges, for example, are not thrilled that Isa is marrying down, in a way, by accepting Louis, and even his later successes do not satisfy their snobbery. But whatever insecurity these factors may have caused for Louis, the turning point of his whole life—and that of his wife and children—comes because of thwarted love. As is Mauriac's custom, he connects the life of his characters with nature. The region of Les Landes, where most of his novels take place, is subject to sudden downpours, and its extensive pine forests regularly suffer from flash fires. Many readers have noted that these phenomena give Mauriac images of human emotions. But at the most delicate moment of this novel, Mauriac chooses more subtle imagery. When Louis and Isa are out courting one day, Louis rubs some fennel between his hands, and, though he has been an unbeliever all his life, the distinctive smell sets off an unexpected experience: "I suddenly had an intense feeling, an almost physical certitude, that another world existed, a reality of which we knew nothing but the shadow."[111] This is a moment of insight comparable to the one Proust famously linked to his protagonist's sudden access of memory while eating a *madeleine* in *À la recherche du temps perdu*.

That opening seems to promise much. But a short time after their marriage, as they lie in a shuttered bedroom with lime branches rustling against the house and giving the impression of someone breathing across the room, Isa reveals that she was briefly in love with another man before she met Louis. Though she claims it was not serious and even that she prayed at Lourdes for a good husband (and immediately recognized Louis was the answer to her prayers), he interprets her earlier infatuation in a way fatal to their happiness: "It was all a sham.... She lied to me, I am not set free. How could I have thought that any girl would fall in love with me? I am a man whom nobody can love."[112] That one moment, which plays

[111] Ibid., 34.
[112] Ibid., 44.

on Louis' self-doubts even more than does the snobbish social order, undoes their unity. They will have several children. But Louis constructs, not entirely correctly, the belief that his wife, at bottom, has no real interest in him.

The usual sins follow. He takes mistresses and treats them as paid slaves. She turns from him to her children. He hates his family; they fear him. His consolation is to make a name for himself and a great deal of money, but he laments when he wins one of his greatest cases, "If I had had, at that moment, a wife who loved me, to what heights might I not have risen?"[113] And not only professional heights. It might have also freed him from the thwarted love that took the form of avarice and, later, the desire for revenge on his family through blocking their inheritance. Instead, not only does he cheat on his wife repeatedly, he deliberately insults his wife's piety at every turn, making it clear that he sees through the mere formalities of religion to the pride, avarice, and lack of charity beneath the conventional practices. He even throws the Dreyfus affair in the family's face as proof of the Church's willingness to accept open injustice to protect her social position. More cruelly still, when their young daughter, Marie—loved specially by them both—dies, Isa blames her husband for having been too stingy to call in a specialist, and he reproaches her for her despair, despite her religious faith.

A vipers' tangle, indeed. But as he writes down all this for his wife to read—part of his revenge—something unanticipated begins to take hold of him: love. There is a certain mysterious and—be it said—slightly implausible quality to the second part of the novel, in which this vipers' tangle has to be cut in order to free those bound by it. The children try to thwart Louis' plot to disinherit them. By chance, he finds out and outsmarts them. But the game no longer seems worth the trouble, and he reflects: "The horror of old age is that it is the sum-total of a life—a sum-total of which one cannot change a figure. I have spent sixty years creating this old man dying of hatred. I am what I am. I should have to become somebody else. Oh God, oh God—if only You existed!"[114] And then an even more surprising thing happens: Isa dies before she can read Louis' diary.

[113] Ibid., 60.
[114] Ibid., 151.

As his children make excuses for why they did not call him in time, he comes to an important insight: "At that moment, I realised that my hatred was dead—and that my desire for revenge was dead with it. It had been dead, perhaps, for a long time. I had stoked up my resentment, I had spurred myself on." He even feels himself "quite suddenly ... detached"[115] from his fortune—and relieved: "After all, what had I been doing, for years, except trying to get rid of that fortune, load it upon somebody who was not of my own family? I have always been mistaken about the object of my desires. We do not know what we desire. We do not love what we think we love."[116]

This echo of the opening epigraph from Teresa of Avila leads to a kind of freedom and, at sixty-eight, a feeling of being "born again". It even causes him to understand that, in fact, his wife had not been indifferent to him. She had been distressed by his anger and their estrangement for decades—hardly a sign of indifference. He had taken people at their worst and had not realized that you have to break through appearances really to reach them—the very thing Dr. Courrèges had recommended to his cynical son. But for such a breakthrough, help must come from elsewhere: "Even the elect do not learn to love all by themselves. To get beyond the absurdities, the failings, and above all the stupidity of people, one must possess a secret of love which the world has forgotten.... I seek Him Who alone can achieve that victory; and He must Himself be the Heart of hearts, the burning centre of all love."[117] The saints have known this—and also have known their own imperfection—which is why they had such humble opinions of themselves. Louis now knows that his life-long low view of himself was in a way correct. He just had not seen that it is the universal human condition and points to the need for a remedy. And in this recognition of himself he decides that he now must penetrate through to a similar truth about at least one other person before he dies.

He finds that person in his granddaughter, Janine, and shows the new depth of understanding he has achieved on the very last page of his diary. A sudden heart attack ends his life mid-sentence. His children

[115] Ibid., 163.
[116] Ibid., 167.
[117] Ibid., 177.

are suspicious of his newfound altruism and generosity and attribute it all to senile self-deception. But Janine—herself suffering from another tangle involving a wayward husband—has perceived the truth. At the end, her grandfather had seen through the conventions to the reality: "Grandfather is the only religious man I have ever met."[118] He had been dreadful but "a great light shone upon him in his last days."[119] And the pious family had actually been greedy, while the grandfather, for all his evils, had been devoted to an unfulfilled love.

Told baldly, this would be a conventional and therefore unconvincing "Catholic" ending. But it is part of the power of Mauriac's literary genius that a bald account of events cannot convey what he achieved. Louis' conversion has to be appreciated in the light of the details of the vipers' tangle in his heart and in his family to see that such a late-life release, however implausible, might just, through some miracle, be possible. It is a big risk for any modern artist to try to portray a change of heart to selfless love. It is much easier and less risky to portray the evils in society and individuals, which are undeniable. It is difficult for many people even to admit the old categories of virtues and holiness, let alone to believe them. Louis' cynical children take the more common view. But though Mauriac may not entirely succeed in making the conversion believable at every point, he comes close enough that *Vipers' Tangle* has to rank among the very greatest Catholic novels in the twentieth century for its depiction of both evil and good.

That depiction mattered to Mauriac because, like most people, he did not respond to abstract theology and philosophy. He claimed to be incapable of either, but that is not strictly true. He was quite capable of reasoning very carefully and with a novelist's sharp eye for parts of reality that are invisible to most people. He had an instinctive power for sensing life. It is difficult to say—he did not always know himself—whether his novels have an evangelical effect, and the whole question of whether novels should be engaged in such an enterprise is, of course, a vexed one. Mauriac and Maritain traded opinions on the question, Maritain saying that even in dealing with evil it was necessary to "purify the source", Mauriac not necessarily

[118] Ibid., 194.
[119] Ibid., 198.

disagreeing but reminding Maritain that, along with his characters, the Christian novelist himself is implicated in the very same sinfulness as all other men. Paradoxically, Maritain thought that, strictly speaking, the insight and opening to new realities in literature, while important, are separate from the truths of faith. Yet the Bible, Dante, and many other Christian texts assume that what we regard as "literature" may play an important role in faith and must do so because most people are "incapable" of philosophy, as Aquinas says in several places. As with the early Christians, faith has to come by hearing—conversation and story—not by rational speculation, or at least not at the beginning.

Such storytelling has to conform to rules of its own and cannot be the abstract, idealized spiritual vision certain Christians assume it should be. If Mauriac is right—and it would be self-defeating for a Christian to deny his point—a Christian literature is going to reflect both greater lows and greater highs than a merely humanist one. André Gide, a sometime friend of Mauriac's, attacked an earlier novel by Mauriac, *Destins* (*Lines of Life*), for what Gide regarded as his use of salacious material to sell books. Mauriac replied intelligently in his book *Dieu et Mammon* (*God and Mammon*),[120] but he also argued that a real novelist—even a Catholic novelist—does not always have control over the material that wishes to come to birth through him. Mauriac even partly conceded something that Gide often said, that the devil is a "collaborator" in literature. To make the attraction of evil understandable—and a Christian novelist must make due allowance for the great presence of evil in the world—its power must come through to us in literature. Mauriac wrestled with this problem without entirely solving it. He dispelled Gide's main charges but became more careful about his work afterward. On a humbler plane, Mauriac knew, of course, that all writers, including himself, want to be read. Otherwise, they would not write. And everyone has to earn a living. But Gide's suspicion that the playing off of Mammon and Christ was the key to Mauriac's work is off target. Mauriac was not the kind of author—or man—who primarily seeks money and fame. In fact, Mauriac's willingness to say unpopular things became clearer as the political situation grew dangerous in

[120] Mauriac, *God and Mammon*; Gide's letter is translated on pp. 55–57.

the 1930s and 1940s, and he adopted views that were often unwelcome, especially among Catholics.

Before World War II, he was highly outspoken about the rise of Fascism and Nazism and was particularly disgusted by General Franco's combination of Catholicism and violence in Spain. Along with Maritain, he was one of the few Catholics who supported the Republican forces against the "Catholic" Nationalists, even though the Republicans had strong Communist ties. During the occupation of France, Mauriac's journalism was virulently anti-Nazi, so much so that he published under the pseudonym "Forez" and late in the war had to go into hiding. After the war, though he had risked his own life speaking out, he took the position, unpopular on all sides, that so-called "collaborators" ought—except for the most notorious cases—to be treated with charity. Many of those most thirsty for blood, like Jean-Paul Sartre, had been passively complicit during the occupation. Albert Camus, who had better credentials with the Resistance, initially opposed Mauriac, but later, when he had seen what the *épuration* became, admitted, "In our quarrel, it was Monsieur François Mauriac who was right."[121]

Mauriac's position on this question seemed, in the complex politics of France, to be right-wing. In fact, his politics were never partisan but almost always an expression of Christian principles colored by a deep French nationalism. Mauriac did not hesitate during the bloody Algerian war to take what appeared left-wing positions in opposing violent repression of Arabs. For the strict partisans, this seemed inconsistent. But the deeper consistency lay in a desire to see a France restored and unified in basic Christian and democratic principles, both of which forbade repression. His voice was very influential. It is said that a single article by him stopped police brutality in Algeria for two or three months.[122] Mauriac's friendship with de Gaulle and overall support of the general's policies (they disagreed on

[121] Quoted in Tony Judt, *Past Imperfect: French Intellectuals 1944–1956* (Berkeley: University of California Press, 1992), 71. Judt's book is a useful guide to situating Mauriac's public positions in the postwar period. On Sartre's own collaborationism, see the amusing essay by Clive James, *Cultural Amnesia: Necessary Memories from History and the Arts* (New York: Norton, 2007), 669–79.

[122] Robert Speaight, *François Mauriac: A Study of the Writer and the Man* (London: Chatto & Windus, 1976), 197.

particular matters) reflected the novelist's view that only de Gaulle had the historical, almost mythical, power to bring the various strands of the nation together, even if it had to be under a kind of "consular" regime. Many viewed this as a conservative stance, but again it might be truer to say that Mauriac's seeming oscillation between "conservative" and "liberal" views shows his deeper commitment to a vision of man and of France that could be only partially incarnated by either of the usual competing political factions.

During this period of turmoil, Mauriac was noticeably less interested in literature. As he confessed in his *Bloc-notes*, "At my age, the conflict between the Christian and the novelist has moved on to another plane. It's much less a question of the Jansenist scruples that used to trouble me in describing the passions than a kind of disenchantment with everything to do with art in general, and with my own art in particular. A feeling that art is literally an idol, that it has its martyrs and its prophets, and that for many people it is a substitute for God. And not art alone, but the word—the word that has not been made flesh."[123] The conflict between "the Christian and the novelist" here echoes another controversy into which Mauriac was drawn. In 1939, the young Jean-Paul Sartre, before he became well known, mounted an attack on Mauriac in *La Nouvelle Revue française*. Sartre accused Mauriac of playing God with his characters in the novel *La fin de la nuit*, tailoring their fates to a preestablished Christian template and making absolute statements about them that no man can claim to know. Sartre ended the sometimes insightful critique with the infamous remark, "God is not an artist; and neither is M. Mauriac."[124]

The basis of Sartre's complaint was that Mauriac allegedly introduced absolute judgments on things happening that only God could know, particularly in a relativistic "Einsteinian" universe. This effectively turned his human characters into things determined by circumstances and eliminated their freedom (a rather stiff literary application of Sartre's later distinction between the *en soi* and the *pour soi*). A Christian novelist more than anyone—witness Dostoyevsky, says Sartre—is well situated to write of free beings. *La fin de la nuit* is not

[123] Quoted in ibid., 193–94, from *Bloc-notes I*, 40.

[124] An English version of this essay appears in Jean-Paul Sartre, *Literary Essays*, trans. Annette Michelson (New York: Philosophical Library, 1957), 7–23.

the best of Mauriac's novels, partly because Thérèse Desqueyroux, a complex character who is in several of Mauriac's stories, put in an appearance. This woman—who in an early incarnation tried to murder her husband and later went through many complex changes—obsessed Mauriac, but he could not determine finally what to do with her. That indecision caused him to flutter around her in his writing. Sartre notes this fluctuation in point of view and makes some insightful comments about clumsy passages in the book where Mauriac wrongly intrudes himself. But to blame "the omniscient author" entirely for lording it over his characters means to banish all general remarks of a factual nature from fiction. Dickens and Balzac, who are novelists if anyone is, make such remarks without fatal consequences. And even preestablished Christian templates have not been fatal to literature: among the poets, they do not seem to have hampered unduly writers like Dante or Claudel. Sartre's criticism, a half century later, seems just when aimed at poor construction but vastly overblown when it tries to dictate to novelists what they can and cannot do. As in much of his work, Sartre also draws too sharp a distinction between human freedom and the often limiting circumstances of our lives as embodied creatures.[125]

Mauriac took some of Sartre's better points into account in his later work. But consistent with his view of Christian literature as possessing greater highs and lows than the secular view, his basic vision was truer than Sartre's. Mauriac suggested strongly that much of the evil we do is inherited and may not entirely entail personal responsibility. (Father Donissan in Bernanos' *Sous le soleil de Satan* made the same observation when he was given the gift of reading souls.) In Mauriac's books, that evil is pervasive, even cosmic, in addition to being transmitted at times by the more everyday vehicles of family and community. Robert Speaight has observed of this particular point: "If Sartre's criticism was well founded, Mauriac would not have been

[125] To be fair, a more mature Sartre conceded as much, even after decades of public feuding with Mauriac. In 1960, asked by Madeleine Chapsal in an interview about Mauriac, he remarked: "I think that I would be more flexible today, since the essential quality of the novel must be to provide involvement and interest, and I would be much less finicky about the methods employed.... You always find a way to say what you want, and the author is always present": trans. by and quoted in David O'Connell, *François Mauriac Revisited* (New York: Twayne, 1995), 175.

the first Christian to be caught by the problem of predestination and free will, nor the first to find it insoluble."[126] Linked as it largely is to sex and money in provincial France, Mauriac's is a somewhat narrow literary world. But those provincials reveal much that is universal in human existence. And those universals are more starkly present in the provinces than they might appear in more sophisticated settings. Further, in his classical economy of presentation and profound knowledge of people, Mauriac has few peers. Among his Catholic contemporaries, perhaps only Graham Greene is on a par.

In terms of Catholicity, Mauriac had the advantage over Greene in that he remained firmly Catholic. Pascal was the one who kept him upright through the challenges and outright personal rebellion he experienced living in his day in France. The institutional Church, he confessed, not only left him cold but induced doubts for several reasons. First, even in early youth he had been repelled by the bourgeois element in the provinces. People there were nominally Catholic, seemingly devoted to maintaining faith and morals, but secretly using those pieties as a cover for selfishness with little concern about justice and the poor, as appears in many of the novels. The local parishes seemed to do nothing to remedy this situation. Furthermore, when the Church condemned movements like Marc Sagnier's *Le Sillon*, to which Mauriac had belonged in his youth, it seemed to set up a barrier between the Catholic faith and modern society. Leo XIII, as we have seen earlier, had encouraged the *Ralliement* to the Republic; Catholics were to participate in modern life while bringing distinctive perspectives. But for Mauriac, Pius X's 1907 encyclical *Pascendi* had seemed to cut off other experiments seeking to enter into dialogue with the modern world and left him very much at sea. And, of course, there was the general intellectual skepticism toward traditional belief.

Pascal helped with all of this, as Mauriac explained in his late and wise book *What I Believe*.[127] There, he shows a calm confidence won after decades of struggle, struggle not only against the usual temptations but also with uncongenial elements in the Church. Mauriac says, for instance, that after *Pascendi*, "I testify today that it was the

[126] Speaight, *François Mauriac*.

[127] François Mauriac, *What I Believe*, trans. and with an introduction by Wallace Fowlie (New York: Farrar, Straus & Giroux, 1963).

Christ of Pascal who said to me, in those hours, 'Stay with me.' "[128] Already visible here is the Mauriac who would welcome the Second Vatican Council, in which "Peter is no longer that old man isolated and even imprisoned by his servants. I see him surrounded by all his sons, and even by those who had asked for their part of the inheritance and who had withdrawn from him."[129] Mauriac felt "vague resentment"[130] under every pope except Pius XI. But this statement should not be read anachronistically as supporting movements that appeared after the Council. In 1968, when Paul VI issued *Humanae Vitae*, the encyclical that repeated the Church's condemnation of contraception, for example, six hundred French priests signed a letter of protest. Mauriac signed a letter of loyalty to the pope.[131] Jacques Maritain's *Paysan de la Garonne* appeared a few years later and slammed the abuses of the Council that were leading to wholesale abandonment of Catholic principles. Mauriac read it and agreed that the earlier desired liberalization had taken a radically wrong turn. His hopes for the pastoral openings inaugurated at the Council reveal the gentleness and tenderness that Mauriac identified with the Pascalian heart of Catholicism—despite his admitted ferocity as a polemicist after World War II when the bulk of his work consisted in widely followed and very influential journalism.[132]

His Pascalian stance is close to von Balthasar's *Love Alone Is Credible,* which appeared in 1963, three years after Mauriac's *What I Believe*. Pascal's very person, in Mauriac's eyes, refuted many of the modern materialist objections: "If God does not exist, where does Blaise Pascal come from? Could blind inert matter have engendered that thought and language and insatiable heart?"[133] To those who argue that Pascal is not a normal thinker, he says:

> He is not like philosophers and, according to Paul Valéry, he is the opposite of a philosopher. He was a man who believed that truth exists and is Someone. He claimed he knew truth and tried to persuade others, and did so not in an obscure language demanding an initiation but

[128] Ibid., 106.
[129] Ibid., 137.
[130] Ibid.
[131] Speaight, *François Mauriac*, 218.
[132] This has been collected in four volumes of *Bloc-notes* (Paris: Seuil, 1993).
[133] Mauriac, *What I Believe*. 113.

> in an ordinary language an ordinary man can understand, the most precise and the purest language spoken in France, which never lost sight of the creature formed by nature and customs he wanted to convince. "He sees in a superior way what anyone can see!" Valéry says scornfully. Yes! But what if this were the sign of genius?[134]

Mauriac the novelist knows there are many self-deceptions and much wishful thinking among Christians seeking consolation—himself included—but he seems convinced that he can trust in Christ as "the only one who gave forth the gentleness which all the others had refused me, a gentleness that was strong and without affectation, and which only a God has the power to join with infinite force."[135]

This is a powerful way of putting the case. But, as Mauriac knows, it is of course open to the usual objection that it is wishful thinking imprinted deep in us during childhood. But for him this thinking paradoxically seems to be a key to truthfulness. And these sorts of paradoxes actually seem to have aided his work as a novelist; as for instance, he says, "The light I have received, to which I have consented, made me attentive, for as long as I live, to [the] contradiction in myself and in all men."[136] Yet he will not allow that a Christian can remain content with the "mysteries" of who we are, where we come from, where we are going.[137] The secularists who deny any sense to these questions are the ones who have forbidden a search into the truth. We admittedly do not know the answers, but God does and gradually shows us, sometimes after many years of willful blindness and hurt. Louis' thirty and more years of wounded love in *Vipers' Tangle* is hardly a unique case and may even be more like the rule in certain respects even for the professed Christian. Yet that light exists, and Mauriac claims that, in his own small way, he saw the light from the burning fire of which Pascal talks in his famous mystical "Memorial", even as a young child. It seems the simple truth to say that, whatever turns took place in his literary life, that light was what he offered in his novels—as did those of his countryman Bernanos—as a lifeline to all the children of thwarted loves.

[134] Ibid., 111.
[135] Ibid, 89.
[136] Ibid., 36.
[137] Ibid., 28.

Chapter 11

The Motley Society and After

In 1925, a twenty-three-year-old Englishman was swimming out to sea—whether to kill himself or just to take out his frustrations was never entirely clear. He was stung by a swarm of jellyfish—which forced him back to shore. Thus, God or his creation spared the life of a man who has a good claim to being the greatest English novelist of the twentieth century; Evelyn Waugh. If Hopkins presents a modern poetic sensibility struggling with the agony and ecstasy of human life, Waugh offers a stiletto-like satire on the vapid modern world as it began to emerge in England after the First World War. His portrait of that world in the early novels is as merciless as it is hilarious. When he became a Catholic, about four years after his suicide attempt, his work shifted somewhat to richer themes. But throughout his career, there is an unusual combination of hatred and love at play in virtually everything Waugh wrote. In his very earliest years, he was known to his family as a particularly satirical child. But in those same years, he was early attracted to religious ritual, even reenacting high Anglican rites at home. It might not be too strong to suggest that he returned from his possible suicide attempt even more himself: with some special stinging capacity all his own, as the early novels attest, but also with a growing inclination toward Christianity—and Catholicism, which he had decided quite early was the only real Christianity left.

Waugh and soon his longtime friend Graham Greene were the first Catholic novelists in England really to address the modern social world, the one that emerged in England and elsewhere after the catastrophe of World War I. By contrast, Chesterton and Belloc were products of a far older age. By the time the Great War ended, both were well into their forties and had been formed in controversies that were starting to change into something quite different. The wildly hedonistic England of the "Bright Young Things" after the war and the chaos following the withdrawal of the Western Christian order form the subject of Waugh's early novels. *Decline and Fall* (1927) and *Vile Bodies* (1930) in particular are among the most hilarious and inventive representations of the "motley society"[1] of the modern world. Waugh brings a dizzying, headlong energy to these stories. The very names of the characters are strokes of comic genius: Lady Metroland, the Countess of Circumference, Mrs. Blackwater, Mr. Outrage, Fanny Throbbing, Alastair Digby-Vaine-Trumpington, the Chasm family, Sir Humphrey Maltravers, Miles Malpractice, Miss Runcible, Mrs. Melrose Ape (a lady evangelist who wrote the famous hymn "There Ain't No Flies on the Lamb of God"), and on and on. In lesser hands, this kind of satire might soon pale. But Waugh had the unflagging satirical sense of P. G. Wodehouse—whom he greatly admired—and something more serious besides.

The more serious side is a kind of oddity in the Catholic literature of the twentieth century. Many converts came to the Church because of some personal crisis, a few by the kind of sense of civilizational order Belloc and Chesterton had seen disappearing along with the faith. Waugh is rather unusual in that his sense of the absurdity of the modern world seems to have been firmly there from the beginning—long before he made any serious turn toward religion, his youthful attraction to Christian liturgy notwithstanding. Indeed, there may never have been such an odd combination of love of order and beauty alongside a merciless flaying of outer chaos in all of literature. But as Graham Greene brilliantly observed, Waugh's satire is the obverse side of his Romanticism. He was deeply dismayed by what he found to be the English society of his time—a society of which, as a young man at least, he was also a part—and a kind of disappointed love lies behind the savage satire. The same was also largely true of Waugh's account of army life, another institution that

[1] What exactly is this "motley society"? One scholar has characterized it as follows: "This is a social space in which the mixture of types (social, ethnic, psychological) is complete and ostentatious, in which randomness in action prevails, the power of causes is weak, indifference overshadows morality, nature is absent or evil, the present devours the past as well as the future, individuals are passive and do not claim control over themselves or over society, spurts of energy alternate jerkily with bouts of sullen inertia, cultural syncretism provides a general background for the action": Virgil Nemoianu, "Evelyn Waugh and Motley Society", *CLIO*, vol. 12, no. 3 (1983): 233–34.

proved to be far different from what he experienced during World War II. The comic account he provides in *Sword of Honor*, a novel in three parts that may actually be his greatest work of all, is in its way a lament for the lack of chivalry and sacrifice that warriors, at their best, might embody.

Like Chesterton, Waugh started out wanting to be a painter. Charles Ryder, the narrator of Waugh's great later Catholic novel *Brideshead Revisited*, is—not coincidentally—a painter as well. Waugh's father was a director of a publishing house, so the young Waugh was at home among literary and artistic figures from the first. The painting career never really took off, but sometime—maybe at Oxford—Waugh fell in love with the Pre-Raphaelite movement and the British painters who belonged to it. His first book was a study of Dante Gabriel Rossetti, a notable poet, translator of Dante, and one of the leading lights among the Pre-Raphaelites. It is significant that Waugh's tastes ran in that direction rather than toward the modernism in painting that was then everywhere in vogue. In Waugh, there is never the feeling—as in some other Catholic authors—that the turn to the past and to the Church is merely a flight from modernity. His tastes and critical faculties seem joined from the beginning: the modern world does not drive him to the Pre-Raphaelites. Their canvases are merely, self-evidently *better* than what is currently on offer. And in similar fashion, he sees clearly into and can draw sharp portraits of the energetic but empty 1920s.

Decline and Fall, his first novel, tells the story of Paul Pennyfeather, an Oxford theology student who has his pants stripped off by friends during a bout of drinking and is expelled from the university. Forced to support himself, he takes a job—as Waugh himself did after coming down from Oxford—at a boy's prep school in Wales, sonorously named Llanabba Castle. (It was after Waugh's failure at this desperate employment and after the promise of a job by C.K. Scott Moncrieff, the well-known translator of Proust and Catholic convert, fell through that Waugh may have attempted suicide.) Pennyfeather's fellow teachers are a collection of odd birds, and the whole stable of characters is a wickedly *louche* set. The headmistress, Mrs. Beste-Chetwynde (later Lady Metroland), with whom Paul falls in love, is a madame with a large and profitable stable of prostitutes in South America. Paul goes to jail on her behalf, before returning to Oxford by pretending to be his own cousin, where he pursues studies of Christianity again with a decided preference for the early figures with the strictest attitudes toward the least deviations from orthodoxy. This book was a great critical success, although Chesterton—who later influenced Waugh immensely via *The Everlasting Man*—wrote a harsh review, perhaps not understanding that it was really a satire against a new form of English society with which he had no contact.

Among the various uproarious scenes is one in which a retired army colonel Grimes, to make ends meet, reduced to teaching the young boys, receives a letter that might have taken him away from his misery. The owner of a local brewery writes him:

> We employ a certain number of travellers to go round to various inns and hotels to sample the beer and see that it has not been diluted or in any way adulterated. Our junior traveller, who was a friend of mine from Cambridge, has just developed D.T.'s and has had to be suspended. The salary is two hundred a year with car and travelling expenses. Would this attract you at all? If so, will you let me know in the next few days. Yours sincerely.

Grimes turns to Paul: "God's own job, and mine for the asking!"[2] But like all the other characters, he is prevented by previous circumstances from escaping from his current fallen state. It is no wonder that page after page of this sort of invention convinced the vast run of critics that here was a major new literary talent.

But Waugh really came into his own with the sequel, the novel *Vile Bodies*. In all literature, there has never been a more headlong satire of the social whirl. It begins with a nausea-inducing crossing of the English Channel by most of the main characters—an obvious image of the lurching instability in the England of the Bright Young Things. And it closes with a chaotic motorcar race in which the very machinery of the race cars and the perilous race circuit—crashes and injuries everywhere—suggest a whole society riding a technological achievement with no real purpose that perhaps is actually taking the humans into the ditch. Several ditches, actually. By a comic misunderstanding, a drunken Agatha Runcible winds up as substitute driver

[2] Evelyn Waugh, *Decline and Fall* (London, Chapman & Hall, 1928), 122.

in unlucky Car 13. She pushes serious drivers off the track and winds up in a crash in a town miles away—as well as in a mental hospital, where she repeats to herself in terror, "*Faster, faster*".

There is much else of simple and outright hilarity, of course. The main "plot", if the book may be said to have one, is the effort of Adam Fenwick-Symes—a nobleman, but also a gossip journalist like several of his friends—to find enough money to marry Miss Nina Blount, an airheaded woman of his set. In the second half of the story, she abandons Adam abruptly for a childhood friend who has made a great fortune abroad. They have a quick affair, then marry, then head off by "aeroplane" on a honeymoon:

> Ginger looked out of the aeroplane: "I say, Nina," he shouted, "when you were young did you ever have to learn a thing out of a poetry book about: '*This scepter'd isle, this earth of majesty, this something or other Eden*'? D'you know what I mean? '*this happy breed of men, this little world, this precious stone set in the silver sea.*[3]

She vaguely remembers that it occurred in a play in which she once acted: "Well, they may have put it into a play since. It was in a blue poetry book when I learned it." The point clearly is that these two privileged representatives of the upper class retain a vestigial sense—but very indistinct—of the greatest lines of poetry ever written about their country, "This blessed plot, this earth, this realm, this England", which Shakespeare put into *Richard II.*

No brief summary can convey the rushing energy with which Waugh executed this satire. Critics have noticed that it became sharper and more savage midway through the book because in his own life he experienced something similar to what had happened to Adam Fenwick-Symes: his first marriage abruptly ended when his wife of a few years deserted him, without warning, for a rather shabby friend. *Vile Bodies* also contains a devastating portrait of a scheming priest, Father Rothschild, S.J., who seems to know everyone and every scheme afoot in the "best" social circles. Still, he also has some spiritual insight into the current crisis: "Perhaps it is all in some way historical? I don't think people ever *want* to lose their faith either in

[3] Evelyn Waugh, *Vile Bodies* (Boston: Little, Brown, 1977), 283.

religion or anything else. I know very few young people, but it seems to me that they are all possessed with an almost fatal hunger for permanence. I think all these divorces show that. People aren't content just to muddle along nowadays.... They say, 'if a thing's not worth doing well, it's not worth doing at all.' It makes everything very difficult for them."[4] But if Waugh was not above mocking a certain type of priest at this point, it was to the Catholic Church that he finally turned in 1930, the very year in which *Vile Bodies* appeared.

Like many before him, he turned to Farm Street Church and none other than the famous Father Martin D'Arcy, who has left a striking record of Waugh's way of taking instruction. He had, of course, read a great deal of theology and history on his own. Father D'Arcy comments that Waugh had "come to learn and understand what he believed to be God's revelation, and this made talking with him an interesting discussion based primarily on reason. I have never myself met a convert who so strongly based his assents on truth.... Hard, clear thinking had with the help of grace given him the answer for which he had been searching, and one can see its effect in his subsequent writings."[5] (When Waugh came to write *Helena*, his 1950 novel about Emperor Constantine's mother, who discovered the True Cross in Palestine, he concluded with the observation that the relics of the Cross are welcomed "because it states a fact", and Helena is honored because "she makes one blunt assertion. And there is hope."[6]) That this well-known maker of converts had never met a candidate so bent on truth says a great deal about Waugh. And D'Arcy was right that the conversion affected his later works, though not until several other wicked satires, such as *Black Mischief*, *A Handful of Dust*, and *Scoop*, had appeared.

Waugh, too, has left some indications of his state of mind at the time. As noted above, he had earlier come to believe that Catholicism was the "only genuine" form of Christianity. And he was as sharply aware, perhaps even more so than Belloc since things had

[4] Ibid., 183–84.

[5] David Pryce-Jones, ed., *Evelyn Waugh and His World* (Boston: Little, Brown, 1973), 61–64.

[6] Evelyn Waugh, *Helena* (Boston: Little, Brown, 1950), 247. Waugh sometimes claimed that he regarded this his best novel. Few would agree with him, though it is a gently imaginative presentation of a little-known figure.

decayed even more in Waugh's day, that Christianity was the essential and formative constituent of Western culture. The difficulties lay not there, but in personal awareness, something many have accused Waugh of lacking. He kept personal matters well hidden, but of his conversion, he wrote openly, "the trouble is that I don't feel Christian in the absolute sense. The question seems to be must I wait until I do feel this ... or can I become a Catholic when I am in such an incomplete state—and so get the benefit of the sacraments and receive faith afterwards?" Father D'Arcy clearly advised acting. As Waugh put it, he wanted "just to get the seed in anyhow & hope it would come up".[7]

It "came up" in stages over time. Besides satire, in the 1930s Waugh wrote a biography of the Jesuit martyr Thomas Campion and a series of travel books. In the latter, an unapologetic assertion of the superiority of Western civilization and Christianity came to the fore. And this sometimes savage strain became more and more pronounced in Waugh's life. According to an often-repeated anecdote, Nancy Mitford once said to Waugh, who was a guest at her home in Paris, that she could not understand how he could behave so unkindly and call himself a Catholic. Waugh replied, "You have no idea how much nastier I would be if I was not a Catholic. Without supernatural aid, I would hardly be a human being."[8] In later years he would use an ear trumpet and it was said he even took up a pose as an out-of-touch hater of his times, although Graham Greene claimed that in the years of their acquaintance he had only once observed such behavior by Waugh.[9]

Whether the personal behavior was sincere or affected, Waugh's views about the modern world were deep-seated and openly stated. In a well-known passage in *Mexico: An Object Lesson* (published in England as *Robbery under Law*), he deplores the persecution of Christians in that country, which like Graham Greene he visited during a particularly bad period, and lays out a kind of secular profession of faith from which he never significantly faltered:

[7] Selena Hastings, *Evelyn Waugh: A Biography* (Boston: Houghton Mifflin, 1995), 225.

[8] Quoted in Clifton Fadiman, André Bernard, eds., *Bartlett's Book of Anecdotes* (Boston: Little, Brown, 2000), 563.

[9] Graham Greene, *Ways of Escape: An Autobiography* (New York: Simon & Schuster, 1980), 270–71.

> Let me, then, warn the reader that I was a Conservative when I went to Mexico and that everything I saw there strengthened my opinions. I believe that man is, by nature, an exile and will never be self-sufficient or complete on this earth; that his chances of happiness and virtue, here, remain more or less constant through the centuries and, generally speaking, are not much affected by the political and economic conditions in which he lives; that the balance of good and ill tends to revert to a norm; that sudden changes of physical condition are usually ill, and are advocated by the wrong people for the wrong reasons; that the intellectual communists of today have personal, irrelevant grounds for their antagonism to society, which they are trying to exploit. I believe in government; that men cannot live together without rules but that they should be kept at the bare minimum of safety; that there is no form of government ordained from God as being better than any other; that the anarchic elements in society are so strong that it is a whole-time task to keep the peace. I believe that the inequalities of wealth and position are inevitable and that it is therefore meaningless to discuss the advantages of elimination; that men naturally arrange themselves in a system of classes; that such a system is necessary for any form of co-operation work, more particularly the work of keeping a nation together. I believe in nationality; not in terms of race or of divine commissions for world conquest, but simply thus: mankind inevitably organizes itself in communities according to its geographical distribution; these communities by sharing a common history develop common characteristics and inspire local loyalty; the individual family develops most happily and fully when it accepts these natural limits....
>
> A conservative is not merely an obstructionist,... a brake to frivolous experiment. He has positive work to do.... Civilization has no force of its own beyond what it is given from within. It is under constant assault and it takes most of the energies of civilized man to keep going at all.... Barbarism is never finally defeated; given propitious circumstances, men and women who seem quite orderly, will commit every conceivable atrocity....
>
> Unremitting effort is needed to keep men living together at peace.[10]

Three years earlier, traveling in Abyssinia, which had recently been occupied by Mussolini's troops, he had praised the Fascists, not

[10] Evelyn Waugh, *Robbery under Law: The Mexican Object Lesson* (Boston: Little, Brown, 1939), 16–17.

for their violence, but for, in his estimation, the fact that they were at least bringing civilization and clarity where only barbarism and chaos had reigned: "Along the roads will pass the eagles of ancient Rome, as they came to our savage ancestors in France and Britain and Germany, bringing some rubbish and some mischief: a good deal of vulgar talk and some sharp misfortunes for individual opponents; but above and beyond and entirely predominating, the inestimable gifts of fine workmanship and clear judgment—the two determining qualities of the human spirit, by which alone, under God, man grows and flourishes."[11] Though Mussolini was admired by a wide spectrum of figures in Britain at the time for an energy and discipline they believed was lacking in their own country, this was a highly Romantic view of things, especially from a writer who was so sensitive to the depths of Western corruption and frivolity—and the political illusions to which they gave rise.

It was in the books that came after World War II, especially *Brideshead Revisited* and *Sword of Honor*, that Waugh achieved his most mature vision. *Brideshead* in particular was very popular and was even made into a splendid video version in the 1980s, though the later book may be the greater work. Waugh looks back in these stories to the 1930s and the war years with a combination of criticism and regret. Though his keen eye is still ready to draw black humor out of the incongruities of life in modern Britain, there emerges in these stories an appreciation for what civilization has slowly built up over time and a realization of how easily it could be thrown away, even by people who were not as shallow and flighty as the characters in the earlier novels.

For the first time, the Catholic Church is also a serious force in his stories, though she, too, has a mixed influence. In *Brideshead Revisited*, for example, the Church is largely identified with Lady Marchmain, a pious noblewoman who drives her husband and son Sebastian to drink—and then to flight (the family name is Flyte). At the same time, there is a redemptive element to this Catholicism, though it must play out over long times and distances. At a

[11] Evelyn Waugh, *Waugh in Abyssinia* (Baton Rouge, La.: Louisiana State University Press, 2007), 253. This is a reprint of the 1933 original. Excerpts of several of Waugh's travel books have been collected in *When the Going Was Good* (New York: Penguin, 2012), a reprint of several earlier editions.

crucial point in the story, Lady Marchmain is reading aloud from one of Chesterton's Father Brown detective stories, in which the priest explains how he caught a criminal. But the point also has to do with the wayward members of the family and people in general. Cordelia, one of Lady Marchmain's daughters and—like King Lear's daughter Cordelia—a truth-teller, recalls the episode later:

> "D'you know what Papa said when he became a Catholic? ... He said ...: 'You have brought back my family to the faith of their ancestors.' ... The family haven't been very constant, have they? There's him gone and Sebastian gone and Julia gone. But God won't let them go for long, you know. I wonder if you remember the story Mummy read us the evening Sebastian first got drunk—I mean the *bad* evening. Father Brown said something like 'I caught him' (the thief) 'with an unseen hook and an invisible line which is long enough to let him wander to the ends of the world and still to bring him back with a twitch upon the thread.'"[12]

The novel's subtitle, "The Sacred and Profane Memories of Captain Charles Ryder", indicates the main thread of the story. Ryder, whose name subtly suggests a kind of knight, meets Sebastian Flyte at Oxford, where they become fast friends and perhaps even homosexual lovers, as many men did in Waugh's Oxford. Sebastian exudes boyish charm, and that personal quality, coupled with the opulence of his family's home and way of life, captivates Charles and offers him a kind of romantic dream of a life he has never anticipated could exist. The charm and family faith, however, conceal many troubles, in particular the way in which Lord Marchmain abandoned the family out of guilt—and then took a mistress in Venice. As Sebastian heads down a similar path, Charles finds himself resenting Catholicism because of the way it destroys lives. But all this is a prelude to a process by which he himself will wind up in the Church.

A decade and more after Oxford, Charles is married with children and is an established painter of England's great houses and other safe subjects. But he is deeply unhappy and somehow frozen out of the

[12] Evelyn Waugh, *Brideshead Revisited* (Boston: Little Brown, 1945), 220.

dreams he once entertained. Sebastian is a drunk lost somewhere in Arab lands. Charles' wife is unfaithful to him, which sends him to Mexico and Central America in search of exotic subjects to stimulate his imagination. He returns with many completed canvases, but Anthony Blanche, a flagrant but highly entertaining homosexual who was a friend at Oxford, shows up at his exhibit. He has come, he tells Ryder, to see what his old friend has wrought:

> "I found, my dear, a very naughty and very successful practical joke. It reminded me of dear Sebastian when he liked so much to dress up in false whiskers. It was charm again, my dear, simple, creamy English charm, playing tigers."
>
> "You're quite right," I said.
>
> "My dear, of course I'm right. I was right years ago—more years, I am happy to say, than either of us shows—when I *warned* you. I took you out to dinner to warn you of charm. I warned you expressly and in great detail of the Flyte family. Charm is the great English blight. It does not exist outside these damp islands. It spots and kills anything it touches. It kills love; it kills art; I greatly fear, my dear Charles, it has killed *you*."[13]

This is Anthony Blanche speaking, not Evelyn Waugh, but it is hard not to detect here an element that did not exist in the earlier books: charm as a spiritually deadening agent, a truly novel perception.

But Anthony has not seen all. Charles met Julia, Sebastian's sister, on shipboard traveling back from New York to England. During the crossing, he realizes that Sebastian was, like John the Baptist, only the precursor and that this woman, who greatly resembles her brother, is the destined love of his life. They begin an adulterous affair, and love, as it always does, begins to lead everyone new directions. God and all mankind seem arrayed against them, they say, but they resolve to hold onto their happiness in spite of everything. For two years, they enjoy bliss at Brideshead Castle, "not a day's coldness or mistrust or disappointment".[14] But all that seeming peace—and the anticipation of a lifetime more when their divorces are finalized and they are able to marry—is about to be destroyed for a larger peace.

[13] Ibid., 273.
[14] Ibid., 278.

What follows has sometimes been criticized as sentimentality, even by some Catholics. A series of crises leads to everyone's being reconciled to God, most notably and dramatically, Lord Marchmain. The critics, as is often the case, remain unconvinced by the fictional presentation of conversion. But that is precisely where Waugh's artistry shows itself at its strongest. For instance, when Julia flies into a fit of hysteria about "living in sin" and forever being cut off from God, Charles tries to tell her it is all bosh. But she replies with a remarkable litany of connections that suggest the depth of faith in a particular soul:

> "A word from so long ago, from Nanny Hawkins stitching by the hearth and the nightlight burning before the Sacred Heart. Cordelia and me with the catechism, in Mummy's room, before luncheon on Sundays. Mummy carrying my sin with her to church, bowed under it and the black lace veil, in the chapel; slipping out with it in London before the fires were lit; taking it with her through the empty streets, where the milkman's ponies stood with their forefeet on the pavement; Mummy dying with my sin eating at her, more cruelly than her own deadly illness.
>
> "Mummy dying with it; Christ dying with it, nailed hand and foot; hanging over the bed in the night-nursery; hanging year after year in the dark little study at Farm Street with the shining oilcloth; hanging in the dark church where only the old charwoman raises the dust and one candle burns; hanging at noon, high among the crowds and the soldiers; no comfort except a sponge of vinegar and the kind words of a thief; hanging for ever; never the cool sepulcher and the grave clothes spread on the stone slab, never the oil and spices in the dark cave; always the midday sun and the dice clicking for the seamless coat.
>
> ". . . No way back; the gates barred; all the saints and angels posted along the walls. Thrown away, scrapped, rotting down; the old man with lupus and the forked stick who limps out at nightfall to turn the rubbish, hoping for something to put in his sack, something marketable, turns away with disgust.
>
> "Nameless and dead, like the baby they wrapped up and took away before I had seen her."[15]

[15] Ibid., 381.

Here of course, it is Waugh who has created the poetry of attachment to the faith, but it is very nearly unparalleled as a description of that attachment in modern literature.

The other scene, the dramatic conversion of Lord Marchmain after a quarter century living away in adulterous flight, is heightened by perhaps even greater artistry. He returns, gravely ill, to Brideshead because of World War II and has had his sickbed set up in the highly ornate "Chinese drawing room". Further, he asks that the "Queen's bed" with a canopy like "a Baldachino" be brought down.[16] And it is within this sumptuous staging that his slow decline, struggles with the fear of death, and last interactions with his estranged family transpire. Among the other turmoil, the "religious question" arises. The women—Julia, Cordelia, his mistress Cara—as well as his strict son Bridey want him to see a priest. But he is frightened and politely turns the local pastor away the first time he comes. The next time he is *in extremis*, doubtfully even conscious, when the final decision must be made.

Charles sees all this, as would many then and since, as taking advantage of the weakness and fear of an old man. He mocks the efforts bitterly—and in retrospect concedes that taking possession of the grand house as Julia's husband was one of his selfish motives for wanting things not to change radically. And perhaps there is, subconsciously, a fear of what God may do to his own life. Daughter Julia and mistress Cara kneel at the foot of the bed as the priest enters. He begins to anoint Marchmain and in his ear asks the dying man to make some sign to indicate he is sorry for offending God. Marchmain seems unconscious:

> *Ego te absolvo in nomine Patris* ... and saw the priest make the sign of the cross. Then I knelt, too, and prayed: "O God, if there is a God, forgive him his sins, if there is such a thing as sin," and the man on the bed opened his eyes and gave a sigh, the sort of sigh I had imagined people made at the moment of death, but his eyes moved so that we knew there was still life in him.
>
> I suddenly felt the longing for a sign, if only of courtesy, if only for the sake of the woman I loved, who knelt in front of me, praying, I knew, for a sign. It seemed so small a thing that was asked, the bare

[16] Ibid., 315.

acknowledgment of a present, a nod in the crowd. All over the world people were on their knees before innumerable crosses, and here the drama was being played again by two men—by one man, rather, and he nearer death than life; the universal drama in which there is only one actor.

The priest took the little silver box from his pocket and spoke again in Latin, touching the dying man with an oily wad; he finished what he had to do, put away the box and gave the final blessing. Suddenly Lord Marchmain moved his hand to his forehead; I thought he had felt the touch of the chrism and was wiping it away. "O God," I prayed, "don't let him do that." But there was no need for fear; the hand moved slowly down his breast, then to his shoulder, and Lord Marchmain made the sign of the cross. Then I knew that the sign I had asked for was not a little thing, not a passing nod of recognition, and a phrase came back to me from my childhood of the veil of the temple being rent from top to bottom.

It was over; we stood up; the nurse went back to the oxygen cylinder; the doctor bent over his patient. Julia whispered to me: "Will you see Father Mackay out? I'm staying here for a little."

Outside the door Father Mackay became the simple, genial man I had known before. "Well, now, and that was a beautiful thing to see. I've known it happen that way again and again. The devil resists to the last moment and then the Grace of God is too much for him. You're not a Catholic I think, Mr. Ryder, but at least you'll be glad for the ladies to have the comfort of it."[17]

After such a moment, Charles and Julia cannot ever be together again, of course. And they part.

The entire story of *Brideshead Revisited* is told by Charles in retrospect, stirred by his "revisiting" Brideshead Castle years later. The circumstances are quite odd. To his great surprise, his British Army unit has been sent there to wait for further orders during the Second World War. He reveals very little about what the last scene and the parting with Julia meant to him, though he says that all the others seem to have reconciled with the Church and one another. As he goes through the now disordered mansion, he reflects:

There was one part of the house I had not yet visited, and I went there now. The chapel showed no ill-effects of its long neglect; the

[17] Ibid., 338–39.

> art-nouveau paint was as fresh and bright as ever; the art-nouveau lamp burned once more before the altar. I said a prayer, an ancient, newly learned form of words, and left, turning towards the camp; and as I walked back, and the cook-house bugle sounded ahead of me, I thought:—
>
> The builders did not know the uses to which their work would descend; they made a new house with the stones of the old castle; year by year, generation after generation, they enriched and extended it; year by year the great harvest of timber in the park grew to ripeness; until, in sudden frost, came the age of Hooper; the place was desolate and the work all brought to nothing; *Quomodo sedet sola civitas*. Vanity of vanities, all is vanity.[18]

And yet, this may be a bit of a literary conceit rather than the truth of the case. So he ruminates further in the very last words of the novel:

> And yet, I thought, stepping out more briskly towards the camp, where the bugles after a pause had taken up the second call and were sounding *Pick-em-up, pick-em-up, hot potatoes*—and yet that is not the last word; it is not even an apt word; it is a dead word from ten years back.
>
> Something quite remote from anything the builders intended, has come out of their work, and out of the fierce little human tragedy in which I played; something none of us thought about at the time; a small red flame—a beaten-copper lamp of deplorable design, relit before the beaten-copper doors of a tabernacle; the flame which the old knights saw from their tombs, which they saw put out; that flame burns again for other soldiers, far from home, farther, in heart, than Acre or Jerusalem. It could not have been lit but for the builders and the tragedians, and there I found it this morning, burning anew among the old stones.
>
> I quickened my pace and reached the hut which served us for our ante-room.
>
> "You're looking unusually cheerful today," said the second-in-command.[19]

A military setting also marks the other great novel of Waugh's maturity. *Sword of Honor* is actually a trilogy of novels—*Men at Arms*, *Officers and Gentlemen*, and *Unconditional Surrender*—published from 1952 to 1961, and deals with the experiences of Guy Crouchback,

[18] Ibid., 350–51.
[19] Ibid., 351.

the childless heir of an old Catholic recusant family living alone in Italy after his wife divorced him. Actually, those experiences reveal a great deal more than might be expected. Though Waugh declared in a later preface to the republication of the three books in a single volume that it was not a Catholic novel, his assertion was not strictly true. The whole arc of the narrative moves from Guy's realization at the time of the Molotov-Ribbentrop Pact that the twin evils of the modern world—Communism and Fascism—had declared themselves open allies, to his belief that he can now take up a heroic crusade like his forefathers. Experience of the absurdities of army life and Guy's own incapacities as a middle-aged man—which Waugh's satirical gift handles with mature deftness—expose the unreality of that dream and the mixed moral nature of the Allies themselves. The various personal and military fiascoes he encounters lead Guy to realize that the Christian life is really about personal acts of charity and kindness in a world that, in peace as well as war, is wildly out of our control.

At the outset, we learn that Guy confesses his obvious sins regularly but also realizes: "There was no risk of his going deeper than the denunciation of his few infractions of the law, of his habitual weaknesses. Into that wasteland where his soul languished he need not, could not, enter. He had no words to describe it. There were no words in any language. There was nothing to describe, merely a void."[20] As an expression of the soul of many people, before the war gave them a palpable purpose again, this shows great insight. Guy lives in a town where a statue of Roger of Waybroke, an English knight stranded on his way to the Second Crusade, is prominently displayed, "his arms five falcons. His sword and one gauntlet still lay beside him." In his dreams of possible heroism, he identifies with that distant forebear and his sword of honor.

But much later, in the final installment of the trilogy, a Croatian Jewish woman tells him an uncomfortable truth:

> "Is there any place that is free from evil? It is too simple to say that only the Nazis wanted war. These communists wanted it too. It was the only way in which they could come to power. Many of my people

[20] Evelyn Waugh, *Men at Arms* and *Officers and Gentlemen* (New York: Dell, 1966), 14.

> wanted it, to be revenged on the Germans, to hasten the creation of the national state. It seems to me there was a will to war, a death wish, everywhere. Even good men thought their private honour would be satisfied by war. They could assert their manhood by killing and being killed. They would accept hardships in recompense for having been selfish and lazy. Danger justified privilege. I knew Italians—not very many perhaps—who felt this. Were there none in England?"
> "God forgive me," said Guy. "I was one of them."[21]

So it is this remedy for his own spiritual emptiness, and that of many others, that lies behind a subconscious desire for war.

Along the way, of course, Waugh derides the illusion of military virtues and preparedness, the ambition and political interests intertwined in the conduct of the war, the manipulation of the press for propaganda and personal gain. Much of this is territory he has worked before, but now set in the larger context of what otherwise seemed noble purposes. The foil to all this human corruption and egoism is a single, seemingly negligible figure: Guy's father. Mr. Gervase Crouchback is described as having preserved not only good humor but, despite many misfortunes, a "mysterious and tranquil joy". The reasons for this joy are carefully elaborated. He has no class consciousness—because the division he makes between people falls into only two parts:

> On one side stood the Crouchbacks and certain inconspicuous, anciently allied families; on the other side stood the rest of mankind, Box-Bender, the butcher, the Duke of Omnium (whose onetime wealth derived from monastic spoils), Lloyd George, Neville Chamberlain—all of a piece together. Mr. Crouchback acknowledged no monarch since James II. It was not an entirely sane conspectus but it engendered in his gentle breast two rare qualities, tolerance and humility. For nothing much, he assumed, could reasonably be expected from the commonalty; it was remarkable how well some of them did behave on occasions; while, for himself, any virtue he had came from afar without his deserving, and every small fault was grossly culpable in a man of high tradition.[22]

[21] Evelyn Waugh, *Unconditional Surrender* (Boston: Little Brown, 2012), 300.
[22] Waugh, *Men at Arms*, 35–36.

This mildly mad view of the world seems relatively sane and perhaps even saintly in a world at war.

Guy himself has to learn similar lessons in humility—at least the wisdom of not expecting too much from fallen humanity and of recognizing how little the good we are able to do is from our own merit.

But all this must reckon with a world in which large-scale evils walk abroad. For instance, a second "sword of honor" appears in the third volume—the Sword of Stalingrad, forged to commemorate the Soviet resistance to the Germans outside that city. This new sword also represents, however, an unholy pact of convenience between the Allies and the Soviets. Still, amid many betrayals and atrocities and disasters, discrete acts of honor and charity are possible. In the very scene in which Guy learns he was one of those who unconsciously wanted war, he is trying to help some Jews left in the region. Others just take their plight as one among many thousands of such cases, and the Allied command has basically given up on Serbia:

> Guy had not dismissed the Jews from his mind.... Here again, in a world of hate and waste, he was being offered the chance of doing a single small act to redeem the times. It was, therefore, with joy that he received the signal: Central Government approves in principle evacuation Jews stop.[23]

This is a realistic Guy whose "single small act" conforms with a true humility. In the end, Guy's previously formal faith comes together with this human dimension. The world is still mad, but there are a few sure points of light within it.

All of Waugh's work operates within a sense of Catholicism as settled and unchanging, perhaps even unchangeable. And he believed this a precious good in a very bad world. The large intellectual ferment, even within the more settled Thomist circles, that was traced in earlier chapters of the present work basically passed him by. (He noticed the dissident Hans Küng, however; "not Chinese, central European; a heresiarch who in happier days would be roasted".)[24] It was a great shock to him, therefore, when John XXIII convened

[23] Evelyn Waugh, *The End of the Battle* (Boston: Little, Brown, 1961), 251.

[24] *The Letters of Evelyn Waugh*, ed. Mark Amory (New Haven: Ticknor & Fields, 1980), 608.

Vatican II. Indeed, it may have killed him. He liked the pope, "but there is an instinctive and (I find) uncontrollable antipathy towards anyone whose photograph one sees twice a day."[25] Paul VI was a different matter. When Pope Paul visited Israel in 1964, Waugh let fly in a private letter: "It has been a sad disappointment to me that the Pope escaped from Palestine with a buffeting. I hoped for assassination. He has two very fine houses of his own in Italy. I think it very vulgar of him to go touring with the television. All this talk of ecumenicism is exceedingly painful to my sour & crusty nerves."[26]

Paul, of course, was also the pope responsible for suppressing the Latin liturgy, which Waugh had come to revere, and replacing it with a flat English substitute lacking the numinous. That same year, Waugh invited a friend to Rome for Easter, "to avoid the horrors of the English liturgy". The following Easter, he accused British Cardinal Heenan of being two-faced for having claimed, in a private dinner, to favor the old Mass but in public having defended the new one. He entered into a public dispute about the matter, observing, "This was the Mass for whose restoration the Elizabethan martyrs had gone to the scaffold. St. Augustine, St. Thomas à Becket, St. Thomas More, Challoner and Newman would have been perfectly at their ease among us; were in fact, present there with us."[27] He confessed in a letter to a priest, "I find the new liturgy a temptation against Faith, Hope and Charity but I shall never, pray God, apostatise."[28]

In a preface he wrote in the 1960s to a revised version of *Sword of Honor*, although (as noted above) he disavows that it is a Catholic book, he says that in revising the text he has found something "outside my original intention":

> I had written an obituary of the Roman Catholic Church in England as it had existed for many centuries. All the rites and most of the opinions here described are already obsolete. When I wrote *Brideshead Revisited* I was consciously writing an obituary of the doomed English upper class. It never occurred to me, writing *Sword of Honor*, that the Church was susceptible to change. I was wrong and I have seen a

[25] Ibid.

[26] Ibid., 617.

[27] Quoted in Joseph Pearce, *Literary Converts* (San Francisco: Ignatius Press, 2006), 334.

[28] Amory, *Letters*, 631.

> superficial revolution in what then seemed permanent. Despite the faith of many of the characters, *Sword of Honor* was not specifically a religious book. Recent developments have made it, in fact, a document of Catholic usage of my youth.[29]

Waugh's children reported that around this time his declining health and dismay at changes in the Church caused him to begin to pray for death. A bit of an exaggeration, perhaps, but it is quite clear from Waugh's correspondence that the consolation he had once found in the Church, living in an age he despised, had evaporated. "The Vatican Council has knocked the guts out of me", he wrote.[30] In his last letter, he explained:

> Easter used to mean so much to me. Before Pope John and his Council—they destroyed the beauty of the liturgy. I have not yet soaked myself in petrol and gone up in flames, but I now cling to the Faith doggedly without joy. Church going is a pure duty parade. I shall not live to see it restored. It is worse in many countries.[31]

On Easter morning, April 10, 1966, after hearing a Latin Mass by special arrangement, Waugh had a heart attack and died.

Travels in Greeneland

In his heyday, Waugh often expressed his astonishment that everyone did not become a Catholic. It seemed to be deeply ingrained in his nature to see everything outside the clear truths of the faith as laughably empty. It was either "the motley society" and a muffled despair or the Catholic Church and ultimate certitude: "Conversion is like stepping across the chimney piece out of a Looking-Glass world, where everything is an absurd caricature, into the real world God made; and then begins the delicious process of exploring it limitlessly."[32] The exception in his work, *Brideshead Revisited*, seems

[29] Evelyn Waugh, *Sword of Honor* (Boston: Little, Brown, 2012), preface.

[30] Amory, *Letters*, 638.

[31] Ibid., 639.

[32] Quoted in Pearce, *Literary Converts*, epigraph.

to allow that there are some steady and seductive alternatives—in the great families and houses of England, in friendship, in high art, in romantic love—even though they all prove unsatisfactory in the long run. By contrast, Waugh's contemporary and sometime friend Graham Greene put the relationship between the Church and the world into a far more complex and, at times, excruciating tension, bordering on psycho-pathology. Greene's character Wilson in *The Heart of the Matter* seems to have come out of his own experience: "He had long since become incapable of anything so honest as madness; he was one of those condemned in childhood to complexity."[33] There was little even by way of satiric laughter in that world.

The biographers[34] of Greene have noted his feeling of being a divided personality from very early on, and it has been argued that he suffered from bipolar disorder, which led to several suicide attempts, including playing at Russian roulette as a way "to escape from boredom". He once wrote to his fiancée that there seemed nothing worth doing except to "get killed somehow in an exciting manner".[35] In addition, all his life Greene felt compelled to risky behavior and attracted to those engaged in it. In *A Sort of Life*, his autobiography, he wrote that if he had to select an epigraph for all his work, it would be these lines from Robert Browning's "Bishop Blougram's Apology":

> Our interest's on the dangerous edge of things.
> The honest thief, the tender murderer,
> The superstitious atheist, demi-rep
> That loves and saves her soul in new French books—
> We watch while these in equilibrium keep
> The giddy line midway.[36]

[33] Graham Greene, *The Heart of the Matter* (New York: Bantam, 1967), 181.

[34] Norman Sherry's three-volume *The Life of Graham Greene* (New York: Viking, 1984–2004) is the standard biography, though marred in places by Sherry's personal relationship with Greene. W.J. West, *The Quest for Graham Greene* (New York: St. Martin's Press, 1997), tries to dig into some of the questions that Sherry avoided.

[35] Norman Sherry, *The Life of Graham Greene*, vol. 1. *1904–1939* (London: Penguin, 1989), 221.

[36] Graham Greene, *A Sort of Life* (New York: Pocket Books, 1973), 103.

Though Greene was never exactly an atheist once he had converted, he manifested various superstitions, including never writing more or less than five hundred words a day—and to do that, he would, at times, have to go out into the street and see a certain combination of numbers on a car's license plate before he could begin. But the "dangerous edge of things" was his native country, and his fiction, he said, was a kind of "guided dream" that came from deep within. The result, however troubled, was very powerful, and it is only because he was an open Catholic that he never won the Nobel Prize.

Robert Louis Stevenson was the cousin of Greene's mother, and there was something of Stevenson's adventurousness in Greene. Greene's father was headmaster of Berkhamsted School in Hertfordshire, which he attended. He seems to have felt great tension between his loyalty to the family and desire to be just another one of the boys—and harassment by the other boys did not help matters. But lots of people find themselves in similar circumstances without showing the same degree of dividedness. It would not be mere speculation to suggest that some fundamental fracture in Greene's soul was reflected—not caused—by his early life circumstances. Indeed, it may be that Greene's psychological problems gave him a more vivid sense than the average of the ways that all souls have been sundered by sin, original and actual. And that overarching theme plays a central role in virtually every one of his serious literary works.

In his early years, Greene wrote "entertainments", which is to say, lighter fiction meant to amuse readers as movies were beginning to do for the masses. *Stamboul Train*, *England Made Me*, *The Confidential Agent*, and *The Ministry of Fear*, all written in the 1930s and early 40s, show a sharp narrative eye and developing sense of the pacing of a story. And he continued sporadically in this vein, most notably with the satire about British intelligence operatives—Greene himself had been in MI6 during World War II and seems to have remained ambivalently active in British intelligence gathering until quite late in life—*Our Man in Havana* (1958). Several of them were turned into films, and Greene encouraged other writers to learn from the visual attractions of movies. In addition, he wrote film scripts, the most famous probably for Orson Welles' *The Third Man*. These all retain a certain fascination, but Greene's lasting reputation must depend on his serious novels, beginning with *The Power and the Glory* (1940), his story of a "whiskey priest" being hunted by the revolutionary government of twentieth-century Mexico. Greene's great period extended from that debut through *The Heart of the Matter* (1948), *The End of the Affair* (1951), and finally *A Burnt-Out Case* (1960).

Each of these novels is marked by an ambivalence—in the sense of an internal division—toward the Catholic faith unlike that of any other major Catholic writer of the time. Mauriac and Bernanos depict a world in thrall to the devil as no English-language writer was ever to do. But Greene depicts fault lines within the soul of the believer that later start to give away, so that faith itself is lost—either in despair or in outright unbelief. Greene wrote in the early days of the Catholic literary revival, which owed its origins to the great John Henry Newman's conversion and intellectual dominance of the nineteenth century. But his particular brand of faith-*cum*-doubt struck a new chord in Catholic literature. In several ways, his ambivalence anticipates a trait that would become more common among Catholics just before, during, and after the Second Vatican Council—particularly in novelists like Anthony Burgess, David Lodge, and Brian Moore, who were lapsed though still viscerally attached to Catholicism.

It is difficult to say what exactly changed to make this possible. Greene had become a Catholic in 1926 while courting his future wife, herself a convert whom he met when she wrote him at Oxford to tell him he had misrepresented Catholic teaching in one of his articles. When they became engaged, Greene—then living in Nottingham—decided to speak with a local priest, a Father Trollope, in order at least to understand his future wife's beliefs. Not only was Greene prejudiced in the usual Protestant ways against Catholic practices, but like many people in the modern world, he did not think he could even believe in God: "I had no intention of being received into the Church. For such a thing to happen I would need to be convinced of its truth and that was not even a remote possibility."[37]

Father Trollope was a large man, a convert himself, as well as a former actor. Greene approached him with the assumption that he was some sort of self-indulgent gourmand and secret voluptuary: "It was quite a while before I realized that my first impression was totally false and that I was facing the challenge of an inexplicable goodness." Still,

[37] Ibid., 143.

there may have been something of Greene's old love of the danger of forbidden borderlands in his approach:

> I didn't disbelieve in Christ [or the date of the Gospels, the historical evidence for the existence of the man Jesus Christ]—I disbelieved in God. If I were ever to be convinced in even the remote possibility of a supreme, omnipotent and omniscient power I realized that nothing afterwards could seem impossible. It was on the ground of a dogmatic atheism that I fought and fought hard. It was like a fight for personal survival.[38]

In the end, Father Trollope—and God—won this struggle, and Greene became convinced of the truth of God's existence and of the Catholic Thing, as Belloc and Chesterton (both later influences) had put it. In his later life, Greene would sometimes say that he was converted to Catholic truth at this point, but those truths did not touch his emotions or inner life until he visited Mexico and confronted the persecution of the Church there by the forces and ideas of modernity. But there is some inconsistency in this account. Certainly, the old divisions within persisted over the years and may have eventually carried him outside Catholicism. Still, he describes his first confession in terms that seem to involve both mind and heart:

> The first General Confession, which precedes conditional Baptism and which covers the whole of a man's previous life, is a humiliating ordeal. Later we may become hardened to the formulas of Confession and skeptical about ourselves: we may only half intend to keep the promises we make, until continual failure or the circumstances of our private life finally make it impossible to make any promises at all and many of us abandon Confession and Communion to join the Foreign Legion of the Church and fight for a city of which we are no longer full citizens. But in the first Confession a convert really believes in his own promises. I carried mine down with me like heavy stones into an empty corner of the Cathedral, dark already in the early afternoon, and the only witness of my Baptism was a woman who had been dusting the chairs. I took the name of Thomas—after St. Thomas the doubter and not Thomas Aquinas—and then I went

[38] Ibid., 145.

on to the *Nottingham Journal* office and football results and the evening of potato chips.

I remember very clearly the nature of my emotion as I walked away from the Cathedral: there was no joy in it at all, only a somber apprehension. I had made the first move with a view to my future marriage, but now the land had given way under my feet and I was afraid of where the tide would take me. Even my marriage seemed uncertain to me now. Suppose I discovered in myself what Father Trollope had once discovered, the desire to be a priest? At that moment it seemed by no means impossible. Only now after more than forty years I am able to smile at the unreality of my fear and feel at the same time a sad nostalgia for it, since I lost more than I gained when the fear belonged irrevocably to the past.[39]

There is much compressed and passed over here. In the years before he seemed to pass outside the Church, Greene enjoyed the guidance of two distinguished Dominican priests, Dom Bede Jarrett, O.P. (who died suddenly at an early age) and Thomas Gilby, O.P., a great English Thomist, as well as social acquaintance with countless other Catholics. In fact, he was quite generous in supporting Catholic artists and writers and philanthropic causes—and more engaged in the Church than the retrospective glance might suggest.

But his faith was under constant assault by unruly passions—sexual ones in the first place, but others as well, most notably a wanderlust and virtual phobia about the regularities of home life. Even his later flirtation and more than flirtation with Marxism and anti-Western regimes may have had something to do with the psychological need always to be on some kind of dangerous frontier. He married Vivien Dayrell-Browning (herself a Catholic convert) in 1927, but he was not a faithful husband and began trips to exotic and dangerous places—Liberia, Mexico, Vietnam, the Congo, Haiti, Cuba, and many more—that it seems were preferable to life at home, almost any home. In *A Sort of Life*, he compares these journeys to the Russian roulette he played to escape boredom and offers a psychological insight he probably thought universal but that seems mostly applicable only to himself: "From terror one escapes screaming, but fear has an odd seduction. Fear and the sense of sex are linked

[39] Ibid., 146–47.

in secret conspiracy."[40] He eventually abandoned his wife completely in 1948, though they never divorced and he never remarried. During the 1950s, as was clear in his fiction, his relationship with the Church continued, but largely on his own terms, which began to turn toward highly eccentric views on God as "Omega Point" and the cooperation of Church and Communism, far outside Catholic orthodoxy, which a Jarrett or Gilby might have corrected. One thing that seemed to have remained fairly constant, however, was Greene's sense that only the religious view of the world gives human personality, real or fictional, any depth. For the next decade, he was able to draw on that spiritual dimension, however unsettled.

The truth of this contention is quite visible in what will probably remain Greene's most read book: *The Power and the Glory*. It is set in Mexico during the persecutions of the Church in the 1930s, and Greene confessed that this experience in Mexico added an emotional attachment to his earlier intellectual attachment to the Church. In the novel, a priest in the state of Tabasco is being hunted by the local authorities, particularly a puritanical and ruthless revolutionary officer—an idealist in his own murderous way—who plans on executing him since priests have been outlawed. In his flight from death, the priest has discovered the fragility—and falseness—of his former, easy life in the Church. He was drinking heavily, and, in a moment of weakness, he fathered a child with a woman he had met. But he has not fled or apostasized, as almost all the other priests have done.

Typically for one of Greene's serious novels, the protagonist is torn between God and the devil—in the form of despair over his discovery of his own weakness. Yet also typical of Greene's world, there is a kind of purer spirituality that emerges from the temptations themselves. Father Montez, the whiskey priest, may redeem himself in a way, first, because at the beginning of the story he willingly misses a boat that would have taken him out of Mexico and into safety in order to hear a dying person's confession, and again, toward the end of the novel, when he does the same for another person knowing that he will most likely be captured and shot—which is precisely what happens.

[40] Ibid., 28.

The Vatican was not pleased at the time. In a later introduction to the novel, Greene recounted how the Archbishop of Westminster read him a condemnation by the Holy Office because the novel was "paradoxical" and "dealt with extraordinary circumstances".[41] Pius XII later told Greene that he did not approve of certain attributes of the whiskey priest but that the novel was acceptable. The matter eventually just dissipated when Greene refused to rewrite it. Still, questions lingered long about what he was up to with this close relationship between sinfulness and saintliness. No less a figure than Hans Urs von Balthasar thought Greene a great writer but balked at the way he promulgated a "mystique of sin": "the thesis set forth under the pretext of sincerity and anti-pharisaism, that guilt itself, when assumed voluntarily (in solidarity with another sinner), contains a redemptive element, which is today perhaps the decisive element; this plainly and necessarily contradicts true redemption."[42]

Von Balthasar's point is, of course, true. We do not come to redemption through sinning. But it may not exactly be applicable to Greene's work. Father Montez sins out of weakness and fear, not solidarity. The solidarity comes with his recognition that he is a sinner, not a special person set apart from others, even though his priestly office is something special and sacred. The true danger on which von Balthasar is trying to focus involves the reader, who may come to believe that only by sinning and running the risk of sinning can he fully comprehend the Christian life. That is a point worth recognizing—and rejecting. Still, it is a common experience to virtually every Christian that humility and self-knowledge often come to us through our failures.

In all the novels of Greene's "great period", perhaps only Scobie in *The Heart of the Matter*—the novel many consider Greene's finest—comes close to von Balthasar's description of the theological problem. Scobie is a British police officer in West Africa, known for his integrity and fairness toward all the racial and ethnic groups within his authority. He is married to an unattractive, whiny, and deeply unhappy woman and feels guilty because he believes his marriage

[41] Graham Greene, *The Power and the Glory* (New York: Viking/Compass, 1968), 5.

[42] Hans Urs von Balthasar, *The Christian and Anxiety*, trans. Dennis D. Martin and Michael J. Miller (San Francisco: Ignatius Press, 2000), 113.

vows have made him responsible for her unhappiness. He first compromises himself by borrowing money from a shady Syrian in order to send her away from dismal circumstances to start a new life in South Africa. But in her absence, he then begins an affair with a woman thirty years younger, who survived an ordeal at sea in which she lost her husband, after her ship was sunk by Nazi submarines.

At the beginning of *The Divine Comedy*, Dante says he found himself in a dark wood but does not know how he got there, "I was so full of sleep when I abandoned the true way" (*Inf.* I, 11–12). It is a common Christian experience. Scobie understands a little better in retrospect, but he begins to stray because he feels pity for the poor young woman and begins visiting her, as he often does others in the village, with benevolent intentions. Further, both of them think that their difference in age removes questions of romance and allows a pure friendship. But after an incident, they kiss: "What they had both thought was safety proved to have been the camouflage of an enemy who works in terms of friendship, trust and pity."[43] It seems that this particular relationship has been misconstrued by many readers, including von Balthasar, as some kind of justification of sin under the guise of sympathy. The sentence just quoted, however, makes it clear that the devil can operate even via "friendship, trust, pity". But there is nowhere in *The Heart of the Matter* where Greene seeks to excuse Scobie's fault. In fact, he said later that he had been writing of Scobie's "corruption by pity"—pity and real compassion being very different things. And there are signs all through the novel that Scobie's despair and, later, suicide may be something a Christian may understand and learn from, but—absent extenuating circumstance and God's mercy—they remain a grave and perhaps unpardoned sin.

Von Balthasar was onto something, however, in his remark about Greene's "mystique of sin". Greene does seem inclined to put his characters into situations of sin or near despair because it is only in those dire straits that certain spiritual truths emerge from everyday categories. But he is hardly alone and, in fact, is in good company (Dante's, for example), so far as that is concerned. What some of the more strictly theological and philosophical readers may object to is that there is not always a "good" resolution of these situations. Father

[43] Greene, *Heart of the Matter,* 173.

Montez is shot by a firing squad, much like Father Miguel Pro, a real-life saint, and he comes to a certain humility before God and fellow sinners, though we do not know whether his repentance is sufficient. But then again we would not anyway, no matter what Greene or any other novelist says about a character, since we do not know whether anyone except for the canonized saints is saved—or damned.

Similarly, though Scobie's suicide is not strictly called for by his circumstances, not even because of the sacrilege he has committed by taking Communion in a sinful state, Greene may be showing a man in the grip of madness—as he himself nearly was when he was married with two mistresses. In a moment of clarity, Scobie hears a striking voice as he nears committing the act:

> You say you love me, and yet you'll do this to me—rob me of you for ever. I made you with love. I've wept your tears. I've saved you from more than you will ever know; I planted in you this longing for peace only so that one day I could satisfy your longing and watch your happiness. And now you push me away, you put me out of your reach. There are no capital letters to separate us when we talk together. I am no Thou but simply you, when you speak to me; I am humble as any other beggar. Can't you trust me as you'd trust a faithful dog? I have been faithful to you for two thousand years. All you have to do now is ring a bell, go in a box, confess.... The repentance is already there, straining at your heart. It's not repentance you lack, just a few simple actions.

Scobie replies, perhaps more candidly than most of us, "No. I don't trust you. I've never trusted you.... I can't shift my responsibility to you."[44]

Greene quotes Charles Péguy as an epigraph to *The Heart of the Matter:* "The sinner is at the very heart of Christianity.... No one is as competent as the sinner in Christian affairs. No one, except the saint." Some readers thought that the honorable police officer Scobie in that novel was meant as a portrait of a saint. But perhaps what comes though here is pride—that was certainly Greene's own judgment of Scobie—and a disturbing insight into the kind of obsessiveness and confusion, even in the face of calm recognition of truth,

[44] Ibid., 290.

that often in fact accompany sin. As Greene put it in the face of criticism, "Suicide was Scobie's inevitable end; the particular motive of his suicide, to save even God from himself, was the final twist of the screw of his inordinate pride. Perhaps Scobie should have been a subject for a cruel comedy rather than for tragedy."[45]

Similar insights emerge in other works. Without breaking off either his marriage or his affair with his longtime mistress Dorothy Glover, in 1946 Greene began a simultaneous affair with a stunningly beautiful Catholic convert, Catherine Walston (he was her sponsor when, as an adult, she converted to Catholicism). He dedicated *The End of the Affair* to her. In that novel, a writer is having an affair with a neighbor's wife. He and the neighbor have a strange friendship, as did Greene and Catherine's husband. When a German bomb hits the building where the lovers are meeting during World War II, the woman spontaneously prays to God that she will change her life if only her lover is not dead. Mysteriously—miraculously?—he is not. But this sets off a titanic tug-of-war in several characters' souls about the relative claims of human and divine love. And hatred. The writer tells us on the first page, "This is a record of hate far more than of love." And on the last page, his mistress dead and denied him by her vow, he tells us, "I wrote at the start that this is a record of hate.... I found the one prayer that seemed to serve the winter mood. O God, You've done enough. You've robbed me of enough. I'm too tired and old to learn to love. Leave me alone forever."[46] Bleak, but again, probably an honest confession of how many people look at God but are afraid to admit.

The End of the Affair was a scandalous success, so much so that some Catholic wags complained that it gave the impression Christ had said: "If you love me, break my commandments." Greene and Walston were certainly busy doing that. Greene began rationalizing the affair, even getting advice from liberal priests that it was all right to go to confession again and again, knowing he would immediately resume the liaison. Greene's earlier sense of the acute tension between earthly and heavenly impulses gradually slid into a much more lax Catholicism. This character flaw weakened his art, as he himself might have

[45] Greene, *Ways of Escape*, 126.

[46] Graham Greene, *The End of the Affair* (New York: Viking, 1967), 1 and 167.

predicted. One of his central contentions as a literary critic was that after the seventeenth century the novel had degenerated because of a lack of religious seriousness. Only in the nineteenth century, when orthodox religious belief reappeared, were the fullness and depth of the human soul again available to writers. For all their vagaries about religion, Dickens, Hardy, Conrad, Lawrence, and James had all benefited from it. By contrast, he argued, Virginia Woolf's and E. M. Forster's characters "wandered like cardboard symbols through a world that was paper-thin".[47]

Politics began to replace the drama of the soul in Greene's writings by the 1950s. *The Quiet American* (1955) is set in war-torn Vietnam and, though not as purely anti-American as often thought, does foreshadow a growing indulgence toward Communism, especially in the developing world. *Our Man in Havana* (1958) pokes fun at the world of espionage. Behind this "entertainment", however, hangs a sense of foreboding about British, American, and other shadowy intelligence forces. Greene was primed for the advent of Fidel Castro, whom he would later defend. Greene's only other truly important novel, *A Burnt-Out Case,* is set in a leper colony in Africa, where the architect Querry (read: query) has fled following the failure of his gift as a designer of churches. Believing in nothing, he tries to help with the patients and is mistakenly characterized as a saint by the European media. Perhaps Greene was feeling unworthy of veneration himself. *A Burnt-Out Case* was the last gasp of a great talent—and Evelyn Waugh told Greene "I don't think you can blame people who read the book as a recantation of faith"[48] as well. The later novels—*The Honorary Consul* (1973), *The Human Factor* (1978), *Monsieur Quixote* (1982)—all lack the spiritual depth and emotional fireworks of vintage Greene. They lapse into a soggy ideology and gestures toward a vague liberation theology.

Greene himself, normally a man possessed of a fair amount of self-knowledge, disputed that he had made a major turn with *A Burnt-Out Case,* but he conceded that he felt his life as a writer had come to an end with the book. In the second volume of his autobiography, he argued—directly against Waugh—that it

[47] Graham Greene, *Collected Essays* (New York: Random House, 2010), 115.

[48] Amory, *Letters,* 559.

should be possible for a Catholic to write a novel about a character whose faith lapses, while the author remains unlapsed. But the situation was not quite so simple, and he must have known it. The longstanding tensions between what he believed and what he practiced—especially the sexual irregularities and multiple mistresses (sometimes simultaneously)—were bound to take their toll. When they were in fairly equal balance, they led to some remarkable works. And one of the reasons why Catholics were attracted to them is that they, too, could identify with a faith, hemmed in by doubts and counterclaims in the modern world, that still went on believing. Typically, as a Catholic matures—and if he really remains Catholic—the difficulties and challenges recede and are resolved in a kind of acceptance, which may still involve a good deal of searching. Greene chose another common path—to continue with his way of life and to cease going to confession, while slowly redefining Catholicism in myriad ways, which he knew to a friend like Evelyn Waugh was clearly "heretical". And as he moved away from the Church in her fullness, especially what he derided as a kind of "suburban" smugness, he moved away from much that constituted average human life in the free societies of the West.

This side of Greene has puzzled Catholics and non-Catholics alike. At MI6, he was a colleague of the notorious British traitor Kim Philby, who passed secrets to the Soviet Union and eventually ended up there when his activities were discovered. Greene had already taken a somewhat anti-American position in his 1955 novel *The Quiet American*, though, as usual, the story is complicated by sex and jealousy. And in *The Human Factor*, a later novel (1978), he seems to have abandoned all religious belief and even any confidence in Western institutions compared with Communist ones. He would regain some unorthodox Catholic perspective through the intervention of a Spanish priest, Leopoldo Durán, who indulged Greene's heterodoxy but also seems to have argued with him about his Communist sympathies.

In a 1987 speech he gave in Moscow, for example, Greene claimed to have observed a new thing: "We are fighting—Roman Catholics are fighting—together with the Communists, and working together with the Communists. We are fighting together against the Death Squads in El Salvador. We are fighting together against the Contras in Nicaragua. We are fighting together against General Pinochet in Chile."[49] Mikhail Gorbachev, who was present at the speech, was only two years away from pulling the plug on the Latin Communists, their Catholic sympathizers, and his own USSR. Greene concluded: "I even have a dream, Mr. General Secretary, that perhaps one day before I die, I shall know that there is an Ambassador of the Soviet Union giving good advice at the Vatican."[50]

W.J. West, one of Greene's biographers, raises the possibility that Greene may have been working as a double agent with British Intelligence all this time, giving the impression of left-wing sympathies for information-gathering purposes. But that seems quite improbable on West's own showing. Just before the reelection of Ronald Reagan in 1984, for example, Greene told Father Durán that, if he died, he wanted it known that he would have become a Communist if Reagan were returned to office. Around the same time, Greene told Malcolm Muggeridge that Russia only destroyed the Church's body, while America destroyed her soul. (Greene satirized Muggeridge, who had become a Catholic apologist after years of atheism and immorality, in the guise of one of the characters of *The Human Factor*.) Norman Sherry, Greene's authorized biographer and a friend, nonetheless remarks about these late developments in utter bewilderment, "How could his subtle mind engage in such intellectual folly?"[51]

In the end, it is baffling. Greene's insight into the human soul could be as acute as any contemporary's. But his trajectory presents a cautionary tale. Before Communism started to break up, Greene had openly admired those Polish Catholics who collaborated with the Communist regime in the PAX group. Such political misjudgments, along with his desire to absolve himself of his own sins, made him unsympathetic to the vision of man held up by John Paul II. It comes as no surprise that Greene characterized that pope's views on sexual matters—which is to say, standard Catholic teaching—as "unimaginative and unkind". This of the pope who developed the "theology of the body"? Greene's character flaws and Cold War

[49] Graham Greene, *Reflections*, selected and introduced by Judith Adamson (Toronto: Lester & Orpen Dennys, 1990), 316–17.

[50] Ibid., 317.

[51] Norman Sherry, *The Life of Graham Greene*, vol. 2: *1935–1955* (New York: Penguin, 2004), 492.

fantasies led to the extinction of a great gift. He went from being the premier novelist of the soul in English to an enabler of later and lesser lights who let their appetites and resentments rule their talents. Someday, we will be in a better position to winnow the wheat from the chaff in Greene's rich oeuvre. For the moment, however, he is a sad reminder of much that went awry within Catholicism—from great strengths and imaginative work to relative inconsequence—in the second half of the twentieth century.

The Best Book of the Millennium

A future literary critic—say two thousand years from now—coming upon the work of J. R. R. Tolkien and needing to date it by internal evidence alone would be hard put to see that it was contemporary with the great books by a Waugh or Greene. Further, if Sigrid Undset presents an epic medieval setting in which the Catholic elements are unmistakable, Tolkien uses some of the same heroic material, but in far less obviously religious fashion, to build up what is very likely the most influential and powerful Catholic story written during the twentieth century. Readers who doubt the Catholicity of the tale are often referred to Tolkien's exchange of letters with Robert Murray, S.J., in which he remarks that, "The Lord of the Rings is of course a fundamentally religious and Catholic work; unconsciously so at first, but consciously in the revision. That is why I have not put in, or have cut out, practically all references to anything like 'religion', to cults or practices, in the imaginary world. For the religious element is absorbed into the story and the symbolism."[52] In the same letter, he commends the priest for having noticed that the elf Lady Galadriel was inspired by images of the Virgin Mary. But the fact that the question was raised at all stems from the fact that the Catholic inspiration is not at all obvious and the immense popularity the work has enjoyed has reached far beyond Catholic audiences to many who were probably utterly unaware of the author's own sense of how the "religious element is absorbed into the story".

[52] J. R. R. Tolkien, *The Letters of J. R. R. Tolkien*, selected and ed. Humphrey Carpenter with the assistance of Christopher Tolkien (Boston: Houghton Mifflin, 1981), 172.

About the appeal, however, there can be no doubt. Since its publication, *Lord of the Rings* (LOTR) has sold more than 150 million copies, been made into one of the most successful film series in cinema history, and been voted the most influential book of the twentieth century in several surveys. Customers of the online bookseller Amazon chose it—with boldness beyond their likely competence—the best book of the millennium. If we take Tolkien's words about its religious element as true (as we will try to show below) and also note the undeniable fact that the story is also deeply informed by the heroic sagas of the northern European medieval tradition, of which Tolkien as a trained philologist had a profound knowledge, a mystery arises. Quite apart from what we know after the fact, how is it that such a work should have such great appeal in Europe, the Americas, and around the world—a modern world, after all, much of which Tolkien did not admire and even seeks, in his indirect way, to oppose? The only answer is that the appeal is to some universal human element that will have to be examined more closely.

Tolkien's work emerged from an unusual background. He was born in South Africa to British parents, but his father died when he was only four. His mother returned to England and, along with her sister, converted to Catholicism. The rest of the family shunned the two sisters, who also brought up their children as Catholics. In part owing to the financial and emotional strains this produced, Tolkien's mother died within a few years, leaving her two boys to be raised by a family friend, Father Francis Xavier Morgan, an Oratorian priest who had worked under the great Cardinal Newman at the Birmingham Oratory. Exotic African memories, love for the English countryside in the suburb of Edgbaston, and an early fascination with making up languages all came together in the course of Tolkien's life. A brilliant student, he entered Oxford, where he studied languages, adding Sanskrit, Gothic, Old Bulgarian, Lithuanian, Russian, Old and Middle English, Finnish, Old Norse, Old Saxon, Old and Middle High German, Icelandic,[53] and other exotic tongues to the more typical Latin, Greek, French, German, etc.

[53] Humphrey Carpenter, *J. R. R. Tolkien: A Biography* (Boston: Houghton Mifflin, 1977), 55.

But as with his soon-to-be friend C. S. Lewis, his academic work became an added advantage in creating works of the imagination involving medieval saga and romance in a way that spoke to contemporary readers.

Before Tolkien and Lewis, this might have seemed an unlikely combination, but it proved a potent brew. How so? To begin with, there is something in the Middle Ages that belongs to a simpler and, to modern eyes, more authentic, form of life. Medieval people were, of course, as sophisticated and intelligent as their modern counterparts in various classes and professions. Yet some of the fundamental questions of human existence seemed to emerge in starker form in their circumstances. Indeed, some have criticized Tolkien for making his Middle-earth a Manichaean realm in which all evil is aligned with Mordor and all good with the hobbits of the Shire and their allies in the great battles against the forces of Sauron. This is, even in mere factual terms, a mistake—since temptations to evil, not always resisted, appear among the "good" characters in Tolkien as well. The battle between good and evil is, as always, fought out in every human heart. But the sides *are* more clearly defined than in most modern literature. And the reason it appeals to us may have something to do with an observation Christopher Dawson—whom Tolkien read and admired—once made: "Why is a stockbroker less beautiful than a Homeric warrior or an Egyptian priest? Because he is less incorporated with life, he is not inevitable, but accidental, almost parasitic?"[54] In modern terminology, there is a sharper *existential* struggle at stake for the warrior or priest than for the financial operator, however necessary the latter may be in a modern economy.

It is also relevant that the comfort and wealth that are the goal of most modern social activity, while harmless in themselves, are a kind of mask of the ultimate struggles for good and evil, life and death, in which every human being is engaged. And we have to free ourselves from the exclusive pursuit of material goods before we can enter into a larger world of human meaning and truth. That seems to be what Tolkien meant by his remark about the religious element being incorporated into his stories. LOTR is both an adventure saga and

[54] Christopher Dawson, *The Dynamics of World History*, ed. John J. Mulloy (Wilmington, Del.: ISI Books, 2002), 69.

a pilgrimage. The hobbits journey from a comfortable life in their pastoral Shire through many battles, in which they must engage both to defend their homeland and to restore Middle-earth. There is no shirking this responsibility, which can be traced a bit more easily at first in *The Hobbit*, which Tolkien published in 1937, a kind of simpler prelude to *The Lord of the Rings*.

Many readers see *The Hobbit* as merely a children's book, a fairy tale about a small race of beings, similar to children themselves, who are drawn into a typical adventure involving the slaying of a dragon, Smaug, and the liberation of the peoples whom the dragon oppressed. The story may be read in that way: millions of parents have read *The Hobbit* to their children at bedtime, and the children have no difficulty following the clear lines of the story. Tolkien had a profound appreciation of fairy tales, which he did not regard as a lesser form of literature but, rather, as one of the literary genres that enable us to see the primordial sense of wonder that the earlier ages of men preserved in their own storytelling. In an uncanny appropriation of that sense of wonder, Tolkien is able to reproduce the sense of the transcendent operating in the world itself to which Christopher Dawson and many others had pointed in early peoples. And in that regard, he recovers something valuable for all of us. Not merely for children. So it seems no mere literary device in Tolkien when archaic beings from the beginnings of the world wander into stories or men who shape-shift into animals make their appearance or animals talk or trees uproot themselves and walk about in order to take part in large cosmic struggles.

In his stunning lecture "On Fairy Stories", he replies to those who regard them as an inferior literary form when compared with more "realistic" fiction:

> There are profounder wishes: such as the desire to converse with other living things. On this desire, as ancient as the Fall, is largely founded the talking of beasts and creatures in fairy-tales, and especially the magical understanding of their proper speech. This is the root, and not the "confusion" attributed to the minds of men of the unrecorded past, an alleged "absence of the sense of separation of ourselves from beasts". A vivid sense of that separation is very ancient; but also a sense that it was a severance: a strange fate and a guilt lies on us. Other

> creatures are like other realms with which Man has broken off relations, and sees now only from the outside at a distance, being at war with them, or on the terms of an uneasy armistice.[55]

That is one of the larger contexts in which fairy stories convey something to us. Even at a more mundane level, however, Tolkien says that they help rescue us from a cramped world and a "disease of language" that mocks imaginative writing as unreal. The disease has really reduced our sense of the world to a flat, dull, practical materialism: "It was in fairy-stories that I first divined the potency of the words, and the wonder of the things, such as stone, and wood, and iron; tree and grass; house and fire; bread and wine."[56] But both the words and the wonder require that we become "enchanted" again in order to see—as Chesterton also urged—the miraculousness in ordinariness.

There is no mechanical formula for creating an enchanted world, says Tolkien. The writer who succeeds depends on a certain "elvish craft" of which he is not the master but the servant, because all true "sub-creation" is an imitation of *the* Creation and the Creator and properly derives from them. His great appeal to many different audiences clearly stems from his gift of enchanting while telling tales in which timeless human struggles with good and evil are in play. That is certainly what readers encounter in *The Hobbit* and in *The Lord of the Rings*. The hobbits living in Hobbiton are living a snug, comfortable life. But the Faery world, like the real world, does not dispense us from the large questions of good or evil or the pilgrimage of earthly life every man must make. Both those challenges require that we learn to sacrifice ourselves for something greater than the self—a truth that the desire for comfort and many modern philosophies would deny. Materialism inevitably must say that a great abundance and variety of *things* are all that we can hope for in life and that the enjoyment of them as much as possible is the only goal of each individual—with perhaps the proviso that we do so without harm to others. But a story like the ones Tolkien concocted disputes that understanding at its very root and brings out the truth that just the opposite is the case: we can only properly enjoy the good things of

[55] The essay was originally the Andrew Lang Lecture given at the University of St. Andrews and reprinted in J. R. R. Tolkien, *Tree and Leaf* (Oxford: Oxford University Press, 1969), 66.

[56] Ibid., 59.

the creation when we do not make them the goal, only the product of a different activity.

The desire for wealth and comfort is what Tolkien, in *The Hobbit*, calls "the dragon sickness". The dragon Smaug sleeps on the pile of gold and jewels and other precious objects he has looted from the surrounding peoples. They are of no real use to him other than as a gratification of his blind greed. By a number of subtle but unmistakable indications, the story also suggests that even that comfort we think of as such a normal human impulse, one that might rest untroubled in a lovely place like the Shire, participates in the dragon sickness. The remedy is the one the Christian tradition has always upheld: "But seek first his kingdom and his righteousness, and all these things shall be yours as well" (Mt 6:33). That injunction puts things in their right order without denying, as some purely "spiritual" religions might, that the created goods are real goods.

In *The Hobbit*, Bilbo will slowly learn this lesson by growing in maturity and risking his own goods and even his life so that the main evil may be defeated—and the men, hobbits, dwarves, elves, and other beings subject to its terrors shall be freed. Unlike the central figures in heroic sagas, however, he does not do this by virtue of his own courage and strength—and in *Lord of the Rings* his nephew Frodo will undergo a similar experience. Both hobbits put themselves in harm's way for the sake of the good, though it goes against the respectable ethos of the Shire, where everyone knows that adventures are "uncomfortable things". Such weak creatures only succeed because elements of "chance" or good luck—Providence, really—are present. We are not, Tolkien subtly teaches via this element in the story, complete masters of our own fates. Far from being an extraneous "Christian" dimension tacked on to a heroic saga, providential guidance is a realistic representation of something any reflective person will recognize as true to life.

As many readers have noticed, it is because Bilbo and later Frodo and Sam Gamgee spare the life of the slitheringly treacherous but pitiable creature Gollum that they receive help at key moments. Here, it might be argued, Tolkien *does* introduce a Christian theme that some might dispute. Many acts of compassion, mercy, and kindness are performed that are never reciprocated. And malefactors, far from being grateful or repentant, may continue wreaking havoc if they are spared. But Tolkien's handling of this theme is very deft and is convincing because his "elvish craft" does not render the connection explicit or abstract. And in the end, there *are* instances of compassion bearing unintended good consequences that a narrow "realism" would not have anticipated.

The elvish craft also appears in the humorous way Tolkien can have Bilbo picked up by a gang of dwarves as a "burglar" who will help them in their efforts to defeat Smaug. In fact, his ability to help defeat Smaug depends upon his finding "by chance" the Ring of power that Gollum once held, which enables him to act without being seen. It was highly unlikely that this unimportant hobbit would come to possess this very important source of power, but the wizard Gandalf, a wise and ancient figure, explains it much later in *Lord of the Rings* to Frodo without really explaining: "There was something else at work, beyond any design of the Ring-maker. I can put it no plainer than by saying that Bilbo was *meant* to find the Ring, and *not* by its maker. In which case you also were *meant* to have it. And that may be an encouraging thought."[57]

This power is very different from that sought through the industrial machinery (something Tolkien abhorred in real life) that some of the evil beings in Middle-earth have made. He says, "Goblins are cruel, wicked, and bad-hearted. They make no beautiful things, but ... many clever ones"[58]—an obvious reference to the evil powers Tolkien saw growing in the world in the years before, during, and after World War II. By contrast, the journey depends on cooperation with enigmatic forces in nature—earth, moon, light, stone, birds—and the delicate hints in ancient prophecies.

The last element may seem odd, but Tolkien, as became clearer after his death, had created a whole "secondary world" with its own mythology. His earlier unpublished texts about the origins of that world and developments within it have since appeared under the title *The History of Middle-earth* and fill a dozen volumes.[59] Most important in this context is his creation story, *The Silmarillion*, in which the Creator, Ilúvatar, like the biblical God, must deal with a fallen

[57] J. R. R. Tolkien, *The Lord of the Rings*, 50th Anniversary, one-vol. ed. (Boston: Houghton Mifflin, 2005), 56.

[58] J. R. R. Tolkien, *The Hobbit* (London: HarperCollins, 2011), 73–74.

[59] Christopher Tolkien, ed., *The History of Middle-earth* (Boston: Houghton Mifflin, 1984–1996).

angel, Melkor. The description of the fallen angel echoes biblical themes but transposes them into the language about the "music" of Ilúvatar's great creation: "But as the theme progressed, it came into the heart of Melkor to interweave matters of his own imagining that were not in accord with the theme of Ilúvatar; for he sought therein to increase the power and glory of the part assigned to himself." But Ilúvatar comments: "And thou, Melkor, shalt see that no theme may be played that hath not its uttermost source in me, nor can any alter the music in my despite. For he that attempteth this shall prove but mine instrument in the devising of things more wonderful, which he himself hath not imagined."[60]

All this is played out in both books in ways that cannot be presented in detail here. But the details are enhanced by the unique way in which Tolkien, perhaps alone among modern authors and non-moderns, is able to create a sense of a realm existing across immense ages—"the abyss of time", as he sometimes called it—in which the general story of good and evil is played out amid many specific stories in the past and on into the future. C. S. Lewis said of this aspect of his friend's "sub-creation":

> Not content to create his own story, he creates, with an almost insolent prodigality, the whole world in which it is to move, with its own theology, myths, geography, history, paleography, languages, and orders of beings—a world "full of strange creatures beyond count". The names alone are a feast.... You can hardly put your foot down anywhere ... without stirring the dust of history.[61]

Sub-creation is an imitation of the Creation that "we make still by the law in which we're made", as Tolkien writes in the poem "On Fairy Stories".[62] But it avoids the blasphemy of the artist who thinks of himself as a pure creator, not dependent on what God has provided first, as much as it rejects the dull materialism of the everyday world in the modern West.

Fully conscious of those who think of this as escapism, Tolkien embraces the term—and celebrates it in some of its forms:

[60] J. R. R. Tolkien, *The Silmarillion* (New York: Ballantine Books, 2002), 6.
[61] C. S. Lewis, *Essay Collection and Other Short Pieces* (London: HarperCollins, 2000), 519.
[62] Tolkien, "On Fairy-Stories", 54.

> Why should a man be scorned if, finding himself in prison, he tries to get out and go home? Or if, when he cannot do so, he thinks and talks about other topics than jailers and prison-walls? The world outside has not become less real because the prisoner cannot see it. In using Escape in this way the critics have chosen the wrong word, and, what is more, they are confusing, not always by sincere error, the Escape of the Prisoner with the Flight of the Deserter.[63]

Furthermore, the very language we now use has to be reenchanted to capture lost dimensions of reality that are there, only ignored now because of our assumptions about the world.

Tolkien is quite prepared to connect this world of fantasy, which he says exists in every culture because it is part of human nature, with the story of stories in the Incarnation:

> It may be a far-off gleam or echo of *evangelium* in the real world.... The Gospels contain a fairy-story, or a story of a larger kind which embraces all the essence of fairy-stories. They contain many marvels—peculiarly artistic, beautiful, and moving: "mythical" in their perfect, self-contained significance;... and among the marvels is the greatest and most complete conceivable eucatastrophe. But this story has entered History and the primary world; the desire and aspiration of sub-creation has been raised to the fulfilment of Creation. The Birth of Christ is the eucatastrophe of Man's history. The Resurrection is the eucatastrophe of the story of the Incarnation. This story begins and ends in joy. It has pre-eminently the "inner consistency of reality." There is no tale ever told that men would rather find was true, and none which so many sceptical men have accepted as true on its own merits. For the Art of it has the supremely convincing tone of Primary Art, that is, of Creation. To reject it leads either to sadness or to wrath.... This story is supreme; and it is true. Art has been verified. God is the Lord, of angels, and of men—and of elves. Legend and History have met and fused.[64]

Still, even after Christ's triumph on the Cross, evil is never finally defeated in this life, and that is why the struggle between good and

[63] Ibid., 60.
[64] Ibid., 71–72.

evil goes on until the end of time. The story repeats itself with different figures and in differing circumstances. But it is a story that is always singular and always universal because of the eternal as well as the temporal elements within it. And one of the larger cycles of such a struggle forms the matter of *The Lord of the Rings*, which takes place in the very next generation of hobbits, with Bilbo's nephew, Frodo, now taking center stage in the drama of Middle-earth. The story is vast—usually published in three large volumes: *The Fellowship of the Ring*, *The Two Towers*, and *The Return of the King*. Each is filled with dozens of memorable scenes and developments within the general arc of a very simple story: the need for Frodo, as "ring bearer" now, to journey along with his traveling companions (Gandalf, other hobbits, elves, dwarves, men—in the last category, notably, Aragorn, the true king of Middle-earth) from Rivendell, home of the elves, to Mount Doom, where he will destroy the ring by casting it into a fiery crevice—thereby frustrating the "Dark Lord" Sauron's power.

Readers enchanted by the story feel this to be a long, almost timeless, journey—but the whole of the story transpires essentially over only three months, beginning with the departure of the fellowship from Rivendell on December 25 and ending with the final destruction of the ring on March 25. These dates are traditionally, of course, Christmas and the Feast of the Annunciation (in the Middle Ages, also the day of the crucifixion). So by a subtle introduction of dates, Tolkien covertly inscribes his story within the sacred history of the Bible. But this is no simple allegory—a form that has one-to-one correspondences between Christian truths and persons or events. Tolkien was writing a much larger kind of "sub-creation", one that imitated the Creator's own complex world by introducing a sense of a past stretching back into impenetrable mists and a rich present with proliferating events within the overall Creation-Fall-Redemption story. It is all done with such power that readers who "get" LOTR find themselves regularly rereading or rethinking their understanding of the story.

Despite Tolkien's mostly true claim that the book was not an allegory, it did have some concrete connections to issues in contemporary life, not least a profound regret over and rejection of the mechanized modern industrial civilization. The evil beings in Middle-earth are the ones who create the powerful machines—precisely because their dark magic seeks power over others and willful domination. Industrialism, whether in tolerably good or deeply insidious form, entails a certain treatment of nature itself—creation, viewed from another angle—as mere matter and energy to be redirected for creaturely purposes. All human work reshapes nature to some extent, of course, for human purposes, but in Tolkien's Mordor a whole ideology of disregard for the earth seems to be drawn together: no living thing, no natural landscape seems to have any value in itself—or any wisdom to teach us except for its usefulness for our own dragon-inspired purposes. There is an early Catholic environmentalism implied in this representation, of course, but also a deep connection to Catholic social doctrine in which rule over others is for *their good*, not the good of the ruler. And all authority, and therefore rule, comes from God and must be held accountable to his wishes for Middle-earth.

But as beautifully as this overarching truth is presented in LOTR, no simplistic "back to the land" or anti-modern program emerges from the story. That is because the story involves a profound rending of the created order going back behind the appearance of Middle-earth. Tolkien once described human history as "a 'long defeat'—though it contains some samples or glimpses of final victory",[65] and that accurately describes the way of his sub-created world as well. The battle against evil must be undertaken again and again, with differing partial victories and defeats, until some transformation takes place that cannot be represented within Middle-earth itself. In its own way, Middle-earth must await the Return of the King, who is not only Aragorn or some other just ruler, but a power who can resolve the root problem: Ilúvatar, the Father of All himself.

Such truths, of course, have been expressed many times throughout biblical history, from the Hebrew Scriptures down to modern theology. But they usually appear only as ideas, though the OT stories reflect something of the history of partial victories and defeats that Tolkien presents. What is most remarkable about LOTR is the way in which it is able to present a warrior's sensibility—the necessity of a hardiness in facing natural and supernatural challenges—with gentle,

[65] Tolkien, *Letters*, 255.

deeply enchanted delicacy of feeling toward nature and living beings. At the same time, it is able to combine both in the way that two of its characters, like Christ, pass through death to great triumphs. Gandalf the Grey dies fighting a dragon at the Bridge of Khazad-dûm and is resurrected later with even greater powers, now as Gandalf the White, because of his self-sacrifice. The human Aragorn risks passing through the Paths of the Dead in the hope of thereby arriving in time to win a battle against Mordor and became a true king. The "dead" souls who emerge with him help turn the battle to victory. It is typical of Tolkien's Catholicism that death and life—both parts of the creation—collaborate in the resolution of the story.

Tolkien did not make many comments on the Church, but some of his most significant ones came during Vatican II. Like Evelyn Waugh and other traditionalists, he did not much like the changes, though he expressed support for "those developments that are strictly 'ecumenical'". But in the same letter he warns his son Michael against:

> the "protestant" search backwards for "simplicity" and directness, which, of course, though it contains some good or at least intelligible motives, is mistaken and indeed vain. Because "primitive Christianity" is now and in spite of all "research" will ever remain largely unknown; because "primitiveness" is no guarantee of value, and is and was in great part a reflection of ignorance. Grave abuses were as much an element in Christian "liturgical" behaviour from the beginning as now. (St. Paul's strictures on Eucharistic behavior are sufficient to show this!) Still more because "my church" was not intended by Our Lord to be static or remain in perpetual childhood; but to be a living organism (likened to a plant) which develops and changes in externals by the interaction of its bequeathed divine life and history—the particular circumstances of the world in which it is set. There is no resemblance between the "mustard-seed" and the full-grown tree. For those living in the days of its branching growth the Tree is the thing, for the history of a living thing is part of its life, and the history of a divine thing is sacred.[66]

This view clearly has some affinities with Newman's notions of "development", which Tolkien may have absorbed in his early years

[66] Ibid., 394.

with Father Morgan of the Oratorians. But it does not solve many questions about true and false steps in history or show how to discern them. Still, there is a "hermeneutic of continuity" in Tolkien, and, bewildered as many were in the 1960s by both secular and religious upheaval, he counseled Communion—daily, if possible—as the only sure way of dealing with the situation.

Perhaps the deepest Christian echoes come forth in LOTR as Frodo, the ring bearer, and Sam, his faithful companion, near Mount Doom, where they hope to destroy the ring. A much-quoted passage encapsulates one of the founding truths of the whole of Middle-earth. As Frodo and Sam are taking evening rest near the end of their long struggle to defeat evil, Sam muses: "There, peeping among the cloud-wrack above a dark tor high up in the mountains, Sam saw a white star twinkle for a while. The beauty of it smote his heart, as he looked up out of the forsaken land, and hope returned to him. For like a shaft, clear and cold, the thought pierced him that in the end the Shadow was only a small and passing thing: there was light and high beauty for ever beyond its reach."[67] This kind of insight is powerful precisely because it transpires on the other side of much death and suffering, which is to say, it is a vision of peace that has faced the worst the world has to offer.

But Tolkien's hobbits will not succeed in the task, any more than any of his other creatures, because of their own merits. Sam bravely carries Frodo up the mountain when the ring-bearer's strength has failed and he can climb no farther. But there is a great surprise in store at the final moment: Frodo after all this time *cannot part* with the ring. His own will, like that of all the creatures in the fallen Middle-earth, is incapable of freeing itself. And it is Gollum—who appears suddenly at this very last moment—the Gollum spared by both Bilbo and Frodo in earlier episodes despite his many crimes, who commits one last crime. He bites off Frodo's finger and the ring with it: " 'Precious, precious, precious!' Gollum cried. 'My Precious! O my Precious!' And with that, even as his eyes were lifted up to gloat on his prize, he stepped too far, toppled, wavered for a moment on the brink, and then with a shriek he fell. Out of the depths came his last wail *Precious*, and he was gone."[68]

[67] LOTR, 901.
[68] Ibid., 925.

A lesser creator would have ended the story there, mission accomplished. But Tolkien continues on for two hundred pages more, inscribing the whole into the effect it then has on the kingdom of Aragorn, the Shire, and the larger cycle of advance and retreat in the struggle between good and evil. And on Frodo and Sam. The former after all his experiences must travel away forever to the Grey Lands. The latter returns to the Shire, where, after cleaning up the dragon-disease that has taken over in his absence, he marries, founds a family, and lives happily—not ever after, but in the temporary peace afforded to him and the whole Shire by the successful battle against the most recent incarnation of evil. This satisfies our sense that good must triumph in a fantasy story, but it also leaves the whole saga firmly situated in what Tolkien often called "the abyss of time", the long stretch before and after any mortal creature's earthly life that gives us a glimpse of the eternal.

Readers for decades have been enchanted by Tolkien's powers in this regard. No less astute a critic than C. S. Lewis said in a letter to Tolkien after reading the final product:

> In two virtues I think it excels: sheer sub-creation—Bombadil, Barrow Wights, Elves, Ents—as if from inexhaustible resources, and construction. Also in *gravitas*. No romance can repel the charge of "escapism" with such confidence. If it errs, it errs in precisely the opposite direction: all victories of hope deferred and the merciless piling up of odds against the heroes are near to being too painful. And the long *coda* after the eucatastrophe, whether you intended it or no, has the effect of reminding us that victory is as transitory as conflict ... and so leaving a final impression of profound melancholy. It will rank, along with the *Aeneid* as one of what I call my "immediately sub-religious" books.[69]

It is one sign of some continued Christian cultural vitality that Tolkien and Lewis himself exerted such a profound influence, as did other members of their Oxford literary group, the Inklings. As a journalist has argued: "The Inklings, a 1930s Oxford drinking club, has been a more powerful force than the Bloomsbury Group, the Algonquin set in New York, Hemingway's Paris set or the W. H. Auden/Christopher

[69] C. S. Lewis, *The Collected Letters of C. S. Lewis*, vol. 2 (New York: Harper One, 2004), 990–91.

Isherwood group of writers of the 1930s."[70] Such things are, of course, difficult to assess with much accuracy, but that such a claim is entirely plausible says a great deal about the potential for the Christian reenchantment of the world well into the twenty-first century.

The Ecstatic Pessimist

> I am no more than a secretary of the invisible thing
> That is dictated to me and a few others.
> Secretaries, mutually unknown, we walk the earth
> Without much comprehension. Beginning a phrase in
> the middle
> Or ending it with a comma. And how it all looks when
> completed
> Is not up to us to inquire, we won't read it anyway.[71]

Czesław Miłosz died in August 2004, almost twenty-five years after winning the Nobel Prize in Literature and at the age of ninety-three. A Catholic born before World War I in an obscure corner of Europe (the multiethnic Grand Duchy of Lithuania, then part of Czarist Russia), even after more than thirty years living in the United States, he insisted on writing his poetry in Polish, a language little-known outside its "natural habitat". Yet in spite of Miłosz's own modesty and self-deprecating humor ("I know what was left for smaller men like me: / A feast of brief hopes, a rally of the proud, / A tournament of hunchbacks, literature"),[72] he not only spans the twentieth century in terms of time but occupies a large and central place in modern culture and the world. If J. R. R. Tolkien was the most popular Catholic writer in the latter half of the twentieth century, Miłosz was the most culturally sophisticated and wide-ranging.

By a curious paradox, it was precisely Miłosz's remote origins on the East-West border that gave him a unique and powerful

[70] Nigel Reynolds, *Daily Telegraph*, January 20, 1996.

[71] Czesław Miłosz, "Secretaries" in *Selected Poems, 1931–2004* (New York: Ecco/Harper-Collins, 2006), 141.

[72] Czesław Miłosz, "A Confession", in *Polish Poetry of the Last Two Decades of Communist Rule: Spoiling Cannibal's Fun* (Evanston, Ill.: Northwestern University Press, 1991), 30.

perspective. That, and the fact that, like many of his compatriots, he had been tried in the refiner's fire of successive waves of Nazism and Communism. Another poet might have retreated into an aesthetic dreamland, a tactic Miłosz deplored in Western or Eastern European writers. Or he might have turned into the kind of *engagé* intellectual quite common in Europe after World War II. But Miłosz found those fashionable figures, whose drug of choice was most often Communism or existentialism, equally "talking in their sleep". Miłosz moved with simple ease and at great depth through the most thorny modern cultural questions without flinching, seeking a more livable world for the human race in what he did not hesitate to call reality.

One sign of his sheer intellectual power is that instead of paralysis, the common malady, he turned the very contradictions and challenges into a source of insight. Though he never wrote a single great work like *The Divine Comedy* or *Paradise Lost*, he produced hundreds of pages of poetry objectively recording the full range of perceptions of someone who had witnessed the titanic struggles and intellectual dead ends of the twentieth century. One of the more political poems was so powerful that some of its lines were chiseled decades later on a monument in Gdansk to slain members of Poland's heroic union *Solidarity*: "You who wronged a simple man.... Do not feel safe. The poet remembers. / You can kill one, but another is born. / The words are written down, the deed, the date."[73] In many other poems, though, he is more concerned to capture ignored truths and moments of insight that may lead to a different kind of life, even if he is wary and ironic about the culture that has to sustain that life:

> Treasure your legacy of skills, child of Europe,
> Inheritor of Gothic cathedrals, of baroque churches,
> Of synagogues filled with the wailing of a wronged people.
> Successor of Descartes, Spinoza, inheritor of the word
> "honor,"
> Posthumous child of Leonidas,
> Treasure the skills acquired in the hour of terror.[74]

[73] Czesław Miłosz, "You Who Wronged", in *New and Collected Poem, 1931–2001* (New York: HarperCollins, 2001)103.

[74] Czesław Miłosz, "Child of Europe", in ibid., 84.

A Catholic of a unique personal cast, despite recurrent doubts and personal obsessions, he was repelled early on by the right-wing Polish Catholicism that he often deprecates as merely a "national rite" and deeply marred by anti-Semitism—a trait that did not exist with the same virulence in the more easygoing and diverse Wilno (his preferred name for Vilnius) of his younger days, with its large and vibrant Jewish community. Another great modern Polish poet, Adam Zagajewski, has explained the religious dimension of Miłosz's work as a defense of "our right to infinity" despite all the well-known contemporary objections: "The telegram Nietzsche sent to inform Europeans of God's death reached him, of course, but he refused to sign the receipt and sent the messenger packing."[75] Witty, but perhaps slightly misleading. Miłosz had gotten a good education in Vilnius and had taken deeply to heart the perennial philosophical and theological disputes in the Western tradition. So he was not particularly susceptible to facile disbelief any more than he was to blind belief: "My imperviousness to the usually rather shallow progressive-atheist arguments was like the chess-player's contempt for cards."[76] This was the main reason, perhaps, why he and John Paul II admired one another and seemed at times on a similar wavelength. Miłosz thought the pope a great man, one of the rare public figures who could have played one of Shakespeare's kings. But there were challenges of many other kinds all the same.

He was to be deeply shaken by political atrocities and perversions that destroyed the social and natural worlds he had loved as a boy. Miłosz's mature work tenderly preserves a highly colored and detailed memory of the Lithuanian countryside and his passionate attachment to it, perhaps with even more emotion because of his exile. But Miłosz's active intelligence did not allow him to indulge in mere nostalgia. Miłosz always displayed strong masculine energy combined with great poetic sensitivity about nature and human value. His unashamed defense of his childhood experience had to confront something that he came to realize quite early, even before the political upheavals: the very structure of nature—quite apart from

[75] Adam Zagajewski, "On Czeslaw Milosz (1911–2004)", *New York Review of Books*, September 23, 2004: 65.

[76] Czesław Miłosz, *Native Realm: A Search for Self-Definition*, trans. Catherine S. Leach (Garden City, N.Y.: Doubleday, 1968), 117.

what we do to one another—seemed to him pitiless, as did, at times, its Creator. Nature was morally innocent, because its destruction of humanity and Darwinian survival of the fittest was mechanical, not malicious. But any honest look at our situation had to allow for the indifference of the world, the passing of all things, the fragility of memory, which was precious and to be cultivated while it lasted, but even so unable to prevail over time. That perception lies behind his often expressed sympathy for the Manichaeans, the early Christian heretics and their successors who believed that this world must have been created by an evil *daimon*. Goodness and a good God would have to lie beyond this world with its undeniable evils.

Miłosz was not much impressed, therefore, with Theodor Adorno's later remark that it was impossible to write poetry after Auschwitz. The *Shoah*, the attempted genocide of the Jews, was a special evil, but we are deluding ourselves if we do not see that nature herself is continually committing innocent outrages. If the voice of poetry is to be stopped by the mere fact of great evils, then poetry would not be possible in any age. And yet, something in him did not think that this bleak vision of nature was all there was to be said: "Nothing could stifle my inner certainty that a shining point exists where all lines intersect."[77] Miłosz regularly experienced and recorded in his poetry moments of natural transcendence, even—in fact, especially—when he contemplated nature. To pick only one example out of hundreds, he duly recorded in "Gift" a day when he was sixty and living in Berkeley:

> A day so happy.
> Fog lifted early, I worked in the garden.
> Hummingbirds were stopping over honeysuckle flowers.
> There was no thing on earth I wanted to possess.
> I knew no one worth my envying him.
> Whatever evil I had suffered, I forgot.
> To think that once I was the same man did not embarrass me.
> In my body, I felt no pain,
> When straightening up, I saw the blue sea and sails.[78]

[77] Ibid., 87.

[78] Czesław Miłosz, *Selected and Last Poems, 1931–2004*, trans. Anthony Milosz (New York: Ecco, 2011), 108.

Somehow he had experienced similar moments even during the terrifying years before and during World War II, so it was not mere literary affectation when he stated "I was always an ecstatic pessimist."[79]

The significance of all this for Miłosz as poet is probably best seen in his 1980 Nobel Lecture. Happily, unlike many such texts before and since, Miłosz offered no grandiose philosophical sermon on that occasion. In fact, if there is an overarching point to this witty and humane discourse, it is that in our time it is a blessing to be from a small, obscure, and particular place and culture. If you are writing in a language little known in France or the United States (as Miłosz did), it keeps you faithful to "a certain ideal image of a poet, who, if he wants fame, he wants to be famous only in the village or the town of his birth."[80] While this sounds like a sure formula for provinciality to Western ears, it really leads to a serious engagement with concrete things instead of a slavery to literary fashion. Such a poet is forced into a dialogue between past and present as he looks for a way to adapt an inherited poetic language to express unprecedented circumstances. In Miłosz's view, this endeavor has much larger repercussions than most of us think.

To begin with, the poet must avoid the twin dangers of mere traditionalism, on the one hand, or an empty avant-gardism, on the other (the totalitarians, Miłosz pointed out elsewhere, were quite indulgent of avant-gardism because of its ultimate powerlessness—it was the poet who approached reality whom they censored). The perpetually unsettled state of such a poet makes him a restless seeker: "And it may happen that leaving books behind as if they were dry snake skins, in a constant escape forward from what has been done in the past, he receives the Nobel Prize. What is this enigmatic impulse that does not allow one to settle down in the achieved, the finished? I think it is a quest for reality. I give to this word its naive and solemn meaning, a meaning having nothing to do with philosophical debates of the last few centuries."[81] Instead, as a child of Eastern Europe in the first half of the twentieth century, Miłosz thinks this pursuit of reality—however much derided in more sophisticated milieus—has a central human importance.

[79] Miłosz, *Native Realm*, 163.
[80] Ibid.
[81] Ibid.

The great prestige of science and technology in the nineteenth and twentieth centuries gave rise to regimes based on scientific notions of society that, in their total confidence in themselves, murdered tens of millions around the globe. One mark of the totalitarian systems was their fear of realities beyond the reach of their systems: "Precisely for that reason, some ways of life, some institutions became a target for the fury of evil forces, above all, the bonds between people that exist organically, as if by themselves, sustained by family, religion, neighborhood, common heritage. In other words, all that disorderly, illogical humanity, so often branded as ridiculous because of its parochial attachments and loyalties."[82] Much, of course, depends on the quality of those loyalties, but dismissing them out of hand as "unscientific" led to far greater atrocities than the old order ever produced.

Resisting the Captive Mind

The intellectual background to all this is clearest in a book published in 1953 with which most people who lived through the Cold War have some familiarity—Miłosz's analysis of the state of intellectuals' souls under socialism, *The Captive Mind.* That prose work expanded his visibility enormously in Europe and America. To reread it now, decades after the fall of Soviet Communism, is to be astonished, page after page, not only by the sheer genius of the exposition, but also by the almost superhuman refusal of the then-recent defector to indulge in simplistic hatred or bitterness. There is nothing even remotely like it in world literature except, perhaps, for Octavio Paz's *The Labyrinth of Solitude*, which also combines a poet's sensitivity and intuitiveness with a powerful but sympathetic intelligence about a whole society, of which the writer cannot deny he is a part.

The continuing interest of *The Captive Mind* lies not in its revulsion at a discredited system but in its penetrating portraits of people—Miłosz uses several friends as matter for analysis. Their pseudonyms already tell much: Alpha, the Moralist; Beta, the Disappointed Lover; Gamma, the Slave of History; and Delta, the Troubadour. To begin

[82] Czesław Miłosz, Nobel Lecture, December 8, 1980, www.nobelprize.org/nobel_prizes/literature/laureates/1980/milosz-lecture.html.

with, they were all vulnerable—even the ones who considered themselves Catholics—to the creeping nihilism of European thought in recent centuries, a nihilism that had been unintentionally reinforced by Western science and technology. They were horrified by Nazism, whose concrete effects they had seen in their own country. And they did not like Russia very much, even before the old Russian inferiority complex, the deep source of its messianism, was transformed into the New Faith of Communism. At the same time, they had no confidence in a Western Europe that had self-destructed because it was willing to accept slavery in order to survive. Even America, though the first society that had provided material welfare for most of its people and one that still possessed some of the virtues needed to face totalitarianism, was quite naïve about the threats in the world.

Miłosz allowed that intellectuals in those circumstances actually had some advantages over their Western counterparts. For one thing, they did not suffer gladly the triviality of some forms of thoughts and art from the West: "In the intellectuals who lived through the atrocities of war in Eastern Europe there took place what one might call the *elimination of emotional luxuries*. Psychoanalytic novels incite them to laughter. They consider the literature of erotic complications, still popular in the West, as trash. Imitation abstract painting bores them. They are hungry—but they want bread, not hors d'oeuvres."[83]

But the political dimension of the twentieth century is only one side of Miłosz's work, as it is only one side of human life. Two of Miłosz's autobiographical efforts—*Native Realm: A Search for Self-Definition* (1968) and *The Land of Ulro* (1977)—continued to mine the personal dimension, but not for subjective purposes. In these very rich memoirs, which often provide a highly detailed starting point for reflections on the task of poetry and the state of the human race in the late twentieth century, it becomes possible to see the permanent contribution Miłosz made to modern thinking and the continuing invitation to live out some difficult truths—difficult in the sense that they do not come naturally to us in modern societies. For him, the West, like the East, suffered from a reductionist view of man rooted in the flat and mechanical world of Newtonian physics. Both of his reflections point toward the urgency of finding a different way

[83] Czesław Miłosz, *The Captive Mind*, trans. Jane Zielonko (New York: Vintage, 1990), 41.

of experiencing and conceptualizing the world. Toward the end of *Native Realm*, he formulates it in terms of poetry: "Poetic discipline is impossible without piety and admiration, without faith in the infinite layers of being that are hidden within an apple, a man, or a tree; it challenges one through becoming to move closer to what *is*."[84]

While this may appear to be a hopelessly abstract statement, in fact it expresses a whole program of life that avoids alike the deadening vision of materialism and its literary opposite, the unreal fantasies of Romanticism. Miłosz spelled this out quite openly in *The Land of Ulro*. There he lays out a kind of modern pantheon of poets and writers who sought to break the deadly stranglehold of the dead Newtonian universe on the human imagination. The first was Goethe, who in both his poetry and his writings on science waged "a Thirty Years War against Newton". Along with him, Miłosz identified William Blake (from whose work he got the name Ulro, the world of mechanism), the Swedish mystic Emanuel Swedenborg, the great Polish Romantic poet Adam Mickiewicz, and, in a slightly different way, the modern French thinker Simone Weil. But for Miłosz, the most influential representative of this tradition was a distant relative, Oscar V. de L. Miłosz, himself a powerful poet, whom he met in Paris during his twenties. Oscar Miłosz's work, Czesław humbly reported, "without exaggeration, decided my intellectual career".[85]

To list these poets and their concerns risks reducing a very complex argument to what seems like merely "a fall into mysticism", a phrase Miłosz says was used in Polish literary circles to signify that a writer had uncritically embraced the tenets of religion and was thus no longer intellectually interesting. Miłosz's pantheon is quite the opposite. They all seem to be seeking the space to imagine something difficult to formulate in merely scientific terms. In the old Newtonian system, the world was essentially an infinite billiard table on which balls randomly collided. In such a world, how could human value—or even an appreciation of the beauty of the world—truly be imagined? The Nazis had tried to use force, the Communists the magic trick of the dialectic of history, to derive value from

[84] Miłosz, *Native Realm*, 280.

[85] Czesław Miłosz, *The Land of Ulro*, trans. Louis Iribarne (New York: Farrar, Straus, and Giroux, 1984), 187.

what had no values. Even in the West, which loudly proclaimed human dignity, good intentions were undermined by a vision of reality that provided no substantial support for all the most humane things, that in fact hollowed out such proclamations even as they were being made. Miłosz came to believe that the Einsteinian universe, which the poets partly anticipated, with its insistence on the demonstrable relatedness of things rather than on relativity in the moral sense and its new view of space as a self-involved phenomenon rather an empty expanse, offered a chance to reimagine the things he had cherished since boyhood. His post-humous last book of poetry, *Second Space*, is his attempt to explore that realm himself.

American and Polish

It was an oddity of history that this man, so deeply rooted in particular memory and experience in the East, should have spent many of his mature years—indeed from 1961 until he returned to Poland in 1991—in the West, teaching at Berkeley. He admired the dynamism of the United States. (He once wrote of his stint as cultural attaché, "The air in America, even summer in Washington with its 98° humidity, did not make me lethargic. It exhilarated me."[86] And of the American countryside, "it restored me ... to my boyhood.")[87] But he also deplored America's a-historical existence and materialism. He had a wide circle of friends among American poets, but his strongest attractions among American writers were, significantly, to Walt Whitman and, among more modern writers, Robert Frost and Robinson Jeffers, whom he translated. The Manichaean in him resonated with the dark strain in the latter two poets. Jeffers, who had isolated himself in what was in his day the sleepy fishing town of nearby Carmel, in particular exerted a fascination over Miłosz's imagination, but one that he strove to resist. The cruel and impersonal nature of Jeffers' universe and his "inhumanism", a worship of Darwinian survival of the fittest, came dangerously close to Miłosz's

[86] Miłosz, *Native Realm*, 259.
[87] Ibid., 260.

pessimistic perceptions of the world. But the Pole would not give total assent to this worship of necessity. In a poem to Jeffers, he allows that the poet is powerful, "And yet you did not know what I know. The earth teaches / more than does the nakedness of elements." Miłosz concludes:

> Better to carve suns and moons on the joints of crosses
> as was done in my district. To birches and firs
> give feminine names. To implore protection
> against the mute and treacherous might
> than to proclaim, as you did, an inhuman thing.[88]

One of the distinctive characteristics of all Miłosz's work is his deep and constant perception that hardheaded, discursive reason neither explains nor offers a solution to our circumstances. He came to and developed this understanding precisely through his own great intelligence. Philosophy and theology alike have wandered into miasmal swamps in our day, so the knowledge poetry can bring to us, he realized, becomes more urgent. It was no accident that, in his old age, Miłosz decided to translate the Book of the Apocalypse into Polish and even learned Hebrew in order to translate some of the Old Testament as well. He frequently spoke about his *daimonion*, a term Plato used for the voice that guided Socrates and that Miłosz seems quite literally to have thought of as a kind of muse, an inspiration from some part of the human mind or spirit to which most of us have little access but that is wiser than we usually are.

In the very last poem ("Orpheus and Eurydice") of his posthumous volume *Second Space*, written after he had moved back to Kraków following the fall of Communism, Miłosz restated his belief in the poet as a channel for a voice of reality: "He submitted to the music, yielded / To the dictation of a song, listening with rapt attention, / Became, like his lyre, its instrument." And what was the content of that song? The answer shows that, to the very end, Miłosz's *daimonion* did not abandon him:

[88] Quoted in Leonard Nathan and Arthur Quinn, *The Poet's Work: An Introduction to Czesław Miłosz* (Cambridge, Mass.: Harvard University Press, 1991), 8.

He sang the brightness of mornings and green rivers,
He sang of smoking water in the rose-colored daybreaks,
Of colors: cinnabar, carmine, burnt sienna, blue,
Of the delight of swimming in the sea under marble cliffs,
Of feasting on a terrace above the tumult of a fishing port,
Of the tastes of wine, olive oil, almonds, mustard, salt.
Of the flight of the swallow, the falcon,
Of a dignified flock of pelicans above a bay,
Of the scent of an armful of lilacs in summer rain,
Of his having composed his words always against death,
And of having made no rhyme in praise of nothingness.[89]

A fitting epitaph, which also perhaps explains why Miłosz is buried in the crypt of Kraków's Wawel Cathedral among Poland's great artists, kings, and saints. His "having made no rhyme in praise of nothingness" may seem a modest enough note on which to bring this brief examination of Catholic literature in the twentieth century to a close. But in a time when great ideals of human dignity and worth were often proclaimed in insincere words and dishonored in practice, when nihilism, skepticism, relativism, ideology-driven humanisms of several kinds produced tens of millions of corpses, and worldwide systems of oppression, it is a larger and more consequential achievement than it seems.

[89] Czesław Miłosz, *Second Space: New Poems*, trans. Czesław Miłosz and Robert Hass (New York: HarperCollins, 2004), 100.

CONCLUSION

The Pathos of the Catholic Intellectual Tradition

[GOD Speaks:]
Having once seen Saint Louis on his knees, one no longer desires to see
Oriental slaves prone on the earth
All stretched out flat on their bellies on the earth. To be freely loved,
Nothing can weigh as much, nothing can cost as much.
It is certainly my greatest invention.
When one has tasted the joy
Of being freely loved
What remains is nothing but subservience....
When Saint Louis loves me
I know, I understand what it is to be loved.
(And that is everything). Doubtless he fears God,
But it is a noble fear, all filled, all swelled,
All replete with love, like a fruit swollen with juice,
In no way a cowardly, a base fear, an indecent fear
Gripping the belly. But a great, but a high, but a noble fear,
The fear of displeasing me because he loves me, and of disobeying me because he loves me,
And because he loves me, the fear
Of not being found pleasing
And loving and loved in my sight. No infiltration in that noble fear
Of an evil fear and a pernicious and vile cowardice.
And when he loves me it is true. And when he says he loves me it is true. And when he says that he would rather
Have leprosy than fall into mortal sin (he loves me so much), it is true.
With him I know it is true.

It is not only true because he says it. It is true because he is
true. He does not only say it to sound well.
He does not say it because he has seen it in books nor because
he has been told to say it.
He says it because it is so.[1]

This is already a long book and, if it has been at all successful, should convince the reader that it could—usefully, perhaps—have even been much longer. From Leo XIII's renewal to John Paul II's and Benedict XVI's public witness, from the flight of the Maritains from materialism to Czesław Miłosz's resistance to totalitarianism, across the speculations of Guardini, de Lubac, Rahner, von Balthasar, and the creative work of Claudel, Bernanos, Mauriac, Hopkins, Waugh, Graham Greene, and many more, the Catholic intellectual tradition carried out important labors in the twentieth century, even as it bequeathed many ongoing questions—not to say outright problems—to our own time. The dialogue of faith and reason is never concluded, as John Paul II wrote in his encyclical *Fides et Ratio*. But that ongoing conversation is, on both fronts, crucial to the preservation, not only of Catholic things, but of all the truly human things today.

Because it is primarily in the Catholic intellectual vision, which John Paul II described as having "exceptional philosophical density",[2] that the very humanness of humanity still finds a substantial defense. During a large part of the twentieth century, the threat to humanity came from political systems that denied human freedom and defined human existence in ideological terms that essentially abolished human things. For the past quarter century or so, those same threats have continued, but in less crudely political, more subtly cultural forms. For example, the eminent American philosopher (and atheist) Thomas Nagel published in 2012 a slim book entitled *Mind and Cosmos: Why the Materialist Neo-Darwinian Conception of Nature Is Almost Certainly False*,[3] in which he merely argues, while still remaining a non-believer, that we need some different view of

[1] Charles Péguy, *The Mystery of the Holy Innocents*, trans. Pansy Parkenham (New York: Harper, 1956), 101–2; available online at http://www.centropeguy.org/cachepeguy7.htm.

[2] *FR* 80.

[3] Thomas Nagel, *Mind and Cosmos: Why the Materialist Neo-Darwinian Conception of Nature Is Almost Certainly False* (New York: Oxford University Press, 2012).

matter—a richer materialism, so to speak—if we are to preserve not only the mind but all the human truths. For this single but important qualification—and for arguing that there may be a kind of "natural teleology" in the cosmos—he was savagely attacked. One of his defenders argued that Nagel was being crucified because he had committed "the sin against the Holy Ghost that pious scientists are taught never to forgive".[4]

The scientific materialism that is now the default setting in modern culture, however, faces more than one blank wall. Not only can it not account for human things—the Neo-Darwinist effort to attach thought, emotion, and morality to advantages for group survival is one of the silliest ideas in the modern world—but it cannot account for, indeed, is tending toward the utterly self-refuting, radically self-defeating denial of, ideas and thought, which are not material things. Naturally, most people are not aware of the full consequences of these "scientific" arguments and would recoil from them if they were. But at the same time they tend to think that these things are "true". So the Catholic intellectual tradition finds itself in the delicate position of needing to affirm things that the most common and most militant contemporary forms of "reason" now tend to deny, if we want to save reason from itself.

In a similar vein, human freedom—the very existence of free will—is under siege. Neuroscientists—going beyond their own discipline into fields of value and philosophy—want to identify the mind with the brain and have taken to referring to traditional ideas of free will as "folk" belief. So, mind, spirit, emotion, heart, freedom, responsibility, courage, nobility—all those words we use to mark out what is especially human and cannot be found in any other being in our world—are put under a similar interdict, a truly bizarre impulse to eliminate not only God but human nature in slavish adherence to a self-destructive scientific method. As C. S. Lewis once remarked, materialistic scientists hold a view that makes their own work no different from the salivating of a dog. You do not have to deny the many limits on our freedom, both internal and external, to know that this is a human dead end that threatens the scientists and secularists alike. As John Paul II remarked on the eve of the third

[4] David Gelerntner, "The Closing of the Scientific Mind", *Commentary*, January 2014: 18.

millennium, "Truth and freedom either go together hand in hand or they perish together in misery."[5]

This is the deep metaphysical background that Catholicism must defend in order to preserve both the truly divine and the truly human things. And though on this score it did well in the twentieth century—witness how Karl Rahner and Edith Stein and others dealt brilliantly with the whole Continental tradition as it existed in Heidegger, Husserl, and other great thinkers; and how Elizabeth Anscombe and Alasdair MacIntyre replied creatively to the whole Wittgensteinian and Anglo-American tradition—Catholicism is no longer a significant part of the cultural dialogue, as it was in the first half of the twentieth century. Indeed, rifts have entered the Catholic tradition itself from the secular world that make it less coherent and effective in making its own case.

Besides the deep philosophical questions, there are more immediate pragmatic and political challenges as well. The many self-contradictory elements in contemporary secularism add up, I believe, to what might be called the *pathos of secularism*—a sincere desire to respect others and promote human happiness, combined with a radical and painful lack of foundations for belief in the dignity of all men.[6] One consequence of the failure to find metaphysical and ethical groundings for belief in human dignity is an inability to carry that belief into action without falling into a kind of self-contradiction that violates human dignity and freedom. Many—and not only Catholics—have recognized this *pathos*. In *The Rebel*, Albert Camus points out how, since the French Revolution, the desire for absolute freedom and absolute justice rooted in nothing but men themselves has led, inexorably, to widespread tyranny and injustice. That is perhaps inevitable because, from a profound Christian point of view, the way of Babel, the desire to erect something perfect, a soaring human construct, without reference to the true God—who is also the fundamental reality behind everything—always ends in self-destruction.

[5] *FR* 90.

[6] For an example of a sincere, sophisticated, and self-aware secular effort to provide foundations for humane action despite defensible foundations, see Luc Ferry, *A Brief History of Thought*, trans. Theo Cuffe (New York: Harper Perennial, 2011). Ferry's book was a runaway best seller in several countries, attesting to a hunger for what he attempts to provide, despite the fact that he ultimately fails.

You have to give over a lot of power to Caesar if you want him to establish a kingdom of absolute freedom and justice. And as Charles Péguy once remarked, the one thing that has produced more wars than injustice is the wild pursuit of justice.

Catholic thinkers dealt quite creatively and, often enough, effectively with such challenges in the twentieth century. We no longer face the open tyrannies of Communism, Nazism, or Fascism, on account of which Christian Democracy—as developed by Maritain, Simon, and others—emerged as an effective alternative in its day. As all those distorted views of man showed rather quickly—and our own Western materialism with its self-destructive abortion, contraception, and consequent demographic collapse may soon illustrate as well—civilizations rooted in mistaken notions of man or the thin soil of rationalism do not long endure. The challenge now that that century has passed is whether a new generation will find a way to deal with less obvious but equally insidious threats to both human and divine things.

Whether that attempt will succeed, however, depends on something we noted in Péguy's stance at the very outset. Unlike other intellectual traditions, the Catholic intellectual tradition has to withstand scrutiny by two different sets of criteria. It must, of course, be true to itself as an *intellectual* enterprise, which is to say, it must be able to hold its own in terms of self-consistency, rigor, and human scope, and at the same time—impossible though it may seem—answer to the demand that in its ultimate results it correspond to the simplicity of the gospel itself. As T. S. Eliot once noted, we live in a complicated age, and the only simplicity that seems valid to us lies on the other side of complexity. In part, that is what the great Cardinal Newman—who developed spectacular theories of doctrinal development, the "idea" of a university, and assent to faith still worthy of study—meant when he spoke of Christian theology as "knowledge carried to the heart".

Measured on these dual grounds, some clear challenges appear. Perhaps the most significant from the faith side of the dialogue is that the sheer welter of contemporary thought, secular as well as religious, seems to overwhelm any fixed notion of truth or morality in the modern world. This is a phenomenon that cannot be attributed to any one cause, and it afflicts religious groups and others making truth claims outside the Catholic orbit as well.[7] Many people—popes, philosophers, theologians, moralists, politicians, even media figures—decry the obvious threats to a humane existence posed by such common attitudes as relativism, skepticism, and a shallow pragmatism or technologism. Any clear observer will notice the loss of connection to high culture and the degradation of popular culture, the ignorance of the past and homelessness in the present, that are conspicuous features of our world. John Paul II added that a further threat is *eclecticism*,[8] a tendency to welcome differing perspectives, without an adequate concern for how partial they may be, how in need of serious correction from other views, and, ultimately, how they may be made to fit together, because truth is one. In what may indicate a kind of *pathos* within the current Catholic tradition itself, John Paul II raised this issue in the very same encyclical in which he affirmed that there is no official Catholic philosophy and that the various intellectual disciplines must be free to pursue their investigations in light of their own criteria.

In the end, however, a truly Catholic intellectual tradition must be aware of its responsibility to foster what John Paul II called "interior unity":

> I am well aware that these requirements which the word of God imposes upon philosophy may seem daunting to many people involved in philosophical research today. Yet this is why, taking up what has been taught repeatedly by the Popes for several generations and reaffirmed by the Second Vatican Council itself, I wish to reaffirm strongly the conviction that the human being can come to a unified and organic vision of knowledge. This is one of the tasks which Christian thought will have to take up through the next millennium of the Christian era. The segmentation of knowledge, with its splintered

[7] This was brought home to me personally some years ago when I was involved in a Catholic-Jewish dialogue at a synagogue outside of Washington, D.C., where I live. I urged the audience, including a very wise old female rabbi, who had organized the event, not to take seriously the idea that everything a Catholic might say is taught by the Church: "You Jews, with your tradition of learning, wouldn't believe how utterly ignorant of our tradition most Catholics are. Surveys show that large percentages of Catholics, even after a dozen or more years of Catholic schooling, can't even list the Ten Commandments." I hadn't finished speaking before she was shaking her head and saying how Jewish congregations are finding the same thing among their young people.

[8] *FR* 86.

> approach to truth and consequent fragmentation of meaning, keeps people today from coming to an interior unity. How could the Church not be concerned by this? It is the Gospel which imposes this sapiential task directly upon her Pastors, and they cannot shrink from their duty to undertake it.[9]

If this is so—and it seems hard to deny—there are "pastoral" tasks to be carried out in the way of firm teaching about truth that for a long time, especially since Vatican II, were thought to belong only to the older "legalistic" Church. We may not return to the Thomist categories of the past, but we need something like them—something substantial and comprehensive—probably along the lines MacIntyre has described, if we hope to have any chance to meet the challenge.

With the election of the highly charismatic Pope Francis in 2013, who immediately captured worldwide attention for his humility and simplicity, many Catholics and others assumed that he was discarding the old efforts to affirm Catholic faith and morals. In fact, from his very early days as pope, he showed, not an abandonment of the older truths, but a strategy to present them in a new, more effective key:

> 34. If we attempt to put all things in a missionary key, this will also affect the way we communicate the message. In today's world of instant communication and occasionally biased media coverage, the message we preach runs a greater risk of being distorted or reduced to some of its secondary aspects. In this way certain issues which are part of the Church's moral teaching are taken out of the context which gives them their meaning. The biggest problem is when the message we preach then seems identified with those secondary aspects which, important as they are, do not in and of themselves convey the heart of Christ's message. *We need to be realistic and not assume that our audience understands the full background to what we are saying*, or is capable of relating what we say to the very heart of the Gospel which gives it meaning, beauty and attractiveness.
>
> 35. Pastoral ministry in a missionary style is not obsessed with the disjointed transmission of a multitude of doctrines to be insistently imposed. When we adopt a pastoral goal and a missionary style which would actually reach everyone without exception or exclusion, the

[9] Ibid., 85.

> message has to concentrate on the essentials, on what is most beautiful, most grand, most appealing and at the same time most necessary. *The message is simplified, while losing none of its depth and truth, and thus becomes all the more forceful and convincing.*[10]

That evangelizing perspective provides what should be a touchstone for all Catholic intellectual work.

Modern intellectual life tends to exalt research, discovery, new practical applications via technology, and so on. And in their proper place, these are all useful, even essential, qualities of the life of the mind. Religious knowledge and practice—"faith and morals" in the older language—do not consist primarily in such an attitude, however. Though we may hope that philosophy and theology, Scripture studies and social thought, artistic creation and literature may bring us unexpected riches from the tradition, they also have as their primary foundation a rootedness in and fidelity to that tradition. As Chesterton, ever wise on this and many other points, argued, the only progress possible in the Christian tradition is greater progress into and toward the fullness of Christian truth. In a certain perspective, this is a paradox: a kind of conservative innovation or creative traditionalism. But after the various revolutions and counter-revolutions of all kinds in the twentieth century, truth itself seems exhausted, and only truths of a fragmented, humble, postmodern sort—typically applying to some personal issue or technological problem—seem all that remains. Reason itself, as Pope Saint John Paul II, Pope Benedict XVI, and Pope Francis have argued, can both see this problem and understand its responsibility to address it.

It has long been a Catholic contention that revelation exists, particularly the coming of Christ into the world, precisely to free us from our self-generated weaknesses and limitations. In this sense, revelation actually frees reason to be more fully itself. While modern rationalists regard revelation and even metaphysics as illegitimate, it is faith that has the broader view here. Science and technology have suggested that certain things are out of bounds, such as all the classical "why" questions: Why does the world exist, what are we, what can we hope for in this life and after? When Spinoza said that we should

[10] Pope Francis, Apostolic Exhortation *Evangelii Gaudium* (November 24, 2013), nos. 34–35 (emphases added).

focus on this life, he may have been correcting an excessive focus on the next. But what kind of human wisdom is it—even the ancients at their best took this seriously—that does not keep before our eyes the fact that we are mortal and die? Or that does not ask what conclusions are to be drawn from that truth?

In the first pages of the present work, we pointed out that at the Second Vatican Council, the Church rightly sought to orient herself differently toward the modern world. The more legalistic and institutional emphasis of the earlier part of the century gave way to a greater focus on the pastoral and personal side of the Mystical Body of Christ. In several respects, the latter emphasis almost obliterated the former, when what was needed was the perennial Catholic emphasis on "both-and" rather than "either-or". But it has also become clear over the past half century that there is a radical call in Catholicism for a personal choice: either a person believes in Jesus as the only begotten Son of God and the Church as the fullest expression of his will for the world, or he does not. Consequences flow from that choice. For too much of the past half century, it seemed that almost anything was compatible with Catholicism. There is an urgent need to respect differences and complexity, but also to recover the ancient wisdom that certain choices place you within the household, others outside. So while for Catholics "both-and" is often the rule, there is no getting around the fact that at some points we are faced with an "either-or".

That may be *the* single most neuralgic attitude in this new Christian millennium. It will take a great deal of work, intellectual work, just to make clear how Catholicism's No to certain questions is not narrowness and exclusion. A real "no" on some partial question occurs in the context of a "yes" to a fuller, indeed, the fullest truth. And this play of yes and no is not merely some harsh authoritarianism. It can even be a heartfelt fidelity that knows the choice will lead to suffering and yet reflect the highest human sentiment. Or, to recall again, what God himself inspired one poet, struggling to be faithful, to write to Our Lady of Chartres in the twentieth century:

> When we sit down at the cross formed by two ways
> And must choose regret along with remorse
> And dual fate forces us to pick one course
> And the keystone of two arches fixes our gaze,

You alone, mistress of the secret, attest
To the downward slope where one road goes.
You know the other path that our steps chose,
As one chooses the cedar for a chest.

And not for virtue, which we don't possess.
And not for duty, which we do not love.
But, as carpenters find the center of
The wood, to seek the center of wretchedness.

And to approach the axis of distress,
And for the dumb need to feel the whole curse,
And to do what's harder and to suffer worse,
And to take the blow in all its fullness.

Through that sleight-of-hand, that very artfulness,
Which will never make us happy anymore,
Let us, O Queen, preserve at least our honor,
And along with it our simple tenderness.[11]

[11] Charles Péguy, "Prière de confidence", in *Les Tapisseries* (Paris: Gallimard, 1968), 132 (author's translation).

ACKNOWLEDGMENTS

A book like this cannot be born without the collaboration of many friends, first among them Michele and Donald D'Amour, whose exceptional generosity and patience were essential to a project that grew far beyond what any of us imagined when it all started. Dr. Patrick Powers and Mr. Paul Jackson, who manage the Fides et Ratio Seminars at the Faith & Reason Institute (of which I have had the honor of serving as president since its founding in 1999), along with the hundreds of participants in the seminars from scores of Catholic institutions both here and abroad, have affected my whole view of the modern Catholic intellectual tradition. James Perry, Robert Odle, James Lucier, Ann and Bill Burleigh, Sean Fieler, George Marlin, and Michael Crofton in varying ways contributed material and moral support. Father James Schall, S.J., as well as Father Robert Sokolowski, both the wisest of counselors, helped at crucial points. Virgil Nemoianu, a mentor since my graduate studies, expanded my horizons early on. My intellectual debts to many others must here remain heartfelt, if silent, so as not to burden the reader who is already facing a big book. Brad Miner, my friend and reliable partner in editing *The Catholic Thing*, read portions of the manuscript and provided advice out of his long experience in book publishing. Father Joseph Fessio, S.J., and Ignatius Press including Mark Brumley, Carolyn Rae Lemon, and Anne Englund Nash, did as professional a job handling this prickly manuscript as any author has a right to expect. And to my wife, Veronica, and family, who know from sad experience what writing a book does to a person and those around him, love and gratitude.

INDEX